THE CLIMAX OF PROPHECY

THE CLIMAX OF PROPHECY
Studies on the Book of Revelation

Richard Bauckham

T&T CLARK
EDINBURGH

T&T CLARK LTD
59 GEORGE STREET
EDINBURGH EH2 2LQ
SCOTLAND

First Published 1993

British Library Cataloguing-in-Publication Data
A catalogue record for this book
is available from the British Library

ISBN 0 567 09620 3

Typeset by Trinity Typesetting, Edinburgh
Printed and bound in Great Britain by Biddles Ltd, Surrey

For my mother

Contents

Introduction

The Apocalypse of John is a work of immense learning, astonishingly meticulous literary artistry, remarkable creative imagination, radical political critique, and profound theology. Yet, among the major works of early Christianity included in the New Testament, it remains the Cinderella. It has received only a fraction of the amount of scholarly attention which has been lavished on the Gospels and the major Pauline letters. The present volume is a contribution to remedying this neglect.[1]

The essays in this volume are products of my own fascination with and study of the Apocalypse over a period of twenty years. Some have been published before, in various journals and volumes, and are here collected and re-published in revised (in most cases very thoroughly revised) form. About two-thirds of the contents of the volume have not been previously published. Each chapter can be read as a self-contained essay, but they are also interconnected (and cross-references help the reader to make the connexions). They belong to a single sustained enterprise of understanding both the form and the message of the Apocalypse in its literary and historical contexts. While writing the previously unpublished essays in this volume, over the past two years, I was also writing a shorter, systematic account of the theology of the Apocalypse.[2] Many of the lines of interpretation advanced in the latter are explored and justified in much greater detail in the present volume. While

[1]For surveys of recent research on Revelation, see Vanni (1980); Schüssler Fiorenza (1985) chapter 1; Böcher (1988).
[2]Bauckham (1993).

the other volume focuses on the theology of the Apocalypse, the present volume, though not neglecting theology, devotes more attention to the literary and historical questions which are in the end inseparable from the Apocalypse's theological message. Thus the two volumes are complementary.

The approach to understanding the Apocalypse which unites the essays in this volume has at least four major aspects. In the first place, close attention to the literary composition of the work is essential. Revelation has been composed with such meticulous attention to the detail of language and structure that scarcely a word can have been chosen without deliberate reflection on its relationship to the work as an integrated, interconnected whole. The source-critics of the nineteenth and early twentieth centuries, who divided Revelation into a number of disparate sources incompetently combined by an editor, could do so only by crass failure to appreciate the specific literary integrity of the work as it stands. This has been widely recognized in more recent study, which has stressed the literary and ideological unity of the book. But there has still been little enough investigation of the distinctive literary techniques by which Revelation conveys meaning. Here the insights of modern literary criticism are of limited use, since they have been developed with reference to very different kinds of literature. The literary features of Revelation are to some extent indebted to the techniques of contemporary Jewish exegesis and apocalyptic writing, to some extent the distinctive contribution of the author's own literary genius. Revelation demands literary appreciation in its own terms. Again and again in these essays we shall find that close attention to literary composition opens up a remarkable density of meaning in the text, which has been so crafted as to be capable of yielding its full meaning only to repeated reading and appropriate study.

Secondly, Revelation's use of the Old Testament scriptures is an essential key to its understanding. The pattern of almost continuous allusion to the Old Testament throughout the book is not a haphazard use of Old Testament language by a writer so soaked in the Old Testament that he naturally uses its language, as some scholars have mistakenly thought. It is a pattern of disciplined and deliberate *allusion* to specific Old Testament texts. Reference to and interpretation of these texts is an extremely important part of the meaning of the text of the Apocalypse. It is a book designed to be read in constant intertextual relationship with the Old Testament. John was writing what he understood to be a work of prophetic scripture, the climax of prophetic revelation, which gathered up the prophetic meaning of the Old Testament scriptures and disclosed the way in which it was being and was to be fulfilled in the last days. His work therefore presupposes and conveys an extensive interpretation of large parts of Old Testament prophecy. Allusions are meant to recall the Old Testament context, which thereby becomes part of the meaning the Apocalypse conveys, and to build up, sometimes by a network of allusion to the same Old Testament passage in various parts of the Apocalypse, an interpretation of whole passages of Old Testament prophecy. The interpretation is highly disciplined, employing contemporary methods of Jewish exegesis, especially the technique of *gezērâ šāwâ*, by which passages sharing common words or phrases are interpreted in relation to each other. Frequently in these essays we shall find that obscure passages in Revelation become clear and that passages regularly misunderstood by the commentators can be correctly understood when the Old Testament allusions are identified and John's interpretation of the Old Testament reconstructed in terms of Jewish exegetical practice.

Thirdly, Revelation is an apocalypse, whose primary literary context is the tradition of Jewish and Christian apocalypses. Both in form and in content it is heavily indebted to this tradition. Its relation to the non-canonical apocalypses is different from its relation to the Old Testament. The latter forms a body of literature which John expects his readers to know and explicitly to recall in detail while reading his own work. Frequent specific reference to it is integral to his literary strategy. In the case of the non-canonical apocalypses, on the other hand, the relationship is such that we cannot be sure that John knew any particular apocalypse or expected his readers to do so. The traditions he shares with many of them cannot be pinned down to specific texts to which he makes allusion. Yet the tradition of apocalyptic literature is the living literary tradition to whose forms and content he is most indebted. This has, of course, long been recognized. But since the important work of scholars of a previous generation, such as R. H. Charles and I. T. Beckwith, very little fresh work has been done by way of comparing and contrasting Revelation with the rest of the apocalyptic literature, or of tracing the specific literary conventions and apocalyptic traditions which occur both in Revelation and in other apocalypses. Despite the major advances in our knowledge and understanding of the Jewish and Christian apocalypses during the last two decades, much scholarly writing on Revelation gives the impression that all the relevant parallels were pointed out long ago and that interpreters of Revelation have no need to engage in firsthand study of other apocalypses. In these essays we shall frequently draw on the results of firsthand study of Jewish and Christian apocalypses other than Revelation, and demonstrate that floods of fresh light can still be thrown on Revelation in this way. This is not at all to deny the individual distinctiveness of Revelation. On the contrary, precisely this method will show how John often uses common apocalyptic traditions in highly creative ways and develops the conventions of the literary genre for his own purposes and by means of his own literary genius. Similarly, for example, his non-Christian Jewish contemporary, the author of 4 Ezra, made his own use of the genre to create a very different kind of literary masterpiece. The creative individuality of such examples of the genre is often obscured by secondhand generalizations about apocalyptic literature not based on firsthand acquaintance with that literature.

Fourthly, if Revelation's meaning is intertextual (in relation to the Old Testament) it is also contextual (in relation to its contemporary world). At this point, there is both a Scylla and a Charybdis to be avoided in the interpretation of the book. On the one hand, justice cannot be done to the Apocalypse by an interpretative approach which treats it as a self-contained aesthetic object, for the understanding of which the world in which John and his first readers lived is irrelevant. This would deprive the work of its true character: as a prophetic critique of the political idolatry and economic oppression intrinsic to

Roman power in the late first century, and as a call to its readers to bear witness to the truth and righteousness of God in the specific circumstances — religious, political, social and economic — in which they lived in the cities of the Roman province of Asia. The world created by the text is intended as an interpretation of the real world in which John and his readers lived, and so, despite its visionary form, makes frequent reference to quite specific features of that world. On the other hand, Revelation should not be reduced, by simplistic application of sociological theory, to a sociologically determined function. Justice must be done to its character as a sophisticated literary work of individual genius, embodying a highly reflective vision of the impact of the divine purpose on the contemporary world. Its social strategy — a call to radical dissociation from structural evil — is based on a perception of the Roman Empire as an oppressive system, characterized by political idolatry and economic exploitation. But, while it is John's prophetic theological vision of God's righteous rule which brings to light, by contrast, the evil of the Roman system, the latter is also conveyed, as we shall see in some of the essays in this book, by very precise and accurate reference to the political and economic realities of the late first century world. The political and economic history of Revelation's context becomes essential to its adequate interpretation.

Chapter 1 of this book ('Structure and Composition') broaches in general some of the literary questions which recur throughout the book in relation to specific passages of Revelation. It analyses the literary structure of Revelation by identifying the structural markers which the book itself highlights, and it provides a preliminary account of two highly characteristic literary techniques which have been scarcely noticed in previous study of Revelation. Chapter 2 ('The Use of Apocalyptic Traditions') shows, by study of a series of specific examples of Revelation's indebtedness to traditions which also occur elsewhere in apocalyptic literature, that John did not borrow such traditions from other apocalypses, but knew them, as other apocalyptists must have done, in some form, probably oral, independently of their incorporation in actual apocalypses. An attempt to locate the social context in which such traditions were transmitted throws some light on John's membership of a circle of Christian prophets. The examples also show how tracing such traditions in other literature can have significant results for the exegesis of Revelation. From John's use of apocalyptic traditions common to Jewish and Christian apocalypticism, chapter 3 ('Synoptic Parousia Parables and the Apocalypse') turns to his use of Gospel traditions. Revelation's allusions to the parables of the Thief and the Watching Servants are placed in the context of the tradition of these and related parables, as seen in other early Christian literature, and conclusions are drawn with regard to the relationship of early Christian prophets to the Gospel tradition.

In chapters 4 and 5 questions of literary composition and the use of apocalyptic traditions are pursued in relation to two major aspects of the theology of Revelation. Chapter 4 ('The Worship of Jesus') discusses a striking but relatively neglected feature of the christology of Revelation, showing how John combines the attribution of divine worship to Jesus Christ with a sensitivity to the question of the relationship of worship to monotheistic faith. He uses apocalyptic traditions and imagery to express one of the highest christologies in the New Testament, and shows how, within an entirely Jewish Christian world of ideas, belief in the divinity of Christ was integrated into deliberate loyalty to the Jewish monotheistic tradition.[3] Chapter 5 ('The Role of the Spirit') shows that Revelation has a more sophisticated and more extensive pneumatology than its rather few references to the Spirit might at first suggest.[4]

Chapter 6 ('The Lion, the Lamb and the Dragon') and chapter 7 ('The Eschatological Earthquake') draw attention to another literary feature of Revelation, its profusion of visual imagery, and focus on some of the major images which recur through the visions and which function as bearers of concentrated symbolic meaning: the messianic images of the Lion and the Lamb, the portrayal of the devil as the Dragon,

[3]For a more comprehensive account of the christology of Revelation, see Bauckham (1993) chapter 3.

[4]For the pneumatology of Revelation, see also Bauckham (1993) chapter 5.

and one of Revelation's dominant images of the end: the earthquake. Study of the range of association which these images would carry for John's first readers shows how they can be both intertextual and contextual, i.e. they both allude to the Old Testament and also resonate with aspects of contemporary culture and history in the environment of the seven churches. By comparison with apocalyptic traditions which provide more or less precedent for these images, John's development and use of them are seen to be once again highly creative.

Chapter 8 ('The Apocalypse as a Christian War Scroll') investigates Revelation's use and interpretation of another set of images drawn from apocalyptic tradition: those which relate to holy war and are applied in Revelation to the participation of Christians in God's eschatological victory over evil. Study of the holy war motif in Revelation has been previously largely limited to the idea of God's (and the Lamb's) war against and victory over evil. This chapter shows that John carefully takes up Jewish expectations of a messianic war in which God's people are to fight and to win a military victory over their enemies, and reinterprets them, substituting faithful witness to the point of martyrdom for armed violence as the means of victory. Though military means are repudiated, the imagery of holy war is employed in the interests of active participation by Christians in the divine conflict with evil, following up the decisive victory which their Messiah, the Lamb, has already won.

This issue of the role which Revelation expects the church to play in God's purpose of establishing his rule on earth is taken further in chapter 9 ('The Conversion of the Nations'). Chapter 8 leaves unresolved the crucial question of the kind of result which the suffering witness to which Revelation calls its readers is expected to have. Will the church's witness to the nations lead, as most interpreters have supposed, only to the destructive judgment of the nations, or will it convert them to the worship of the true God, as a few interpreters have suggested? Will God's kingdom come by eliminating all who presently join the dragon and the beast in opposing it, or will it come by winning them to and including them in God's rule? Chapter 9 argues in detail that Revelation takes up from the Psalms and the later Old Testament prophets the most universalistic form of Jewish eschatological hope: that all the nations of the world will acknowledge the one true God and become his peoples. It also argues that the central message of the Apocalypse is its revelation of the way in which this is expected, in the purpose of God, to occur: by the participation of the Lamb's followers in his faithful witness to the truth sustained to the point of death and subsequent vindication. This is, in essence, the content of the sealed book of the divine purpose which the Lamb opens so that John may make it known in his prophecy.

This chapter 9 is much the longest because it is also probably the most important and original contribution made here to the understanding of the message of the Apocalypse. The title of the present book is explained by this chapter. John, it is argued, understood his prophecy to be the climax of the tradition of Old Testament prophecy, because in the revelation made to him by Jesus Christ was disclosed the secret of the divine purpose for the final coming of the kingdom of God. Whereas the prophets had predicted the conversion of all the nations to the worship of the true God and obscurely foreseen the oppression of God's people by pagan power in the last days, John's prophecy reveals that the former is to be the consequence of the latter, and that the key to both is the task of faithful witness in the face of all opposition, to which the followers of the Lamb, his readers, are now called. The argument of this chapter hinges on Revelation's use of the Old Testament. The cumulative case is built up by detailed study of a whole series of key allusions to the Old Testament. John's central message has gone largely unrecognized because the way in which he conveys it, by subtle and disciplined allusion to the Old Testament, has not been appreciated.

The last two chapters, 10 and 11, turn to Revelation's portrayal and critique of the Roman system of oppression, against which it calls the churches to witness to the truth and righteousness of God. The system has two major aspects, which Revelation portrays as the harlot of Babylon, representing the city of Rome in her corrupting influence over and economic exploitation of the empire, and the beast from the sea, which represents the imperial power, in its military and political dominance of the empire, supported by the political religion which absolutizes power through idolatrous worship. Thus these two chapters focus on the contextuality of the Apocalypse's message in the Roman Empire as seen from the cities of Asia at the end of the first century. Chapter 10 ('The Economic Critique of Rome in Revelation 18') highlights, for the first time, not only the extent to which Revelation condemns Rome for its economic oppression, but also the accurate detail with which Revelation 18 depicts the economic relations between Rome and her empire. Chapter 11 ('Nero and the beast') argues that the figure of Nero (who is identified as the beast by its number 666) is a major key to understanding Revelation's portrayal of the imperial power as the beast. Although it has been widely recognized that Revelation alludes to the expectation of Nero's return, an accurate understanding of precisely how Revelation takes up and adapts this expectation has been lacking. Careful study of the forms this expectation took, in pagan, Jewish and Christian literature, in comparison with Revelation, shows that John has in fact made highly creative use of two different forms of the legend, creating out of them a history of the beast in parodic antithesis to the history of Jesus Christ. In his symbolic vision of the past, present and future of the Roman empire he brings together accurate references to the apparent contemporary realities of Roman power and prophetic perception of the hidden reality of divine power.

Details of previous publication

Part of section 3 of chapter 2 also appears in: 'Resurrection as Giving Back the Dead: A Traditional Image of Resurrection in the Pseudepigrapha and the Apocalypse of John,' in J. H. Charlesworth and C. A. Evans ed., *The Pseudepigrapha and the New Testament* (JSPSS; Sheffield: JSOT Press, 1993).

Chapter 3 was previously published as: 'Synoptic Parousia Parables and the Apocalypse,' *NTS* 23 (1976-77) 162-176; and 'Synoptic Parousia Parables Again,' *NTS* 29 (1983) 129-134.

Chapter 4 is a revised version of: 'The Worship of Jesus in Apocalyptic Christianity,' *NTS* 27 (1980-81) 322-341.

Chapter 5 is a revised version of: 'The Role of the Spirit in the Apocalypse,' *EQ* 52 (1980) 66-83.

Chapter 6 is a revised version of: 'The Figurae of John of Patmos,' in A. Williams ed., *Prophecy and Millenarianism: Essays in Honour of Marjorie Reeves* (London: Longman, 1980) 107-125.

Chapter 7 was previously published as: 'The Eschatological Earthquake in the Apocalypse of John,' *NovT* 19 (1977) 224-233.

Chapter 8 is a revised version of 'The Book of Revelation as a Christian War Scroll,' *Neot* 22 (1988) 17-40.

Chapter 10 was previously published as: 'The Economic Critique of Rome in Revelation 18,' in L. Alexander ed., *Images of Empire* (JSOTSS 122; Sheffield: JSOT Press, 1991) 47-90.

I am grateful to these journals and publishers for permission to republish material.

1

Structure and Composition

The book of Revelation is an extraordinarily complex literary composition,[1] as not only this chapter but also other chapters in this volume will help to make clear. This complexity has rarely been fully appreciated. The major literary study of Revelation which will do justice to it has yet to be written. The present chapter has only modest purposes. In the first section an analysis of the literary structure of the book will be offered. In the second and third sections, two very distinctive literary techniques which permeate the composition of the whole book will be discussed. The extent and significance of the use of these techniques has not been previously recognized. The discussion of them here will therefore be pioneering and preliminary.[2]

Revelation was evidently designed to convey its message to some significant degree on first hearing (cf. 1:3), but also progressively to yield fuller meaning to closer acquaintance and assiduous study. It is important to realise that the essential structure of the book, without recognition of which it would be

---

[1]The more Revelation is studied in detail, the more clear it becomes that it is not simply a literary unity, but actually one of the most unified works in the New Testament. The evidence discussed in this chapter should be sufficient to refute theories which divide the book into disparate sources. Theories of this kind have largely been discredited, but are still sometimes advanced: e.g. Kraft (1974); Ford (1975).

[2]One immensely significant feature of the composition of Revelation which is not discussed in this chapter is the use of the Old Testament. The most important work on this is now Jan Fekkes' unpublished dissertation: Fekkes (1988). See also Beale (1988) (with further bibliography) and chapter 9 below.

incomprehensible, must have been intended to be perceptible in oral performance. In the first section of this chapter we are therefore primarily concerned with literary features which are relatively obvious. In the second section we turn to features which might or might not take part in the initial impact of the text in oral performance. They help to create that reservoir of meaning in the text which could certainly not be exhausted at first acquaintance but remains to be progressively tapped by attentive rereading and study. In the third section of the chapter we enter the sphere of hidden meaning which only assiduous study could be expected to uncover. Not that this is a question of an esoteric meaning distinct from the more accessible message of the book. The meaning concealed in the text by the literary technique discussed in this section is no different from, but reinforces the message that lies on the surface of the book.[3] Revelation is in no sense a sealed book (22:10), but its meticulous literary composition has given it an unusual depth and density of meaning which yields itself only to proper understanding of its literary character.

1. Structure

There have been many divergent attempts to discern the structure of Revelation by identifying its major divisions.[4] The difficulty that has been experienced in these attempts results partly from the fact, as Barr puts it, that 'whereas our concern is to divide the book, John's concern was to bind it together'.[5] As we shall see, John has taken considerable care to integrate the various parts of his work into a literary whole. But he has also indicated a clear structure of the kind that is necessary for

[3]For further discussion of this kind of hidden meaning in Revelation, see chapter 11 section 1 below.

[4]Significant discussions of the structure of Revelation include Farrer (1949) chapters 2-3; Vanni (1971); Yarbro Collins (1976) chapter 1; Strand (1976); Lambrecht (1980); Schüssler Fiorenza (1985) chapter 6; Mazzaferri (1989) 330-374.

[5]Barr (1984) 43.

hearers or readers to find their way through his vision. This structure is intimately connected with the meaning his work conveys, but we must expect it to be signalled by linguistic markers. John, it is important to remember, was writing in the first place for *hearers* (1:3), even though he must also have expected some readers who would study his work at leisure. In a text intended for oral performance[6] the structure must be indicated by clear linguistic markers.

Major divisions of the book

Revelation has a prologue (1:1-8) and an epilogue (22:6-21). The prologue contains an epistolary opening, marking Revelation as a letter (1:4-6),[7] and the epilogue ends with an epistolary conclusion (22:21). Both also contain prophetic oracles. That the epilogue begins at 22:6 is probably indicated by the strong verbal echoes of 1:1-3 in 22:6-7.

The whole of the book between prologue and epilogue is recounted as a single visionary experience which took place on Patmos on the Lord's Day (1:9). The technical phrase ἐγενόμην ἐν πνεύματι (1:10)[8] indicates the beginning of this whole visionary experience. The words ἐν πνεύματι recur three times later in the book (4:2; 17:3; 21:10), indicating three major transitions within the whole vision. At 4:2 there is the same phrase as in 1:10: ἐγενόμην ἐν πνεύματι, while in both 17:3 and 21:10 the phrase used is καὶ [ὁ ἄγγελος] ἀπήνεγκέν με ἐν πνεύματι.[9] The divisions thus indicated are as follows. At 1:9-10 begins John's inaugural vision of the risen Christ who gives the seven messages to the churches (2-3). At 4:1-2a John is taken up

---

[6]On the importance of this, see Barr (1986).

[7]On the genre of Revelation, see Bauckham (1993) chapter 1.

[8]On the phrase, see chapter 5 section 1 below.

[9]We should also notice that on all four occasions the phrase ἐν πνεύματι is in close proximity to the verb λαλέω (1:12; 4:1; 17:1; 21:9, 15). This seemingly ordinary word is reserved by John for special use with reference to *revelatory* speech (also used in 10:3, 4 [twice], 8; and for the satanic parody of revelation in 13:5, 11, 15), just as he reserves the verb δείκνυμι for visionary revelation (1:1; 4:1; 17:1; 21:9, 10; 22:1, 6, 8). The uses of neither verb have structural significance as such (*contra* Mazzaferri [1989] 297-299), but the occurrences of λαλέω in close proximity to ἐν πνεύματι reinforce the structural significance of the latter.

into heaven for a kind of second beginning of his visionary experience: an inaugural vision of heaven (4-5), from which develops the whole sequence of judgments down to the end of chapter 16. In 17:3 and 21:10 the corresponding phrases we have noticed belong to a broader linguistic parallelism between 17:1-3 and 21:9-10:

(17) ¹Καὶ ἦλθεν εἷς ἐκ τῶν ἑπτὰ ἀγγέλων τῶν ἐχόντων τὰς ἑπτὰ φιάλας, καὶ ἐλάλησεν μετ' ἐμοῦ λέγων, Δεῦρο, δείξω σοι... ³καὶ ἀπήνεγκέν με εἰς ἔρημον ἐν πνεύματι...

(21) ⁹Καὶ ἦλθεν εἷς ἐκ τῶν ἑπτὰ ἀγγέλων τῶν ἐχόντων τὰς ἑπτὰ φιάλας τῶν γεμόντων τῶν ἑπτὰ πληγῶν τῶν ἐσχατῶν, καὶ ἐλάλησεν μετ' ἐμοῦ λέγων, Δεῦρο, δείξω σοι... ¹⁰καὶ ἀπήνεγκέν με ἐν πνεύματι ἐπὶ ὄρος μέγα καὶ ὑψηλόν ...

These very clearly parallel openings of the two visions are matched by equally clearly parallel conclusions: 19:9b-10 and 22:6-9:

(19) ⁹... καὶ λέγει μοι, Οὗτοι οἱ λόγοι ἀληθινοὶ τοῦ θεοῦ εἰσιν. ¹⁰καὶ ἔπεσα ἔμπροσθεν τῶν ποδῶν αὐτοῦ προσκυνῆσαι αὐτῷ. καὶ λέγει μοι, "Ορα μή· σύνδουλός σού εἰμι καὶ τῶν ἀδελφῶν σου τῶν ἐχόντων τὴν μαρτυρίαν Ἰησοῦ· τῷ θεῷ προσκύνησον. . .

(22) ⁶Καὶ λέγει μοι, Οὗτοι οἱ λόγοι πιστοὶ καὶ ἀληθινοὶ... ⁸...ἔπεσα προσκυνῆσαι ἔμπροσθεν τῶν ποδῶν τοῦ ἀγγέλου τοῦ δεικνύοντός μοι ταῦτα. ⁹καὶ λέγει μοι,"Ορα μή· σύνδουλός σού εἰμι καὶ τῶν ἀδελφῶν σου τῶν προφητῶν καὶ τῶν τηρούντων τοὺς λόγους τοῦ βιβλίου τούτου· τῷ θεῷ προσκύνησον.

These structural markers delimiting two parallel sections — 17:1-19:10 and 21:9-22:9 — are so clear that it is astonishing that so many attempts to discern the structure of Revelation have ignored them. Moreover, the two sections are thematic parallels: they deal respectively with the two cities that John portrays as women. In 17:1-19:10 he sees the harlot of Babylon and her fall; in 21:9-22:9 he sees the bride of the Lamb, the New

Jerusalem, which comes down from heaven. Together these two sections form the climax towards which the whole book has aimed: the destruction of Babylon and her replacement by the New Jerusalem. The intimate connexion between the two parallel sections is further indicated by the announcement of the Lamb's marriage to his bride at the end of the rejoicing over the fall of Babylon (19:7-9a).[10]

That we have identified 22:6-9 both as the conclusion to the major section 21:9-22:9 and as the beginning of the epilogue is no problem. To insist on assigning these verses only to one or other of these sections, as most previous scholars have done,[11] is to misunderstand John's literary methods, among which are the overlapping and interweaving of the sections of his work. John has skilfully formed this section as both the conclusion to the vision of the New Jerusalem and the beginning of the epilogue. Those parts of 22:6-9 which are not verbally parallel to 19:9b-10 are verbally parallel to 1:1-3. Into the repeated incident of John's attempt to worship the angel John has woven allusions to the beginning of his whole work. The result is that, whereas in 19:9b-10 the true words of God to which the angel refers are the immediately preceding beatitude (19:9a), in 22:6-9 they are the words of the prophecy of the whole book of Revelation, as in 1:3, and the angel himself is revealed as the angel to whom 1:1 referred. Whereas no reader could expect the conclusion to the vision of the fall of Babylon to be the end of the whole prophecy, the conclusion to the vision of the New Jerusalem *must* be also the conclusion to the whole prophecy.

Between the two sections 17:1-19:10 and 21:9-22:9 comes a section which must be understood as a single section describing the transition from one to the other. It describes the events which intervene between the fall of Babylon and the descent of the New Jerusalem. Yarbro Collins' attempt[12] to divide this section into seven visions, each introduced by καὶ εἶδον, fails

---

[10]On the structural and thematic parallels between the two sections, see especially Giblin (1974).

[11]A notable exception is Giblin (1991) 214-217, though his explanation differs slightly from mine.

[12]Yarbro Collins (1976) 15-16, following Farrer (1949) 57.

because, although she explains the καὶ...εἶδον of 21:2 as not an instance of this introductory phrase, she completely ignores the καὶ εἶδον of 20:12, which clearly is such an instance. There are therefore, not counting 21:2, eight occurrences of this phrase in this section (19:11, 17, 19; 20:1, 4, 11, 12; 21:1), which would make eight, not seven, visions, if this phrase is intended to mark the division between distinct visions. In fact, these eight visions would be such an unsatisfactory way of dividing the section that it is not conceivable that John intended the formula καὶ εἶδον as a structural marker. In any case, when John intends a *number* of sections to have a structural significance he makes the enumeration explicit, as with the seven seals, the seven trumpets, the seven bowls, the three woes (8:13; 9:12; 11:14) and the three angels flying in midheaven (14:6-11). In a text intended for oral performance he had to do so.

So far we have identified as the major divisions of the book: (1) the inaugural vision of Christ, including the seven messages to the churches (1:9-3:22); (2) the inaugural vision of heaven (4-5) leading to the sequences of judgment (6-16); (3) Babylon the harlot (17:1-19:10); (4) the transition from Babylon to the New Jerusalem (19:11-21:8); (5) the New Jerusalem the Bride (21:9-22:9). We have noticed how the fifth of these sections overlaps the epilogue (22:6-21). We should also notice how John has forged literary links between the other sections. In 4:1 the voice which summons him to heaven is said to be the same voice he had heard at the outset of his whole visionary experience in 1:10-11, marking 4:1 as a transition within the single visionary experience introduced in 1:9-11. Another link between 1:9-3:22 and the chapters which follow is made by 3:21: 'To the one who conquers I will give a place with me on my throne, just as I myself conquered and sat down with my Father on his throne.' This is the last of seven promises made by Christ to 'the one who conquers' (cf. 2:7, 11, 17, 28; 3:5, 12), but whereas the others are framed in terms appropriate to the church addressed, this last promise seems to be placed last, not because of any special appropriateness to the church at Laodicea, but rather because it anticipates chapter 5. Christ's own 'conquest' and his consequent enthronement with his Father in heaven is what John sees announced and celebrated in chapter 5.

The sequence of judgments in chapters 6-16 reaches its climax and completion in the series of seven bowls of God's wrath poured out on the earth by the seven angels in chapter 16. It is one of these angels who is introduced as John's guide both at the beginning of the Babylon section (17:1) and at the beginning of the New Jerusalem section (21:9). In this way these two sections are tied into the sequence of judgments. They are the dual conclusion to which the whole process of judgment from chapter 6 onwards has been leading. But there is also another device which links these two sections with what precedes. The triumphant divine cry 'It is done!' (Γέγονεν Γέγοναν) is heard twice in the book, a few verses before the beginning of each of these sections (16:17; 21:6). In the first case it refers to the accomplishment of the judgment of evil, completed in the fall of Babylon; in the second place, it refers to the new creation, completed in the descent of the New Jerusalem from heaven. This creates a parallelism between the end of the sequence of judgments (chapters 6-16), which briefly describes the fall of Babylon, and the end of the section on the transition from Babylon to the New Jerusalem (19:11-21:8), which briefly describes the descent of the New Jerusalem. The two parallel sections on Babylon and the New Jerusalem (17:1-19:10; 21:9-22:9) then appropriately follow these two parallel conclusions.

The series of sevens

The section chapters 6-16 is the most structurally complex part of the book, but precisely for that reason John has made his structural markers prominent and emphatic. It is therefore important to base our understanding of the structure on these emphatic markers. Most obvious are the three series of sevens: the seven seal-openings, the seven trumpets, the seven bowls. (The seven thunders of 10:3-4 are a cancelled series of judgments[13] which do not therefore become a structural feature of the book.) Each series is explicitly numbered. Moreover, the seventh of each series is linked to the others and to the vision

---

[13]See chapter 9 section 3 below.

of the throne of God in chapter 4 by a literary device which is discussed in detail elsewhere in this volume.[14] It consists of a formula which is expanded on each occurrence, thus:

4:5:   ἀστραπαὶ καὶ φωναὶ καὶ βρονταί

8:5:   βρονταὶ   καὶ φωναὶ καὶ ἀστραπαὶ καὶ σεισμός

11:19   ἀστραπαὶ καὶ φωναὶ καὶ βρονταὶ   καὶ σεισμὸς καὶ χάλαζα μεγάλη

16:18-21: ἀστραπαὶ καὶ φωναὶ καὶ βρονται   καὶ σεισμὸς... μέγας καὶ χάλαζα μεγάλη

The formula, whose core is an allusion to the Sinai theophany (Exod 19:16; cf. Jub 2:2; LAB 11:4), is expanded by the addition of an extra item in 8:5 and 11:19, while in 16:18-21 the earthquake and hail are described at some length. In 4:5 the formula describes a theophany confined to heaven, which in the later instances becomes a theophany resulting in judgment on earth. Thus the formula serves to anchor the divine judgments of chapters 6-16 in the initial vision of God's rule in heaven in chapter 4. It also creates a particular kind of relationship between the three series of seven judgments. The judgment of the seventh seal-opening, the climax of the first series, described by this formula in 8:5, encompasses the whole course of the judgments of the seven trumpets, and similarly the judgment of the seventh trumpet, described by this formula in 11:19b, encompasses the whole series of bowl judgments, climaxing in the final, fullest elaboration of the formula in 16:18-21. Thus the formula indicates that it is the same final judgment which is reached in the seventh of each of the three series. With each of the first two sevenths we attain a preliminary glimpse of the final judgment, which the following series then approaches again from closer range, as it were. The expansion of the formula corresponds to the intensification of the judgments in each series.

   The precise way in which the three series of sevens are linked to each other differs. The seven seal-openings are linked to the seven trumpets by the technique of overlapping or

---

[14]See chapter 7 section 2 below.

interweaving.[15] When the Lamb opens the seventh seal in 8:1 there is silence for about half an hour. This is the silence in which God hears the prayers of the saints (8:3-4), to which his response is the judgment on the earth as described in 8:5.[16] But between the reference to the silence and the offering of the prayers of the saints, John introduces the seven angels with their trumpets (8:2), in preparation for 8:6.

In the case of the seven trumpets and the seven bowls, the seventh trumpet (11:15-19) is separated from the first appearance of the seven angels with the bowls (15:1) by chapters 12-14. The link is therefore forged by the fact that the first part of 11:19 ('God's temple in heaven was opened, and the ark of his covenant was seen within his temple') is echoed in 15:5-6 ('the temple of the tent of witness in heaven was opened, and out of the temple came the seven angels with the seven plagues'), which introduces the account of the seven bowls, while the second part of 11:19 is, as we have already seen, expanded in the account of the seventh bowl (16:17-21). Thus, despite the intervention of chapters 12-14, the whole sequence of bowls is clearly marked as a development of the seventh trumpet.

The three series of seven judgments are distinguished, by means of the structural markers John uses, from the seven messages to the churches (chapters 2-3). The churches are not numbered in sequence, only named. It is important that they are seven (1:11, 20), but the order in which they occur is determined by geography (the route John's messenger would follow, starting from Ephesus). Since they do not form in any other sense a sequence, it is not important that the hearer be made aware of the numerical progression: first, second, third, etc. In the case of the three series of judgments, however, this

---

[15]On this technique, which she calls 'interlocking', see Yarbro Collins (1976) 16-18. Schüssler Fiorenza's discussion of 'intercalation' ([1985] 172-173) confuses this technique, by which the end of one section is interlocked into the beginning of the next section, with the quite different technique of intercalation, in which a section is interrupted by the intercalation of a passage of different character (e.g. the intercalation of chapter 7 into the series of seven seal-openings).

[16]See chapter 2 section 4 below.

is important, because these are sequences progressing towards the final judgment in the seventh of each series. Therefore not only is the number of each series stated before it begins, with an emphasis that increases with each of the three series (5:1, 5; 8:2, 6; 15:1, 6-16:1), but also the numerical sequence in each series is carefully stated by means of a standard formula for each series (seals: 6:1, 3, 5, 7, 9, 12; 8:1; trumpets: 8:7, 8, 10, 12; 9:1, 13; 11:15; bowls: 16:2, 3, 4, 8, 10, 12, 17).

Another difference between the seven messages as a group and the three series of seven judgments is that, whereas in all three series of seven judgments there is a 4 + 3 structure which we shall examine shortly, the series of seven messages to the churches has a 3 + 4 structure. The latter appears in the fact that at the conclusions to the messages, in the first three the refrain 'Let anyone who has an ear listen to what the Spirit is saying to the churches' (2:7a, 11a, 17a) precedes the promise to the one who conquers (2:7b, 11b, 17b), whereas in the last four the refrain (2:29; 3:6, 13, 22) follows the promise to the one who conquers (2:26-28; 3:5, 12, 21).[17] This clear structural difference between the first three and the last four messages is ignored by Farrer in his unconvincing attempt to find subtler indications of a 4 + 3 structure in the seven messages.[18] Since it is difficult to discern any reason within the messages for this distinction between the first three and the last four churches, it may be that the intention is simply to distinguish this series of seven as different in kind from the three series of seven judgments. Consequently, we should not attach any structural significance to the fact that there are *four* series of sevens in Revelation, or attempt to find correlations between the seven messages and the three series of seven judgments.[19] The set of seven messages is in a different category from the three series of judgments.

The three series of seven judgments have a 4 + 3 structure, but this is much more pronounced in the case of the first two

[17]For the internal structure of the seven messages, see Aune (1983) 275-278; (1990).

[18]Farrer (1964) 70-83.

[19]As Farrer (1964) 83-86; Sweet (1979) 44-45, do.

series (the seal-openings and the trumpets), which are also distinguished from the third (the bowls) in having an intercalated passage between the sixth and seventh judgments, so that their structure could be described as 4 + (2 + intercalation + 1). In the case of the seal-openings (6:1-8:5), a closely similar wording introduces each of the first four judgments, whose content is in each case a horse and its rider (6:1-8). No hearer would be in doubt that these four form a set, whereas the longer accounts of the fifth, sixth and seventh seal-openings have only a slightly varying, much shorter introductory formula in common with the first four and with each other (6:9, 12; 8:1). The intercalation between the sixth and seventh seal-openings is chapter 7. Although it interrupts the series, it is closely linked to the sixth seal-opening, because it answers (especially in 7:9) the question at the end of 6:17, which thus proves not to be merely rhetorical.[20]

In the case of the trumpets (8:2, 6-11:19), the first four do form an obvious group, but more emphasis is placed on the last three as a group. This is done by the introduction, between the fourth and fifth trumpets, of the vision of the eagle proclaiming a threefold 'Woe' on the inhabitants of the earth (8:13). Although it has occasionally been questioned whether the third woe is the seventh trumpet, 8:13 in fact leaves no doubt that the three woes are identical with the judgments that occur at the blast of the three last trumpets. The woes, with the emphatic formulae in 9:12 and 11:14 signalling their sequence, provide an additional method, alongside the numbering of the trumpets, of keeping the hearer aware of the sequence of the fifth, sixth and seventh trumpet judgments. One might wonder why such emphasis is necessary. The reason must be partly that this sequence leading to the final judgment, as both the seventh trumpet and the third woe, is peculiarly important for John's purpose in these chapters (cf. 10:6-7). But the enumeration of the woes, by indicating the end of the second

---

[20]It is also linked to the fifth seal-opening by the themes of the number of the elect (6:11; 7:4-9), their white robes (6:11; 7:9, 13-14) and their death (6:9, 11; 7:13).

woe (11:14), also helps to keep the long intercalation (10:1-11:13) in its proper place in the sequence. It is to be connected with the sixth trumpet rather than the seventh, since its significance is to be understood in terms of its connexion with the passage it immediately follows (9:20-21), recording the failure of the judgment of the sixth trumpet to evoke repentance. The repentance which has not occurred in 9:20-21 does occur, as a result of the events of the intercalation, in 11:13.[21] The formula signalling the sequence of the woes in 11:14 then indicates that the period in which there is opportunity for repentance is rapidly coming to an end as the third and last woe, the final judgment, approaches 'soon'. The words ἔρχεται ταχύ here clearly recall Christ's declaration of his imminent coming to judgment: ἔρχομαι ταχύ (2:16; 3:11; 22:6, 12, 20), which in 2:16 had been linked with the need for repentance before he comes.

The two intercalations between the sixth and seventh seal-openings (7:1-17) and between the sixth and seventh trumpets (10:1-11:13) have no literary links between them, but are clearly placed in parallel by the structure of the two series and the way in which each deals with the issue raised at the end of the account of the sixth judgment in each series (6:17; 9:20-21). These lengthy interruptions in the sequence of judgments *delay* the final, seventh judgment, and such delay would be particularly felt in oral performance. They serve to incorporate the issue of the delay of judgment into the structure of the book. This is also why the first four judgments and the last three are sharply distinguished in the series of seals and the series of trumpets. In each case, the first four judgments follow each other rapidly and in a literary pattern which makes the sequence seem smooth and inevitable. Thereafter the sequence becomes more problematic. The fifth seal explicitly raises the issue of delay (6:10); the sixth seal, with its imagery of final judgment and its assertion that the great day of God's wrath has come (6:17), seems to bring us to the very brink of the final judgment; but the sequence is then interrupted by a passage which

---

[21]See chapter 9 section 5 below.

announces delay (7:3). In the trumpet series, the issue of delay is again explicitly raised within the intercalation (10:3-7). As well as symbolizing the delay of judgment, the two intercalations are distinguished from the series of judgments themselves in being concerned with the people of God. In the first intercalation (7:1-17), the delay is for the sake of protecting the people of God from the judgments, so that they may triumph in heaven, while in the second intercalation (10:1-11:13) the delay is for the sake of the prophetic witness of the people of God. The relationship between the first two series of judgments and the two intercalations is the structural means by which John is able to relate the story of God's judgment on an unbelieving world to the story of God's people in an unbelieving world and their witness to that world.

Before leaving the two intercalations, we should note that John creates literary links between each and the vision of the victorious Lamb in chapter 5. I have argued elsewhere that the vision of the victory of the Lamb's followers in 7:4-14 is constructed deliberately in parallel to the vision of the victorious Lamb in 5:5-14.[22] In the case of the second intercalation, the literary link is more obvious: it is by comparison with the ἄγγελον ἰσχυρόν of 5:2 that the angel of 10:1 is ἄλλον ἄγγελον ἰσχυρόν. The open scroll which he holds (10:2) must therefore have some connexion with the sealed scroll about whose opening the angel of 5:2 asks. Moreover, the passage in which John then eats the scroll (10:8-10) is modelled on Ezekiel 3:1-2, the second part of an account, the first part of which (Ezek 2:9-10) formed the Old Testament basis for the description of the scroll in 5:1. Although almost all commentators have thought the two scrolls different, it will be argued at length later in this volume that they are in fact the same.[23] The scroll which has been opened by the Lamb through the opening of the seven seals (6:1, 3, 5, 7, 9, 12; 8:1) is then brought down from heaven by the angel for John to consume, so that he may reveal its contents as prophecy (10:11). He does so initially in 11:1-13, more fully from chapter 12 onwards.

[22]See chapter 8 section 3 below.
[23]See chapter 9 section 2 below.

Thus John has very skilfully linked all parts of chapters 6-11 into the vision of heaven in chapters 4-5. The two series of sevens — the seal-openings and the trumpets — develop sequentially out of the vision of the Lamb and the scroll in chapter 5: the Lamb opens each of the seven seals of that scroll, and the seventh seal-opening entails the following sequence of trumpet-blasts. Moreover, both series at their climactic conclusions (8:5; 11:19) are linked back to the vision of the divine throne in chapter 4 (4:5). But the two intercalations within the two series (7:1-17; 10:1-11:13) also have their own literary links with chapter 5. In particular, the second intercalation turns out to contain the event to which chapter 5 looks forward: the revelation of the contents of the scroll.[24]

In the third series of judgments, the bowls, there is no intercalation. There is, it is true, a brief interruption within (not after) the account of the sixth bowl: a prophetic oracle in which Christ addresses his people (16:15). In being concerned with the people of God this has a somewhat comparable role to the intercalations in the first two series of judgments. But it does not signal a delay. Quite the opposite: it emphasizes the suddenness of the Lord's final coming to judgment. It therefore points up the fact that there is *not* in this series of judgments the intercalation which the first two series might have led us to expect. This series moves with unimpeded rapidity to the seventh and final judgment. Humanity's failure to repent, which is noticed in connexion with the fourth and fifth bowls (16:9, 11) as it was in connexion with the sixth trumpet (9:20-21), now raises no question of delay. The time for repentance is past (cf. 10:6-7). The structural difference makes it clear that this third series of judgments is the final series.

Without an intercalation, the 4 + 3 structure in this series becomes much less marked and important. But it can still be discerned, in that the first four judgments apply to the same four divisions of creation (earth, sea, fresh waters, heavens) as the first four trumpets did, whereas the last three bowls are

---

[24]For further discussion of the structure and significance of 10:1-11:13, see chapter 9 sections 3-5 below.

concerned with the judgment specifically of the beast and his city. This fourfold division of creation (different from the fourfold division used in 5:13) is significant because it occurs also in 14:7. The angel there calls on all people to 'worship him who made heaven and earth, the sea and the springs of water.' In the judgments of the first four bowls, the worshippers of the beast are shown the evidence that God the Creator, not the beast, is God. Thus the 4 + 3 structure retains some significance in the series of seven bowls, but in order that it may not suggest a break in the continuous series of seven judgments precisely the fourth and fifth judgments are given a striking degree of literary parallelism (16:9, 11).

Chapters 12-14
Most attempts to discern the structure of Revelation have found it particularly difficult to see how chapters 12-14 fit into the overall structure. The beginning of chapter 12 seems an uncharacteristically abrupt fresh start, devoid of literary links with anything that precedes. The formula used in 12:1 and 12:3 (καὶ σημεῖον μέγα ὤφθη ἐν τῷ οὐρανῷ...καὶ ὤφθη ἄλλο σημεῖον ἐν τῷ οὐρανῷ ...) is a quite fresh introductory formula, unlike any John has used before, and the two protagonists it introduces, the woman and the dragon, have not been mentioned in the book hitherto. Chapter 12 cannot be read as a continuation of the account of the seventh trumpet (11:15-19) because we know that the imagery of 11:19b describes the final judgment and concluded the account of the seventh seal in 8:1-5. There are not even the kinds of literary links backwards to preceding sections of the book which John provides elsewhere at major transitions which might otherwise seem like entirely fresh beginnings (4:1; 17:1; 21:9). It seems we must accept that the abrupt transition is intentional. John has made it abrupt precisely in order to create the impression of a fresh start.

The fresh start is required because the narrative of the woman and the dragon begins chronologically earlier than any previous part of his visionary narrative. It recalls the enmity between the woman and the serpent (Gen 3:15) and portrays the people of God (Israel) as mother of the Messiah. The story

of the conflict between the dragon and the woman leads into
an account of the contemporary conflict between the people
of God (the church) and the enemies of God. This account
ends with the vision of the conquerors of the beast triumphant
in heaven (15:2-4), which is the upshot of the confrontation
between the beast (chapter 13) and the followers of the Lamb
(14:1-5). But if John has not integrated this section into the rest
of his book at the beginning of the section, he has done so at
its end. He links it to the account of the seven bowls which
follows by the same technique of overlapping or interweaving
as he had used to link the series of seal judgments to the series
of trumpet judgments. The vision of the people of God
triumphant over the beast in heaven (15:2-4) is sandwiched
between the introduction of the seven angels with the seven
last plagues (15:1) and the account of their preparation for
pouring out the bowls on the earth (15:5-8). Moreover, the
seven angels are introduced by a variation of the formula which
has previously been used only to introduce the dragon and the
woman at the beginning of chapter 12: καὶ εἶδον ἄλλο σημεῖον
ἐν τῷ οὐρανῷ μέγα καὶ θαυμαστόν (15:1). This clearly makes
the series of seven bowls a continuation of the narrative begun
at the beginning of chapter 12. We have already noticed how
15:5 echoes 11:19a and 16:17-20 expands 11:19b, making the
seven bowls a fuller version of the seventh trumpet. This means
that chapter 15 is the point where the narrative begun in
chapter 12 with the dragon's threat to the pregnant woman
converges with the narrative begun in chapter 5 with the Lamb
receiving the scroll in order to open it. Both narratives reach
a provisional conclusion in the sequence of seven bowls
(pending a further conclusion in 19:11-21:8). The convergence
of the two narratives is shown by the fact that the seven bowls,
a sequence of judgments which continues and completes the
two previous sequences of seven judgments, refers, as the
previous sequences had not, to the forces of opposition to God
in the terms which have been introduced in chapters 12-14:
those who had the mark of the beast and worshipped its image
(16:2), the throne and the kingdom of the beast (16:10), the
dragon, the beast and the false prophet (16:13), Babylon the
great (16:19).

The main function of chapters 12-15 is to deal much more fully with the subject that was adumbrated in the two intercalations (7:1-17; 10:1-11:13): the people of God in their conflict with the forces opposed to God. The links with the two intercalations are thematic rather than structural, but it is worth noting the most important: the 144,000 (7:4) reappear in 14:1, the apocalyptic period of the church's suffering and witness (11:2-3) reappears in 12:6, 14; 13:5, the beast who appears very enigmatically in 11:7 is properly introduced in chapter 13, where he makes war on the saints and conquers them (13:7) as he had already in 11:7.

As with the passage 19:11-21:8, Yarbro Collins sees 12:1-15:4 as an unnumbered series of seven visions,[25] but again this is not very satisfactory. She understands the terms ὤφθη (12:1, 3) and καὶ εἶδον (13:1, 11, 14:1, 6, 14; 15:1, 2) as introductory indications of a new vision. This would appear to divide the section into nine visions, but she rightly observes that in 12:1, 3 the repeated ὤφθη does not introduce two distinct visions, but two major figures in a single vision. She also discounts 15:1, as introducing, not a vision in this series, but the sequence of the seven bowls, with which this unnumbered series of visions is interlocked by the occurrence of its seventh vision (15:2-4) between the introduction to the seven bowls (15:1) and its continuation (15:5). She is correct, as we have already seen, in recognizing the overlap at this point, but she ignores the fact that 15:1 (καὶ εἶδον ἄλλο σημεῖον ἐν τῷ οὐρανῷ μέγα καὶ θαυμαστόν) echoes the terminology of 12:1 (καὶ σημεῖον μέγα ὤφθη ἐν τῷ οὐρανῷ) and 12:3 (καὶ ὤφθη ἄλλο σημεῖον ἐν τῷ οὐρανῷ), thus integrating the bowls sequence into the series of visions begun in chapter 12. It seems unlikely that John is counting visions here, and even if he were, the number would not be of major structural significance, since in oral performance hearers would not be counting a series of visions of this kind. By contrast, explicit numbering is used in 14:8, 9, to enable hearers to perceive the three angels (14:6-11) and their messages as a group.

[25]Yarbro Collins (1976) 14, following Farrer (1949) 47-49.

What would probably be more significant in enabling hearers to perceive major transitions in the passage 12:1-15:4 would be not simply the use of καὶ εἶδον, but the use of καὶ εἶδον along with a reference to *place*. Thus the passage starts with two portents *in heaven*, introducing a narrative in which movement from heaven to earth and to the wilderness is very explicit (chapter 12). Then the occurrences of καὶ εἶδον are combined with indications of place thus: from the sea (13:10), from the earth (13:1), on mount Zion (14:1), in mid-heaven (14:6), on a white cloud (14:4), in heaven (15:1), on the sea of glass (15:2).

From the parousia to the new creation

We need now to return to the passage 19:11-21:8, which we identified as demarcated by the parallel visions of Babylon (17:1-19:10) and the new Jerusalem (21:9-22:9). We observed how the end of this passage, by its reference to the new Jerusalem (21:2) and the divine saying 'It is done!' (21:6), forms a parallel to the end of chapter 16, with its reference to Babylon (16:19) and the divine saying 'It is done!' (16:17). This gives the end of the section 19:11-21:8 an important structural relation to what follows. But we have not yet accounted for the way the passage begins.

At first sight it might seem that the beginning is as abrupt, as unconnected with anything that precedes, as the beginning of chapter 12. There may perhaps be an intended parallel with 4:1: in 4:1 a door in heaven is open so that John may ascend; in 19:11 heaven is open so that the divine Warrior may ride out to battle. The parallel would be apt, in that 19:11 marks the end of the visions and auditions of events in heaven which have been so prominent a part of the whole narrative from 4:1 to 19:10. After 19:11 nothing is seen or heard of anything that happens in heaven. Henceforth all the action takes place on earth, as it did before 4:1. But this parallel would only mark 19:11 as an abrupt transition, without as yet integrating the new section into anything that precedes, in the way that 4:1 continues by referring back to 1:10 and thereby establishing a link across the transition.

In fact, the peculiarity of 19:11-21:8 is not that it begins completely afresh, as 12-15 does, but that it very quickly acquires links not just to one but to several previous passages. John has skilfully placed his vision of the parousia so that it does not appear continuous with the preceding narrative — it is the point at which the divine no longer acts from heaven but breaks into the world — but does appear as the climax toward which the whole of what precedes has pointed. To this end he has planted in the preceding chapters a series of pointers to which the vision of the parousia now refers back. The most important are:

(a) 6:15: The list of those who hide from judgment because the great day of the wrath of God and the Lamb has come (6:17) is reproduced (with some variation characteristic of the way Revelation varies repeated phrases) as the list of those whose flesh the birds are to eat when they have been slain in the battle (19:18). The judgment they anticipate in 6:17 is at last described in 19:11-21.

(b) 12:5: The child who is to rule all nations with a rod of iron (ποιμαίνειν πάντα τὰ ἔθνη ἐν ῥαβδῷ σιδερᾷ) was snatched up to God. He returns to do just that (19:15: ποιμαινεῖ αὐτοὺς [τὰ ἔθνη] ἐν ῥαβδῷ σιδερᾷ).

(c) 14:20: In the two parallel visions of the judgment as a corn harvest and a vintage (14:14-20), the harvest is carried out by 'one like a son of man' (14:14), who is certainly Christ (cf. 1:13, and the allusion in both passages to Dan 7:13),[26] but the vintage seems incongruously to be only the responsibility of angels. But this is because, whereas the gathering of the grapes into the wine press is carried out by an angel (14:18-19), the subject of the crucial action of the treading of the winepress is not stated (14:20). The passive ἐπατήθη ('was trodden') serves as a divine passive, alluding to Isaiah 63:3, but also prepares for the revelation of the one who will tread the winepress in 19:15. Moreover, the horses of 14:20 — for the horses' bridles (τῶν χαλινῶν τῶν ἵππων) are not simply an abstract measure of height (NRSV wrongly: 'as high as a horse's bridle'), but the actual cavalry horses in a battle ('as high as the horses' bridles')[27] — appear in 19:18.

---

[26]See chapter 9 section 6 below.
[27]See chapter 2 section 1 below.

(d) 16:14, 16: The demonic spirits 'gather [the kings] for the battle of the great day of God the Almighty' (16:14: συναγαγεῖν αὐτοὺς εἰς τὸν πόλεμον τῆς ἡμέρας τῆς μεγάλης τοῦ θεοῦ τοῦ παντοκράτορος; cf. 16:16: συνήγαγεν). The precise divine title 'God the Almighty' occurs in Revelation only here and in 19:15, while the gathering of the kings (which alludes to Ps 2:2) is clearly echoed in 19:19:συνηγμένα ποιῆσαι τὸν πόλεμον.

(e) 17:14: The Lamb's title, as conqueror of the beast and the kings, reappears in 19:16 (with a verbal variation characteristic of Revelation) and his followers reappear as the armies of heaven in 19:14.

All these passages have raised expectations which are met in the vision of the parousia. It is, incidentally, this kind of skilful crossreferencing between the various parts of the book (of which there are many other examples) that makes the literary unity of Revelation certain. We may also note that the description of Christ in 19:11-16 contains several allusions back to the vision of Christ in chapter 1 and the descriptions of him in the messages to the churches (faithful and true: 3:14; eyes like a flame of fire: 1:14; 2:18; sharp sword from his mouth: 1:16; 2:12, 16; to rule the nations with a rod of iron: 2:26-27).

We may note two other ways in which the section 19:11-20: 15 is integrated into the structure of the book. In the first place, the principal enemies of God and his people make their first appearance in the book in this order:

Death and Hades (6:8)
the dragon (12)
the beast and the false prophet (13)
Babylon (17)

(The anticipatory reference to the beast in 11:7 can be discounted, as should probably also be the anticipatory references to Babylon in 14:8 and 16:9.) The order in which their destruction occurs is the reverse, creating a chiastic arrangement:

Babylon (18)
the beast and the false prophet (19:20)
the dragon (20:1-10)
Death and Hades (20:14).

Secondly, the song of the twenty-four elders in 11:18 proclaims that with the blast of the seventh trumpet the time has arrived 'for judging the dead, for rewarding your servants ... , and for destroying those who destroy the earth.' This programme is also carried out roughly in reverse order. The destruction of the destroyers of the earth begins in chapter 16 and is continued in 19:11-21; 20:7-10. The rewarding of the servants of God is the function of the millennium (20:4-6). The judgment of the dead takes place in 20:11-15. Thus the judgment announced by the seventh trumpet actually extends to the end of chapter 20.

Summary

We have been concerned in this section only with the macro-structure of Revelation. Of course, the various sections of the book which we have delineated also have their own internal structure, to which we have referred only when it has significance for the interrelation of these major sections.[28]

The subtleties of the structure of Revelation, with its complex interlinking of the major sections of the book, make it virtually impossible adequately to represent the structure in a diagram. The following is no more than a simplified division of Revelation into the sections established by the preceding discussion:

1:1-8	Prologue
1:9-3:22	Inaugural vision of Christ and the churches including seven messages to the churches
4:1-5:14	Inaugural vision of heaven leading to three series of sevens and two intercalations:
6:1-8:1; 8:3-5	Seven seals, numbered 4 + 1 + (1 + intercalation) + 1
8:2; 8:6-11:19	Seven trumpets, numbered 4 + 1 + (1 + intercalation) + 1

---

[28]For an analysis of the structure of the section 17:1-19:10, see chapter 10 section 1 below. Giblin (1991) gives a good deal of attention to the structure of specific sections of Revelation. See also n.17 above.

2. Repetition and variation of phrases

A remarkable feature of the composition of Revelation is the way in which very many phrases occur two or three times in the book, often in widely separated passages, and usually in slightly varying form. These repetitions create a complex network of textual cross-reference, which helps to create and expand the meaning of any one passage by giving it specific relationships to many other passages.[29] We are dealing here not with the writing habit of an author who saved effort by using phrases more than once, but with a skilfully deployed compositional device. One reason we can be sure of this is that such phrases almost never recur in precisely the same form. The author seems to have taken deliberate care to avoid the obviousness of precise repetition, while at the same time creating phrases which closely allude to each other.

The phenomenon we are considering must be distinguished from cases of repetition (many of them noticed in section 1 above) which serve as structural markers, highlighting sequential or parallel passages. For example, the formulaic introductions to each of the seven messages (2:1, 8, 12, 18; 3:1, 7, 14) are unvarying, as is the refrain which calls attention to what the Spirit says (2:7, 11, 17, 29; 3:6, 13, 22). (But it is

[29]Speaking rather more generally (not just of this literary technique), Mealy (1989) 5, refers to 'the extensive network of cross-references and allusions which affect the interpretation of virtually every passage in Revelation.'

noteworthy that when the first part of this refrain occurs again, *without structural significance*, in 13:9, its form varies.) In section 1 we noted the precise verbal correspondence between 17:1 and 21:9, marking clearly the beginnings of the two parallel visions of Babylon and the New Jerusalem. The sequence of each of the series of seven judgments (seal-openings, trumpets, bowls) is marked by formulae which show some variation but also much precise repetition. The precise verbal agreement between 1:1 and 22:6 (δεῖξαι τοῖς δούλοις αὐτοῦ ἅ δεῖ γενέσθαι ἐν τάχει) probably also has a structural significance, marking the beginnings of the prologue and the epilogue. For structural markers to be effective in oral performance they needed to employ such precise verbal repetition.[30]

However, such precise verbal repetition is virtually limited to structural markers. If we leave aside divine designations (such as κύριος ὁ θεὸς ὁ παντοκράτωρ) and short phrases which recur often (such as οἱ βασιλεῖς τῆς γῆς) there are exceedingly few phrases which recur without any variation whatever. Since it is difficult to find a special reason for the very few that do, they are probably accidental exceptions to John's deliberate practice of varying such phrases. Such exceptions are

1:14-15:   οἱ ὀφθαλμοὶ αὐτοῦ ὡς φλὸξ πυρός, καὶ οἱ πόδες αὐτοῦ ὅμοιοι χαλκολιβάνῳ
2:18:   τοὺς ὀφθαλμοὺς αὐτοῦ ὡς φλόγα πυρός, καὶ οἱ πόδες αὐτοῦ ὅμοιοι χαλκολιβάνῳ

22:7 = 22:10 = 22:18: τοὺς λόγους τῆς προφητείας τοῦ βιβλίου τούτου

14:8 = 18:2: ἔπεσεν ἔπεσεν Βαβυλὼν ἡ μεγάλη

1:15   ὡς φωνὴ ὑδάτων πολλῶν
14:2:   ὡς φωνὴν ὑδάτων πολλῶν
19:6:   ὡς φωνὴν ὑδάτων πολλῶν

---

[30]Note also the skilful balance of repetition and variation in the parallel accounts of the three groups of mourners for Babylon: (1) 18:9-10; (2) 18:11, 15-16; (3) 18:17b-19.

Even in these examples, the extremely formulaic nature of the words in 14:8; 18:2 (echoing Isa 21:9) may explain the precise repetition. Although the quoted phrase in 1:15; 14:2; 19:6 is identical, it is notable that the latter two verses continue with a similar but not identical phrase:

14:2:   ὡς φωνὴν ὑδάτων πολλῶν καὶ ὡς φωνὴν βροντῆς μεγάλης

19:6:   ὡς φωνὴν ὑδάτων πολλῶν καὶ ὡς φωνὴν βροντῶν ἰσχυρῶν

It looks as though John concentrated on securing the variation between these two passages and neglected the parallel with 1:15.

In any case, such precise repetitions are very rare, while repetition with variation is normal. In some cases, only the word order varies:

2:14:   φαγεῖν εἰδωλόθυτα καὶ πορνεῦσαι

2:20:   πορνεῦσαι καὶ φαγεῖν εἰδωλόθυτα

1:9:   διὰ τὸν λόγον τοῦ θεοῦ καὶ διὰ τὴν μαρτυρίαν Ἰησοῦ

20:4:   διὰ τὴν μαρτυρίαν Ἰησοῦ καὶ διὰ τὸν λόγον τοῦ θεοῦ[31]

4:8:   καὶ ἀνάπαυσιν οὐκ ἔχουσιν ἡμέρας καὶ νυκτός

14:11: καὶ οὐκ ἔχουσιν ἀνάπαυσιν ἡμέρας καὶ νυκτός

12:3:   ἔχων κεφαλὰς ἑπτὰ καὶ κέρατα δέκα

13:1:   ἔχον κέρατα δέκα καὶ κεφαλὰς ἑπτά[32]

16:6:   αἷμα ἁγίων καὶ προφητῶν

18:24: αἷμα προφητῶν καὶ ἁγίων

6:11:   χρόνον μικρόν

20:3:   μικρὸν χρόνον

---

[31]Cf. also 6:9.
[32]Cf. also 17:3, 7.

Sometimes one word differs:

14:8: ἐκ τοῦ οἴνου τοῦ θυμοῦ τῆς πορνείας αὐτῆς πεπότικεν πάντα τὰ ἔθνη

18:3: ἐκ τοῦ οἴνου τοῦ θυμοῦ τῆς πορνείας αὐτῆς πέπωκαν πάντα τὰ ἔθνη

7:17: καὶ ἐξαλείψει ὁ θεὸς πᾶν δάκρυον ἐκ τῶν ὀφθαλμῶν αὐτῶν

21:4: καὶ ἐξαλείψει πᾶν δάκρυον ἐκ τῶν ὀφθαλμῶν αὐτῶν

But there are many other forms of variation. For example:

17:14: κύριος κυρίων ἐστὶν καὶ βασιλεὺς βασιλέων

19:16: βασιλεὺς βασιλέων καὶ κύριος κυρίων

12:9: ὁ δράκων ὁ μέγας, ὁ ὄφις ὁ ἀρχαῖος, ὁ καλούμενος διάβολος καὶ ὁ Σατανᾶς

20:2: τὸν δράκοντα, ὁ ὄφις ὁ ἀρχαῖος, ὅς ἐστιν διάβολος καὶ ὁ Σατανᾶς

2:9: ἐκ τῶν λεγόντων Ἰουδαίους εἶναι ἑαυτούς, καὶ οὐκ εἰσὶν ἀλλὰ συναγωγὴ τοῦ Σατανᾶ

3:9: ἐκ τῆς συναγωγῆς τοῦ Σατανᾶ, τῶν λεγόντων ἑαυτούς Ἰουδαίους εἶναι και οὐκ εἰσὶν ἀλλὰ ψεύδονται

14:11: καὶ ὁ καπνὸς τοῦ βασανισμοῦ αὐτῶν εἰς αἰῶνας αἰώνων ἀναβαίνει

19:3: καὶ ὁ καπνὸς αὐτῆς ἀναβαίνει εἰς τοὺς αἰῶνας τῶν αἰώνων

13:10: ὧδέ ἐστιν ἡ ὑπομονὴ καὶ πίστις τῶν ἁγίων

14:12: ὧδε ἡ ὑπομονὴ τῶν ἁγίων ἐστίν

13:8: οἱ κατοικοῦντες ἐπὶ τῆς γῆς, οὗ οὐ γέγραπται τὸ ὄνομα αὐτοῦ ἐν τῷ βιβλίῳ τῆς ζωῆς τοῦ ἀρνίου τοῦ ἐσφαγμένου ἀπὸ καταβολῆς κόσμου

26   *The Climax of Prophecy*

17:8: οἱ κατοικοῦντες ἐπὶ τῆς γῆς, ὧν οὐ γέγραπται τὸ ὄνομα ἐπὶ τὸ βιβλίον τῆς ζωῆς ἀπὸ καταβολῆς κόσμου

1:14: οἱ ὀφθαλμοὶ αὐτοῦ ὡς φλὸξ πυρός
2:18: τοὺς ὀφθαλμοὺς αὐτοῦ ὡς φλόγα πυρός
19:15: οἱ δὲ ὀφθαλμοὶ αὐτοῦ φλὸξ[33] πυρός

1:16: καὶ ἐκ τοῦ στόματος αὐτοῦ ῥομφαία δίστομος ὀξεῖα ἐκπορευομένη[34]
19:15: καὶ ἐκ τοῦ στόματος αὐτοῦ ἐκπορεύεται ῥομφαία ὀξεῖα

3:12: τῆς πόλεως τοῦ θεοῦ μου, τῆς καινῆς Ιερουσαλημ ἡ καταβαίνουσα ἐκ τοῦ οὐρανοῦ ἀπὸ τοῦ θεοῦ μου
21:2: τὴν πόλιν τὴν ἁγίαν Ιερουσαλημ καινὴν εἶδον καταβαίνουσαν ἐκ τοῦ οὐρανοῦ ἀπὸ τοῦ θεοῦ
21:10: τὴν πόλιν τὴν ἁγίαν Ιερουσαλημ καταβαίνουσαν ἐκ τοῦ οὐρανοῦ ἀπὸ τοῦ θεοῦ

13:18: ὧδε ἡ σοφία ἐστίν. ὁ ἔχων νοῦν ...
17:9: ὧδε ὁ νοῦς ὁ ἔχων σοφίαν[35]

12:17: τῶν τηρούντων τὰς ἐντολὰς τοῦ θεοῦ καὶ ἐχόντων τὴν μαρτυρίαν Ἰησοῦ
14:12: οἱ τηροῦντες τὰς ἐντολὰς τοῦ θεοῦ καὶ τὴν πίστιν Ἰησοῦ

1:6: καὶ ἐποίησεν ἡμᾶς βασιλείαν, ἱερεῖς τῷ θεῷ καὶ πατρὶ αὐτοῦ
5:10: καὶ ἐποίησας αὐτοὺς τῷ θεῷ ἡμῶν βασιλείαν καὶ ἱερεῖς

[33]A few manuscripts have ὡς φλόξ, but our evidence of John's stylistic technique of varying phrases strengthens the case for regarding this reading as assimilation to 1:15.

[34]Cf. also 2:12.

[35]These passages are discussed in chapter 11 section 1 below.

19:20: εἰς τὴν λίμνην τοῦ πυρὸς τῆς καιομένης ἐν θείῳ
20:10: εἰς τὴν λίμνην τοῦ πυρὸς καὶ θείου
21:8:   ἐν τῇ λίμνῃ τῇ καιομένῃ πυρὶ καὶ θείῳ

14:11: οἱ προσκυνοῦντες τὸ θηρίον καὶ τὴν εἰκόνα
        αὐτοῦ, καί εἴ τις λαμβάνει τὸ χάραγμα τοῦ
        ὀνόματος αὐτοῦ
19:20: τοὺς λαβόντας τὸ χάραγμα τοῦ θηρίου καὶ τοὺς
        προσκυνοῦντας τῇ εἰκόνι αὐτοῦ

17:4:   περιβεβλημένη πορφυροῦν καὶ κόκκινον, καὶ
        κεχρυσωμένη χρυσίῳ καὶ λιθῳ τιμίῳ καὶ μαργαρίταις
18:16: περιβεβλημένη βύσσινον καὶ πορφυροῦν καὶ
        κόκκινον, καὶ κεχρυσωμένη ἐν χρυσίῳ και λιθῳ
        τιμίῳ καὶ μαργαρίτῃ³⁶

22:7 = 22:10 = 22:18: τοὺς λόγους τῆς προφητείας τοῦ
        βιβλίου τούτου
22:19: τῶν λόγων τοῦ βιβλίου τῆς προφητείας ταύτης

1:13:   περιεζωσμένον πρὸς τοῖς μαστοῖς ζώνην χρυσᾶν
15:6:   περιεζωσμένοι περὶ τὰ στήθη ζώνας χρυσᾶς

Doubtless many other examples could be found. Perhaps the most remarkable is the following phrase (which will be discussed in detail in chapter 9 section 10 below), which occurs seven times, never in the same form twice:

5:10:   φυλῆς καὶ γλώσσης καὶ λαοῦ καὶ ἔθνους
7:9:   ἔθνους καὶ φυλῶν καὶ λαῶν καὶ γλωσσῶν
10:11: λαοῖς καὶ ἔθνεσιν καὶ γλώσσαις καὶ βασιλεῦσιν
11:9:   λαῶν καὶ φυλῶν καὶ γλωσσῶν καὶ ἐθνῶν
13:7:   φυλὴν καὶ λαὸν καὶ γλῶσσαν καὶ ἔθνος
14:6:   ἔθνος καὶ φυλὴν καὶ γλῶσσαν καὶ λαὸν
17:15: λαοὶ καὶ ὄχλοι εἰσὶν καὶ ἔθνη καὶ γλῶσσαι

---

³⁶See chapter 10 section 3 below.

We should also notice the similar variation in lists. The list of eight types of sinners in 21:8 and the list of six types of sinners in 22:15 have four items in common, occurring in a different order, while each list concludes with a different way of describing the same category of sinners. The list of types of humanity in 6:15 is varied to make a list of types of participant in battle in 19:18.[37] The qualities ascribed to God in doxologies occur in ever varied combinations, never the same for more than two items in succession (4:9, 11; 5:12, 13; 7:12; 19:2).

14.11 is a striking example of the effect of the web of cross-references which is created by this literary technique. In its immediate context there is an obvious contrast, which no doubt first-time hearers would notice, between the worshippers of the beast who 'have no rest' (οὐκ ἔχουσιν ἀνάπαυσιν) and the Christian martyrs who 'will rest (ἀναπαήσονται) from their labours' (14:13). But for those who become more familiar with the book, there is a subtler parallel to be discovered, between the worshippers of the beast 'who have no rest day or night' (οὐκ ἔχουσιν ἀνάπαυσιν ἡμέρας καὶ νυκτός) and the four living creatures, who are the central worshippers of God in heaven, who also 'have no rest day or night' (ἀνάπαυσιν οὐκ ἔχουσιν ἡμέρας καὶ νυκτός) (4:8). This parallel continues the ironic parallel between the worship of God and the worship of the beast which has run through chapter 13. In 14:11 the irony is savage, for behind the formal parallel created by the identity of language lies a material contrast: between the unceasing joy of the worshippers of God and the unceasing torment of the worshippers of the beast. There are further cross-references between 14:11 and 19:3 and between 14:10-11 and 20:10, which establish that the fate of the worshippers of the beast is the eventual fate of all evil: the devil, the beast, the false prophet and Babylon the great. Those who worship the beast

[37]The variation is not arbitrary. 19:18 relates more closely to Ezek 39:18, 20, to which its context also alludes. The two categories in 6:15 which are omitted in 19:18 (οἱ μεγιστᾶνες, οἱ πλούσιοι) may well be thought to belong more appropriately among the mourners for Babylon (see especially 18:3, 15, 19, 23) than in the armies of the beast in 19:18.

throw in their lot with the forces and the institutions of evil, and must expect to share their fate.

One way of understanding John's literary technique of repeating phrases is to relate it to the Jewish exegetical technique of *gezērâ šāwâ*, which John, like many of his Jewish contemporaries, used to interpret the Old Testament Scriptures.[38] This technique depended on observing verbal coincidences between scriptural texts. Texts containing the same words or phrases could be used to interpret each other. In effect, Scripture was treated as containing the same kind of network of internal cross-reference by repetition of phrases (often, of course, in somewhat varying form) as John has created in his own work. Since John certainly understood himself to be writing the same kind of inspired, prophetic work as the prophetic scriptures he studied, the parallel is surely not accidental. John wrote a work to which he expected the technique of *gezērâ šāwâ* to be applied, a work which would yield much of its meaning only to the application of this exegetical technique.

3. Numerical composition

In section 1 we have discussed those numerical features, mainly the four series of seven (the seven messages to the churches and the three series of seven judgments), which are structural features of Revelation. But there are other examples of numerical composition which do not have any structural significance. They would not have been noticed by hearers of the book and are not noticed by the majority of careful readers of the book. One of these which has been frequently noticed is the series of seven beatitudes (1:3; 14:13; 16:15; 19:9; 20:6; 22:7, 14). This is unlikely to be accidental, but it has no significance for the structure of the book. Each beatitude belongs in its place in the book for reasons unconnected with the fact that it is one of seven. But anyone who troubles to count

---

[38]For the use of *gezērâ šāwâ*, in Revelation, see chapter 9 sections 7-9 below.

them finds that the number of beatitudes is the number symbolic of completeness, seven.[39] Moreover, this discovery gives the beatitudes greater meaning. Together they spell out the adequate response to John's prophecy (reading/hearing and keeping: 1:3; 22:7; faithfulness as far as death: 14:13; 22:14; readiness for the Lord's coming: 16:15) and the fullness of divine blessing that attends that response (rest from labours: 14:13; invitation to the Lamb's marriage supper: 19:9; participation in the first resurrection: 20:6; the tree of life and entry into the New Jerusalem: 22:14; but these are only *representative* of the complete blessing indicated by the number seven). The seven beatitudes comprise a kind of summary of Revelation's message.

It is part of John's meticulous literary artistry that he has worked into his work symbolic features which are not easily noticed. This is not surprising. He was writing a book which he intended to have a status comparable to the Old Testament prophetic books, and he could expect some readers to study it with the same intensity with which he himself studied Old Testament prophetic books. His work would convey sufficient meaning in oral performance in the worship meetings of the churches of Asia, but it would also have much more to offer those, such as his fellow prophets in the circle of prophets in those churches,[40] who pondered it with prayerful and scripturally learned attention. Moreover, the process of great literary creation does not necessarily calculate what readers will notice.

The most significant numbers in Revelation are seven, four, three and twelve (and in some cases, multiples of these).[41] Seven, as we have noted, is the number of completeness, a symbolic significance which suits all of its occurrences in Revelation. It means that a list of seven can be representative of all: the seven churches of Asia *stand for* all the churches. Also

---

[39] For seven as the number of completeness, see chapter 11 n. 34 below.

[40] See chapter 2 section 5 below.

[41] Two has a rather limited significance, as the number of witness (11:3-13). For some other symbolic numbers in Revelation, see chapter 11 section 1 below.

quite clear in its symbolism is the number four, which is the number of the world. The earth has four corners (7:1; 20:8) and four winds (7:1). The created world can be categorized in four divisions. One such division is used in 5:13, where 'every creature in heaven and on earth and under the earth and in the sea' offers to God and the Lamb a fourfold doxology ('blessing and honour and glory and might'). (All other doxologies in Revelation are either sevenfold [5:12; 7:12] or threefold [4:9, 11; 19:2].) Revelation makes greater use of an alternative fourfold division of creation: earth, sea, (rivers and) springs, heaven (8:7-12; 14:7; 16:2-9). These four parts of creation are respectively the targets of the judgments of the first four trumpets (8:7-12) and the first four bowls (16:2-9). Such judgments, demonstrating God's power over his whole creation, should have brought sinners to repentant acknowledgement of their Creator (14:7), whereas in fact they admit his power but curse him (16:9). We can now see that the 4 + 3 pattern which characterizes all three series of seven judgments (seal-openings, trumpets, bowls) is partly determined by the fact that in each case the first four judgments form a set of judgments on the earth or the world. We can also see the appropriateness of the *four* series of seven judgments which there would have been had the seven thunders not been rescinded (10:3-7).[42] A *complete* set of judgments on the *whole* world would be appropriately: 4 x 7.[43]

It is certainly no accident that the list of cargoes which Babylon (Rome) imports from 'the merchants of the earth' (18:11-13) comprises twenty-eight (4 x 7) items. They are listed as representative of *all* the products of the whole *world*.[44]

Since, as we shall see, the number of occurrences of divine titles in Revelation is usually significant, it is probably not insignificant that one of them occurs four times: 'the one who lives for ever and ever' (4:9, 10; 10:6; 15:7). Four is appropriate because it designates God the eternal Creator who is sovereign

---

[42]For the cancellation of the seven thunders, see chapter 9 section 3 below.

[43]Note also that the threat of sevenfold punishment occurs four times in Leviticus 26 (vv. 18, 21, 24, 28).

[44]For the contents of the list, see chapter 10 section 3 below.

over his creation (cf. 4:11; 10:6). In connexion with one of the occurrences of this designation, however, John uses, unusually, a threefold division of the created world: heaven, earth, sea (10:6). Probably he does so in order to anticipate and to make a connexion with his use of the same threefold division in chapters 12-13. It is used in those chapters (cf. also 21:1) because the satanic trinity who there contest God's sovereignty over his creation originate respectively from these three divisions of creation: the dragon from heaven (12:3), the beast from the sea (13:1) and the second beast from the earth (13:11). But the Creator of heaven, sea and earth will bring a speedy end to their opposition (10:6-7; 15:7).

Three seems to be a number without a consistent symbolic significance. It has a different kind of meaning in relation to one of Revelation's most important designations of God, John's original variation on the Old Testament divine name: 'the one who was and who is and who is to come' (4:8).[45] The God who thus exists and comes to his creation in three tenses is worshipped with the Trishagion (4:8: 'Holy, holy, holy') and threefold doxologies (4:9, 11; cf. 19:2). But the full set of occurrences of this divine designation and its variations is significant:

1:4:   the one who is and who was and who is to come
1:8:   the one who is and who was and who is to come
4:8:   the one who was and who is and who is to come
11:17: the one who is and who was
16:8:   the one who is and who was.

The shorter versions (11:17; 16:8) occur at points in the vision which anticipate the end, when God will have 'come' in his eschatological kingdom. The expectation of his coming is now fulfilled. But the significance for our purpose is that the threefold form of the formula occurs three times and the twofold form twice. The satanic parody, the beast 'that was and is not and is to come,' also occurs (in this and two varying forms) three times (17:8a, 8b, 11).

---

[45]On this divine designation, see Bauckham (1993) chapter 2.

Other titles for God which are most characteristic of Revelation and most important for the theology of Revelation occur seven times each. Especially in the circumstances of ancient writing, this would not have been easy to achieve. It is further evidence of the meticulous composition of the book. In placing just seven occurrences of these divine titles within his work, John was not just playing a literary game. It was one of the ways in which he wrote theological meaning into the detail of the composition of his work. We could say that he buried in the literary composition of his work theological significance which few readers have subsequently unearthed, though it may well be that, among his first readers, at least his fellow-prophets would know better than later readers what to look for. Just as the seven beatitudes scattered throughout the book express the fullness of divine blessing on those who obey the message of the prophecy, so the seven occurrences of a divine title indicate the fullness of the divine being to which that title points.

The full title 'the Lord God Almighty' (κύριος ὁ θεὸς ὁ παντοκράτωρ), John's equivalent of the Old Testament's Yahweh Sabaoth, occurs in that full form just seven times (1:8; 4:8; 11:17; 15:3; 16:7; 19:6; 21:22), while the shorter form ὁ θεὸς ὁ παντοκράτωρ occurs twice (16:14; 19:15). These two occurrences themselves perform a literary function, helping to link 16:12-16 to 19:11-21, in which the battle the former passage presages takes place, but they also allow the number of occurrences of the full title to be the number of completeness, seven. Another important designation for God which occurs seven times is 'the one who sits on the throne' (ὁ καθήμενος ἐπὶ τοῦ θρόνου: 4:9; 5:1, 7, 13; 6:16; 7:15; 21:5).[46] Variations on this phrase are also found (4:2, 3; 7:10; 19:4; 20:11), but it looks as though John used these variations quite deliberately in order to keep the number of occurrences of the precise phrase to seven.

The divine title 'the Alpha and the Omega' (used in the only two speeches attributed directly to God: 1:8; 21:6) and its equivalents occur as self-designations by God and by Christ as follows:

[46]On both these divine designations, see Bauckham (1993) chapter 2.

God: I am the Alpha and the Omega (1:8)
Christ: I am the first and the last (1:17)
God: I am the Alpha and the Omega, the beginning and the
        end (21:6)
Christ: I am the Alpha and the Omega, the first and the last,
        the beginning and the end (22:13)

Not only is this pattern significant for John's Christology.[47] It also means that the title and its equivalents are used in all seven times in divine self-declarations (excluding 'the first and the last' in 2:8, where it is not a self-declaration).

The statistics of major christological titles are also significant. The word Χριστός (including occurrences of Ἰησοῦς Χριστός) occurs seven times in the book, and the name Ἰησοῦς fourteen times, seven of these in connexion with μαρτυρία or μαρτύρων (1:2, 9; 12:17; 17:6; 19:10 [twice]; 20:4). (Revelation's characteristic association of 'Jesus' with 'witness' might perhaps explain why Ἰησοῦς occurs 7 x 2 times, since two is the number of witness [11:3-13].) The word ἔρχομαι, spoken by Christ as a promise or threat of his parousia, occurs seven times (2:5, 16; 3:11; 16:15; 22:6, 12, 20). But the most important of Revelation's christological terms is 'the Lamb'. This occurs twenty-eight (7 x 4) times. Seven of these are in phrases coupling God and the Lamb together (5:13; 6:16; 7:10; 14:4; 21:22; 22:1, 3). Since it is through the Lamb's conquest that God's rule over his creation comes about, the 7 x 4 occurrences of 'Lamb' appropriately indicate the worldwide scope of his complete victory. Corresponding to the 7 x 4 occurrences of the Lamb, are the *seven* occurrences of the *fourfold* phrase by which Revelation designates the nations of the world ('peoples and tribes and languages and nations': the phrase varies each time it occurs but is always fourfold: 5:9; 7:9; 10:11; 11:9; 13:7; 14:6; 17:15). It designates all the nations of the world, who, despite their present allegiance to Babylon and the beast, it is the object of the Lamb's conquest to bring into God's kingdom. The first occurrence of the fourfold phrase (5:9), following the

---

[47]See Bauckham (1993) chapter 3.

first two of the twenty-eight appearances of the Lamb (5:6, 8), establishes its close connexion with the Lamb's victory.[48]

References to the divine Spirit in Revelation fall into two distinct categories: those which refer to 'the seven Spirits' and those which refer to 'the Spirit'. There are *four* references to the *seven* Spirits (1:4; 3:1; 4:5; 5:6), because they represent the fullness of the divine power 'sent out into all the earth'. These four references to the seven Spirits correspond to the seven occurrences of the fourfold phrase for the nations of the earth. It is as the power of the church's prophetic witness to all the nations that they are sent out into all the earth.[49] They also correspond to the 7 x 4 references to the Lamb, since the seven Spirits are very closely associated with the victorious Lamb (5:6). The four references to them indicate that the Lamb's victory is implemented throughout the world by the fullness of the divine power. (Continuing the 7 x 4 pattern, we should also notice that there are *four* references to the *seven* churches [1:4, 11, 20 (twice)], suggesting that they represent all the churches of the world.)

As well as these four references to the seven Spirits, there are also fourteen to 'the Spirit',[50] perhaps (since 'the witness of Jesus is the Spirit of prophecy': 19:10) deliberately corresponding to the fourteen references to Jesus. Seven of these references to the Spirit occur in the refrain repeated in each of the seven messages to the churches (2:7, 11, 17, 29; 3:6, 13, 22). This leaves seven other references, four in the phrase ἐν πνεύματι (1:10; 4:2; 17:3; 21:10), two citing words of the Spirit (14:13; 22:17), one in the phrase 'Spirit of prophecy' (19:10). It is worth noticing that the word προφητεία also occurs seven times (1:3; 11:6; 19:10; 22:7, 10, 18, 19).

There are far too many of these numerical patterns for them to be accidental. Of course, there are probably a few coincidences to be found. It is unlikely to be intentional that the word ἄβυσσος occurs seven times (9:1, 2, 11; 11:7; 17:8;

---

[48]For a full study of the phrase, see chapter 9 section 10 below.

[49]See further Bauckham (1993) chapter 5.

[50]The word πνεῦμα also occurs in 11:11; 22:6, which I judge not to be references to the divine Spirit, and in 13:15; 16:13, 14; 18:2, which clearly are not.

20:1, 3), while it is hard to tell whether the seven references to the θυσιαστήριον in heaven (6:9; 8:3 [twice], 5; 9:13; 14:18; 16:7, excluding the reference to the θυσιαστήριον on earth in 11:1) are significant. But it may very well be intentional that the word δρέπανον (sickle) occurs seven times (all in 14:14-19). The completeness of the judgment of the world would be thereby signalled. Moreover, it is worth noticing that, whereas significant terms for God, Christ and the Spirit seem all to occur a symbolically significant number of times, no such pattern appears to apply to the powers of evil: δράκων occurs thirteen times, Σατανᾶς eight times, διάβολος five times, ὄφις four times (excluding 9:19), θηρίον thirty-eight times (excluding 6:8) and Βαβύλων six times. It seems as though the numbers seven and twelve are deliberately *avoided*, just as the two lists of types of sinners excluded from eschatological salvation (21:8; 22:15) comprise respectively eight and six times, deliberately falling either side of seven. It seems that only when parodying the divine are the significant numbers three (16:13) and seven (12:3; 13:1; 17:3, 7, 9-11) attributed to the powers of evil. The list of categories of humanity who fear the wrath of God and the Lamb in 6:15 may be of seven items (unless πᾶς δοῦλος καὶ ἐλεύθερος is regarded as a single item), representing *all* the classes of humanity. But when the list is adapted in 19:18 (cf. Ezek 39:18, 20) to describe all those who make up the armies of the beast at the battle of Armageddon it is certainly no longer sevenfold (cf. also 13:6).

Twelve is the number of the people of God (7:4-8; 12:1; 14:1; 21:12, 14), squared for completeness, multiplied by a thousand to suggest vast numbers (7:4-8; 14:1; 21:17). So obviously important is the number twelve in the account of the New Jerusalem, that it is surely significant that the number can be found to occur twelve times in 21:9-22:5, if, as well as the ten occurrences of the word δώδεκα, one counts as two further occurrences the four threes of 21:13 and the list of the ordinals up to the twelfth in 21:19-20.[51] Perhaps it is also significant that the words θεός and ἀρνίον each occur seven times within the

---

[51]Giblin (1991) 203 and n. 145, achieves the same result by a slightly different calculation.

same portion of text (θεός: 21:10, 11, 22, 23; 22:1, 3, 5; ἀρνίον: 21:9, 14, 22, 23, 27; 22:1, 3).[52]

We do not yet know whether John was original in his technique of numerical composition. Evidence of the technique in other apocalyptic writings has not yet been found and may be difficult to find, since the noncanonical apocalypses have in most cases not been preserved in their original languages and have been transmitted with far less concern to preserve their precise textual form unchanged. Giblin[53] has shown that techniques of numerical composition somewhat comparable to those used in Revelation can be found in Joshua 24:1-25. It is not likely that John modelled his technique on this passage in particular. It would be consistent with our conclusion at the end of section 2 to suppose that, in this case also, John has reproduced a scriptural technique of literary composition in his own prophetic composition. But we should need evidence of the more widespread presence of numerical composition in other parts of the Old Testament before we could confidently conclude this.

[52]Pointed out by Giblin (1991) 203-204.
[53]Giblin (1964).

2

The Use of Apocalyptic Traditions

The relationship between the Apocalypse of John and the extracanonical Jewish apocalypses has been variously understood. At one extreme are those who see Revelation as a typical Jewish apocalypse, whose admittedly Christian authorship makes little significant difference,[1] while at the other extreme are those who distinguish sharply between prophecy and apocalyptic and minimize Revelation's resemblances to the Jewish apocalypses in order to classify it as a Christian prophecy in continuity with Old Testament prophecy.[2] This discussion has often not sufficiently recognized the diversity of the Jewish apocalypses, both in themes and in literary forms. Nor has it sufficiently distinguished the various dimensions of Revelation's possible relationship to them. Thus one could ask whether John is indebted to Jewish apocalyptic for the literary forms he uses, for theological ideas,

---

[1]Ford (1975) offers one version of the view, which was more popular in a past era of source criticism, that Revelation in fact originated as a Jewish apocalypse (among the followers of John the Baptist, according to Ford), to which some Christian additions have been made. The rather common view that Revelation is 'more Jewish than Christian' (cf. Bultmann's famous statement: 'The Christianity of Revelation has to be termed a weakly christianized Judaism': Bultmann [1955] 175) rests on the untenable presupposition that early Christianity was something different from Judaism, whereas in fact first-century Christianity was a distinctive form of Judaism.

[2]Most recently, Mazzaferri (1989). His case for Revelation's continuity with OT prophecy is excellent, but unfortunately his account of Jewish apocalyptic is a caricature. Schüssler Fiorenza (1985) chapter 5, rightly refuses the alternative of prophecy or apocalyptic.

for symbolic images, for the ways in which he interprets Old Testament scriptures. In each of these aspects he may be more or less distinctive while also being indebted to apocalyptic tradition. His distinctiveness may be comparable to that of one Jewish apocalypse in relation to others[3] or it may be due to his deliberately Christian prophetic consciousness and message. We should probably reckon with both types of distinctiveness.

One aspect of Revelation's relationship to the Jewish apocalypses which has been little enough explored is Revelation's use of specific items of apocalyptic tradition which also appear in Jewish apocalypses and sometimes also in later Christian apocalypses. Where these have been noticed they have often been taken to show that John was actually borrowing from a particular Jewish apocalyptic work, such as 1 Enoch.[4] Although it is *a priori* quite likely that John had read some of the Jewish apocalypses which we know, it seems to me impossible to prove his specific literary dependence on any such work. The traditions in question usually turn out to be attested in a variety of works, Jewish and Christian, in such a way that a chain of literary dependence is very difficult to reconstruct and it seems more plausible to think of traditions which were known, independently of their use in particular apocalypses, in circles, Jewish and Christian, which studied and produced apocalyptic literature.

The detailed study of particular items of apocalyptic tradition as they appear in Revelation and in other Jewish and Christian writings is laborious — no doubt one reason why it has rarely been undertaken. But it is essential to the understanding of the background and composition of apocalyptic literature, and can yield significant exegetical results. In this chapter, we shall engage in four case studies.[5] (Other examples of Revelation's

---

[3] For some rarely noted differences between Revelation and the major Jewish apocalypses, see chapter 6 section 1 below.

[4] E.g. Charles (1920) 1.lxv, lxxxii-lxxxiii; and for discussion, cf. Mazzaferri (1989) 48-49.

[5] Another important area of study would be of parallels between Revelation's interpretations of specific Old Testament texts and those in other apocalypses, in order to trace traditions of scriptural exegesis in apocalyptic circles. The traditions studied in the present chapter have been deliberately chosen as examples of traditions which are *not* interpretations of the Old Testament.

use of traditions which can be found also in other apocalyptic
literature are studied elsewhere in this volume: see especially
chapter 4; chapter 8; chapter 11 sections 2-3.) Following these
case studies, we shall raise the question of the social context in
which such traditions could have been transmitted.

1. Blood and horses (Revelation 14:20b)

We begin with a collection of texts which are clearly related in
some way:

(A) Revelation 14:20b:
καὶ ἐξῆλθεν αἷμα ἐκ τῆς ληνοῦ ἄρχι τῶν χαλινῶν τῶν
ἵππων, ἀπὸ σταδίων χιλίων ἑξακοσίων.

...and the blood flowed from the winepress, up to the
bridles of the horses, for 1600 stadia.

(B) 1 Enoch 100:3:
And the horse will walk up to its chest in the blood of
sinners, and the chariot will sink up to its height.[6]

(C) 4 Ezra (6 Ezra) 15:35-36:
*...et erit sanguis a gladio usque ad ventrem equi et femur hominis
et suffraginem cameli.*[7]

...and there shall be blood from the sword as high as a
horse's belly and a man's thigh and a camel's hock.

(D) Ginza:
Then comes that king, lets his horse loose, and it walks
over them [the kings] up to the saddle in blood, and the
whirlpool of blood reaches up to its nostrils.[8]

[6]Translation from Knibb (1982) 234.
[7]Text from Bensly (1895) 75.
[8]German translation in Lidzbarski (1925) 417, from the Aramaic text in
Petermann (1867) 390-391.

(E)[9] y. Ta'an. 4:8:
They killed among them until the horse sank up to the nostrils in blood. And the blood rolled along rocks of 40 *se'ah* in weight, until it reached four miles into the sea.

Lam. R. 2:2:4:
They killed among them until the horse sank up to its nostrils in blood, and the blood rolled along stones of 40 *se'ah* [in weight] and flowed four miles into the sea.

b. Giṭṭ. 57a:
They slew in it [Bethar] men, women and children, until their blood flowed and poured into the great Sea.

(F) Prayer of Rabbi Shimon ben Yoḥai 9:
...Legions will join them [the Edomites] from Edom, and they will come and make war [against the Ishmaelites] in the plain of Acre, until the horse sinks to its thighs in blood.[10]

Poem 'On that Day':
Edom and Ishmael will fight in the valley of Acre
Till the horses sink in the blood and panic.[11]

---

[9]See the German translation of these three texts in Schäfer (1981) 138-139, 146, 153, and the brief discussion of them on pp. 178-179. He describes them as 'a typically hyperbolic Aggadah', but fails to recognize that they employ a motif also found elsewhere.

[10]Translation from Lewis (1950) 316; cf. also the translation in Buchanan (1978) 412. The passage has often been thought to refer to the events of the Third Crusade, in the thirteenth century, but Lewis argues that this part of the Prayer is a tenth-century apocalypse. His notes on chapter 9 (pp. 336-337) show that there are some problems with this date.

[11]Translation from Lewis (1974) 199. This is obviously closely related to the passage in the Prayer of Rabbi Shimon ben Yoḥai, and has been included here for that reason. The poem has been dated at the beginning of the twelfth century, at the time of the First Crusade, but Lewis supports a seventh-century date. If there is a direct literary relationship between the poem and the Prayer of Rabbi Shimon ben Yoḥai, it must be the poem that is dependent on the Prayer, since only the latter retains the traditional motif that the blood will reach the thighs of the horses.

(G) Greek Tiburtine Sibyl 183-184:
καὶ γενήσονται αἱματοχυσίαι πολλαὶ ὥστε γενέσθαι τὸ
αἷμα εἰς τὸ οτῆθος τῶν ἵππων τοῦ συγκερασθῆναι τὴν
θάλασσαν.

And there will be much shedding of blood, so that the
blood will reach the chest of the horses as it is commingled
with the sea.[12]

(H) Greek Apocalypse of Daniel 4:6-8 = 6:1-3:[13]
Καὶ γενήσεται πόλεμος καὶ αἱματοχυσία μεγάλη, οἷα οὐ
γέγονεν ἀπὸ καταβολῆς κόσμου. συγκερασθήσεται γὰρ
τὸ αἷμα ἐν τῇ θαλάσσῃ οταδίους δώδεκα. καὶ ἐν ταῖς
ῥύμαις τῆς πόλεως ἵπποι βαφήσονται τὸ αἷμα
ἐπιπνιγόμενοι.[14]

And there will be war and great bloodshed such as has not
been since the foundation of the world. For the blood will
be mixed in the sea for 12 stadia. And in the streets of the
city horses will be submerged, drowning in the blood.

(I) Prophecy of Daniel about the island of Cyprus:
καὶ μέχρι οτήθους τῶν ἵππων αἷμα ῥεύσει·[15]

And blood will flow up to the chests of the horses.

(J) Oracles of Leo the Wise 1:283-288:
Καὶ πληθύνει δὲ τὸ αἷμα
τῶν ἐλθῶν καὶ εὐσεβῶν τε,
[καὶ] τὴν θάλασσαν κεράσει

---

[12]Text and translation (slightly altered) from Alexander (1967) 20, 28.

[13]The first reference is according to the chapter and verse division in the
translation by Zervos (1983); the second reference is according to the chapter and
verse division in the text, German translation and full commentary by Berger
(1976A).

[14]Text from Berger (1976A) 13-14. Zervos (1983) 765, translates a slightly
differing text.

[15]Text from Klostermann (1895) 123 line 22.

σταδίους τετρακοσίους·
καὶ πνιγήσονται καὶ ἵπποι,
ἀναβάται δὲ σύν τούτοις.[16]

And the blood of Gentiles and the blood of godly people
will abound, and it will mingle with the sea for 400 stadia,
and the horses will drown and the riders with them.

(K) Prophecy of Themation about Constantinople:
There will be a massacre of men... so that all the hollows
and all the land of the city will be filled with blood, so that
even a three-year-old cow will drown in the blood, and the
blood will run into the sea about 18 stadia.[17]

This collection of texts, ranging in date from the second or first
century B.C. (B) to the medieval period, from Jewish, Christian
and (in one case) Mandean (D) works, clearly shows that
Revelation 14:20 makes use of a *topos* which was widely used to
indicate slaughter, in war, of exceptional proportions.[18] In
most cases it occurs in the context of apocalyptic prophecy.
Most appropriately it is used with reference to the last battle of
history, in which sinners will destroy each other on an
unprecedented scale (so B),[19] but in many of the later
apocalypses it describes an earlier battle in the sequence of
events which lead to the end of history. In some cases, the battle
which, from the fictitious standpoint of the pseudepigraphal
prophecy, is set in the future may be an event already in the past
from the standpoint of the author and his readers (F?, H?): the
process of redaction of early medieval apocalypses often results

[16]Text from Legrand (1875) 42.

[17]Translation from Berger's German in Berger (1976A) 75. I have not had
access to the Greek text of this work. For the reference to the three-year-old cow,
cf. GkApDan 4:3 = 5:15. For passages in other Byzantine apocalypses related to
texts G - K, see Berger (1976A) 75; and Slavonic Vision of Daniel 4, translated in
Alexander (1985) 68.

[18]Cf. the parallel images of blood in SibOr 5:372, 472-473.

[19]Cf. also Lactantius, *Div. Inst.* 7.19, which is probably a remnant of this
tradition.

in the back-dating of material which originally referred to the final events of history. But the texts in E (three very closely related versions of the same tradition, part of a complex of traditions about the fall of Bethar) are the only case where the *topos* is used not in a prophecy but in an account of the past: the slaughter of the inhabitants of Bethar by the Romans at the end of the Bar Kokhba war (135 A.D.). This may be a case of borrowing a motif from apocalyptic traditions to describe a historical event. Certainly the extreme hyperbole of the *topos* makes it most appropriate to the apocalyptic future.

Only one of the texts (B) can be securely dated prior to Revelation, and only one other (C) could possibly be dated prior to or as early as Revelation. The work from which this text comes (6 Ezra, i.e. the last two chapters of 4 Ezra in its Latin version, which were not originally part of 4 Ezra) has been most often dated in the late third century A.D., on the basis of supposed references to the events of that period,[20] but some scholars have suggested that it is a pre-Christian Jewish work.[21] The issue need not detain us, since the texts most relevant to Revelation will turn out to be some of those which are unquestionably later in date than Revelation. This has not previously been noticed, because scholars are normally, of course, hesitant to interpret a text on the basis of evidence much later than it. Consequently, not only has 1 Enoch 100:3 often been regarded as the only relevant parallel to Revelation 14:20, but also Revelation 14:20 has sometimes been regarded as actually dependent on 1 Enoch 100:3.[22] This is certainly not the case, as consideration of some of the other texts in our collection, late though they be, will demonstrate.

Revelation 14:20b makes two points about the blood: (i) it reaches to a remarkable height (up to the bridles of the horses), and (ii) it flows for a remarkable distance (1600 stadia). Only the first of these points is paralleled in 1 Enoch 100:3 (B), as also in texts C, D, F and I. But the second element also, as well as the first, is paralleled both in the texts about the

---

[20]E.g. Myers (1974) 349-353; Erbetta (1981) 319; cf. Duensing (1965) 690.

[21]Schrage (1964); Harnisch (1973) 72-74.

[22]E.g. Mazzaferri (1989) 49.

slaughter at Bethar (E) and in the group of Byzantine apocalypses (H, J, K) related to the Greek Tiburtine Sibyl (G). The distance given in these texts varies and is always much shorter than in Revelation, but, just as in Revelation, a specific distance is given. Moreover, the rabbinic tests (E) and the Byzantine texts (G, H, J, K) share a further feature which is missing in Revelation: that the blood flows into the sea and the distance given is the distance for which the blood flows into the sea. This correspondence also enables us to see that texts G and H, whose verbal resemblances show them to be closely related, are each in some respect closer than the other to the tradition which must lie behind them: whereas only G states that the blood reaches the chest of the horses, only H states a distance for which the blood flows into the sea. Thus they must depend on a common source. The Greek Apocalypse of Daniel (H) was dated to the years 801-802 A.D. by its editor, Klaus Berger,[23] but Mango[24] rejects Berger's argument for this date in favour of a date in the winter of 716-717 A.D. In any case, like all the Byzantine apocalypses, it was certainly composed on the basis of earlier material. The Greek Tiburtine Sibyl (G) is dated by its editor, Paul Alexander, as early as the fifth or sixth century A.D.[25] If this is correct, then the tradition on which both depend must be earlier. However, these uncertain dates are not important for our argument. That these late texts preserve a very early apocalyptic motif can be demonstrated independently of their precise date.

We cannot rule out the possibility of borrowing between Jewish and Christian traditions during the Christian centuries. The medieval Hebrew apocalypses, such as the Prayer of Rabbi Shimon ben Yoḥai from which one of the texts in F comes, may sometimes have been influenced by Byzantine apocalypses,[26] such as those from which texts G - K come.[27] On the basis of the

---

[23]Berger (1976A) 36-37; followed by Zervos (1983) 756.

[24]Mango (1982) 310-313.

[25]Alexander (1967) 7, 41-42.

[26]Cf. Berger (1976A) 4.

[27]With the reference by the texts in F to the Ishmaelites, cf. the Third Greek Apocalypse of Daniel, quoted by Berger (1976A) 75: Ishmaelites and Romans.

texts in F alone, it would be hazardous to conclude that they *must* derive from a Jewish apocalyptic tradition which pre-dates Revelation. But it is highly improbable that the rabbinic tradition about the slaughter at Bethar (E) was influenced by or influenced Christian apocalyptic texts. Its resemblance to Revelation 14:20 cannot be due to dependence on Revelation. If this rabbinic tradition were not known, then perhaps the Byzantine texts (G - K) might be conjectured to be ultimately dependent on Revelation, though they show no verbal resemblance to Revelation beyond the unavoidable words ἵππων and αἷμα and betray no knowledge of the context of Revelation 14:20b. But the fact that they (G, H, J, K) share with the rabbinic tradition (E) the feature that the blood flows into the sea, which is not in Revelation, demonstrates that they must be dependent not on Revelation but on a very early tradition to which the rabbinic tradition about the slaughter at Bethar is also indebted. Thus the resemblance between Revelation 14:20b and texts E, G, H, J, K, in specifying a distance for which the blood flows, must derive from a Jewish tradition pre-dating Revelation, on which all these texts are ultimately dependent. Thus Revelation 14:20b is certainly dependent not on 1 Enoch 100:3, but on a fuller form of the *topos* than appears in 1 Enoch 100:3: a form in which reference was also made to the distance the blood flowed. Since in all the texts except Revelation this distance is obstinately connected with the idea that the blood flows into the sea, we must suppose that in all probability this connexion was always present in the *topos* when it specified a distance and has been deliberately omitted by the author of Revelation. The point of the reference to the sea is preserved most clearly in y. Ta'an 4:8 and Lam. R. 2:2:4 (E), with their additional mention of the great boulders rolled along by the blood until it reaches the sea. The idea is evidently that so much blood has to form a river which flows down to the sea, and becomes so mighty a river that it flows a very long way out into the sea.

In most versions of the *topos* which mention horses it is clear that they are the horses of the warriors in the great battle (text H may be an exception). This is also the case in Revelation 14:20. The height of the blood is not measured by a purely theoretical standard (so, wrongly, NRSV: 'as high as a horse's bridle') but by the horses actually standing in it ('as high as the bridles of the horses'). They are the horses of 19:18, on which the armies of the beast and his allies ride to do battle against the King of kings at Armageddon. Thus the use of the *topos* in Revelation 14:20 enables John to combine the image of a vintage (14:17-20) with that of a battle, anticipating the more fully described battle-scene of 19:11-21. That blood flows from the winepress would indicate slaughter, but that it reaches the bridles of the horses indicates more precisely slaughter in a battle.

That the horses drown in the blood (along with their riders, according to text J) is stated only in texts H and J (cf, K). It should be regarded as a secondary development of the *topos*, distinctive of these late Byzantine texts. It is not the point in Revelation 14:20, and so it is a mistake to see in that verse an allusion to the Exodus, when the horses of the Egyptian army were submerged and drowned in the Red Sea (Exod 14:28; 15:1),[28] though this precedent might be in view in text J. In Revelation the point is not the destruction of the horses, but the vastness of the slaughter of the humans in whose blood their surviving horses stand up to their bridles.

John's image of the winepress, to which he attaches the *topos*, alludes to Joel 3[4]:13 (which explains why the winepress is 'outside the city': 14:20, cf. Joel 3[4]:12) and to Isaiah 63:1-6. It may have been with reference to Isaiah 63:6 ('I will pour out their lifeblood on the earth/land') that he felt the *topos*'s reference to blood flowing *into the sea* inappropriate. But he followed the *topos* in specifying a distance (cf. texts E, H, J, K), as a second indication of the unprecedented scale of the slaughter. The symbolic appropriateness of the distance he specifies (much greater than in any other instance of the *topos*) may lie in its being a multiple of ten and four, numbers which relate to the kings (17:12-14) of the whole earth (16:14)[29] who gather their armies for the battle. It is the blood of their armies

---

[28]Corsini (1983) 271.
[29]For four as the number of the earth, see chapter 1, section 3 above.

which flows over the whole length of the land of Israel, which might be calculated as 1600 stadia[30] and which John might have taken Isaiah 63:6 to indicate.

This study is an interesting case where the relevance of much later texts to the study of early Jewish and Christian apocalypses can be not merely suggested but actually demonstrated. Such relevance is possible because the apocalyptic tradition in Judaism and Christianity was a continuous and relatively conservative tradition over the course of many centuries, throughout which material in earlier texts was constantly being reused in later texts and a repertoire of traditional ideas and images was in continuous use.[31] Of course, there were also innovations, and so great care is needed in arguing for the early origin of motifs in late texts. Moreover, much more detailed study of the later apocalypses is needed before their relationship to earlier apocalyptic tradition can be properly understood. The example we have studied suggests that biblical scholars should not underestimate the importance of such study.

2. Completing the number of the martyrs (Revelation 6:9-11)

(A) Revelation 6:9-11:
When he opened the fifth seal, I saw under the altar the souls of those who had been slaughtered for the word of God and for the testimony they had given; [10]they cried out with a loud voice, 'Sovereign Lord, holy and true, how long will it be before you judge and avenge our blood on the inhabitants of the earth?' [11]They were each given a white robe and told to rest a little longer, until the number would be complete both of their fellow servants and of their brothers and sisters, who were soon to be killed as they themselves had been killed.

(B) 1 Enoch 47:1-4:
And in those days the prayer of the righteous and the

---

[30]Charles (1920) 2.26.
[31]Cf. Berger (1976B) 14-15.

blood of the righteous will have ascended from the earth before the Lord of Spirits. [2]In those days the holy ones who dwell in the heavens above will unite with one voice, and supplicate, and pray, and praise, and give thanks, and bless in the name of the Lord of Spirits, because of the blood of the righteous which has been poured out, and (because of) the prayer of the righteous, that it may not cease before the Lord of Spirits, that justice may be done to them, and (that) their patience may not have to last for ever. [3]And in those days I saw the Head of Days sit down on the throne of his glory, and the books of the living were opened before him, and all his host, which (dwells) in the heavens above, and his council were standing before him. [4]And the hearts of the holy ones were full of joy that the number of righteousness had been reached, and the prayer of the righteous had been heard, and the blood of the righteous had been required before the Lord of Spirits.[32]

(C) 4 Ezra 4:35-37:
Did not the souls of the righteous in their chambers ask about these matters, saying, 'How long are we to remain here? And when will the harvest of our reward come?' [36]And the archangel Jeremiel answered and said, 'When the number of those like yourselves is completed; for he has weighed the age in the balance, [37]and measured the times by measure, and numbered the times by number; and he will not move or arouse them until that measure is fulfilled.'[33]

(D) 2 Baruch 23:4-5a:
For when Adam sinned and death was decreed against those who were to be born, the multitude of those who would be born was numbered. And for that number a place was prepared where the living ones might live and where the dead might be preserved. [5]No creature will live

---

[32]Translation from Knibb (1978) 132-133.
[33]Translation from NRSV.

again unless the number that has been appointed is completed.[34]

The relationship between these four texts is of special interest because they occur in four apocalypses (one Christian and three Jewish) which are roughly contemporaneous. (In the case of the passage from 1 Enoch, the apocalypse in question is the Parables of Enoch, i.e. chapters 37-71 of 1 Enoch.) All four probably date from the late first century,[35] though their precise chronological order cannot be determined. Moreover, the four works, especially Revelation, 4 Ezra and 2 Baruch, share other resemblances and common traditions. That there are close links between 4 Ezra and 2 Baruch is well-known. All three possible relationships (dependence of 4 Ezra on 2 Baruch, dependence of 2 Baruch on 4 Ezra, common tradition) have been proposed, but no finally decisive argument for any of them has been advanced.[36] However, there are also some very striking links between 4 Ezra and Revelation, which have been much less discussed. Bogaert is correct to claim that the relationship between 2 Baruch and 4 Ezra should not be considered without consideration also of the relationships of both these Jewish works to the Christian apocalypse of John.[37] In the case we are considering, the relationship between 4 Ezra

---

[34]Translation from Klijn (1983) 629. Further allusions to the idea of a predetermined number of the elect which must be completed are in 1 Clem 2:4; 58:2; 59:2; Didascalia 21; Pistis Sophia 23; 26; 27; 45; 86; 96; 98; 125. The passages in the Pistis Sophia are studied by van Unnik (1963). Of special interest is Justin, *1 Apol.* 45:1: 'until the number of those who are foreknown by him as good and righteous is complete, on whose account he has delayed the consummation'. This relates the necessity of completing the number to the delay until the eschaton in the same way as our texts A, C and D do. It seems most likely to be an independent witness to the tradition, not dependent on these texts.

[35]The Parables of Enoch (1 Enoch 37-71) is the most difficult of the four works to date. In favour of a date in the late first century A.D., see Knibb (1980); Dunn (1980) 77; Charlesworth (1985A) 108; Schürer (1986) 256-259; but for proposals of a date earlier in the first century, see Schürer (1986) 259; Nickelsburg (1981) 221-223; Collins (1984) 143. For the question of the relative dates of the other three apocalypses, see Bogaert (1980) 49.

[36]Cf. Stone (1990) 39.

[37]Bogaert (1980) 50, 67.

and Revelation is much closer than that between 4 Ezra and 2 Baruch.

What the four texts have in common is the idea of a 'number' of people which will be 'completed' at the eschatological moment. It could also be said that in all four texts this idea is advanced as an answer to the question (explicit or implicit), 'How long?' (i.e. how long will it be until the eschatological intervention of God?). The question is explicitly asked in Revelation and 4 Ezra, but it could also be said to be implicit in 1 Enoch in the prayer of the righteous that 'their patience may not have to last for ever'. Moreover, the question, 'how long?', though it does not occur in the text quoted from 2 Baruch, does occur in the context (21:19). It is, in fact, the question by Baruch to which the quoted text (23:4-5a) is the central part of God's response. Similarly, in 4 Ezra, Ezra himself first asks the question, 'How long?' (4:33), and receives from the angel Uriel an answer of which the quoted text (4:35-37) is the major part. The question, 'How long?' also occurs elsewhere in both 4 Ezra (6:59) and 2 Baruch (81:3).[38] It had long been the question asked in the face of God's apparent non-intervention or delayed intervention on behalf of his people (Ps 6:3; 13:1-2; 74:10; 79:5; 80:4; 89:46; 90:13; 94:3; Jer 12:4; Hab 1:2; cf. Isa 6:11), whence it became a question asked by apocalyptic writers about the time which must pass until the decisive, eschatological intervention of God (Dan 8:13; 12:6). It seems that our tradition, at least as known to the authors of Revelation, 4 Ezra and 2 Baruch, was associated with this question. It was known as a traditional answer to the traditional question, 'How long?'

However, apart from these very basic resemblances between all four texts, there are also major differences. It is notable that the people whose number is to be completed are different in each case: in Revelation they are those who have been put to death for their witness to God, in 1 Enoch they are the righteous who have been killed by their powerful oppressors

---

[38]On the question of eschatological delay in 2 Baruch, see Bauckham (1980) 14-19.

(cf. ch. 46), in 4 Ezra they are simply the righteous (however they might have died), and in 2 Baruch they are all people who have lived. In each case, the category relates to a concern of the whole work: to Revelation's concern with the faithful witness of Christians to the point of death, to the concern of the parables of Enoch with the suffering of the righteous at the hands of the rich and powerful, to 4 Ezra's specific concern with the fate of the small number of righteous Israelites, and to 2 Baruch's repeated reference to the divinely predetermined number of human beings (cf. 21:10; 48:6).[39]

Turning to resemblances shared by some but not all of the four texts, we may note first of all that in Revelation, 1 Enoch and 4 Ezra, but not in 2 Baruch, the tradition takes the form of a scene in which a question is asked or a prayer offered by the righteous people who desire the eschatological intervention of God and some kind of answer is given, related to the idea of the completion of the number of people. In 2 Baruch the idea is not dramatized in this way, but simply asserted by God.

Other resemblances link only two of the four texts. Perhaps most striking are those between Revelation and 4 Ezra:

(a) In both texts a question in the form, 'How long...?', is asked.
(b) In both texts it is asked by righteous dead people.
(c) In both texts an answer is given to them, which is in effect: Until the number of those in the same category as yourselves is completed. (In each text the idea of people 'in the same category as yourselves' is expressed in terms characteristic of the work as a whole: for 4 Ezra, cf. 8:51, 62 [also 2 Bar 21:24]; for Revelation, cf. 11:18; 19:2, 5, 10; 22:9).

However, there are also striking resemblances between Revelation and 1 Enoch:

[39]The idea is also found in rabbinic literature, e.g. Gen. R. 24:4: 'The son of David will not come until all those souls which are destined to be born will be born'; cf. other references in Stone (1990) 97 n. 40.

(a) Both texts concern people of God who have been put to death by the wicked.
(b) In both cases these people address a prayer to God (whereas in 4 Ezra the question of the righteous does not seem to be addressed to God).
(c) The prayer is for God's justice in avenging their blood.[40]

Resemblances between 4 Ezra and 2 Baruch are:

(a) In both cases the text forms the answer (by God or his angel) to the question, 'How long?' asked by the seer in the context (4 Ezra 4:33; 2 Bar 21:19).
(b) In both cases the eschatological expectation is not focussed on the avenging of the righteous (as in Revelation and 1 Enoch), but on the resurrection and its accompanying reward for the righteous (though in 2 Baruch the judgment of the wicked is also in view: 24:1).
(c) In both cases the divine predetermination of the number of people is stressed, in accordance with the emphasis of both these works on the divine determination of the time of the end, whereas in Revelation and 1 Enoch it is assumed rather than stressed.

There is one resemblance between 1 Enoch and 2 Baruch: in both cases the tradition is associated with a divine judgment scene in which 'the books' are 'opened' (in 2 Baruch, the scene follows the quoted text, in 24:1). Between 1 Enoch and 4 Ezra the only resemblance is that in both cases the people in question are called 'the righteous'.

If we assume that the resemblances between 1 Enoch and 4 Ezra and between 1 Enoch and 2 Baruch are not significant enough to need explanation, it would be possible to account for the pattern of other resemblances by a chain of literary dependence: Parables of Enoch → Revelation → 4 Ezra → 2 Baruch.

---

[40]We could add that, although the answer to the prayer is postponed in the immediate context in Revelation, it occurs in response to the prayers of the saints in 8:3-5, following the completion of the number of the righteous in chapter 7, as it does in 1 Enoch 47:3-4.

This particular set of literary relationships between the four works is the only one which would account for the phenomena without positing hypothetical common sources (oral or written). But it is rather improbable. Fully to assess it, it would be necessary to investigate other passages in which any of the four works seem to share common traditions. Bogaert, investigating a series of other common traditions in Revelation, 4 Ezra and 2 Baruch has proposed the following chain of interary dependence: 2 Baruch → Revelation → 4 Ezra. The rather extensive dependence of 4 Ezra on Revelation which he posits he explains as a form of polemical response by the author of 4 Ezra to the Christian apocalypse.[41] However, the position of 2 Baruch makes the relationship he proposes between the three works irreconcilable with the one required by the tradition we have studied.

It seems best to conclude that the relationships between the four texts we have studied do not result from direct literary dependence between them, but on a common tradition which had already taken different forms in the sources used by each.

John presumably knew the tradition in a form which already had the features which Revelation 6:9-11 shares with 1 Enoch 47:1-4 and also those it shares with 4 Ezra 4:35-37. This means that the tradition already supplied the main shape of the scene depicted in Revelation 6:9-11. It is probable that a little of the vocabulary, including ἕως πότε (cf. 4 Ezra 4:35), δεσπότης (only here in Revelation; cf. 4 Ezra 4:38), πληρωθῶσιν (the verb is otherwise used in Revelation only in 3:2; cf. 4 Ezra 4:36; 2 Bar 23:5), comes from the tradition, but for the most part it is characteristic of Revelation (e.g. θυσιαστηρίου, cf. 8:3-5; 9:13; 11:1; 14:18; 16:7; ἐσφαγμένων, cf. 5:6, 9, 12; 6:4; 13:3, 8; 18:24; διὰ τὸν λόγον τοῦ θεοῦ, cf. 1:9; 20:4; διὰ τὴν μαρτυρίαν ἣν εἶχον, cf. 1:9; 12:11; 19:10; 20:4; τῶν κατοικούντων ἐπὶ τῆς γῆς, cf. 3:10; 8:13; 11:10; 13:8, 14; 17:8; στολὴ λευκή, cf. 7:9, 13, 14; ἀναπαύσωνται, cf. 14:13; χρόνον μικρόν, cf. 20:3; σύνδουλοι...

---

[41]Bogaert (1980). In Bogaert (1969) 26-27, he argued for the dependence of 4 Ezra on 2 Baruch. Although he does not make this clear in Bogaert (1980), he presumably continues to think that 4 Ezra is directly dependent on 2 Baruch as well as on Revelation.

ἀδελφοί, cf. 19:10; 22:9). Many of these characteristic expressions are of more than stylistic significance. They forge links between this passage and the theme of martyrdom elsewhere in Revelation. Especially worth noticing are the way the image of the altar (which we naturally take to be the altar of sacrifice, but for which John uses the word he elsewhere uses for the altar of incense) serves to link this scene with the passages in which the martyrs' prayers for vengeance are seen to be fulfilled (8:3-5; 9:13; 14:18; 16:7), and the image of the white robe links this scene with that in which the completed number of the martyrs are seen triumphant in heaven (7:9-17). John has therefore integrated the tradition into his own interpretation of the themes of martyrdom and judgment throughout his book.

He has also brilliantly integrated the understanding of eschatological delay — the main point of the tradition — into the way in which he has used the whole series of seven seal-openings to deal with this theme.[42] At the openings of the first four seals, traditional judgments represented by the four horsemen are executed upon the world. But they are notably moderate, affecting only a quarter of the earth. Hearers expecting the coming of God's rule over the earth, which chapter 4 has led them to expect, will fully understand the martyrs' cry 'How long?' With the opening of the sixth seal, expectation will mount again: the familiar apocalyptic imagery of 6:12-17 heralds the actual arrival of the day of judgment, when the blood of the martyrs will be avenged on their oppressors. But again John holds his hearers in suspense, inserting a long parenthesis (chapter 7) before the opening of the seventh seal.[43] This parenthesis dramatizes precisely the delay which has been explained to the martyrs (6:11). The full number of the martyrs (144,000) is completed in this interval between the very approach of judgment (6:17) and the scene at the opening of the seventh seal, when all heaven is silent so that God may listen to the prayers of the saints and at last avenge their blood (8:1, 3-5: see section 4 below). Thus John has made use of the tradition about the completion of the

---

[42]Cf. Bauckham (1980) 28-36.

[43]On Revelation 7, see below: chapter 8 section 3; chapter 9 section 3.

number of the martyrs and integrated it into the sequence of seven seal-openings in order to raise, for the first time, a major theme of his prophecy: that the remaining interval before the coming of God's kingdom is the period in which God's faithful people must bear witness to the point of suffering and death. The tradition John has used in 6:9-11 did not explain why this should be, other than to appeal to the predetermined plan of God. But in the rest of his work John goes on to share the prophetic revelation which has been given to him as to the meaning of this delay. It is not just that there is an arbitrarily decreed quota of martyrs to be completed. It is so that the witness of the martyrs may play a key role in God's purpose of establishing his universal kingdom.[44]

3. Giving up the dead (Revelation 20:13)

(A) Revelation 20:13:
καὶ ἔδωκεν ἡ θάλασσα τοὺς νεκροὺς τοὺς ἐν αὐτῇ,
καὶ ὁ θάνατος καὶ ὁ ῞Αιδης ἔδωκεν τοὺς νεκροὺς τους
ἐν αὐτοῖς...

And the sea gave up the dead which were in it,
And Death and Hades gave up the dead which were in them...

(B) 1 Enoch 51:1:
And in those days the earth will return that which has been entrusted to it,
and Sheol will return that which has been entrusted to it, that which it has received,
and destruction [Abaddon] will return what it owes.[45]

---

[44]See chapter 9 below.

[45]Translation from Knibb (1978) 135. Isaac (1983) 36, prefers a form of the Ethiopic text with only two main clauses:

> In those days, Sheol will return all the deposits which she had received and hell [Abaddon] will give back all which it owes.

Isaac discusses the textual variants in this verse in (1983A) 408, where he argues that the three-clause form of the text is a secondary scribal harmonization with 4 Ezra 7:32 (our text C). However, the three-clause form of the text of 1 Enoch 51:1

(C) 4 Ezra 7:32:
Et terra reddet qui in eam dormiunt
et pulvis qui in eo silentio habitant
et promptuaria reddent quae eis commendatae sunt animae.

And the earth shall give back those who sleep in it,
and the dust those who dwell silently in it,
and the chambers shall give back the souls which have
    been committed to them.

(D) Pseudo-Philo, LAB 3:10:
...Et vivificabo mortuos, et erigam dormientes de terra.
Et reddet infernus debitum suum
et perditio restituet paratecen suam...

...And I will give life to the dead, and raise from the earth
    those who sleep,
and Sheol will give back what it owes,
and Abaddon will restore what has been entrusted to it...

(E) 2 Baruch 21:23:
Therefore, reprove the angel of death, and let your glory
    appear, and let the greatness of your beauty be known,
and let the realm of death [Sheol] be sealed so that it may
    not receive the dead from this time,
and let the treasuries of the souls restore those who are
    enclosed in them.[46]

(F) 2 Baruch 42:8:
And dust will be called, and told,
'Give back that which does not belong to you
and raise up all that you have kept until its own time.'[47]

---

is closer to LAB 3:10 (our text D), with which it shares the same three terms for the
place of the dead (the earth, Sheol, Abaddon). Since LAB is not extant in Ethiopic,
this correspondence cannot have originated within the Ethiopic textual tradition.
Therefore most probably the three-clause form of the text of 1 Enoch 51:1 is
original.

[46]Translation from Klijn (1983) 628.
[47]Translation from Klijn (1983) 634.

(G) 2 Baruch 50:2:

For the earth will surely give back the dead at that time;
it receives them now in order to keep them, not changing
     anything in their form.

But as it has received them so it will give them back.

And as I have delivered them to it so it will raise them.[48]

(H) 4 Ezra 4:41b-43a:

In inferno promptuaria animarum matrici adsimilata sunt.

*Quemadmodum enim festinavit quae parit effugere necessitatem
     partus,*

sic et haec festinat reddere ea quae commendata sunt ab initio.

The chambers of the souls in Sheol are like the womb.

For just as a woman in travail hastens to escape the pains
     of childbirth,

so also do these places hasten to give back what has been
     entrusted to them from the beginning.

(I) Pseudo-Philo, LAB 33:3:

*...infernus accipiens sibi deposita non restituet nisi reposcetur ab
     eo qui deposuit ei...*

...Sheol which has received what has been entrusted to it
     will not restore it unless it is reclaimed by him who
     entrusted it to it...

(J) Apocalypse of Peter 4:3-4:

He will command Gehenna to open its gates of steel and
     to give back all who are in it.

He will command the beasts and the birds to give back all
     the flesh that they have eaten,

because he wills that (all) humankind appear...[49]

---

[48]Translation from Klijn (1983) 638.

[49]Translation by Julian Hills. This translation of the Ethiopic version of the
Apocalypse of Peter, which I use by permission of the translator, will be published
in A. Yarbro Collins and M. Himmelfarb ed., *New Testament Apocrypha*, vol. 2
(Sonoma, CA: Polebridge Press, 1993?).

(K) Apocalypse of Peter 4:10-12:

See and understand the seeds that are sown, dry and lifeless, upon the ground, and come to life and bear fruit. The earth gives back as it were the deposit with which it has been entrusted. That which dies is the seed that is sown upon the ground, and comes to life, and is given for the life of humankind. How much more, on the day of judgment, will God raise up those who believe in him, and his elect, for whose sake he made (the world).[50]

(L) Apocryphal quotation in Tertullian, *De Res.* 32.1:

Et mandabo piscibus maris
et eructuabunt ossa quae sunt comesta,
et faciam compaginem ad compaginam et os ad os.

And I will command the fish of the sea,
and they shall vomit up the bones that were consumed,
and I will bring joint to joint and bone to bone.

(M) Midrash on Psalms 1:20:

R. Berechiah taught: It was the wilderness which said, *I am the rose of Sharon* (Cant 2:1): 'I am the one beloved by the Holy One, blessed be He, for all the good things of the world are hidden within me, and God has bestowed his blessing upon me, for He said, *I will plant in the wilderness the cedar, the Shittah tree, and the myrtle, and the oil-tree; I will set in the desert the fir-tree, and the pine, and the box-tree together* (Isa 41:10). And when the Holy One, blessed be He, requires it of me, I shall return to God what He laid away with me, and I shall again blossom as the rose, and shall sing a song to Him, for it is said, *The wilderness and the parched land shall be glad; and the desert shall rejoice, and blossom as the rose* (Isa 35:1).'

---

[50]Translation by Julian Hills. The idea of the earth giving back the dead also occurs in the Ethiopic version of 4:13 ('On the day of judgment the earth will give back all things...'), but has probably been introduced here by the Ethiopic translator. It does not occur in the original Greek of this verse which has survived in a quotation in Macarius Magnes, *Apocritica* 4.6.16 (ἡ γῆ παραστήσει πάντας τῷ θεῷ ἐν ἡμέρᾳ κρίσεως...).

The Rabbis taught that it was the earth which said *I am the rose of Sharon:* 'I am the beloved one in whose shadows all the dead of the world are hidden. But when the Holy One, blessed be He, requires it of me, I shall return to Him what He laid away with me, as it is said, *Thy dead shall live, my dead bodies shall arise — Awake and sing ye that dwell in the dust* (Isa 26:19), and I will blossom as the rose, and sing a song to God, as it is said, *From the uttermost part of the earth have we heard songs: "Glory to the Righteous"* (Isa 24:16).'[51]

(N) Midrash Rabbah on Canticles 2:1:2:
R. Berekiah said: This verse (Cant 2:1) is spoken by the wilderness. Said the wilderness: 'I am the wilderness, and beloved am I, for all the good things of the world are hidden in me, as it says, *I will plant in the wilderness the cedar, the acacia tree* (Isa 41:19); God has placed them in me for safe keeping, and when God requires them from me, I shall return to Him His deposit unimpaired. I also shall blossom with good deeds, and chant a song before Him, as it says, *The wilderness and the parched land shall be glad* (Isa 35:1).' In the name of the Rabbis it was said: This verse is said by the land [of Israel]. It says: 'I am it, and I am beloved, since all the dead are hidden in me, as it says, *Thy dead shall live, my dead bodies shall arise* (Isa 26:19). When God shall require them from me I shall return them to Him, and I shall blossom forth with good deeds like a rose, and chant a new song before Him, as it says, *From the uttermost parts of the earth have we heard songs* (Isa 24:16).'[52]

(O) Pirqe de R. Eliezer 34:
Rabbi Ishmael said: All the bodies crumble into the dust of the earth, until nothing remains of the body except a spoonful of earthy matter. In the future life, when the

---

[51]Translation from Braude (1959) 28-29. Braude's note explains the first paragraph as referring to the generation that died in the wilderness wanderings and were buried in the desert, but another possibility is suggested by 1 Enoch 61:5.
[52]Translation from Freedman and Simon (1939) 92.

Holy One, blessed be He, calls to the earth to return all the bodies deposited with it, that which has become mixed with the dust of the earth, like the yeast which is mixed with the dough, improves and increases, and it raises up all the body. When the Holy One, blessed be He, calls to the earth to return all the bodies deposited with it, that which has become mixed with the dust of the earth, improves and increases and raises up all the body without water.[53]

(P) Pesiqta Rabbati 21:4:
Another comment [on Ps 76:9]: R. Phinehas taught in the name of R. Johanan: If the earth is said to have *feared*, why *still?* And if *still*, why *feared?* The explanation of the earth's fear is in what the earth said: 'It may be that the time of the resurrection of the dead has come and the Holy One, blessed be He, requires of me what He has deposited with me, as it is written, *The earth also shall disclose her blood and shall no more cover her slain* (Isa 26:21).' But then when she heard God say, *I*, she grew still.[54]

I have discussed the tradition represented by these texts in greater detail elsewhere.[55] Here we shall focus on what is most relevant for the understanding of the place of Revelation 20:13 within the tradition. It is noteworthy that, just as the texts discussed in the previous section probably all date from the late first century A.D., so most of the texts with which we are concerned in this section are roughly contemporary in date. With the exception of the rabbinic texts (M-P), in which the tradition survives at a later date, all the texts given (A-L) most probably date from the period 50-150 A.D.[56] But as with the texts in the previous section, so it seems clear that the recurrence

---

[53]Translation from Friedlander (1965) 258.
[54]Translation from Braude (1968) 419.
[55]Bauckham (1993A).
[56]For the date of the Parables of Enoch, see n. 35 above. For the date of the Apocalypse of Peter (during the Bar Kokhba war: 132-135 A.D.), see Bauckham (1985A); Bauckham (1993B) chapter 2.

of the tradition with which we are now concerned in a variety of Jewish and Christian works from the first and second centuries A.D. cannot be explained purely by literary relationships among these works.[57] We must be dealing with a rather widespread traditional formula which all these writers probably knew independently of its occurrence in any specific literary work.

The tradition in all these texts makes use of one fundamental image of resurrection: *the place of the dead will give back the dead.* In a large number of the texts (B, C, D, F, H, I, K, M, O, P), this basic image is further expressed by means of a legal metaphor: *the place of the dead will return what has been entrusted to it.*[58] Probably this legal metaphor belongs to the most original form of the tradition, and is implicit even where not explicitly expressed. The full legal terminology is clearest in text I (LAB 33:3). The idea is that God has entrusted the dead to the place of the dead for safekeeping. The place of the dead does not therefore own them, but owes them to God and must return them when he reclaims them at the time of the resurrection. The point of the metaphor is that the place of the dead has no absolute right to the dead so that it may retain them for ever. It has only a temporary right, a kind of custodianship of the dead, granted it by God. The dead actually belong to God; he entrusts them to Sheol for safekeeping, but retains the right to reclaim them. The idea therefore represents a powerful step beyond the old Israelite idea that in death a person falls out of the sphere of God's sovereignty into the power of Sheol. The metaphor of God's entrusting the dead to Sheol for safekeeping is an assertion of God's sovereignty over the realm of the dead, and therefore of his power to demand that Sheol surrender the dead back to life.

The image of resurrection which the tradition embodies is what we might call a unitary, rather than dualistic, image of

[57]Black (1985) 214, regards LAB 3:10 as 'a clear allusion' to 1 Enoch 51:1, but the full range of parallels makes common tradition at least as likely.

[58]The same legal metaphor is used differently in the idea that a person's soul is entrusted to him or her by God and must be returned at death: GkApEzra 6:3, 17, 21; ApSedr 9:2; Hermas, *Mand.* 3:2.

resurrection. It imagines the dead person returning from the place of the dead to life on earth. It makes no distinction between the dead person (as shade or spirit or soul) in Sheol or Hades and the dead body in the grave. More dualistic images of bodily resurrection in the Jewish and Christian tradition had to imagine the reunion of these two elements: the soul brought from Sheol is reunited with the body raised from the grave. But our tradition originates from what was no doubt the earlier Jewish concept, in which there was no sharp distinction between Sheol and the grave or between the dead person and the dead body. Rather the bodily person who died is imagined as returning from the place of the dead to resume bodily life.

That our tradition expresses this unitary image of resurrection can be seen clearly in text B (1 Enoch 51:1), whose three lines repeat the same thought in synonymous parallelism. The three terms 'earth', 'Sheol', and 'Abaddon', are used synonymously for the place of the dead. The thought of the whole verse is simply that the place of the dead will give back the dead who have been entrusted to it. Some have interpreted this text (as well as other texts in our collection) according to the dualistic understanding of resurrection, according to which the body must be recovered from one place, the soul from another, in order to be reunited. The earth restores the body, Sheol and Abaddon the soul. But in that case one would have expected two lines rather than three. R. H. Charles thought that Sheol and Abaddon represent two different places from which the righteous and the wicked souls respectively come,[59] but there is no evidence of such a distinction between the terms Sheol and Abaddon in Jewish literature.[60] In Old Testament texts they occur in synonymous parallelism as alternative terms for the place of the dead (Job 26:6; cf. Prov 15:11; 27:20; 1QH 3:19). It is best to interpret the whole verse in continuity with Old Testament thought, according to which the *dead person* is

[59]Charles (1912) 99.
[60]Stemberger (1972) 46. In AscIsa 10:8, Abaddon is the lowest part of the underworld, below Sheol, but there is no indication that it contains a distinct class of the dead.

in the earth or Sheol or Abaddon.[61] The personification of the place of the dead is also rooted in Old Testament usage (e.g. Job 24:19; 28:22; Isa 5:14).

Comparison of text B (1 Enoch 51:1) with the other texts printed at the beginning of our collection (A, C - E) shows that there was a traditional formulation, whose basic structure is three lines of synonymous parallelism expressing the thought that the place of the dead will give back the dead. The persistence of the threefold form indicates that in none of these cases are we likely to be justified in distinguishing a place of the body and a place of the soul: the idea expressed in this form remains the simple one of the return of the dead. The various terms for the place of the dead which are used in these texts can be understood, largely from an Old Testament background, as synonyms for Sheol.

As well as the three terms for the place of the dead in text B (1 Enoch 51:1) — the earth, Sheol, Abaddon — which recur exactly in text D and two of which recur individually in some other texts (earth: texts C, D, K, M, N, O, P; Sheol/Hades: texts: A, E, H), the following terms are also used in these texts to describe the place or the power which gives back the dead: the dust (texts C, F), the chambers or treasuries of the souls (texts C, E, H), the sea (text A), Death (text A), the angel of death (text E), and Gehenna (text J). The last is surprising, especially as the text refers to the iron gates which are elsewhere those of Sheol/Hades,[62] and must be understood as the Ethiopic translation's rendering of Hades in the original Greek of the Apocalypse of Peter.[63] The references in texts F and H to animals which are commanded to give back the dead represent a special form of the tradition, designed to meet a concern about the fate of those who have died but were not buried — and so, according to the traditional notion which did not

---

[61]For the earth as synonymous with Sheol, see 1 Sam 28.13.

[62]Isa 38:10; Wisd 16:13; 3 Macc 5:51; PsSol 16:2; Matt 16:18; cf. Ps 107:16; OdesSol 17:10.

[63]Cf. Buchholz (1988) 293. This is confirmed by SibOr 2:228-229, which is dependent on this verse of the Apocalypse of Peter and refers to 'the gates of Hades'.

sharply distinguish between Sheol and the grave, could not easily be located in Sheol with the rest of the dead (cf. also 1 Enoch 61:5; SibOr 2:227-237).[64]

Of the remaining terms for the place of the dead, 'the dust' (texts C, F) is used as in Isaiah 26:19 and Daniel 12:2, two key passages for the Jewish concept of resurrection, as well as in other Old Testament passages (e.g. Job 17:16; 20:11; Pss 22:29; 30:10), for the place of the dead. 'The angel of death' in text E (2 Bar 21:23) may be Abaddon, who is 'the angel of the abyss' in Revelation 9:11. The personification of Abaddon in Job 28:22 could have led to the idea that he is the angel in charge of the underworld and therefore the angelic power to whom God entrusts the dead.

The term 'the chambers of the souls' (texts C, E, H) occurs frequently in 4 Ezra, twice in 2 Baruch (21:23; 30:2), once in Pseudo-Philo (LAB 23:13; cf. 21:9), and occasionally in the Rabbis, to designate the place where the righteous dead await the resurrection. (LAB 15:5 also speaks of the 'chambers of darkness' where the wicked are kept.) It may have originated as an interpretation of Isaiah 26:20.[65] Whether or not the original text of 4 Ezra 4:41 (text H) explicitly located the chambers of the souls in Sheol, there can be little doubt that both 2 Baruch and 4 Ezra imply that the chambers are in Sheol. So the phrase 'the chambers of the souls' is another equivalent to Sheol, the place of the dead, at least with reference to the righteous dead.

In this context 'souls' *need* mean no more than the dead in Sheol, the shades. It need not imply the distinction of body and soul in death and resurrection as the reunion of the two. Certainly, this dichotomous view of death and resurrection

---

[64]For this form of the tradition, see Bauckham (1993A) section IV; and for the concern, see Lieberman (1974) 527-529.

[65]This is how the chambers (ταμεῖα) Isa 26:19 are understood in 1 Clem 50:4, which gives a composite quotation of Isa 26:19 and Ezek 37:12. (On this quotation, see Daniélou [1964] 95; Daniélou [1965] 221, 225.) That the chambers of Isa 26:19 are in Sheol could have been concluded by comparison with Prov 7:27, according to the midrashic technique of *gezērâ šāwâ*.

seems not to be found in 2 Baruch, which can describe the resurrection either as the coming forth of the souls from the chambers (chapter 30) or as the restoration of the dead by the earth in the same bodily form in which they died (chapter 50). These are surely not two distinct aspects of resurrection, but alternative ways of describing the same event: the return of the dead to bodily life. 2 Baruch never speaks of death as the separation of soul and body or of resurrection as the reunion of the two.

4 Ezra, however, does explicitly speak of death as the separation of soul and body (7:78, 88-89, 100).[66] Presumably, therefore, for this author resurrection must be the reunion of body and soul, and Stemberger argues that he actually describes it in those terms in 7:32 (our text C), though his use of the traditional formulation hampers him in doing so. According to Stemberger, the first two lines of this text are intended to describe the return of the body from the earth, the third line the return of the soul from the chambers.[67] He argues that the third line is set apart from the first two by the change from the simple pronoun (*qui*) 'to 'the souls which' (*animae quae*).[68]

However, it remains more plausible to interpret all three lines as synonymous parallelism, as elsewhere in this tradition. In each line the author uses a traditional description of the dead which is appropriate to the place of the dead as specified in that line. Thus in the first line, the earth gives back those who sleep in it, because 'those who sleep in the earth' is a traditional description of the dead (Dan 12:2; 2 Bar 11:4; 21:24), while in the second line the dust gives back those who dwell silently in it, because 'those who dwell in the dust' is another traditional description of the dead (Isa 26:19; cf. Job 7:21; Dan 12:2; 1QH 6:34).[69] When in the third line the author uses 'souls' to describe the dead, this is not meant to distinguish this line from

---

[66]On 4 Ezra's anthropology, see Stemberger (1972) 79-81.

[67]Stemberger (1972) 75, 82.

[68]Stemberger (1972) 74.

[69]For Sheol as a place of silence, cf. Pss 94:17; 115:17.

the first two, but simply to correspond to the conventional phrase 'the chambers of the souls'. When 'the chambers' is used for the place of the dead, the appropriate term for the dead is 'souls', just as when 'the earth' is used for the place of the dead, the appropriate term for the dead is 'those who sleep in it'. Thus 4 Ezra has not broken the rule that the three lines of the traditional form are synonymous, and although the author himself probably understood resurrection as the reunion of soul and body, the language of the traditional form he uses in itself expresses no more than the simple idea of the return of the dead from the place of the dead. The only texts in our collection in which the tradition has been adapted to express a more dualistic image of resurrection are those few in which it is explicitly the bodies of the dead which will be returned (texts J, K, O). In these few texts an apologetic concern with particular problems in the notion of bodily resurrection is clear and accounts for the shift from traditional language.

In Revelation 20:13 the three places of the dead are the sea, Death and Hades. The third is not surprising, but the other two terms are unique in the tradition represented by our collection of texts. However, the personified Death may be compared with 'the angel of death' (text E), and may well be John's substitute for Abaddon, since he has used the latter name for the king of the demons (rather than the ruler of the dead) in 9:11 (cf. also 4QBer^a 2:7). Death and Hades are a standard pair in Revelation (1:18; 6:8; 20:13-14; cf. also LAB 3:10b) and may represent the Old Testament pair Sheol and Abaddon, though there is also Old Testament precedent for the pair Death and Sheol (Hos 13:14). More problematic is the sea. It is not plausible to introduce a distinction between body and soul into this verse, so that sea is the place from which the bodies of those who have died at sea are recovered, while Death and Hades surrender their souls. In this case, the earth as the place where the bodies of other people are to be found would surely have to be mentioned too. But in any case, the object of both clauses is 'the dead' (τοὺς νεκρούς). The language is clearly not intended to distinguish soul and body, but simply to speak of the return of the dead. There seem then to be two possible explanations for the reference to the sea. It may be the place for a special category of the dead: those who have died at sea.[70] It is true that, like other categories of dead people who have not been buried, those who have died at sea are sometimes a special concern in texts about resurrection (within our tradition, see text L; cf. also 1 Enoch 61:5; SibOr 2:233). But if these people are in mind in Revelation 20:13, then the distinction must be between those who are buried in the earth, who are thought of as being in Sheol/Hades, and those who die at sea, who are thought of as being in the subterranean ocean. But there seems to be no other evidence for this distinction.[71] So more probably, and in the light of several Old Testament passages which closely associate the subterranean ocean with Sheol (e.g. 2 Sam 22:5-6; Job 26:5; Ps 69:15; Jon 2), the sea is here simply another synonym for Sheol. This is the more probable because it brings Revelation 20:13 into line with the rest of the tradition in which three terms for the place of the dead are used synonymously (texts B-E). Revelation 20:13 preserves the synonymous parallelism exhibited by the tradition as found elsewhere.

Texts A-E all preserve to some extent the threefold formula, using three synonymous terms for the place of the dead, which we must suppose to be original to the tradition. The other texts, though employing the same image of resurrection, use only one term for the place of the dead. However, even within the group of texts A-E, the threefold formula appears in its pure form only in texts B and C: three lines, each of which states that the place of the dead will give back the dead who were entrusted to it. Text A (Rev 20:13) has abbreviated the form: it

---

[70]Charles (1920) 2.195-196, thinks this is the meaning of the present text, though he considers the original text to have read τα ταμεῖα rather than ἡ θάλασσα. Daniélou (1964) 24-25, suggests that according to the original text of 4 (5) Ezra 2:31 God will bring the dead from the 'depths of the earth' and 'the depths of the sea': but this reconstruction of the original text is highly conjectural.

[71]Cf. Swete (1907) 273; Kiddle (1940) 406; Caird (1966) 260. These writers depend on a passage in Achilles Tatius (fifth century A.D.), cited by Wetstein, to the effect that those who die at sea have no access to Hades. I do not know the basis for the claim by Ford (1975) 359, that 'there was a tradition that only those who died on dry land would rise from the dead'.

has three terms for the place of the dead, but couples the last two in one line. It has also dropped the legal metaphor, and with this omission the idea of giving *back* the dead has receded from prominence. Text D retains the legal metaphor and the same three terms for the place of the dead as are found in text B. However, the first line no longer speaks of the earth returning the dead but of God raising them. This change has probably been made in order to adapt the form to its context here in a divine speech and to emphasize the divine initiative in the act of resurrection. A similar motivation may account for the more drastic modification in text E, which is in the context of a prayer to God. Here the idea of the place of the dead restoring the dead is found only in the last clause, but the three terms (angel of death, Sheol, treasuries of the souls) may indicate that the threefold formula still lies behind this text.

In conclusion we return to John's use of the tradition in Revelation 20:13. In the context of an account of the last judgment (20:12-13), the tradition functions to evoke the resurrection of the dead for judgment. Since there is no interest here in the form of resurrection, the tradition, which asserted simply that the dead will return from death, served John's purpose well. The tradition's three lines of synonymous parallelism he has reduced to two, making 'Death and Hades' the joint subject of the second verb, but the remaining repetition serves to emphasize the universality of resurrection so that all may be judged. It was perhaps because John always refers to 'Death and Hades' together (1:18; 6:8; 20:14) that he wished to keep them together in 20:13, in parallel with 'the sea', but it may also be that he wanted to state the resurrection in two clauses in order to make the climactic third clause of the sentence the statement about the judgment.

The use of the term 'the sea' for the place of the dead (or probably better understood, in parallel with 'Death and Hades', as the power which holds the dead in death) was probably not in the tradition as John knew it. It reflects his image of the sea as the primeval chaos from which opposition to God derives (13:1). By referring to it in 20:13 he prepares the way for the reference to it in 21:1. As Death and Hades are destroyed (20:14), so in the new creation there will be no more sea. Thus by varying the tradition's terms for the place of or power over the dead, John has integrated the tradition into his own work.

4. Silence in heaven (8:1)[72]

The 'silence in heaven for about half an hour' which follows the opening of the seventh seal (8:1) has long puzzled the commentators. Suggestions as to its significance include: a dramatic pause in the action,[73] a temporary cessation of revelation,[74] the expectant awe of the heavenly hosts as they await the events of God's final judgment revealed by the opening of the seal,[75] and an allusion to the primordial silence which preceded creation and which now precedes the new creation.[76] It was R. H. Charles who, in 1913, adumbrated the correct interpretation.[77] He made two observations. One was that v. 1 belongs closely with vv. 3-4: the silence is that during which the angel burns the incense on the altar to accompany the prayers of the saints. Charles could only appreciate this connexion by regarding v. 2 as interpolated into the original sequence, but he failed to appreciate that v. 2 is an example of the characteristic 'interlocking' by which John links the sections of his vision together:[78] the seven angels with their trumpets are introduced in the midst of the account of the opening of the seventh seal in order to indicate that the account, which follows (8:6-11:19), of the seven trumpet blasts is in some sense included in the events that follow the opening of the seventh seal.

---

[72]My discussion of rabbinic and Hekhalot texts in this section is very much indebted to Professor Philip S. Alexander.

[73]Mounce (1977) 179.

[74]Swete (1907) 106-107.

[75]Beckwith (1919) 550.

[76]Rissi (1966) 3-6, followed by Sweet (1979) 159.

[77]Charles (1913) 153-155; cf. Charles (1920) 1.223-224.

[78]See chapter 1 section 1 above.

Charles' second observation was that a key to the meaning lies in a rabbinic tradition about the seven heavens, according to which the fifth heaven contains 'companies of Ministering Angels, who utter [divine] song by night, and are silent by day for the sake of Israel's glory, for it is said: *By day the Lord doth command his lovingkindness, and in the night his song* [i.e. the song of the angels] *is with me* [Ps 42:9]' (b. Ḥag. 12b).[79] The meaning is that the angels in heaven praise God throughout the night, but, out of his gracious love for Israel, God silences them during the day so that the prayers of Israel on earth may be heard by him in heaven.[80] The angels give way to Israel for the sake of the honour of Israel (a frequent theme in rabbinic literature).[81] Charles concluded that in Revelation 8:1, 3-4, 'The praises and thanksgivings of the heavenly hosts are hushed, in order that the prayers of the suffering saints on earth may be heard before the throne of God.'[82] Revelation, which portrays continuous praise of God[83] by the living creatures and the elders in heaven (4:8-11), clearly does not share the notion of a daily cessation of the angelic singing, but uses the same general idea in order to indicate the special role which the prayers of the church for judgment are given in God's purpose. At the climax of history, heaven is silent so that the prayers of the saints can be heard, and the final judgment occurs in response to them (v. 5).

It is important that the tradition in the Babylonian Talmud, attributed to the third-century Resh Laqish (Rabbi Shimon ben Laqish), is a tradition about the contents of the seven heavens.[94] It therefore belongs to the apocalyptic tradition of

[79]Although b. 'Abod. Zar. 3b, cited by Caird (1966) 106, also cites Ps 42:8 to indicate that God listens to the praises of the *ḥayyot* by night, it does not draw the conclusion that they are silent by day.
[80]See the comments in Grözinger (1982) 94.
[81]In relation to the worship of God, see Grözinger (1982) 86-98, 326-329.
[82]Charles (1913) 153.
[83]For the continuous praise of God in heaven, see also 1 Enoch 39:12; 41:7; 2 Enoch 21:1 (J); TLevi 3:8; LadJac 2:15; ApConst. 7.35.3; 8.12.27; Hek. Rab. 26:2. Cf. Gruenwald (1988) 159-160.
[84]Two other versions of the tradition, one of which gives a much more elaborate account of the worship of the angels, are given in translation in Grözinger (1982)

speculation about the contents of the seven heavens, which is evidenced also by such apocalypses as 2 Enoch and 3 Baruch. But it is not the only place where such an idea is to be found in Jewish literature. Hekhalot Rabbati, one of the early medieval Merkabah texts which have important connexions with ancient apocalyptic, describes how every day at the approach of dawn God sits on his throne and blesses the *ḥayyot* (the 'living creatures' associated with the throne: Ezek 1:5-14; Rev 4:6-8). At the end of the blessing, he commands: 'Let the voice of my creatures, which I have created [i.e. the *ḥayyot*], be silent for me, and let me hear and give ear to the prayer of my sons [i.e. Israel].'[85]

Also connected with the *ḥayyot* of Ezekiel is a tradition in Midrash Rabbah on Genesis, to the effect that when Israel says the Shemaʿ, the angels are silent until Israel's praise is completed (Gen. R. 65:21).[86] This is presented as an interpretation of Ezekiel 1:24: 'When they [the *ḥayyot*] stood [בעמדם] [i.e. stood still, stopped], they dropped their wings.' There was a well-established tradition that in heaven only God sits and all the angelic beings always stand (in the case of the *ḥayyot* this was thought to be implied by Ezekiel 1:7). Therefore, it is argued in the midrash, בעמדם cannot really mean, 'when they stood', since they are always standing. Instead, using the exegetical technique of *ʾal tiqrê*, בעמדם is read as בָּא עַמְדֹם: '[when] the people [of Israel] come, be silent'. In other words, when Israel comes to pray, God commands the *ḥayyot* to be silent.[87]

93-94. By contrast with b. Ḥag. 12b, they agree in saying that the angels worship throughout the day and are silent at night, apparently adopting a different interpretation on Ps 42:9.

[85]Translation by P. S. Alexander from the Hebrew text in Schäfer (1981A) §173 (MS Oxford 1531); cf. the German translation in Schäfer (1987) 112-113; and cf. Gruenwald (1980) 154-155.

[86]This text is discussed in Halperin (1988) 137-140, but, because he does not recognize that the idea of silence in heaven so that God may hear the prayers of Israel has precedents in Rev 8:1 and TAdam 1:12 (see below), he supposes this to be the author's original interpretation of the silence he knew from Tg. Ezek 1:24-25; b. Ḥag. 12b.

[87]For another version of this tradition in Midrash Tanḥuma: see Grözinger (1982) 88. This makes explicit the point that the *ḥayyot* sing with their wings, so that the dropping of the wings indicates their silence (see below).

Since the sound of the wings of the *ḥayyot* is heard when they move and therefore they were usually thought to sing with their wings,[88] it is a natural interpretation of Ezekiel 1:24 to suppose that the dropping of their wings when they stop indicates their silence. This is the interpretation found in the Targum to Ezekiel 1:24-25 ('When they stood still, they silenced their wings')[89] and in 4QShirShabb (4Q405 20-21-22). The latter text, which belongs to a description of the praises of the angels in the heavenly temple before the throne of God, reads: 'when they settle, they [stand] still. The sound of glad rejoicing falls silent, and there is a stillness of divine blessing in all the camps of the godlike beings, [and] the sound of praises' (lines 12-13).[90] The meaning seems to be that when the angels who cause the movement of the chariot throne stop still, the sound of glad rejoicing which they make while moving ceases, and then the praises of the angels in all their camps can be heard.[91] Although there is no question here of human prayers, this text does show how Ezekiel 1:24 could easily give rise to the idea that at certain times the *ḥayyot* fall silent, so that the voices of others praising God may be heard.[92]

The tradition in Genesis Rabbah which we have just discussed is one of three traditions cited in Genesis Rabbah 65:21 in order to prove that 'the voice of Jacob [i.e. of the people of Israel]... is the voice that silences both celestial and terrestrial beings.' The second of these traditions is also of interest for our purposes. It is an interpretation (also found in b. Ḥull 91b) of

---

[88]b. Ḥag. 13b; 3 Enoch 22:15; Hek. Rab. 11:4; Hek. Zuṭarti (Halperin [1988] 388-389); Pesiqta de Rab Kahana 9:3; Pirqe de Rabbi Eliezer 4 (end); Paris Magical Papyrus, line 3061 (Halperin [1988] 59 n. 20). Halperin (1988) 59, argues that the idea is already found in LXX Ezek 1:23-24; 3:23, but his argument is questionable.

[89]Tg. Ezek 1:25 explains this silence as required for God's revelation to be spoken to the prophets. The same idea is found in b. Ḥag. 13b. Cf. also Halperin (1988) 404.

[90]Translation from Newsom (1985) 307.

[91]On the more general theme of the silent praise of the angels in 4QShirShabb, see Allison (1988).

[92]On 4Q405 20-21-22 as interpretation of Ezekiel, see Newsome (1987).

Job 38:7 ('when the morning stars sang together and all the sons of God shouted for joy'). 'The morning stars' are taken to be Israel, and the text is understood to mean that only after Israel has given praise to God on earth do the angels give praise in heaven.[93] Though the main point is that Israel takes precedence over the angels, it is presupposed that the angels must be silent if the prayers of Israel are to be heard in heaven. The theme is developed in some of the Hekhalot texts, which depict the angels wanting to say the liturgy but having to be silenced by God so that he may first listen to the prayers of Israel:

> Happy are Israel, since they are beloved before the Omnipresent more than the ministering angels! For in the hour when the ministering angels seek to say song and praise above, they surround the throne of glory like mountains upon mountains of fire, and like hills upon hills of flame. But the Holy One, blessed be he, says to them: 'Be silent every angel, every seraph, every living creature, and every wheel which I have created, till I hear and give ear first to all the songs, praises, and sweet psalms of Israel.'[94]

In view of the role of the angel who conveys the prayers of the saints before the throne of God in Revelation 8:3-4, it is worth noticing that the same texts refer to the role of the angel Shemu'el (or Shom'i'el) who stands at the windows of the lower heaven in order to hear the prayers of Israel and to convey them to the highest heaven. The angels in each of the heavens may begin to sing the Trishagion only when they have heard the praises of Israel ascending to God.[95]

A final passage from rabbinic literature uses the same idea of silence in heaven so that the prayer of God's people on earth may be heard in a rather different way. The Targum to the

[93]See Grözinger (1982) 87-88.
[94]Translation by P. S. Alexander from the Hebrew text in Schäfer (1981A) §529.
[95]Schäfer (1981A) §§527-529; cf. §§787-789, 807-809; Grözinger (1982) 328-329.

Song of Songs includes a catalogue of ten songs to which Scripture refers. The fifth is the song of Joshua (Josh 10:12):

> The fifth song was recited by Joshua the son of Nun, when he waged war against Gibeon and the sun and the moon stood still for him for thirty-six hours. They ceased reciting [their] song, and he opened his mouth and recited [his] song, as it is written, 'Then sang Joshua before the Lord' [Josh 10:12].[96]

This interpretation of Joshua 10:12-14 depends on understanding דמם ('to be still') in vv. 12, 13, not (as in the English versions) as 'to stand still', but in its more usual sense: 'to be silent'. Thus Joshua's command is: 'Sun, be silent in Gibeon, and you moon in the valley of Aijalon'. The sun and the moon are understood as angelic beings[97] who sing the praises of God in their movements through the heavens. It seems their movement itself creates their song, so that when they stop (Josh 12:13: עמד, as in Ezek 1:24) they are silent. There is perhaps an echo of the idea of the music of the spheres, or perhaps the angels of the sun and the moon, like the *ḥayyot*, sing with their wings, so that when they drop their wings and stand still, they fall silent.

The Targum distinguishes between the words of Joshua commanding the sun and the moon to be silent (Josh 10:12b) and the song of Joshua, which was addressed to God (10:12a). The latter was a prayer for God's help in the battle, which God heard and answered (10:14). The point is therefore that the sun and the moon must fall silent in order that Joshua's song may be heard by God in heaven. Thus the theme which in the other texts we have examined applies to the regular liturgical worship of God by Israel is here applied to a specific salvation-historical event. There has to be a period of silence in heaven so that a prayer for God's vengeance on the enemies of his people (cf. Josh 10:13) can be heard by God. This makes an interesting parallel to Revelation 8:1-5, where the prayer of the

---

[96]Tg. Cant 1:1: translation by P. S. Alexander.
[97]Cf. AscIsa 4:18; 3 Bar 6-8; 2 Enoch 11-12; TAdam 4:4; 3 Enoch 17:4-5.

saints is for God's eschatological vengeance on their oppressors (cf. 6:10), which occurs as a result (8:5).

The parallel is instructive, but we cannot base too much on this specific tradition in this relatively late Targum. However, in the case of the general theme of the other texts we have examined, it is possible to be sure that it dates back to New Testament times. Although b. Ḥagigah 12b differs from the others in supposing that the worship of the angels ceases for the whole of the daytime, whereas in the other texts the angels are silent only for the time that it takes Israel to say the liturgical prayers, there is also agreement between b. Ḥagigah 12b, Hekhalot Rabbati and (since the Shemaʿ was said at dawn [m. Ber. 1:2] as well as in the evening) Genesis Rabbah 65:21 in the idea that the worship of the angels ceases at dawn, when the praises of Israel begin. They seem to be variations on a traditional theme. Since all these texts date from after the destruction of the temple, it is not surprising that none of them applies this tradition specifically to Israel's worship in the temple, but another text which is clearly related to these enables us to take this tradition back to the time of the second temple. This is the first part of the Testament of Adam (known as the Horarium), which describes the diurnal cycle of the worship of God, by various parts of his creation, at each of the twelve hours of the night and the twelve hours of the day.

The Testament of Adam exists in several versions, of which the most important are the Syriac (in three recensions), and (for the Horarium only) the Greek and the Armenian. The original language (Hebrew, Greek or Syriac) is debated. The most thorough recent examination of the issue by Robinson concluded that the extant Greek text is dependent on the third Syriac recension, and that the first Syriac recension provides the best text of the work.[98] However, he was not able to take into account the Armenian version of the Horarium, now published by Stone.[99] The Armenian is closest to the Greek, but also has

[98]Robinson (1982) 102-104.
[99]Stone (1982) 39-80. Robinson (1989), which purports to give an 'updated' account of scholarship on the Testament of Adam, in fact concludes with Robinson's own work of 1982 and makes no mention of Stone (1982) except in the bibliography.

agreements with the Syriac against the Greek.[100] Stone argues that, in the light of the Armenian version, neither the Syriac nor the Armenian-Greek form of the text of the Horarium can be regarded as primary, but that both are reworkings of common primary material. He also questions the evaluation of the first Syriac recension as the best form of the Syriac tradition.[101] In the light of this significant reopening of the question, it seems best to consider the texts of all three Syriac recensions and of the Greek and the Armenian on their merits. However, one significant overall difference between the Syriac, on the one hand, and the Greek and Armenian, on the other, should be borne in mind. Whereas the Syriac tradition is exclusively concerned with the praise of the various creatures of God at each hour of the day and the night, the Greek-Armenian tradition gives the magical names of each hour and is interested in the spells and talismans appropriate to each. It is plausible that the former is the more original, and that the Greek-Armenian form of the text is an adaptation in the interests of Hellenistic magic.[102]

The section in which we are interested is the account of the eleventh and twelfth hours of the night. The various versions in translation are as follows:

Syriac I:
The eleventh hour: joy in all the earth while the sun is rising from paradise, and shining forth upon creation.
The twelfth hour: the awaiting of incense and the silence which is imposed upon all the ranks of fire and of wind[103] until all the priests burn incense to his divinity. And at that time all the powers of the heavenly (places) are dismissed.[104]

---

[100]Stone (1982) 52-54.
[101]Stone (1982) 54-55.
[102]Cf. Robinson (1982) 18, 141.
[103]Cf. Ps 104:4.
[104]Translation from Robinson (1982) 57; cf. Robinson (1983) 993.

Syriac II:
The eleventh hour: joy in all the earth while the sun is rising from the paradise of the living God, above his creation and shining forth upon all the earth.
The twelfth hour: the waiting and silence imposed on all the orders of fire and spirit until the priests burn incense to God. And at that time all the orders and powers of his heaven are dismissed.[105]

Syriac III:
The eleventh hour: the joy of all the earth while the sun is rising from the paradise of God and shining forth upon creation.
The twelfth hour: the burning of incense and the silence imposed in heaven on all the seraphim and the fiery and spiritual (beings).[106]

Greek:
The eleventh hour is called *glṭw*, in which the gates of heaven are opened and a man praying in contrition will be readily heard. In this (hour) the angels and cherubim and seraphim fly with noisy wings and (there) is joy in heaven and (on) earth; and the sun rises from Eden. The twelfth hour is called *'lṣy,* or *'lṣyn,* in which the fiery ranks rest (ἀναπαύονται).[107]

Armenian:
Concerning the eleventh hour which is called Alfadu. At that time the gate of heaven is opened for prayers. He who makes an upright prayer to God and beseeches him, whatever forgiveness of sins you ask of God, at that time God has mercy upon you.
Concerning the twelfth watch which is called Šačʿšami. At that time the angels of heaven rest. At that time whatever talismans you conjoin, man cannot be released from it.[108]

---

[105]Translation from Robinson (1982) 73.
[106]Translation from Robinson (1982) 95.
[107]Translation from Robinson (1982) 125, 127.
[108]Translation from Stone (1982) 77.

The material which the Greek and Armenian have under the eleventh hour but which is missing from the Syriac recensions occurs in the latter under the tenth hour. However, the Greek also has the substance of the Syriac recensions' account of the eleventh hour, which is missing from the Armenian. We may be certain therefore that a description of the dawn was original to the account of the eleventh hour, and that the twelfth hour of the night is in fact to be understood as the first hour after dawn.[109]

At the twelfth hour, the brief comment common to the Greek and the Armenian (that the fiery ranks/angels of heaven rest) is intelligible as a brief summary of the fuller account common to the Syriac recensions (ἀναπαύονται should be translated 'cease', i.e. from worship). In two other places (seventh hour of the night, tenth hour of the day) the Greek and Armenian agree in omitting references to priests which are found in the Syriac. Since in these places the activity of the priests described is thaumaturgical, it was of interest to the Greek-Armenian tradition, and so is retained (in both cases by the Greek, in one by the Armenian), but is ascribed to anyone, not a priest. It is plausible that at the twelfth hour of the night, a desire in the Greek-Armenian tradition to omit all reference to the activity of priests simply eliminated the reference to the burning of incense altogether. Since this leaves the 'rest' of the angels without explanation, whereas the Syriac recension explains it in a way consistent with the traditions we have been examining earlier in this section, it is plausible that the Syriac form of the account of the twelfth hour of the night is the more original, and that the Armenian and the Greek represent a secondary abbreviation. This conclusion will be supported by the evidence we shall now adduce for regarding this account in the Syriac as of very early origin.

The reference to an incense offering by the priests at dawn can only be to the early morning service in the temple in Jerusalem, in which the burning of incense on the altar of incense soon after dawn took place between the slaughter of

[109]Cf. ApPaul 7.

the sacrificial lamb and its offering as the daily morning burnt-offering (Exod 30:7; Philo, *Spec. Leg.* 1.171, 276; m. Tam. 3:2; 4-7; cf. m. Yom. 3:5).[110] There was no such practice of burning incense at dawn in Christian churches[111] and so the reference cannot be the work of the Christian editor who (in the Syriac version) combined the Horarium with the prophecy of Adam, which forms the second part of the Testament and is very largely, if not entirely, Christian. In the morning service in the temple, on the other hand, the offering of incense was a high point, perhaps *the* high point,[112] of the ritual, preceded by the sound of an instrument that could be heard throughout Jerusalem (m. Tam. 5:6). While the priests were offering the incense, the congregation assembled in the temple were at prayer (Luke 1:10). (It was also the time of prayer for Jews not present in the temple.) No doubt the ascending smoke of the incense was seen as symbolizing and assisting the ascent of prayers to God in heaven. It is entirely natural that it should be the incense offering which is mentioned as requiring the silence of the angels, so that the prayers of Israel might be heard.

This passage must date from before A.D. 70. It is surprising that the relevance of this passage to the date and origin of the Horarium is not noticed by Robinson, who points out that the Horarium has no indubitably Christian features[113] and concludes that it is an originally Jewish work,[114] probably no

---

[110]Cf. Schürer (1979) 302-307. For the reliability of the account in m. Tamid, see Sanders (1992) 116, 507 n. 16.

[111]There is no evidence for the liturgical use of incense by Christians before the late fourth century (Fehrenbach [1922] 6-8; Atchley [1909] 81-96). In eastern Christian practice, which would be relevant to the Testament of Adam, incense was used, at least from the fifth century, during the eucharist (Fehrenbach [1922] 10-11), but there is nothing to indicate that it had any peculiar importance, such as to account for the exclusive mention of this element of the worship in TAdam 1:12.

[112]According to Schürer (1979) 305 n. 49, it was the most solemn moment, but it is not at all clear that the evidence cited for this (Philo, *Spec. Leg.* 1.275-276) provides more than Philo's own rather rationalizing interpretation.

[113]Robinson (1982) 156.

[114]Robinson (1982) 156-158; cf. Robinson (1983) 990 ('may date from considerably before the third century A.D.').

later than the third century A.D., perhaps earlier.[115] It is hard to see how the account of the twelfth hour of the night could have been composed by anyone other than a Jew before the destruction of the temple, and so probably the Horarium as a whole dates from the period of the second temple.[116]

The relevance of this text for the understanding of Revelation 8:1 goes further than attesting at an early date the idea that silence is required in heaven so that the prayers of God's people might be heard. The association of this idea with the incense offering in the temple also makes this materially the most relevant parallel to Revelation 8:1, 3-4. What happens in vv. 3-4 is clearly the heavenly parallel, enacted by an angelic priest in the heavenly temple, to the offering of incense in the temple in Jerusalem. The latter no longer took place when Revelation was written. But Revelation portrays the heavenly reality which the earthly ceremony had symbolized. The incense in heaven accompanies the prayers of God's people and ensures that they reach the throne of God. The early Jewish belief that the angels bring human beings' prayers to God (Tob 12:12, 15; 1 Enoch 47:1-2; 99:3;[117] [cf. 104:1]; 3 Bar 11-16; TLevi 3:7?) is here dramatized in terms of the liturgy of the heavenly temple.[118]

---

[115]Robinson (1982) 152. Note also the points of resemblance to 4QShirShabb, which Robinson (1985) points out.

[116]Ri (1990) argues that the Testament of Adam is a writing supplementary to the Cave of Treasures (a Syriac Christian work), showing features of an exegesis of the text of the Cave. (This is in part a revival of the argument of M. Kmosko.) But (at least as far as the Horarium goes) the argument is unconvincing. The link Ri proposes with Cave of Treasures 5:1 (Ri [1990] 115-116) is not cogent: the Horarium seems to have nothing to do with the hours of prayer observed in early Christianity.

[117]Note the special relevance of 1 Enoch 47:1-2; 99:3, where the prayers of the righteous, assisted by the angels, lead to the eschatological judgment on the wicked, as in Rev 8:3-5.

[118]4QShirShabb indicates that equivalents to the burnt-offerings in the temple were thought to be offered by the angels in the heavenly temple which is the model for the earthly (cf. also TLevi 3:5-6; b. Ḥag 12b). It is probably only an accident of the survival of the fragments that the incense offering is not mentioned in the extant texts of 4QShirShabb. For another point of contact between the depictions of the heavenly temple in Revelation and 4QShirShabb, see Allison (1986). For the offering of sacrifices on the altar in the heavenly temple, see b. Ḥag. 12b;

In Revelation 8:5 the imagery of the incense offering in the heavenly temple is given an apparently original and ingenious development. To indicate that the prayers of the saints are answered by the eschatological judgment of God on the earth, the angel takes fire, symbolizing judgment, from the altar and throws it on the earth. The image derives from Ezekiel 10:2, 6, where an angel (the man clothed in linen) is commanded to take fire from under the divine chariot-throne, between the cherubim, and to throw it on the city, symbolizing judgment. This follows the marking of the righteous on the forehead for protection (Ezek 9:4), just as the judgment in Revelation 8:5 does (7:3). But it is also of interest that the fire which burns under the divine throne, between the cherubim, is more fully described in Ezekiel 1:12-13, where lightning is said to issue from the fire.[119] This is one source of the image in Revelation 4:5, where 'lightnings and voices and thunders' — the symbols of theophany — issue from the throne (cf. also Exod 19:16). In Revelation 8:5, the throwing of fire on the earth is accompanied by an expanded version of this formula (the first of three: cf. 11:19; 16:18-21): 'thunders and voices and lightnings and an earthquake'. By the addition of the earthquake, the theophany in heaven becomes also judgment on earth.[120] These echoes of Ezekiel's visions of the divine throne in 8:5 (and the related 4:5) suggest that, although there is no explicit allusion to Ezekiel in Revelation's reference to silence in heaven (8:1), exegesis of Ezekiel 1:24, which we have seen to be the source of this idea in some Jewish traditions, may lie behind the idea as it appears in Revelation.

Finally, we must consider the duration of the silence: ὡς ἡμιώριον (8:1). Although the usual translation, 'for about half an hour', is what the phrase would normally mean, it is possible

---

b. Men. 110a; Aptowitzer (1989) 14-19. According to the Alphabet of Ben Sira (quoted in Aptowitzer [1989] 15), while the temple stood, when the high priest offered sacrifice and incense, so did Michael in heaven, but he does so no longer. The offering of incense by angels in ApMos 33:4 seems to take place on earth.

[119] 4QShirShabb (4Q405 20-21-22) associates Ezek 1:12-14 and 10:2, 6: see Newsom (1987) 25-26.

[120] See chapter 7 section 2 below.

that ὡς is used as in 4:6; 5:6; 6:1; 8:8; 9:7; 13:3; 14:3 (v. l.); 19:1, 6, where it is virtually a technical idiom of visionary experience. In that case, we should translate: 'for what seemed like half an hour' or 'for, as it were, half an hour'. But the specification of half an hour is puzzling. The use of 'one hour' to symbolize a very short period of time (17:10; 18:10, 17, 19; cf. 3:10) is understandable, as is the use of 'hour' to indicate not a period, but a point of time (3:3; 9:15; 11:13; 14:7), but it is not easy to relate the 'half an hour' of 8:1 to any of these occurrences of 'hour' in Revelation. The suggestion that it is half the eschatological hour of God's judgment (3:3; 14:7)[121] misunderstands the latter as indicating a period rather than simply the time at which God's judgment occurs, and there seems no reason why the half hour of silence should be half of the 'hour of trial' (3:10, probably equivalent to the three-and-a-half year period of 11:2, 3; 12:6, 14; 13:5) or the 'one hour' of 17:10; 18:10, 17, 19. Probably it is better to think of liturgical time, such as the context of worship in the heavenly temple suggests. It is plausible to suppose the offering of incense in the morning ritual in the temple at Jerusalem (as described in m. Tam. 6) took about half an hour. Revelation 8:1 refers to the heavenly equivalent.

5. The context of the transmission of apocalyptic traditions

Our four case studies of apocalyptic traditions in Revelation suggest that the author's use of such traditions is not to be explained by his dependence on Jewish apocalypses known to us. Probably he knew them as traditions which in some form, oral or written, circulated independently of the apocalypses (and other works) in which we now have access to them. This confirms other indications that the writers of apocalypses, Jewish and Christian, customarily incorporated preexisting items or blocks of traditional material.[122] Such traditions might

---

[121]Prigent (1981) 130.
[122]Cf. Stone (1990) 21-22; Bauckham (1993B) chapter 2.

be reproduced very conservatively (as in, for example, the Apocalypse of Peter)[123] or they might be adapted in highly creative ways to the author's own purposes (as is usually the case in the Apocalypse of John).

If such traditions circulated independently of the literary works in which we know them, whether as oral traditions or perhaps in the notebooks of the learned people who composed apocalypses, the question arises as to the sociological context in which the transmission of such traditions could have occurred. It is most natural to think of circles of Jewish and Christian teachers who used such traditions in their oral teaching and to which the authors of the apocalypses belonged. But in the case of Revelation we can probably be more specific. It was most likely in the circle of Christian prophets of the seven churches and their area, of which John was an eminent member (perhaps in some sense the leader), that such traditions circulated.

In Revelation the Christian prophets are prominent members of the Christian community (referred to in 11:18; 16:6; 18:20, 24; 22:6, 9,[124] though in 10:7 the reference is to the Old Testament prophets,[125] and the two prophets of 11:10 represent the faithful church as a whole).[126] Faithful Christians are described generally as 'the prophets and the saints' (11:18), 'saints and prophets' (16:6), 'the saints and the apostles and the prophets' (18:24), or 'prophets and saints' (18:24). Moreover, John is placed in a special relationship with other prophets in 22:9, where the angel calls himself 'a fellow-servant with you and with your brothers and sisters the prophets and with those who keep the words of this book'. The parallel between this verse and 19:10, as well as the concluding words of 19:10, also show that in 19:10 John's 'brothers and sisters who hold the testimony of Jesus' are also the Christian

---

[123]Bauckham (1993B) chapter 2.

[124]For the view that these references are to Christian, not Old Testament prophets, see Hill (1972) 408-411; Aune (1989) 109.

[125]See below chapter 9 section 3.

[126]See below chapter 9 section 5.

prophets.[127] The fact that in 22:9 the prophets are coupled with 'those who keep the words of this book' (cf. 1:3; 22:7) shows that in both these passages the prophets in question must belong to the churches of Asia to which Revelation is immediately addressed.

Following Hill[128] and others,[129] David Aune has argued in some detail that the ὑμεῖς who are addressed in 22:16a ('I Jesus have sent my angel to you [ὑμεῖς] with this testimony for the churches') are the circle of Christian prophets, who are envisaged as mediating John's prophetic message to the seven churches.[130] In that case they may have functioned as the envoys who took copies of the book to the churches and as the readers who read it aloud to the churches (1:3).[131] Aune also argues that the 'servants' of God to whom 1:1 and 22:6 refer are the Christian prophets.[132] In that case, the chain of revelation set out in 1:1 (God — Jesus Christ — angel — God's servant John — God's servants) reaches only the prophets. Only then in 1:3 is it extended to reach all Christians who hear the book read by the prophets, so that in 1:4, 9 John addresses the seven churches as 'you'. The chain of revelation then recurs in abbreviated form in 22:16a: Jesus — angel — you [prophets] — churches. Just as in 1:1 John includes himself among the prophets who mediate his prophecy to the churches by calling himself 'God's servant' and the prophets 'God's servants', so in 22:16a he includes himself with his brothers and sisters the prophets (22:9) in the 'you' addressed by Jesus. However, it remains very uncertain whether the servants of God to whom 1:1 and 22:6 refer are the prophets rather than all Christians. The term can undoubtedly refer to all Christians (2:20; 7:3; 19:5; 22:3; and almost certainly in 11:18, where the parallel with 19:5 shows that it is not the prophets alone who are called 'your servants', but that 'the prophets and the saints' are

---

[127]Aune (1989) 109.
[128]Hill (1972) 413.
[129]Listed in Aune (1989) 112-113 n.7.
[130]Aune (1989).
[131]Aune (1989) 107-108, 111.
[132]Aune (1989) 110.

subdivisions of the general category 'your servants').[133] It refers
unambiguously to prophets only in 10:7, where the phrase
'your servants the prophets' refers to the Old Testament
prophets and deliberately alludes to Amos 3:7[134] (cf. Moses as
'the servant of God' [15:3], a deliberate echo of Exod 14:31).
Thus we cannot be at all sure that the prophets are designated
as the recipients of the revelation in 1:1 and 22:6, but the
possibility that they are addressed in 22:16a remains.

If the prophets were intended to mediate John's prophecy
to the churches, then we might expect that they would do more
than read it aloud. They would also have explained and
expounded it. The meticulous care with which John has
composed his work, packing it with meaning that can only be
uncovered by a process of exegesis similar to that which he and
other Jewish exegetes applied to the Old Testament prophets,
must mean that he intended it to be, not merely read, but
studied. The prophets, who may have learned with him to
interpret the Old Testament in the ways that lie behind much
of the text of Revelation and who were familiar with the same
apocalyptic traditions that he reinterprets in his work, would
form the obvious group of students who could study and
interpret in the Spirit what John had written in the Spirit.

Revelation refers to only one specific Christian prophet
other than John himself: the Thyatiran woman whom he calls
Jezebel and considers a false prophet (2:20). But of a circle of
Christian prophets in the churches of Asia at this time one
other trace remains. We know from Papias[135] and Polycrates[136]
that Philip the evangelist, whose four daughters were prophets
(Acts 21:8-9), migrated to Asia, with at least three of the
daughters. Two lived and died, like their father, at Hierapolis,
another at Ephesus. Since these prophets, like their father
(Acts 6:5), must have been originally members of the Jerusalem
church, they may well have brought Jewish and Jewish Christian

---

[133]This view was rightly argued by Aune (1983) 206, but in Aune (1989) 110,
115-116 n. 40, he changes his mind.

[134]See below chapter 9 section 3.

[135]Eusebius, *Hist. Eccl.* 3.39.9.

[136]Eusebius, *Hist. Eccl.* 5.24.2. On this passage, see Bauckham (1993C).

apocalyptic traditions from Palestine into the circle of Christian prophets in Asia.

Another Christian apocalypse roughly contemporary with Revelation may also be used cautiously as evidence for the way in which early Christian prophets could form a prophetic circle in which prophetic traditions might be shared. This is the Ascension of Isaiah.[137] It is of particular interest in this context since Revelation and the Ascension of Isaiah show major common dependence on some of the same apocalyptic traditions (discussed in chapter 4 and chapter 11 sections 2-3 below). The Christian community from which the Ascension of Isaiah comes evidently valued Christian prophecy (3:19, 27). They also seem to have understood it, as John also understood his own prophetic role (cf. especially Rev 10:1-11, and chapter 9 below), on the model of Old Testament prophecy. The accounts of Isaiah and the prophetic circle around him, in the Ascension of Isaiah, seem to bear some relation to the prophetic experience of the author's circle, even though he has certainly also thought himself back imaginatively into an Old Testament situation.

In the Ascension of Isaiah's account of the reign of king Manasseh and Isaiah's confrontation with him and the false prophet Belkira, which results in Isaiah's martyrdom, there are a number of references to the group of prophets associated with him ('the prophets who were with him': 3:1, 6-7; 5:13). These include other named prophets — Micah, Joel, Habakkuk, the aged Hananiah, and Isaiah's son Jashub (3:9; cf. 4:1; 6:7, 17; 7:1; 8:24; 11:16) — as well as a larger group (3:9-10), who in the time of Israel's apostasy under Manasseh lived an ascetic life together with Isaiah in the wilderness (3:8-11). However, in the happier reign of the godly king Hezekiah, a gathering of the prophets at court is described (chapter 6), in the context of which Isaiah's great vision of the coming of Christ was received

[137]On the depiction of prophecy in the Ascension of Isaiah and its implications for the practice of early Christian prophecy, see Bori (1980); Bori (1983); Acerbi (1989) chapter 7; Hall (1990). These authors rightly treat the Ascension of Isaiah as a whole as a Christian work. Whatever its Jewish sources may have been, they have been thoroughly integrated into a Christian composition.

(chapters 7-11). When they heard that Isaiah was coming to Jerusalem, 'forty prophets and sons of the prophets' gathered there from neighbouring parts of the country to meet him (6:3). The distinction between 'prophets' and 'sons of the prophets' (the Old Testament term for a school of prophets gathered around a master prophet, known as their 'father': cf. 1 Sam 10:12; 1 Kings 20:35; 2 Kings 2:3, 5, 7, 12, 15; 4:1, 38; 5:22; 6:1; 9:1; Amos 7:14; and cf. Isa 8:16) is perhaps between the named prophets (6:7: Micah, Hananiah, Joel, Jashub) and their disciples. In that case, several groups of prophets, each with a leader, are here envisaged.[138] They gather in order to hear Isaiah's words of prophecy, but also so that he may lay hands on them and he may hear their prophecy (6:4-5). The picture is of a group experience of prophetic inspiration in which prophecies are exchanged. In response to a shared experience of heavenly revelation, the prophets worship together (6:8-9). In this context, while Isaiah is uttering inspired prophecy, he falls into a trance, in which he experiences the vision which he afterwards narrates to Hezekiah and the prophets (6:10-7:1; 11:36).[139]

We cannot simply transfer all details of the account from its imagined Old Testament context to the circle of early Christian prophets from which the Ascension of Isaiah comes. For example, the important role which king Hezekiah plays in the account cannot correspond to anything in the early Christian context. The fact that the court officials and the people, who are present at the prophesying session until Isaiah goes into trance, are removed from the room before he recounts his vision to the king and the prophets (6:17), belongs to the apocalyptic literary convention of a secret revelation (contrasted with the canonical book of Isaiah which he 'prophesied openly': 4:20). It has to be kept secret until the last generation of world history, when at last people will read it (11:37-40). We should

---

[138]It may be that 'Jezebel' and 'her children' (Rev 2:20, 23) compose such a group.

[139]As Alexander (1983) 248-249, points out, the account resembles that of the Merkabah conventicle in Hekhalot Rabbati 13-20.

not conclude that the Christian prophets of the Ascension of Isaiah's community kept their own prophetic revelations secret from the rest of the church. Their generation was the last generation of history. Their practice may well have been more like that at the beginning of the account of the prophetic gathering in chapter 6, where the people are present to witness the group of prophets exchanging prophecies. This corresponds roughly to the practice in the Corinthian church, where Paul expects a group of prophets to prophesy in turn for the benefit of the assembled church (1 Cor 14:29-33).

With due allowance for historical imagination, the emphasis on corporate prophetic experience is so strong in the Ascension of Isaiah that it must reflect something about the Christian prophetic experience in the Ascension of Isaiah's community.[140] We can see how prophets scattered about the churches might form a circle which would gather from time to time, perhaps around a leader such as John, to experience prophetic inspiration as a group and to exchange prophecies which might then be conveyed to their various churches. In such a context apocalyptic traditions, taken up in one prophet's prophecy, would be passed on to others and become part of the common stock of prophetic material. We should also notice the strong hint in the Ascension of Isaiah (4:19-22) that the Christian prophets engaged in interpreting the prophetic meaning of Old Testament Scripture.

John's visionary experiences, we might suppose, would ordinarily have taken place in the context of a gathering of his fellow-prophets (probably also in the larger context of a church gathered for worship). He would relate the vision to them orally and they would later recount it to other churches. In the case of his written prophecy, which he has composed in isolation on Patmos in order to produce something much more elaborate and definitive, no doubt incorporating revelations received over a long period of prophetic ministry, conceived as equivalent to and surpassing the written works of the Old Testament prophets, he nevertheless follows the same

---

[140]OdesSol 7:16b-20 may be another piece of evidence for an early Christian prophetic group: see Aune (1982) 448-449.

pattern of communication. He conveys the prophecy to his fellow-prophets for them to communicate to the churches (22:16a).

For the social context in which apocalyptic traditions were transmitted in non-Christian Jewish circles the evidence is even more elusive. Were there circles of Jewish apocalyptists which functioned in a similar way to the way we have argued circles of Christian prophets did? Michael Stone has argued that the social context of 4 Ezra can be inferred to be rather similar to that portrayed in chapter 6 of the Ascension of Isaiah. Although Ezra is recognized as a prophet by the people (12:42), his apocalyptic revelations, contained in his book, are to be communicated only to 'the wise among your people, whose hearts you know are able to comprehend and keep these secrets' (12:37). Similarly, in chapter 14, Ezra receives a public revelation, to be made known to all (i.e. the books of canonical Scripture) and a secret revelation only for 'the wise among your people' (14:26, 45-46). Stone also points out that a group of five scribes accompany Ezra when he receives these revelations (14:24). He draws the parallel with the Ascension of Isaiah in that in both cases there are (a) the seer, recognized as a prophet by the people; (b) an inner group who accompany the seer and are to some extent privy to his experiences; (c) the people, who are set apart from (a) and (b). In both cases, part of the seer's revelation is communicated to the people, part restricted to the inner circle.[141] However, the parallel is not wholly convincing. The five scribes in 4 Ezra are merely scribes: their role is to write down the revelation Ezra receives. Their equivalents in Ascension of Isaiah 6 are not the prophets, but perhaps the three secretaries (6:17), if their function is to write down Isaiah's account of his vision. The 'wise' to whom Ezra's secret revelations are to be confined (cf. also 1 Enoch 82:2) do form a significant inner circle, but there is no suggestion that they do more than receive and understand the revelation communicated to them in Ezra's apocalypse. They suggest an esoteric group of students of apocalypses, but not of apocalyptists. Even less like the group of prophets in the

---

[141]Stone (1991) 75-77.

Ascension of Isaiah are the group of leaders of the people to whom Baruch speaks in 2 Baruch 44-46.

The groups in first-century Judaism in which at least some of the apocalypses circulated and were valued evidently thought of themselves as 'the wise' among the people (1 Enoch 82:2; 4 Ezra 12:37; 14:46; cf. Dan 11:33, 35; 12:3), a relatively distinct group with revelation known only to them. But such groups are the equivalents of the Christian churches, not of the circles of Christian prophets within the churches. We can only guess that within these groups there were teachers, some of whom were the visionaries who composed the apocalypses, and who formed schools of teachers in which apocalyptic traditions were transmitted. It would not be at all surprising if some of these apocalyptic teachers became Christian prophets and thereby facilitated the continuity of apocalyptic traditions between Jewish and Christian circles.

3

Synoptic Parousia Parables
and the Apocalypse

I

In the discussion of the possible role of Christian prophets in the formation of the tradition of the words of Jesus,[1] reference has quite often been made to the relevance or irrelevance of the words of the exalted Christ transmitted by the prophet John in the Apocalypse. They remain the only undisputed example from the first century of prophetic utterances made in the name of Christ in the first person, and for advocates of the creative activity of the Christian prophets they are therefore invaluable evidence that such utterances could be made.[2] Their use as evidence for the role of prophecy in the formation of Synoptic traditions involves, admittedly, additional assumptions not easily demonstrable. We must suppose that John's prophecy is typical of the content of early Christian prophecy in general, and also that this late first-century work

---

[1]E.g. Boring (1972); Hill (1974). More recent literature includes Dunn (1978); Aune (1983) chapter 9; Boring (1983). Since the present chapter was first published (in 1976) a considerable literature has been published, both on this issue and on the parables discussed, which it has not been practical to take into account in the revision of the chapter.

[2]E.g. Bultmann (1963) 127: 'We can see with complete clarity what the process of reformulation of such dominical sayings was like in sayings like Rev 16^{15}... or like Rev 3^{20}...' Cf. Jeremias (1971) 2.

is faithfully representative of the earlier prophets whom alone we can suppose to have been responsible for originating *logia* which actually entered the Synoptic tradition. Some have maintained the uniqueness of John's prophetic status vis-à-vis other prophets,[3] and it seems at least hazardous to infer otherwise unattested characteristics of Christian prophecy in general from the contents of the Apocalypse alone. In any case the Apocalypse is surely untypical in being a lengthy and closely integrated literary composition, with its own very distinctive stylistic traits. Partly for this reason the words of Christ reported in it[4] are for the most part quite unsuitable for transference to the lips of the Jesus of the Synoptic tradition, at least without substantial adaptation. They deal specifically with the situation of the churches (the greater part of the seven messages to the churches) or they are phrased in imagery peculiarly characteristic of the visions of the Apocalypse (e.g. 22:14). But a small number of *logia* which are apparently detachable from their context may be found,[5] and it is upon a close examination of these that the weight must rest in any argument for citing the Apocalypse as evidence for the relation of Christian prophecy to the tradition of the words of Jesus. These 'detachable' *logia* fall into two categories: those which are closely modelled on Old Testament texts (1:7; 3:19a; 22:12, 13),[6] and those which (as we hope to show) bear some relationship to Synoptic sayings (2:7a etc.; 3:3b, 20; 16:15).[7] Here we shall be content to note the existence and possible relevance of the first category, for certainly some Synoptic *logia*

---

[3]Hill (1972).

[4]Rev 1:17-3:22; 16:15; 22:7, 12-16, 20.

[5]According to Boring (1972) 504, the Apocalypse 'contains individual sayings which could be taken from their present context and inserted into the synoptic tradition where they would fit quite well'; he does not specify.

[6]Comparison of Rev 22:12 with 1 Clem 34:3 (cf. also Barn 21:3) probably indicates common dependence on a *testimonia* collection (evidence for Revelation's use of which may also be found in Rev 1:7; Matt 24:3); cf. Grant and Graham (1965) 12; Hagner (1973) 62, 93, 270-271.

[7]The only obvious exception to these two categories is the repeated (ἰδοὺ) ἔρχομαι ταχύ (3:11; 22:7, 12, 20). For Rev 3:21 as a 'detachable' *logion*, see Bultmann (1963) 159 n. 4; but this absolute use of νικάω is an idiom peculiar to the Apocalypse.

(notably in the Synoptic apocalypse) might seem to be classifiable with it. Its scope, however, would be severely limited and it cannot be treated as evidence for the freely creative role ascribed to the Christian prophets. Sayings in the second category (notably 3:20 and 16:15) have been so treated, and it is therefore with an examination of these sayings and their relationship to the Synoptic tradition that this chapter is concerned.

II

Most commentators on the Apocalypse have assumed that in the case of some or all of the four sayings in our second category John is dependent on existing traditions of the words of Jesus. The whole question of Revelation's relationship to Synoptic traditions is of considerable interest, not least because it seems almost certain that John knew these traditions in forms independent of our written Gospels.[8] As in the case of Paul[9] there is wide disagreement on the extent to which Revelation alludes to dominical sayings.[10] We shall here be concerned

[8]This is shown most clearly by the form of Rev 3:5c (cf. Matt 10:32 // Luke 12:8) and the form of the formula ὁ ἔχων οὖς ἀκουσάτο (2:7): while the Synoptic versions of this are various, all have ὦτα rather than οὖς cf. Swete (1907) 29. The only systematic treatment of Revelation's relation to the Synoptic tradition is Vos (1965). But Vos hardly engages with the question of the activity of prophets in forming the tradition (cf. 223-224), and his general conclusion that Revelation demonstrates a 'fixed tradition' of the sayings of Jesus, while by no means wholly unjustified, is something of an overreaction to the idea of a very fluid tradition, and precludes him from considering how the modification of Synoptic *logia* in the Apocalypse might correspond to similar processes discernible in the Gospels.

[9]Cf. Dungan (1971); Wenham (1981); Allison (1982); Tuckett (1983); Wenham (1985); Richardson and Gooch (1985).

[10]Passages which are probable allusions to the Synoptic tradition are Rev 3:5c (cf. Matt 10:32 // Luke 12:8); Rev 3:21 (cf. Matt 19:28 // Luke 22:28-30); the sequence of woes in the seven seal-openings (cf. the Synoptic apocalypse, especially in its Lukan form). Also perhaps Rev 1:3 (cf. Luke 11:28); Rev 1:7 (cf. Matt 24:30); Rev 11:2 (cf. Luke 21:24); Rev 13:10 (cf. Matt 26:52); Rev 1:7 (cf. Matt 10:38 etc.); Rev 19:9 (cf. Matt 22:1-14). The case for treating 19:9 as an allusion to a form of the parable of the Great Supper has some support from the observation that the comparison of believers with wedding guests is characteristic of Jesus' teaching,

almost exclusively with the four detachable *logia,* but the probability of more extensive allusion should be borne in mind as reinforcing the case for Revelation's dependence on Synoptic traditions in these four instances. One of these other allusions must be briefly mentioned, for Revelation 3:5c is a clause which, both in its Synoptic context (Matt. 10:32 // Luke 12:8)[11] and in its context here of one of the promises to the conquerors, forms the apodosis of just such a sentence of eschatological divine law as Käsemann has identified as characteristic of early Christian prophetic pronouncements.[12] There is no doubt that the Apocalypse uses both the stylistic form of these 'sentences of holy law', and also the idea of 'eschatological *jus talionis*' in purer forms than are found in the promises to the conquerors (e.g. Rev 11:18; 16:6; 22:18-19), though this in itself cannot prove that such pronouncements were peculiar to prophetic utterance in the early church.[13] From Revelation 3:5c itself, however, we may conclude only that John is dependent on earlier tradition. In adopting the clause into the context of one of his own ὁ νικῶν sayings, he has destroyed the verbal correspondence of protasis and apodosis that characterized the Synoptic *logion,* though it is

whereas elsewhere in early Christian teaching they are the bride: Jeremias (1972) 174 n.2. For a longer list of possible Synoptic allusions in Revelation, see Charles (1920) 1.lxxxiv-lxxxvi (Charles thought Revelation dependent on Matthew and Luke); and Swete (1907) clvi-cvii, has a few other suggestions. All those which have any probability are discussed at length by Vos (1965). Boring (1972) 503 n.7, finds Synoptic sayings 'clearly reflected' only in 3:5 and 2:7 (etc.). But this insistence on explicit quotation ignores the generally allusive character of references to the sayings of Jesus at this period: cf. Dungan (1971) 149; Davids (1985) 68-69; Bauckham (1985B) 383. We hope here to make a case for 3:3, 20; 16:15; a finally demonstrable case for the less obvious allusions is not possible, but they become more plausible in the light of a significant number of clearer allusions.

[11]For the general scholarly consensus that this saying is related to the Synoptic saying, see references in Vos (1965) 86 n.128.

[12]Käsemann (1969) 77, 79, identifies specifically both this Synoptic saying and the promises to the conquerors as sentences of eschatological divine law of the type he is concerned to illustrate, but he makes no reference to Rev 3:5c in particular. Perrin (1967) 186, adduces Rev 3:5c (i.e. evidence of use by a Christian prophet) in support of treating the Synoptic saying as belonging in the tradition of pronouncements which Käsemann identified.

[13]See Hill (1974) 271-273.

possible that he intended his readers to recall the original protasis. Whether the saying was known to John and his churches as prophetic pronouncement from the exalted Lord or as a word of the earthly Jesus cannot be determined from this context, but it is clear that John is dependent on a saying deeply rooted in the Synoptic tradition. His use of it has little relevance to the question of its authenticity.

The same may be said of the first of our four detachable *logia*: ὁ ἔχων οὖς ἀκουσάτω. This occurs in each of the seven messages to the churches (2:7 etc.) and again (in slightly different form) at 13:9. There can be little doubt that it echoes the saying which is scattered through the Synoptics (where it performs the same function as a formula calling attention to what has been said).[14] The additional clause τί τὸ πνεῦμα λέγει ταῖς ἐκκλησίαις in the seven messages is designed to refer it unambiguously to the words of the exalted Lord through his Spirit. It is worth noticing that this adaptation, presupposing a difference between words of Jesus in the Gospel tradition and prophetic words of the exalted Christ, was thought necessary.

The relation of Revelation 3.3, 20; 16:15 to the Synoptic tradition is somewhat less generally admitted and more problematic. We hope to show that these sayings are dependent on the Synoptic parables of the Thief and the Watching Servants, and in the next section will turn aside first to consider certain aspects of the tradition of those parables before returning to the Apocalypse.

III

The parables of the Watching Servants and the Thief are found in their Lukan versions together in Luke 12:35-40, where they form two of a group of three *parousia* parables (with the Servant in Authority: 12:42-48). All three are evidently intended to

---

[14]Matt 11:15; 13:9, 43; Mark 4:9, 23; (7:16); Luke 8:8; 14:35. Only Matt 13:9; Mark 4:9; Luke 8:8 are in parallel passages.

focus on the unexpectedness of the *parousia*, though in different ways. One form of unexpectedness is common to everyone: noone knows when the Son of man will come: hence the exhortation to live in a state of constant preparedness (12:40). For those who are not so living, however, there is a further, menacing form of unexpectedness (12:36). The Watching Servants focuses on the *parousia* as blessing to those who are found ready; the Thief focuses on the *parousia* as threat to the unprepared.[15] The double aspect of the master's return as blessing or judgment is spelt out in the third parable. The application of the Watching Servants and the Thief is specifically to readiness (12:35-36, 40). Luke in this context includes no actual command to 'stay awake' (the common early Christian metaphor for preparedness in view of the *parousia*),[16] though such a command may be inferred from 12:37. Nor is the Thief in Luke's version explicitly given a night setting.

Comparison with Matthew 24:43-44 shows that Luke's version of the Thief must be nearly *verbatim* Q. Matthew's modifications are limited to providing the parable with an explicit night setting. He substitutes φυλακῇ for Luke's ὥρᾳ and adds ἐγρηγόρησεν, probably deriving these elements from Q's Watching Servants (Luke 12:38, 37), which he has omitted. A night setting is also given to the parable in 1 Thessalonians 5:2, 4—independently, we may assume. The association of burglars with night is obvious enough (and was also so in the ancient

---

[15]Jeremias (1972) 49, finds 'the application of the parable to the return of the Son of Man strange,' for the disaster of a burglary is hardly comparable with the joyful event of the *parousia*; but Rev 3:3 is sufficient evidence that, even for Christians, the *parousia* may be regarded as threat. Whether this parable was a *parousia* parable on the lips of Jesus cannot be determined here, but it undoubtedly had this significance in the earliest traceable tradition. The phraseology in 1 Thess 5:2, 4 and 2 Pet 3:10 may reflect reluctance to compare Jesus himself with the thief, but the day of the Lord is not in those passages distinct from the *parousia* (cf. Best [1972] 205). The versions in GThom 21b, 103, are not evidence for a tradition of the Thief which lacked Q's christological interpretation, as Jeremias thought. Probably the *parousia* has there disappeared because of Gnostic reinterpretation: cf. Gärtner (1961) 177-182; cf. Smitmans (1973) 53-54, 64.

[16]For a full study of the use of this metaphor and related imagery, see Lövestam (1963).

world), and a desire to introduce into this parable the motif of staying awake at night is readily intelligible in view of the currency of this metaphor in early Christian discourse. Matthew 25:13 — an otherwise inappropriate conclusion to a parable in which wise as well as foolish virgins sleep — is a further example of the tendency to extend the use of this image, whose only original *parabolic* context was perhaps the Watching Servants.

Luke's group of three *parousia* parables was probably already collected as a group in the sayings source. Matthew extends the collection considerably but omits both the Watching Servants and the Markan parable of the Doorkeeper (Mark 13:33-37), which occurs in Mark at the point corresponding to the beginning of Matthew's collection of *parousia* parables. Matthew 24:42 is probably a relic of one of these. The Doorkeeper (whose relation to the Q parables has been variously understood) is perhaps best explained as a conflation of the Servant in Authority and the Watching Servants. The expectation (Mark 13:35-36) of the master's return at night is unexpected after 13:34a, where he is represented not as going out for the evening (as in Luke 12:36) but as making arrangements with the servants for a prolonged absence (as in Luke 12:42). The phrase ἄνθρωπος ἀπόδημος (Mark 13:34) is a standard way of beginning a parable (Matt 25:14; Mark 12:1 pars.), and is a natural enough beginning for the Servant in Authority, although not actually used in the Q version.[17] But the motif of staying awake at night, which has no original place in the Servant in Authority, has been drawn into the story by its common association with the theme of preparedness for the *parousia* and with it have come details from the Watching Servants (Mark 13:35).[18] Thus we may suppose that in the

[17] It is quite unnecessary to treat it as introduced from the parable of the Talents, though it is often done: e.g. Dodd (1961) 122; Jeremias (1972) 54; Beasley-Murray (1957) 112.

[18] That it is the doorkeeper alone who watches, rather than all the servants (as in Luke), is more true to life and may be more original, as Jeremias (1972) 54, argues. Lövestam (1963) 84-91, probably overinterprets the night symbolism in this parable, but it may be true that the attraction of the motif of staying awake at night involved the metaphorical significance of the night itself as well as of wakefulness. It was not only at night that doorkeepers might fall asleep (2 Sam 4:6 LXX).

tradition behind Mark 13:33-37 as well as in the Q tradition *parousia* parables were closely associated through affinity of subject-matter. Further evidence of such association may be found in Gospel of Thomas 21b and 103, both of which conflate the Thief and the Watching Servants, and in Didache 16:1 (to be discussed below).

IV

Besides the tendency to association, and in some cases conflation, the tradition of these parables also shows a tendency which we shall call 'deparabolization'. Deparabolization occurs when the application of the parable breaks down the literary structure of the parable as story. Neither applications appended to parables nor allegorical features within parables produce a breakdown of narrative form;[19] this occurs rather when application intrudes into the parable in such a way as to replace narrative by metaphorical statements or commands drawn from the imagery of the story but in fact applied directly to the audience. Many short sayings are in 'deparabolized' form (e.g. Matt 7:6),[20] but Luke's Watching Servants and Mark's Doorkeeper provide the only extensive examples of deparabolization within the Synoptic tradition.

Mark's Doorkeeper has only one verse of narrative (Mark 13:34), after which the parable breaks into direct address to the listeners (vv. 35-36), not as an application additional to the narrative (which is also provided in vv. 33 and 37) but actually in place of narrative. The listeners already become the doorkeepers before the story is told. Similarly Luke's Watching

[19]Some of those features of the tradition of these parables which we shall identify as 'deparabolization' have been previously noticed as 'allegorization'. The partially allegorical nature of these parables (whether original or secondary) does facilitate but is nevertheless no more than a prerequisite for deparabolization. A wholly allegorical story may have perfect narrative structure.

[20]The term is not of course intended to imply that such sayings may not originate in 'deparabolized' form.

Servants begins (Luke 12:35) with metaphorical exhortation,[21] moves into narrative in verse 36, but continues in the form of two beatitudes (vv. 37-38). The beatitude form, temperately used, need not break up narrative structure (cf. 12:43), but in this case the beatitudes certainly function in favour of direct application. Luke 12:37a might be lifted out of the parable and still remain intelligible merely in terms of the commonest of early Christian metaphors. The two beatitudes in the Watching Servants (12:37-38) and that in the Servant in Authority (Luke 12:43 // Matt 24:46) are the only beatitudes to be found in the context of Synoptic parables.

The literary phenomena which we have here identified as the result of deparabolization have been differently construed. That part of Mark's Doorkeeper which has been 'deparabolized' is the part which corresponds to the Watching Servants, and some suspicion might arise as to whether there was ever such a parable. Bultmann indeed regarded Mark 13:33-37 as 'an unorganic composition'[22] and Luke 12:36-38 as 'some gathered fragments of the tradition which in their form and content are secondary and show themselves to be community formulations'.[23] That the existing state of the parables derives from a breakdown of an original narrative structure rather than from a collection of fragments of extended metaphor and allegory is indicated by (a) the recognition that even the differences between the two versions are best explicable in terms of development from a common basis,[24] together with (b) the observation that although, on this view, both versions have been heavily deparabolized, the form of deparabolization is different in each case.

---

[21]Because of its *form* it is common to treat verse 35 as 'a piece of homiletic matter, not originally part of the parable' (Dodd [1961] 121), but the images are entirely appropriate to the story (see Lövestam [1963] 93-94). The lamps are not derived from the Wise and Foolish Virgins, where their function is different.

[22]Bultmann (1963) 119, 173-174; cf. Taylor (1966) 524: 'a homiletical echo of several parables'.

[23]Bultmann (1963) 118.

[24]This is the burden of the argument in Jeremias (1972) 53-54; and cf. Dodd (1961) 120-121.

The extensive deparabolization of this parable must be explained both by intensive use of it in the churches and by the peculiar susceptibility of its contents to this treatment. Given a christological interpretation, the major parts of the story fall readily into place as metaphors which were in any case in common Christian use: servants waiting for a returning master, keeping awake during the night, the time of the lord's return unknown. The ease with which the parable might be dissolved into these metaphors could have resulted in its entire disappearance from the tradition. Its survival in the Lukan and Markan versions was doubtless partially ensured by the additional features peculiar to these versions: in Mark the opening scene (Mark 13:34) which results from conflation with the Servant in Authority, in Luke the detail of the master's waiting on the servants at table after his return (Luke 12:37b). Even so, the story has not disappeared and minor elements survive which belong purely to the story: the banquet from which the master returns in Luke 12:36, the house which is clearly the scene of the action and which remains stubbornly non-allegorical until the Gospel of Thomas.[25] In particular, the door of the house, which Luke's servants open to their master when he knocks and at which Mark's θυρωρός keeps watch, will later concern us. While exhortations drawn from the imagery of the parable seem to have had independent currency in the churches, the parable as story continued to be known, and such exhortations might be expected to gain imaginative force from their original parabolic setting. Thus the seemingly commonplace metaphor of a command to keep awake (1 Cor 16:13; 1 Thes 5:6; 1 Pet 5:8; Ignatius, *Pol.* 1:3) or to gird the loins (1 Pet 1:13; Polycarp, *Phil.* 2:1) might suggest a picture of servants waiting up for their master, lamps still burning and the servants ready to open as soon as he knocks. Matthew 24:42 shows how deparabolization could be carried to the point of eliminating features peculiar to the story entirely: if it is based on Mark 13:25 Matthew has substituted ὁ κύριος ὑμῶν for ὁ κύριος τῆς οἰκίας and ποίᾳ ἡμέρᾳ for the time of night. Yet

---

[25] In GThom 21 this becomes 'the house of his kingdom'.

both here and in the parallel part of Didache 16:1 (see below) the language may remain reminiscent of the parable.[26]

Deparabolization has not affected the Q version of the Thief, a parable which clearly offers less scope for such a treatment. Gospel of Thomas 103, however, recasts the Thief into beatitude form, while in 1 Thessalonians 5:2, 4 and 2 Peter 3:10 the simile ὡς κλέπτης (ἐν νυκτί) suffices to convey the message of the parable.[27] Moreover the Q application of the Thief takes its place, detached from the parable, in the mosaic of sayings about wakefulness which is found in Didache 16:1. This passage may now be compared with the Synoptic traditions:

Didache 16:1	Synoptic parallels
γρηγορεῖτε ὑπερ τῆς ζωῆς ὑμῶν·	γρηγορεῖτε (Matt 24:42; cf. Mark 13:35-36)
οἱ λύχνοι ὑμῶν μὴ σβεσθήτωσαν,	ἔστωσαν ὑμῶν αἱ ὀσφύες περιεζωσμέναι
καὶ αἱ ὀσφύες ὑμῶν μὴ ἐκλυέσθωσαν,	καὶ οἱ λύχνοι καιόμενοι (Luke 12:35)
ἀλλὰ γίνεσθε ἔτοιμοι·	καὶ ὑμεῖς γίνεσθε ἔτοιμοι (Matt 24:4 // Luke 12:40)
οὐ γὰρ οἴδατε τὴν ὥραν ἐν ᾗ ὁ κύροις ὑμῶν ἔρχεται.	ὅτι οὐκ οἴδατε ποίᾳ ἡμέρᾳ ὁ κύριος ὑμῶν ἔρχεται. (Matt 24:42; cf. Mark 13:35; Matt 24:50 // Luke 12:46)

[26]Note that in the surrounding verses (24:37, 39, 44) Matthew speaks of the coming of the Son of man, and uses similar language of the coming of the Lord only in 24:46, 50, where the reference is to the master in the Servant in Authority.

[27]Doubts are possible as to the relation of this phrase to the Q parable. Though they can hardly be independent, the possibility cannot be dismissed out of hand that the latter could have been expanded from the former: cf. Best (1972) 205. But a strong argument in favour of the priority of the Q version is its surprising failure to employ the image of staying awake at night: ἔτοιμος is used in the New Testament of readiness for the *parousia* only in Luke 12:40 // Matt 24:44. See also Jeremias (1972) 48-50; Lövestam (1963) 96-97; Smitmans (1973) 54-55; Dodd (1959) 114-15.

Whether the writer of Didache 16 had access to our Gospels is not very relevant to our purposes. As Audet pointed out, the process by which, working with the Gospels in front of him, he could have compiled this patchwork of sayings is incredible.[28] Nonetheless, in view of the close parallel with Matthew 24:42 it is unlikely that his tradition was wholly independent of the specifically Matthean redaction. The significant feature of the passage is the combination of detachable exhortations not only from Matthew 24:42 but also from Luke 12:35 (both already deparabolized parts of the Watching Servants) and from the application of the Thief. The association of these exhortations in quotations from memory is most easily explicable by the writer's mental association of the parables from which they derived.

V

The preceding discussion has shown:

(1) *Parousia* parables were widely used and familiar in the primitive church. The evidence for this in the cases of the Watching Servants and the Thief is remarkably good.[29]

(2) *Parousia* parables were collected and associated from a very early stage. This again is especially well attested for the Watching Servants and the Thief, and to a lesser extent also for the Servant in Authority. Allusion to one of these two or three parables might be expected to suggest its well-known companion(s) also.

(3) Owing both to extensive usage and to amenable subject-matter, the Watching Servants and (to a lesser extent) the Thief suffered from deparabolization. Either as simile ('the day of the Lord will come like a thief') or as metaphorical exhortation ('Let not your lamps be extinguished') the imagery of the parables was therefore absorbed into ordinary Christian discourse and could be used independently of its parabolic context.

---

[28]Audet (1958) 180-182; cf. Draper (1985) 280.
[29]See also further evidence in the Additional Note at the end of this chapter.

(4) This independent usage would seem, however, to have coexisted with the continued popularity of the parables as stories. The common metaphors of spiritual wakefulness and eschatological readiness we may suppose to have been frequently reinforced by the popularity of parables which gave vivid narrative settings for such imagery.

(5) We may add that the *Sitz im Leben* of the tradition of these parables in the churches is evidently (as has often been noticed) the kind of 'eschatological paraenesis' of which the epistles provide abundant examples: Christian living in expectation of the *parousia*, for which the metaphor 'keep awake' so frequently recurs. Didache 16 provides an unquestionable example of precise reference to these parables in paraenetic material from probably late in the New Testament period, while 1 Thessalonians 5 corresponds at the earliest point to which we have access.[30]

VI

It is within this pattern of tradition in the church that the references to these parables in Revelation 3:3, 20; 16:15 are to be understood. The content of Revelation 3:3b is close to the Q version of the Thief (both parable and application), except that John introduces the motif of staying awake at night, as Paul and Matthew had done. In keeping with the context in a speech of the Lord, deparabolization takes the form not only of the simile ὡς κλέπτης but also of recasting the parable into an 'I' saying. The reference of the image, faithful to the Q tradition, is to the *parousia* as judgment, the menacing unexpectedness of the Lord's coming for the unrepentant Christians at Sardis. Where the image recurs in 16:15 it is combined with a beatitude pronounced on the man who is prepared. Unfortunately the precise sense of this beatitude is not clear (and the commentators signally fall to elucidate it). The absurd image (adopted by the REB) of the man who

---

[30]See Dodd (1959) 112-116, especially 115-116.

undresses but stays awake in order to guard his clothes from the possibility of theft is surely not to be allowed.[31] The picture must be of the man who stays awake, fully clothed, contrasted with the man who sleeps and will therefore be caught naked when surprised in the night. This image has no connexion with that of the thief, for the hazards of a burglary are not principally those of being caught without one's clothes. Rather the image of the thief, having been used to suggest the sudden and unexpected nature of the *parousia* and the danger of the Christian's being caught unprepared, introduces the familiar metaphor of staying awake but is then forgotten as the beatitude develops a novel variation of that metaphor.

The beatitude is possibly an expansion of that in Luke 12:37-38[32] and the image may be intended to recall Amos 2:16,[33] which has some appropriateness in the context of the gathering of armies for the battle of the great day of God. Though we might otherwise be tempted to treat it as a simple non-allegorical image of eschatological readiness, the case for allegory seems decided by τηρῶν τὰ ἱμάτια, which cannot naturally mean 'keeps on his cloths' (NEB). If that is the meaning, then 'the verb is governed by the metaphor: the garment is equivalent to the state of salvation, which is to be maintained'.[34] The beatitude is certainly a creative development from no more than the metaphor of staying awake in the Synoptic tradition, but in the light of its meaning — intimately linked with the allegory of 3:18 — it is doubtful whether it is quite such an easily detachable *logion* as at first appeared.

---

[31]REB: 'Happy the man who stays awake, and keeps his clothes at hand so that he will not have to go naked and ashamed for all to see!'; cf. Farrer (1964) 178: 'The caretaker who undresses and sleeps may have his garments stolen, to his great disgrace when he runs out crying for help.' The suggestion (Hendrikson [1962] 164; Vos [1965] 84) that τηρῶν τὰ ἱμάτια means 'keeps his garments unspotted' (cf. 3:4) turns the beatitude into a string of intolerably mixed metaphors. The same consideration tells against the transposition of 16:15 into the message to Sardis (so Charles [1920] 2.49; Lohmeyer [1953] 136-137), for the danger there is of defiling clothes, not losing them.

[32]Vos (1965) 84, unconvincingly suggests it may be a paraphrase of Luke 12:43.

[33]So Bruce (1973) 341.

[34]Riesenfeld (1972) 143.

A clear and intentional allusion in Revelation 3:20 to the parable of the Watching Servants has been only occasionally proposed, notably by J. Jeremias,[35] though similarities of imagery have not infrequently been noticed by the commentators (more often with Luke 12:36 than with Luke 12:37). Our suggestion that the verse be interpreted as an application of the parable presupposes (a) that the parable would have been sufficiently familiar in John's churches for readers to be expected to catch the allusion, and (b) an eschatological interpretation of the verse. For the first presupposition we would appeal to the conclusions in section V above, especially (1) and (2), together with the fact of John's use of the Thief in 3:3. The imagery there is self-contained, in the sense that though greater force would doubtless be given by recollection of the parable, the verse would nevertheless be wholly intelligible without reference to the parable. The allusion to the Watching Servants in 3:20, if such it be, is somewhat more dependent on its ability to recall the parable itself, but it should be noticed that this is a type of allusion which is common in Revelation's use of the Old Testament. As an example from the seven messages to the churches, the language of 3:9 could not be fully appreciated by readers who failed to recognize and to recall the context of the allusion to Isaiah 60:14. A similarly allusive use of a dominical parable in 3:20 is wholly of a piece with John's literary techniques throughout the Apocalypse.

On the question of the eschatological reference of 3:20 the commentators are divided.[36] Most of those who oppose it recognize an allusion to the messianic banquet, but by way of analogy only: the joys of intimate communion with Christ in the next world are anticipated for the repentant Laodicean Christian in this.[37] Similarly a direct, rather than analogical reference to the eucharist has been generally felt inappropriate because of the individualism of the verse.[38] These commentators

[35]Jeremias (1972) 55; (1965) 178; also Vos (1965) 97-100; cf. Kiddle (1940) 60.
[36]An eschatological reference is accepted by Bousset (1906) 233; Swete (1907) 63; Lohmeyer (1953) 39; Lohse (1960) 32; Vos (1965) 95; Sweet (1979) 109.
[37]E.g. Farrer (1964) 83; Bonsirven (1951) 126. Such a view need not be incompatible with recognizing an allusion to the Watching Servants in this verse.
[38]Caird (1966) 58; but cf. Minear (1968) 57-58; Allo (1921) 45.

take the image of opening the door as representing the repentance commanded in verse 19, while the major image of the verse is found to be Christ as the guest in the house of the believer. Even those who refer the verse to the *parousia* adopt this latter interpretation,[39] though such a setting for the messianic banquet or even the eucharist (both of which are the Lord's feast to which believers are invited) is remarkable.

In favour of the eschatological interpretation of the verse in general and the reference to the parable of the Watching Servants in particular, we would argue:

(1) A reference to the *parousia* is to be expected at this point in the message to the Laodicean church. In three previous messages — to Ephesus, Pergamum, and Sardis — the church is commanded to repent, and this command is in each case followed by an announcement of the imminent *parousia* (2:5, 16; 3:3; cf. also 3:22-23); 3:20 occupies the analogous position in the message to Laodicea. Moreover, without the eschatological interpretation of 3:20 this one of the seven messages would be lacking in any reference to the impending eschatological crisis which pervades the rest of the seven and provides their major link with the rest of the Apocalypse. Revelation 16:15, which develops the imagery of 3:18, makes it clear that the Laodiceans' need for repentance has eschatological urgency: they must not be found naked at the *parousia*. The argument up to verse 20 leads one to expect a reference to eschatological readiness, and the introduction of imagery from the Watching Servants at that point is as natural as the introduction of imagery from the Thief at 3:8.

(2) A further argument has been based on the sequence of 3:20-21 compared with the probable basis for the image of 3:21 in the Synoptic *logion* Luke 22:28-30 // Matthew 19:28.[40] In its Lukan version this includes reference to eating and drinking at the Lord's table in the coming kingdom, and while we would

[39]Including, unaccountably, Jeremias (1965) 178; cf. Beckwith (1922) 491: 'Here the Messiah is represented as coming to the houses of his people.' Beckwith finds no analogous image of the *parousia* other than John 14:23.

[40]For a fuller discussion of this relationship, see Vos (1965) 100-104, with references to previous literature.

regard the Watching Servants (Luke 12:37) as the primary source of this image in Revelation 3:21, its recurrence in Luke 22:30 may well have suggested the basis for Revelation 3:21.

(3) A reference to the parable eliminates the difficult image of Christ the guest. He is, on the contrary, pictured as the master whose servants are expected to be ready to open to him at his return. The house is his own in which he graciously and remarkably (cf. Luke 17:7-8) condescends to dine with his servants. There is no need to allegorize either the house or the door[41] (so often expounded as the door of the believer's heart); they are non-allegorical features of the parable, the necessary setting for this peculiarly vivid image of readiness for the Lord's return. In 3:19 the Lord commands repentance; 3:20 opens with an announcement of his imminent coming;[42] the repentant Laodicean Christian is then pictured as the servant ready to receive his returning master; the verse concludes with a promise of remarkable blessing on that servant (the master will share a meal with him).

The note of individual application in the verse, which might be thought out of place in a reference to the *parousia*, is entirely in keeping with the tendency of *parousia* parables to focus on the individual's condition of preparedness or otherwise (Luke 12:43; cf. Rev 16:15), as also with the context of the promises to the conquerors, which are an individualized form of eschatological promise. John's use of the pair of parables, the Thief and the Watching Servants, corresponds precisely to the difference of emphasis which we noted in the Lukan versions. The *parousia* may come either as judgment or as blessing. The conditional clauses in 3:3 and 3:20 do not of course make the *parousia* itself conditional on the repentance or continued unrepentance of Christians; they do make its character as judgment or blessing conditional on the state in which Christians are then found. The change from threat (in 2:5, 16; 3:3) to promise (in 3:20) is unexpected, but also fitting.

---

[41]In the door Vos sees an allusion to the saying in Mark 13:29; Matt 24:33; cf. Jas. 5:9. But this is both inappropriate and unnecessary.

[42]For ἰδού and the vivid present, cf. Rev 1:9; 2:22; 22:7, 12.

Laodicea, unique among the churches in having no good word to be said about it, receives a sentence of severest judgment in 3:16. The note of loving reproof in verse 19 is necessary to encourage the repentant, and verse 20 therefore appropriately continues with the promise of blessing rather than judgment at the Lord's coming for those who heed the call to repent.

Deparabolization by means of an 'I' saying is carried further in 3:20 than in 3:3 or 16:15. In 3:20 the Lord does not come ὡς κύριος (!), but wholly assumes the role of the master in the parable. The difference corresponds to the extent of christological allegory in the parables as we already have them in Luke. The *parousia* is like a burglary for those who are unprepared, but the allegory cannot be pressed to any closer identification of the Son of man with the thief. In the Watching Servants the allegory is more thorough-going.

VII

To what extent has creative development occurred in the tradition of these parables as we have traced it in the Synoptics, 1 Thessalonians, 2 Peter, Revelation and the Didache? Conflation of *parousia* parables has occurred (Mark 13:33-37) and the motif of staying awake at night has found its way into the Thief (Matt 24:43; 1 Thes 5:4-7; Rev 3:3; 16:15) where it was not originally explicit. Allegory is hardly present in the tradition of the Thief, neither in the Q version[43] nor in the epistles nor in the Apocalypse. In all its three versions the Watching Servants (Luke 12:35-38; Mark 13:33-37; Rev 3:20; and cf. Matt 24:42) is quite extensively (though not wholly) allegorical, and for this reason was heavily subjected to the kind of deparabolization we have observed. If the allegory is secondary it was at any rate present in the tradition prior to this process of deparabolization, which presupposes it, and no more

[43]Note that the Q interpretation (Matt 24:44 // Luke 12:40) is not strict allegory. Whereas the householder would only have been ready for the thief had he known when the thief was coming, Christians are to be ready *because* they do *not* know when the Son of man is coming.

extensive development of the allegory is present in the later than in the earlier versions. There is some reason to regard Luke 12:37b as secondary to the parable;[44] it was probably not in the version conflated in Mark 13:33-37 and perhaps not in the version for which Matthew may have substituted Matthew 24:42. But it was probably a pre-Lukan addition to the parable,[45] and the version of the parable known to John and the seven churches of Asia had at least something comparable. It is hardly possible to tell which form of the meal is the more original: John may have eliminated the motif of the serving Lord as having no other place in his eschatological imagery.

Both in 1 Thessalonians 5:4 - 7 and in Revelation 16:15 the parable of the Thief provided the starting-point for the development of further extended metaphors, but these have little integral relationship to the imagery of the parable. The symbolism of light and darkness in the one case and of clothes and nakedness in the other has been suggested by the metaphor of wakefulness and by favourite symbolic images of each writer. In the case of 1 Thessalonians 5 some influence on the Synoptic tradition elsewhere may have been exerted by Paul's development of the metaphor, though the relation to Luke 21:34-36 is debatable.[46] Both passages (1 Thes 5:4-7 and Rev 16:15) are suggestive as to the treatment of the parables of Jesus in the teaching of the church, but from neither can we conclude that the tradition of the parables themselves was affected by this treatment. Deparabolization, a process which affects only the formal literary structure of the parables, appears to have been the only process through which the tradition of these parables was significantly affected by their use in the churches.

Furthermore it should be noted that Revelation's use of the tradition is distinctive in no other way than its formulation of the sayings as 'I' sayings in speeches of the exalted Lord. John's prophetic consciousness apparently allows him a no less

[44]Jeremias (1972) 53-54. This does not mean that the image itself cannot derive from Jesus' teaching.
[45]Jeremias (1972) 54 n.18.
[46]See, e.g., Dodd (1961) 115-116.

conservative treatment of the existing tradition of Jesus' teaching than that by, say, Matthew or the author of Didache 16. If the Apocalypse may be allowed to imply anything about the role of Christian prophets in the formation of the Synoptic tradition, then it must be that this role was not a distinctive one, no different in kind from that of teachers or preachers who did not speak directly in the name of the Lord.

The process of deparabolization is the principal process by which the paraenesis of the church has affected the tradition of these *parousia* parables. The paraenetic material of the epistles is non-parabolic, and (left to their own devices) the teachers and the prophets of the early church apparently employed metaphorical exhortations rather than extended illustrative stories. The tradition of the parables of Jesus must have been used in the teaching of the church, but it has to be admitted that such a *Sitz im Leben* (together with its alleged influence on the tradition) has usually remained a mere postulate. The parables of the Watching Servants and the Thief provide a concrete example of two-way interaction between the church's own paraenesis and its tradition of the remembered sayings of Jesus, with evidence available from both types of material. The effect of this interaction on the Synoptic tradition appears to have been formal modification rather than substantial formulation; the effect on the church's paraenesis was a somewhat meagre enrichment of metaphor rather than a stimulus to creative imitation. Naturally the conclusions to be drawn from this example are limited — certainly to parabolic material. No comparable evidence of interaction is available *from both sides* in the case of other parables,[47] but this (to the extent that it is not merely accidental) may argue that others were actually less affected by their use in the churches. The attempt to reconstruct the history of the Synoptic tradition must at least be subject to the checks provided by such evidence

---

[47]Even the possible allusions suggested by Moule (1952) 76-78 (= Moule [1982] 51-53), are somewhat tenuous with regard to parables. Cf. Brown (1963) 25: 'Epistolary parallels to the *parables* are relatively few.'

external to the Gospels as may be found. This may be thought unduly restrictive, but it was precisely out of a methodological need to find external evidence for the creative role of the Christian prophets in the tradition that appeal to the evidence of the Apocalypse was made. That appeal cannot be upheld.

Additional note

The purpose of this note is to consider five further allusions to the *parousia* parables, which have scarcely been noticed in the literature on the parables.[48] They will confirm the arguments of this chapter about the process of deparabolization, and throw some valuable additional light on the tradition-history of these parables.

(1) Ascension of Isaiah 4:16:

> The Lord... will serve those who have kept watch in this world.[49]

This statement, which follows the depiction of the *parousia* in a lengthy passage of eschatological prophecy, is a striking allusion to the parable of the Watching Servants (Luke 12:37). It is most unlikely that the author knew Luke's Gospel, to which neither this section nor the rest of the Ascension of Isaiah seems to allude elsewhere. This verse therefore confirms the view, taken above,[50] that Luke 12:37b belongs to the pre-Lukan text of the parable.[51]

----

[48]Nos. 2, 3 and 4 are included in the parallels listed by Resch (1895) 333-338. No. 4 is briefly discussed by Smitmans (1973) 55 n. 55, 65 n. 102.

[49]Translation from Knibb (1985) 162.

[50]Against Schneider (1975) 34-35.

[51]Perhaps it might be suggested that AscIsa 4:16 preserves the original context of the saying, whence Luke has inserted it into the parable. To this I would reply: (a) The reference to 'watching' in AscIsa 4:16 comes from the parable, not from Luke 12:37b alone. (b) In AscIsa 4:16 the saying is hardly intelligible except as an allusion to material familiar from another context. (c) SibOr 2:177-183 (quoted below) similarly alludes to the parables of the Watching Servants in a context like that of AscIsa 4, but its allusions are to other parts of the parable.

The allusion is a deparabolized one: 'the Lord' is not the master in the parable but the Lord Jesus (already mentioned in the context), who serves, presumably at the messianic banquet, those who have kept awake, not in the master's house, but 'in this world'.[52] But presumably the allusion (like that at Rev 3:20) would still call the parable to mind; only if this remarkable image of the serving Lord were familiar to readers from the parable could it be so abruptly introduced here.

(2) Sibylline Oracle 2:177-183:

ὕψιστος πάντων πανέπισκοπος αἰθέρι ναίων
ὕπνον ἐπ' ἀνθρώποις σκεδάσει βλέφαρ' ἀμφικαλύψας.
ὦ μάκαρες θεράποντες, ὅσους ἐλθὼν ἀγρυπνοῦντας
εὕροι ὁ δεσπόζων· τοὶ δ' ἐγρήγορθαν ἅπαντες
πάντοτε προσδοκάοντες ἀκοιμήτοις βλεφάροισιν.
ἥξει δ' ἀτρεκέως καὶ ἔσσεται ὡς ἀγορεύω. [53]

The Most High, who oversees all, living in the sky,
will spread sleep over men, having closed their eyes.
O blessed servants, as many as the master, when he comes,
finds awake; for they have all stayed awake
all the time looking expectantly with sleepless eyes.
For he will come, at dawn, or evening, or midday.
He will certainly come, and it will be as I say.[54]

This passage, again in the context of a long eschatological prophecy, is probably dependent on Luke 12:37-38. The variation of vocabulary is only to be expected in this kind of poetic paraphrase.[55] But, like Ascension of Isaiah 4:16, it is additional evidence of the remarkable popularity of the parable of the Watching Servants in the eschatological teaching of the

---

[52]The addition of 'in this world' recalls GThom 21b ('watch for the world'), but the latter is a gnosticizing interpretation; cf. Schrage (1964A) 68.

[53]Text in Geffcken (1902) 35-36. The work should be dated in the mid- or late second century.

[54]Translation from Collins (1983) 349.

[55]Cf. the paraphrase of Mark 13:17 (par.) in lines 190-193.

early church. It is also striking confirmation of the remark made earlier in this chapter about the deparabolizing effect of the beatitude in Luke 12:37a: 'Luke 12:37a could be lifted out of the parable and still remain intelligible merely in terms of the commonest of early Christian metaphors.' This is exactly what has happened in Sibylline Oracle 2:179-181. The adaptation of Luke 12:38 in line 182 is a further deparabolizing step: it is no longer a question of staying awake for the master's return *during the night.*

(3) Methodius, *Symposium* 5:2:

οἱ λύχνοι ὑμῶν μὴ σβεννύσθωσαν, καὶ αἱ ὀσφύες ὑμῶν μὴ λυέσθωσαν. διὰ τοῦτο καὶ ὑμεῖς ὅμοιοι γίνεσθε ἀνθρωπους προσδεχομένοις τὸν κύριον αὐτῶν, πότε ἀναλύει ἐκ τῶν γάμων, ἵνα ἐλθόντι καὶ κρούσαντι αὐτῷ εὐθέως ἀνοίξωσι ἐστε, ὅτι ἀνακλινεῖ ὑμᾶς καὶ παρελθών διακονήσει· κἂν τῇ δευτέρᾳ, κἂν τῇ τρίτῃ, μακαρίοί ἐστε.[56]

The most important aspect of this version of the parable of the Watching Servants is its opening sentence, which closely resembles, not Luke 12:35, but Didache 16:1: οἱ λύχνοι ὑμῶν μὴ σβεσθήτωσαν, καὶ αἱ ὀσφύες ὑμῶν μὴ ἐκλυέσθωσαν. This agreement cannot be accidental, but it is hard to be sure how it should be explained. Methodius' text could be influenced by the Didache, or it may be independent testimony to the same non-Lukan version of the saying which the Didache quotes. In that case it would confirm the Didache's independence of our Gospels at this point.

The rest of the parable follows the Lukan version fairly closely,[57] but it should be noticed how naturally the two beatitudes have been further deparabolized. No longer applied to the servants in the parable, they are now addressed directly

---

[56]Text from Bonwetsch (1917) 54-55. The work dates from the end of the second century.

[57]The words διὰ τοῦτο ὅμοιοι γίνεσθε ἀνθρώποις (cf. Luke 12:36: καὶ ὑμεῖς ὅμοιοι ἀνθρώποις) look as though they have been influenced by Matt 24:44: διὰ τοῦτο καὶ ὑμεῖς γίνεσθε ἕτοιμοι.

to the hearers in the second person. When it is seen how easily deparabolization has affected the various parts of the parable in these later versions, the argument that it had already affected Luke 12:35 and Mark 13:35-36 in the tradition before the Gospels[58] becomes irresistible.

(4) Epiphanius, *Haer.* 69:44:1:

γίνεσθε ἕτοιμοι, αἱ ὀσφύες ὑμῶν περιεζωσμέναι, καὶ αἱ λαμπάδες ὑμῶν ἐν ταῖς χερσὶν ὑμῶν, καὶ ἔσεσθε ὡς καλοὶ δοῦλοι, προσδοκῶντες τὸν ἴδιον δεσπότην· ὡς γὰρ λῃστής ἐν νυκτί, οὕτως παραγίνεται ἡ ἡμέρα.[59]

This text may be only a quotation from memory of Luke 12:35-40, which has been influenced by 1 Thessalonians 5:2. In the next sentence Epiphanius goes on to quote from 'the holy apostle' a somewhat loose version of 1 Thessalonians 5:4: οὐκ ἐστε σκότους τέκνα, ἀλλὰ ἡμέρας, ἵνα ἡ ἡμέρα ὑμᾶς μὴ ὡς κλέπτης καταλάβῃ.

On the other hand, the passage contains some variations of vocabulary which *might* be translation variants: λαμπάδες (Luke 12:35: λύχνοι; cf. Matt 25:1-8: λαμπάδες); ἐν ταῖς χερσὶν ὑμῶν (cf. Luke 12:36 Vulg.: *in manibus vestris*); προσδοκῶντες (Luke 12:36: προσδεχομένοις; cf. SibOr 2:181: προσδοκάοντες); τὸν ἴδιον δεσπότην (Luke 12:36: τὸν κύριον ἑαυτῶν; cf. SibOr 2:180: ὁ δεσπόζων); λῃστής (Luke 12:39: κλέπτης). Of these the most interesting are δεσπότην and λῃστής. The use of κύριος in Luke 12:36-37 (cf. Matt 24:42) is one of the features of the parable which made it so easily deparabolized: it immediately suggests Christ. δεσπότης, however, is only very rarely used of Christ;[60] to substitute it for κύριος would be

---

[58]This is in effect also how Mark 13:35-36 is explained by Dupont (1970) 106, though he does not, of course, use the term 'deparabolization'.

[59]Text from Holl (1933) 191. The work was completed in 377.

[60]Jude 4; 2 Pet. 2:1; Melito, *Peri Pascha* 96-97; Martyrdom of Justin (Rec. B) 5:6; Clement of Alexandria, *Strom.* 4:7; cf. Julius Africanus, ap. Eusebius, *Hist. Eccl.* 1.7.14 (the relatives of Jesus as οἱ δεσπόσυνοι). For the christological use of δεσπότης, see Bauckham (1990A) 282-284, 303-307. The word is used in a Synoptic parable only in P[75] at Luke 13:25.

contrary to the deparabolizing tendency. On the other hand, it may be simply Epiphanius' reminiscence of οἰκοδεσπότης (Luke 12:39) in the parable of the Thief. All the New Testament references to the parable of the Thief use κλέπτης (Matt 24:43; Luke 12:39; 1 Thes 5:2; 2 Pet 3:10; Rev 3:3; 16:15), but ληστής is used in the Coptic of Gospel of Thomas 21b and 103.[61]

Whether this is sufficient evidence to claim this passage as an independent tradition of the parables of the Watching Servants and the Thief, or to sustain Resch's argument that this is the version of the Thief which Paul quotes in 1 Thessalonians 5:2[62] is doubtful. If it were an independent tradition, it would be further evidence of the close association of the two parables throughout their transmission. In this case the association is such that the application of the Thief (γίνεσθε ἕτοιμοι) has become an introduction to both parables.

(5) Epistle of the Apostles 43:1-2:

Ethiopic	*Coptic*
Be as the wise virgins who kindled the light and did not slumber and who went with their lamps to meet the lord, the bridegroom, and have gone in with him into the bridegroom's chamber. But the foolish ones who talked with them were not able to watch, but fell asleep.	You will be like the wise virgins who watched and did not sleep, but [went] out to the lord into the bride-chamber. But [the foolish] were not able to watch, but fell asleep.[63]

---

[61]Also in the Greek translation of ActsThom 146 (see Smitmans [1973] 65 and n.102) and presupposed in the Bohairic version of Matt 24:43 (see Schrage [1964A] 68 n.6).

[62]Resch (1904) 405-406. His argument is rejected by Smitmans (1973) 55 n.55.

[63]Translation from Hills (1990) 149.

This early second-century version of the parable of the Wise and Foolish Virgins is followed by a detailed allegorical interpretation.[64] Its interest for our purposes, however, is twofold. First, its introductory formula (at least in the Ethiopic version) has become an exhortation. This is the same mildly deparabolizing step as has already been taken in the Watching Servants in Luke 12:36.[65] Secondly, the story differs from that in Matthew 25:1-13. In the Matthean version, the contrast is not between wise virgins who stay awake and foolish virgins who sleep, but between those who have their oil ready and those who have not. They all fall asleep. The consequent inappropriateness of the exhortation to watch in the application of the parable (Matt 25:13) has often been noticed. In the Epistle of the Apostles, however, we have a version to which the Matthean application would be wholly appropriate. What has happened is that the popularity of the image of watching in Christian eschatological teaching, which already affected the Matthean version by producing the application (Matt 25:13), has here affected the story itself and transformed it into a story about staying awake. This confirms our previous identification of a tendency to extend the use of the motif of watching to parables where it did not originally belong, including the Matthean version of the Thief (Matt 24:43).

[64]For a study of the whole passage, see Hills (1990) chapter 6.

[65]It is possible that Luke 13:25 is a more drastically deparabolized version of the Wise and Foolish Virgins, as Dodd (1961) 128-129, argued in effect.

4

The Worship of Jesus

In the development of Christology in the primitive church, the emergence of the worship of Jesus is a significant phenomenon. In the exclusive monotheism of the Jewish religious tradition, as distinct from some other kinds of monotheism, it was worship which was the real test of monotheistic faith in religious practice. In the world-views of the early centuries A.D. the gap between God and humanity might be peopled by all kinds of intermediary beings — angels, exalted human beings, hypostatized divine attributes, the Logos — and the early church's attempt to understand the mediatorial role of Jesus naturally made use of these possibilities. In the last resort, however, Jewish monotheism could not tolerate a mere spectrum between God and humanity; somewhere a firm line had to be drawn between God and creatures, and in religious *practice* it was worship which signalled the distinction between God and every creature, however exalted. God must be worshipped; no creature may be worshipped.[1] For Jewish monotheism, this insistence on the one God's exclusive right to religious worship was far more important than metaphysical notions of the unity of the divine nature. Since the early church remained — or at least professed to remain — faithful to Jewish monotheism, the acknowledgement of Jesus as worthy of

---

[1]Hayman (1991), who questions the appropriateness of 'monotheism' as a description of early Judaism, nevertheless agrees essentially with this point: 'For most Jews, God is the sole object of worship, but he is not the only divine being' (15). On Jewish monotheism, cf. Rainbow (1991) 79-81; Dunn (1991) 19-21; Sanders (1992) 242-247.

worship is a remarkable development.[2] Either it should have been rejected as idolatry — and a halt called to the upward trend of christological development — or else its acceptance may be seen with hindsight to have set the church already on the road to Nicene theology.

Of course, it may be argued that early Christianity developed from a kind of Judaism which was *not* as strictly monotheistic as later rabbinic Judaism. Early Christianity could with considerable plausibility be seen as a variety of the 'two powers in heaven' heresies against which the Rabbis later argued.[3] Or, again, it might be held that the worship of Jesus emerged in Gentile Christianity influenced by hellenistic syncretism, and therefore not in the context of a strict distinction between God who must be worshipped and creatures who may not be worshipped.

Either of these explanations would make the worship of Jesus more readily explicable, but they do not fit the evidence. Some of the most interesting evidence is that contained in two early Christian writings which are among the most explicit in their treatment of Jesus as worthy of divine worship, and yet at the same time seem to be alert to the dangers of infringing monotheism by worshipping creatures: the Apocalypse of John and the Ascension of Isaiah.[4] These two works, despite some notable differences, seem to belong to broadly the same kind of Christianity, a Christianity which expressed its faith in terms drawn from the tradition of Jewish apocalyptic and Merkabah

---

[2]For an account of the evidence for and significance of the worship of Jesus in early Christianity, see Bauckham (1992); cf. also France (1982); Hurtado (1988) 11-15 and chapter 5; and for a different view of some of this evidence: Dunn (1991) 204-206.

[3]Cf. Segal (1977).

[4]The Ascension of Isaiah is widely admitted to be roughly contemporary with Revelation: see Charles (1900) xliv-xlv (late first century); Burkitt (1909) 60 (early 2nd century); Daniélou (1964) 12-13 (late first century); Knibb (1985) 149-150 (late first-early second century); Acerbi (1989) 281-282; Hall (1990) (early second century). Against the older source-critical theories (still perpetuated by Knibb [1985]), I agree with the Italian research team (cf. Pesce [1983]; Norelli [1991]) that the Ascension of Isaiah is a unitary work of Christian origin. However, this issue is not important for the discussion in this chapter, which concerns only chapters 6-11.

mysticism.[5] Both works contain (a) a vision of the worship of Christ in heaven, and (b) a prohibition of the worship of angels. Since there seems to be no direct literary dependence between the two works, it is likely that this combination was typical of the apocalyptic Christian circles which they represent. It is the purpose of this chapter to study this interesting combination of motifs.

1. The angel refuses worship: an apocalyptic tradition

The Apocalypse of John relates, in almost identical terms, two episodes (Rev 19:10; 22:8-9) in which the seer prostrates himself before the interpreting angel to worship him; the angel interposes, 'You must not do that! I am a fellow-servant with you and with your brothers and sisters who hold the testimony of Jesus. Worship God!' (19:10; cf. 22:9). A similar episode occurs in the Ascension of Isiah, where on reaching the second heaven Isaiah falls down to worship the heavenly being who occupies the throne in that heaven. His angelic guide forbids him: 'Worship neither throne nor angel from

---

[5]For the relationship between apocalyptic and Merkabah mysticism, see various comments in Scholem (1955) chapter 2; Scholem (1965) chapter 3; Rowland (1975) (including discussion of Rev 4); Gruenwald (1980); Rowland (1982) chapters 11-12; Alexander (1983) 235-236; Himmelfarb (1988); Morray-Jones (1991) 1-4. In using the term 'Merkabah mysticism' with reference to the first and second centuries A.D., I do not of course intend to imply that all features of the medieval Merkabah texts can be read back into that period. I use the term to identify the continuity which can be demonstrated between descriptions of ascent to the throne of God in earlier texts (among which the Ascension of Isaiah is prominent) and the literature of medieval Merkabah mysticism.

The similarities between the Ascension of Isaiah and Gnostic literature, pointed out by Helmbold (1972), do not show the Ascension of Isaiah to be Gnostic, since these features are also to be found in Jewish apocalyptic; they show rather that Christian Gnosticism was indebted to the kind of Jewish and Jewish Christian apocalypticism that the Ascension of Isaiah represents. There are no distinctively Gnostic features in the Ascension of Isaiah.

On the Ascension of Isaiah as a work of Jewish Christian apocalyptic, see Daniélou (1964) 12, 173-6; Himmelfarb (1986); Acerbi (1989); on its relationship to Merkabah mysticism, see Gruenwald (1980) 57-62; Alexander (1983) 248-249; and below, section 3.

the six heavens, from where I was sent to lead you, before I tell you in the seventh heaven. For above all the heavens and their angels is placed your throne, and also your robes and your crown which you are to see' (7:21-22).[6] Later, when Isaiah calls his guide 'my Lord', the angel insists, 'I am not your Lord, but your fellow-servant' (8:5).[7]

It is highly unlikely that the Ascension of Isaiah is dependent on the Apocalypse[8] or *vice versa*, but the coincidence of ideas is striking. Both forbid worship of angels on the grounds that only God (in the seventh heaven) may be worshipped and that angels are not the seer's superiors but his fellow-servants.[9] It looks as though both reflect a common tradition in apocalyptic Christianity, just as they elsewhere reflect common traditions about Antichrist (Rev 11-13; AscIsa 4:2-14).[10] To understand this tradition we must first examine the standard pattern of response to angelophanies in apocalyptic and other Jewish literature.

There seem to be two similar but distinguishable types of reaction to angelophanies. In both cases the glorious apparition of the heavenly being provokes fear and prostration. But in one case the fear is extreme and the prostration is involuntary: the visionary falls on the ground in a faint 'as one dead'. In the other case the fear is less extreme and the prostration voluntary: the visionary bows down before the angel in a gesture of awed reverence. A simple example of the first category occurs in the Testament of Abraham: when the archangel Michael appeared to Abraham, 'he fell upon his face on the ground as one dead'

[6]Translation of the Ethiopic version (which is here to be preferred to the Latin and Slavonic) from Knibb (1985) 167.

[7]For this translation, see Charles (1900) 54-55, with note justifying the translation 'fellow-servant' rather than 'companion' (Knibb); the original Greek of the angel's reply is preserved in the Greek Legend 2:11: οὐκ ἐγὼ Κύριος, ἀλλὰ σύνδουλός σου εἰμί. For the address 'lord' to an angel (in an account of ascent through the seven heavens of a kind similar to the Ascension of Isaiah), see 3 Bar 5:1; 6:4, 9; 11:2, 3, 8; 12:2.

[8]There are few indications that Ascension of Isaiah is dependent on any New Testament writings.

[9]For angels as 'fellow-servants' of the righteous, cf. also Teachings of Silvanus (CG VII, 4) 91:25-33.

[10]See chapter 11 section 3 below.

(Rec. A: 9:1). A more graphic account occurs in 3 Enoch 1:7: when R. Ishmael entered the seventh heavenly Hall: 'As soon as the princes of the chariot (Merkabah) looked at me and the fiery seraphim fixed their gaze on me, I shrank back trembling and fell down, stunned by the radiant appearance of their eyes and the bright vision of their faces'.[11] An example of the secondary category is 2 Enoch 1:7 (J): when two angels appeared to Enoch, 'I bowed down to them and was terrified; and the appearance of my face was changed because of fear'.[12] Both types of reaction occur in the resurrection narratives of the Gospels: 'for fear of him the guards trembled and became like dead men' (Matt 28:5); 'they were frightened and bowed their faces to the ground' (Luke 24:5).

Of course neither reaction need constitute worship and neither was originally regarded as reprehensible in apocalyptic literature. Prostration (προσκύνησις), though it could denote divine worship[13] and occurs as a response to theophanies,[14] was also a normal gesture of respect, acceptably given to human superiors.[15] The gesture in itself was not an indication of

[11]Translation from Alexander (1983) 256. Other examples: 4 Macc 4:10-11; Rev 1:17; Hek. Rab. 24:2-3. Fainting is probably the sense in Dan 8:18; 10:8-9. In some accounts of angelophanies only fear is mentioned: TAbr 13:4 (Rec. B); 2 Enoch 20:1; cf. Mark 16:5, 8; Luke 24:37.

[12]Other examples: Num 22:31; Josh 5:14; Dan 8:17; JosAs 14:10-11.

[13]E.g. Exod 20:5; 23:24; Deut 5:9; ApMos 27:5; 33:5; ApAbr 17:5; 2 Enoch 66:2, 5 (J); Matt 4:9-10.

[14]Gen 17:3; Ezek 1:28; 3:23; 43:3; 44:4; 1 Enoch 71:11; 2 Enoch 22:4; LAE 26:1; 28:1; cf. 1 Enoch 14:24. 1 Enoch 60:3; 71:2 seem to be generalised reactions to the vision of the throne of God and its surrounding angels.

[15]E.g. Gen 18:2; 19:1; 23:7, 12; 33:2, 1 Sam 28:14; 1 Kings 2:19; 2 Kings 2:15; Isa 45:14; Rev 3:9; TIsaac 6:2. In Moses' vision in the *Exagōgē* of Ezekiel the Tragedian, the stars prostrate themselves before him (lines 79-80): for discussion, see Hurtado (1988) 57-59. For examples of προσκύνησις as an acceptable gesture of respect by a human being to an angel, see LAB 18:9; TIsaac 2:3. In 3 Enoch 4:9; 14:5, the angels prostrate themselves before Metatron; and in 3 Enoch 18 there is elaborate description of how each rank of angels shows respect for its superiors: 'they remove the crown of glory from their head and fall on their faces' (cf. also Hek. Rab. 23:3). On προσκύνησις and worship, see Greeven (1968); Moule (1977) 175-176; Mastin (1973). When Greeks objected to προσκύνησις to a living man, it was not because it was blasphemous, but because it was servile: see Charlesworth (1935), especially 16-20.

worship such as belongs to God alone. Terror and fainting commonly characterize the visionary's response to the vision or voice of God,[16] but also to other kinds of visionary phenomena.[17]

Nevertheless in both reactions a potential danger of angelolatry might be seen to lurk. The gesture of prostration came to be unacceptable to Jews in contexts which gave it idolatrous overtones, such as reverence for monarchs who claimed divinity.[18] Arguably angelophanies were a comparable context, since polytheists worshipped similar beings,[19] and apocalyptic always walked a somewhat dangerous tightrope in its relationship with oriental and hellenistic syncretism, borrowing so much and yet needing to distinguish itself sharply from non-Jewish religion.[20] It would not be surprising if the need for the apocalyptic tradition to safeguard monotheism sometimes took the form of prohibiting προσκύνησις to angels. Furthermore, the *fear* which is a primary ingredient in both types of reaction to angelophanies, and becomes uncontrollable terror in one, comes very close to the essentially religious response to the numinous. Accounts of angelophanies depict

---

[16] 1 Enoch 60:3; 65:4; ApAbr 10:2; LadJac 2:1; Matt 17:6.

[17] Dan 5:6; 7:15, 28; 8:27; 1 Enoch 14:9, 13-14; 4 Ezra 10:30; cf. 3 Bar 7:5.

[18] The earliest Jewish instance of a refusal to prostrate oneself is Est 3:2, which is interpreted as a monotheistic objection to προσκύνησις in the LXX Additions to Est 13:12-14 ('I will not bow down to anyone but you, who are my Lord'), the Aramaic prayer of Mordecai ('for I feared thee, O God of Ages, and would not give the glory due to thee to any son of man made of flesh and blood') and the Second Targum to Est 3:3 ('I will not bow down, except to the living and true God'): see the discussion (with these and other texts cited) in Paton (1908) 195-197; Moore (1977) 204-207. The question became acute in relation to those Roman Emperors who demanded explicit divine honours: cf. Philo, *Leg. Gai.* 116. For the monotheistic rejection of προσκύνησις, see also Acts 10:25-26: for Cornelius, his action is the reverence due to a human messenger of God, but Peter regards it as inappropriately given to a mere man.

[19] If it is true that Jewish angelology is indebted to Zoroastrianism, it is relevant to note that in Zoroastrianism both the Bounteous Immortals and the *yazads* were worshipped. Jewish angels certainly also had an older relationship to the gods of the Canaanite pantheon.

[20] On the relationship of apocalyptic to non-Jewish culture, see Bauckham (1978) 10-23.

the angels radiant with the divine glory they share, and many of the accounts of the visionaries' reactions seem to exemplify precisely that mixture of terror and fascination which Rudolf Otto described as humanity's basic, primitive response to the numinous Other, which lies at the root of all religious worship.[21] It is easy to see that the prominent role of angels in apocalyptic visions could come to require some safeguard against the danger to monotheism.[22]

To provide such a safeguard was the purpose of the tradition in which an angel is represented as refusing worship. Several texts besides those already cited in the Apocalypse of John and the Ascension of Isaiah are evidence of this tradition. The earliest and mildest version is in

(a) Tobit 12:16-22.
When the archangel Raphael revealed his identity, Tobit and Tobias

> were shaken; they fell face down, for they were afraid. But he said to them, 'Do not be afraid; peace be with you. Bless God forevermore. As for me, when I was with you, I was not acting on my own will, but by the will of God. Bless him each and every day; sing his praises.... So now get up from the ground, and acknowledge God. See, I am ascending to him who sent me....' And he ascended. Then they stood up and could see him no more. They kept blessing God and singing his praises, and they acknowledged God for these marvellous deeds of his, when an angel of God had appeared to them.[23]

Here Raphael refuses obeisance ('get up from the ground'), making it clear that he is no more than a servant of God, and

[21]Otto (1923) chapter 4.

[22]Williams (1909); Simon (1977); Hurtado (1988) 22-35, 82-85 (but cf. also the criticism of Hurtado in Rainbow [1991] 83), discuss the main evidence alleged for Jewish angelolatry and rightly conclude that there was no cult of angels in Judaism, though prayer to angels may have been an occasional feature of popular piety, and invocation of angels a Jewish contribution to hellenistic magic.

[23]NRSV, translating the text in Sinaiticus.

emphatically directs all attention to God, to whom all praise is due.

(b) Apocalypse of Zephaniah 6:11-15[24]
The seer has encountered a hideous and terrifying angel (later identified as the accusing angel, Satan). He faints and prays to God to deliver him (6:8-10). Then

> I arose and stood, and I saw a great angel standing before me with his face shining like the rays of the sun in its glory since his face is like that which is perfected in its glory. And he was girded as if a golden girdle were upon his breast. His feet were like bronze which is melted in a fire. And when I saw him, I rejoiced, for I thought that the Lord Almighty had come to visit me. I fell upon my face, and I worshipped him. He said to me, 'Take heed. Don't worship me. I am not the Lord Almighty, but I am the great angel Eremiel,[25] who is over the abyss and Hades...[26]

Whether the Apocalypse of Zephaniah is an originally Jewish or Christian work is still debated,[27] but it seems probable that it has received only minimal Christian editing, if any. In any case, it is unlikely that our passage is dependent on Revelation. It is certainly striking that all three items in the description of the angel recur in the longer description of Christ in Rev 1:13-16, but each of the three also occurs in other angelic

---

[24]This passage is from the Akhmimic text, which has sometimes been known (following Steindorff [1899]) as the 'anonymous Apocalypse,' but is now commonly (as by Wintermute [1983]) identified as part of the Apocalypse of Zephaniah on the grounds of its close affinity with the Sahidic fragment of an Apocalypse of Zephaniah. I have expressed some doubts about this identification (Bauckham [1986] 101-102), but the issue is not important in the present context.

[25]Eremiel is the angel Jeremiel of 4 Ezra 4:36.

[26]Translation from Wintermute (1983) 513.

[27]Wintermute (1983) 501, supports a Jewish origin, Diebner (1993?) a Christian origin. Himmelfarb (1983) discusses the work in relation to the Jewish and Christian tradition of tours of hell: its place in this tradition probably indicates a fairly early date.

descriptions.[28] A Christian author or editor is unlikely to have created a description of an angel modelled on one of Christ. Even if Revelation 1:13-16 were the source of the description here, the account of the seer's worship and the angel's rejection of it is sufficiently different from that in Revelation 19:10; 22:8-9 to be probably independent of the latter. Probably, therefore, this text is evidence of a more widespread common tradition on which both the Apocalypse of John and the Ascension of Isaiah also depended.

(c) Joseph and Aseneth 15:11-12

> And when the man had finished speaking these words, Aseneth rejoiced exceedingly with great joy about all these words and fell down at his feet and prostrated herself face down to the ground before him, and said to him, 'Blessed be the Lord your God the Most High who sent you out to rescue me from the darkness and to bring me up from the foundations of the abyss, and blessed be your name forever. What is your name, Lord; tell me in order that I may praise and glorify you for ever and ever.' And the man said to her, 'Why do you seek this, my name, Aseneth? My name is in the heavens in the book of the Most High, written by the finger of God in the beginning of the book before all (the others), because I am chief of the house of the Most High. And all names written in the book of the Most High are unspeakable, and man is not allowed to pronounce nor hear them in this world, because those names are exceedingly great and wonderful and laudable.'[29]

---

[28]Face shining like the sun: 2 Enoch 1:5; 19:1; 4 Ezra 7:97; 3 Enoch 48C:6; Rev 10:1; ApPaul 12; cf. TAbr 7:3; 16:6 (Rec. A); JosAs 14:9; QuEzra A20; 1 Enoch 14:20; 106:10; 2 Enoch 39:5 (J); ApPet 1:7; 15:2.

Girded with golden girdle: Dan 10:5; Rev. 15:6; ApPaul 12; cf. QuEzra A27.

Feet like brass in the fire: Ezek 1:4, 7; Dan 10:6; JosAs 14:9.

[29]Translation from Burchard (1985) 227.

Aseneth's request to know the name of the angel (who is the archangel Michael: cf. 14:8) and his response are modelled on Judges 13:17-18, but it is surely significant that the terms of Manoah's request there ('What is your name, so that we may honour [LXX: δοξάσομεν] you when your words come true?')[30] are heightened in Aseneth's ('in order that I may praise and glorify you for ever and ever'). It looks as though she is represented as wishing to offer divine worship to the angel,[31] and that the angel's refusal to divulge his heavenly name, which cannot be known or uttered on earth,[32] is an oblique way of refusing worship.[33] In the course of his speech he makes clear that, though he is the chief of the house of the Most High, he is not the Most High.

(d) Apocalypse of Paul (Coptic version)

And companies of singers were singing and ascribing blessing to the Father, and tens of thousands of thousands of angels were standing before him, and thousands of thousands of angels were surrounding him, saying, 'Honourable is thy name and splendid is thy glory, O Lord'; and the Cherubim and the Seraphim said, 'Amen'. And when I Paul saw them I quaked in all my members, and I fell down upon my face. And, behold, the angel who accompanied me came to me and raised me up, saying, 'Fear thou not, O Paul, thou beloved of God; rise up now and follow me, and I will shew thee thy place'.[34]

---

[30]Cf. also TLevi 5:5, but there Levi wants to know the angel's name so that he may call on his assistance when he needs it.

[31]In 17:9 it is not clear whether Aseneth refers to him as 'a god' or as 'God,' perhaps recognizing him as 'the angel of Yahweh' (cf. Judg 13:21-22) who in the Old Testament is in some sense identified with Yahweh. However, post-biblical Jewish literature consistently takes the Old Testament's 'angel of Yahweh' to be an angel who acts for God but is not to be identified with God or worshipped: cf. LAB 42:10 in relation to Judg 13:21-22.

[32]For such secret names, cf. AscIsa 7:4; 8:7; 9:5; and Smith (1985) 701 n. 10.

[33]Hurtado (1988) 81, 84.

[34]Translation from Budge (1915) 1078.

Although the context of this incident is somewhat obscure, its significance seems to be that Paul should not fear or prostrate himself before the angels in the third heaven because he is not inferior to them; his own throne, as he subsequently sees, is set up for him, with those of the prophets, the other apostles, and the martyrs, in paradise, where the angels honour them. This text therefore particularly resembles Ascension of Isaiah 7:21-22.

(e) Apocryphal Gospel of Matthew 3:3

Then Joachim adored the angel, and said to him: 'If I have found favour in thy sight, sit for a little in my tent, and bless thy servant.' And the angel said to him: 'Do not say servant, but fellow-servant (*conservum*); for we are servants of one Master.'[35]

This late Christian text, included for the sake of completeness, is likely to be dependent on Revelation 19:10; 22:8-9.

This completes the evidence for the tradition in which an angel refuses worship. There are also, however, some other texts which counter the danger of angelolatry in somewhat different ways. These texts are additional evidence that the traditional forms of response to angelophanies were felt by some within the apocalyptic tradition to run the risk of infringing strict monotheism.

(f) Ladder of Jacob 3:3-5

And Sariel[36] the archangel came to me, and I saw (him), and his appearance was very beautiful and awesome. But I was not astonished by his appearance, for the vision which I had seen in my dream was more terrible than he. And I did not fear the vision of the angel.[37]

---

[35]Translation from Walker (1873) 21; Latin text in de Santos Otero (1988) 183.
[36]For the archangel Sariel, see 1 QM 9:14-15; 1 Enoch 9:1; 10:1; 20:6; Tg Neof Gen 32:25; ApPet 7:10; 9:1; 11:4 12:3 (cf. Bauckham [1993B] chapter 3 section 8).
[37]Translation from Lunt (1985) 408.

The Ladder of Jacob is certainly a Jewish apocalypse[38] (with a Christian addition in chapter 7), whose affinities with the Apocalypse of Abraham suggest a date around 100 A.D. In our passage the possibility that the awe-inspiring appearance of the archangel should inspire in Jacob a fear akin to divine worship is negated by the fact that Jacob has already seen the far more terrifying face of God himself in his vision (1:4, 6).[39]

(g) 3 Enoch 16:1-5

Rabbi Ishmael said: The angel Metatron, Prince of the Divine Presence, the glory of highest heaven said to me: At first I was sitting on a great throne at the door of the seventh palace, and I judged all the denizens of the heights, the *familia* of the Omnipresent, on the authority of the Holy One, blessed be he. I assigned greatness, royalty, rank, sovereignty, glory, praise, diadem, crown, and honour to all the Princes of Kingdoms, when I sat in the heavenly court. The Princes of Kingdoms stood beside me, to my right and to my left, by authority of the Holy One, blessed be he. But when Aher came to behold the vision of the Merkabah and set eyes on me, he was afraid and trembled before me. His soul was alarmed to the point of leaving him because of his fear, dread and terror of me, when he saw me seated upon a throne like a king, with ministering angels standing beside me like servants, and all the Princes of Kingdoms crowned with crowns surrounding me. Then he opened his mouth and said:

---

[38]Lunt (1985) 404, is too cautious in speaking of 'the possibly original Jewish document'. Moreover, Charlesworth (1983), (1985) is wrong to classify it among 'Expansions of the "Old Testament" and Legends' (in Charlesworth [1985]) rather than among 'Apocalyptic Literature and Related Works' (in Charlesworth [1985]). It is generically an apocalypse. The interpretation of Jacob's vision at Bethel as an apocalyptic revelation of the future is of a piece with the common Jewish exegetical practice of finding apocalyptic revelations in the accounts of visions in the Old Testament histories (cf. also ApAbr).

[39]The face of God is 'as of a man, carved out of fire' (1:4), 'of fire, including the shoulders and arms, exceedingly terrifying' (1:6); cf. the descriptions of the face of God in 2 Enoch 22:1 (J); 39:3-4 (A), 5 (J).

'There are indeed two powers in heaven!' Immediately a heavenly voice came out from the presence of the Shekinah and said: 'Return, backsliding children — except Aher!' Then 'Anafi'el YHWH, the honoured, glorified, beloved, wonderful, terrible, and dreadful Prince came at the dispatch of the Holy One, blessed be he, and struck me with sixty lashes of fire and made me stand upon my feet.[40]

Another version of this story is in b. Ḥag. 15a,[41] but the version in 3 Enoch is the more interesting for our purposes, because here the reason for Aher's heretical conclusion that there are two powers (i.e. divinities) in heaven is the God-like splendour of Metatron, enthroned as the heavenly vicegerent of God (the 'lesser YHWH': 12:5). Aher's terror should be noted, because it is in this response to Metatron's royal appearance — the traditional response to angelophanies — that Aher's apprehension of Metatron as a second divinity consists. The version in b. Ḥag. 15a omits both the God-like appearance of Metatron and Aher's terror, and represents Metatron as the heavenly scribe rather than the heavenly grand vizier. In one recension of b. Ḥag. 15a (probably the older)[42] the reason for Aher's conclusion that 'there are two powers' is obscure, while in the other it is because he sees Metatron seated, but in his role as scribe, not like a king, as in 3 Enoch. Probably, as Morray-Jones has argued,[43] 3 Enoch preserves the more original, pre-talmudic tradition.[44] This version must derive from the early

[40]Translation from Alexander (1987) 63-64.

[41]This passage is discussed in Segal (1977) chapter 3; Alexander (1977) 177-178; Rowland (1982) 334-339. In fact, the three differing texts of this passage represent two recensions of the story, as Alexander (1987) 54-63, argues. For the three texts, with translations, see Alexander (1987) 54-55, 59-60, 61-62.

[42]Alexander (1987) 62-63.

[43]Morray-Jones (1991) 17-36, against Alexander (1987) 54-66 (who argued that 3 Enoch's version is a secondary development from b. Ḥag. 15a).

[44]Morray-Jones (1991) 34 admits that the text of 3 Enoch 16:1-5 itself shows signs of dependence on the Talmud, but this dependence consists in additions to an originally independent tradition.

Merkabah mystical circles themselves[45] and served to counter the danger to monotheism which could be incurred by the extreme exaltation of the figure of Metatron or the lesser YHWH. The talmudic tradition is a bowdlerized version from redactors who were much less sympathetic to the Metatron tradition, and anxious to suppress any reference to the speculation about Metatron as the lesser YHWH enthroned in heaven.[46]

(h) Cairo Genizah Hekhalot A/2, 13-18

> A youth [i.e. Metatron] comes out to meet you from behind the throne of glory. Do not bow down to him — for his crown is as the crown of his King, and the sandals on his feet are as the sandals of his King, and the robe upon him is as the robe of his King...; his eyes blaze like torches, his eyeballs burn like lamps; his brilliance is as the brilliance of his King, his glory is as the glory of his Maker — Zehobadyah is his name.[47]

Here the Merkabah mystic is warned not to mistake Metatron for God, and therefore not to perform obeisance which in these circumstances would be worship. The mistake was no doubt peculiarly easy to make in the case of Metatron, but the glory of all angels to some extent resembles the glory of their Maker: this is why the danger of idolatry was always present in circles which devoted as much attention to angels as apocalyptic and Merkabah mysticism did.

Since the role of Metatron in these Merkabah texts presents a closer parallel to the role of Christ in early Christianity than

---

[45]Odeberg (1928) introduction: 85-86, believed 3 Enoch 16 to emanate from 'early opponents to the Metatron-speculations of the mystics'; but by comparison with the version in b. Hag. 15a its demotion of Metatron is moderate. It is therefore better to see it as an attempt at self-correction from within the Metatron tradition.

[46]Morray-Jones (1991) 30-32, 33.

[47]Translation from Alexander (1983) 268 n.a., from the text published by Gruenwald (1969) 362-363. On 'the youth' resembling God, see also Halperin (1988) 405.

any other figure in Jewish religion,[48] it is interesting to notice how the worship of Metatron in heaven is here explicitly excluded,[49] whereas the worship of Christ in heaven is explicitly portrayed in the Apocalypse of John and the Ascension of Isaiah.

These texts, (g) and (h), from the Hekhalot literature are, of course, much later than the Apocalypse of John and the Ascension of Isaiah, but they belong to a tradition which was in some respects continuous with the older Jewish apocalyptic tradition and with which, as we shall see, the Ascension of Isaiah has particular affinities. They illustrate again how the role of mediating heavenly beings could be felt to endanger monotheism, and how the tradition itself sought to safeguard monotheistic worship from such danger.

In taking up the traditional motif of the angel who refuses worship, the authors of the Apocalypse of John and the Ascension of Isaiah showed themselves alert to this kind of danger and sensitive to the implications of Jewish monotheism in the sphere of worship. We must now examine the specific use they made of the tradition.

---

[48]For some of the parallels, see Murtonen (1953) 409-411, though his view that the figure of Metatron has been influenced by the Christian view of Jesus is improbable. Even less tenable is the view that 'Metatron is a rough draft of which Jesus is the marvellous finished product': Couchoud (1932) 65.

[49]Were there Merkabah mystics who *did* worship Metatron? Presumably the warnings against the danger of this presuppose that the danger was sometimes realised, though perhaps those who did 'worship' Metatron would not have regarded it as worship. In b. Sanh. 38b (discussed in Urbach [1975] 138-139; Segal (1977) 68-71; Alexander [1977] 177; Hurtado [1988] 32) R. Idi disputes with a *min* who argues from Exod 24:1 that there is a second divine figure who should be worshipped. Since it is R. Idi who calls this figure Metatron we cannot be quite sure that the *min* is an adherent of the Metatron-Merkabah traditions. Urbach thinks it 'most likely that the reference is actually to a Christian sectarian' ([1975] 139), while Segal supposes that Metatron was the rabbinic name for a variety of mediating beings in heresies, and finds no convincing evidence that Merkabah mystics were ever called heretical ([1977] 200). On the other hand, the warnings against the worship of Metatron make it quite possible that some Merkabah mystics strayed into 'two powers' heresy.

2. The tradition in the Apocalypse of John

The usual explanation for the inclusion and repetition of the incident in Revelation 19:10; 22:8-9 is that John intended to counter a tendency to angel-worship in the Asiatic churches to which he addressed his work.[50] In that case it is surprising that no reference to this aberration is made in the seven messages to the churches,[51] but it is possible that the prophetess 'Jezebel' (2:20) justified her teaching by appeal to visionary revelations given by angels.

A more adequate understanding of the function of the two passages will be reached by examining their role in the structure of the Apocalypse. A literary artist as skilful as John will not have duplicated this incident other than by careful design. In fact, the two parallel passages 19:9-10 and 22:6-9 form the parallel conclusions to two visions (17:1-19:10 and 21:9-22:9) which also have closely parallel openings (17:1-3; 21:9-10). It is clearly John's intention in this way to mark out these two visions as comparable and contrasting segments of his work: they portray the two cities Babylon the harlot and Jerusalem the bride, the judgment of the one and the subsequent establishment of the other.[52]

The parallel openings and closings of the two visions raise and answer the question of the authority on which John receives and communicates these prophetic revelations. As so often in apocalyptic visions it is in each case an angel who shows John the vision (17:1-3; 21:9-10), though in both cases John also adds that this occurs while he is ἐν πνεύματι (17:3; 21:10; cf. 1:10; 4:2), i.e. in a condition of visionary rapture attributed to the action of the divine Spirit.[53] It is as the giver of prophetic

---

[50]So, e.g., Bousset (1906) 493; Swete (1907) 249, 304; Kiddle (1940) 382, 449; Peake (1920) 355 n. 1; Morris (1969) 228; Preston and Hanson (1949) 120, 143-144; Sweet (1979) 280.

[51]So Caird (1966) 237.

[52]The structure of these passages and its theological significance is studied in detail by Giblin (1974). The following two paragraphs are much indebted to his analysis.

[53]On the significance of the phrase ἐν πνεύματι, see chapter 5 below.

revelation that John is tempted to worship the angel (22:8), but in rejecting worship the angel disclaims this status: he is not the transcendent giver of prophetic revelation, but a creaturely instrument through whom the revelation is given, and therefore a fellow-servant with John and the Christian prophets, who are similarly only instruments to pass on the revelation.

Instead of the angel, John is directed to 'worship God' (19:10; 22:9) as the true transcendent source of revelation. In the first version of the incident, the angel's rejection of worship is further justified by the explanation, 'For the witness of Jesus is the Spirit of prophecy' (19:10c). The divine Spirit who gives John the visionary experience in which he may receive revelation communicates not the teaching of an angel but the witness which Jesus bears.[54] The second version of the incident (22:6-9) lacks a precise verbal parallel to 19:10c, but a similar point is made in the verses which follow it. For this second version of the incident functions both as a conclusion to the vision of the New Jerusalem (21:9-22:9) and also as the beginning of the epilogue to the whole book (22:6-21). For this reason the question of the authority for revelation in 22:6-9 is no longer limited to the immediately preceding vision, but expands, as the language of those verses indicates, to include the revelation given in the whole book. For the same reason the angel is no longer merely the angel of 21:9 but the angel who 'showed' John the whole of his prophetic vision (cf. 1:1; 22:6b). The angel's rejection of worship now functions, therefore, to claim for the whole book the authority, not of an angel, but of God himself (hence 22:18-19), to whom alone worship is therefore due. The equivalent of the reference to 'the witness of Jesus' in 19:10 is now found in the words of the epilogue, in which the angel disappears from view and Jesus testifies directly: 'I Jesus have sent my angel to you with this testimony for the churches.... He who testifies to these things says, "Surely I am coming soon"' (22:16, 20). The angel is mere intermediary, Jesus is the source of the revelation.[55]

[54] For the subjective genitive in μαρτυρία Ἰησοῦ, cf. 1:2; 22:20. In a subordinate sense both John (1:2) and the angel (22:16) bear witness to Jesus' witness.
[55] Cf. in more detail, Giblin (1974) 496-498.

Thus John has used the traditional motif of the angel who refuses worship in order to affirm the divine source of his prophecy and play down the role of the angelic intermediaries. What is interesting from the point of view of Christology is that for John it seems that Jesus is the source, not the intermediary, of revelation. It is true that Jesus is subordinate to God and receives the revelation from God. The title of the apocalypse (1:1) sets out a chain of communication of the revelation: God, Jesus, angel, John, Christians. But when it comes to distinguishing the giver of revelation from the instrument of revelation it is clear that for John Jesus belongs with God as giver, while the angel belongs with John as instrument. Implicitly the monotheistic prohibition of the worship of angels does not prohibit the worship of Jesus.

John had chosen to make his point about the authority for his prophecy by using a tradition about *worship*. There was good reason for this. In a sense the theme of his whole prophecy is the distinction between true worship and idolatry, a distinction for which Christians in the contemporary situation needed prophetic discernment. The 'eternal Gospel' is summarised in the words 'Fear God and give him glory... and worship him' (14:6), and the conflict between God and Satan takes historical form in the conflict of human allegiances manifest in *worship*. The Apocalypse divides mankind into the worshippers of the dragon and the beast (13:4, 8, 12, 15; 14:9, 11; 16:2; 19:20; 20:4; cf. the emphasis on idolatry in 2:14, 20; 9:20) and those who will worship God in the heavenly Jerusalem (7:15; 14:3; 15:3-4; 22:3; cf. 11:1). This contrast reaches its climax in the two visions of Babylon the harlot in 17:1-19:10 (where the metaphor of harlotry probably has the overtone of false worship, even if this is not the primary meaning;[56] cf. also 2:20-22), and Jerusalem the bride in 21:9-22:9, with its picture of the city in which God himself dwells as its temple (21:22) and his servants do him priestly service (22:3). The message of these two visions is emphasised by their parallel conclusions (19:10; 22:8-9), which enable John to end both with the

[56]See chapter 10 section 2 below.

injunction 'Worship God!' The angel's refusal of worship
reinforces the point: Do not worship the beast, *do not even
worship God's servants the angels,* worship God!

Such deliberate treatment of the question of true and false
worship implies that when John portrays the worship of Christ
in heaven in chapter 5 he cannot be doing so in forgetfulness
of the stringent claims of monotheism in the sphere of worship.
In that chapter John — like many an apocalyptic seer and
Merkabah mystic — has been admitted to the heavenly throne-
room of God, not, as was perhaps sometimes the case in
Merkabah mysticism, for the sake of a merely private experience
of heavenly worship, but rather, in the old prophetic tradition
continued by the apocalyptists, in order to be present at the
heavenly council-meeting to learn God's plans for his action in
history. The divine purpose of establishing his kingdom John
sees entrusted to Christ, who has proved himself, by his
redeeming death, to be the only one worthy to execute it. Since
it is he who has achieved salvation on the cross it is he who must
bring it to completion in the final eschatological events by
which evil is destroyed and the reign of God established. The
question of the angel, 'Who is worthy...?' (5:2) — which
follows an ancient pattern of procedure in the heavenly council
(1 Kings 22:20-21; Isa 6:8)[57] — elicits the important information,
not only that the Lamb is worthy, but also that *no one else is worthy*
(5:3). This establishes Christ's unique role in distinction from
all angels who act as the instruments of God's purpose. Such
angels appear frequently in the visions in which John portrays
the Lamb's execution of his commission: at every point before
the parousia itself (19:11-16) it is angels who actually implement
the divine purposes in history. But this instrumental role of the
angels — for which no special worthiness is required and no
praise given — is distinguished sharply from the role of Christ
as the divine agent of salvation and judgment, even though
that role is the subordinate one of executing the Father's will.
For his acceptance of that unique role Christ receives the
worship of the heavenly host (5:8-12).

[57]Jörns (1971) 45-46, following Müller (1963).

The distinction between Christ and the angels which John establishes in chapter 5 with regard to the work of establishing God's reign is therefore strictly parallel to the distinction we have observed John using with regard to the giving of revelation. Just as the angels are only fellow-servants with the Christian prophets in the communication of revelation and may not be worshipped (19:10; 22:8-9), so the angels who implement the divine purpose in history are only fellow-servants with the prophets and martyrs who bear the witness of Jesus in the world. In both cases, however, Christ, although he receives the revelation from God (1:1) and the scroll from God (5:7), is not classed with the servants who may not be worshipped but with God to whom worship is due.[58]

There can be no doubt that in 5:8-12 John portrays explicit divine worship paid to Christ: the parallels between 4:9-11 and 5:8-12 make this clear.[59] The setting, it should be remembered, is the heavenly throne-room in which the apocalyptic and Merkabah traditions portrayed the ceaseless angelic worship

[58]Mention should be made of the argument of Rowland that in Jewish apocalyptic literature the principal angel, described in terms of divine glory, is evidence of a kind of incipient binitarianism in the Jewish doctrine of God, a 'bifurcation' of divinity, and that the description of Christ in Rev 1:13-16 identifies him with this angelic figure who was already, in Jewish thought, a kind of aspect of divinity: see Rowland (1980); (1982) 94-113; (1983); (1985). But against the idea of a Jewish 'bifurcation' of divinity, see Hurtado (1988) 85-90 (also against the parallel arguments of Fossum); Dunn (1991) 215-219. I would agree with these criticisms, and would also question whether the terms of the description of Christ in Rev 1:13-16 are necessarily either divine or angelic. Such terms were used generally to describe glorious heavenly beings, whether God or angels or glorified humans, and there are many more parallels in Jewish and Christian apocalyptic and other literature than Rowland notices. In any case, as Hurtado (1988) 82-85, points out, in those Jewish works in which the exalted angelic figures to which Rowland draws attention appear, *worship* is strictly reserved for God.

[59]Cf. Kiddle (1940) 105 (on 5:11-12): 'Nowhere else in the New Testament is Christ adored on such absolutely equal terms with the Godhead'; Swete (1907) 127 (on chapter 5): 'This chapter is the most powerful statement of the divinity of Christ in the New Testament, and it receives its power from the praise of God the Creator which precedes it.'

of God.[60] The hymn of 5:12,[61] in its accumulation of doxological terms, resembles on a minor scale the more elaborate hymns of the Hekhalot texts.[62] Of course, never in the Jewish texts are such angelic hymns sung to any except God.[63]

At 15:13 the climax of the throne-vision is reached as the circle of worship expands to encompass the whole creation

[60]For the hymns sung in heaven, see ApAbr 17; 1 Enoch 39:12-13; 4QShirShab; 2 Enoch 21:1; 3 Enoch 1:12; 19:7; 20:2; 39:2; 40:1-2; 48B:2. Also Odeberg (1928) introduction: 183-7; Scholem (1965) chapter 4.

[61]The three hymns using the formula ἄξιος... λαβεῖν (4:11; 5:9, 12) have sometimes been called 'acclamations'. It is not, however, likely that the formula derives, as Peterson argued, from Greek secular acclamations: see the most recent discussions in Jörns (1971) 56-73; van Unnik (1970); Carnegie (1982) 255. Jörns prefers to see the three 'Axios-Strophes' as antiphonal responses.

This is not to deny, however, that in view of John's polemic against Emperor-worship, a parallel and contrast with the acclamations of the Emperor may be intended: cf. Carnegie (1982) 255-256. It is interesting to compare Mekhilta de-Rabbi Ishmael, Shirta 1, where doxological hymns to God are very explicitly compared with acclamations of human kings: see Goldin (1971) 80-81.

[62]Cf., e.g. Hek. Rab. 28:1; also the hymns in Mekhilta de-Rabbi Ishmael, Shirta 1, with the attempt at reconstruction in Goldin (1971) 81. There is some discussion of the heavenly hymns in Jewish apocalyptic literature, Revelation and the Hekhalot literature in Gruenwald (1988).

[63]Perhaps the closest parallels are 3 Enoch 22:1: 'Above them (the Hayyot) there is one prince, noble, wonderful, strong, and praised with all kinds of praise. His name is Kerubiel...'; Hek. Rab. 23:2: 'Anaphiel-YHVH, Lord of Israel — a revered, awesome, terrifying, noble, glorified, powerful, mighty, and valiant prince whose name is mentioned before the Throne of Glory three times a day, in the heavens, from the day the world was created until now, in praise, because the signet ring of the heavens and of the earth is given into his power' (translation in Blumenthal [1978] 76). The prostration of angels before superior angels is described in 3 Enoch 4:9; 14:5; 18; Hek. Rab. 23:3. There is certainly also a tendency in the Hekhalot texts to dwell on the glory of the angels, in terms which almost become doxological (Hek. Rab. 23:2, 4; 3 Enoch 17:1; 19:1; 20:1; 26:1; 28:1) — precisely the tendency against which the texts in section 1 are aimed. But notice: (a) such passages are no doubt intended to enhance the glory of God by describing the glory of the creatures whose purpose is to glorify God; and (b) even this tendency does not lead to doxologies addressed jointly to God and the angels, like the doxology of God and Christ in Rev 5:13.

The Parables of Enoch mention several times the 'worship' of the Son of Man or Elect One (most clearly: 1 Enoch 48:5; 62:6, 9), but always as the eschatological subjection of people to God's vicegerent, never as worship by angels in heaven (unless 61:7 refers to this).

and the doxology is addressed to both God and the Lamb, uniting the praise of God (4:9-11) and the praise of the Lamb (5:9-12) in a single hymn which anticipates the goal of God's purpose through Christ, the universal worship in the new heaven and earth. The conjunction of God and the Lamb (cf. 7:10; 11:15; 14:4; 20:6; 21:22; 22:1) in this verse illustrates how John, while holding Christ worthy of worship, remains sensitive to the issue of monotheism in worship. Christ cannot be an alternative object of worship alongside God, but shares in the glory due to God. So the specific worship of Christ (5:9-12) leads to the joint worship of God and Christ, in a formula in which God retains the primacy. Although elsewhere John represents Christ as sharing God's throne (3:21; 22:1, 3), here God alone is called 'he who sits on the throne'.[64]

Probably the same concern leads to a peculiar usage in other passages of the Apocalypse, where mention of God and Christ together is followed by a singular verb (11:15) or singular pronouns (6:17;[65] 22:3-4).[66] It is not clear whether the singular in these cases refers to God alone or to God and Christ together 'as a unity'.[67] John, who is very sensitive to the theological implications of language and even prepared to defy grammar for the sake of theology (cf. 1:4), may well intend the latter. But in either case, he is evidently reluctant to speak of God and Christ together as a plurality.[68] He never makes them the

[64]Beskow (1962) 140-141: but he exaggerates the subordination of Christ in Revelation by ignoring 5:9-12.

[65]Probably in 6:17 the reading word αὐτοῦ should be preferred, since it is easier to understand correction of αὐτοῦ or αὐτῶν than *vice versa*.

[66]20:6 is hardly in the same category, since αὐτοῦ rather obviously refers to Christ (cf. 20:4).

[67]Beasley-Murray (1974) 332 (on 22:3); cf. 189 (on 11:15); Swete (1907) 142 (on 11:15); Mounce (1977) 231 (on 11:15); Holtz (1962) 202-3. God and Christ take a singular verb in 1 Thes 3:11.

[68]At 5:14 (where the reading ζῶντι εἰς τοὺς αἰώνων might conform to the usage just noticed, but is much too poorly attested to be original) John probably deliberately avoided specifying the object of worship, since 5:13 would require it to be plural (elsewhere when he uses the same terms, in 4:10; 7:11; 11:16; 19:4, the object of worship is specified as God; cf. 5:8, of the Lamb). Holtz (1962) 202 (following Lohmeyer), suggests that the repeated αὐτοῦ in 1:1 is another example of a singular pronoun for both God and Christ.

subjects of a plural verb or uses a plural pronoun to refer to them both. The reason is surely clear: he places Christ on the divine side of the distinction between God and creation, but he wishes to avoid ways of speaking which sound to him polytheistic. The consistency of his usage shows that he has reflected carefully on the relation of Christology to monotheism. It is significant that one of the passages in question (22:3-4) again concerns worship.

Arguments that the heavenly liturgy of the Apocalypse reflects an earthly liturgy practised in John's churches[69] can probably not be sustained.[70] John's eschatological perspective is such that he reserves for the New Jerusalem the church's participation in the angelic liturgy in the face-to-face presence of God.[71] But the worship of Christ in the Apocalypse is nevertheless 'highly suggestive of the devotional attitude of the Asiatic Church... towards the Person of Christ'.[72] The doxology in 1:5-6, whether or not based on a traditional formula,[73] is evidence enough that John's churches offered praise to Christ comparable with that offered by the angels in heaven.[74] Doxologies, with their confession that glory belongs exclusively to the One who is addressed, were a Jewish form of praise to the one God. There could be no clearer way of ascribing to Jesus the worship due to God.[75]

3. The tradition in the Ascension of Isaiah

The Ascension of Isaiah is more closely related to the traditions

[69]Piper (1951) 10-22; Mowry (1952) 75-84; Shepherd (1960). O'Rourke (1968) finds only fragments of pre-existing hymns (and none in chapter. 5).

[70]Jörns (1971) 178-84; Carnegie (1982) 243-247.

[71]Schüssler Fiorenza (1973) 577-479; Schüssler Fiorenza (1976) 175.

[72]Swete (1907) 84; cf. Carnegie (1982) 247.

[73]Schüssler Fiorenza (1974) 223-227, thinks John has turned a traditional confessional formula into a hymn of praise by adding the doxology; but cf. Carnegie (1982) 249.

[74]Doxologies addressed to Christ also appear in 2 Tim 4:18; 2 Pet 3:18; perhaps 1 Pet 4:11; Heb 13:21; 1 Clem 20:12; 50:7. Cf. also Pliny's report that Christians 'carmen Christo quasi deo dicere secum invicem' (*Ep.* 10.96). For doxologies to Christ in second-century literature, see Bauckham (1992) section 2.

[75]For other aspects of the Christology of Revelation which identify Christ with God, see Bauckham (1993) chapter 3.

of Merkabah mysticism than is the Apocalypse of John. It shows a great many remarkable similarities to the later Hekhalot literature, including features not otherwise attested in the older Jewish and Christian apocalypses. It describes, for example, Isaiah's ascent through the seven heavens, each with its hosts of angels, in progressively increasing glory.[76] From the vision of the descent of Christ through the heavens we learn that each heaven has its door-keepers who demand seals to be shown before permitting entry (10:24, 25, 27, 29): a striking correspondence with the Hekhalot literature.[77] Isaiah's entry into the seventh heaven is challenged by an angel before he is admitted (9:1-5).[78] In each heaven Isaiah is transformed into the glory of the angels of that heaven (7:25; 9:3, 33).[79] He joins the angels in their worship of God (8:17; 9:28, 33).[80] The angels in heaven cannot bear to see the glory of God (9:37) but the righteous behold the glory of God 'with great power' (9:38).[81]

---

[76]The seven heavens in AscIsa resemble the seven halls of the later Hekhalot texts rather than the seven heavens of TLevi 2-3; 2 Enoch; 3 Baruch; or even Visions of Ezekiel. Cf. also the Apocalypse of Zephaniah quoted by Clement of Alexandria, *Str.* 5.11.77.

[77]Cf. 3 Enoch 18:3; Hek. Rab. 17; 19; 20:5-21:3; 22:2; 23; Hekhalot Zuṭarti §§415-416. According to the Ethiopic version of AscIsa, Christ 'gave the password' at each gate; but the Latin has *ostendebat characterem* (10:25) and *dedit signum* (10:29) (Slavonic in Bonwetsch's Latin translation, has *ostendebat signa* and *dedit signum*). Evidently the Greek had χαρακτήρ, meaning the impress on a seal, corresponding to Hek. Rab. 19, where at each gate seals imprinted with the names of angels had to be shown. This motif is not otherwise known from the older apocalypses, but is found in the Naassene psalm quoted by Hippolytus, *Ref.* 5.10.2-8; and in Ophian teaching as reported by Origen, *C. Cels.* 6.31 (but cf. Himmelfarb [1988] 83). Cf. also the gatekeepers (called 'toll collectors') of the heavens in ApPaul (CG V, 2) 20:16, 20-23; 1ApJas (CG V,3) 33:7-15.

[78]Cf. 3 Enoch 2:2-4; 4:7-9; 6:2-3; Gruenwald (1980) 147.

[79]Cf. 2 Enoch 22:10; 3 Enoch 15:1; 48C:6. On the transformation of the visionary in apocalyptic and the Hekhalot literature, see now Himmelfarb (1991).

[80]Cf. 1 Enoch 39:9-10; 71:11; ApAbr 17; ApZeph 8:2-4; 3 Enoch 1:11-12; Hek. Rab. 5:3; 25.

[81]Sometimes in the Hekhalot texts the angels cannot behold God but the mystic can: Hek. Rab. 24:5; Lesser Hekhalot, as quoted by Scholem (1955) 63 ('God who is beyond the sight of his creatures and hidden to the angels who serve him, but who has revealed himself to Rabbi Akiba in the vision of the Merkabah'). On

All these are features of the literature of ascent (or descent) to the Merkabah.[82]

On the other hand, by comparison with the Merkabah texts, the angelology is restrained. This may be due in part to the abbreviation which all versions of the work seem to have suffered,[83] but it is still noteworthy that no angel except Michael is named,[84] few specific angels are singled out,[85] and there is relatively little mention of the various classes and ranks of angels. More definitely, there is a statement that the secret names of angels cannot be known by any human being before death (7:4-5; cf. 8:7; 9:5, of the name of Christ): this must be a deliberate rejection of the techniques of Merkabah mysticism, in which it was essential for the mystic to know the names of the angelic doorkeepers he must pass and to be able to invoke the

whether God may be seen, according to the Hekhalot literature, see Elior (1989) 108-110. For a variety of views in earlier texts on whether God may be seen by angels or humans, see 1 Enoch 14:21; 2 Enoch 22; 4 Ezra 7:98; QuEzra A24-26; ApAbr 16:3; TLevi 5:1; 3 Bar 16:4 (Slav.). The versions of AscIsa seem confused as to whether Isaiah himself was able to see God (9:37, 39; 10:2; 11:32; cf. 3:9): it seems that in the original he could only bear the sight momentarily. The confusion in the versions may be due to a doctrinal difference.

For the idea of 'power', cf. 1 Enoch 71:11; 3 Enoch 1:10-12; Ma'aseh Merkabah §§557-558; Alexander (1987A) 59.

[82]Cf. also Scholem (1965) 30, 129; Alexander (1983) 248-249.

[83]Such abbreviation is apparent from comparison of the versions, and the Greek Legend, and perhaps also from the quotation of 9:35-36 preserved in Epiphanius, *Haer.* 67.3 (Charles [1900] 67): but on the latter, see Acerbi (1984) 42-47, arguing that the differences in Epiphanius' text are largely due to theological reworking. The Greek Legend seems to show traces of a richer angelology: cf. the lists in 2:40: ἄγγελοι, ἀρχαί, ἐξουσίαι, καὶ πᾶσαι τῶν οὐρανῶν αἱ δυνάμεις (the corresponding verse, AscIsa 10:15, has shorter lists in Latin and Slavonic), and 2:22, quoted below. More suggestive of Merkabah mystical interest is the mention of ὑποθρόνια ζῷα in Greek Legend 2:20.

[84]Michael is named at 3:16 ('the chief of the holy angels'), and, in Slavonic and Latin but not Ethiopic, at 9:23, 29, 42. On Michael in the AscIsa, see Norelli (1980) 340-343.

[85]Apart from Michael and 'the angel of the church' (3:15), only Isaiah's guide (7:2 etc.), the angel who presides over the worship in the sixth heaven (9:4), and the angel of 9:21 (identified as Michael by Slavonic and Latin at 9:23).

names of other angels as protection during his ascent.[86] Any suggestion that Isaiah's ascent could be an example of what a would-be mystic could accomplish on his own initiative by the theurgic use of angelological lore is thereby countered. Isaiah is able to ascend only because God himself has sent an angel from the seventh heaven to conduct him there as an exceptional privilege, so that he may receive the prophetic revelation of the descent of Christ into the world (6:13, 7:4-5, 8; 8:8-10; 11:34). For the righteous in general the ascent to heaven is possible only after death (7:23; 8:11; 11:34).[87]

The Ascension of Isaiah therefore seems to be deliberately rejecting a form of Merkabah mysticism (whether Jewish or Christian is not clear) in which angels were reverenced and invoked both as obstacles and as aids in the mystical ascent to heaven. The author saw this as a dangerous obsession with angels, bordering on idolatry, and in order to oppose it head-on he also used the traditional motif, already developed as a safeguard for monotheism in apocalyptic and Merkabah mystical circles, in which the seer attempts to worship an angel and is forbidden. With the version of this in the Ethiopic (to which the Slavonic and Latin are similar) at 7:21-22, should be compared the rather different version preserved in the so-called Greek Legend 2:21-22:

> And he took me up into the sixth heaven,[88] and I could no longer bear the splendour and the lights, and I was greatly

---

[86]Hek. Rab. 16:4-5; 17; cf. Scholem (1955) 50-51; Alexander (1977) 178. No doubt this is why the technique of passing the gatekeepers is mentioned in Christ's descent (10:24, 25, 27, 29), not in Isaiah's ascent: presumably Isaiah's guiding angel deals with this for him. The difference is not an indication of distinct sources, *contra* Himmelfarb (1988) 84.

[87]Perhaps there is also some polemic against the Enoch traditions, though a moderate polemic, in view of 9:9. The author does not deny Enoch's translation, though he equates it with the post-mortem ascensions of the other righteous people of the Old Testament (9:7-9); he does seem to deny Enoch's visit to heaven before his translation.

[88]In AscIsa the incident occurs in the second heaven, while in the sixth heaven occurs the exchange in which the angel refuses to be called 'Lord'. The Greek Legend has moved the latter back to the firmament below the first heaven (2:10-

afraid and fell on my face. And the angel of God who was
with me said: 'Listen, prophet Isaiah, son of Amos: do not
worship (προσκυνήσῃς) angels or archangels nor
dominions (κυριότητας) nor thrones, until I tell you.'
And seizing me by the hand, he strengthened the spirit
which is in me.[89]

In view of the abbreviation which all versions of the Ascension
of Isaiah have suffered, it may well be that the additional
material here is original. Certainly, the dazzling, overwhelming
effect of the angel's glory, the visionary's fear and trembling,
and the angel's action to bring him to his feet and strengthen
him, are all authentic parts of the response to angelophanies
in the apocalyptic and Hekhalot literature.[90] The further
incident in Ascension of Isaiah 8:6 (also in the Greek Legend
2:10-11), where the angel refuses to be called κύριος because he
is Isaiah's fellow-servant (σύνδουλος), makes a similar point to
that made in Revelation 19:10; 22:8-9: the interpreting angel is
not the source of the revelation given to Isaiah, but only a
servant of God sent to guide him through the heavens.

In the Ascension of Isaiah the prohibition of the worship of
angels is more directly linked with the vision of the worship of
God in heaven than it is in the Apocalypse of John. Throughout
his passage through the six lower heavens Isaiah's attention is
directed upwards to the seventh (cf. 7:27).[91] The sole function

11) and replaced it in the sixth heaven by the prohibition of angel-worship. It is
perhaps possible that the original included two versions of the seer's attempt to
worship angels and its prohibition, one in the second and one in the sixth heaven.

[89]Greek text in Charles (1900) 144. (The Greek Legend is a much abbreviated
and rewritten version of AscIsa, but it frequently preserves the original Greek of
the latter.)

[90]Dan 8:17-18; 10:10, 18; ApAbr 10:2; 3 Enoch 1:7-9; Hek. Rab. 24:2-3.

[91]There is a very similar theme in 3 Baruch, where, on seeing the wonders of the
lower heavens, Baruch is told by his angelic guide, 'Wait and you will see the glory
of God' (6:12; 7:2; 11:2; 16:4 [Slav.]; cf. 5:3). In my view (cf. Bauckham [1990] 371-
374) these statements anticipate a vision of God in the seventh heaven, which
Baruch reached in the original form of this apocalypse, but which has been lost
(except for the minimal summary in 16:4 [Slav.]) in the extant, abbreviated forms
of the work. Dean-Otting (1984) 136-148, interprets this theme in 6:12; 7:2 as
countering the danger of worship of Helios, the sun-god interpreted by Jews as the
angel of the sun (cf. the prayer to Helios in Sefer ha-Razim, quoted by Dean-Otting

of all the angels in the lower heavens is to praise God and his Beloved and the Holy Spirit (7:17; 8:18) in the seventh heaven. Similarly Isaiah is not to worship the angels in these lower heavens, because his place is in the seventh heaven, participating in the worship of God there (7:21-22). The angel forbids Isaiah to worship 'before I tell you in the seventh heaven' (7:22), a clause which functions explicitly to link the prohibition in the second heaven with the angel's commands to worship, when Isaiah reaches the seventh heaven (9:31, 36; cf. 'Worship God' in Rev 19:10; 22:9).

It is therefore the more remarkable that these commands to worship are commands to worship Christ (the pre-existent Christ, most often called 'the Beloved' in the Ascension of Isaiah) and 'the angel of the Holy Spirit'. The worship which is prohibited in the case of angels is commanded in the case of Christ and the Holy Spirit. The carefully structured form of the account of the trinitarian worship in the seventh heaven should be noticed. It is set out in the following pattern:

A. Worship of Christ
  1. the righteous worship and Isaiah joins them (9:28)
  2. the angels worship (9:29)
  3. the guiding angel's command 'Worship this one' (9:31) and identification of the object of worship, 'This is...' (9:32).

B. Worship of the Holy Spirit
  1. the righteous worship and Isaiah joins them (9:33)
  2. the angels worship (9:34)
  3. the guiding angel's command 'Worship him', and identification of the object of worship, 'This is...' (9:36).

[1984] 146; and, for awareness of the danger of sun-worship, cf. ApAbr 7:7-8; LadJac 12:12). The recurrence of this theme in 11:2, in relation to Michael, suggests that the polemic against angelolatry is broader and includes a concern that the principal angel, Michael, should not be worshipped. The prominence of the theme of glory, in relation to the seven heavens and to God, in both 3 Bar and AscIsa shows that they share a common approach to the problem of angelolatry. On glory in AscIsa, see Pesce (1983) 67-68.

C. Worship of God
   1. Christ and the Holy Spirit worship (9:40)
   2. the righteous worship (9:41)
   3. the angels worship (9:42)
      and the praises of the six heavens ascend (10:1-5)
   4. the guiding angel's identification of the object of worship,
      'This is...' (10:6).[92]

The fact that Christ and the Holy Spirit are here represented as worshipping God (9:40)[93] is just as noteworthy as the fact that they are themselves worshipped. This subordination, though it takes a different form from the subordination in the Apocalypse of John, manifests the same desire to ensure that all worship is ultimately directed to God the Father. Christ and the Holy Spirit share in this worship but are not rival objects of worship alongside the Father, and to express that they themselves worship him.

The Ascension of Isaiah has commonly been held to embody an angel-Christology. The two figures of the Beloved and 'the angel of the Holy Spirit', on the right and left hand of God respectively (9:35-36; 11:32-33),[94] have been identified either with Michael and Gabriel,[95] or with the two Seraphim of Isaiah 6:2-3, whom Origen identified as Christ and the Holy Spirit (*Princ.* 1.3.4).[96] The former identification has very little to recommend it, for: (a) in spite of Daniélou's argument, when Michael is named in 3:16[97] he cannot be a name for Christ; (b)

---

[92]The need for a specific command to 'Worship God' was perhaps redundant here, though it is not clear why Isaiah is not stated to have joined in the worship of God.

[93]Cf. also Irenaeus, *Demonstratio* 10.

[94]The positions in 9:35-40 are clearer in the version in Epiphanius, *Haer.* 67.3; see Charles (1900) 67.

[95]So Daniélou (1964) 127-129, followed by Stead (1974) 514. Against Daniélou's identification of the angel of the Holy Spirit with Gabriel, see Norelli (1983) 215-220.

[96]So Werner (1957) 132; cf. Kretschmar (1956) 73, 78; Acerbi (1989) 186-187. On Origen's identification, see Daniélou (1964) 134-6; Kretschmar (1956) 64-8; and for a similar identification in Irenaeus, see Daniélou (1964) 138.

[97]On the text of 3:15-16, and against the view that the Greek text originally named the angel of the Holy Spirit Gabriel, see Norelli (1980) 320-324; Verheyden (1989) 248-250.

the addition of Michael in the Slavonic and Latin versions at 9:23, 29, 42, may well be original;[98] (c) 11:4 does not identify the 'angel of the Holy Spirit' with Gabriel, since the angel there is the angel of Matthew 1:20, not Gabriel of Luke's account, of which this section is ignorant;[99] (d) the evidence that Michael and Gabriel were represented as placed on either hand of God is inadequate (cf. 2 Enoch 24:1). The identification with the Seraphim cannot be refuted, but nor is there anything in the text to support it.

This is not to say that there may not be elements of an angel-Christology behind the Ascension of Isaiah.[100] Both 9:27 (cf. 9:21) and the description of the Holy Spirit as 'the angel of the Holy Spirit'[101] suggest that Christ and the Holy Spirit are conceived as heavenly beings analogous to the angels. The theme of the descent and ascent of the Lord (10:7-11:32) probably has an angelological background.[102] But angelic features are thrust into the background[103] by the rigorous differentiation between Christ and the angels. Christ is 'the Lord of all the glories [i.e. angels][104] which you have seen' (9:32), 'the Lord with me [God] of the seven heavens and of their angels' (10:11), worshipped by the angels of all the heavens (7:17; 8:18; 10:19; 11:26-32). The Christology of the Ascension of Isaiah is less aptly defined in terms of an angel-Christology, than in terms of worship, the combination of the

---

[98]These points (a) and (b) are neglected by Pesce (1983) 68, who supposes that there is no reference to a principal angel in AscIsa, and therefore that the Beloved has been cast in that role. On Michael in 9:23, 29, 42, see Norelli (1980) 342-343; Norelli (1983) 217-218.

[99]For the probability that 11:2-22, though only in the Ethiopic version, belongs to the original text, see Charles (1900) xxii-xxiv; Vaillant (1963) 111-112. On the angel of 11:4, see Norelli (1983) 211.

[100]Knight (1991) relates the Christology of the AscIsa to other possible traces of angelomorphic Christology in the New Testament and early Christian literature.

[101]On this term, see Norelli (1980) 343-364; Norelli (1983).

[102]Talbert (1976) 422-426.

[103]Cf. also Simonetti (1983) 185-193, 203; Acerbi (1989) 187-189 and chapter 6, who in different ways both show that the Christology of the AscIsa transcends a mere angel-Christology.

[104]This is certainly the sense of 'glories' (Lat. *gloriarum*) here: cf. Jude 8; 1QH 10:8; 2 Enoch 22:7, 10.

prohibition of the worship of angels with the command to worship Christ. Finally, it should be noticed that here Christ's status as worthy of worship already belongs to him in his pre-existence (9:27-32), though it is apparently his redemptive work which leads to his enthronement (11:32).

4. Conclusion

The worship of Jesus in early Christianity could neither be easily rejected, since it was a natural response to his role in the Christian religion, nor unreflectively permitted, since it raised the relationship of Christology to monotheism in its acutest form. No doubt the latter consideration, combined with the conservatism of the liturgy, which so largely followed Jewish models, accounts for its absence from the formal liturgies which have survived from the pre-Nicene period.[105] That it occurred at least in hymns and spontaneous worship, however, cannot be doubted,[106] and the Christological significance of this should not be underrated. That the highest Christology, including the direct ascription of the title 'God' to Jesus, seems to have occurred earliest in contexts of worship, has often been noticed,[107] but sometimes with the implication that it should therefore be taken less seriously. In fact, on the contrary, if it is in worship that monotheism is tested in religious practice, the devotional attitude to Jesus in worship is the critical test of Christology.

There may have been early Christian circles in which a general neglect of the limits of monotheism in worship

---

[105]Jungmann (1965). It is important to notice that the liturgies are more conservative, in the area of prayer to and worship of Jesus, than the evidence of the New Testament suggests was true of Christian worship towards the end of the first century: cf. the doxologies addressed to Christ cited in n. 74 above. The extent to which prayer is addressed to Jesus in the New Testament has been frequently underestimated (Delay [1949]); note especially John 14:14, which lays down a general principle.

[106]See Rawlinson (1926) 135-136; Martin (1964) 31; Jungmann (1965) chapter 10; Hengel (1983); Bauckham (1992) section 3.

[107]E.g. Segal (1977) 215.

accompanied the emergence of the worship of Jesus. But the importance of the material studied in this chapter lies in its sensitivity to the issue of monotheism in worship. So far from endorsing a general tendency to reverence intermediary beings, these writers emphasised a traditional motif designed to rule out angelolatry. At the same time they depicted the worship of Jesus in the throne-room of heaven. This combination of motifs had the effect, probably more clearly than any other Christological theme available in their world of ideas, of placing Jesus on the divine side of the line which monotheism must draw between God and creatures.

5

The Role of the Spirit

References to the Spirit of God in the Apocalypse can be divided into three categories: four occurrences of the phrase ἐν πνεύματι (1:10; 4:2; 17:3; 21:10); ten other references to the Spirit (2:7, 11, 17, 29; 3:6, 13, 22; 14:13; 19:10; 22:17); and four references to the seven Spirits (1:4; 3:1; 4:5; 5:6).[1] The first three sections of this chapter will consider these three categories in turn, while the fourth will discuss two passages which illuminate the way the activity of the prophetic Spirit gives the church its eschatological perspective.

1. The Spirit of vision

Under this heading we shall consider the four occurrences of the phrase 'in the Spirit' (ἐν πνεύματι) (1:10; 4:2; 17:3; 21:10). Though in each case the reference is to John's experience as a prophetic visionary, we shall find that the precise meaning is not the same in each case.

In early Christian literature the phrase ἐν πνεύματι commonly means 'in the Spirit's control,' with various connotations. Frequently it denotes temporary experience of the Spirit's power in prophetic speech or revelation,[2] without specifying

---

[1]On the numerical symbolism in the numbers of references to the Spirit, see chapter 1 section 3 above.

[2]Matt 22:43; Luke 1:7; 2:27; Acts 19:21; 1 Cor 12:3; Martyrdom of Paul 1; cf. also prayer in the Spirit (Eph 6:18; Jude 20); worship in the Spirit (John 4:23-24). The phrase can be used of the Christian's permanent experience of the indwelling

any particular mode of the Spirit's operation. When Polycrates writes that one of the daughters of Philip (who were prophets) 'lived entirely in the Holy Spirit' (ἐν ἁγίῳ πνεύματι πολιτευσαμένη) and that Melito 'lived entirely in the Holy Spirit' (ἐν ἁγίῳ πνεύματι πάντα πολιτευσάμενον: ap. Eusebius, *Hist. Eccl.* 5.24.2, 5) he presumably means that they enjoyed a lifelong experience of prophetic inspiration. In Didache 11:7-9, however, the phrase ἐν πνεύματι would seem to be a theologically neutral term for ecstatic speech, for the prophet who speaks ἐν πνεύματι is assessed as true or false by other criteria than this. It may be that through indiscriminate use the phrase had lost the theological assessment originally implicit in it and become merely phenomenological in this context, or it may be that the prophet who speaks in ecstasy is considered inspired, but not by the Spirit of God (cf. 1 John 4:1-6). In either case the primary reference is here not to the source of inspiration but to the phenomenon of ecstatic speech.

It has sometimes been thought that ἐν πνεύματι in Revelation refers to John's human spirit (cf. Rev 22:6): it would then indicate that this rapture into heaven (4:2) and transportation (17:3; 21:10) were 'in the spirit' rather than 'in the body'. The phrase would be equivalent to Paul's ἐκτὸς τοῦ σώματος (2 Cor 12:2) and John's experience similar to that in the Ascension of Isaiah (which will be discussed below).[3] But we shall see that this cannot be the sense in 17:3; 21:10, and reference to the divine Spirit in 1:10; 4:2 therefore makes John consistent both with his own and with early Christian usage.

Spirit: Rom 8:9. Note also the expression, 'to see in the Holy Spirit,' used in the Targums (McNamara [1972] 113) and rabbinic literature (e.g. Lev. R. 9:9; 21:8; 37:3; other examples in Abelson [1912] 259, 263, 265-266; Davies [1948] 211, 213), with reference to prophetic knowledge, supernaturally given (apparently in mental perception rather than literal vision). Martyrdom of Paul 1 seems to be a Christian use of this Jewish expression.

[3] Cf. also 1 Enoch 71:1, 5, where Enoch's spirit is translated into heaven, and 1 Cor 5:3-4; Col 2:5 for metaphorical use of the idea that the spirit may be where the body is not. For examples of translation both in and out of the body, see Russell (1964) 166-168. Acts 12:7-11 recounts a visionary experience ἐν πνεύματι (cf. 12:11) which is no mere vision (12:9) but the medium of transportation in the body; cf. also Acts 8:39.

In 1:10; 4:2, the expression γενέσθαι ἐν πνεύματι, though not precisely attested elsewhere, is best understood as a technical term for the visionary's experience of 'rapture' by the Spirit. It is probably to be taken as both phenomenological and theological, denoting both the visionary experience as such and the Spirit's authorship of it. For visionary experience Luke prefers the more strictly phenomenological γενέσθαι ἐν ἐκστάσει (Acts 22:11; cf. 10:10), with its opposite, γενέσθαι ἐν ἑαυτῷ (Acts 12:11), although Luke certainly understands the Spirit to be the agent of visions (Acts 2:17; 7:55). When someone ceases to be ἐν ἑαυτῷ and becomes ἐν ἐκστάσει, he loses his outward consciousness. Instead the Spirit takes control of his faculties: he becomes ἐν πνεύματι. Thus Josephus describes Balaam prophesying as one who was no longer ἐν ἑαυτῷ but overruled by the divine Spirit (τῷ θείῳ πνεύματι νενικημένος: *Ant.* 4.118). Similarly, according to Pseudo-Philo, the Holy Spirit which came upon Kenaz and indwelt him 'took away his bodily sense (*extulit sensum eius*) and he began to prophesy' (LAB 28:6). Such language may suggest a kind of bodily possession more readily associated with those pagan prophets of antiquity who became in a trance the wholly passive mouthpieces of the god. Perhaps this is what Josephus intends, but it need not be the meaning of Pseudo-Philo. Certainly it was not John's experience. He remains a free agent throughout his visions. But the visionary experience is nonetheless necessarily a suspension of normal consciousness. John was ἐν πνεύματι in the sense that his normal sensory experience was replaced by visions and auditions given him by the Spirit.

The experience of trance-like suspension of normal consciousness is vividly described in the Christian apocalypse known as the Ascension of Isaiah, a work which may date from only shortly after Revelation:

> And while he [Isaiah] was speaking with the Holy Spirit in the hearing of them all, he became silent, and his mind was taken up from him, and he did not see the men who were standing before him. His eyes indeed were open, but his mouth was silent, and the mind in his body was taken

up from him. But his breath was (still) in him, for he was seeing a vision. And the angel who was sent to show him (the vision) was not of this firmament, nor was he from the angels of glory of this world, but he came from the seventh heaven. And the people who were standing by, apart from the circle of prophets, did [not] think that the holy Isaiah had been taken up. And the vision which he saw was not from this world, but from the world which is hidden from the flesh (6:10-15).[4]

This may be taken as an accurate phenomenological account of the kind of visionary experience John intends by the expression γενέσθαι ἐν πνεύματι. The Ascension of Isaiah goes on to interpret the prophet's experience as a real translation of his spirit out of his body through the seven heavens, thus opting for the latter of the two possibilities suggested by Paul in 2 Corinthians 12:2. But such an interpretation is presumably only possible of a vision which, like Isaiah's, can be understood as a realistic sight of the heavenly realms. In John's case, not only is he silent as to the bodily or spiritual nature of his translation to the heavenly court (chapter 4), but also his visions are clearly not intended to be realistic. They are symbolic representations of happenings present and future, heavenly and earthly. In many cultures trances, and also dreams, have been understood as the absence of the spirit from the body, and this interpretation of visionary rapture is to be found in other apocalyptic works besides the Ascension of Isaiah,[5] but there is no need to attribute it to John.

The expression γενέσθαι ἐν πνεύματι is used in somewhat different ways in Revelation 1:10 and 4:2, and it is difficult to find a translation which fits both its occurrences. 'I fell into a trance' (Caird) is the sense of 1:10, though it misses the agency of the Spirit. But this cannot be the sense of 4:2. The technical terminology of vision in 4:1 shows that 4:2 cannot be the

---

[4]Translation from Knibb (1985) 165. On AscIsa 6, see chapter 2 section 5 above.
    [5]1 Enoch 71:1, 5; TLevi 2-6. Russell (1964) 167 n.1, understands 'Come up here!' (Rev 4:1) as indicating a translation of the spirit; but the same words in Rev 11:12 refer to bodily translation.

beginning of a second trance: John is already ἐν πνεύματι. The context requires that 4:2 refer to John's rapture to heaven. This is an experience which the apocalyptic seers commonly described in more elaborate terms,[6] and it may be significant that John prefers an expression which attributes it to the agency of the Spirit. 'I was caught up by the Spirit' (NEB) is perhaps the most adequate translation. The two remaining occurrences of ἐν πνεύματι (17:3; 21:10) are instances of transportation 'in the Spirit', and will be discussed further below.

We must first enquire into the precedents in Jewish literature for John's understanding of the Spirit as the agent of visionary experience. His extensive use of Old Testament language and imagery and his writing within the genre of Jewish apocalyptic vision make such precedents particularly relevant. The idea of the Spirit of God as the agent of visionary experience is occasional in the Old Testament (Num 24:2; cf. vv 4, 16-17), though probably also implied in general references to ecstatic prophecy (Num 11:24-29; 1 Sam 10:6, 10). More important are the prominence of the Spirit in Ezekiel's experiences of visionary rapture (3:12, 14; 8:3; 11:1, 24; 37:1; 43:5; cf. also Elijah in 1 Kings 18:12; 2 Kings 2:16), and the specification of dreams and visions as the manifestation of the eschatological outpouring of the Spirit in Joel 2:28. In later Jewish literature, the Spirit inspires prophetic speech (e.g. 1 Enoch 91:1; Jub 25:14; 31:12; Pseudo-Philo, LAB 18:11; 32:14; 4 Ezra 14:22) more commonly than visions (Sir 48:24).[7] This is despite the frequency of visions in the Jewish apocalyptic works, but in line with the rarity of references to the Spirit in these works. But the apocalyptists do occasionally mention the Spirit as the agent of visionary transportation (2 Bar 6:3; Hebrew ApEl) and possibly once as the agent of translation into heaven (1 Enoch 70:2) — these are the ideas which recur in Revelation 4:2; 17:3; 21:10.

John's translation into the heavenly court (4:3) was the common experience of apocalyptic visionaries, but in the

---

[6]E.g. 1 Enoch 14:8; 39:3; TAbr A 10:1; ApAbr 15:2-4; 2 Enoch 3:1; 3 Bar 2:1-2.
[7]Cf. also the Spirit inspiring dreams: TAbr A 4:8-9; LAB 9:10.

extant, unquestionably Jewish literature[8] the only possible reference to the Spirit as the agent of such a translation is in reference to Enoch's final assumption: 'he was lifted on the chariots of the spirit, and his name vanished among them' (1 Enoch 70:2).[9] It seems likely, however, that we should understand: 'chariots of the wind'. The terminology recalls Elijah's translation in a chariot of fire and a whirlwind (2 Kings 2:11), and reflects the fact that on the basis of Elijah's experience the chariot of fire and the whirlwind had become the common means of translation to heaven in the post-biblical Jewish literature.[10] The two are probably identified in Sirach 48:9, and the chariot also became identified with the 'chariot of the cherubim'. It was on this chariot, God's own chariot, that Abraham (TAbr 9-10) and Adam (LAE 25:3) experienced temporary raptures to heaven, and on this chariot Job's soul was taken up to heaven after his death (TJob 52:9). Life of

---

[8]Perhaps Jewish is the Apocalypse of Zephaniah of which only a fragment is extant, quoted by Clement of Alexandria, *Str.* 5.11.77. It begins: 'And a spirit took me and brought me up into the fifth heaven.' *Pace* Wintermute (1983) 500, it seems very unlikely that this quotation is from the same work as the much more extensive Coptic fragments of an Apocalypse of Zephaniah, and it is impossible to tell whether the work is of Jewish or Christian origin, though it certainly belongs to the Jewish and Christian apocalyptic genre of ascents through the seven heavens. Since the quotation goes on to refer to 'the Holy Spirit', the πνεῦμα which transports the visionary to the fifth heaven seems not to be the divine Spirit (cf. 2 Bar 6:3; Hermas, *Vis.* 1:1:3; 2:1:1, quoted below). In a similar context in an apocalyptic tour of the heavens, is a passage in the Gnostic Apocalypse of Paul (CG V,2), presumably based on a Jewish or Christian apocalypse: 'Then the Holy [Spirit] who was speaking with [him] caught him up on high to the third heaven' (19:20-24: translation from Robinson [1977] 240). This passage is evidently closely related to Apocalypse of Paul 11: 'And after that I saw one of the spiritual beings beside me and he caught me up in the Holy Spirit and carried me up to the third part of Heaven, which is the third heaven' (translation from the Syriac in Duensing [1965A] 763). All three passages use the same kind of language of visionary transportation, derived from Ezekiel, as the passages quoted in the next paragraph below.

[9]Translation from Knibb (1978) 165.

[10]Whirlwind: 1 Enoch 39:3-4; 52:1; cf. also 1 Enoch 14:8; ApAbr 15:4; and Widengren (1948) 108-110, with the passage there cited from the *Ginza*: 'Winds, winds led away Shitil the son of Adam; storms, storms led him away, made him ascend...'

Adam and Eve 25:3 calls it 'a chariot like the wind'.[11] These parallels make it probable that 1 Enoch 70:2 originally referred to 'chariots of the wind'. At the same time the ambiguity of wind/Spirit and the association of Spirit and fire might well have suggested the agency of the Spirit in translation to heaven, as they did in some early Christian writers.[12] It may therefore be only an accident of survival that we have no such Jewish parallels to Revelation 4:2. What is certainly clear is that most apocalyptists preferred more graphic descriptions.

Parallels to transportation ἐν πνεύματι (Rev. 17:3; 21:10) are somewhat easier to find. While Elijah's translation provided the model for descriptions of translation to heaven, Ezekiel's experiences were the principal model for accounts of visionary transportation from place to place. The language of 17:3; 21:10 should be compared with the following passages from Jewish and early Christian writings:

1 Kings 18:12; 2 Kings 2:16.

Ezekiel 3:12, 14; 8:3; 11:1, 24; 37:1; 43:5.

Bel 36 (Theodotion): 'The angel of the Lord took (ἐπελάβετο) Habakkuk by the crown of his head, and carried (βαστάσας) him by the hair of his head, and with the blast of his breath (ἐν τῷ ῥοιζῷ τοῦ πνεύματος αὐτοῦ) set him down in Babylon above the pit.'[13]

2 Baruch 6:3: 'And behold, suddenly a strong spirit lifted me and carried me above the wall of Jerusalem'.[14]

---

[11]Cf. also 3 Enoch 24:2; ApMos 38:3. Chariot, cherubim, winds, clouds were all associated on the basis of such texts as Pss 18:10; 68:4; 104:3; Ezek 1.

[12] AscIsa 7:23: Christians 'at their end' will ascend to heaven 'through the angel of the Holy Spirit'; OdesSol 36:1: 'I rested on the Spirit of the Lord, and she raised me up to heaven'; Gregory of Nyssa, *In Cant.* 10: 'Like Elijah, our mind is taken up in the chariot of fire and carried through the air to the glories of heaven — by fire we understand the Holy Spirit.'

[13]LXX lacks the reference to the angel's πνεῦμα.

[14]Translation from Klijn (1983) 622.

Hebrew Apocalypse of Elijah: 'The Spirit of God took me up and brought me to the south of the world.... Again the Spirit took me up and brought me to the east of the world.... Again the Spirit took me up and brought me to the west of the world....'[15]

Acts 8:39-40: 'The Spirit of the Lord snatched Philip away (ἥρπασεν); the eunuch saw him no more, and went on his way rejoicing. But Philip found himself at Azotus....'

Gospel of the Hebrews (*ap.* Origen, *In Joann.* 2.12): [Jesus said:] 'Even so did my mother, the Holy Spirit, take (ἔλαβε) me by one of my hairs and carry me away (ἀπήνεγκε) onto the great mountain Tabor.'

Hermas, *Visions* 1:1:3: 'And a spirit took me and carried me away (ἔλαβεν καὶ ἀπήνεγκε) through a pathless region....'

Hermas, *Visions* 2:1:1: 'And again a spirit took me (αἴρει) and carried me away (ἀποφέρει) to the same place....'[16]

Most of these passages copy the language of Ezekiel. It should be noticed that, while in some of them it is by no means clear whether it is *the* Spirit *of God* that is intended, in no case is the reference to the human spirit of the prophet. The closest parallels to these verses of Revelation are Ezekiel 37:1 and Bel 36, and these suggest that ἐν πνεύματι may be instrumental in Revelation 17:3; 21:10 (as it clearly is in Ezek 37:1 LXX: ἐξήγαγέ με ἐν πνεύματι Κύριος). John's usage is seen to be conventional terminology for visionary transportation, though again it might be significant that in 21:10, obviously modelled on Ezekiel 40:2, he prefers ἐν πνεύματι to 'in visions of God', which is found in that verse of Ezekiel. His stress on the Spirit's agency in his visionary experience is a little stronger than

---

[15]On this passage, see Bauckham (1990) 362-364.

[16]The *Visions* of Hermas are probably contemporary with Revelation: see Bauckham (1974) 28-29.

appears to have been normal in the Jewish apocalyptists, but the terminology itself is stereotyped and unremarkable. It might even be thought that, by introducing the interpreting angel in 17:3; 21:10, he has permitted apocalyptic stylistic conventions to mar the more expressive image of the wind which caught up Ezekiel, the sudden gust of mysterious divine power sweeping the prophet off his feet. But John's language probably conveyed as much to his readers, as did Bel 36, which sounds almost comic today. John's language affirmed economically the divine source of his visions; but that this was more specifically the Spirit of Jesus appears not from the phrase ἐν πνεύματι alone, but from its context in the Apocalypse as a whole.

John is much less interested than many other apocalyptists in describing psychologically his visionary experience.[17] His purpose was not so much to describe how he received the revelation as to communicate it to his readers. Certainly that there are these particular four occurrences of ἐν πνεύματι and no others has literary rather than psychological significance. The parallel formulae of 17:3 and 21:10, reminiscent of Ezekiel's vision of the new temple, are clearly intended to highlight the antithesis of Babylon and Jerusalem. They are strategically placed for literary effect and theological significance, rather than to show that the Spirit played a special role at these points and not others. For the purpose of passing on the revelation John needed only to indicate that the whole revelation came to him ἐν πνεύματι — which was a theological claim as much as a psychological statement.

The claim must certainly be taken as indicating that real visionary experience underlies the Apocalypse, but should not be taken to mean that the book is a simple transcript of that

---

[17]For details of the apocalyptists' psychic experiences, see Russell (1964) chapter 6; Rowland (1982) chapter 9. For the character of John's visionary experience, it may be noteworthy that, again unlike many apocalyptists, he does not speak of dreams or visions at night or waking from sleep (cf. Dan 7:1-2; Zech 1:8; 4:1; 2 Bar 53:1; 4 Ezra 3:1; 11:1; 12:3; 13:1, 14; TLevi 2:5; 5:7; 1 Enoch 83:3, 6; 85:1; 86:1; 90:40).

experience, as someone might recount their dreams on a psychiatrist's couch. That would take no account of the literary conventions John employs or the complex literary composition of his book. Out of his visionary experience John has produced a work which enables the reader, not to share the same experience at secondhand, but to receive its message transposed into a literary medium. For, in distinction from such purely personal experiences as that of Paul (2 Cor 12:1-4), who heard unutterable words in paradise, John's visions were *prophetic* experience. What he heard and saw was 'the revelation of Jesus Christ which God gave him to show to his servants what must soon take place' (1:1). Experiences of rapture to heaven and visionary transportation were not uncommon in Jewish apocalyptic mysticism and pagan religious experience, and the authentication of John's message therefore lies not in the experience as such but in the claim that it took place under the control of the Spirit and came to him through Jesus Christ from God.[18]

In primitive Christianity prophetic vision ἐν πνεύματι was a manifestation of the outpouring of the Spirit in the last days (Joel 2:28): it is itself an aspect of the church's living in the age of eschatological fulfilment.[19] But like all the Spirit's activity it is also eschatologically directed: it orientates the church's life towards the parousia. Purely personal experiences like Paul's rapture to heaven might do this on a personal level. John's visions were to do so for the seven churches of Asia in their specific historical circumstances in the reign of Domitian. They were to show the meaning in those circumstances of living towards the coming of Christ.

---

[18]The attempt by Jeske (1985) to reject any reference in the phrase ἐν πνεύματι to John's ecstatic condition and to find its primary significance to refer to John's shared experience of the Spirit in the churches I do not find at all convincing. I agree that the phrase highlights John's *reception* of his message, but not that this reception (indicated by ἐν πνεύματι) is shared with his readers. The phrase highlights John's *distinctive* experience as a prophet who passes on the message to the churches. The Spirit in this phrase is community-related, not with regard to John's participation with others in the Spirit, but by inspiring John's reception, in the Spirit, of a prophetic message to be given to the others.

[19]On visionary experience in early Christianity, see Dunn (1975) 177-179, 213-216.

2. The Spirit of prophecy

In post-biblical Judaism, as is well known, the Spirit is especially the Spirit of prophecy, the Spirit who speaks through the prophets.[20] In Revelation also the Spirit is almost exclusively the Spirit of prophecy. This observation, however, is not especially helpful without an understanding of the meaning of 'prophecy' in Revelation. We shall see that it carries probably rather broader connotations than might at first be thought.[21]

Parts of the Apocalypse are explicitly said to be the words of the Spirit: the seven messages to the churches; 14:13b; and 22:17a. The seven messages are 'what the Spirit says to the churches,' equated with the words of the exalted Christ. The significance of 14:13b would seem to be that the words of the Spirit are the Spirit's response, speaking through John, to the heavenly voice. As John obeys the command to write the beatitude, the Spirit inspiring him adds an emphatic endorsement of it. In 22:17a, Ἔρχου is certainly (*pace* the majority of commentators) addressed by the Spirit and the Bride not to the one who thirsts, but to Christ. It is the response to Christ's promise in 22:12, just as the same promise and response recur in 22:20. Again in all probability 'the Spirit' is equivalent to the inspired utterance of the Christian prophets, here in the form of Spirit-inspired prayer.

Thus the Spirit of prophecy speaks through the Christian prophets bringing the word of the exalted Christ to his people on earth, endorsing on earth the words of heavenly revelations, and directing the prayers of the churches to their heavenly Lord. These are the special functions of the Christian prophets, whom Revelation distinguishes as a special group within the churches (11:18; 16:6; 18:20, 24; 22:9). The doctrine of the Spirit in the Apocalypse has sometimes been felt to be deficient in that the Spirit is *only* the Spirit of prophecy, rather than moral or life-giving power in Christian life. There is a real distinction here from some other New Testament writers

---

[20]See, e.g., Sjöberg (1968) 381-383; Hill (1967) 227-228.

[21]For a fuller treatment of the subject of this section, see Bauckham (1993) chapter 5.

(notably the Fourth Gospel and Paul), but it should be remarked that the Spirit of prophecy is envisaged as having life-giving and life-changing effects. For the Spirit brings to the churches the powerful word of Christ, rebuking, encouraging, promising and threatening, touching and drawing the hearts, minds and consciences of its hearers, directing the lives and the prayers of the Christian communities towards the coming of Christ.

Is Spirit-inspired prophecy a function which the Apocalypse confines to the Christian prophets or is there a sense in which the church as a whole has a prophetic vocation?[22] One reason for suspecting the latter is the relationship between prophecy and the phrase 'the witness of Jesus' (μαρτυρία Ἰμσοῦ), which, along with some related expressions, is very frequent in the book. In this expression Ἰησοῦ seems to be always a subjective, not an objective genitive, so that the phrase always means, in some sense, 'the witness Jesus bore'. Thus, when 19:10 says that 'the witness of Jesus is the Spirit of prophecy', this difficult statement must mean that the witness Jesus bore is the content of Spirit-inspired prophecy. It is therefore also the content of John's own prophecy, the Apocalypse itself (1:2): the word of God which John's prophecy communicates is attested primarily by Jesus himself (22:20), as also by the angel who communicates it to John (22:16) and by John (1:2). In essence, this word of God is also that to which Jesus bore witness in his earthly life (1:5) and to which his followers now bear witness in the world (1:9 etc.). Witness in Revelation is verbal (see especially 11:7; 12:11), though it is linked with obedience to God's commandments (12:17; cf. 14:12) and its *consequence*, in the circumstances envisaged in Revelation, is expected to be martyrdom (2:13; 6:9; 17:6; 20:4). Those who bear the witness of Jesus are certainly not just the prophets (19:10) but Christians in general (12:17). Yet in 11:3, where the faithful church in its witness to the world is portrayed under the image of 'my two witnesses' who 'prophesy' (cf. 11:10), prophecy and witness seem to be equated. The characterization of the Christian

---

[22]For discussion, see Hill (1972) 411-414; Aune (1983) 206-208.

community as 'those who bear the witness of Jesus' seems therefore to attribute a prophetic role to the whole church.

Probably a distinction is to be drawn between the special vocation of the Christian prophets to declare the word of God within the Christian community, and the general vocation of the Christian community as a whole to declare the word of God in the world. The former will then subserve the latter. The Spirit speaks through the prophets to the churches and through the churches to the world. However, as far as specific references to the Spirit go, those we have so far examined concern exclusively the Spirit's inspiration of Christian prophecy addressed to the churches. For the Spirit's activity in the church's missionary role in the world, we must turn to a distinct category of references to the Spirit which we have not yet considered.

3. The seven Spirits

The third and last category of references to the Spirit in Revelation are those to the seven Spirits (1:4; 3:1; 4:5; 5:6). The identity of these seven Spirits, called in 1:4 'the seven Spirits who are before [God's] throne' (cf. 4:5), is debated.[23] They have sometimes been identified, not as the divine Spirit, but as the seven principal angels who, in Jewish angelology, stand in the presence of God in heaven (cf. Tob 12:15; 1 Enoch 20 [Greek]; 4QShirShabb).[24] But Revelation itself refers to these seven angels (8:1) in terms quite different from the way it refers to the seven Spirits. Moreover, although the term 'spirit' could certainly be used of angels (as frequently in the Dead Sea Scrolls), it very rarely has this meaning in early Christian literature and never in Revelation.

The seven Spirits are a symbol for the divine Spirit, which John has chosen on the basis of his exegesis of Zechariah 4:1-14, a passage which lies behind not only the four references to

---

[23]Dix (1926); Jouon (1931); Skrinjar (1935); Bruce (1973).
[24]Most recently by Giblin (1991) 71-72.

the seven Spirits but also the description of the two witnesses in 11:4. It seems to have been the key Old Testament passage for John's understanding of the role of the Spirit in the divine activity in the world. If we wonder why he should have attached such importance to this obscure vision of Zechariah, the answer no doubt lies in the word of the Lord which he would have understood as the central message of the vision: 'Not by might, nor by power, but by my Spirit, says the LORD of hosts' (Zech 4:6). The question to which the message of Revelation is the answer was: Given the apparently irresistible might and worldwide power of the beast, how is God going to establish this rule of earth? Zechariah 4:6 indicates that it will not be by worldly power like the beast's, but by the divine Spirit.

In Zechariah's vision he is shown a golden lampstand on which are seven lamps. John could not have failed to connect this with the seven-branched lampstand that stood in the holy place in the temple (cf. Exod 25:31-40; 40:4, 24-25). Beside the lampstand are two olive trees (Zech 4:3). As John no doubt understood the narrative, Zechariah asks first about the identity of the seven lamps (4:4-5) and then about the identity of the olive trees (4:11-13). His first question is not immediately answered directly. First he is given the oracle just quoted ('Not by might, nor by power, but by my Spirit': 4:6), followed by further words of the Lord which expand on this point (4:7-10a), and then his question is directly answered: 'These seven are the eyes of the LORD, which range through the whole earth' (4:10b). John evidently took this sequence to mean that the seven lamps symbolize the seven eyes of the Yahweh, which are the divine Spirit. We postpone for the moment the question of the identity of the olive trees.

In John's vision of heaven he sees seven lamps burning before the divine throne, which he identifies as the seven Spirits (Rev 4:5). Since the heavenly sanctuary was understood as the model on which the earthly sanctuary was constructed and in John's visions it therefore contains the most important contents of the earthly sanctuary (cf. 8:3-5; 11:19; 15), these seven lamps correspond to the seven lamps which burned 'before the LORD' (Exod 40:25) in the earthly sanctuary. They are the lamps of Zechariah's vision. No doubt a lampstand is presupposed, but it is probably significant that John does not mention it: the lampstands he mentions are on earth (1:12-13, 20; 2:1, 5; 11:4). As the seven lamps before the throne in heaven, the seven Spirits belong to the divine being. This is why the reference to them in the trinitarian blessing of 1:4-5a is also to 'the seven Spirits who are before his throne'.

But if these references associate the seven Spirits with God, in 5:6 they are very closely associated with the Lamb, who is said to have 'seven horns and seven eyes, which are the seven Spirits of God sent out into all the earth'. The echo of Zechariah 4:10b is clear. In Revelation the eyes of Yahweh are also the eyes of the Lamb. This has an exegetical basis in Zechariah 3:9, where John would have taken the 'stone with seven eyes' to refer to Christ and the seven eyes to be the same as those of Zechariah 4:10b.

Probably Revelation 5:6 identifies the seven Spirits with *both* the seven horns *and* the seven eyes of the Lamb.[25] It is important to realise that the eyes of Yahweh in the Old Testament indicate not only his ability to see what happens throughout the world, but also his ability to act powerfully wherever he chooses. The message of the prophet Hanani in 2 Chronicles 16:7-9, which makes verbal allusion to Zechariah 4:10b (16:9: 'the eyes of the LORD range throughout the entire earth'), clearly understands this verse, as John did, in connexion with Zechariah 4:6 ('Not by might, nor by power but by my Spirit'). Hanani rebukes King Asa for having relied on the power of an army instead of on Yahweh, whose eyes range throughout the world to help those who rely on him (cf. the very similar passage Ps 33:13-19; cf. also Ps 34:15; Sir 34:15-16). This connexion between God's all-seeing eyes and his power John makes explicit by adding seven horns, the well-known symbol of strength, to the seven eyes. Probably he noticed that in Zechariah the power of Yahweh is opposed to the power of the nations inimical to God's people, symbolized by four horns (Zech 1:18-21). Similarly, in Revelation, the seven horns of the Lamb[26] are the divine power

---

[25]Cf. Bruce (1973) 334 n.6.
[26]For the horns of the Messiah, cf. also Deut 33:17; 1QSb 5:26; 1 Enoch 91:38.

set against the horns of the dragon and the beasts (Rev 12:3; 13:1, 11; 17:12-13). The crucial question, however, is the nature of this divine power.

The seven horns and the seven eyes belong to the description of the Lamb when he first appears in Revelation: as the slaughtered Lamb who has conquered (5:5-6). They represent the power of his victory. The seven Spirits are sent out into all the earth to make his victory effective throughout the world. How do they do so? The answer is best found in the implicit relationship that exists between the seven Spirits and the two witnesses of Revelation 11:3-13. The relationship depends again on allusions to Zechariah 4, which John is continuing to interpret in 11:3-4. The two olive trees of Zechariah's vision are said to be 'the two anointed ones [literally: 'sons of oil'] who stand by the Lord of the whole earth' (Zech 4:14). Revelation's two witnesses are 'the two olive trees and the two lampstands that stand before the Lord of the earth' (11:4). If 'the two olive trees' have a significance for John more than simply as a way of referring to Zechariah's vision, it is probably that the two are prophets (cf. 11:3, 10), anointed with the oil of the Spirit. But in identifying them with two lampstands, he has modified the symbolism of Zechariah's vision. He must mean that they are lampstands bearing the lamps which are the seven Spirits, though since he has chosen to have only two witnesses, according to the biblical requirement for valid witness (Num 35:30; Deut 17:6; 19:15), and therefore only two lampstands, he cannot refer to the seven Spirits without confusing the imagery intolerably. Nevertheless, the implication is clear that the seven Spirits are the power of the church's prophetic witness to the world, symbolized by the ministry of the two witnesses. The universality of this witness is suggested by the phrase John borrows from Zechariah, that they 'stand before the Lord of the earth', which also relates their universal witness to God's or Christ's lordship of the world. It is therefore through their prophetic witness that the seven Spirits are sent out into all the earth. The horns and the eyes of the Lamb are the power and discernment of their prophetic witness, which is their faithfulness to the witness Jesus bore. Through this witness of the church to the world the seven Spirits make the victory of the Lamb effective universally.

If we now relate the two lampstands (11:4), which represent the churches in their faithful witness to the world, and the seven lampstands (1:12-13, 20),[27] which represent the seven churches of Asia, to which John's prophetic message is addressed, we can see once again that the ministry of Christ by the Spirit in the churches ('walking among the seven golden lampstands': 2:1) is directed towards their effectiveness as those who bear his witness in the world (11:3-4). The messages of the Spirit speaking through the Christian prophets in the churches (e.g. chapters 2-3) are intended to give the churches themselves 'power to prophesy' (11:3).

4. The Spirit and the eschatological perspective

We have seen that the varied terminology of the Spirit's activity reflects the various aspects of 'prophecy' broadly understood. The Spirit mediates the activity of the exalted Christ in and through his church, declaring Christ's word to his people in vision and prophetic oracle, leading the prayers of his people, inspiring his people's missionary witness to the world. In all of this, the Spirit's role is eschatological, constituting the Christian churches the community of the age to come. As it is from the victory of Christ in his death and resurrection that this eschatological activity of the Spirit in the world derives (5:6), so it is towards the fulfilment of this victory in the eschatological future that the Spirit's activity in and through the churches is directed.

This eschatological role of the Spirit in the Apocalypse is not simply that of predicting the events of the end. The purpose of John's prophecy was to enable the Christians of the seven churches to bear the witness of Jesus, and this could only be done by directing their sight and their lives toward the coming

[27]No doubt it is implied, through not stated, that the seven Spirits are sent out into the world as the lamps on the seven golden candlesticks. A relationship between the seven churches and the seven Spirits is suggested in 3:1.

of the Lord. The point was not so much to enable them to foresee the future as to enable them to see their present from the perspective of the future.[28] The implications of this may be illustrated from an examination of two passages in which the Spirit is specifically mentioned.

(a) Revelation 22:17

To understand this verse we must be careful about identifying the Bride. The Bride is not the sum of the Christian communities observable in the world at the end of the first century: the churches of Ephesus, Smyrna, Pergamum and the rest. The Bride is the New Jerusalem, which comes down out of heaven from God (21:2), the church at the consummation of history. The Bride is the church which the Lamb, when he comes, will find ready for his marriage, arrayed in the fine linen of righteous deeds (19:7-8). The Bride is the church seen from the perspective of the *parousia*.

Very different were the seven churches addressed in the Apocalypse. The 'soiled clothes' of the Christians at Laodicea (3:17) contrast with the pure linen of the Bride. The general unpreparedness for the Lord's coming at Ephesus, Pergamum, Sardis (2:5, 16; 3:3) contrasts with the Bride's ardent prayer for the Bridegroom's coming (22:17). The contrast is not really between the unfaithful and the faithful within the churches. It is not that those few at Sardis who had not 'soiled their clothes' constitute the Bride while the others do not. The contrast is rather between present and eschatological reality, between the churches as they are and the churches as they must become if they are to take their place at the eschatological nuptial banquet. Every hearer of the prophecy is 'invited to the marriage supper' (19:9); all the churches are summoned by the voice of prophecy to become the Bride.

The church which prays for the Lord's coming in 22:17 is therefore the eschatological church, the church which will be at the *parousia*. In this prayer it is led by the voice of the Spirit speaking through the prophets, for the function of the Spirit is to direct the churches towards their eschatological reality,

---

[28]Cf. Schüssler Fiorenza (1985) 46-51.

Hearers of the prophecy are then invited to join in this prayer of the Spirit and the Bride, and as they join their own voices to that of the Spirit the eschatological church is becoming present reality already — in the congregations at Ephesus, Smyrna or wherever. By eliciting this response the Spirit is making ready the Bride for the arrival of the Bridegroom.

The prayer for the *parousia* is at the heart of Christian living according to the Apocalypse. Christian life must be lived under the Spirit's direction towards the eschatological future out of which the Lord is coming. Commentators have great difficulty with 22:17, for if the 'Come' of the first two clauses is addressed to Christ, the transition to an invitation to the thirsty to come, in the third clause, is thought painfully abrupt. It is, in fact, a natural progression of thought.[29] People who join the Spirit's prayer for the *parousia* are directing their lives in faith towards that promise. The invitation to the thirsty is also a call towards the eschatological future. For the promise of the water of life without price belongs to the new creation (21:6): the river of the water of life flows through the street of the New Jerusalem (22:1-2). There is no taking the water of life without a turning towards the eschatological future.

There can be no question that 22:17c really does mean that the water of life, the life of the new creation, is available to people in the present. But it is nonetheless the life of the new creation, coming to people from the future. Entry into the New Jerusalem is not a possibility with which people's past provides them; with their first taste of that city's water they are beginning to live out of the new possibilities of the future which the pure promise of God opens before them. The focus of that promise is the Lord's 'I am coming soon,' three times repeated in this epilogue to the Apocalypse (22:7, 12, 20), and the promise is also the Lord's invitation into the New Jerusalem.

(b) Revelation 11:3-13

The reference to the Spirit here is in 11:8, where πνευματικῶς

---

[29]Swete (1907) 310, speaks of 'a remarkable change of reference'. But in any case, Didache 10:6 is good evidence of the early church's ability to set side by side a prayer for the *parousia* and an invitation to the believer to 'come'.

does not mean 'allegorically' or 'figuratively' but something more like 'prophetically' (NRSV). It refers to Spirit-given perception. The great city is called Sodom and Egypt through the Spirit of prophecy, who thus makes plain its real character as a city ripe for judgment and a land from which God's people are redeemed.

The story of the witnesses is to be read neither as simple prediction (history written in advance) nor as allegory (history or future history written in code symbols). Rather it is a story through which the churches are to perceive imaginatively, through the perspective granted them by the Spirit, their vocation and their destiny. Like 22:17, the story functions as a summons towards the eschatological future. It is not so much a story which predicts the future as a story which creates the future.

The story makes wide-ranging reference to many Old Testament situations of prophetic witness and of conflict between God's witnesses and the world. The following figures have all contributed to the imagery:

Joshua and Zerubbabel, standing for the hope of a new Jerusalem amid the ruins of the city which the Gentiles had trampled;[30]
Elijah, who procured three and a half years of drought and called down fire from heaven to consume his enemies, and whose prophetic ministry ended in assumption;[31]
Moses, who turned the Nile to blood and smote the earth with every plague, and, according to some in the first century, was taken up to heaven in a cloud;[32]
Jeremiah, in whose mouth God's word was a fire to devour

---

[30]Rev 11:2, 4; cf. Zech 4.

[31]Rev 11:5-6, 12; cf. 2 Kings 1:9-12; 2:1-11; and for the traditional three and a half years of the drought (cf. Rev 11:3), see Luke 4:25; Jas 5:17. For the strong association between Elijah's ministry and the drought, see LAB 48:1.

[32]Rev 11:6, 12; cf. Exod 7:14-25 (the first of the ten plagues); and for Moses' ascension, cf. Josephus, *Ant.* 4.326; Clement of Alexandria, *Str.* 6.15.2-3.

[33]Rev 11:5; cf. Jer 5:14. For Jeremiah's martyrdom, see LivPro 2:1; 4 Bar 9:25-32.

the people, and traditionally a martyr;[33]
Isaiah, martyred, according to tradition, by his people
because he 'called Jerusalem Sodom'.[34]

The story therefore provides a paradigm of faithful prophetic
witness. Echoing many an historical precedent, it portrays the
power of the true prophet's message, his rejection and
martyrdom, and his hope of eschatological vindication issuing
both in judgment, and also, more prominently, in salvation for
the world which rejected and triumphed over him (11:13). This
is the pattern for the churches, who are called to the prophetic
ministry of the last days. Or perhaps we should express the
message as an *a fortiori: how much more* is this the pattern for those
whose witness is a greater thing even than Moses' or Elijah's and
against whom the beast musters greater forces than the witnesses
of God had ever faced before? The story functions as a call to the
churches to fulfil this pattern in their own witness. It is not so
much prediction as potential prediction, fulfilled to the extent
that it secures the churches' identification with the witnesses of
the story. It is primarily a summons and a promise, which belong
inseparably together, a dramatized version of the Lord's word to
the church at Smyrna: 'Be faithful until death, and I will give you
the crown of life' (2:10).

The role of the Spirit in directing Christian life towards the
parousia and the role of the Spirit in inspiring those who bear
the witness of Jesus come together in this story which crystallizes
one of the major messages of the prophecy. Bearing the witness
of Jesus is a matter of sharing 'in Jesus the persecution and the
kingdom and the patient endurance' (1:9): it leads to suffering,
rejection and death. To a citizen of Pergamum who viewed
σαρκικῶς the martyrdom of Antipas, this way was merely the
way to death; and so, according to the beast's way of seeing the
world, the death of the witnesses was his victory (11:7). But
viewed πνευματικῶς, from the perspective of the *parousia*, it is
the way to life.[35] Faithful bearing of the witness of Jesus depends

---

[34]Rev 11:8; cf. AscIsa 3:10; Isa 1:9-10.

[35]Rev 11:11 alludes to Ezekiel's vision of resurrection: Ezek 37:10; cf. also TAbr
A 18:11.

on an outlook formed by the hope of the *parousia*, in the light of which martyrdom is called the *martyr's* victory (12:11; 15:2). The eschatological perspective alone creates the paradox in which the invitation to new life is also, so it must have seemed in the churches of Asia in the 90s, a summons to death.

There is also a further dimension to the story of the witnesses. It is clear that it follows not only precedents from Old Testament history but also rather more closely the history of Jesus, who shared the fate of the prophets before him. The witnesses' resurrection after three and a half days (an apocalyptic modification of 'on the third day') and their ascension in a cloud recall Jesus' resurrection and ascension. The phrase 'where their Lord was crucified' (11:18) is a strikingly matter-of-fact, historically specific statement, quite uncharacteristic of the visions of the Apocalypse.[36] It resembles the equally specific reference to the martyr Antipas (2:13).[37] Despite appearances, John's prophetic imagination does not really carry him away from the world of concrete human existence, or at least does so only to bring him back to it with new Spirit-given perception. The story of the witnesses is rooted in the specific historicity of Jesus' crucifixion and is intended to take root in the lives of those who bear the witness of Jesus in the streets of the cities of Asia.

In this way the story permits a vivid representation of the faithful witness's identification with Jesus in his witness and death, and also in his vindication. The pivotal role which the history of Jesus plays in the Apocalypse does not detract from, but rather reinforces, the eschatological outlook of the book. The corollary of eschatological hope in the Apocalypse is certainly not the meaninglessness of present existence. The present takes its meaning from the redemption already accomplished (1:5-6; 5:9) which guarantees the future hope, defines its content (the coming Lord is Jesus who was crucified, who was dead and is alive for ever: cf. 1:18) and also provides the model for positively living towards the *parousia* meantime.

---

[36] Cf. Rev 5:5-6 for a symbolic vision of Jesus' death.

[37] Jesus and Antipas are the only post-Old Testament persons (apart, of course, from himself) to whom John refers by their personal names.

The followers of the Lamb must follow his way through death to life (cf. 14:4), and in so doing they may know that it is the way through death to life primarily because it was so for him. In their knowledge of the risen and exalted Jesus they have a preview of the perspective from the parousia.

Finally, we must ask about 'the great city' which the Spirit identifies as Sodom and Egypt (11:8). The phrase, 'where also their Lord was crucified,' seems to identify it as Jerusalem, but 'the great city' is Revelation's otherwise consistent terminology for Babylon (Rome) (14:8; 17:18; 18:2, 10, 16, 18-19, 21).[38] We need to realise that the Spirit's identifications are not simple allegories, but define present situations seen in eschatological perspective.[39] In its rejection of Jesus, Jerusalem forfeited the role of holy city (11:2), which John therefore transfers to the New Jerusalem (21:2, 10). But as the pattern of Jesus' witness and death is extended across the empire in the person of his followers who bear his witness, so the cities of the empire and especially Rome herself play Jerusalem's role — not her true vocation as the holy city, but her apostate role as the harlot city (Isa 1:21) and Sodom (Isa 1:9-10). Jerusalem, where the Lord was crucified, behaved in that action just as every other city in the world was to behave, became in a sense the model for the rest. So on Jerusalem, the murderer of prophets, came 'all the righteous blood shed on earth' (Matt 23:35), while in Babylon the great city 'was found the blood of prophets and of saints, and of all who have been slaughtered on earth' (Rev 18:24).

The identification of the city therefore belongs to the pattern set out by the story of the witnesses. The story is set in Jerusalem because Jerusalem's treatment of the prophets and especially of Jesus is paradigmatic: this is what those who bear the witness of Jesus may expect from the world. Any and every city in whose streets the corpses of the witnesses lie is *thereby* identified, its character seen in the Spirit, as Sodom and Egypt. The value of this identification as part of the Spirit's message

---

[38]The term is only very occasionally used of Jerusalem: SibOr 5:154, 226, 413; cf. TAbr A 2:6 (of the heavenly Jerusalem); ApEl 4:13 (dependent on Rev 11:8). These instances cannot count against the force of Revelation's own usage.

[39]In relation to this chapter, the point is well made by Minear (1966).

to the churches is that it enables them to characterize situations of conflict in their true perspective, to distinguish appearances from underlying reality, to see through the apparent success of the hostile world and the apparent failure of faithful witness. This example of the function of one passage in Revelation[40] may serve to illustrate how the apocalyptic imagery functions as a vehicle of the eschatological perception which the Spirit imparts through the prophets.

[40]For further discussion of Rev 11:3-13, see chapter 9 section 5 below.

6

The Lion, the Lamb and the Dragon

1. The images of the Apocalypse

Study of the images of the Apocalypse has often been impeded or even forestalled completely by too hasty acquiescence in the assumption that they are of a piece with the imagery of the apocalyptic writings in general. This assumption tends to carry with it such unexamined judgments as that apocalyptists always related visionary experiences full of 'grotesque' or 'bizarre' imagery, and that this was either a mannered literary convention or an elaborate code-language designed to dress up or to conceal the message. Judgments vary widely as to the visual effectiveness of the imagery. While D. H. Lawrence complained of the Apocalypse: 'If it is imagery, it is imagery which cannot be imagined,'[1] E. F. Scott was impressed that John was 'able to turn everything into a picture, and the pictures are so vividly drawn that we seem often to be seeing the thing itself'.[2] It is certainly not always easy to know how to read the apocalyptic images. When we read in John's opening vision of the risen Christ that his head and his hair were white as white wool and white as snow (Rev 1:14), are we to visualize this feature as part of an attempt to share John's visual impression of the resplendant figure? Or are we to treat it as a conventional item

---

[1]Lawrence (1974) 7.
[2]Scott (1941) 143.

in literary descriptions of heavenly beings (cf. ApAbr 11:2; 1 Enoch 71:1; 106:2; 2 Enoch 1:5; Hermas, *Vis.* 4:2:1)? Or are we to recall that in Daniel 7:9 (cf. 1 Enoch 71:10) this feature belongs not to the Son of man but to the Ancient of Days, and so conclude that the transference reflects John's high Christology? Or should the white hair be allegorized as a symbol of Christ's eternal preexistence? Such questions cannot be answered without rather careful and sensitive study both of the use of imagery in the apocalypses in general and of the use of imagery in the Apocalypse of John in particular.

It is correct to recognize that John's images need to be understood within the context of the tradition of apocalyptic writings, but such a recognition does not of itself take us very far. The apocalyptic literature is a more diverse collection of material than is commonly recognized by the commentators on the Apocalypse. Symbolic visions are common within it, but are not consistently prominent and vary considerably in character. Sources of imagery and genres of visions need to be studied and distinguished. Unimaginative allegories in which the figures are merely conventional or quite arbitrary can be found as well as richly evocative symbols which defy any straightforward deciphering. The most cursory comparative study will reveal that John selects certain apocalyptic genres and not others, revivifies forms which are almost unexampled since Old Testament prophecy, and creates and uses images in ways which one suspects to be entirely fresh. By comparison with many examples of ancient apocalyptic literature, most readers must be impressed by the vitality and profusion of John's images. There is much to be said for the view that he changed apocalyptic 'into a vehicle for great thoughts and imagination, much as Shakespeare took a dull old play and transformed it into *Hamlet*.'[3]

An obvious difference between the Apocalypse and most of the other apocalyptic works is the sheer quantity of the visionary matter. Most of the book recounts what John 'saw', though the visions are so recounted as to incorporate much in the way of

[3]Scott (1941) 181.

hymns, speeches, authorial comments and allusive reference to Old Testament scripture. In Jewish apocalyptic, visual images were by no means the only, or even always the primary, vehicle of revelation. Narrative prophecy, for example, held an important place, as in Daniel 9:24-27; 11:2-12:4, sometimes (as there) on the lips of an angel, often in more or less symbolic terms. John has comparatively little of this,[4] replacing it with visionary material. While the apocalyptists sometimes predict the plagues of the last days, for example (e.g. ApAbr 30:2-8), only John recounts visions of these plagues. Again, the symbolic visions of the apocalyptists are frequently the kind of allegory which requires interpretation: the apocalyptic seer is characteristically puzzled or disturbed by his vision until the interpreting angel explains it (e.g. Dan 7:15-16; 4 Ezra 10:27-40), and such an explanation may be as long and quite as important as the vision. The genre often resembles that of the allegorical dream (Gen 40-41; Dan 2; 1QGenApoc 19) or the prophetic parable (Ezek 17). John uses it sparingly:[5] his images are usually meant to carry their own significance given the context of mental associations which he shared with his readers. They are commonly symbols which transcend allegorical significance. The shallow interpretation of the Apocalypse as mere code-language might be a fair judgment on some (not all) Jewish apocalyptic allegories, but it is a misunderstanding of John's intention which cannot survive serious comparative study of the apocalyptic visions. John's visions were directed by a desire, not to mystify either the Christians or the imperial authorities, but to promote spiritual insight. They were to manifest that 'most important characteristic of symbols, namely their power to direct our thinking and our orientation towards life.'[6]

---

[4] The only extended passages are 11:4-13; 20:7-10; cf. also 18:9-19. There are short comments of a non-visionary prophetic type: e.g. 9:6, 20-21; 21:24-27; 22:3-5. Chapter 13 moves between vision and prophetic narrative in the style of Daniel 8:3-14.

[5] Only in 7:13-14; 17:6-18; cf. 1:20. He frequently adds explanatory clauses of his own: e.g. 4:5; 5:6, 8; 12:9; 13:6; 16:14; 19:18.

[6] Fawcett (1970) 32.

The richness of John's visual imagination is all the more striking when the Apocalypse is compared with the two great Jewish apocalypses of the same period: 2 Baruch and 4 Ezra. These perhaps suggest that the visual imagination of the apocalyptic tradition was on the decline by the end of the first century A.D. Discourses rather than visions predominate as the means of revelation. Each of these two lengthy works has only three visions, occupying only 36 verses of the 693 verses of 2 Baruch and only about 100 verses of the 718 verses of 4 Ezra.[7] In 2 Baruch especially, despite the book's outstanding literary quality in other respects, the symbolism of the visions is curiously lacking in vitality: the vision of the waters (chapter 53) seems little more than a peg on which to hang the long 'interpretation' of it (56-74). After the first century both Jewish and Christian apocalyptists moved in a different direction, concentrating attention on narrations of journeys through the seven heavens. In such a context it seems best to eschew theories of literary sources incorporated in the Apocalypse: the uniqueness of its imaginative quality is more easily understood if it is all John's own. One last indication of the book's uniqueness may be noticed. By the standards of the apocalyptic tradition it is hard to know whether to classify the Apocalypse as one vision or a series of visions, for the typical apocalyptic vision is short and self-contained.[8] If an apocalypse contains a number of visions, the imagery does not normally overflow from one vision to another. As an integrated sequence of visionary material, architectonically planned, creating one world of images kaleidoscopically presented, the Apocalypse of John is unique.

One fruitful approach to the imagery of the Apocalypse is to concentrate on major distinct images. Naturally this cannot be an exclusive method, for John's work is a continuous developing whole, but it will direct attention to aspects neglected even in

---

[7] The interpretations of the visions occupy a further 145 verses of 2 Baruch and 72 verses of 4 Ezra.

[8] The exceptions are those apocalypses (e.g. 3 Baruch) which describe a visionary's tour of the other world, in which he views its contents.

the approach of those scholars most sensitive to the imagery of the book. Austin Farrer's work, for example, directs attention primarily to John as an exegete of the Old Testament scriptures, comparing the Apocalypse to 'a fresh and continuous scriptural meditation, conceived in the very words in which it is written down; as though, in fact, the author were thinking with his pen'.[9] Certainly John was an exegete as well as a visionary, and it is true that the Apocalypse as he wrote it is a supremely literary achievement whose effect is by no means equivalent to a series of pictures: to Dürer's woodcuts of the Apocalypse, for example, or to the great medieval Spanish manuscript illustrations to the Beatus Apocalypse.[10] It is not a transcript of visionary experience as someone might tell a psychiatrist his dreams, but neither is it sufficient to treat the visions as literary convention. Though we cannot hope to penetrate very far into the nature of John's inspiration, it is at least congruous with the impression the imagery makes on the reader to suppose that John's repeated use of the stereotyped formulae of apocalyptic vision, his repeated 'I saw' and 'behold', reflects experience of heightened visual imagination, in which images were 'given' to him out of which new avenues of spiritual insight opened. Perhaps John first envisioned them in the process of writing, but it is in some ways easier to suppose that some at least of the major images of the book existed in his mind prior to writing. This may explain what Beckwith noticed as a trait of his manner: 'the introduction of an object not previously mentioned, as if already familiar to the reader'.[11] Its recognition will also enable us to catch the early anticipations of great themes which are fully introduced later: so that, for example, in the harlot queen Jezebel (2:20) we can see a minor reflection,

[9]Farrer (1964) 24. Farrer's account of the way John uses the Old Testament is often very speculative and is insufficiently based on comparison with other post-biblical Jewish literature, but his introductory section on 'The Nature of John's Visionary Experience' (23-29) is very perceptive.

[10]For a fine selection of illustrations of the Apocalypse, see Quispel (1979).

[11]Beckwith (1919) 247. Not all Beckwith's examples of this are equally valid: e.g. 'the second death,' introduced without explanation at 2:11, was a current Jewish term (known from the Targums).

the Thyatiran representative, of the image of the great harlot (chapter 17); or the rider on the white horse of the first seal-opening (6:2) may be seen to stand in antithetical parallelism to the Rider of 19:11.

The study of the images of the Apocalypse can usefully proceed only through reconstruction of their resonances in their historical context. Whatever truth there may be in the idea that they embody archetypal images, in Jung's sense,[12] their full significance is not appreciable apart from the range of association they were capable of evoking in the seven churches of Asia in the late first century A.D. In the rest of this chapter we shall attempt to put suggestions into practice with reference to just two images: the Lamb and the Dragon.

2. The Lamb

The figure of the Lamb is introduced in Revelation 5:5-6. The manner of its introduction is very significant. The contrast of the Lion (v. 5) and the Lamb (v. 6) has usually been noticed by the commentators, but variously understood. H. B. Swete was certainly wrong to suggest 'the unique combination of majesty and meekness which characterized the life of Jesus Christ,'[13] for this mistakes the symbolic value of the animals. G. B. Caird is nearer the mark: 'It is almost as if John were saying to us ...: "Wherever the Old Testament says 'Lion' read 'Lamb'." Wherever the Old Testament speaks of the victory of the Messiah or the overthrow of the enemies of God, we are to remember that the gospel recognizes no other way of achieving these ends than the way of the Cross.'[14]

The juxtaposition of more than one image with a single referent is a characteristic of John's visions. Two examples which closely resemble the technique in these verses are 7:4-9 and 21:9-10. In 21:9 the angel promises to show John the bride

[12]Dudley (1967) 38.
[13]Swete (1907) 78.
[14]Caird (1966) 75.

of the Lamb, but what he actually shows him is not a young woman (such as Hermas saw),[15] but the city of the New Jerusalem.[16] In this case, however, though the literary technique is similar, the element of surprise is less than in 5:5-6, for the two images have already been associated in 21:2 and they do not contrast as do the Lion and the Lamb. In 7:4-8 John hears the number of the sealed, twelve thousand from each tribe of Israel, but what he sees (v. 9) is so unexpectedly contrasting that many commentators refuse to admit the identity of the two groups. The procedure, however, is doubly similar to 5:5-6, for it both juxtaposes contrasting images and does so as a means of expressing John's Jewish Christian reinterpretation of Jewish hopes.[17]

The contrast of Lion and Lamb was certainly intentional on the part of a writer as attentive to his symbols as John, and is reinforced by remembering their natural enmity, by which the helpless lamb commonly falls prey to the hungry lion (1 Sam 17:34-35; Jer 49:19-20; 50:17, 44-45; Amos 3:12). But it should not be stressed to the neglect of the third image in these verses: the Root of David. The mention of David recalls the situation of controversy with the non-Christian Jews in the letter to the church at Philadelphia (3:7). Both at Smyrna and at Philadelphia the Christian communities were the object of enmity from 'those who say they are Jews but are not,' Jews who asserted their privilege as the people of God by birth against the Christian claim to inherit the Old Testament promises through Jesus Christ. Polemic against these Jews was a concern of John's as well as polemic against the imperial cult: he takes up the question of the true Messiah here (5:5-6) and again in 22:16.[18]

The Lion of Judah is from Genesis 49:9; the Root of David is from Isaiah 11:1, 10. Both Old Testament texts were *loci classici*

---

[15]Hermas, *Vis.* 4.2.1-2.

[16]In 4 Ezra 9:38-10:54, Ezra sees Mother Zion as a mourning woman who changes into a city; but there the point is the contrast between Zion's present distressed condition and the future heavenly glory to which she is to be transformed.

[17]See further chapter 8 section 3 below.

[18]On 22:16, see chapter 9 section 9 below.

of Jewish Messianic hopes in John's time. They were evidently favourites at Qumran, where the Messiah of Israel is described in terms of both Isaiah 11:1-5 and Genesis 49:8-10 in 4Q Patriarchal Blessings, and 1QSb 5:20-29; and again as the Isaianic 'Branch of David' in 4QFlor 1:11-12; 4QpIsa^a Frag. D. Both texts characterize the Messiah as the warrior prince who will conquer the enemies of Israel. In the Isaiah passage, attention often focused on 11:4b, paraphrased in Psalms of Solomon 17:27 as: 'He shall destroy the godless nations with the word of his mouth.' At Qumran the Branch of David was to 'smite the peoples with the might of your hand and ravage the earth with your sceptre; may you bring death to the ungodly with the breath of your lips' (1QSb 5:24). It is Isaiah 11:4 that John himself also applies to Christ in Revelation 19:11, 15 (there combined, as in PsSol 17:26-27, with a reference to Ps 2:9). His reference to the Root of David is clearly a reference to the messianic conqueror of the nations.

The 'Lion of the tribe of Judah' is not attested as a messianic title in pre-rabbinic literature, but there are two significant instances of messianic application of the lion image from Genesis 49:9.[19] In 1QSb 5:29 the Messiah is addressed: 'you shall be as a lion; and you shall not lie down until you have devoured the prey which nought shall deliver... .' (Here the image is drawn from Numbers 23:24 and Micah 5:8 as well as from Genesis 49:9.) In the vision of 4 Ezra 11-12 the great eagle, which represents the power of Rome, is reproved for its wickedness by a lion and consequently destroyed (11:37-12:3). The interpretation explains that the lion is the Messiah 'from the seed of David', who will rebuke and destroy the rulers of the empire (12:31-33). Conquest by judicial sentence has now replaced conquest by military might, as was envisaged at Qumran, but clearly in both cases the figure of the lion is the symbol of destructive power.

This is the principal force of the image of the lion as very frequently employed in the Old Testament: whether of powerful

---

[19]By contrast, the Targums and Gen. R. 98:7-8 refer Gen 49:9 to the tribe, and only verse 10 to the Messiah.

enemies,[20] of Israel triumphant over her enemies,[21] or of the destructive wrath of God.[22] The lion suggests ferocity, destructiveness and irresistible strength.[23] 'The lion has roared; who will not fear?' (Amos 3:8). The lion is 'a hero among beasts, who will not turn tail for anyone' (Prov 30:30). Judas Maccabaeus was appropriately praised as 'like a lion' in his military prowess and success (1 Macc 3:4). When John appropriated a messianic symbol which was perhaps less than common in his time, he did so because it embodied concisely the Jewish hope of a great conqueror of the enemies of God. It strongly reinforced the connotations of destructive power which the more familiar designation Root of David also carried, and it made possible the striking contrast of the Lion and the Lamb. If John was familiar with a tradition like that in 4 Ezra 11-12, then the Lion has even greater appropriateness, for there its role is to conquer the eagle, the symbol of the fourth world-empire. 4 Ezra 11-12 belongs to the traditional apocalyptic genre of the four world-empires vision, in which the kingdom of the Messiah and the saints succeeds the last great tyranny of the Gentiles,[24] and this is a genre which John also adapted to his purpose, modelling his sea-beast (Rev 13:1-3) on the four beasts of Daniel 7. Like Ezra's eagle, the sea-beast embodies the oppressive power of Rome and is to be destroyed by the

---

[20]E.g. Pss 7:2; 10:9; 17:12; 22:13, 21; 35:17; 57:4; 58:6; Isa 5:29; Jer 4:7; 5:6; 50:17.

[21]E.g. Num 23:24; Deut 33:20; Mic 5:8; 2 Macc 11:11.

[22]E.g. Isa 38:13; Jer 25:38; Lam 3:10-11; Hos 5:14; 13:7-8.

[23]The fearlessness of the lion is the point in 2 Sam 17:10; Prov 28:1; Isa 31:4. In Hos 11:10 the comparison seems to be simply with the strength of the lion's roar. There is little evidence for the view that the lion symbolized royalty; though cf. Prov 30:30-31; 1 Kings 10:19-20; 2 Chron 9:18-19; Goodenough (1952-1968) 7.80 n. 426. In ApEl 2:7, the king who 'will run upon the sea like a roaring lion,' may be compared with the lion for the sake of its messianic association, but more probably the image refers to the king's success in bloody battle (2:8).

[24]The genre begins with the vision of Daniel 7, on which subsequent examples are based, sometimes very explicitly (4 Ezra 12:11-12; Rev 13:1-2). Examples are 2 Bar 39-40; 4 Ezra 11-12; SibOr 4:49-101; and the unpublished fragment of an apocalypse of four trees from Qumran (see Milik [1956] 411 n.2); cf. also TNapht 5:6-8; Bogaert (1969A) 17; Stone (1968) 303.

Messiah. At Revelation 5:5-6 John is introducing the sea-beast's conqueror: the Lion of Judah who appears as a Lamb.

It is not likely that John's readers were tempted to zealotism, expecting God-given success for a military uprising against the Roman oppressor.[25] Temptations seem to have been rather in the opposite direction: towards compromise with the imperial cult. Any polemic John intended against militaristic messianism would have been aimed in the direction of non-Christian Jews, perhaps especially the refugees from Palestine who poured into the cities of Asia after the Jewish War. John writes about the victory of the Messiah and his people, often in the traditional militaristic imagery of the messianic war.[26] But that the victory in question is not a military victory over the godless nations, nor even the destruction by judicial sentence that 4 Ezra expected, John establishes once and for all by representing the messianic conqueror as a sacrificial Lamb.

The hopes embodied in the messianic titles of Revelation 5:5 are not dismissed by the vision of the Lamb. Insofar as John's Jewish contemporaries were not merely nationalists but looked for the victory of God over all who opposed him, their aspirations were those of the Apocalypse too. In Revelation 22:16 the Root of David is one of the titles Christ gives himself. But the notion of messianic conquest is reinterpreted. Jesus Christ *is* the Lion of Judah and the Root of David, but John 'sees' him as the Lamb. Precisely by juxtaposing these contrasting images, John forges a symbol of conquest by sacrificial death, which is essentially a new symbol.

There is no substantial evidence that the Lamb was already established as a symbol of the messianic conqueror in pre-Christian Judaism. The verse commonly cited from Testament of Joseph 19:8 has so evidently been rewritten — if not entirely composed — by a Christian editor, that it is no longer possible to tell whether the victorious lamb was already present in a

---

[25]Rev 13:10 might be taken to imply this, but in that case the silence of the seven messages to the churches is very surprising.

[26]See further chapter 8 below.

Jewish version.[27] It is true that horned lambs, probably representing the Maccabees, appear in 1 Enoch 90:9 and, if a widely accepted emendation of the text is correct, the Messiah appears as a lamb with 'big black horns' in 1 Enoch 90:30.[28] But these figures belong within the complicated animal allegory of 1 Enoch 85-90, where David and Solomon also appear as lambs before they become rams on ascending the throne (89:45, 48). In the terms of the allegory, the people of Israel are sheep, their leaders sheep or rams, and their young leaders therefore lambs. Any of John's readers who happened to have read this Apocalypse of the Beasts might associate John's horned Lamb with the Enochic symbols of powerful leaders of the people of God, but they would still be entirely unfamiliar with the notion of a *sacrificial* lamb as a conqueror.

Again, from the Christian tradition the portrayal of Jesus as Lamb was undoubtedly already familiar (cf. John 1:29, 36; Acts 8:32; 1 Cor 5:7; 1 Pet 1:19), as was the understanding of his death as victory (Col 2:15). The novelty of John's symbol lies in its representation of the sacrificial death of Christ as the fulfilment of Jewish hopes of the messianic conqueror. Doubtless the Lamb is intended to suggest primarily the passover lamb, for throughout the Apocalypse, and in a passage as close as 5:10, John represents the victory of the Lamb as a new Exodus, the victory which delivers the new Israel. It is to be noticed that he deals in symbols rather than explanations: how it was possible for the death of Christ to be such a victory is not explained. The vision of the Lamb therefore portrays the manner of Christ's victory: through death. A later vision, that of the Dragon, reveals the cosmic scope of the victory.

Both the Lamb, and also, as will be seen, the Dragon, are characteristic of many of John's visionary images in that they are visualized forms of metaphorical figures. Where Paul may speak of 'Christ our passover lamb' (1 Cor 5:7), John 'sees' the

---

[27]In any case, the same remarks apply to this lamb as to those in 1 Enoch 90:9, 38 (see below): it belongs within a larger animal allegory, and it is not a sacrificial lamb.

[28]See Knibb (1978) 216; and a full discussion in Lindars (1976).

Lamb. Another good example is the harlot of 17:3-6, where the common prophetic metaphor of harlotry is translated into vision. Where Jeremiah, for example, spoke of Jerusalem dressed in scarlet and decking herself with ornaments of gold (Jer 4:30), John 'sees' Babylon as an ostentatiously dressed harlot. In 14:14-20 he 'sees' the metaphors of Joel 3:13 enacted in two scenes representing the judgment of the world as harvest and vintage. Jeremiah's acted parable in Jeremiah 51:63-64 is adapted to a visionary image of angelic action in Revelation 18:21. Such a list could easily be extended. The images of the Apocalypse are in many cases a form of sharply perceived metaphor, and their purpose is to sharpen the readers' perception of the object in view, enabling them in a peculiarly vivid way to share the visionary's perception of it.

3. The Dragon

John was concerned, in common with contemporary Jewish apocalypses, about the victory of God over the forces of evil as they manifested themselves in his contemporary world. The oppressive power of Rome, the imperial cult, the corrupt civilization of Rome are all portrayed, in a series of vivid images, as enemies who fall before the conquering Lamb and his people. The genre of the four world-empires vision served John well as a basis for this theme. He wished, however, to root his own version of the traditional theme in the deeper theme of Christ's conquest of all evil through his death. The conquest of the Beast of Rome must be through the blood of the Lamb because it was Christ's death which struck the decisive blow at the forces which inspire the Beast. To represent this in visual symbol John portrayed the fall of Satan himself, the 'great red dragon' (12:3). This was unprecedented in Jewish apocalyptic vision, though Jesus himself saw Satan fall 'like lightning' (Luke 10:18). The Jewish hope was certainly for the defeat of Satan, with and through the conquest of his earthly representatives (1QM 18:1-3; TMos 10:1); but John, while sharing this hope for the future (Rev 20), placed the decisive encounter already in the past. The dragon, then, must first appear in person and suffer defeat in heaven, before marshalling his forces to do battle on earth.

The defeat of the Dragon (12:7-9) is doubtless the same event as the victory of the Lamb (5:5-6), and both are to be historically located in the death and resurrection of Jesus Christ (continued in the witness and martyrdom of his followers: 12:11). John's visions, however, are not historical narrative but vehicles of the cosmic significance of historical events, and for this reason they often resemble the images of myth, while retaining the historical reference that genuine myths lack. Early Jewish apocalyptic has been characterized as a movement of 're-mythologizing the long-since de-mythologized religion' of Old Testament Israel;[29] for the imagery of ancient myths which had been suppressed or historicized beyond recognition revived in the apocalyptic visions, not as pure myth, but as means of pointing the theological significance of history and especially of representing the end of history. The mythical quality of John's vision of the Woman and the Dragon in Revelation 12 has for a long time provoked scholars to search out its mythical origins, and the recognition that apocalyptic imagery sometimes derived from very ancient Canaanite myth suggests the possibility that John's Dragon is Leviathan, the seven-headed primeval sea-monster, the Ugaritic Lōtān whom Baal or 'Anat conquered in a famous mythical battle.[30] The problem about this identification is that of ascertaining to what extent this myth of God's battle with the sea-monster was still a living myth in the world of the first century A.D.

In the Old Testament period there seems no doubt that the myth was a living one, and the dragon Leviathan therefore a powerful symbol of opposition to God. References to Leviathan or the dragon (תנין) show close relationships with the Ugaritic texts in which the Canaanite myths are known to us. Leviathan

---

[29] Koch (1972) 27; cf. Hanson (1975).

[30] For the Canaanite origin of Leviathan, see Wakeman (1973) chapter 4; Day (1985) 4-7, 13-18; Uehlinger (1990). On the Canaanite myth, see also Binger (1992). Emerton (1982) proposes that the Ugaritic *ltn* be vocalized Lītān(u), rather than, as usually, Lōtān. It can now be regarded as established that the Old Testament dragon myth is of Canaanite, not Babylonian origin.

and other sea monsters represent the forces of chaos defeated by God in his primeval act of creation (Job 7:12; 41:1-11; Ps 74:13-14;[31] cf. Job 26:12-13; Ps 89:11).[32] The myth could also be historicized and used to depict God's defeat of Egypt at the Exodus (Isa 51:9-10).[33] So the chaos dragon could become an image of the God-opposing power of Israel's contemporary political enemies: Egypt (Isa 30:7; Ezek 29:3-5; 32:2-8) or Babylon (Jer 51:34). The image conveys the assurance of God's defeat of these powers who oppose him (Ezek 29:4-5; 32:3-8; Jer 51:37, 44; cf. Isa 51:9-11).[34] In Isaiah 27:1, where the description of Leviathan is a verbally exact reflection of the references to Lōtān in the Ugaritic texts,[35] the creation myth has been transformed into an eschatological myth. It symbolizes the eschatological victory of God ('on that day') over the forces that oppose him. Commentators generally suppose that (as in Jer 51:34; Ezek 29:3-5; 32:2-8) the dragon must here be a symbol of whatever political power was oppressing Israel in the prophet's time (the very uncertain date of the passage makes identification debatable).[36] But in this 'proto-apocalyptic' passage, which envisages the defeat of heavenly as well as earthly powers (24:21-23) and the resurrection of the dead (24:19), it seems quite possible that the potent mythological symbol of the chaos dragon represents the ultimate forces of evil behind all political manifestations of opposition to God.[37]

[31]On these passages see Pope (1965) 60-61, 276-278; Wakeman (1973) 62-68; Day (1985) 43-44, 62-87, 21-25.

[32]On these passages, referring to Rahab, see Wakeman (1973) 56-62; Day (1985) 38-39, 25-28. Raham is very probably another name for Leviathan (see especially Job 26:12-13, where 'Rahab' is parallel to 'the twisting serpent' = Leviathan [Isa 27:1]): see Wakeman (1973) 79; Day (1985) 6.

[33]On this passage, see Day (1985) 91-93.

[34]On these passages, see Day (1985) 89-90, 93-95, 109.

[35]Lōtān is called 'the twisting serpent ... the crooked serpant' (CTA 5.I.1-2 = KTU 1.5.I.1-2) and 'the dragon [*tnn*] ... the crooked serpent' (CTA 3.IIID.37-39 = KTU 1.3.III.40-42), quoted in Pope (1965) 276; Day (1985) 13-14, 142. Compare Isaiah 27:1: 'Leviathan the twisting serpent, Leviathan the crooked serpent... the dragon that is in the sea' (for the translation, see Day [1985] 5 n.8).

[36]Day (1985) 142-145.

[37]Cf. Kaiser (1974) 223.

In any case, the text is open to such an interpretation by later readers.

Whether the myth of God's victory over the chaos dragon remained alive independently of these scriptural texts is very uncertain. The one clear indication that at any rate some knowledge of the myth survived independently is the fact that the dragon was known to have seven heads. Lōtān had seven heads,[38] but the Old Testament alludes only to several heads of Leviathan, not specifying the number (Ps 74:14).[39] Yet the dragon of Revelation 12:3, like his deputy the sea monster (13:1), both of whom, as we shall see, bear some relation to Leviathan, has seven heads,[40] as has the dragon defeated by Christ according to Odes of Solomon 22:5. A few other texts, Jewish and Gnostic (b. Kidd. 29b; Pistis Sophia 66; 67; ApocrJn [CG 2, 2] 11:30-31; cf. TAbr A 17:14; 19:5, 7),[41] though not referring to *the*dragon, retain the image of a serpent with seven heads. Although mythological dragons commonly have more than one head,[42] the figure seven is characteristic of Jewish tradition and works indebted to it. Of course, it was *the* symbolic number in Jewish tradition. The many-headed Leviathan (Ps 74:14) could easily have been assumed to have seven heads, even if the fact that he originally did have seven were not

---

[38]CTA 3.IIID.39 = KTU 1.3.42; CTA 5.I.3 = KTU 1.5.I.3, quoted in Day (1985) 13-14. Note also the depiction of seven-headed monsters on Mesopotamian seal cylinders (Fontenrose [1980] 154), including one of gods attacking a monster with seven heads (illustrated in Fontenrose [1980], opposite 148; the caption to the partial illustration of this seal, in Ford [1975] opposite 169, very misleadingly identifies the figure as 'the seven-headed Egyptian dragon'), and the plaque of unknown origin described in Pope (1965) 277.

[39]But in Job 41 Leviathan seems to have only one head.

[40]For the dragon's red colour (Rev 12:3) a specific mythological source is unlikely. The Greek Python and the Egyptian Typhon were multicoloured (Fontenrose [1980] 185); the Egyptian Set (whether or not in dragon form) was red (Fontenrose [1980] 185). But blood-red seems to have been widely regarded as a suitable colour for dangerous mythological dragons: see Homer, *Iliad* 2:308 (δαφοινός); Virgil, *Aeneid* 2:207 (*sanguinis*). Revelation's dragon may be red from the blood of the martyrs.

[41]Cf. also the Mandean *Ginza*: in Foerster (1974) 223-224.

[42]See, e.g., Fontenrose (1980) 80-82 (100 heads), 209 n. 52 (3 heads), 243 (50 heads), 356 (9 heads), 500 (8 heads).

known. But probably we should conclude that some extra-biblical information about Leviathan survived from the old myth.[43]

However, there is little else to indicate that the myth survived as a living myth independently of exegesis of the Old Testament texts. Virtually everything about Leviathan in post-biblical Jewish literature can be understood as interpretation of those texts. A possible exception is the appearance of Leviathan in the lost Book of Giants, which once formed part of the Enoch literature. It seems that here Leviathan was associated with the giants (the sons of the angelic Watchers who descended from heaven before the Flood and mated with women) and so connected with the Enoch literature's primary myth of the origin of evil (the fall of the Watchers). The Book of Giants apparently depicted a great battle between one of the giants and Leviathan, in which both were at length destroyed by the archangel Raphael.[44] The association of Leviathan with a myth of primeval evil is suggestive in relation to Revelation 12, but in the Book of Giants Leviathan is certainly very far from being the principal supernatural opponent of God, as the dragon is in Revelation 12.

Other appearances of Leviathan or the dragon in post-biblical Jewish literature fall into two categories. First, there is the legend of the two monsters Leviathan and Behemoth, which appears in the Jewish apocalypses (1 Enoch 60:7-10, 24; 2 Bar 29:4; 4 Ezra 6:49-52; cf. ApAbr 21:4)[45] and survived in later rabbinic literature.[46] The two monsters were the first animals to be created by God, on the fifth day of creation. Leviathan was

---

[43]So Day (1985) 24.

[44]Milik (1967) 299; cf. 320. References to Leviathan on Aramaic incantation bowls (Milik [1976] 320, 338; Wakeman [1973] 67) speak of 'the curse, the decree, and the ban which I brought down upon Mount Hermon and upon the dragon Leviathan and upon Sodom and Gomorrah': the reference to Mount Hermon (cf. 1 Enoch 6:6) shows that probably Leviathan is here known from the Enoch traditions.

[45]On these passages, see Caquot (1975); Delcor (1977) 159-167, 170-172.

[46]Ginzberg (1913-1938) 1.27-28; 5.43-46; Caquot (1975) 115 nn.1-3, 119 nn.1-2; Jacobs (1977); Stone (1990) 187 nn.39-40.

given the sea to live in, Behemoth part of the land. God has preserved them in order to feed them to his people at the end-time. This legend can be understood almost entirely in terms of exegesis of Old Testament texts. Behemoth and Leviathan (Job 40:15-41:34) are the sea-monsters (תנינם) who were the first animals created on the fifth day (Gen 1:21).[47] According to 4 Ezra 6:49-50, Behemoth was originally a sea monster, later transferred to the land, because according to Job 40:19 Behemoth was the 'first of the works of God' and therefore one of the תנינם of Genesis 1:21. Behemoth's domain has a thousand mountains (4 Ezra 6:51): an interpretation of Psalm 50:10b (cf. Job 40:20). The slaughter of the two to provide food for the eschatological people of God is based on Psalm 74:14.[48] Later rabbinic tradition depicts the hunt for Leviathan, in which the monster is captured by Gabriel and slaughtered by God himself (b. B. B. 74b-75a),[49] but this seems to be the result of interpretation of Job 40:19; 41:1-2; Isaiah 27:1, rather than (as has been suggested)[50] an independent survival of the old creation myth.

The significant point, for our purposes, about this interpretation of Leviathan is that (along with Behemoth) he is understood as the mightiest and fiercest of the animal creation.[51] He is not a supernatural power of evil. To essentially the same tradition of interpretation belong the references to Leviathan in the Apocalypse of Abraham, where Leviathan is the great monster of the deep (21:4), restrained from doing too much damage by the archangel Jaoel, 'because [says Jaoel]

[47]This interpretation is also in Tg. Ps.-Jon. Gen 1:21 ('the great sea monsters, Leviathan and his mate'), and presupposed in Jub 1:11 (which, while not naming Leviathan or Behemoth, echoes Job 40:19).

[48]Cf. Theodotion's rendering: τῷ λαῷ τῷ ἐσχάτῳ.

[49]See also the passage from Midrash Alpha Bethoth, given in translation in Jacobs (1977) 8. In another form of the tradition (Pesiqta de Rab Kahana 29), clearly influenced by the fights between wild animal staged in the Roman amphitheatres, Leviathan and Behemoth fight and slaughter each other: Jacobs (1977) 5-8.

[50]Jacobs (1977).

[51]This view is essentially found already in the Old Testament: Gen 1:21; Ps 104:26; cf. Job 40:15, 19.

through me is subjugated the attack and menace of every reptile' (10:10; cf. Job 7:12).[52]

Secondly, there are a few texts which continue the tradition of Jeremiah and Ezekiel, in which the dragon represents a great political power or ruler opposed to God. In Psalms of Solomon 2:25-29, the arrogant dragon who aspires to divine lordship, is probably the Roman general Pompey, who conquered Jerusalem.[53] In the Apocalypse of Elijah 3:33, it is the last political enemy of God and his people, the Antichrist, who 'will perish like a serpent'.[54] Probably also, though not immediately so clearly, a reference to God's judgment of the last great human political opponent of his will is Ladder of Jacob 6:13:

> And the Lord will pour out his wrath against Leviathan the sea-dragon; he will kill the lawless Falkon with the sword, because he will raise the wrath of the God of gods by his pride.[55]

This is clearly based on Isaiah 27:1. The puzzling name Falkon, evidently used as another name for Leviathan, is explained by Lunt as a corruption of the rare Hebrew word עֲקַלָּתוֹן ('crooked'), which is used in Isaiah 27:1, was understood as a name and so transliterated in the Greek original of the Ladder of Jacob and corrupted to Falkon in Slavonic.[56] Another possibility is that it is a corruption of δράκων (rendering תַּנִּין in Isa. 27:1). Leviathan/

---

[52]Cf. perhaps the role of Gabriel in 1 Enoch 20:7.

[53]On this passage, see Efron (1987) 246-260.

[54]Cf. also CD 8:10; SibOr 5:29 (Nero); 6 Ezra 15:29, 31. The dragon seems to be used as a symbol of political power in Mordecai's dream in the Additions to Esther (11:6). The interpretation of the two dragons as Haman and Mordecai (10:7) seems inappropriate, and so it may well be that the dream preexisted this interpretation. They may originally have been two Gentile political powers, who fight each other and over whom Israel, as God's people, prevails. See Moore (1973) 388-390; (1977) 176, 180-181, 248-249. But his comment ([1977] 176) that in 'apocalyptic literature a *drakōn* is a major figure and is symbolic of evil rather than good,' is scarcely justified (his references to 2 Bar 29:3-8; 4 Ezra 6:52 do not support it).

[55]Translation from Lunt (1985) 410.

[56]Lunt (1985) 404.

Falkon's pride may derive from Job 41:34 (cf. 40:12; PsSol 2:25), though it is also worth noticing that Rahab, the other Old Testament name for the sea monster, was often understood to mean 'pride'.[57] However, the reference to 'the God of gods' makes an allusion also to the God-defying arrogance of the king in Daniel 11:36 certain.[58] This shows that Leviathan is here understood as the last human political ruler who will oppose God and oppress God's people, the last ruler of Rome ('the kingdom of Edom': 6:15; cf. 5:12), who is described in 6:1, 3, and probably already in the obscure passage 5:14-15, where the name Falkon seems to occur again in an unintelligible context (5:15).[59]

Finally, it is possible that Testament of Asher 7:3 ('crushing the head of the dragon in the water'), which gives an eschatological interpretation of Psalm 74:13, belongs in this category. The dragon (the plural תנינים of Ps 74:13[60] reduced to one) may be the Gentile oppressor of the people of Israel.[61] But, on the other hand, it is very uncertain whether this phrase should really be isolated, as a Jewish substratum, from the patently Christian references to the incarnation which surround it. As a Christian text, it can only refer to Jesus' conquest of Satan at his baptism.[62]

Both these Jewish traditions of interpreting Old Testament texts about Leviathan made some contribution to Revelation,

---

[57]Kiessling (1970) 171-173. Note especially Ps 89(88): 11 LXX, Vulg.; Job 26:12 Vulg.; Isa. 30:7 Vulg.; Isa. 51:9 Vulg. The interpretation (perhaps correctly: so Day [1985] 6) relates the name רהב to the Hebrew root רהב, 'to act arrogantly'.

[58]Revelation 12:4 may show that a similar connexion between Leviathan and Daniel 8:10 lies behind Revelation's image of the dragon.

[59]See Lunt (1985) 404, 409 note m.

[60]Against the suggestion that this be read as singular (Wakeman [1973] 68 n. 5), see Day (1985) 24-25.

[61]Cf. Delcor (1977) 168-169.

[62]Cf. Cyril of Jerusalem, *Catech.* 3:2, quoted in Daniélou (1964) 225: 'Since, therefore, it was necessary to break the heads of the dragon in pieces, he went down and bound the strong one in the waters.' For several other patristic and liturgical texts applying Ps 74:13b to the baptism of Christ, see Harris and Mingana (1920) 327-328, and note that in most cases there is a singular dragon, as in TAsher 7:3.

but the contribution they made was to the portrayal of the two beasts of chapter 13,[63] not to the image of the Dragon in chapter 12. The first beast, the sea monster (13:1-2), derives immediately from Daniel 7:2-7, where the four beasts, whose characteristics John combines in the picture of his beast, represent the world empires. Coming out of the chaotic sea (Dan 7:2-3), they are in some sense sea monsters, and John must have recognized their affinity to Leviathan used as a symbol of the final God-defying political power destined to be overthrown with the coming of God's kingdom. Accordingly, he gives his sea monster (13:1-2) a corresponding earth monster (13:11), a Behemoth to accompany Leviathan. So, in chapter 13, he gives the legend of the two great monsters a political-eschatological interpretation, using them to represent the Roman power and the imperial cult of his time.

The figure of the Dragon, however, though he inspires the beasts (12:18-13:4; 13:11), transcends the political sphere. He represents the primeval and ultimate power of supernatural evil: 'that ancient serpent, who is called the Devil and Satan, the deceiver of the whole world' (12:9; cf. 20:2). We have found no Jewish precedent for this representation of ultimate evil, the devil, as 'the great dragon' (12:9). As 12:9 shows, this image of the devil as the Dragon has been made possible by the identification of Leviathan, the dragon who is destined to eschatological defeat by God, with the serpent of Genesis 3. The latter is recalled explicitly in 12:9, but also by the enmity between the Dragon and the Woman (12:1-4, 13-16) and the enmity between the Dragon and her children (12:4, 17), alluding to the curse on the serpent in Genesis 3:15. The serpent of Genesis 3 was certainly already associated or identified with the devil in Jewish interpretation (Wisd 2:23-24; 1 Enoch 69:6; ApAbr 23:7, 11), but for any hint, outside Revelation, of an identification of this serpent with Leviathan we have only two Christian texts. Romans 16:20 assures Paul's readers that 'the God of peace will shortly crush Satan under your feet'. The use of 'crush' (συντρίψει) suggests that behind this text may lie

---

[63]Cf. Wallace (1948).

an association of Psalm 74:13-14 ('... you broke [שברת; LXX συνέτριψας] the heads of the dragons in the water; you crushed [רצצת; LXX συνέτριψας] the heads of Leviathan ...') with Genesis 3:15, perhaps in connexion also with Psalm 91:14. In a later text, Odes of Solomon 22:5, Christ is represented as saying:

> He who overthrew by my hands the dragon with seven heads,
> and placed me at his roots that I might destroy his seed.[64]

The first line refers to Leviathan, the second to the serpent's seed in Genesis 3:15.[65] Thus it may be that Revelation 12 stands in some kind of exegetical tradition, but its exegetical basis for identifying Leviathan and the serpent of Genesis 3 is probably Isaiah 27:1, where Leviathan is described both as נחש (LXX: ὄφις) and as תנין (LXX: δράκων). That Isaiah 27:1 lies behind Revelation 12 is confirmed by the proximity of the image of Israel as a woman in the throes of childbirth (Isa 26:17-18; cf. Rev 12:2).[66] But characteristically, John does not rest content with exegesis. He does what no one had done before: he brings the Old Testament text to imaginative life in the visionary figure of a great red dragon.

If Leviathan had largely, by the first century A.D., lost his ancient mythological role as the primeval opponent of God, the identification of him with the serpent in the garden of Eden largely restores it. Probably, however, this does not exhaust the range of reference in the symbol. Much of the

---

[64]Translation from Charlesworth (1985) 754.

[65]Harris and Mingana (1920) 329-330.

[66]Cf. Rissi (1966) 36-37; Court (1979) 112. Whereas Isa 27:1 calls Leviathan 'the dragon that is in the sea', the dragon in Revelation falls from heaven to earth, and is certainly not a sea monster. However, the reference to the sea is omitted in Isa 27:1 LXX, and although John is normally dependent on the Hebrew text of the Old Testament, not the LXX, it is possible that the LXX here follows a variant Hebrew text which omitted אשר בים. The association of Leviathan with heaven could result in part from the influence of Isa 24:21. Mealy (1989) chapter 5, argues for the influence of Isa 24:20-23 on Rev 12:4, 7-9; 19:19-20:3. Note also Job 26:13.

significance of the Dragon's role depends on the reader's recognition, from the moment of his first appearance in the heavens (12:3), that the Dragon is doomed to defeat at the hands of the divine Dragon-slayer. The story of this defeat is given unexpected twists and is not finally achieved until 20:10, but the reader's expectation of the final victory is an aid both to the structure of the book and also to the intelligibility of the story. The defeat of the Dragon may be expected once he is recognized as the dragon of Isaiah 27:1, and once the enmity between the Dragon and the Woman is seen to reflect the curse of Genesis 3:15. It may also be expected on the more general ground that it is the common lot of mythological dragons to be slain, especially dragons who attack divine heroes. For this aspect we must turn to the question of pagan mythological allusions.

For the readers of the Apocalypse some symbols would have not only scriptural associations but also various pagan mythical associations. In attempting to trace these it is important to keep as close as the evidence allows to the local forms of cult and myth in the area of the seven churches of Asia, an area where indigenous religious traditions were strong and often distinctive.[67] Common to the whole hellenistic world, but strikingly evident from the coinage and other evidence of this area in particular, was the association of serpents with divinity. The serpent was the symbol of the cult of Asklepios, perhaps once a divine snake himself, and represented by a real snake in the healing rites.[68] Snakes were also used to represent the god in the Dionysiac mysteries[69] and the rites of the Phrygian Sabazios: they symbolized sexual and mystical union with the god. Serpents were associated with the cult of Isis, whether or

[67]With reference to Rev 2-3 in particular, the importance of local associations in the imagery has been demonstrated by Hemer (1986).

[68]The serpents of Asklepios appeared very frequently on coins of the area, especially Pergamum: Wroth (1892) 127-131, 136-137, 141; but cf. also, for Laodicea, Head (1906) 302; for Thyatira, Head (1901) cxxix; for Philadelphia, Head (1901) 202, 205, 207.

[69]The serpents of Dionysos regularly appeared on the *cistophori*, the coins of the Attalids of Pergamum: for examples from Pergamum, Laodicea and Sardis, see Wroth (1892) 123-126; Head (1906) 278-282; Head (1901) 236-238.

not actually used in her mysteries,[70] and with the cult of the local goddess (Cybele) at Sardis[71] and at Hierapolis, where the ἔχιδνα was a dominant force in religious life.[72] Pergamum, where the serpent was associated with all three major cults, of Asklepios, Dionysos and Zeus, has been said to be 'obsessed with the symbol of the serpent.'[73]

These associations cannot be easily dismissed as irrelevant, for in the image of the snake John appears to have selected precisely the most pervasive image of pagan divinity in the area of his churches and he cannot have been unaware of the fact. K. H. Rengstorf saw in Revelation 12 a reflection of Christian opposition to the Asklepios cult,[74] but it is unlikely that, prominent though Asklepios was in Asia, John would have represented the arch-enemy of God in so particular a form. However, that he intends a broader polemic against the pagan cults of the seven cities seems quite possible.[75] The serpent symbol of pagan divinity therefore adds significant local dimensions to the Dragon.

There was, however, a certain ambiguity about the serpent symbol in pagan religion, an ambiguity which John exploits. The serpent featured not only as the cultic symbol of the god but also in well known myths as the opponent of the god or the hero who slays it. In these cases the serpent represented, if not evil, at least hostility to the god.[76] The stories most likely to

[70]Witt (1971) 83; cf. a coin from Laodicea (reign of Augustus) in Head (1906) 288 no. 61.

[71]Hemer (1986) 139.

[72]Ramsay (1895) 87, 94.

[73]Blaiklock (1965) 105; cf. Hemer (1986) 85, 104.

[74]Rengstorf (1953) 24-27.

[75]Hedrick (1971) 173, objects to Rengstorf's theory on the grounds that for John the arch-enemy of the church was not Asklepios but the Roman Empire. But the imperial cult was not the only form in which pagan religion affected the seven churches: the problem at Thyatira was evidently one of compromise with the ordinary socio-religious life of the city trade guilds. John was fighting on several fronts, and in chapter 12 required a symbol of evil more fundamental than the imperial cult.

[76]The serpent as symbol of evil is rare in the hellenistic world. Of the many examples of snake symbolism to be found in Goodenough (1952-1968), only the Jewish magical amulets discussed in 2.228-232, use the serpent as a symbol of evil. These are perhaps to be connected with the victory of Horus over Typhon: cf. Griffiths (1960) 113-115.

come to the minds of John's readers are Heracles and the Hydra, Apollo and the Python, perhaps also Horus and Typhon. Heracles was a favourite figure at Sardis,[77] Apollo was well known throughout the cities of Asia, and the popularity of the story of Apollo's birth and his defeat of the Python is well attested by coins of the area.[78] In a form of this story which was current by John's time,[79] the dragon threatens and pursues Apollo's mother Leto at the time of his birth and is later slain by the god. Because of the dragon's connexion with Apollo's birth, the case for supposing that Revelation 12:1-4 was deliberately intended to recall this story seems a good one, the best of many suggestions of specific myths supposed to underlie this chapter.[80] The allusion is then partly an artistic device, identifying the Dragon as the enemy whom the divine Child will eventually slay. Having set out in 12:1-4 an approximation to the opening of the Apollo story, John is free to diverge from

[77]Hemer (1986) 138-139.

[78]Hedrick (1971) 112; Ramsay (1895) 90; Wroth (1892) 11 no. 21.

[79]Hedrick (1971) chapter 4, shows that the two myths of Apollo's birth and his defeat of the Python were originally distinct, and only in the combined myth was the Python associated with Apollo's birth. (This is version D, in the classification of the Apollo-Python myths by Fontenrose [1980] 21; cf. 18.) The combined myth, first found in Lucian and Hyginus in the second century A.D., was probably known in Asia in John's time: Hedrick (1971) 110-114.

[80]The Leto-Apollo-Python myth was first suggested as a source of Revelation 12 by Dieterich (1891), and the suggestion is supported by Saffrey (1975) 416-417; Yarbro Collins (1976) 63-67; Giblin (1991) 127; cf. Fontenrose (1980) 210. The case for Revelation's dependence on this myth is well argued by Hedrick (1971), but his negative evaluation of all other suggestions is marred by his assumption that John must be reproducing a complete myth, rather than creatively exploiting existing symbolism. The relevance of Babylonian myth (Marduk and Tiamat) and Zoroastrian myth (Atar and Azhi Dahaka) is really put in doubt primarily by the lack of evidence that these were available to John and his readers. (Appeal to hellenistic syncretism or an elusive 'international myth' — as by Beasley-Murray [1974] 192 — is no substitute for such evidence.) The Egyptian myth of Horus and Typhon (Set) is perhaps more relevant: as early as Herodotus (2:156-157) it was assimilated to the story of Apollo and Python, and it may have been known in Asia through the Isis cult, though it was certainly not prominent in the cult. If it was known, we cannot be sure in which of its various forms, some of which are closer to Revelation 12 than others.

it as far as his purposes dictate, while keeping up the expectation
of the proper end of the story, the final defeat of the Dragon.
The allusion may also be to the significance of the pagan story,
though that significance in this period is not easy to recover.
Was it by this time no more than a story, or (as in Hyginus'
version) an aetiological myth of the origin of Apollo's oracle at
Delphi? Or did it suggest the triumph of the sun-god over the
forces of darkness, a myth revitalized in the first century by the
Emperor's assumption of the role of Apollo? The evidence is
slight,[81] but it may be that in the myth of the defeat of the
Python John encountered a living local equivalent of the old
Semitic myth of the victory over Leviathan. Just as in 5:5-6 he
showed the crucified Christ as the unexpected fulfilment of
Jewish hopes of a messianic conqueror, so he was ready to take
up also whatever pagan symbol might embody an aspiration for
divine triumph over evil and show the crucified Christ as the
Dragon-slayer. There is no contradiction here with his
simultaneous use of the serpent symbol to brand the pagan
cults as satanic. Similarly Jews who oppose Christ and his
followers can be called 'the synagogue of Satan' (2:9; 3:9).

The Dragon is a symbol whose power derives from a variety
of associations. He is the ancient serpent who initiated
humanity's estrangement from God with the bait of becoming
like gods. He is the symbol of the false gods of Asian paganism,
who made the same promise to their worshippers in the
mysteries while actually making them as unlike gods as
themselves. He is the dragon who lies in wait for the birth of the
divine hero who will return to slay him. He is the twisting
serpent Leviathan whom the sword of God will destroy at the
final elimination of evil. He derives not so much from a single
living myth on which John depended, as from a fresh
combination of associations creating a new symbol. The Dragon
is a fine example of John's capacity to envision the figures of
Old Testament texts and to raise them to new imaginative life
by exploiting the vital symbolism of his readers' environment.

[81]Caird (1966) 147; cf. Stauffer (1955) 139, 151-153, 177.

7

The Eschatological Earthquake

I

The earthquake is one of the major images of the End in the Apocalypse, far too often passed over as a conventional apocalyptic image of no great interest. A study of its background and use will show that, like other symbols in the Apocalypse, it is intended to exploit a range of conceptual associations and to play a distinctive role in the structure of the book.

In very many Old Testament and later Jewish texts an earthquake accompanies a theophany. Very frequently this earthquake is part of a cosmic quake: the whole universe, firmament, heavenly bodies, earth, sea and the foundations of the world tremble at the coming of God (Sir 16:18-19; Judith 16:15; TLevi 3:9). Frequently the creation shakes before the coming of God as warrior, leading his hosts to battle against his enemies (Judg 5:4-5; Joel 2:10; Mic 1:4; Ps 78:7-8), before the coming of God to reign over the nations (Pss 97:5; 99:1), before the coming of God to judge the wicked (Isa 13:13; 24:18-20; 34:4; Jer 51:29; Ezek 38:20; Nah 1:5). These aspects are all found together in the apocalyptic descriptions of the great cosmic quake which will accompany the eschatological theophany (1 Enoch 1:3-9; 102:1-2; TMos 10:1-7; 2 Bar 32:1).

Among the Old Testament accounts the Sinai theophany is of particular interest. In Exodus 19-20 the quaking of the mountain (19:18) is not especially prominent. It is entirely absent from the account in Deuteronomy 6. But in the Old Testament poetic descriptions it has a larger place, and there the theophany imagery of thunderstorm and earthquake is extended to cover the whole Exodus event from the Red Sea to the Jordan (Pss 68:8; 77:17-18; 114; Isa 64:3; Hab 3). By 4 Ezra 3:18, which describes God's descent from heaven to Sinai, the Sinai earthquake has become a cosmic quake: 'You bent down the heavens [cf. Ps 18:9; LAB 23:10] and shook the earth, and moved the world, and caused the depths to tremble, and troubled the times [or, better: "universe"].' Similarly, the account of the Sinai theophany in the Biblical Antiquities of Pseudo-Philo, having quoted Exodus 19:16-17 (LAB 11:4), continues: 'And behold the mountains burned with fire, and the earth quaked, and the hills were disturbed, and the mountains were rolled about, and the abysses boiled, and every habitable place was shaken, and the heavens were folded up, and the clouds drew up water, and flames of fire burned, and thunderings and lightnings were many, and winds and storms roared, the stars gathered together, and angels ran on ahead, until God should establish the law of his eternal covenant' (LAB 11:5).

Alongside the Exodus traditions, the Old Testament uses very similar language in other descriptions of divine intervention — either in the past (Judg 5:4-5; 2 Sam 22:8-16 = Ps 18:7-15; cf. LAB 32:7-8) or at the day of the Lord (Joel 2:1-2, 10; Mic 1:3-4; Nah 1:3-6). In this latter context especially the notion of the cosmic quake which shakes both heaven and earth becomes explicit (Isa 13:13; 24:18-23; 34:4; Joel 2:10).

In apocalyptic writings the eschatological theophany, the day of the Lord, is clearly portrayed as a new Sinai theophany. The expectation of a new act of divine intervention on the pattern of the Exodus deliverance and including the image of the great earthquake is already to be found in Habakkuk 3 and Isaiah 64. The clearest examples of this development are in 1 Enoch 1:3-9 and Testament of Moses 10:1-7. Lars Hartman has shown the underlying Old Testament bases for these passages: in 1 Enoch the most important include Exodus 19:11-18 and Deuteronomy 33:2 as well as Micah 1:3-4; Habakkuk 3:3-4; Daniel 7:10. But Hartman is wrong to suggest that the Pentateuchal allusions and the explicit mention of Sinai (1 Enoch 1:4) have been influenced solely 'via identity of keywords and similarity of motif.'[1] The identifications of the eschatological theophany as a new Sinai theophany belongs to the apocalyptists' understanding of salvation-history, whereby God's redemptive acts in the future are portrayed on the model of his past acts. It may also be true, as Otto Betz argues, that 1 Enoch and the Qumran community read Deuteronomy 33:2-5 as eschatological prophecy.[2] Though there is no clear allusion to Deuteronomy 33:2 in Testament of Moses 10, it may nevertheless be behind the passage, since the Testament of Moses is based on the common understanding of Deuteronomy 31-34 as a prophecy of the future history of Israel,[3] and Deuteronomy 33:29 is undoubtedly echoed in 10:8.

In these passages the earthquake accompanies the expected coming of God as King and Judge. But the earthquake may also itself form part of the final judgment on the enemies of God's people, as in Sibylline Oracle 3:675-693. This passage is an expanded poetic paraphrase of Ezekiel 38:19-23;[4] but whereas in Ezekiel the earthquake seems to retain its traditional function of merely heralding God's coming (with the actual judgments on Gog described subsequently in 38:21-22), in the Sibylline Oracle the earthquake becomes part of the judgment.[5] A different development of the function of the great earthquake is in texts where its main purpose seems to be the destruction of the old cosmos to make way for the new (4 Ezra 6:11-16; 1 Enoch 83:3-5; cf. Heb 12:27). Finally, from these traditions of the last great earthquake we should distinguish sharply another role which earthquakes play in apocalyptic literature. We find them included, simply as one among many other natural and human-made disasters, in catalogues of 'signs' of the End or in series of preliminary judgments which lead up to the End (Matt 24:7; Mark 13:8; Luke 21:11; 2 Bar 27:7; 70:8; 4 Ezra 9:3;

---

[1]Hartman (1966) 114.
[2]Betz (1967) 91.
[3]Harrington (1973) 56-68.
[4]This is amply proved by Hartman (1966) 91-94.
[5]Cf. also Isa 29:6; Amos 9:1, for earthquakes as an instrument of divine justice. The concept is rare in the Old Testament.

ApAbr 30:6). The earthquake in these contexts has no special role as accompaniment of the eschatological theophany. The two roles seem to be both present in the series of ten last plagues in Apocalypse of Abraham 30, where an earthquake is included in the fifth plague (30:6), and the last plague, reminiscent of the Sinai theophany and of Revelation 16:18, consists of 'thunder, voices and destroying earthquakes' (30:8).

II

Earthquakes in the Apocalypse of John play no part in the preliminary judgments. Their role, as we shall see, is the more traditional Old Testament one of heralding the coming of God in judgment. In three cases (8:5; 11:19; 16:18) there is clear allusion to the Sinai theophany, as in the tenth plague of Apocalypse of Abraham 30:8. This has been commonly noticed, but John's characteristic creation of a progressive series of references to Exodus 19 has oddly gone unnoticed. The deliberate stylistic device is obvious once the following four texts are compared:

4:5:	ἀστραπαι και φωναι και βρονται
8:5:	βρονται καὶ φωναὶ καὶ ἀστραπαι καὶ σεισμός
11:19:	ἀστραπαὶ καὶ φωναὶ καὶ βρονταὶ καὶ σεισμὸς καὶ χάλαζα μεγάλη
16:18-21:	ἀστραπαὶ καὶ φωναὶ καὶ βρονραὶ καὶ σεισμὸς … μέγας… καὶ χάλαζα μεγάλη

In 8:5 and again in 11:19 the formula is simply expanded by the addition of an extra item; in 16:18-21 the earthquake and the hail are described at some length. Clearly the earlier references are intended to point forward to this full description, which is the seventh of the seven last plagues of Revelation 16.

In 4:5 the language brings together the Sinai theophany (Exod 19:16; cf. LAB 11:4) and the chariot vision of Ezekiel (Ezek 1:13). The threefold expression 'voices and thunders and lightnings' occurs in Jubilees 2:2 (in an account of the creation of the angels)[6] and would seem a stereotyped phrase: the voices are phenomena of the thunderstorm. The seven torches (λαμπάδες) of fire in the latter part of 4:5 should perhaps also recall not only Ezekiel 1:13 but also the λαμπάδες which were visible on Sinai according to Exodus 20:18 LXX. The theophany is confined to heaven, judgment on earth is not yet in view, and so the earthquake would be inappropriate. But the later references back to 4:5 serve to anchor the expectation of God's coming to judge and rule the world in this initial vision of his rule in heaven.

In 8:5, Ezekiel (10:2) and Exodus (19:16, 18) are again combined. Fire from heaven is cast in judgment on the earth in response to the prayers of the saints, and 8:5b should be taken as a summary statement of the whole course of the judgments of the seven trumpets which follow. The seventh trumpet, the final achievement of God's kingdom on earth (11:15), is similarly described in 11:19. We should probably recall that the voice of the trumpet accompanied the thunder and lightning on Sinai (Exod 19:13, 16, 19; 20:18). The earthquake (Exod 19:18) is not in the Septuagint version of Exodus, but John's allusions to the Old Testament are normally to the Hebrew text,[7] and in any case we have seen that the earthquake was widely treated as a major feature of the phenomena at Sinai (cf. also Heb 12:26).

In 11:19 the signs of the theophany follow the opening of the heavenly sanctuary. Later, in 15:5, it becomes clear that the opening of the temple is so that the power and glory of God might be manifested on earth in the final judgment of the nations. In 11:19 itself the immediate purpose is apparently so that the ark of the covenant may be seen, establishing another connexion between the judgments and the Sinai covenant. The ark in the heavenly sanctuary must be the throne of God which chapter 4 describes, but its description here as the ark of the covenant makes possible an explicit allusion to the Sinai

---

[6] The Hebrew text in 4QJub[a] (4Q216) appears to have only 'voices' (הקולות): for the text and discussion, see VanderKam and Milik (1991) 257-260.

[7] Cf. Vanhoye (1962); Trudinger (1963).

covenant, prefacing the formula which recalls the Sinai theophany.

Just as the theophany formula in 8:5 encompasses the whole series of trumpet judgments up to its recurrence in 11:19, so a comparison of 15:5 and 16:17-21 with 11:19 suggests that the whole series of the seven last plagues is summed up in 11:19. At each point John uses the allusion to Sinai to suggest that the End has been reached, though not yet exhaustively described. The progressive expansion of the formula accords with the increasing severity of each series of judgments, as the visions focus more closely on the End itself and the limited warning judgments of the trumpets give place to the seven last plagues of God's wrath on the finally unrepentant.

The inclusion of a 'great hail' in the formula at 11:19 suggests that John's mind is now moving towards a fusion of the Sinai references with other Old Testament allusions. Hail is an expected intensification of the description of a great thunderstorm (cf. Isa 30:30; Ps 18:12-13), but an examination of 16:18-21 will indicate that John has in mind especially the hailstorms of Exodus 9:8-24; Ezekiel 38:22 and perhaps also Joshua 10:11.

III

In the description of the last plague and the fall of Babylon in Revelation 16:17-21 a number of Old Testament allusions converge. The series of seven plagues in chapter 16 are fairly closely modelled on the ten last plagues of Egypt. The fact that Apocalypse of Abraham 30 has a series of ten last plagues on the Gentiles and ends with an allusion to the Sinai theophany like Revelation 16:18 may be evidence that there was already, before John wrote, an apocalyptic tradition of paralleling the last plagues with the plagues of Egypt, in accordance with the well-established treatment of the End as a new Exodus. The new Exodus symbolism appears in Revelation in many forms,[8]

---

[8]E.g. cf. 15:3 with the eschatological interpretation of Exod 15:17-18, attested in 4QFlor.

and John's allusions both to the Egyptian plagues and to Sinai are of a piece with this. But the order of the plagues in chapter 16 bears no relation to Exodus, where the Egyptian plague of hail is the seventh of the ten, and the plague of darkness, which becomes John's fifth, is the ninth of the ten. Why should John have selected the hail as his last?

The primary reason is surely that he required his last plague to be characterized by the allusion to Sinai and in particular to include the great earthquake. He found the earthquake which accompanies God's final judgment on the nations already linked to a plague of hail in Ezekiel's description of the judgment on Gog (Ezek 38:19-22). Like the author of the third Sibylline Oracle, he made the earthquake itself part of the judgment, but the association with Sinai and the language of 16:20 ensure that it remains also the sign of a theophany. The creation trembles and flees from the presence of God coming in wrath to judgment (cf. also 6:14; 20:11; Ps 97:1-5 etc.).

Peculiar to John among the apocalyptists is the effect of his earthquake in causing the fall of cities. This is primarily because he has summed up his picture of human wickedness in the image of the great city Babylon. To his account of the fall of Babylon many Old Testament nations and cities have contributed: Egypt, Babylon, Tyre, Edom, the cities of Plain. But when in 16:19 (and also in 11:13) he described the fall of Babylon in an earthquake, he could have had none of these precedents in mind. If he had an Old Testament precedent it could only have been Jericho. There is some reason to suppose that the fall of Jericho may have played a part in his composition, though there are no verbal allusions. The sevenfold circuit of Jericho, the seven trumpets and the multiplication of the seventh circuit by seven, the ark accompanying the march (cf. Rev 11:19; 16:17), all suggest parallels with John's trumpet and bowl visions. Perhaps also his thought ran ahead from the fall of Jericho to the rain of great hailstones on the Amorites (Josh 10:11). Like the psalmists he thought of the whole Exodus event from the plagues of Egypt to the conquest of Canaan as one great manifestation of God's power to judge the nations and to deliver his people.

It may be that we should also at this point attend more closely to Revelation's temporal and geographical context. The Greco-Roman world took earthquakes seriously as signs of divine displeasure, and the first-century world, Asia Minor in particular, experienced devastating earthquakes in which great cities, including some of the seven of Revelation, suffered severely. Sardis was catastrophically hit by the great earthquake of A.D. 17, which called forth imperial aid for the twelve Asian cities affected, including also Philadelphia.[9] Laodicea suffered a ruinous earthquake in A.D. 60. Further afield there were notable earthquakes in Cyprus in 76, and the eruption of Vesuvius which destroyed Pompeii in 79 would have included both earthquake and a hail of stones quite adequate to the description in Revelation 16:21.[10] Both the Roman world's attitude to and its experience of destructive earthquakes are reflected in the Jewish Sibylline Oracles, in which earthquakes are a standard form of God's judgment on cities.[11] Sibylline Oracle 5:438 even predicts that Babylon (not here a cipher for Rome) will be levelled by an earthquake. Probably in the early second century, Sibylline Oracle 5:286-297 foretold the fall of the cities of Asia in terms which must have seemed wholly credible after the experience of the previous century. The fourth Sibylline, written about a decade before Revelation, in the aftermath of Vesuvius and in expectation of Nero's return (lines 130-139), contained *post eventum* prophecies of the recent earthquakes in Cyprus and Asia Minor (lines 107-113, 128-129).

Set in its first-century Asian context Revelation's image of the fall of the great city in an earthquake had greater power than the Old Testament alone could have given it. H. B. Swete's comment on the words οἷος οὐκ ἐγένετο ἀφ' οὗ ἄνθρωπος

---

[9]Hemer (1986) 144, 150, 156-157, 166, 175. 'Its impact [at Sardis] was evidently such that it seemed an event of almost apocalyptic scale. The literary allusions suggest that something unusually catastrophic happened at Sardis' (134).

[10]For a description of the eruption of Vesuvius designed to bring out its 'apocalyptic' qualities, see Stauffer (1955) 147-148.

[11]Besides the references in the rest of this paragraph, see SibOr 3:401-413, 449, 457, 459; 4:99-100; 5:128-129. See also Hemer (1986) 193-194.

ἐγένετο ἐπὶ τῆς γῆς... (16:18) is entirely justified: 'Writing in a century remarkable for the number and severity of its earthquakes, and to men whose country was specially subject to them, St John is careful to distinguish this final shock from even the greatest hitherto known.'[12] This expression in 16:18 was something of an apocalyptic technical term, derived from Daniel 12:1 (which is echoed in TMos 8:1; 1QM 1:11; Matt 24:21; Mark 13:19; cf. also 1 Macc 9:25). John will certainly also have noticed the similar terminology used with reference to the Egyptian plagues of hail and locusts (Exod 9:18, 24; 10:6), the great cry at the death of the firstborn (Exod 11:6), Joel's locust plague (Joel 2:2) and the great day of the slaughter of the Amorites (Josh 10:14). But the technical apocalyptic formula, describing the End events as the unprecedented climax of all previous history of divine judgments, corresponded to a more everyday hyperbole, the natural tendency to describe a remarkable event as unprecedented.[13] Josephus described the earthquake in Judaea in 31 B.C. as 'such as had not happened at any other time' (*Ant.* 15.121), and Pliny called the earthquake in Asia in A.D. 17 the greatest in human memory (N.H. 2.86). Revelation 16:18 both alludes to whatever its readers were accustomed to recall as the greatest earthquake ever, and projects that experience into the apocalyptic future which will surpass any known disaster.

IV

Evidently to be compared with 16:19 is the earthquake of 11:13. The parallelism of these verses and the otherwise consistent symbolism of Revelation are good reason for regarding this earthquake too as heralding the End. If the great city of chapter 11 has some of the characteristics of Jerusalem, it also has those of Babylon: John's purpose here is

[12]Swete (1907) 210.
[13]Other Old Testament examples of this kind of language are Deut 4:32; 2 Kings 18:5; 23:25; Jer 30:7. Cf. also Josephus, *BJ* 1.12.

to merge rather than to distinguish the two cities.[14] In this case the contrasts of 11:13 and 16:19-21 are instructive. The earthquake of 11:13 accompanies the resurrection and ascension of the two witnesses, whose careers are modelled on those of Moses and Elijah and also Jesus Christ. The shaking of the heavens at the assumption of Moses (2 Bar 59:3) and the record of Elijah's assumption ἐν συνσεισμῷ (LXX 4 Kingdoms 2:11) may be rather remote parallels. Nor can we be sure that the tradition of the earthquake at the resurrection of Jesus (Matt 28:2) was known in the seven churches of Asia at this date. But clearly the divine intervention which the earthquake signals is here described not purely in terms of judgment, but also in terms of the vindication of the people of God. Those whose eyes are opened to this aspect of the eschatological events repent and glorify God, by contrast with the people in 16:21 who, seeing nothing but the wrath of God, curse him. The contrast is no contradiction for John is not concerned to forecast the proportions of the converted and the finally unrepentant; he simply moves the focus of attention from one to the other.

Two passages remain to be considered. Both 6:12-17 and 20:11 are explicitly passages in which the earthquake accompanies the theophany of God the Judge. Moreover in these two cases John employs the tradition of the cosmic quake, in which the heavens as well as the earth flee from God's presence. The first passage echoes several Old Testament descriptions of the Day of the Lord. The second seems to include the notion of the destruction of the old cosmos to be replaced by the new (cf. 21:1). The first passage refers, and is the first reference in Revelation, to the same final earthquake to which 8:5; 11:13, 19; 16:18 also refer. In the case of 20:11, however, the earthquake is located on the far side of the millennium. It has often been noticed that John uses some of the same images twice, on either side of the millennium: the bride adorned for the eschatological marriage, the gathering of the nations to battle, with allusions to Ezekiel's vision of God in both 19:17-18 and 20:8. It may be that the duplication of

---

[14]Cf. Minear (1966) 89-105.

cosmic quakes should be seen as part of the same pattern. Or it may be that the whole sequence 19:11-20:15 should be seen as another instance of John's method of expanding earlier images in later visions. Just as the seven last plagues are summed up in 11:19, so perhaps 19:11-20:15 does not take us on beyond the earlier images of the End but expands them. The clearest indication of this would be the echo in 20:11 of earlier earthquake descriptions in 6:14 and 16:20. The vision of the sixth seal may then be intended already to point forward as far as the Last Judgment.

V

The eschatological earthquake in the Apocalypse is not the tired apocalyptic cliché so many commentators have thought it to be. It is rich in Old Testament and contemporary allusion, and carries considerable theological weight. With the author of Hebrews John shares the expectation that the God whose voice shook Sinai will once again shake heaven and earth (Heb 12:25-29), and to the unrepentant his coming can only be fearful. Revelation's images are flexible, theologically significant and not intended to be pieced together into a single literal picture of what will happen at the End. Besides the great earthquake, there are many other images of the End: the harvest, the vintage, the last great battle, the Lamb's wedding banquet. Only the insensitively literalistic will be puzzled that John can describe the fall of Babylon first in the great earthquake and then at the hands of the armies of the beast, or that in the last of the seven plagues we find an earthquake instead of the battle of Armageddon which the penultimate plague had led us to expect. As one image among many, the earthquake will not of course tell us everything John has to say about the End. In particular it does not reveal that the coming of God which it heralds is to be a Christophany, the manifestation to the world of the Lamb who conquered on the cross (1:7; 19:11-16).

8

The Apocalypse as a Christian War Scroll

1. Introduction

In Jewish eschatological expectation the theme of the holy war plays a prominent role.[1] The future will bring the final victory of the divine Warrior over his people's and his own enemies. But the tradition of an eschatological or messianic holy war can be divided into two forms, in one of which the victory is won by God alone or by God and his heavenly armies and in the other of which his people play an active part in physical warfare against their enemies. The former tradition has a kind of precedent in the Old Testament holy war traditions, since the paradigm of a divine victory over the enemies of Israel could be taken to be the Exodus, in which God alone overthrew the Egyptians while Israel looked on (Exod 14:13-14). The deliverance of Jerusalem from the armies of Sennacherib (2 Kings 19:32-35; Isa 37:33-36; cf. Ezek 39:2-4; Zech 14:12) set another precedent, and the account of the great victory in the reign of Jehoshaphat (2 Chron 20, especially vv. 15-17; with vv. 22-24, cf. Ezek 38:21; Hag 2:22; Zech 14:13; 1 Enoch 56) embodies this ideal kind of holy war in which the divine Warrior requires no human assistance. In the proto-apocalyptic

---

[1] In general, see Leivestad (1954) 3-18; Collins (1975), (1977); Yarbro Collins (1977); Brownlee (1983); Heard (1986).

passages of the Old Testament it is this kind of holy war which seems to emerge as the expectation for the future: God fights alone (Isa 59:16; 63:3) or with his heavenly army (Joel 3:11b; Zech 14:5b). In apocalyptic proper this tradition predominates. In Daniel and the Testament of Moses the conflict becomes a dualistic one between supernatural forces of both good and evil, and the real victory is achieved by Israel's angelic patron Michael in the supernatural sphere. God's earthly people play no military role (although the function of martyrdom will have to concern us later). In the later apocalypses of 2 Baruch, 4 Ezra and the Parables of Enoch the victory of the Messiah over the pagan oppressors of Israel is prominent, but the idea of a victory by judicial sentence takes precedence over military language (2 Bar 40:1; 1 Enoch 62:2-3; and especially 4 Ezra 12:31-33; 13:9-11, 37-38).

In most cases where the idea of a military Messiah occurs in the early post-biblical Jewish literature, his army is not mentioned, even if it may sometimes be implied (cf. PsSol 17:22-24; 2 Bar 72:6; SibOr 3:654, 689; 5:418-419). This is surprising since the dominant Old Testament tradition of the holy war in which God's people certainly fight, though the heavenly armies may fight with them and the victory is undoubtedly due to God, is prominent in the Maccabean literature and must have inspired the Jewish resistance movements against Rome in the first and second centuries A.D. In the later Hebrew apocalypses of the medieval period the expectation of a Messiah who would lead the troops of Israel in a holy war against her enemies is common, but in the Jewish apocalypses of the earlier period almost absent (cf. 1 Enoch 90:19). It is possible that in this respect the extant ancient apocalypses are not entirely typical of the apocalyptic literature of the period. It must be remembered that most of the ancient Jewish apocalypses have been preserved only by Christians, who in the early centuries largely repudiated apocalyptic militancy. If there were apocalypses which inspired the Zealots or the Bar Kokhba revolt, it is perhaps not surprising that they have not survived.

The one work — not preserved by Christians — which does give us detailed evidence of ideas about an eschatological holy war in which Israelite armies will fight is the War Scroll from Qumran (1QM). When Matthew Black suggested, rather incidentally, that the book of Revelation could be described 'as a kind of "War Scroll" of Christianity,' the feature of the book of Revelation he had in mind was the idea of a holy war waged by Christ with 'the sword of his mouth'.[2] I wish to take up the suggestion in a different way, to draw attention to the emphasis on *human participation* in the eschatological holy war as the book of Revelation presents it. As many scholars have noticed, holy war imagery permeates the book,[3] but it is usually only to the war against the forces of evil as waged by God and Christ that these scholars draw attention.[4] The more distinctive feature, by comparison with other extant apocalypses of the period, is the participation of Christians in the war. I hope to show that John shows detailed knowledge of a kind of military messianism which must have been common in some Jewish circles of his time, of which we have only hints, for the most part, but for which 1QM provides our best evidence. Questions of the source criticism and date of 1QM[5] need not greatly concern us, since it is for the kind of holy war traditions found in it rather than for its specific history within the Qumran community that we shall make reference to it.

My suggestion that the book of Revelation be considered — from one point of view, at least — as a 'Christian War Scroll' is not, of course, intended to suggest any similarity of *genre* between Revelation and 1QM. But the question of genre may highlight an important aspect of the comparison. 1QM is not, in literary form, an apocalypse, even though its contents have some affinities with apocalyptic literature.[6] In its present form at least it is a 'rule', which, in the context of a description of the eschatological war, provides instructions on the conduct of the war. It is orientated to human participation in the war, providing its readers with religious encouragement, as well as practical

---

[2]Black (1984) 293.
[3]See especially Yarbro Collins (1976); Ford (1975); and now Giblin (1991).
[4]An exception is Leivestad (1954) 212-38.
[5]For surveys of views, see Dimant (1984) 516-517; Duhaime (1984) 68-70.
[6]Rowland (1982) 39-42; especially Duhaime (1984); Duhaime (1988).

military rules and plans, as they prepare to engage in the war. The book of Revelation *is* an apocalypse in form, but it also has a formal peculiarity in that it combines the genres of apocalypse and *letter* (see especially 1:4-5). As a letter, directly addressed to a group of churches, it incorporates, as introduction to the apocalypse proper, seven individual messages from Christ to the seven churches, which give the whole work a more explicitly exhortatory function than is usual in apocalypses. At the end of each of the seven messages the promises to 'the one who conquers' (2:7, 11, 17, 26; 3:5, 12, 21) link these messages with the vision of the new Jerusalem which ends the Apocalypse (cf. 21:7). They function to invite the readers to participate in the eschatological war which is described in the central part of the book, where the vocabulary of conquest (νικᾶν) is frequent, and so gain their place in the new Jerusalem. The visions of God's conflict with the forces of evil do not represent events of which the readers are to be mere spectators: they represent a struggle for which, as the seven messages reveal, many of the readers may be unprepared or which they may be inclined to evade, but in which they are called to participate. Since, as we shall see, John reinterprets the holy war traditions and makes the warfare metaphorical rather than literal, there is not the concern with practical military matters which we find in 1QM. But in religious function there is a certain parallel between the two works.

Since our aim is to show, not simply that John uses the metaphor of warfare in a general way for Christian witness and martyrdom, but that he takes up and reinterprets specific traditions about the messianic war, detailed exegesis is necessary. In a full treatment examination of all the passages in which Christians are represented as participating in the holy war would be necessary, but within the present limits of space we shall confine ourselves to the three passages (5:5-6; 7:2-14; 14:1-5) on which the main weight of the case must rest.

2. The conquering Messiah (5:5-6)

This passage introduces, in a programmatic way, the notion of the Messiah as military victor and John's distinctive reinterpretation of that idea. Since I have discussed the passage in detail elsewhere[7] and since our primary interest is now not in the passage for its own sake, so much as its significance as background for John's understanding of the messianic army, the treatment here will be brief. The key point to be noticed is that, in the contrast between what is said to John (5:5) and what he sees (5:6), he first evokes the idea of the Messiah as the Jewish nationalistic military conqueror and then reinterprets it by means of the notion of sacrificial death for the redemption of people from all nations (cf. 5:9-10). The juxtaposition of the contrasting images of the Lion and the Lamb expresses John's Jewish Christian reinterpretation of current Jewish eschatological hopes.[8]

Revelation 5:5 draws two titles (the Lion of Judah and the Root of David) for the Davidic Messiah from Genesis 49:9 and Isaiah 11:1-5, both classic texts for Jewish messianic hopes in the first century (for both passages combined, see 4QPBless; 1QSb 5:20-29; 4 Ezra 12:31-32; for the Shoot of David, see 4QFlor 1:11-12; 4QpIsa[a] Frag. A; PsSol 17:24, 35-37; 4 Ezra 13:10; 1 Enoch 49:3; 62:2; TJud 24:4-6). Current interpretation of both focussed on the Messiah as conqueror of the nations, destroying the enemies of God's people. Both passages were evidently favourites at Qumran, and the interpretation given in the Qumran literature is strongly militaristic:

'May you smite the peoples with the might of your hand and ravage the earth with your sceptre; may you bring death to the ungodly with the breath of your lips' (1QSb 5:24,[9] alluding to Isa 11:4);

'[God] shall strengthen you with his holy name, and you shall be as a lion; and you will not lie down until you have devoured the prey which nought shall deliver' (1QSb 5:29,[10] alluding not only to Gen 49:9, but also to the 'lion of Jacob' passages in Num 23:4; Mic 5:8).

[7]Bauckham (1980) 112-116.
[8]Cf. Caird (1966) 75.
[9]Translation from Vermes (1987) 237.
[10]Translation from Vermes (1987) 273.

There seems little doubt that Revelation 5:5 strongly and deliberately evokes the image of the Messiah as a new David who wins a military victory over the enemies of Israel.

The vision of the slaughtered Lamb (5:6) recalls other Old Testament motifs: the lamb led to the slaughter in Isaiah 53:7, and, in view of Revelation 5:9-10 and the new Exodus theme which runs right through Revelation, the passover lamb.[11] The portrayal of Jesus' death in these terms was already familiar in Christian tradition, but by placing the image of the sacrificial victim alongside those of the military conqueror, John forges a new symbol of *conquest* by sacrificial death. Insofar as 5:5 expresses Jewish hopes for messianic conquest by *military violence*, 5:6 replaces those hopes; and insofar as 5:5 evokes narrowly nationalistic expectations of Jewish triumph over the Gentile nations, 5:6 replaces those expectations. But insofar as the Jewish hopes, rooted in Old Testament scriptures, were for the victory of God over evil, 5:6 draws on other Old Testament scriptures to show *how* they have been fulfilled in Jesus. Jesus the Messiah has already defeated evil by sacrificial death. He was won a victory, but by sacrifice, not military conflict, and he has delivered God's people, but they are from all nations, not only Jews. The continuing and ultimate victory of God over evil which the rest of John's prophecy describes is the outworking of his decisive victory won on the cross. Our interest now is in the part which Revelation gives the Lamb's followers in this continuing holy war.

3. The messianic army (7:2-14)

The vision of the 144,000 and the innumerable multitude in chapter 7 forms a parallel to that of the Lion and the Lamb in chapter 5. Just as in 5:5-6, John *heard* that the Lion of Judah and the Root of David had conquered, but *saw* the slaughtered Lamb, so in chapter 7 he *hears* the number of the sealed (7:4) but *sees* an innumerable multitude (7:9). It seems likely, therefore, that the relation between the 144,000 and the

[11]Comblin (1965) 22-31.

innumerable multitude is intended to be the same as that between the Lion and the Lamb.[12] Moreover, there are specific links between the Lion and the 144,000 and between the Lamb and the innumerable multitude. To the Lion *of the tribe of Judah* (ἐκ τῆς φυλῆς Ἰούδα: 5:5) corresponds a list of the sealed of the tribes of Israel, headed by those *of the tribe of Judah* (ἐκ φυλῆς Ἰούδα: 7:5). To the Lamb standing (5:6), who has ransomed people from every tribe, tongue, people and nation (5:9), corresponds the multitude from all nations, tribes, peoples and tongues, standing before the Lamb (7:9). The correspondences imply that the 144,000 are the Israelite army of the military Messiah of David, while the international multitude are the followers of the slaughtered Lamb. Having rejected nationalistic militarism from his picture of the Messiah in 5:5-6, John is now equally rejecting it from his picture of the Messiah's followers, whose victory must be of the same kind as that of their leader.

Commentators have usually, correctly, identified the 144,000 as those who are sealed for protection against the impending eschatological plagues (7:1-3; cf. 9:4). The echo of Ezekiel 9:4-6 (to which PsSol 15:6 alludes and which CD [MS B] 19:12 quotes in a similar way, with reference to the eschatological visitation) is clear.[13] But the sealing has a *double* significance: it is a mark of protection because it is also a mark of God's ownership (as becomes even clearer in 14:1). Unlike the angel of Ezekiel 9:2-4, who makes a *mark* (σημεῖον: 9:4, 6; PsSol 15:6) with a pen, John's angel has the *seal* (σφραγίς) of the living God (7:2) with which to *brand* (σφραγίζειν: 7:4-5, 8) his slaves (δούλους: 7:3).[14] They are protected in order to serve him. The

---

[12]So Caird (1966) 96; Sweet (1979) 150-151, though I do not agree with the precise way in which they relate the 144,000 to the innumerable multitude. Other commentators are divided as to whether the two groups are distinct groups or the same group (the whole church) seen from different perspectives. In favour of the latter view, see Beckwith (1919) 534-536.

[13]In view of the new exodus theme which runs through Revelation, there may well be a remoter echo of the sign of protection on the night of the passover (Exod 12:13, 22-23). Melito, *Peri Pascha* 15-17, uses σφραγίζειν in this connexion (no doubt under the influence of a typological reference to baptism).

[14]For the practice of branding slaves, see Betz (1971) 659. The practice of branding recruits to the Roman army seems to have begun at a later date (*ibid.*).

form of service may not be immediately apparent, but it is worth noticing that the faithful Israelites to whom Ezekiel 9:4 is applied in CD [MS B] 19:12 are the members of the community which, according to 1QM, expected not only to be spared in the eschatological wrath, but to be its instruments as members of the messianic army.[15]

That the 144,000 Israelites are those called to serve God in battle is clear from the form of 7:4-8: a *census* of the tribes of Israel. In the Old Testament a census is always a counting up of the *military* strength of the nation.[16] Hence those counted are males of military age: twenty years and over (Num 1:3, 18, 20 etc.; 26:2, 4; 1 Chron 27:23; cf. 1 Sam 24:9; 1 Chron 21:5). Accordingly, it later becomes apparent from Revelation 14:4 that the 144,000 are *adult male* Israelites: those eligible for military service. The only divinely commanded censuses of the people in the Old Testament were those in the wilderness (Num 1; 26), and the first of these in particular is most likely to provide a model for an eschatological census. It looks as though the repeated formula of Revelation 7:5-8 (ἐκ φυλῆς…δώδεκα χιλιάδες) is indeed modelled on that of Numbers (1:21, 23 etc.: ἐκ τῆς φυλῆς…).[17] This link with the census of Numbers 1 is of particular interest, since the account of the organization of the military camp of Israel in the wilderness which this census introduces has considerably influenced 1QM. Israel organized in the wilderness for the conquest of the promised land was readily treated as a model

[15]TJob 5:2 is a very interesting parallel to Rev 7:2-8, but one whose significance is hard to evaluate. Job is sealed (σφραγισθῆναι) by an angel as a mark of divine protection in his struggle with Satan, which is described in terms both of a wrestling match and of a battle (4:4, 10; 27:1-5). It seems likely that ideas of holy war are in the background. Note that Job's victory comes through his endurance (ὑπομενῶ 5:1; cf. 1:5; 4:6); cf. Rev 13:10; 14:12.

[16]At first sight, Exod 30:11-16 might seem to be an exception: a census for the purpose of taxation. But the age of eligibility (30:14) is the military age, and 30:12 is probably to be understood as a reference to the military census of Num 1. The census is not for the sake of the tax; rather, the tax is an atonement in view of the association of divine wrath with a census (cf. 2 Sam 24).

[17]Hence the conclusion Caird (1966) 96, draws from the formula of Rev 7 — that the 144,000 represent only *part* of the church (the martyrs) — is unjustified.

for the eschatological Israel who would come from the wilderness (1QM 1:2-3) to reconquer the promised land in the messianic war.[18]

The number of the Israelite army in Revelation 7 — 12,000 from each of the twelve tribes — is, of course, a symbolic number, a 'square number'[19] of perfection, like the perfect dimensions of the new Jerusalem (Rev 21:16). But we should not too readily suppose that a first-century reader need have taken the number to be *purely* symbolic. It would be quite natural to think of an army of all Israel, assembled for the messianic war, as composed of twelve equal tribal contingents. The small force which Moses sent against Midian was 12,000, composed of 1,000 from each of the tribes (Num 31:4-6; cf. Philo, *Mos.* 1.306). In 1 Chronicles 27:1-15, Israel is divided into twelve equal military divisions (though not tribal divisions) of 24,000 each, each division serving in David's army for a month at a time. The numbers of the army in 1QM (28,000 heavy infantry; 7,000 skirmishers; 6,000 cavalry: but the calculations are obscure and these figures uncertain)[20] are those of the army in the field at any time: a much larger figure for the total military strength of all the tribes of Israel (1QM 2:7-8) is presupposed. Certainly, 144,000 is quite a modest number by comparison with Old Testament texts which envisage an assembly of all the fighting men of Israel (Num 1:46; 26:51; Judg 20:2; 1 Sam 11:8; 15:4; cf. 2 Chron 14:8; 17:13-19; 25:5-6; 26:12-13). It is even possible that, in view of the common use of the term 'thousand' in the Old Testament and later texts (1 Macc 3:55; Josephus, *BJ* 2.20.7), including 1QM (4:2, 16; 5:3),[21] for a military division,[22] we should take Revelation 7:4-8 to

[18]For the influence of Num 1-3, 10, on 1QM, see Davies (1977) 28, 30-31; Yadin (1962) 39, 42-48, 54-56; van der Ploeg (1959) 27-28. According to Davies' analysis of the sources of 1QM, it is the document consisting of cols. 2-9 which bases its account of the army on Numbers.

[19]Farrer (1964) 106.

[20]See Davies (1977) 48-52.

[21]The Qumran community was also permanently organized in units of this size: 1QS 2:21-22; 1QSa 1:14-15, 29; CD 13:1-2.

[22]אלף, as a term for a military unit, may originally have referred to a contingent numbering far fewer than a thousand, but by the time of Revelation was certainly understood to be a unit of a thousand men.

mean that each tribe supplies twelve battalions of a thousand men each.

The notion of a messianic army composed of all twelve tribes of Israel is not at all surprising. Not only was the return of the ten tribes and the reunion of all Israel a traditional element in the eschatological hope (Isa 11:11-12, 15-16; 27:12-13; Jer 31:7-9; Ezek 37:15-23; Sir 36:11; Tob 13:13; 2 Bar 78:5-7; TJos 19:4; cf. Matt 19:28; m. Sanh. 10:3; j. Sanh. 10:6),[23] but there is also evidence for the expectation that the ten tribes would return specifically in order to take part in the messianic war:

(1) Such an expectation could well have been suggested by Isaiah 11:14 in its context (1:11-16). This point is of special relevance in view of the connexion of this passage with 'the Root of Jesse' (Isa 11:10), which John used as a title for the military Messiah of David in Revelation 5:5.

(2) The army in 1QM, modelled on Numbers 1-2, is organized according to the traditional division into twelve tribes (2:2-3, 7; 3:13-14; 14:16; 5:1-2; 6:10).[24]

(3) Sibylline Oracle 2:170-76, which certainly belongs to the Jewish stratum of this book, mentions the return of the ten tribes in a way which implies, rather obscurely, that they will be responsible for reversing the Gentile domination of Israel.

(4) 4 Ezra 13 refers to the return of the lost tribes in the context of a vision of the final military assault of the nations on the Messiah and his destruction of them. The author is clearly concerned to deny that the destruction of the nations will take place by military means (13:9-11, 37-38). His emphatic description of the returning tribes as 'peacable' (*pacificam* 13:12, 39, cf. 47) should therefore be seen not only as contrasting this peaceable multitude with the warlike multitude of the nations (13:5, 8, 11), but also as part of a polemic against

[23] Cf. Geyser (1982) 392: 'Expectation of the ingathering of the tribes was the atmosphere which every pious Jew breathed during the major part of the first century B.C. and up to 70.' I would add that it continued to be so long after 70.

[24] Cf. Yadin (1962) 79-83. 1QM 1:2-3 may indicate that the first six years of the war (in which the land of Israel is liberated) will be fought by the three tribes of Levi, Judah and Benjamin, who will then be joined by the lost tribes for the remainder of the forty years' war: so Davies (1977) 66, 114-115.

apocalyptic militarism. It presupposes a tradition in which the lost tribes arrived, not peaceably after the destruction of the nations, but in time to assist in the military defeat of the nations.

(5) Such a tradition is preserved by the Christian Latin poet Commodian (*Instr.* 1.42; *Carmen apol.* 941-86)[25] in a form which must derive from a Jewish source,[26] and which has sufficient links with 4 Ezra 13 to identify it as the tradition known to and countered by the author of that chapter.[27] Here the lost tribes are led back to Palestine by divine guidance and form an all-conquering army, irresistible because God is with them, coming to rescue Jerusalem from the Antichrist. The latter gathers his forces against them, but is finally defeated through the intervention of angels.[28] One is reminded of the final defeat of the Kittim by divine intervention in 1QM (18:1-3).[29] The whole account is couched in the language and concepts of holy war.

The *list* of the twelve tribes in Revelation 7 has several peculiarities which require comment:

(1) The order of the list corresponds to no other extant list of the tribes. Most significant is the fact that Judah heads the list. This is true of Old Testament lists in which the tribes are

---

[25]Latin text in Commodian (1960). Also derived from this tradition is a passage in the Ethiopic *Acts of Matthew* (Budge [1935] 94-95), but this does not refer to the return of the tribes. Note, however, its curious reference to the 144,000, identified with the innocents massacred by Herod.

[26]No doubt there was a written source, but whether it was a work otherwise known (such as the Apocryphon of Ezekiel, or as James suggested, the Book of Eldad and Modad) there is no way of knowing: cf. James (1893) 90-94; James (1920) 103-106; Schmidt (1967) (though I am not convinced by his identification of an *Essene* source); Daniélou (1977) 116-119 (who oddly misunderstands Commodian as referring to the two and a half tribes in Babylon); Charlesworth (1981) 147-149, 295.

[27]Cf. 4 Ezra 13:43-47, with *Instr.* 1.42.30; *Carmen apol.* 940-944, 959-960. Note also the contacts between *Carmen apol.* 962-972 and the medieval Hebrew *Signs of the Messiah* (tr. Buchanan [1978] 504); but the common factor is the application of Isa 49:9-13 to the returning tribes, an application also attested in y. Sanh. 10:6 and in other later Jewish literature.

[28]The tradition is probably based on Dan 11:44-12:1; 8:25, with the 'tidings from the east and the north' of 11:44 interpreted as the news of the coming of the lost tribes.

[29]Note also 'the kings of the north' (*Carmen apol.* 981), as in 1QM 1:4.

arranged geographically, moving from south to north (Num 34:19; Josh 21:4; Judg 1:2; 1 Chron 12:24), but the list in Revelation 7 bears no other resemblance to the geographical list. The only other Old Testament list of tribes which puts Judah first is that of Numbers 2:3 (followed by 7:12; 10:14), i.e. the tribes in their military order in the camp. But, again, the rest of the order of the tribes in Revelation 7 bears no resemblance to the list in Numbers 2. The best parallel is perhaps to be found in Pseudo-Philo, LAB 25:4: a list of the tribes in a conventional order,[30] but with Judah (properly fourth in this order) moved into first place. This is because Judah was the tribe of Cenez (Kenaz), Israel's military leader at the time (cf. 25:2, 9).[31] Similarly, in Revelation 7 Judah takes precedence as the tribe of Israel's military leader, the Lion of Judah (5:5). The rest of the order is probably best explained as in part an unsuccessful attempt to reproduce from memory the order of the birth of the patriarchs[32] and in part the result of random rearrangement in transmission.

(2) The inclusion of *both* Joseph *and* Manasseh (Rev 7:6, 8) (rather than either Joseph alone or *Ephraim* and Manasseh) is unparalleled and has never been explained.[33] A *possibility* is

---

[30]Dan and Naphtali are accidentally omitted in the text of 25:4, but can be restored in the correct place from the parallel lists in 8:11-14; 25:9-13. The same order (not found in any Old Testament text) is followed by Jub 34:30 and by the Testaments of the Twelve Patriarchs, where it is represented as the order of the birth of the patriarchs. In fact, it is not quite the order of birth (according to Gen 29-30), but the order of birth modified so as to keep all the Leah tribes together. The order is also given, in two of the Targums (Fragm. Tg. Exod 28:17-20; Tg. Neof. Exod 28:17-20; 39:10-13) and in Midrash Rabbah (Exod. R. 38:8-9; Num. R. 2:7), as the order in which the names of the tribes appeared on the high priest's breastplate, which was believed to be the order of birth of the patriarchs (Josephus, *Ant.* 3.169).

[31]There is some reason to think that Psuedo-Philo sees Kenaz, a great military hero, as a type of the Davidic Messiah.

[32]In that case, Reuben, Issachar, Zebulon, Joseph and Benjamin are correctly placed, while the two pairs Gad and Asher, Simeon and Levi are correctly paired, but incorrectly placed. A more detailed attempt to explain the order of the list, by comparison with other extant lists of the tribes, is in Bauckham (1991), which also responds to alternative attempts by Winkle (1989) and Smith (1990).

[33]The only explanation offered by the commentators is that Μανασση is an abbreviation of Δαν (missing from the list as it stands) via the abbreviation Μαν.

that the author had in mind Ezekiel 37:15-23, the classic Old
Testament prophecy of the reunion of the twelve tribes in the
messianic kingdom. In the extant text of 37:16, 19, the name
of Joseph has been glossed with phrases referring to Ephraim,
in such a way that the reader could think that 'Joseph' is here
being used as a name for the *tribe* of Ephraim. 'Joseph' might
therefore seem a suitable name for Ephraim in a list of the
tribes of the eschatological, reunited Israel. Alternatively, the
solution may again lie in the census of Numbers 1, on which we
have argued that Revelation 7:4-8 is partly modelled. The
repeated formula which introduces the number of each tribe
in that chapter is varied once. Whereas, for every other tribe,
it begins: 'for the sons of Reuben...,' 'for the sons of Simeon...,'
etc., in the case of Ephraim, it begins: 'for the sons of Joseph,
for the sons of Ephraim...' (Num 1:32). The rubric, 'for the
sons of Joseph,' should really be understood as covering both
the reference to the sons of Ephraim which immediately
follows and the reference to the sons of Manasseh in verse 34,
but John or his source might have taken it as warrant for calling
the tribe of Ephraim Joseph in a military census.

(3) The tribe of Levi (Rev 7:7) might seem out of place in a
military census. It was excluded from the two Mosaic censuses
(Num 1:49; 2:33; 26:1-51; cf. 1 Chron 21:6), but numbered
separately according to a different, non-military principle
(Num 3:15; 26:62). However, in 1QM, although the priests and
Levites do not fight with weapons, they play an essential part in
the conduct of war, conducting prayers before, during and
after battle, and blowing the trumpets which both direct the
troops and call divine attention to the battle. Without them the
war could not be a *holy* war. Consequently, the tribe of Levi is
organized on the same military pattern as the other tribes
(1QM 4:1-8), and can even be said to fight (1:2). Moreover, in
view of the patriarch Levi's and the archetypal 'zealot'
Phinehas's activities in executing divine vengeance (TLevi 5:3;
Num 25:6-13), as well as the military precedents set by the
Maccabees, the tribe of Levi cannot be excluded from violent
prosecution of a holy war, such as Testament of Simeon 5:5
explicitly predicts.

(5) The omission of Dan from the list must probably be

regarded as arbitrary: one tribe was frequently omitted in order to achieve a list of twelve. The tradition that Antichrist was to come from the tribe of Dan (first found in Irenaeus, *Adv. Haer.* 5.30.2; Hippolytus, *De Antichristo* 14) is unlikely to be pre-Christian,[34] since the Antichrist figures of Jewish apocalyptic are invariably Gentile and pagan. In any case, even this would scarcely account for the exclusion of the whole tribe from the eschatological Israel.[35]

The vision of Revelation 7:9a contrasts with the audition of 7:4-8 in two significant ways: whereas the 144,000 are counted, the great multitude cannot be counted,[36] and whereas the 144,000 are Israelites, the innumerable multitude are from all nations. The innumerability of the multitude can scarcely be an empirical *observation* of the Christian church at the time when Revelation was written.[37] Rather, it echoes God's promise to the patriarchs that their descendants would be innumerable (Gen 13:16; 15:5; 32:12; Hos 1:10; Jub 13:20; 14:4-5; Heb 11:12; cf. Gen 22:17; 26:4; 28:14; Jub 18:15; 25:16; 27:23; LadJac 1:10).[38] Two aspects of Jewish reflection on this promise should be noticed. The first is that the contrast between this promise and the numbering of the people in a census had been noticed: see 1 Chronicles 27:33; Pseudo-Philo, LAB 14:2 (where the relation between the Mosaic census and 1 Kings 3:8 is in view);

---

[34] *Contra* Bousset (1896) 171-174.

[35] TDan 5:4-6 predicts the apostasy of Dan, but 5:9-13 envisages the tribe's restoration and participation in the eschatological salvation of Israel. The idea that Antichrist will be a Danite may have originated as an anti-Jewish interpretation of the common expectation of an Antichrist figure from the East, beyond the Euphrates, which was where the ten tribes were believed to be, combined with the influence of Jer 8:16 and the omission of Dan from Rev 7. Note that *Yalqut Shimoni* (on Gen 49:9) draws from Deut 33:22 the quite opposite conclusion: that the mother of the Messiah of David will be a Danite (quoted in Myers [1974] 302).

[36] Even if the 144,000 are actually only counted by God or an angel, the figure is not large enough to be considered uncountable by a human being.

[37] Consequently, the 144,000 and the innumerable multitude are not, as Caird (1966) 96, suggests, related as 'Scriptural image' and 'historic *fact*'.

[38] So Mounce (1977) 171; Sweet (1979) 150; Ford (1975) 126. On the interpretation of the promises to the patriarchs in early Christian literature, see Norelli (1982).

and, for later reflection, Exod. R. 39:1; Num. R. 2:14, 18. The second is that some seem to have thought the promise would be fulfilled through the growth of the ten tribes to vast numbers in the lands of their exile. Thus Josephus (*Ant.* 11.133) reports that the ten tribes beyond the Euphrates are 'countless myriads whose number cannot be ascertained' — surely an echo of the promise to the patriarchs — while according to Commodian, *Instr.* 1.42.24 the tribes have grown to 'so many thousands', and the now hopelessly corrupt text of Testament of Moses 4:9 probably had some similar reference to the growth of the numbers of the tribes in exile.[39] In 4 Ezra 13 it is the hostile nations of the Gentiles who are repeatedly called an 'innumerable multitude' (13:5, 11, 34; cf. 3:7; 7:140), while the ten tribes are called 'another multitude' (13:12, 39, cf. 47). The implication is that they replace the innumerable multitude of the nations, but probably the author hesitated to call them innumerable because of his emphasis on the fewness of the saved (7:140-8:3) and their determined number (4:36).

By contrast with these non-Christian Jewish reflections, Revelation 7:9 sees the promise fulfilled in the great multitude which exceeds the possibility of a census because it is *international.* This is a distinctively Christian understanding of the promise in which probably it is being interpreted by reference to its other form in Genesis: the promise of a multitude of nations (Gen 17:4-6; 35:11; 48:19; cf. Rom 4:16-18; Justin, *Dial.* 119-120).[40] For this reason, the order in which John's standard four-part expression (ἔθνη καὶ φυλαὶ καὶ λαοί καὶ γλῶσσαι)[41] here occurs may not be arbitrary (cf. the different orders in 5:9; 11:9; 13:7; 14:6; and variations of the list

---

[39]For medieval Jewish examples of the theme, see Buchanan (1978) 106, 504, 512. The 'sons of Moses' in the latter two texts are the mythical nation supposed (on the basis of Exod 32:10) to be with the ten tribes in exile.

[40]Also behind Rev 7:9, though verbal echoes are lacking, may be Isa 11:10-16: note the connexions in this passage between the messianic 'Root of Jesse' (cf. Rev. 5:5; 22:16), the gathering of the nations (ἔθνη) who trust in him, the return of the ten tribes, and a war of reunited Israel against her enemies. Notice also that another element in the promises to the patriarchs — the promise of the land — is taken up in Rev 21:7.

[41]The expression derives from Daniel, especially 7:14. See further chapter 9 section 10 below.

in 10:11; 17:15). The placing of ἔθνους first, together with the grammatical awkwardness (not paralleled in other instances of the expression in Revelation) which sets παντὸς ἔθνους apart from the other three (plural) members, enables 7:9 (ὄχλος πολύς... ἐκ παντὸς ἔθνους) to echo the promise to the patriarchs (Gen 17:4 LXX: πλήθους ἐθνῶν), while φυλῶν in second place echoes the repeated ἐκ φυλῆς of 7:4-8, suggesting perhaps that the tribes of Israel are not excluded, but included in the greater, international multitude of Abraham's and Jacob's 'descendants'. Or perhaps it would be better to say that the redeemed of all nations have been included with them among the 'descendants' of Jacob. Both forms of the patriarchal promise (innumerable descendants, a multitude of nations) were given not only to Abraham but also to Jacob (Gen 32:12; 35:11). So the international multitude of 7:9 are all 'sons of Israel' (7:4), though not all are of the twelve tribes. Thus 7:9 as a reinterpretation of 7:4-8 indicates not so much the replacement of the national people of God as the abolition of its national limits. This is consistent with the picture of the new Jerusalem in chapter 21, where gates inscribed with 'the names of the twelve tribes of the sons of Israel' (21:12) stand open to the nations (21:24-26).

If 7:9a contrasts the great multitude as innumerable and international with the 144,000 Israelites, there is as yet no reinterpretation of the military theme as such. Indeed, ὄχλος could correctly be translated 'army,'[42] and verses 9b-10 can readily be understood as continuing the military theme by depicting the army victorious after battle. The white robes are the festal garments of the victory celebration (cf. Tertullian, *Scorpiace* 12; 2 Macc 11:8), and the palm branches may be compared with those which the holy warriors of Simon Maccabee's army waved in celebration of their recapture of the citadel of Jerusalem (1 Macc 13:51; cf. TNapht 5:4).[43] In 7:10 the victorious army, according to a standard motif of the holy war tradition, ascribe their victory to God: 'Victory to our God...' (ἡ σωτηρία τῷ θεῷ ἡμῶν, which is hebraizing Greek

---

[42]TDNT 5.583.
[43]Other references in Swete (1907) 101-102.

for לאלהינו הישועה [cf. Ps 3:8], where ישועה means 'deliverance, victory,' as frequently in the Old Testament and in 1QM).[44] In 1QM, one of the banners which are to be carried by the army on their return from a victorious battle is inscribed, 'Victories of God' (4:13), while the prayers before and after battle repeatedly stress that it is God alone who gives the victory (10:4; 11:4-5; 14:4-5; 18:7-13; cf. also Deut 20:4; 1 Macc 3:22; 2 Macc 8:18; 13:15).

However, the ascription of victory not only to God but also to the Lamb (7:10) prepares for the revelation that it is a victory *of the same kind* as the Lamb's (cf. 5:6): those whom the Lamb's sacrificial death has ransomed from all nations (5:9) share in his victory through *martyrdom*. Against most of the commentators, this must be the meaning of 7:14, but it is a meaning which emerges only gradually in the course of a verse which at first sight seems simply to continue the theme of holy war.

The 'great tribulation' had become a technical term for the eschatological 'time of trouble' of Daniel 12:1.[45] In view of the interpretation of this Danielic expression in 1QM as the time of the battle against the Kittim (1:11-12; 15:1; cf. also the role of Michael in 17:5-8),[46] 'those who come out of the great tribulation' (Rev 7:14) could be taken to mean 'those who emerge victorious from the eschatological war'. The following clause ('and they have washed their robes') then also fits naturally into a description of victory in a holy war, since the washing of garments was part of the ritual purification required after shedding blood (Num 31:19-20, 24; cf. 19:19) and before participation in worship. Probably 1QM 14:2-3, in which the army, the morning after victory, is to 'launder their garments' before taking part in prayers of thanksgiving, refers to such ritual purification.[47] But in contrast to 1QM's statement that

---

[44]Cf. Caird (1966) 100-101.

[45]See Bauckham (1974) 35.

[46]See von der Osten-Sacken (1969) 33, 97.

[47]So Carmignac (1958) 201. Some scholars argue that, since it would then be less strict than the law of Moses, which prescribes seven days of purification, the reference cannot be to ritual, but merely to ordinary washing: Van der Ploeg (1959) 156; Jongeling (1962) 308. But the liturgical context and the explicit reference to the blood of the slain makes the idea of ritual purification hard to exclude, even if further purification would still be required to fulfil the Mosaic commandment.

they 'shall wash themselves of the blood of the guilty cadavers' (14:2-3), Revelation's further explanation, 'they have made [their robes] white with the blood of the Lamb,' achieves, by its startling paradox, a decisive reinterpretation of the holy war motif.

The key to this final clause of 7:14 is to recognize that, in the context of allusion to Daniel 12:1, it must contain a reference to Daniel 11:35; 12:10. With reference to the 'wise' (מַשְׂכִּילִים) who 'fall'[48] by sword and flame, by captivity and plunder' (11:33, 35), it is said that this is 'in order to refine them, and to purify them, and to make them white' (11:35). The same three verbs recur in a different order in 12:10, where the hithpael form of the first two allows them to be taken in a reflexive sense: 'Many shall purify themselves and make themselves white and be refined.' John has correctly seen here a reference to martyrdom, interpreted as a testing and purifying process. Of the three metaphors used to describe this process,[49] he selects that of whitening (washing or bleaching) clothes because of its link with his favourite image of the white clothes of the conquerors in heaven (Rev 2:4-5, 18; 6:11; 7:9; 19:8, 14) and takes advantage of the possible reflexive sense in Daniel 12:10 to make the washing an activity of the conquerors themselves. The stress is therefore on martyrdom as a voluntary act.

One way to understand the purifying effect to which Daniel 11:35; 12:10 refer would be that Israel is purged of her wicked members, either because they apostatize, for fear of martyrdom,[50] or else because it is they who 'fall' and are thus purged from Israel. Though a difficult interpretation, the latter seems to be how 1QM understands these texts, in line with its understanding of Daniel 12:1 as the time of the

---

[48]The meaning 'be tested' in both 11:33 and 11:35, suggested by Hartman and Di Lella (1978) 271, is unlikely to have been seen by the author of Revelation. LXX has προσκόψουσι ('will stumble') in 11:33.

[49]Cf. also the combination of two of these metaphors, including the one John uses, in Mal 3:2. Note also Rev 3:18, which may be an attempt to illustrate all three of the verbs in Dan 11:35; 12:10.

[50]So the medieval Hebrew *Signs of the Messiah*, interpreting Dan 12:10 in conjunction with Zech 13:9; Ezek 20:38: Buchanan (1978) 498-499.

eschatological victory in battle. The wicked among the army of the sons of light fail the 'test' of battle (the 'crucible' [מצרף], 1QM 17:1, 9; cf. צרף in Dan 11:35; 12:10) and are slain, like Nadab and Abihu (1QM 16:9, 13; 17:1-3; cf. 2 Macc 12:39-45).[51]

John, however, seems to take the purification to be the martyrs' purification of themselves through martyrdom, and so takes the great tribulation of Daniel 12:1 to be the time of persecution in which the people of God triumph not through fighting but through martyrdom.[52] Hence also, whereas Michael's role in Daniel 12:1 is taken in 1QM to be his intervention in the final stage of the battle against the Kittim (1QM 17:5-8), in Revelation Michael's heavenly victory corresponds to the victory of the martyrs on earth (Rev 12:7-11). This interpretation of 7:14 as referring to martyrdom is not contradicted by the final phrase 'in (or: with) the blood of the Lamb,' since the meaning of this need not[53] be controlled by 1:5b; 5:9. These latter texts use Passover-Exodus imagery to refer to the redemption of Christians by the death of Christ:[54] Christians are here purely passive recipients of redemption. But the proper comparison is with 12:11, which refers to the participation of Christians in the death of Christ through faithful witness to the point of martyrdom: here it is a question of an activity by Christians, as in 7:14. 12:11 helps to clarify the sense in which the martyrs share in the Lamb's victory by means of a sacrificial death like his. The victory does not consist in their mere death as such, but in their faithful witness to the

---

[51]Cf. Yadin (1962) 221; Bauckham (1974) 39. 1QM makes no verbal allusion to Dan 11:35; 12:10, but the strong influence of Daniel, especially 11:40-12:1, on 1QM makes it likely that these verses lie in the background to the idea of testing in battle. Source-analysis of 1QM is unlikely to affect this conclusion, since there are clear links between col. 1, which is especially based on Daniel (von der Osten-Sacken [1969] 3-34), and cols. 5-19, where allusions to Daniel are also to be found (Von der Osten-Sacken [1969] 97-99).

[52]Cf. the same interpretation of Dan 12:10 in Hermas, *Vis.* 4:3:4-5. I noticed this in Bauckham (1974) 38, but failed to note that in these verses Hermas takes up all three verbs from Dan 11:35; 12:10: צרף in verse 4, לבן in verse 6a, and ברר (which the Greek versions of Daniel render ἐκλέγειν) in verse 5b.

[53]*Pace*, e.g., Swete (1907) 103.

[54]See especially Schüssler Fiorenza (1985) 68-81.

point of death (cf. 2:13; 11:7), maintaining the witness of Jesus (12:7; 19:10), following in the path of Jesus whom Revelation 1:5 calls 'the faithful witness'. The value of their witness is derivative from his, it is maintaining his witness, and so the victory of their faithful witness as far as death is derivative from his victory. They 'have conquered through the blood of the Lamb' (12:11). In 7:14 John has fused this thought of *victory* (the white robes of 7:9) with that of *purification* (they have washed their robes white; cf. also 19:8). Probably the latter idea is not that their deaths atone for their sins, but that the moral probity of their lives as faithful witnesses is sealed in their martyrdom and is their active participation in the redemption won for them by Christ (1:5b). The holiness of the martyrs we shall see further expounded, again in connexion with holy war imagery, in 14:4-5.

Thus it is the last clause of 7:14 which finally transmutes the meaning of the holy war imagery of the rest of the chapter and brings it into line with the vision of the Lamb in 5:6-10. The messianic army is an army of martyrs who triumph through their martyrdom, because they are followers of the Lamb who participate in his victory by following his path to death.[55]

4. The Lamb and his army (14:1-5)

This passage belongs to a section (12:1-14:5) in which John portrays the combatants in the eschatological war. The satanic trinity of dragon, sea-monster and land-monster are portrayed as successfully prosecuting war against the people of God (12:17; 13:7). But in 14:1 the Lamb and his followers stand to oppose them on Mount Zion. The fact that the latter are here called the 144,000 may seem surprising after their reinterpretation as the innumerable host in 7:9. But the usage is parallel to John's continued use of 'Root of David' as a messianic title for Jesus in 22:16, even after its reinterpretation

---

[55]It also shows the whole vision of chapter 7, with its play on the idea of numbering (7:4, 9), to be the fulfilment of the promise to the martyrs in 6:11.

by the vision of the Lamb in 5:5-6. By reinterpreting the militant Messiah and his army John does not mean simply to set aside Israel's hopes for eschatological triumph: in the Lamb and his followers these hopes are both fulfilled and transformed. The Lamb really does conquer, though not by force of arms, and his followers really do share his victory, though not by violence. The combination of the Lamb and the 144,000 conveys the sense that there is a holy war to be fought, but to be fought and won by sacrificial death.

The reference to Mount Zion is an allusion to Psalm 2 (v. 5), one of Revelation's key Old Testament texts (cf. Rev 2:26-27; 6:15; 11:15, 18; 12:5; 19:15) since it depicts the triumph of the messianic king over the hostile nations.[56] For the same reason, it is on Mount Zion that the Messiah in 4 Ezra 13 takes his stand against the nations gathered to fight him, and destroys them. The shift from vision (Rev 14:1) to audition (14:2) effects a move from earth to heaven in order to portray immediately the triumph, which is always in Revelation in heaven, until the opening of heaven at the parousia (19:11). The account of the heavenly song recalls the earlier accounts of the Lamb's triumph (5:6-14) and his followers' triumph (7:9-12), and, especially with reference to 5:8-9 (harps, new song, ransomed), represents the 144,000 participating in the victory of the Redeemer and so singing his victory song. For comparable accounts of celebration after victory in holy war, see 2 Chronicles 20:28; Psalm 144:9-10; 1 Maccabees 13:51; 1QM 4:4-5. The term 'new song' is holy war terminology for a hymn in praise of a fresh victory of the divine Warrior over his foes (Pss 98:1-3; 144:9; Isa 42:10-13; Jdt 16:2-3).

In the standard form for explaining a vision (cf., e.g., 7:14; 11:4), verse 4 contains three identifying statements. The first has caused the greatest difficulty,[57] but is readily explicable when we remember that the 144,000 are an army fighting the Lord's battle. It is for this reason that they are all adult men (whereas the martyrs whom they *symbolize* of course include

[56]Cf. Farrer (1964) 57-58, 137-41, 160.
[57]See the survey of views in Lindijer (1970).

women and children), and it is for this reason that they keep themselves free of the cultic defilement incurred through sexual intercourse (for μολύνειν of ritual defilement, see, e.g., Isa 65:4 LXX).[58] The reference is to the ancient demand for ritual purity in the Lord's army (cf. Deut 23:9-14), which required David's troops to abstain from all sexual relations while on campaign (1 Sam 21:5; 2 Sam 11:9-13). Similarly 1QM forbids women and boys[59] to enter the camp during the whole period of the campaign (7:3-4), while a man who is accidentally impure on the day of battle may not join in the fighting, 'for holy angels are in communion with their hosts' (7:6).

It might be objected that the language of Revelation 14:4a suggests, not temporary abstention during a military campaign, but lifelong celibacy. But (i) the Essenes' preference for lifelong celibacy has been plausibly connected not only with a wish to be in constant readiness for the physical warfare described in 1QM, but also with their present engagement in a spiritual and ethical war against the forces of evil;[60] (ii) John no doubt similarly views the Christian calling as such to involve readiness for and engagement in the Lamb's holy war. This does not mean that he expects Christians to be literally celibate, like Essenes,[61] but that he uses lifelong celibacy for the sake of ritual purity as a *metaphor* for a characteristic of Christian life.

The first identifying statement establishes a qualification of the 144,000 for the second and third identifying statements. That they follow the Lamb wherever he goes implies their faithfulness as far as death, since the Lamb was led to the slaughter (Isa 53:7; Rev 5:6). Consequently, they are offered as sacrifices to God. The three statements of verse 4 therefore

---

[58]The expression 'to defile themselves with women' is used regularly of the Watchers in 1 Enoch (7:1; 9:8; 10:11; 15:3, 4; 69:5: where extant, the Greek uses μιαίνεσθαι): for the overtones of cultic impurity in this usage, see Suter (1979).

[59]Whether the danger in view is of homosexual relations (Yadin [1962] 71) or simply of the inconvenience of having boys in the camp (Van der Ploeg [1959] 112; Jongeling [1962] 194) is uncertain.

[60]Marx (1971).

[61]*Contra* Yarbro Collins (1984) 130-131, who sees the connexion with holy war, but fails to see that if the fighting is not literal the celibacy need not be.

move from holy war imagery to sacrificial imagery, just as John's original statement about the Lamb's victory (5:5-6) did.

The additional statement in verse 5 deftly ties all three statements of verse 4 together. The cultic purity of the messianic army (v. 4a) is reinterpreted in the way in which early Christianity consistently reinterpreted ritual purity: as moral purity. But the particular form of moral purity is specified in verse 6a in a clause ('no lie was found in their mouth') which echoes Isaiah 53:9. There it describes the suffering Servant who was put to death like a sacrificial lamb. Thus following the Lamb wherever he goes means imitating both his truthfulness, as the 'faithful witness' (1:5; contrast the deceit which is characteristic of the forces of evil: 2:20; 12:9; 13:14; 18:23; 19:20; 20:3, 8, 10; 21:27; 22:15) and the sacrificial death to which this led.

The final phrase (ἄμωμοί εἰσιν) describes moral probity under a metaphor which could apply either to holy warriors or to sacrificial victims. 1QM excludes from the army anyone with a physical defect (7:4), and draws its list of such people from Leviticus 21:17-21, where it refers to defects which disqualify Levites from serving in the priesthood. 1QM is thus demanding for soldiers in the holy war the same ceremonial physical perfection as was required for priests. The word used for 'bodily defect' or 'blemish' in 1QM 7:4 and Leviticus 21:17-18 is מום, translated in the Septuagint of Leviticus 21 as μῶμος. Thus ἄμωμοι ('without physical defect') in Revelation 14:5 could specify the qualification for fighting in the Lamb's army. But it could equally well, of course, refer to the physical perfection required in sacrificial animals (e.g. Exod 29:38; Lev 1:3; 3:1; Heb 9:14; 1 Pet 1:19). In a description of the *Lamb's* soldiers who win their victory through sacrificial death, the ambiguity is surely intended.

5. Conclusion

A Jewish apocalypse nearly contemporary with Revelation — 4 Ezra — carefully repudiates all trace of apocalyptic militarism, no doubt in reaction against the failure of the Jewish revolt. Not only is there no element of human participation in the

Messiah's triumph over the Roman Empire and the Gentile nations which gather to make war against him, but military language is avoided in the account of his destruction of them, which takes place by judicial sentence, not weapons of war (4 Ezra 11-13). By comparison, Revelation makes lavish use of holy war *language* while transferring its *meaning* to non-military means of triumph over evil. Even the vision of the parousia, while sharing with 4 Ezra 13 the concept of the Messiah's victory by his *word* ('the sword that issues from his mouth': Rev 19:15, 21; cf. 1:16; 2:12, 16: the common source is Isa 11:4), nevertheless *depicts* the parousia in military terms as a theophany of the divine Warrior (19:11-16). As we have seen, human participation in the eschatological war is not rejected in Revelation, but emphasized and, again, *depicted* in terms drawn from traditions of holy war, which are then carefully reinterpreted in terms of faithful witness to the point of death. The distinctive feature of Revelation seems to be, not its repudiation of apocalyptic militarism, but its lavish use of militaristic *language* in a non-militaristic *sense*. In the eschatological destruction of evil in Revelation there is no place for real armed violence, but there is ample space of the imagery of armed violence.

No doubt in the Jewish circles with which John and his churches had contact — including Jewish refugees from Palestine who joined the great Jewish communities in the cities of Asia Minor after the fall of Jerusalem — ideas of eschatological holy war against Rome, such as the Qumran community had entertained and the Zealots espoused, were well known. Some Jews disillusioned with such expectations after the fall of Jerusalem may have joined the Christian churches to which John wrote. John's interaction with apocalyptic militancy will therefore have been part of his churches' debate with 'the synagogue of Satan who say they are Jews but are not' (3:9). He is not concerned *simply* to repudiate apocalyptic militancy, since he shares much of its general outlook: a strong critique of Roman power as antithetical to the rule of God, a perception of religio-political issues within an eschatological and dualistic framework in which God and his people are in conflict with the satanic power and destined in the end to triumph, and a conviction of the need for God's people to engage in the conflict with evil by active resistance to the religio-political claims of Rome and pagan society.[62] Therefore, instead of simply repudiating apocalyptic militancy, he *reinterprets* it in a Christian sense, taking up its reading of Old Testament prophecy into a specifically Christian reading of the Old Testament. He aims to show that the decisive battle in God's eschatological holy war against all evil, including the power of Rome, has already been won — by the faithful witness and sacrificial death of Jesus. Christians are called to participate in his war and his victory — but by the same means as he employed: bearing the witness of Jesus to the point of martyrdom. It is misleading to describe this as 'passive resistance': for John it is as active as any physical warfare and his use of holy war imagery conveys this need for active engagement in the Lamb's war.

The seven messages offer no hint that any of John's readers were tempted to take up arms against the Roman authorities, though Revelation 13:10 could be interpreted in the sense of a warning against this. At any rate the principal danger (represented by the Nicolatains and the prophetess 'Jezebel') seems to have been a different one: that of compromise with and assimilation to pagan society. Part of the aim of the book is to alert the readers to the fact that what is going on around them, in the social and political life of their own cities, is part of a conflict of cosmic proportions, the eschatological war of good and evil, the conflict of sovereignty between God and the devil, in which they are called to take sides, to take a firm stand, and by faithful witness to the truth to play their part in resisting the pagan state and pagan society. The message is not, 'Do not resist!', so much as, 'Resist — but by witness and suffering, not by violence'. The active metaphor of warfare serves this purpose better than language of passive resistance.

John's apocalyptic imagery achieves 'a symbolic transformation of the world',[63] i.e. it changes his readers'

---

[62]On affinities between Revelation and the Zealots, cf. Yarbro Collins (1977) 252-4, 256.

[63]Cf. Barr (1984).

perception of the situation in which they live and so enables them to behave differently in response to it. The imagery of holy war provides a most effective vehicle for this purpose because it highlights the issue: when the beast puts the martyrs to death, who is the real victor? The answer, in Revelation, depends on whether one sees the matter from an earthly or a heavenly perspective. From the earthly perspective it is obvious that the beast has defeated the martyrs (11:7; 13:7). To 'those who dwell on earth' — people who see things from an earthly perspective — the power of the beast seems supreme and irresistible, and this is why they worship him. 'Who is like the beast, and who can fight against it?' (13:4), they cry, in a deliberate parody of what Jews said about the divine Warrior (Exod 15:11; Pss 35:10; 71:19; 89:6; 1QH 7:28; 1QM 10:8-9; 13:13), as well as of the name of Israel's champion Michael (which means, 'Who is like God?'). The sheer political and military power of the beast seems divine, and this earthly view of the power-situation was surely one which Christians themselves were tempted to share. They were a tiny minority of powerless people confronted with the apparently irresistible might of the Roman state and the overwhelming pressure of pagan society. To refuse to compromise was simply to become even more helpless victims.

The apocalyptic visions, however, reveal that from a *heavenly* perspective things look quite different. From this perspective the martyrs are the real victors. To be faithful in bearing the witness of Jesus even to the point of death is not to become a helpless victim of the beast, but to take the field against him and win. John can depict the triumph of the martyrs only in scenes set in heaven, because it requires the heavenly perspective — established when the slaughtered Lamb is first seen triumphant before the throne of God (5:6) — to make their triumph apparent, but the heavenly perspective is destined to prevail on earth at the parousia (19:11-21). Thus the heavenly and eschatological dimensions which apocalyptic gives to a perception of the current situation enable John to present a different assessment of it from that which his readers might otherwise be inclined to share with their non-Christian neighbours. It is a different assessment of the same empirical fact — the suffering of faithful Christians at the hands of pagan power — and by taking advantage of the availability of military imagery for *both* assessments — the beast is victorious, the followers of the Lamb are victorious — John is able to pose most effectively the issue of how one sees things. Is the world a place in which political and military might carries all before it, or is it one in which suffering witness to the truth prevails in the end?

It remains, finally, to relate John's understanding to those Jewish traditions which gave martyrdom a place in the holy war. The concept of martyrdom as a form of active resistance is already to be found in a group of writings — both historiographical and apocalyptic — concerned (originally) with the martyrs of the Antiochan persecution: 2 Maccabees, 4 Maccabees, Daniel and the Testament of Moses. In these works, to a greater or lesser extent, non-violent resistance to the point of martyrdom takes precedence over the military resistance of the Maccabees.[64] Military action is (a) accepted, but its efficacy linked with the martyrdoms (2 Maccabees); (b) ignored, though assumed (4 Maccabees); (c) reduced to insignificance (Daniel); or (d) apparently rejected completely (Testament of Moses). On the other hand, martyrdom as a result of faithfulness to the Torah is presented as a form of resistance (cf. Dan 11:32), which, at least in 2 Maccabees, 4 Maccabees and the Testament of Moses (the case of Daniel is less clear), is a kind of human participation in the divine war against the enemies of Israel. The deaths of the martyrs divert the wrath of God from the rest of the nation, which has been suffering for its sins, and call it down in vengeance on their persecutors, who have now spilled innocent blood. However, it is only in 4 Maccabees that the suffering and death of the martyrs is actually described in military language as the waging of holy war. In their faithfulness to God's law to the point of death, the mother and her seven sons fight and conquer Antiochus (e.g. 1:11; 9:24, 30; 16:14). Admittedly, this theme in 4 Maccabees is permeated by the hellenistic concept of the

---

[64]See especially Heard (1986).

triumph of virtuous reason over the passions, in which the martyrs, enduring pain for the sake of righteousness, show themselves superior to the tyrant (e.g. 11:20-21, 24-25, 27; 13:4; 14:1; 16:2), and, characteristically, the military metaphor is combined with that of victory in athletic contests (e.g. 17:11-16). But behind this hellenistic moral philosophy, we must postulate a tradition which had already interpreted the sufferings and deaths of the martyrs as their participation in God's holy war against his enemies.

The evidence therefore suggests that in his martyrological reinterpretation of the holy war John was not entirely innovative. The possibility was available to him in the Jewish traditions he knew; he has taken it up and developed it because it was the only understanding of messianic war consistent with his Christian faith in the crucified Messiah. But is his understanding of the victory of the martyrs therefore the same as that of the Maccabean literature and the Testament of Moses? Do they defeat the beast by calling down divine wrath to avenge their innocent blood? Undoubtedly, something of this idea is present in Revelation (cf. 6:9-11; 18:24; 19:2).[65] But it is not the whole story. The martyrs conquer not by their suffering and death as such, but by their faithful *witness* to the point of death (cf. 12:11). Their witness to the truth prevails over the lies and deceit of the devil and the beast. For those who reject this witness, it becomes legal testimony *against* them, securing their condemnation. This negative function of witness is present in Revelation. But it entails also a positive possibility: that people may be won from illusion to truth. The extent to which this positive possibility is explicitly envisaged in Revelation is a question we shall take up in the next chapter.

---

[65]Yarbro Collins (1981) interprets martyrdom in Revelation purely in this way.

9

The Conversion of the Nations

Whether Revelation envisages the conversion of the nations of the world to the worship of the one true God is a question on which commentators disagree. This in itself is rather surprising. We might have expected that at least on so significant a question about the eschatological future Revelation would be clear. A major part of the explanation for the misunderstandings and confusion of interpreters of Revelation, not only but especially on this issue, lies in a persistent failure to appreciate the precision and subtlety of John's Old Testament allusions.[1] In this chapter we shall demonstrate that the question of the conversion of the nations — not only whether it will take place but also how it will take place — is at the centre of the prophetic message of Revelation. We shall do so primarily by detailed study of the Old Testament allusions in the relevant passages of Revelation, and in this way we shall also demonstrate how one of the principal ways in which Revelation conveys meaning is by very precise reference to the Old Testament.

---

[1]Among recent commentators, Caird (1966) and Sweet (1979) (see also Sweet [1981]), take seriously the indications that John expects the conversion of the nations and are alert to his use of the Old Testament. However, their study of the latter is handicapped by the constraints of relatively brief commentaries on the English text. The present chapter adopts in a general way their approach, but attempts greater methodological rigour in the study of the Old Testament allusions, and as a result frequently differs from their exegesis as well as frequently agreeing with it.

238

1. Universal terminology

Revelation is full of universalistic language, referring to the whole world and its inhabitants. A consideration of some of this language will serve to introduce us to the issue with which this chapter is concerned. There is, for example, the phrase 'the inhabitants of the earth,' which occurs ten times (οἱ κατοικοῦντες ἐπὶ τῆς γῆς: 3:10; 6:10; 8:13; 11:10 [twice]; 13:8, 14 [twice]; 17:8; οἱ κατοικοῦντες τὴν γῆν: 17:2). The variation in 17:2 is probably merely stylistic, but there are two other related phrases where the variation probably is significant, as we shall see: 'the earth and those who inhabit it' (13:12: τὴν γῆν καὶ τοὺς ἐν αὐτῇ κατοικοῦντας), and 'those who sit on the earth' (14:6: τοὺς καθημένους ἐπὶ τὴν γῆς). The phrase 'the inhabitants of the earth' is also common in other apocalypses which are roughly contemporary with Revelation and with which Revelation shows significant affinities in other ways: the Parables of Enoch (1 Enoch 37:2, 5; 40:6, 7; 48:5; 54:6, 9; 55:1, 2; 60:5; 62:1; 65:6, 10, 12; 66:1; 67:7, 8; 70:1), 2 Baruch (25:1; 48:32, 40; 54:1; 55:2; 70:2, 10) and 4 Ezra (3:34, 35; 4:21, 39; 5:1, 6; 6:18, 24, 26; 7:72, 74; 10:59; 11:5, 32, 34; 12:24; 13:29, 30; 14:17). In view of the concern of the apocalypses with universal eschatology, it was natural for the phrase to become a standard apocalyptic usage (cf. also Isa 24:1, 5-6; 26:9; Dan 4:1, 35; 6:25). But whereas in other apocalypses the phrase by no means necessarily carries a negative overtone, in Revelation it seems consistently to do so. The inhabitants of the earth are guilty of the blood of the martyrs (6:10), come under God's judgments (8:13), are the enemies of the two witnesses (11:10), are deceived by the second beast and worship the beast (13:8, 14; 17:8), and are drunk with Babylon's wine (17:2). They are distinguished from God's people (3:10) and above all they are those whose names are not written in the Lamb's book of life (13:8; 17:8). Especially significant is 13:8, which alone refers explicitly to '*all* the inhabitants of the earth,' in order to say both that they worship the beast and that their names are not written in the Lamb's book of life. Evidently equivalent to 'the inhabitants of the earth' is 'the whole world' (ἡ οἰκουμένη ὅλη: 3:10; 12:9; 16:14), which Satan deceives (12:9), and 'the whole earth' (ὅλη ἡ γῆ: 13:3), which follows the beast.

Page 240 — The Climax of Prophecy

The exceptional phrase in 13:12 (τὴν γῆν καὶ τοὺς ἐν αὐτῇ κατοικοῦντας) does not betray a different author, as Charles thought,[2] but is framed in deliberate parallel to 12:12 (οὐρανοὶ καὶ οἱ ἐν αὐτοῖς σκηνοῦντες). As always, the evidence which the source critics took to indicate a variety of sources turns out to be evidence of John's meticulous and subtle use of language. Throughout chapters 12 and 13, the three regions of the heavens, the earth and the sea are in view. Satan is cast out of heaven, but turns his attention to the earth and the sea (12:12). The first beast rises out of the sea, the second out of the earth. Those who are deceived by the second beast and worship the first beast are 'the inhabitants of the earth,' while God's people are symbolized as God's 'dwelling-place, that is, those who dwell in heaven' (13:6: τὴν σκηνὴν αὐτοῦ, τοὺς ἐν τῷ οὐρανῷ σκηνοῦντας). Both here and in 12:12 the contrast with the earth-dwellers is heightened by the use of the theologically resonant verb σκηνόω instead of κατοικέω, which is reserved for the earth-dwellers. It is worth noticing that the same opposition between earth and sea, on the one hand, and heaven, on the other, is found in chapter 18, where those who mourn for Babylon are 'the kings of the earth' (18:9), 'the merchants of the earth' (18:11) and 'all whose trade is on the sea' (18:17), while those who rejoice over her fall, the 'saints and apostles and prophets,' are addressed as 'heaven' (18:20; cf. 19:1-8).

The phrase 'the inhabitants of the earth' is thus clearly used to indicate the universal worship of the beast and the universal corruption of the earth by Babylon (cf. 19:2). This explains why, in 14:6, the idiom is varied: 'those who sit on the earth' (14:6: τοὺς καθημένους ἐπὶ τῆς γῆς). Linguistically, this is no more than an alternative translation of the Old Testament Hebrew phrase יֹשְׁבֵי הָאָרֶץ, since יָשַׁב means both 'to dwell' and 'to sit'. But John will have exploited the possibility of a different translation in order to make a distinction.[3] The inhabitants of

[2] Charles (1920) 1.336.

[3] It is also possible that, whereas his general use of οἱ κατοικοῦντες ἐπὶ τῆς γῆς has no particular Old Testament source, but follows general apocalyptic usage, in 14:6 he is alluding specifically to Ps 98:7. In section 6 below, we shall see that 14:6-7 is based on Ps 96, which forms the first of the closely related group of psalms to which Ps 98 also belongs.

the earth are viewed in 14:6 not merely as worshippers of the beast, but as hearers of the eternal Gospel which calls them to repent and to worship God. They are the same people as those to whom 13:8 refers, but viewed positively rather than negatively. The phrase which also describes them in 13:7 ('every tribe and people and language and nation') recurs, with variation only of order, in 14:6 ('every nation and tribe and language and people'). As we shall see (in section 10 below), this phrase does not in John's usage carry a negative overtone, but refers precisely to the potential for the beast's subjects to become God's.

If 'the inhabitants of the earth' has a consistently negative sense, other universalistic terms are more ambiguous. 'The nations' (τὰ ἔθνη) occurs fifteen times (2:26; 11:2, 18; 16:19; 19:15; 20:3, 8; 21:24, 26; 22:2; and 'all the nations': 12:5; 14:8; 15:4; 18:3, 23), as well as seven times in the fourfold formula just mentioned ('every tribe and language and people and nation,' and variations: 5:9; 7:9; 10:11; 11:9; 13:7; 14:6; 17:16). This formula, of which John makes especially subtle and deliberate use, will be reserved for full discussion in the last section of this chapter. Other references to the nations frequently align them with the powers of evil: they have all drunk Babylon's wine (14:8; 18:3), they have all been deceived by Babylon's sorcery (18:23) and by Satan (20:3), they trample the holy city (11:2) and rage against God (11:18), and so, mustered in the beast's final resistance to God's rule, they become the object of destructive judgment by Christ at his parousia (12:5; 19:15; cf. 2:26). But it is also said that all the nations will worship God (15:4), and in the vision of the New Jerusalem this prophecy is seen realised (21:24, 26; 22:2). To some extent Old Testament usage lies behind the different roles in which the nations appear. A series of references to them (2:26; 11:18; 12:5; 19:15) are dependent on Psalm 2:1-9, in which the rebellion of the nations against the rule of God and his Messiah is violently crushed. The worship of the nations (15:4) and their relation to the New Jerusalem (21:24, 26) reflect other Old Testament texts (Ps 86:9; Isa 60:3, 5, 11). But the references to the nations still leave us with the question: Does Revelation expect the nations to be won from satanic

deception and converted to the worship of God, or does it
expect them to persist in rebellion until they perish under
God's final judgment? In which of these ways does 'the
kingdom of the world' become 'the kingdom of our Lord and
his Messiah' (11:15)? The evidence seems to point both ways
and commentators seem unable to give equal weight to all of
it.

Equally ambiguous are 'the kings of the earth' (1:5; 6:15;
17:2, 18; 18:3, 9; 19:19; 21:24; cf. 'the kings of the whole
world': 16:14), Revelation's term for all rulers. (Since they
are subject to Rome [17:18], they are not only Rome's client
kings, but all the local ruling classes of the Roman Empire.)
The term derives primarily from Psalm 2:2, which explains
its predominantly negative usage, of the rulers of the world
as they are subject to Babylon (17:18), allied with her (17:2;
18:3) and with the beast (19:19) against God and his kingdom.
But the first reference to them (1:5) designates Jesus Christ
'ruler of the kings of the earth' (cf. 17:14; 19:16), a status
which we might suppose takes effect only in crushing their
rebellion and destroying them (19:19-21), were it not for
the last reference to them (21:24), which depicts them
offering their glory to God's glory in the New Jerusalem.
Here John has deliberately assimilated the underlying Old
Testament references to 'kings' (Isa 60:3, 10-11, 16) to the
same term he has used throughout his prophecy for the
rebellious kings.

Other universalistic terminology could be mentioned (see
especially 1:7; 6:15; 11:4; 19:18; 21:3), but most will come up for
discussion at points in the rest of this chapter. The key terms
we have already discussed illustrate the problem with which
this chapter is concerned. Revelation's theme is the transfer of
the sovereignty of the whole world from the dragon and the
beast, who presently dominate it, to God, whose universal
kingdom is to come on earth. How is this to occur? Does
Revelation share the perspective of some of the apocalypses,
often thought to be the typically apocalyptic expectation that
only a faithful minority will be spared the final judgment that
is inexorably coming on the sinful mass of humanity? Or does
it share the much more universalistic hope for the conversion

of the nations to the worship of the true God, which is typical of late Old Testament prophecy and to be found also in some later apocalyptic literature?[4]

2. The scroll

A major key to the correct interpretation of Revelation has been missed by almost all scholars. It is that the scroll which John sees, sealed with seven seals, in the hand of God in 5:1 is the same as the scroll which he sees open in the hands of an angel in 10:2. It is a considerable merit of Mazzaferri's recent work on Revelation that he establishes this point conclusively.[5]

Most scholars have been misled by the fact that in 5:1-9 the word used for the scroll is βιβλίον, whereas in 10:2, 9-10 it is βιβλαρίδιον (which the English versions translate as 'little scroll'). The textual evidence in chapter 10 is confused:[6] there is some manuscript evidence for βιβλίον, βιβλιδάριον and βιβλάριον, as well as βιβλαρίδιον, in verses 1 and 9, and for βιβλίον, βιβλίδιον and βιβλάριον, as well as βιβλαρίδιον, in verse 10, though βιβλαρίδιον seems to have the strongest manuscript support in these verses and so appears in the text of printed editions of the Greek New Testament. In verse 8, however, the strongest attestation is for βιβλίον, which therefore appears in the text of printed editions, but there is also evidence for βιβλαρίδιον, βιβλιδάριον and βιβλάριον. It is likely that John called the scroll of chapter 10 βιβλίον (10:8) as well as βιβλαρίδιον (10:2, 9-10). This in itself strongly suggests that too much importance should not be attached to the distinction between βιβλίον in 5:1-9 and βιβλαρίδιον in 10:2, 9-10.

βιβλαρίδιον, like βιβλίδιον, βιβλιδάριον and βιβλάριον, is in form a diminutive of βιβλίον, but in the Greek of this period

---

[4]E.g. 1 Enoch 10:20-21; SibOr 3:710-723, 767-775. See Jeremias (1958) 55-62; Russell (1964) 297-303; Donaldson (1990).

[5]Mazzaferri (1989) 265-279; cf. also Farrer (1964) 93, 124-125, but he then retreats from identifying the two scrolls (127), as does Sweet (1979) 176-177. Bergmeier (1985) spoils his real insights by a misguided preoccupation with source-criticism.

[6]Details in Mazzaferri (1989) 267.

words which are diminutive in form frequently no longer carry diminutive meaning. None of the diminutive forms in Revelation seem to be intended to be diminutive in meaning.[7] Notably, θηρίον, though formally a diminutive of θήρ, certainly does not mean 'little beast', and ἀρνίον, though formally a diminutive of ἀρήν, certainly does not mean 'little lamb'. Moreover, it so happens that the only other known occurrences of βιβλαρίδιον in Greek literature are in the *Shepherd* of Hermas, another Christian prophet, probably roughly contemporary with John, who clearly uses βιβλαρίδιον interchangeably with both βιβλίδιον and βιβλίον. The context is most interesting. The woman who appears in Hermas's *Visions* and gives him his prophetic revelations is reading a βιβλαρίδιον, whose content she wishes Hermas to communicate to the church. Since its contents are too considerable for him to remember, she gives him the book, now called a βιβλίδιον, for him to copy (*Vis.* 2:1:3). As he describes how he copied it out and it is then removed from him, it is again twice called a βιβλίδιον (2:1:4). Later a man appears to him in a dream and asks him about the identity of the woman from whom he received the βιβλίδιον (2:4:1). She herself then appears and asks Hermas whether he has yet given the book (βιβλίον) to the elders of the church (2:4:2). She is referring to the copy which Hermas had made from the βιβλαρίδιον or βιβλίδιον he borrowed from her. There seems no reason why the latter should be smaller than the copy, which Hermas is at pains to state was an exact copy (2:1:4). The woman is pleased to hear that Hermas has not in fact yet passed on the book to the elders, because she wishes to add more words to it. When she has done so, he is to write two more copies to give to Clement and Grapte: these are again described as βιβλαρίδια (2:4:3).[8]

Hermas's usage not only shows that βιβλαρίδιον, βιβλίδιον and βιβλίον can be used as synonymous. It is also significant

---

[7] Mazzaferri (1989) 268-269.

[8] The only textual variants are in MS. A, whose scribe evidently avoided both βιβλαρίδιον and βιβλίδιον. Instead, it has βιβλιδάριον in 2:1:3, βιβλιδάριον in 2:1:4, βιβλίον in 2:4:1, and βιβλιδάρια in 2:4:3. See the text and apparatus in Whittaker (1956).

that he uses them to describe the prophetic revelation which he is given by a heavenly figure so that he may include it in his own prophetic writing. (Since his *Visions* includes the narrative of how he received the visions, he cannot mean that his own book is simply a copy of the heavenly book: it must incorporate the contents of the latter. He also suggests, in 2:2:1, that the writing in the heavenly book needed some kind of translation into the words of his own prophecy.) His use of the image of the book containing a prophetic revelation is closely parallel to John's image in Revelation 10, where John eats the book so that he may assimilate its content and it may then become the content of his prophecy.[9] If Hermas is not dependent on Revelation (for which there is no evidence) then their common use of the rare βιβλαρίδιον may indicate that this form was used in Christian prophetic circles for books containing prophetic revelation. This might explain why it is in chapter 10 of Revelation, where the scroll is to be given to John as a prophetic revelation, that he uses the word βιβλαρίδιον for it. But this is conjectural. Hermas's usage certainly shows that there is no difficulty in supposing that John calls the same scroll both βιβλίον and βιβλαρίδιον.

This does not show that the scroll of chapter 5 must be the same as the scroll of chapter 10, but it removes the obstacle which has prevented the vast majority of scholars from even considering this possibility. There are several reasons why the two scrolls should be considered identical. In the first place, John creates a very clear literary link between 10:1 and 5:2, indicating that the account which follows in chapter 10 should be read in close connexion with the context of 5:2: the question of the opening of the sealed scroll. The opening words of 10:1, 'And I saw another mighty angel...' (καὶ εἶδον ἄλλον ἄγγελον ἰσχυρόν), echo 5:2: 'And I saw a mighty angel...' (καὶ εἶδον ἄγγελον ἰσχυρόν). The mighty angel of 5:2 is the only one that has been previously mentioned. In itself, this close literary connexion between 5:2 and 10:1 could be taken to indicate only a parallel between the two scrolls, rather than their

---

[9]Cf. also 1 Enoch 81:1-2; 93:1-3, which use the idea of reading the heavenly books and then communicating their content as prophecy.

identity. But it supports the following reasons for concluding their identity.

Secondly, we should take full account of the Old Testament source both for the scroll in chapter 5 and for the scroll in chapter 10. In many parts of this book we have seen that John's use of the Old Testament is not a matter of plucking phrases at random out of contexts, but consists in careful and deliberate exegesis of whole passages. He found reference to a scroll (Ezek 2:8-3:3) within the context of Ezekiel's inaugural vision (1:1-3:11), in which the prophet was both granted a vision of God on his throne and given by God the prophetic revelation which it was his prophetic commission to communicate to the people. In Revelation 4, John's account of his vision of God is considerably indebted to Ezekiel's vision of the divine throne (Ezek 1). Like Ezekiel's vision, this is intended to prepare for the communication of a prophetic message to the prophet. Revelation 5:1 is closely modelled on Ezekiel 2:9-10:

> Ezekiel 2:9-10: I looked, and a hand was stretched out to me, and a written scroll was in it. He spread it before me; it had writing on the front and on the back, and written on it were words of lamentation and mourning and woe.

> Revelation 5:1: Then I saw in the right hand of the one seated on the throne a scroll written on the inside and on the back,[10] sealed with seven seals.

The difference is that, whereas in Ezekiel the scroll is not sealed and is opened by God himself, in Revelation it is sealed and can only be opened, it turns out, by the Lamb (5:2-9). But what follows immediately in Ezekiel is paralleled in Revelation 10. God tells Ezekiel to eat the scroll and gives it to him. When he does so it is sweet as honey in his mouth (3:1-3). Similarly John is told (by a voice from heaven) to take and eat the scroll. When he does so, it is sweet as honey in his mouth (10:8-10). At first sight, there might seem to be a difference, in that John adds that it made his stomach bitter (10:10). But even this additional

---

[10]The reading ὄπισθεν is certainly to be preferred to ἔξωθεν.

detail turns out to be inspired by Ezekiel, for Ezekiel is told to digest the scroll in his stomach (3:2) and the content of the scroll in Ezekiel is said to be 'words of lamentation and mourning and woe' (2:10, quoted above; cf. also Ezek 3:14). It is no doubt for this reason that it is not only, as the word of God, sweet in John's mouth, but also bitter in his stomach, when the message is digested. It is very important to notice that, when he closely echoes Ezekiel 3:1-3 in Revelation 10:8-10, John clearly still has in mind the description of the scroll in Ezekiel 2:10, which he echoed in Revelation 5:1. This strongly suggests that he means to refer to the same scroll in both places: he sees it in God's hand in 5:1, but does not receive it to assimilate as the content of his prophecy until 10:8-10.

The fact that much intervenes between 5:1 and 8:8-10 largely reflects the major difference between Ezekiel's scroll and Revelation's. The scroll in Ezekiel is not sealed, is opened by God and is given directly by God to the prophet. The scroll in Revelation is sealed with seven seals which only the Lamb can open. Therefore there is a longer process by which it reaches the prophet. It is first taken from the hand of God by the Lamb (5:7), who then opens its seven seals (6:1, 3, 5, 7, 9, 12; 8:1). Only when it has been opened by the Lamb in heaven can it be taken from heaven to earth by a mighty angel (10:1-2), who gives it to John to eat (10:8-10). We shall return to the question of the seals and the opening of the scroll. The point here is that the pattern of allusion to Ezekiel's prophetic commissioning in Ezekiel 2:8-3:3 shows that John intends Revelation 5 and 10 to tell a single story of his own reception of a prophetic revelation which is symbolized by the scroll.

Recognition of John's debt to Ezekiel 2:9-3:3 suggests another possible reason why John used the word βιβλαρίδιον in 10:2 for the scroll which he called βιβλίον throughout 5:1-9. In Ezekiel, the scroll, when first seen in the hand of God, is called מגלת־ספר (2:9) and מגלה subsequently (3:1-3). The Greek translators of the Old Testament seem to have had difficulty finding a suitable translation for מגלה on its rare occurrences in the Old Testament. Various Greek words are used. It is possible that John used βιβλίον for Ezekiel's מגלת־ספר and βιβλαρίδιον for Ezekiel's מגלה.

Thirdly, recognizing that the scroll of chapter 10 is the scroll of chapter 5 solves the otherwise insoluble problem of the nature and content of the scroll of chapter 5. It is obvious from 5:1-5 that this is a document whose contents cannot be known until the seals are broken and the scroll unrolled, and whose contents are very important, so that John is distraught to realise that noone can open the scroll to reveal them (5:4). Since the opening is not in order to interpret the contents of the scroll, but simply so that they may be seen (5:4), it is obvious that the scroll cannot represent the Torah or the Old Testament, whose contents were perfectly well known. Nor is there any indication that the scroll is a legal document. Seals were, of course, used on legal documents, but they were also used simply to keep the contents of a document secret for the time being (Isa 29:11; 1 Esd 3:8). The latter is the only purpose indicated here. If the seals were those of witnesses, as some suggest, then we should expect the witnesses to feature in the account. (In Roman law, for example, six witnesses had to sign a will and the will could be opened only when each of the six broke his own seal.) Moreover, it remains quite obscure what kind of legal document the scroll could be.[11] The most attractive suggestion is that it is the Lamb's own last will and testament:[12] its contents would then be, so to speak, the (soteriological or judgmental) effects of his death. But then it is odd that it is the hand of the One who sits on the throne that holds it and that the testator himself should be the only one who can open it. If, as has been suggested, the scroll were a marriage contract or a bill of divorce,[13] there is nothing to indicate this. It is not plausible that the reader should be left to guess the character of a document which is clearly intended to be of key significance in John's visionary narrative.

In fact, once we realise that John's Old Testament allusions are not merely decorative but carry precise meaning, the nature of the scroll is made perfectly clear by the obvious

---

[11]For some suggestions, see Beasley-Murray (1974) 120-123; Yarbro Collins (1976) 22-23.

[12]Beasley-Murray (1974) 121-123.

[13]Ford (1975) 93, 165-166.

allusion to Ezekiel 2:9-10 in Revelation 5:1. It must contain some aspect of the divine purpose, hitherto secret, which will be revealed when the scroll is opened. The analogy with Ezekiel leads us to expect that it is to be revealed to John himself, as a prophet, so that it may become the content of his prophecy. This is why John himself weeps bitterly when he supposes that the scroll's contents are, after all, to remain unrevealed (5:4). Furthermore, chapter 4 already enables us to understand, in a general sense, what the scroll's content must be. Chapter 4 is primarily a revelation of God's sovereignty, as it is manifest and acknowledged in heaven. Only a little acquaintance with prophetic-apocalyptic literature is required for a reader to infer that this vision prepares for the implementation of God's sovereignty on earth, where it is presently hidden and contested by the powers of evil. In other words, the kingdom of God is to come on earth, as it already exists in heaven. This is in fact strongly implied in Revelation's version of the song of the living creatures (4:8), who instead of proclaiming, like Isaiah's seraphim (Isa 6:4), that the earth is already full of God's glory, proclaim God as the One 'who was and who is and who is to come' — i.e. to the world to establish his kingdom. It is a reasonable conclusion, then, that the scroll which the One who sits on the throne holds in his right hand (5:1) is his secret purpose for establishing his kingdom on earth. From chapter 4 we know that God's kingdom must come: the scroll will reveal how it is to come. This also explains why the Lamb alone is worthy to open it. He is the one who has 'conquered' (5:5) and now shares God's throne (5:6; cf. 7:17). In other words, he has already, through his sacrificial death, won the comprehensive victory for God against all evil. The coming of God's kingdom will be the outworking of his victory.

Chapter 5 therefore leads us to expect that the revelation of the content of the scroll will be of major importance to John's prophecy. It would be intolerable if John left it unclear what the content of the scroll is. But commentators are at a loss to identify the contents convincingly. Most think that the contents are progressively revealed as the Lamb opens the seven seals (6:1-8:1). But it would be a very odd scroll to which this could happen. Normally all the seals would have to be broken before the scroll could be opened. Even the fact that Revelation's scroll is an opisthograph, written on both sides, makes no difference to this: no more of the writing would be exposed after the opening of any less than seven of the seals. It is in fact hard to imagine the way in which seals could be used such that part of a scroll could be revealed by the breaking of each. Ford seems to be the only scholar who has a serious suggestion based on the character of ancient documents. She suggests that the scroll is a kind of legal document to which there are some references in rabbinic literature (m. B. B. 10:1-2; m. Giṭṭ. 8:10; b. B. B. 160b; b. Giṭṭ. 81b) and which was apparently folded after every few lines and at each point signed by witnesses on the back.[14] However, in these references there is no indication that each folded section was sealed, so that it could only be read by breaking its own particular seal. The witnesses may have used seals to authenticate their witness, but there is no reason why the seals should have functioned to keep the folds closed.

Ancient readers familiar with sealed scrolls would not suppose that the events which occur when the Lamb opens each of the seals are intended to represent the contents of the scroll. These events simply accompany the opening of the scroll. The progressive opening of the scroll is a literary device which John has created in order to narrate material which prepares us for and is presupposed by the content of the scroll itself. The same must be said of what immediately follows the opening of the last seal (8:1). The silence in heaven (8:1) allows the prayers of the saints to be heard (8:4), to which the divine response is the judgment indicated in 8:5, and spelled out in detail in the judgments of the trumpet-blasts, as is indicated by the interlocking device which introduces the angels with their trumpets already in 8:2 and by the expanded repetition of the imagery of 8:5 at the blast of the seventh trumpet (11:19). There is nothing here to indicate that the trumpets are the content of the scroll. On the contrary, it should now be obvious that the scroll whose last seal is broken at 8:1 then appears opened (ἠνεῳγμένον) at 10:2. As with Ezekiel's scroll, its contents cannot be revealed until ingested by the prophet John.

[14]Ford (1975) 92-93.

Fourthly, there is reason to suppose that for the notion of a *sealed* scroll, containing God's purpose for establishing his kingdom, John was indebted to his interpretation of Daniel, and that this debt to Daniel also links chapters 5 and 10, indicating the identity of the scroll described in each chapter. The idea of closing up (םתס) and sealing (םתח) a scroll occurs several times in Daniel with reference to his visions or his book (8:26; 12:4, 9; cf. 9:24; and for the sealing of scrolls containing prophetic oracles, see also Isa 8:16; 29:11). Modern readers take all these references to mean that the contents of Daniel's visions are to be kept secret until the last days whose events they predict. This is clearly how John read Daniel 8:26 and probably 12:4, as his allusion in Revelation 22:10, which is certainly to Daniel 8:26 and may also be to 12:4, shows:

Daniel 8:26: As for you, close up the vision, for it refers to distant days.

Daniel 12:4: But you, Daniel, close up these words and seal the book until the time of the end.

Revelation 22:10: Do not seal up the words of the prophecy of this book, for the time is near.

Evidently John uses the verb σφραγίζω, in this context, to cover the two actions for which Daniel uses םתס and םתח, i.e. rolling up the scroll and then sealing it. Whereas Daniel wrote for an eschatological future which was far distant from him, that same eschatological future now impinged directly on John and his readers. Therefore while Daniel's visions were to be kept secret until the time to which they applied, John's were to be made public at once.

However, it need not have been obvious to John that Daniel 12:9 has the same significance as Daniel 8:26; 12:4. In 12:5-7, Daniel witnesses a conversation between two angelic figures about the period until the end of history. According to 12:8, Daniel 'heard, but did not understand,'[15] and so enquires

---

[15]Contrast Dan 10:1, which would suggest that it was only this final part (12:7) of his vision in chapters 10-12 that remained mysterious to Daniel.

himself, 'What shall be the end [or: outcome] of these things?' It is to this enquiry that he receives the reply, 'Go your way, Daniel, for the words are closed up and sealed until the time of the end' (12:9). This is not, like the earlier references to closing up and sealing (8:26; 12:4), a command to Daniel. In its context, it could easily be taken to mean, not that what Daniel has written is to be kept secret, but that the *meaning* of what he has written — what he himself has failed to understand — will not be revealed until the time of the end. In this case, the scroll to which 12:9 implicitly refers would not be the book of Daniel itself, but a heavenly scroll containing the divine purpose as it has not yet been revealed even to Daniel.

Revelation 10:5-7 clearly alludes to Daniel 12:7, in a way which we shall consider in more detail later. The angel in Revelation 10 announces that at last the period which leads immediately to the end of history has arrived, i.e. the period predicted in the book of Daniel as 'a time, times, and half a time' (Daniel 12:7). Consequently this time-period appears in Revelation (in several forms: 11:2-3; 12:6, 14; 13:5) only after chapter 10, when John has ingested the scroll and begins to divulge its contents as prophecy. Significantly, it first appears immediately after John has eaten the scroll and been commanded to prophesy (11:2-3). This means that the contents of the scroll are a fuller revelation about the apocalyptic period at the end of history which was predicted in Daniel. The scroll reveals what Daniel himself could not understand (Daniel 12:8). It is therefore the scroll containing God's purpose which, according to Daniel 12:9, was to remain sealed until the time of the end. Thus, the relationship between Revelation 10 and Daniel 12:6-9 shows that John thought of the scroll of Revelation 10 as a scroll which had been sealed, but has now been opened. It follows that the scroll of Revelation 5:1 is sealed because it is this same scroll. In that verse, John follows Ezekiel's description of a scroll (Ezek 2:9-10), but then identifies his scroll as that of Daniel 12:9 by adding: κατεσφραγισμένον σφραγῖσιν ἑπτά. The combination of Ezekiel and Daniel enables John to characterize the scroll both as a prophetic revelation of the divine purpose, given to him to communicate in prophecy, and also as, more specifically, a revelation of

God's purpose for the final period of world history, in which God will establish his kingdom on earth, a revelation which supplements and clarifies what remained obscure in the prophecies of the last days by earlier prophets, especially Daniel.

Fifthly and finally, we must consider the angel who brings the scroll from heaven and gives it to John in Revelation 10. The description of him (10:1-3)[16] is far more elaborate than that of any other angels in Revelation (cf. 15:6; 18:1), though far less elaborate than, and quite distinct from, the description of Christ (1:13-16).[17] This suggests that, as angels go, he is uniquely important in Revelation. The terms in which he is described do not parallel other descriptions of angels to any great extent. With the rainbow on his head (10:1), one might compare the description of the angel Yahoel (ApAbr 11:3). The face shining like the sun is a common feature of descriptions of heavenly beings.[18] But other features are unparalleled. They serve to give him a cosmic stature, towering into the sky as his legs bestride land and sea. In particular, he is associated with all three divisions of created reality, as listed in 10:6: heaven from which he comes (10:1) and the sea and the land on which he stands (10:2). This point is emphasized by the fact that the three divisions of the world appear in 10:5 (sea, land, heaven) and then in reverse order in 10:6 (heaven, land, sea). We shall return to this threefold division later. But here we should notice that the angel's association with the whole cosmos derives from the fact that he brings a message from the Creator of the whole cosmos (10:6). Just as the phrase describing God

---

[16] This description is clearly not, as Beasley-Murray (1974) 170, thinks, based on Dan 10:5-6, as can be seen from comparison with Rev 1:3-16, which is based on Dan 10:5-6.

[17] The only common feature is that the faces of both shine like the sun, but even here a distinction is made: Christ's 'face was like the sun shining with full strength' (ὡς ὁ ἥλιος φαίνει ἐν τῇ δυνάμει αὐτοῦ: 1:16), while the angel's 'face was like the sun' (ὡς ὁ ἥλιος: 10:1). In any case, this is very often said of heavenly beings: e.g. Matt 13:43; 17:2; 2 Enoch 1:5; 19:1; 4 Ezra 7:97; ApZeph 6:11; TAbr A 7:3; 12:5; 16:6; QuEzra A20; 3 Enoch 48C:6; ApPet 1:7; ApPaul 12.

[18] See last note.

as Creator at the beginning of 10:6 relates back to 4:9-10, so the rainbow on the head of the angel recalls the rainbow around the divine throne (4:3). It is from God who reigns in heaven, who created the whole world, and who bound himself to his whole creation in the Noahic covenant, symbolized by the rainbow,[19] that the angel brings the scroll which reveals this God's purpose of establishing his kingdom throughout his creation, over land and sea as well as in heaven.

Once we have recognized that the scroll the angel brings to John is the scroll that John saw in heaven in 5:1-9, we can see that this angel is the angel to whom 1:1 and 22:16 refer. The scroll contains the central and principal content of John's prophetic revelation. It is given to John by an angel (10:1-10), who received it from the Lamb, who opened it after receiving it from the hand of the One who sits on the throne (5:6-7). This chain of revelation, by which the scroll comes from God to John, corresponds exactly to the opening words of Revelation, which function as its title: 'The revelation of Jesus Christ, which God gave him to show his servants what must soon take place; and he made it known by sending his angel to his servant John' (1:1). It is important to notice here that the properly revelatory activity is that of Jesus Christ. God gave him the revelation so that he should show (δεῖξαι) it to God's servants. But Jesus Christ made it known (ἐσήμανεν), and so it is *his* revelation (ἀποκάλυψις).[20] The angel is merely the messenger who communicates Jesus Christ's revelation to John. These roles of God, Christ and the angel correspond exactly to the roles they play in relation to the scroll in chapters 5-10. God gives the scroll to the Lamb, but it is the Lamb who opens it and thereby

---

[19]Farrer (1964) 123-124, thinks the description of the angel also alludes to the Sinai covenant, but this seems more dubious.

[20]It is worth noting a possible linguistic link between John's use of ἀποκάλυψις, for the revelation that Jesus Christ discloses to him by opening the scroll, and Dan 12:9, which, we have argued, is the basis for his image of the sealed scroll. םתס, which in Dan 12:9 (cf. 8:26; 12:4) refers to the 'closing up' of the scroll, could be translated by καταλύπτω (as in Dan 12:9 LXX) or καλύπτω (as in Dan 12:4 LXX). To these Greek words, meaning 'to veil, to cover, to conceal,' the opposite is ἀποκαλύπτω, 'to uncover, to reveal'.

reveals its contents. This is the properly revelatory activity, as the importance attached to the opening of the scroll in 5:1-9 shows. Finally, the angel merely brings the scroll, already opened (10:2, 8), from heaven to give to John. Thus it is only the recognition of the identity of the scroll of chapter 5 with the scroll of chapter 10 that enables us to understand the way John describes his own book in 1:1 and the way that description relates to the content of this book. It is of the greatest importance to recognize that John regards the revelation his prophecy is intended to communicate as that contained in the scroll and that therefore its real content must follow chapter 10. Everything which precedes John's consumption of the scroll is preparatory to the real message of his prophecy.

Only now does it become explicable that, despite the role in communicating the revelation to John which is attributed to Jesus' angel in 1:1 and 22:16, no angel appears as mediating revelation to John until chapter 10. It also becomes clear why the angel of chapter 10 is described in such majestic terms, distinguishing him from all other angels in the book. What remains unclear is whether he appears again, after chapter 10. His mediation of the revelation is complete when he gives the scroll to John (10:10), and there would be no reason to think that he should appear again, if it were not for 22:6-9.

The angel who addresses John in 22:6 is clearly the angel who has shown John the vision of the New Jerusalem (21:9-22:5) and who is described in 21:9 as 'one of the seven angels who had the seven bowls full of the last seven plagues.' This parallels the description of the angel who showed John the vision of Babylon: 'one of the seven angels who had the seven bowls' (17:1). Whether both verses refer to the same angel or to two of the seven angels who had the seven bowls is not made clear. It is immaterial to John's purpose, which is to provide parallel literary introductions to the two visions of Babylon and the New Jerusalem and to tie both closely to the account of the seven bowls in chapter 16, which end with the fall of Babylon. The two visions respectively describe the Babylon which God's final judgment will destroy and the New Jerusalem which will replace her. Not only are the introductions to the two visions (17:1-3; 21:9-10) closely parallel, but so also are the conclusions, in which again the angel who shows John each vision features (19:9-10; 22:6-9). However, as we noticed in a previous chapter,[21] 22:6-9 functions not only as the conclusion to the vision of the New Jerusalem, but also as the beginning of the epilogue to the whole book. This accounts for the clear echo of 1:1 in 22:6 ('the Lord, the God of the spirits of the prophets, has sent his angel to show his servants what must soon take place'), as well as the echo of 1:3 in 22:7. But consequently, in 22:8, 'these things' which John saw are not simply the vision of the New Jerusalem, but the revelation which is the central content of the whole book, and 'the angel who showed them to me' cannot be merely the angel who showed John the vision of the New Jerusalem, even if he were also the angel who showed him the vision of Babylon. The angel of 22:8 must surely be the angel of 1:1, and therefore also the angel of chapter 10. But it is difficult to identify the angel of chapter 10 with one of the seven angels who poured out the seven bowls, described in 15:6 quite differently from the angel of 10:1-2. We must therefore conclude that, despite the parallel with 19:9-10, the angel of 22:8-9 is not the angel who showed John the vision of the New Jerusalem and who addresses John in 22:6. In creating a parallel to 19:9-10, John has deliberately reshaped the material in order to make it a conclusion to the whole of his prophetic revelation. So in 22:6 the angel who has shown John the New Jerusalem speaks of an angel other than himself, the angel of chapter 10. He concludes the vision of the New Jerusalem in terms which also conclude the whole revelation. The 'trustworthy and true' words are those of the whole scroll which had been given to John in chapter 10. By inserting the oracle in which Christ speaks, with its beatitude referring to the whole book (22:7), and then referring to his own reception of the whole revelation (22:8a), John shifts the attention from the angel who speaks in 22:6 to the angel who is spoken of in 22:6. It is this angel, the angel of chapter 10, whom John, having absorbed the whole content of the scroll he received from him, now worships (22:8b), and who now speaks to John (22:9). This reappearance of the angel of chapter 10 in 22:8-9 is very

---

[21]See chapter 1 section 1 above.

important because it enables us to be sure that the contents of the scroll he gives to John in chapter 10 extend a far as 22:5.

3. Eating the scroll (Chapter 10)

Chapter 10, in which the scroll is delivered to John, is carefully placed in the structure of Revelation so that what precedes chapter 10 prepares us to understand the significance of the content of the scroll. We may briefly summarize in four points the way that chapters 4-9 prepare for the contents of the scroll: (1) From the revelation of God's sovereignty in heaven in chapter 4, we know that the scroll will concern the establishment of his kingdom on earth. (2) The Lamb's conquest, which qualifies him to open the scroll, has had the initial result of constituting the Christian church, as a people drawn from all the nations, to be 'a kingdom and priests' (5:9-10). Since the content of the scroll must be the further outworking of the Lamb's conquest, in establishing the kingdom of God, we may guess that the church, as already God's kingdom in a world which contests God's rule, will have some significance for the coming of the kingdom universally. (3) We learn more about the church in chapter 7, which is the interlude that intervenes between the events at the opening of the sixth seal and the opening of the seventh seal. Here the church is depicted, again as drawn from all nations (7:9), but now sharing in the victory of the Lamb through martyrdom.[22] The impression given by chapter 7 is that the church, spiritually preserved from the judgments on the evil world (7:1-3), is delivered from the world through martyrdom. Since chapter 7 is placed at the same point in the series of seal judgments as the section 10:1-11:13 occupies in the series of trumpet judgments, we may expect that there is some relationship between the two passages. The scroll, we may expect, will reveal more fully the significance of the martyrdom to which the church is called. (4) The opening of the scroll is accompanied by two series of judgments on the

[22]See chapter 8 above.

whole world: the judgments of the seals and the trumpets. Both are strictly limited judgments. Those of the seals affect a quarter of the world (6:9), while those of the trumpets affect a third of the world (8:7-12; 9:18). These limited judgments are intended to bring sinful humanity to repentance. This becomes clear in 9:20-21, which indicates that they have failed in this purpose. It is of considerable significance that 9:20-21 immediately precedes the account of the descent of the angel with the opened scroll. That 10:1-11:13, as the interlude between the sixth and seventh trumpets, is to be understood in close connexion with 9:20-21 is indicated by the markers in 9:12 and 11:14, which would be especially important for oral performance of Revelation and serve to bracket the section 10:1-11:13 with 9:13-21, rather than with 11:15-19. The point is that, whereas judgments alone have failed to bring the world to repentance and faith in God, the scroll is to reveal a more effective strategy.

It may be helpful to anticipate what we shall discover in chapters 10-11, as it relates to these four preparatory themes. The church was not redeemed from all nations merely for its own sake, but to witness to all nations. Martyrdom is not simply the church's deliverance from the world, but the culmination of the church's witness to the world. Where judgments alone have failed to bring the nations to repentance, the church's suffering witness, along with judgments, will be effective to this end. Thus God's kingdom will come, not simply by the deliverance of the church and the judgment of the nations, but primarily by the repentance of the nations as a result of the church's witness. The Lamb's conquest, which had the initial effect of redeeming the church from all the nations, has the aim of bringing all the nations to repentance and the worship of God. It achieves this aim as the followers of the Lamb participate in his victory by their suffering witness. This is what the scroll reveals.

However, before the scroll is given to John to eat, its significance is further clarified by 10:3-7. The angel 'gave a great shout, like a lion roaring. And when he shouted, the seven thunders sounded' (10:3). Just as the cries of the four living creatures call forth the riders of the first four seal-openings (6:1-8), so, it seems, the roar of the angel calls forth the seven thunders. They are most naturally understood as a further series of judgments, following those of the seven seal-openings and the seven trumpets.[23] Most probably the idea was suggested by Psalm 29,[24] in which the voice of the Lord, depicted as thunder, is mentioned seven times.[25] The psalm, concerned with God's rule from his throne forever (29:10), is appropriate to Revelation's theme of the establishment of God's kingdom on earth. It is probable that the seven thunders represent a further series of limited, warning judgments, which are revoked. After the judgments of the seal-openings, affecting a quarter of the world, and those of the trumpets, affecting a third of the world, we might expect a series of judgments of even greater severity, affecting half the world.[26] But warning judgments have proved ineffective (9:20-21). There are to be no more series of limited judgments. The next and final series of seven judgments which Revelation depicts are those of the seven bowls (15:1, 5-16:21), which are unlimited in their effect and lead immediately to the final destruction of evil.

John takes the thunders to be a revelation which he should write down as prophecy (10:4). That he does so may be related to the information that the angel's shout was 'like a lion roaring' (10:3). Since there is an undoubted allusion to Amos 3:7 in 10:7, it is likely that this phrase is an allusion to Amos 3:8:

The lion has roared, who will not fear?
The Lord GOD has spoken, who can but prophesy?[27]

---

[23]For discussion of various views of the seven thunders, see Beckwith (1919) 574-575, 577-578.

[24]Kiddle (1940) 169-170; Beasley-Murray (1974) 172. According to Exod. R. 28:6, the voice of God on Mount Sinai was heard as seven thunders (cf. Exod. R. 5:9; b. Shabb. 88b): this may reflect exegesis of Ps 29, which Exod. R. 15:28 understands as referring to seven voices spoken on Sinai.

[25]See Day (1979); Day (1985) 57-60.

[26]Farrer (1964) 125.

[27]Cf. also Hos 11:10; Amos 1:2; Joel 3:16, which would confirm the identification of the lion's roar as the voice of the Lord.

The angel's shout is equivalent to the divine voice of revelation to which the prophet must respond by communicating its message in prophecy. It is important that John responds to the thunders as to a revelation he must write, because this helps to set up a contrast between the seven thunders and the content of the scroll. The seven thunders are not the prophetic revelation given to him to communicate, whereas the content of the scroll is. This contrast is reinforced by the way in which the voice from heaven forbids John to write down the seven thunders: 'Seal up what the seven thunders have said, and do not write it down' (10:4). The idea of sealing is not strictly appropriate here. It should mean that something which has been written is to be kept secret, but instead is used to mean that something should be kept secret by not being written. But the image is used because it makes a contrast between the thunders, which are sealed and so do not become John's prophetic revelation, and the scroll, which has been unsealed so that it may become the content of John's prophecy. The point of the incident of the thunders is to make clear that there are to be no more warning judgments, but *instead* there is to be what the scroll will reveal.

The revocation of the seven thunders is explained by the angel's solemn declaration in 10:5-7. Here we need carefully to observe the allusions both to Daniel 12:6-7 and to Amos 3:7. (Italics indicate allusions to Daniel; underlining indicates allusions to Amos.)

Revelation 10:5-7: Then the angel whom I saw standing on the sea and the land *raised his right hand to heaven and swore by him who lives forever and ever*, who created heaven and what is in it, the land and what is in it, and the sea and what is in it: 'There will be no more delay, but in the days of the sound of the seventh angel, when he is about to blow his trumpet,[28] the mystery of God *will be accomplished*, as he announced to his servants the prophets.

---

[28]This literal translation of the Greek (ἐν ταῖς ἡμέραις τῆς φωνῆς τοῦ ἑβδόμου ἀγγέλου, ὅταν μέλλῃ σαλπίζειν) shows that John avoids saying that there will be no more delay before the seventh angel blows his trumpet. If he had meant that he could have said it more straightforwardly. He leaves room for a period (Daniel's

Daniel 12:6: One of them said to the man clothed in linen, who was upstream, 'How long shall it be until the end of these wonders?' The man clothed in linen, who was upstream, *raised his right hand* and his left hand *toward heaven.* And I heard him *swear by the one who lives forever* that it would be for a time, times and half a time, and that when the shattering of the power of the holy people comes to an end, all these things *would be accomplished.*

Amos 3:7: Surely the Lord GOD does nothing, without revealing <u>his secret</u> (סודו) <u>to his servants the prophets.</u>

The reason why there are to be no more warning judgments is that there is now to be no more delay before the final period of history, Daniel's period of 'a time, times and a half time,' in which the secret purpose (μυστήριον)[29] of God for the coming of his kingdom is to be accomplished. This is the secret purpose which God announced to Daniel and to other prophets of the Old Testament period. But to them it remained mysterious. Daniel did not understand the words of the man clothed in linen (Daniel 12:8) and was told that they were to remain sealed until the time of the end (Daniel 12:9). The full meaning of what Daniel and the other prophets foresaw with regard to the last days of history before the end remained mysterious to them. Only now to John will the scroll of God's purpose for the coming of his kingdom, now unsealed, be given.

Unlike Amos, Revelation does not say that God revealed (נגלה)[30] his secret to his servants the prophets, but that he announced (εὐηγγέλισεν) it. This makes it clear that to the prophets themselves it remained a secret, while also suggesting its character as the good news of the coming of God's kingdom.

three and a half years) which is closely associated with the seventh trumpet, because it is the last period of world history, which leads immediately to the coming of God's kingdom, announced by the seventh trumpet (11:15).

[29] This can be used in Jewish Greek to render both סוד and רז, although the LXX does not use it for the former: see Bockmuehl (1990) 102.

[30] Usually translated by ἀποκαλύπτω.

This is the significance of בשר (translated by εὐαγγελίζομαι in Jewish Greek) in its theologically significant Old Testament occurrences (Isa 40:9; 41:27; 52:7; 61:1; cf. also Ps 40:9 [10]; 68:11; and especially Ps 96:2-3). It is the significance which εὐαγγελίζομαι has in Revelation's only other use of the verb (14:6).

It is quite instructive to compare a passage in the Qumran Habakkuk pesher, commenting on the command to Habakkuk to write down the vision he saw (Hab 2:2):

> God told Habakkuk to write down that which would happen to the final generation, but he did not make known to him when the time would come to an end. And as for that which he said, *That he who reads may read it speedily* [Hab 2:2]: interpreted this concerns the Teacher of Righteousness, to whom God made known all the mysteries (רזי) of the words of his servants the prophets. *For there shall be yet another vision concerning the appointed time. It shall tell of the end and shall not lie* [Hab 2:3a]. Interpreted, this means that the final age shall be prolonged, and shall exceed all that the prophets have said; for the mysteries of God are astounding (1QpHab 7:1-8).[31]

Here there is the idea of something which was hidden from the prophets about the way in which their prophecies would be fulfilled and which has now been revealed to the Teacher of Righteousness (cf. also 1QpHab 2:5-10). Unlike Revelation, however, the secret seems (at least in the immediate context) only to concern the time of the end, which has been delayed longer than the prophets foresaw.[32] Certainly there is a concern

---

[31]Translation from Vermes (1987) 286. See Bockmuehl (1990) 47, for the concepts of mystery and revelation in this passage.

[32]In other respects, John's relation to the Old Testament prophets is not unlike that of the Teacher of Righteousness. This is denied by Schüssler Fiorenza (1985) 136, because she entirely misunderstands and misrepresents Revelation's use of the Old Testament. Certainly, John sees himself as a prophet in the Old Testament tradition of prophecy and receives a revelation given to him as a prophet. But just

with eschatological delay in Revelation 10.[33] Just as Daniel 12:7 answers the question, 'How long?' (12:6), so the angel in Revelation implicitly responds to the question 'How long?' which has been in the reader's mind since it was raised by the martyrs in 6:10. The answer is that there is now to be no more delay before the final period which will bring in the kingdom, the Danielic 'time, times and half a time'. Probably, in chapter 10 we are at John's and his first readers' present:[34] the final period is about to begin in the immediate future. Thus the content of the scroll is 'what must soon take place' (1:1; 22:6). But the scroll will give no more information about the length of the final period than was already given by Daniel. John clearly uses the period of three and a half years indicated by Daniel as a symbolic, not literal, expression for the final period.[35] What the scroll reveals is not further revelation about the time of the end, but further revelation about the nature of the Danielic period, the way in which the events which remained so mysterious in the prophecies of Daniel and the other prophets will contribute to the coming of God's kingdom.

Having digested the scroll, John is given his prophetic commission: 'You must again prophesy about [or: to] many peoples and nations and languages and kings' (10:11). In the first place, this continues the parallel with Ezekiel. After eating the scroll (Ezek 3:3), Ezekiel was given his prophetic commission in these words:

> Son of man, go to the house of Israel and speak my very words to them. For you are not sent to a people of obscure

---

as late Old Testament prophecy already takes up, interprets and develops the authoritative oracles of its predecessors, so John's prophecy gathers up and interprets all the prophecies of the Old Testament prophets which he regarded as relating to the eschatological coming of God's kingdom. Because the Old Testament prophecies are authoritative for him, his fresh revelation cannot be discontinuous with them, but must be closely related to interpretation of them, thereby providing the culmination of the whole prophetic tradition.

[33] See further Bauckham (1980) 29-36.

[34] Caird (1966) 128-129.

[35] Anyone who doubts that all the time-periods in Revelation are symbolic should consider 2:10 and 17:12.

speech and difficult language, but to the house of Israel
— not to many peoples (עמים רבים) of obscure speech and
difficult languages, whose words you cannot understand.
Surely, if I sent you to them, they would listen to you (Ezek
3:4-6).

Unlike Ezekiel, John's prophecy *is* 'to many peoples' — with
the implication, therefore, that they will listen. In fact, of
course, Ezekiel was later commanded quite frequently to
prophesy to various nations (25:2-3; 27:2-3; 28:21-22; 29:2-3;
35:2-3) and their kings (28:2; 29:2-3; 31:2; 32:2). The command
to John (δεῖ σε... προφητεῦσαι ἐπί...) may well reflect the
frequent formula in Ezekiel: הנבה על[36] (which is sometimes
translated 'prophesy against', but cannot consistently be given
this meaning, so that it must mean basically: 'prophesy to,' as
in Ezek 37:4). But the allusion to Ezekiel is combined with one
to Daniel, continuing the combination of Ezekiel and Daniel
that has characterized the whole account of the scroll. Ezekiel's
reference to 'many peoples' (עמים רבים) is expanded by allusion
to Daniel 7:14: 'peoples, nations and languages' (Aramaic:
כל עממיא אמיא ולשניא), to which John adds 'kings'.

The result is a fourfold phrase, one variation of the fourfold
formula he uses seven times in Revelation to refer to all the
nations (5:9; 7:9; 10:11; 11:9; 13:7; 14:6; 17:15). We shall study
the use and variations of this formula in detail in section 10
below. For the moment we note a number of important points
about its form and occurrence in 10:11. In the first place, this
is the only variation of the phrase which uses 'many' (πολλοῖς).
This must be explained from the allusion to Ezekiel 3:6
(whereas Daniel 7:14 has 'all', as also in Dan 3:7, 31 [4:1]; 5:19;
6:25 [26]; Rev 5:9; 7:9; 13:6; 14:6). But 'many' should not be
opposed to 'all' here: John no doubt uses it in the Semitic
manner which contrasts with 'few' rather than with 'all'.
Secondly, this is the only variation of the phrase which uses
'kings' in place of another term (usually φυλή) for the nations
as such. This is explicable on the assumption that in using the

---

[36]LXX: προφητεύω ἐπί.

fourfold formula here, with allusion to Daniel 7:14, John intends to characterize the subject-matter of his prophecy — the contents of the scroll — as that of Daniel 7. Daniel 7 contains the first reference in Daniel to the period of 'a time, times and half a time' (7:25), and puts it in the context of the theme of the coming of God's kingdom (described as the kingdom both of the 'one like a son of man' and of the saints of the Most High). The theme of Daniel 7 is the transfer of sovereignty over 'all peoples, nations and languages' from the world empires, represented as the beasts, to the 'one like a son of man' and the people of the Most High. It is in this way that the phrase is used in Daniel 7:14, which says of the 'one like a son of man' that

> To him was given dominion and glory and kingship,
> that all peoples, nations, and languages should serve him.

Thus John's prophecy — the further explanation of Daniel's prophecy provided by the scroll — is to concern the way this transfer of sovereignty is to occur.

Thirdly, it is important to notice that before 10:11, the fourfold formula had been used to refer, not to the nations themselves for their own sakes, but to the church as drawn from all the nations (5:9; 7:9). 10:11 marks an important transition in the use of the formula. Here and in all its subsequent occurrences (11:9; 13:6; 14:6; 17:15) it refers not to the church, but to the nations themselves. This is not because the church drops out of view as the contents of the scroll are revealed, but because the scroll reveals the role which the church's suffering witness to the nations is to play in the coming of God's universal kingdom. The reason why the church was drawn from all nations (5:9; 7:9) will now be seen to be so that it can bear witness to all nations.

In chapter 11 it will become clear that the role of prophesying to the nations, which 10:11 gives to John, belongs also to the whole church, whose suffering witness to the world is characterized in chapter 11 as prophetic. This makes it difficult – and probably unnecessary – to decide whether προφητεῦσαι ἐπί in 10:11 should be translated 'prophesy to' or 'prophesy about.' John's prophecies from chapter 11 do not take the form of addressing nations and kings directly, as Ezekiel's do (25:2-3 etc.) Thus, 'prophesy about' might be more appropriate. But they concern and serve the church's prophetic witness directly to the nations. John's prophetic commission in 10:11 could be regarded as paradigmatic of the church's.

Finally, the use of 'again' (πάλιν) in 10:1 requires explanation. John has not previously been commanded to prophesy, in so many words, but the command to write the messages to the seven churches (1:19) was implicitly such a command, for the seven messages are certainly prophetic oracles in which the risen Christ speaks through the prophetic Spirit. Thus it is with John's previous prophetic activity in chapters 2-3 that his prophetic activity from 10:11 onwards is compared. The former was to and about the churches, preparing them for the role they are to play in the last days, as the scroll will reveal. The new feature from 10:11 onwards is the concern with the nations and the church's prophetic witness to them.

4. Measuring the sanctuary (11:1-2)

11:1-13 contains the revelation of the scroll *in nuce*. Later chapters of Revelation will greatly expand on it, but the central and essential message of the scroll is given most clearly here. This accounts for its formal distinctiveness, marking it out from the rest of John's visions. The first of its two parts (11:1-2) is highly distinctive in that only here, in the whole book,[37] is John commanded to perform a symbolic prophetic action.[38] This shows that John's fulfilment of his prophetic commission, given in 10:11, now begins. The pattern is again given by

---

[37]With the exception of 10:10.

[38]It is surprising that Aune (1983) does not discuss this passage (merely mentioned: 429 n.96), even though he discusses reports of symbolic actions in the Old Testament prophets (100-101), the Gospels (161-163), Acts (263-264) and Rev 18:21, where the symbolic act (based on Jer 51:63-64) is performed by an angel (284-285). Because he is preoccupied with rather narrowly defined formal features of prophetic speech, he also fails to discuss Rev 11:3-13 as a prophecy.

Ezekiel, whose prophetic commission (Ezek 3) was followed by the first of the symbolic actions in which he acted out his prophetic message (Ezek 4). By following this pattern, John indicates that in 11:1-2 he begins to divulge the contents of the scroll as prophecy. The passage which follows (11:3-13) is also very distinctive, within the whole book, in that it is not a vision or even an interpretation of a vision (as in 17:7-18), but a narrative prophecy (comparable in form with, e.g., Daniel 11). The two passages (11:1-2 and 11:3-13) are linked purely by the time-period, given in different forms in 11:2 and 11:3. This shows that they are both elaborations of the Danielic prophecy of this final period of world history, but they are different, parallel interpretations of it. The time-period links them, but also, by occurring the two different forms, distinguishes them, as also does the quite different imagery used in each.[39]

In 11:1-2 John begins his revelation of the events and significance of the three-and-a-half year period before the end by using symbolism which remains close to the prophecy of Daniel. This passage has never been fully understood because its character as an interpretation of Daniel has not been recognized.[40] John's starting point is the passage to which 10:7 alludes: the answer of the man clothed in linen to the question, 'How long?': 'that it would be for a time, times and half a time, and that when the shattering of the power of the holy people comes to an end, all these things would be accomplished' (Dan 12:7). In order to interpret this, he turns, following common Jewish exegetical practice, to a closely related passage: Daniel 8:13-14. Here again there is a conversation between two human or angelic figures, one of whom asks, 'How long?' and the other of whom replies by giving another version of the standard Danielic time-period (2300 evenings and mornings, i.e. 1150 days). But whereas in Daniel 12:7 the events of the period are described as 'the shattering of the power of the holy people,'

---

[39]Therefore it is in correct to treat 11:1-2 as providing the setting for 11:3-13, as, e.g., Court (1979) 87, does.

[40]Ford (1975) 170, recognizes Dan 8:13-14 as the text most influential on Rev 11:2, but she does not develop this in detail and she does not recognize the allusion to Dan 8:11.

in 8:13b they are described, in rather obscure language, as 'concerning the regular burnt offering, the transgression that makes desolate, and the giving over of the holy place and host to be trampled' (NRSV). It is this verse, along with the clearly closely related 8:11-12, that John has interpreted in Revelation 11:1-2. Unfortunately, Daniel 8:11-12 are probably the most difficult verses in the book of Daniel, and many attempts have been made to correct the Massoretic text,[41] sometimes on the basis of the Greek versions which have significant differences from the extant Hebrew text both in 8:11-12 and in 8:13b. Whether the Greek versions knew a different Hebrew text is debatable, but as far as it is possible to tell the MT represents the text used by John.

John, having been given a measuring rod, is told,

> Rise and measure the sanctuary (ναὸν) of God and the altar and those who worship in it (ἐν αὐτῷ); but throw outside (ἔκβαλε ἔξωθεν) the court which is outside the sanctuary (τὴν αὐλὴν τὴν ἔξωθεν τοῦ ναοῦ) and do not measure it, for it is given over (ἐδόθε) to the nations, and they will trample the holy city for forty-two months (11:1-2).

The sanctuary (ναός) must be the temple building, containing the holy place and the holy of holies. The word was not normally used to include the courts outside the temple building. Therefore 'the court which is outside the sanctuary' (not 'the outer court') does not, as most commentators think,[42] refer to the outermost court of Herod's temple (which is called the court of the Gentiles in modern literature, but was not so called in New Testament times). Nor is it the outer of the two courts of the biblical (Solomon's and Ezekiel's) temples. It must be

---

[41]See especially Montgomery (1929) 335-338; Charles (1929) 1.204-211; Hartman and Di Lella (1978) 222, 225-227; Jeansonne (1988) 87. See also Lacocque (1979) 159, 163-164; Goldingay (1989) 197, who largely accept the MT.

[42]E.g. Swete (1907) 132-133; Beckwith (1919) 599; Charles (1920) 1.277-278; Beasley-Murray (1974) 182.

the court immediately outside the temple building, the innermost of the two courts of the biblical temples or of the several courts of Herod's temple. This court, called in new Testament times the court of the priests, contained the altar of burnt-offering. Therefore the altar to which Revelation 11:1 refers must be the altar of incense, located within the holy place. This is confirmed by the reference to 'those who worship in it,' where ἐν αὐτῷ could perhaps mean 'at the altar,'[43] but most naturally means 'in the sanctuary'. In that case, the altar mentioned between the sanctuary and those who worship in it must be the altar of incense in the holy place. It is true that τὸ θυσιαστήριον, when used without qualification, generally refers to the altar of burnt-offering,[44] but it could be said that John has in fact qualified the term by locating it within the sanctuary. Moreover, he himself uses τὸ θυσιαστήριον without qualification (6:9; 8:3a, 5; 9:13; 14:18; 16:7), as well as with qualification (8:3b; 9:13), to refer to the one altar in the heavenly sanctuary, which corresponds to the altar of incense.[45] Those who worship in the sanctuary must be the priests, who alone could enter the holy place and offer incense on the altar of incense.

Thus it is the sanctuary building, containing the altar of incense and the priests who worshipped there, which John measures, evidently symbolizing its preservation from defilement or destruction by the nations,[46] while the court containing the altar of burnt-offering is given to the nations, who also trample over the whole city of Jerusalem. The most difficult part of the account is the odd expression: καὶ τὴν

[43] Beckwith (1919) 598.

[44] Beckwith (1919) 597; Charles (1920) 1.277.

[45] On this point, see Charles (1920) 1.226-231, against some interpreters who think Revelation refers to two altars in heaven. The heavenly temple has no court outside the sanctuary, where an altar of burnt-offering could be located, and no bloody sacrifices are offered in it.

[46] That the measuring here symbolizes protection is nearly unanimously agreed (one dissenter is Carrington [1931] 182, 185-186). John is most likely dependent on Zech 2:1-2 for the image. Though the measuring there does not strictly signify protection, the idea of protection is prominent in the passage (2:5). Cf. also 1 Enoch 61:1-5. John carefully distinguishes his measuring (11:1) from the angel's measuring of the New Jerusalem (21:15, alluding to Ezek 40:3) by giving himself and the angel different kinds of measuring rod.

αὐλὴν τὴν ἔξωθεν τοῦ ναοῦ ἔκβαλε ἔξωθεν. This curious use of ἔκβαλε has never been explained, because its source in Daniel has not been recognized. The whole phrase is John's translation of the last three words of Daniel 8:11: והשלך מכון מקדשו (literally: 'and the place of his sanctuary was cast down/out'). John has taken the unique phrase מכון מקדשו, which uses the rare (מכון), to mean the court belonging to (i.e. outside) the temple building. שלך would mean 'to cast down, to overthrow' if it referred to the temple itself, but can hardly mean this if, as John supposes, it refers to the court of the temple. However, 'to cast out' (ἐκβάλλω) is an appropriate translation, because John assumes that the reason it has been 'cast out' is that the pagan nations have defiled it. They have removed the burnt offering (Dan 8:11; 11:31; 12:11) and erected the idolatrous 'transgression that makes desolate' (8:13) or 'the abomination that makes desolate' (11:31; 12:11), presumably in place of the altar of burnt-offering. In this sense, idolatrous abominations (שקוץ, as in Dan. 11:31; 12:11) are to be cast away (שלך: Ezek 20:7-8), and in this sense the Lord casts out (שלך) sinners from his presence (2 Kings 13:23; 17:20; 24:20; Jer 7:15; 52:3; Ps 51:13).

Thus John finds no indication in Daniel that the temple building itself is to be given to the Gentiles, but since the daily sacrifices on the altar of burnt-offering are to be abolished (Dan. 8:11; 11:31; 12:11) the court outside the sanctuary must fall into their hands. It is, he says, 'given over' (ἐδόθε) to them. The word is an allusion to Daniel 8:13, which speaks of 'the giving over of both the holy [place] and the host to be trampled' (חת וקדש וצבא מרמס; cf. also 8:12: וצבא תנתן). John also picks up the word 'trampling' (מרמס) from this verse, when he goes on to say that the nations will trample the holy city (cf. Dan 9:24) for the Danielic period of forty-two months (equivalent to the period in Dan 8:14). Perhaps it was the reference to 'the host' (צבא) that caused him to extend the trampling from the temple precincts to the whole city. But certainly also we should see the influence of Zechariah 12:3, which refers to all the nations coming against Jerusalem in the last days. According to the Massoretic text, God 'will make Jerusalem a stone of burden (אבן מעמסה) for all the peoples; all who carry it (כל-עמסיה)

will hurt themselves'. But the Septuagint has: 'I will make Jerusalem a stone trampled (λίθον καταπατούμενον) by all the nations; everyone who tramples it (πᾶς ὁ καταπατῶν αὐτὴν) will utterly mock it.' Clearly, this translates a Hebrew text which had מרמס instead of מעמסה (MT) and כל־רמסיה instead of כל־עמסיה (MT). The occurrence of מרמס in both Daniel 8:13 and Zechariah 12:3, in a similar context of eschatological assault on Jerusalem by pagan powers, would readily associate the two passages in the kind of Jewish exegetical practice that John follows.

The same association of the two passages underlies Luke 21:24: 'Jerusalem will be trampled by the nations, until the times of the nations are fulfilled.' This probably alludes to Daniel 8:13, because of the reference to an allotted time-period (cf. Dan 8:14; 12:7),[47] but it agrees with Revelation 11:2 in referring to 'the nations' (ἔθνη), who are not explicitly the subjects of the trampling in Daniel 8:13, and in making Jerusalem the object of the trampling. These features come from Zechariah 12:3. Whether John knew Luke 21:24 (or Jesus tradition on which it is dependent) is uncertain, but he must certainly have used Daniel 8:13 independently and so it is probable that both passages are indebted to a common exegetical tradition.[48] It is less clear whether 1 Maccabees 3:43, 51; 4:60, which refer only to the trampling of the sanctuary by the nations (though in connexion with the desolation of Jerusalem), are evidence of such a tradition, or only of dependence on Daniel 8:13 (perhaps in connexion with Ps 79:1; Isa 63:18). Psalms of Solomon 2:2, 19; 17:22 (which refer to the trampling of the sanctuary and Jerusalem by the nations) seem to be dependent only on Isaiah 63:18 and Zechariah 12:3, not on Daniel 8:13.

Thus Revelation 11:1-2 results from a quite precise interpretation of Daniel 8:11-14, in connexion with Zechariah 12:3. It is therefore quite unnecessary to suppose, as has often been done, that this passage reproduces an older Jewish

---

[47]Perhaps cf. also Luke 21:24a with Theodotion's version of Dan 8:11a.

[48]The lengthy discussion of the relation of Rev 11:1-2 to Luke 21:24 by Vos (1965) 120-125, is badly marred its failure to recognize the dependence of either passage on Dan 8:13, while Zech 12:3 is quoted (122) only in its MT form.

prophecy, from before A.D. 70, which had not been fulfilled (since in A.D. 70 the sanctuary itself was destroyed by the nations) but which John takes up and uses in a new sense.[49] He may indeed be following an existing Jewish exegetical tradition of interpretation of Daniel 8:11-14, but he himself is here interpreting Daniel 8:11-14. He does so in order to introduce the contents of the scroll, since the scroll is to give further light on what had remained mysterious to Daniel about the events of the period to which Daniel 8:11-14 refers.

It is highly unlikely that in Revelation 11:1-2 John intends to speak literally of the temple which had been destroyed in A.D. 70 and the earthly Jerusalem, in which he nowhere else shows any interest. He understands the temple and the city as symbols of the people of God. This was a possible interpretation of Daniel, for John takes Daniel 8:11-13 to refer symbolically to the same events that Daniel 12:7 calls 'the shattering of the power of the holy people' (cf. also Dan. 7:25). This shattering, which is therefore also the trampling of the holy place (Dan 8:13) and city, John, of course, understands as the great persecution of Christians, which chapter 7 has already foreseen. But his interpretation of Daniel 8:11-13 stresses what is no more than implicit in his reading of Daniel: that the sanctuary, with its altar and the priests who worship in it, is preserved from defilement and trampling by the nations. He is distinguishing the inner, hidden reality of the church as a kingdom of priests (cf. 5:10) who worship God in his presence from the outward experience of the church as it is exposed to persecution by the kingdom of the nations.[50] The church will be kept safe in its hidden spiritual reality, while suffering persecution and martyrdom.[51] This is partially a parallel, using different imagery,

---

[49]E.g. Peake (1920) 291-292; Charles (1920) 1.270-271, 273-278; Beasley-Murray (1974) 176-177; Court (1979) 85-87. Against this view, see Caird (1966) 131.

[50]If John had meant to distinguish the faithful people of God from an apostate part of the people of God, which is rejected, or from the unbelieving world, he would surely not have used the term 'holy city', which is used elsewhere in Revelation only to refer to the New Jerusalem.

[51]Caird (1966) 132; Mounce (1977) 219-221.

to the vision of chapter 7, where the servants of God are kept safe by the seal on their foreheads, but suffer martyrdom.[52] The function of 11:1-2 is not to take us far into the newly revealed significance of the events foreseen by Daniel, but more to provide a link between the Danielic prophecy and the passage which follows (11:3-13). This too can be seen, from the time-period (11:3), to be an interpretation of what happens in the three-and-a-half year period predicted by Daniel, but it employs far less Danielic imagery (only 11:7, alluding to Daniel 7:21). This is because it is designed to convey the distinctive new message of the scroll: the divine intention that 'the shattering of the power of the holy people' (Dan. 12:7) will prove salvific for the nations.

5. The two witnesses (11:3-13)

The story of the two witnesses (11:3-13) is a kind of parable. Two individual prophets represent the prophetic witness to which the whole church is called in the final period of world history, the 1260 days (11:3). That they represent the church is shown by the identification of them as 'the two lampstands that stand before the Lord of the earth'[53] (11:4; cf. Zech 4:1-14).[54] Zechariah's seven-branched lampstand is reduced to two lampstands, but we are at the same time reminded of the seven

---

[52]Chapters 12-13 also portray essentially the same point in different imagery when they show the heavenly woman, kept safe in the wilderness for three and a half years (12:6, 14), while 'her children' (12:16) are attacked and defeated by the beast (13:7).

[53]For this expression, see not only Zech 4:14, but also Ps 97:5, where it is associated with God's universal kingdom. We shall see below that the group of psalms 96-100 was important for John's hope of the conversion of the nations.

[54]It is very often supposed that the allusion to Zech 4 identifies the two witnesses, in some sense, with Joshua and Zerubbabel, thus giving them a priestly and a royal role: e.g. Farrer (1964) 133; Caird (1966) 134; Beasley-Murray (1974) 184; Ford (1975) 178; Court (1979) 92-93; Sweet (1979) 185. But this is to presume that John read Zech 4 in the way modern historical exegesis reads it. It is more probable that John did not recognize the two olive trees in Zechariah as Joshua and Zerubbabel, but took the image as purely prophetic of the eschatological future.

lampstands which represent the seven churches (1:12, 20; 2:1), which in retrospect can be seen to be also derived from Zechariah 4. John is nothing if not consistent in his very precise use of imagery. If the seven lampstands are churches, so must be the two lampstands. But it would be better to say that, if the seven lampstands are representative of the whole church, since seven is the number of completeness, the two lampstands stand for the church in its role of witness, according to the well-known biblical requirement that evidence be acceptable only on the testimony of two witnesses (Num 35:30; Deut 17:6; 19:15; cf. Matt 18:16; John 5:31; 8:17; 15:26-27; Acts 5:32; 2 Cor 13:1; Heb 10:28; 1 Tim 5:19). They are not part of the church,[55] but the whole church insofar as it fulfils its role as faithful witness.

The church's role of witness is appropriately portrayed by a story about two prophets. Just as it would be a mistake to take the story literally, so it would also be a mistake to take it in too strictly allegorical a way, as though, for example, the sequence of events in the career of the two witnesses were intended to correspond to a sequence of events in the history of the church. The story is more like a parable, which dramatizes the nature and result of the church's prophetic witness to the nations. Because it is a parable, it can be taken less as a straightforward prediction than as a call to the churches to play the role which God intends for them.

The story serves to show how it is that the prophetic witness of the church in the final period before the end can achieve a result which the prophecy of the past has not achieved: the conversion of the nations to the worship of the one true God. Old Testament prophets had foreseen that all the nations will finally acknowledge God's rule and worship him (allusions to some such prophecies will be made in later parts of Revelation). But their own prophecy had not brought the nations to faith,[56] nor had they foreseen how this would come about: it is the function of the scroll to reveal how it will. Consequently, the

---

[55]Against Caird (1966) 134.
[56]For the exception of Jonah, see n. 65 below.

two prophets in the story are represented both as significantly continuous with the tradition of Old Testament prophecy and as surpassing it in a way that leads to the conversion of the nations. The story provides the revelation of the scroll *in nuce.*

In 11:5-6 it is clear that the Old Testament models for the two prophets are Elijah and Moses.[57] Elijah is the precedent for the first two supernatural powers attributed to the witnesses (11:5-6a). It was Elijah who was well-known for his power to call down fire from heaven to consume his enemies (2 Kings 1:10-14; Sir 48:3; Luke 9:54). The image is changed in 11:5 to indicate that the power is that of the prophets' *word* of prophetic witness (cf. Sir 48:1; Jer 5:14; 4 Ezra 13:10; Rev 1:16; 2:16; 19:15). It was Elijah who prevented rain from falling (1 Kings 17:1). According to 1 Kings 18:1 the drought lasted less than three years, but Jewish tradition put the duration at three years (LivPro 21:5) or three and a half years (Luke 4:25; Jas 5:17). The latter figure may well be influenced by the Danielic apocalyptic period of 'a time, times and half a time'. Certainly, John has it in mind, when he says that the two witnesses can prevent rain from falling 'during the days of their prophesying' (11:6), i.e. during the 1260 days (11:3) or three and a half years of their prophetic ministry. The remaining two powers of the two witnesses are modelled on those of Moses, who turned the waters into blood (Exod 7:14-24) and 'struck the Egyptians with every sort of plague' (1 Sam 4:8). The turning of water into blood was the first of the ten plagues of Egypt, and is no doubt mentioned as representative, while the general expression which follows sums up the other plagues. (In passing, we may also note that the plagues of 11:6 are so selected and described as to affect the world in the same threefold division as was used in 10:1-6: heaven, waters, earth. The plagues testify to the Creator: cf. 10:6.)

This does not mean that the two witnesses *are* Elijah and Moses. The contrary is indicated by the fact that the powers of

---

[57]The notion that Moses and Elijah represent the law and the prophets has no basis in the text. It is valid only insofar as Moses, as the lawgiver, was the first and greatest of the prophets. It is as a prophet that he sets a precedent for the two witnesses.

each of the Old Testament prophets are attributed to both of
the two witnesses, not divided between them (11:5-6).[58] It has
very commonly been thought that Revelation 11 takes up a
Jewish expectation of the eschatological return of two great
prophets of the biblical past. John will certainly have known of
the expectation that Elijah would return before the end to
preach repentance (Mal 4:5-6; Sir 48:10), as the two witnesses
do. But there is no evidence of a tradition of the return of Elijah
and Moses together.[59] The evidence there is suggests that the
return of Enoch and Elijah, as prophets who would expose the
deceits of Antichrist in the last days, was sometimes expected.
If John does allude to this tradition, he has transformed it, not
only by substituting Moses for Enoch, but also by not interpreting
it literally. Of course, the latter would be of a piece with the way
he has treated Daniel's predictions about the temple in 11:1-
2. One more point about possible tradition behind 11:3-13 is
important. There is no good evidence of traditions from
before the time of Revelation in which returning prophets
were expected to suffer martyrdom. Later apocalyptic traditions
which portray Enoch and Elijah returning to earth, preaching
against Antichrist and suffering martyrdom at his hands, all
show the influence of Revelation 11:3-13.[60]

John's choice of Moses and Elijah as the Old Testament
models for his two witnesses is readily intelligible in terms of his
own work, whatever apocalyptic traditions about eschatological
prophets he may or may not have known. Both were great
prophets (often regarded as the greatest of the prophets) who

---

[58]Minear (1965) 96-97; Giblin (1984) 442.

[59]4 Ezra 6:26 (cf. 7:28; 13:52) refers to the appearance of a larger group of all
those who had been assumed to heaven without dying, including Ezra himself
(14:9) and others to whom Jewish tradition attributed this privilege. Moses may be
included, but it is impossible to be sure, since the tradition that Moses did not die
does not seem to have been very widely accepted.

[60]I demonstrated this point in Bauckham (1976). For further discussion, see
also Berger (1976); Seron (1979); Black (1978); Bauckham (1985). LAB 48:1,
which refers to the death of Elijah (here identified with Phinehas), Enoch and
perhaps others, at their eschatological return to earth, is not a reference to
martyrdom (*contra* Zeron), but to the death which all who are living at the end must
die (4 Ezra 7:29).

confronted pagan rulers and pagan religion. In Moses' case, he confronted Pharaoh and Pharaoh's magicians, who were able to imitate some of his miracles, and later Balak and Balaam (cf. 2:14). (It may be significant that the plague which is specified in 11:6 was one of the two plagues of Egypt which Pharaoh's magicians were able to imitate.[61]) In Elijah's case, he confronted Jezebel (cf. 2:20) and the prophets of Baal. Moses' contest with Pharaoh and his magicians and Elijah's with Jezebel and the prophets of Baal were the two great Old Testament contests between the prophets of Yahweh and pagan power and religion, in which Yahweh's power and authority were vindicated against the claims of pagan gods and rulers. The same is to be true of the great eschatological contest between the two witnesses and the beast, though the vindication will take a different form and have greater consequences. The allusions to Moses have the further importance of integrating the story into the theme of the new Exodus which runs through Revelation. The great city is called Egypt, after the nation which oppressed the Israelites at the time of the Exodus and suffered divine judgment, as it is also called Sodom, after the city renowned for its evil from which righteous Lot escaped when it was judged (11:8). Its fate, however, is to be notably different from that of either Egypt or Sodom (11:13). This is one of the deliberate twists in the story where it takes a different turn from its Old Testament precedents.

The power of the two witnesses to call down fire to consume their enemies (11:5) indicates their immunity from attack for as long as — but no longer than — they need to complete their testimony (11:7). The powers of plague (11:6) are their ability to give signs of divine judgment, commensurate with their preaching of repentance, symbolized by the sackcloth they wear (11:3; cf. Jon 3:4-10; Matt 11:21; Luke 4:13). The reader of Revelation knows very well by now (cf. 9:20-21) that judgments alone do not lead to the repentance. The witness of the two witnesses does lead to repentance, though not independently

---

[61]The miracles of the two witnesses in 11:5-6 are implicitly imitated by the false prophet's miracle in 13:3.

of judgments, but in conjunction with them. The point is not simply that judgments are only intelligible as the judgments of God when accompanied by verbal witness to the true God and his righteousness. It is also that judgments alone do not convey God's gracious willingness to forgive those who repent. Precisely the character of judgments as *warnings* to call sinners to repentance cannot be known from the judgments themselves. Severe as the prophetic ministry of the two witnesses seems to be, it is not essentially a message of judgment, but a call to repentance. As a call to repentance it proves effective, where judgments alone failed.

However, it does so only as a result of the martyrdom and vindication of the witnesses. Their perseverance in witness even at the cost of their lives gives power to their witness, though not immediately. At first, the inhabitants of the world can suppose their message to have been refuted by their death and can rejoice at being relieved of the torment of an uncomfortable call to repent (11:9-10). Only when their witness is seen to be vindicated as the truth (11:11-13), do all who recognize this repent.

There should be no doubt that the end of 11:13 (οἱ λοιποὶ ἔμφοβοι ἐγένοντο καὶ ἔδωκαν δόξαν τῷ θεῷ τοῦ οὐρανοῦ) refers to genuine repentance and worship of God by the pagan world which is symbolized by the great city.[62] The expression corresponds closely to the positive response that is invited by the angel in 14:7 (φοβήθητε τὸν θεὸν καὶ δότε αὐτῷ δόξαν), to the response to God which characterizes the worship of all the nations in 15:4 (τίς οὐ μὴ φοβηθῇ ... καὶ δοξάσει τὸ ὄνομα σου), and to the response which the unrepentant fail to give in 16:9 (οὐ μετενόησαν δοῦναι αὐτῷ δόξαν). Moreover: (1) In Revelation, 'fear' frequently has the positive significance of the Old Testament's 'fear of the Lord,' meaning the proper attitude of worshipful reverence towards God (11:18; 14:7; 15:4; 19:5; but otherwise in 1:17; 2:10; 18:10, 15). When it is linked, as here, with giving glory to God, it must have this positive meaning. (2) 'To give glory to God' always in Revelation refers positively to giving God the worship which is due to him

---

[62]On this point, see especially Trites (1977) 169-170; Sweet (1981) 106-109.

(4:9; 14:7; 16:9; 19:7). It is used in the Old Testament in this sense, and can be used in connexion with repentance (Josh 7:19; Jer 13:16; 1 Esd 9:8; cf. 1 Sam 6:5, of the Philistines' worship of the God of Israel; Dan 4:34 LXX, of Nebuchadnezzar)[63] and in contexts which anticipate the universal worship of God (Ps 96:7-8; Isa 24:15-16; 42:12). (3) 'The God of heaven,' used in Revelation only here and in the contrasting context of 16:11, is peculiarly appropriate with reference to the acknowledgement by pagans of the one true God the Creator. In the Old Testament it occurs almost exclusively in non-Israelite contexts (Gen 24:7; Ps 136:26 are the only exceptions). It is used by Jews speaking to non-Jews or when they are among non-Jews at a pagan court, or it is used by non-Jews acknowledging the God of Israel as the universal God (2 Chron 36:23; Ezra 1:2; 5:11-12; 6:9-10; 7:12, 21, 23; Neh 1:4-5; 2:4; Dan 2:18-19, 37, 44; Jon 1:9). This special appropriateness of the term to a non-Jewish context is clear also in later Jewish literature (Judith 5:8; 6:19; 11:17; Jub 12:4; SibOr 3:174, 286; 4:135). Revelation's very restricted use of the term (11:13; 16:11) accords with this usage, and should make it quite clear that the city of 11:13 is not Jerusalem, and those who are brought to worship the true God are not Jews but pagans.[64]

In 11:13 we see that what judgments alone failed to effect (9:20-21), the witness of the two witnesses does effect. There is a deliberate contrast. After the judgments of the trumpets, 'the rest' (οἱ λοιποί) do not repent (9:20); after the earthquake which accompanies the vindication of the witnesses, 'the rest' (οἱ λοιποί) do repent (11:13). But this remarkable result of the witness of the two witnesses also transcends their Old Testament models. Here it is important to notice that it is with their martyrdom (11:7) that the two witnesses move beyond the prophetic precedents set by Moses and Elijah. Although Jewish tradition had tended increasingly to see the prophets in general as martyrs, this was never the case with Moses or Elijah. Elijah had not even died, and some Jewish traditions affirmed

---

[63]For some later instances of the association of this expression with repentance and conversion, see Haas (1989) 141.

[64]Against, e.g., Beckwith (1919) 604.

this also of Moses. Thus it would not have been possible to choose Old Testament prophets who more emphatically failed to provide a precedent for 11:7-10. But at the point where Moses and Elijah fail to provide the pattern for the story of the two witnesses, another precedent is introduced: the crucifixion of Jesus (11:8). The parallel continues with the resurrection and ascension of the witnesses after three and a half days (11:9, 11). John has converted the 'third day' of the Gospel tradition into 'three and a half days,' just as the tradition he followed with regard to Elijah's drought converted the 'third year' of 1 Kings 18:1 into 'three and a half years'. The fate of the witnesses is given an apocalyptic period appropriate to the allusion to Daniel 7:21 in 11:7, but the Danielic allusion is interpreted by reference to the history of Jesus which provides the model for his faithful followers. The other important respects in which 11:7-12 differs from the model provided by the death and resurrection of Jesus are those which characterize the death and resurrection of the witnesses as public events, witnessed by all the nations of the world (note the emphasis on the events being *seen*: 11:7, 9, 12). This is because the function of the church's prophetic ministry to the world is to bring into universal effect what Jesus achieved in his own prophetic witness, death and resurrection.

Thus the reason why the prophetic ministry of the two witnesses has an effect unparalleled by their Old Testament precedents lies in their participation in the victory of the Lamb.[65] Jesus himself is the faithful witness (1:5; 3:14) because he maintained his witness even to the point of death, beyond which it was vindicated as true witness in his resurrection. In this way, he won a victory over all evil, which, in 5:6-14, was already depicted as leading to the universal worship of God

---

[65]The closest Old Testament prophecy comes to this effect is in the book of Jonah, where Jonah's preaching secures the repentance of the whole of the 'great city' of Nineveh. If John considered this parallel, he might have seen it as prophetic of the ministry of the witnesses, in the sense that Jonah's three days and nights in the belly of the fish prefigure their death and resurrection after three and a half days, but there are no allusions to Jonah in Rev 11:3-13.

and the Lamb. But the way in which his victory takes effect in bringing the nations to repentance and faith is through his followers' participation in his victory. When they too maintain their witness even to death and are seen to be vindicated as true witnesses, then their witness participates in the power of his witness to convert the nations. The symbolic narrative of 11:11-12 need not mean that the nations have to see the literal resurrection of the Christian martyrs before they are convinced of the truth of their witness.[66] It does mean that they have to perceive the martyrs' participation in Christ's triumph over death.

Not only does their following of the precedent of their crucified Lord take the witnesses beyond the precedent of Moses and Elijah, there are also deliberate indications that from the point of their death onwards a kind of reversal of Old Testament precedent occurs. In the first place, the statement that, after the death of the witnesses, 'all the inhabitants of the earth rejoice over them and make merry and send gifts to each other' (11:10) could hardly fail, for Jewish Christians well acquainted with the celebration of Purim, to recall Esther 9:19, 22. But the reversal of application is striking. In Esther, the people of God, threatened with genocide by the nations of the world,[67] are delivered and kill all those who would have killed them. They celebrate this victory with rejoicing and exchange of gifts. In Revelation 11, the witnesses, representing the people of God, are slaughtered by the beast, and the nations of the world rejoice and exchange gifts. In Esther, the victory of the people of God involves the slaughter of their enemies. In

---

[66]The martyrdom, resurrection and ascension of the two witnesses take place at the end of the three-and-a-half year period in which they bear their testimony. But it is most unlikely that John meant that the church, which they represent, would be immune from persecution for the whole final period of world history and suffer martyrdom only at the very end of this period. The three and a half years are the period of the beast's rule, during which Christians continually suffer martyrdom (cf. 13:5-7). But if witness and martyrdom characterize the whole period, so may the vindication of the martyrs and the conversion of the nations.

[67]Ahasuerus' empire, in Esther, is treated as virtually world-wide, as are the empires of Nebuchadnezzar and Darius in Daniel and the empire of the beast in Revelation.

Revelation, the slaughter of the people of God leads to the conversion of their enemies. It may be that this parallel with Esther is continued in 11:11, in the statement that when the two prophets were raised to life, 'great fear fell on all who saw them'. This Semitic expression (cf. Luke 1:12; Acts 19:17) is relatively common in the Old Testament, but is used especially of the fear (whether described as fear of God or fear of God's people) which was inspired in the pagan nations by God in order to protect his people (Gen 35:5; Deut 11:25; Josh 2:9; 2 Chron 17:10; Judith 14:3). In this sense, it is especially notable in connexion with the Exodus (Exod 15:16; Ps 105:38) and the slaughter of their enemies by the Jews in Esther (8:17; 9:2-3). In Revelation, this fear does not intervene to protect the witnesses from slaughter, but is consequent upon their martyrdom and vindication, and thereby proves salvific for their enemies (11:13).

The second, even more notable reversal of an Old Testament motif, occurs in the symbolic arithmetic of 11:13. Almost all commentators have been able to make nothing of these figures except a misleading attempt to relate them to the supposed population of Jerusalem at the time.[68] Only Giblin has recognized their true significance,[69] which is an allusion to the 'remnant' imagery of Old Testament prophecies of judgment. In such prophecies a small faithful remnant of the people was often expected to be spared judgment and to survive when God's judgment fell on the impenitent majority. Such a remnant is sometimes described as a tenth part (Amos 5:3; cf. Isa 6:13, where in its present context the tenth part is the righteous remnant). The figure of seven thousand alludes more specifically to Elijah's prophetic commission to bring about the judgment of all except the seven thousand faithful Israelites who had not bowed the knee to Baal (1 Kings 19:14-18; cf. Rom 11:2-5).[70] These allusions explain why Revelation rather oddly

---

[68]E.g. Charles (1920) 1.291. The population of Jerusalem may well have been somewhat more than 70,000 before A.D. 70: cf. Hengel (1989) 67 n. 38. But it is relevant to ask how likely it is, in any case, that John could have made an accurate estimate.

[69]Giblin (1984) 445-446.

[70]Caird (1966) 140, recognizes the allusion, but misunderstands its point.

gives the figures for those who die in the earthquake, rather than for those who survive and are converted (11:13). In a characteristically subtle use of these Old Testament allusions, Revelation reverses the arithmetic. Only a tenth, only seven thousand suffer the judgment, while the remnant (οἱ λοιποί) who are spared are the nine-tenths. Not the faithful minority, but the faithless majority are spared, so that they may come to repentance and faith. Thanks to the witness of the witnesses, the judgment is actually salvific. In this way, Revelation indicates the novelty of the witness of the two witnesses over against the Old Testament prophets. The contrast, of course, is made in symbolic terms, so that it would be quite inappropriate to wonder why the seven thousand could not also have been converted.

Thus, in a story leading to this remarkable climax in 11:13, the essential message of the scroll is explained. Daniel's prophecies of 'the shattering of the power of the holy people' (12:7), the giving over of the holy place to be trampled (8:13; cf. Rev 11:2), and the defeat of the saints by the beast (Dan 7:21; cf. Rev 11:7) are understood as indicating the way in which other Old Testament prophecies of the conversion of all the nations to the worship of the true God are to be fulfilled. The reason why, in the final period of world history, God will not deliver his faithful people by the slaughter of their enemies, as he did in the days of Moses, Elijah and Esther, but instead will allow them to be slaughtered by their enemies, is that this is the way in which the nations will be brought to repentance and faith, and the sovereignty over them transferred from the beast to the kingdom of God. But this is intelligible only as the way in which the followers of the Lamb participate in his victory, won by his faithful witness, death and vindication, and so give that victory universal effect. Therefore this revelation of the role which the church's suffering witness is to play in the conversion of the nations is the content of the scroll which the Lamb's victory qualified him to open.

6. From first fruits to harvest (Chapter 14)

The story of the witnesses (11:3-13), which occurs roughly at the centre of the whole book and is marked out from the rest of the book by its form as a prediction, not a vision, contains the central statement of the message of the unsealed scroll: the way the church's prophetic witness to the point of death is to lead to the conversion of the nations. The rest of Revelation expands on this theme of the church's witness, setting it in a broader context and elaborating on its results.

Chapters 12-14 form a series of visions reaching from the birth of Jesus Christ (12:1-5), or even from the garden of Eden (12:9) in which the conflict between the woman and the serpent began, to the parousia and the judgment (14:14-20). These chapters have important links with 10:1-11:13, which show they are a more elaborate exploration of the message of the scroll. As we have noticed, there is the Danielic time-period, which occurs, in different forms, in 11:2, 3; 12:6, 14; 13:5, indicating that the same events are portrayed from different points of view. Another important link is the threefold division of the world (heaven, earth, sea), which, as we have observed, is prominent in 10:1-6 and 11:6. This threefold division of the world differs from the fourfold division used for the first four trumpet judgments (8:7-12): earth, sea, rivers and springs, heaven. The latter recurs in the first four bowl judgments (16:2-9). But the threefold division characteristic of chapters 10-11 forms the structure of chapters 12-13, where the dragon confronts the woman in heaven (12:1-4), but is thrown down to earth (12:7-9). His fall calls forth the proclamation: 'Rejoice then, you heavens... But woe to the earth and the sea, for the devil has come down to you...' (12:12). This threefold division is maintained as the devil, fallen from heaven, is assisted by the beast that rises out of the sea (13:1) and the beast that rises out of the earth (13:11). This 'satanic trinity' therefore represents the forces of opposition to God which contest his rule as Creator of heaven, earth and sea (10:6) and oppose his witnesses, with their God-given authority over heaven, earth and sea (11:6). In 14:7 the fourfold division of 8:7-12 reappears in anticipation of its use in 16:2-9: this is an example of the literary interlocking by which the sections of the book are bound together. The use of the threefold division of the world in chapters 12-13 links the section comprising chapters 12-14 back to 10:1-11:13, while the use of the fourfold division in 14:7 links the section forwards to chapters 15-16. But the threefold division recurs in the vision of the fall of Babylon (17:1-19:10: as in 12:12, heaven rejoices [18:20] while the people of earth [18:9, 11] and sea [18:17] mourn), in which the theme of the confrontation between the forces of evil and the witnesses of Jesus recurs.

We can begin to see that what chapters 12-14 add to the account in 11:3-13 is primarily a much fuller exposition of the conflict between the forces of evil and the witnessing church, to which 11:7 briefly alludes (cf. the echoes of 11:7 in 13:1, 7, indicating that 13:1-10 amounts to a fuller explanation of 11:7). The church's witness is given a context in the great cosmic conflict for the sovereignty of the world between God and the forces of evil, a conflict which began in the garden of Eden (12:7) and reaches to the parousia and the judgment (14:14-20). The initially rather enigmatic verse 11:7 is placed in the story of the witnesses in order to anticipate the much fuller development of this theme in chapters 12-14. Thus, in 11:3-13, the church's role in the final period of world history is portrayed primarily by means of the image of prophetic witness, with just a hint of an alternative image: that of warfare (11:7). In 11:3-13, the role of the church is that of faithful witness, following Jesus Christ the faithful witness. But in chapters 12-14 the church's role is portrayed primarily by means of the image of warfare with the forces of evil. The church is the army of the Lamb, the messianic conqueror of evil (14:1-5). This allows a much fuller treatment of the world under the dominion of evil within which and against which the church is called to bear witness. It makes it possible to portray the ambiguity of martyrdom as apparently victory for the beast, but actually victory for the martyrs. We have explored this theme of messianic conquest by martyrdom in some detail in our previous chapter, in which we noted that the church is portrayed in 14:1-5 primarily as the messianic army of the Lamb, triumphant over the beast through martyrdom, but that the end of this section fuses the image of an army with those of faithful witness ('in their mouth no lie was found') and sacrifice ('they are without blemish': 14:5).

Our purpose in the present section is to observe how, just as in 11:3-13 the prophetic witness of the church leads to the conversion of the nations, so in chapters 12-14 the victory of the Lamb's army over the beast leads to the conversion of the nations. Since the dominant image in these chapters is that of warfare, the church cannot in these chapters be portrayed as preaching repentance to the nations, as the witnesses do in 11:3-13. Instead, when the forces of evil (chapters 12-13) have been portrayed on one side and, on the other side, the Lamb and his army have been seen, standing to resist and to triumph on mount Zion (14:1-5), the effect of this confrontation on the nations of the world is symbolized by the messages of the three angels (14:6-11) flying in mid-heaven. This means that they fly between heaven, which since the devil's fall is now the uncontested sphere of God's kingdom, and the earth and the sea, where the devil and the beasts rule. The first angel's message (14:7) is a positive invitation to repentance and worship of the one true God, put in terms which recall 11:13. The other two angels reinforce this message by proclaiming the doom of Babylon (14:8) and therefore the judgment of the unrepentant who continue to drink Babylon's wine and worship the beast (14:9-11). The second angel's message concerns the inevitable fall of that system of human evil that opposes God's kingdom; the third angel's message concerns the judgment of individuals who continue to adhere to the system. Together they constitute the negative warning which underlines the positive invitation of the first angel. The three angels together parallel the preaching of the two witnesses, with their call to repentance (11:3), reinforced by warning judgments (11:5).

What has gone unnoticed in all discussion of this passage is a significant Old Testament allusion in 14:6-7. The first angel has 'an eternal gospel to proclaim' (εὐαγγέλιον αἰώνιον εὐαγγελίσαι). This is notable for the use of the 'gospel' terminology which Revelation elsewhere uses only at 10:7, but the unique phrase εὐαγγέλιον αἰώνιον has never been satisfactorily explained. Unusual and difficult phrases in Revelation frequently turn out to be Old Testament allusions (as we have noticed already in this chapter in one case: 11:2). The phrase we are considering in 14:6 is an allusion to Psalm 96:2b:

Proclaim his salvation from day to day!
(בשרו מיום־ליום ישועתו)
(LXX: Ps 95:2b: εὐαγγελίζεσθε ἡμέραν ἐξ ἡμέρας τὸ
σωτήριον αὐτοῦ)

The verb בשר ('to proclaim good news') is the verb normally translated by εὐαγγελίζομαι. The phrase מיום־ליום ('from day to day') John has taken to mean 'at all times', i.e. eternally. This could be justified by the occurrences of the equivalent phrase יום יום in Psalm 61:9(8) and Proverbs 8:30, where it is used in parallel with expressions which mean 'for ever' or 'always' (respectively לעד and בכל־עת). Thus John has translated the whole phrase בשרו מיום־ליום as εὐαγγέλιον αἰώνιον εὐαγγελίσαι.

That Psalm 96 is the source of the phrase in Revelation 14:6 is confirmed when we consider the whole psalm. The words quoted from 96:2b are followed by:

Declare his glory among the nations,
his marvellous works among all peoples.

We recall that the fourfold formula designating all nations, which varies every time it is used in Revelation, occurs in 14:6 in the form: 'every nation and tribe and language and people'. The terms used in Psalm 96:3 ('nations' and 'peoples') are thus placed first and last to include the others ('tribes' is also used in the Psalm: 96:7). Moreover, the content of the angel's proclamation of the gospel in 14:7 can be found entirely in Psalm 96. There is the call to all nations to fear God, to give him glory, and to worship him:

Ascribe to the LORD, O families of the peoples,
Ascribe to the LORD glory and strength.
Give the LORD the glory due to his name...
Worship the LORD in holy splendour;
Tremble before him, all the earth (Ps 96:7-8a, 9).

There is the contrast between the idols of the nations (cf. Rev 14:9) and the Creator God:

For all the gods of the peoples are idols,
but the LORD made the heavens (Ps 96:5).

There is the announcement of his coming judgment:

He will judge the peoples with equity...
... for he is coming,
he is coming to judge the earth.
He will judge the world with righteousness,
and the peoples with his truth (Ps 96:10, 13).

Moreover, although the theme of God's kingdom is not explicit in Revelation 14:6-7, it is, as the dominant theme of Revelation, certainly implicit: it is God's universal rule that all the nations are called to acknowledge in worship. Therefore it is significant that the message Psalm 96 calls on its hearers to proclaim to all the nations is summed up in the words, 'The LORD is king!' (96:10).

The eternal gospel is therefore the call which Psalm 96 itself contains, the call to all nations to worship the one true God who is coming to judge the world and to establish his universal rule. The theology and language of the psalm is closely akin to the universalistic prophecies of Deutero-Isaiah, which, as we shall see later in this chapter, were also important to John's hope of the conversion of the nations. The early Christian use of εὐαγγέλιον and εὐαγγελίζομαι, for the Christian message of the coming of God's kingdom through Jesus Christ, is usually thought to have been based primarily on Deutero-Isaiah's use of בשר. But it is significant that, whereas in Deutero- (and Trito-)Isaiah's use of the term, the announcement of the good news of Yahweh's reign is made to Jerusalem and Judah (Isa 40:9; 41:27; 52:7; 61:1; cf. 60:6), it is Psalm 96 which uses it of the proclamation of Yahweh's rule to all the nations. Therefore it is Psalm 96 which John has used as the source of his account of the gospel as the church is called to proclaim it to all nations in the final period of world history.

Both Psalm 96 and the very closely related Psalm 98 begin: 'O sing to the LORD a new song'. Presumably therefore it is the message of these psalms — God's victory or salvation (ישועה)

which is to be proclaimed to all nations — which forms the content of the new song which the Lamb's army sings in heaven (14:3). This takes us back also to the new song sung in heaven in celebration of the Lamb's conquest (5:9) and to the victory or salvation of the martyrs which they ascribe to God and the Lamb when they celebrate it in heaven (7:10). God's great victory, in Revelation, is that won by the Lamb in order to establish God's universal kingdom. The Lamb's followers participate in his victory by following him in faithful witness and sacrificial death. His victory, continued in theirs, is celebrated in the new song of Psalms 96 and 98. It is the basis on which God's reign is proclaimed to the nations in the eternal gospel, calling them to acknowledge his rule in worshipping him. Thus, whereas in 5:13 universal worship is anticipated as the direct consequence of the victory of the Lamb, by chapter 14, when the contents of the sealed scroll have been revealed, we know that it is to come about through the participation of the Lamb's followers in his faithful witness as far as death, which was the means of his victory. Hence the new song is now connected with the martyrs' victory (14:3) and the call to universal worship (14:6-7) is consequent on their victory.

Finally, we should note that Psalm 96 is the first of a group of psalms (96-100) which are closely related in language and themes. They all celebrate Yahweh's universal lordship and his coming to judge the world, and they all call on the whole world to worship him. By basing his account of the gospel in 14:6-7 on the first of these psalms, John no doubt intended to allude to the whole group. The eternal gospel to which Psalm 96:2 refers is expounded by this whole group of psalms, which repeat the same themes as Psalm 96. In this way, we can see that John's expectation of the conversion of the nations has one of its Old Testament roots in the remarkably universalistic theology of these psalms. (We shall later notice another allusion to them in Rev 15:4).

As an *invitation* to the nations to worship God, 14:6-7 parallels the witness of the two witnesses, but it does not provide a parallel to the actual effect of the witnesses' witness and vindication in 11:13: the conversion of the nations. For that we must consider another image in chapter 14: the vision of the harvest (14:14-16).

The harvest was a traditional image of the eschatological consummation, but John uniquely presents it in two forms: the grain harvest, called 'the harvest of the earth' (14:14-16) and the grape harvest, called 'the vintage of the earth' (14:7-20). The two images are based on Joel 3:13 (Heb 4:13):

Put in the sickle, for the harvest (קָצִיר) is ripe.
Go in, tread, for the wine press is full.
The vats overflow, for their wickedness is great.

To modern scholars it seems clear that this whole verse refers to the grape harvest, which Joel uses as an image of judgment on the wicked nations (cf. 3:11-12). But John found two images in it: the grain harvest in the first line, the grape harvest in the second. This was no doubt because the word קָצִיר is normally used of the grain harvest (while בָּצִיר is the vintage). He was not the first reader of Joel in New Testament times to find a reference to the grain harvest in these words, as the allusion to them in Mark 4:29 shows.[71] The question which arises, however, is whether, in developing two different images of eschatological harvest from Joel 3:13, John intended them to be alternative images of the same reality, or images of two different aspects of the eschatological consummation. Interpreters of Revelation seem to have found no firm basis for answering this question. But they have neglected important evidence which will decide the matter without difficulty.

The image of treading the grapes in the winepress is a natural image of judgment, and the end of Joel 3:13 makes quite clear that judgment on sinners is in view. We should need good evidence that John intended this image in another sense. Moreover, 14:19 refers to 'the great wine press of the wrath of God,' thereby alluding also to Isaiah 63:1-6 (cf. also Rev 19:15), which depicts God's wrathful judgment of the nations as the treading of a winepress. But it is also worth noticing that the

---

[71]For the possible influence of Gospel traditions on Rev 14:14-19, see Vos (1965) 144-152.

image of the winepress in 14:19 has a relationship with an image used earlier in this same chapter, so that the readers of chapter 14 are already prepared to recognize 14:17-20 as a negative image of God's judgment on the unrepentant nations. The 'great wine press of the wrath of God' (14:19) echoes both 'the wine of the wrath of her fornication' (τοῦ οἴνου τοῦ θυμοῦ τῆς πορνείας: 14:8), which Babylon has made all nations drink, and also 'the cup of the wine of the wrath of God (τοῦ οἴνου τοῦ θυμοῦ τοῦ θεοῦ) poured undiluted into the cup of his anger' (14:10), which God makes all who worship the beast drink. (θυμός, translated 'wrath' in both these phrases, may mean primarily 'passion' in the first [cf. also 18:3], but is clearly meant to link the two phrases.) Babylon's wine is the corrupting way of life which she offered to the nations and thereby enticed them to worship the beast. God's wine is the judgment this inevitably incurs.[72] In the light of these images, the treading of the winepress can only be the act of God's judgment on the nations.

What has gone largely unnoticed is that, if the image of the vintage has an antecedent image earlier in chapter 14, so does the image of the grain harvest. Of the 144,000 (the church in its victory through martyrdom) it is said that 'they have been ransomed from humanity as first fruits (ἀπαρχή) for God and the Lamb' (14:4). The phrase recalls 5:9, addressed to the Lamb: 'by your blood you ransomed for God [people] from every tribe and language and people and nation'. But now we learn that the followers of the Lamb, ransomed by his sacrifice, are to be themselves a sacrifice. Moreover, they are a specific kind of sacrifice: first fruits. The first fruits were the first sheaf which was taken from the harvest before the rest was reaped, and which was then offered to God as a sacrifice (Lev 23:9-14). The connection between the first fruits of 14:4 and the reaping of the whole harvest in 14:14-16 would be obvious to any Jew, who was unlikely to be able to use the image of the first fruits without implying a full harvest of which the first fruits are the

---

[72]In arguing that Babylon's wine and the wine of God's wrath are also the blood of the martyrs (cf. 17:6), Caird (1966) 192-193, muddles John's metaphors.

token and pledge (cf. Rom 8:23; 11:16; 16:5; 1 Cor 15:20, 23; 16:15).[73] Thus the martyrs, redeemed *from* all the nations, are offered to God as the first fruits of the harvest *of* all the nations, whose reaping is depicted in 14:14-16.[74] This must mean that the image of the grain harvest is not an image of judgment, but an image of the gathering of the converted nations into the kingdom of God. It is the positive image which complements the negative image of the vintage.

It is true that firstfruits of grapes were offered (Exod 22:29), as well as of grain, but it would hardly be possible to see the martyrs as the first fruits of the judgment of the nations, which the vintage symbolizes. But this implication may in any case be avoided by an allusion to Leviticus 23:10 in the vision of the grain harvest. That verse, clearly referring to the grain harvest, commands the Israelites:

When you enter the land (הארץ) that I am giving you and you reap its harvest (וקצרתם את־קצירה), you shall bring the sheaf of the first fruits of your harvest to the priest.

The reference to reaping 'its [i.e. the land's] harvest' seems to be picked up and given a new sense in Revelation 14:15: 'reap... because the harvest of the earth (ὁ θερισμὸς τῆς γῆς) is fully ripe'. If John had in mind in this chapter specifically the law of the offering of the first fruits in Leviticus 23:9-14, then it may not be without significance that the first fruits were to be accompanied by the offering of a lamb without blemish (Lev 23:12; cf. Rev 14:4-5).

[73]For arguments to the contrary, see Beckwith (1919) 649; Charles (1920) 2.6; Prigent (1981) 222. It is true that the firstfruits can signify the holy portion (given to God) of a whole, without implying that the rest will also be given to God (e.g. Jer 2:3), but the full harvest as such is nevertheless implied by this use of the metaphor. Therefore the firstfruits ransomed from the earth (14:3-4) are naturally related to the harvest of the earth (14:15-16). It is also true that in the LXX ἀπαρχή by no means always translates ראשׁית, and can frequently mean no more than 'sacrificial offering'. However, all the New Testament instances show that in *metaphorical* use of ἀπαρχή its meaning is not merely 'offering', but 'firstfruits'.
[74]This is seen by Caird (1966) 180-181, 190-192, who makes the mistake, however, of equating the grain harvest and the vintage. (Cf. also, more hesitantly, Sweet [1979] 230.)

The connexion between the martyrs as first fruits and the harvest as the gathering of the nations into the kingdom of God establishes that it is the faithful witness of the church, maintained as far as death, which leads to the conversion of the nations. But the interpretation of the image of the grain harvest not merely in a positive sense, as the eschatological ingathering of the elect,[75] but in a universal sense, as the gathering of the nations of the earth into the kingdom of God, is confirmed by two features of the account of the harvest itself (14:14-16).

In the first place, although the descriptions of the harvest (14:14-16) and the vintage (14:17-20) are in many respects parallel, there is a major difference between them.[76] The grain harvest takes place in only one action: reaping. The vintage comprises two actions: gathering the grapes into the winepress and treading the winepress. These two actions, we learn later in Revelation, correspond to the gathering of the kings of the earth and their armies to Armageddon (16:12-14) and the judgment of the nations at the parousia (19:15, which echoes 14:19 and reveals the identity of the one who treads the winepress, left enigmatic in 14:20). The account of the grain harvest could have been extended in parallel to the vintage, for reaping was followed by threshing (usually performed by animals trampling the grain) and winnowing (in which the good grain was separated from the chaff, which blew away or was burned). Just as treading the winepress is a natural image of judgment, so are threshing and winnowing. But reaping is not. When the harvest is used as an image of judgment, either threshing is the aspect specified (Jer 51:33; Mic 4:12-13; Hab 3:12; Matt 3:12; Luke 3:17; cf. Rev 11:2)[77] or the wicked are

---

[75]So, e.g., Prigent (1981) 233-234.

[76]It has sometimes been argued that the grain harvest is reaped by Christ ('one like a son of man'), while the vintage is conducted by mere angels: e.g. Milligan (1906) 257-258. But this is a mistake. The angel's gathering of the grapes merely prepares for the treading of the winepress. 14:20 leaves the identity of the one who treads the winepress enigmatic (and with patent allusion to Isa 63:1-6, which also leaves the identity of the one who treads the winepress unexpressed), in order to prepare for the revelation of Christ as the warrior and judge in 19:11-16, where he is identified as the one who treads the winepress (19:15).

[77]4 Ezra 4:30, 32, 39, seem to use 'threshing-floor' as an image both of the punishment of evil and of the reward of goodness.

compared with the chaff blown away by the wind or burned (Pss 1:4; 35:5; Isa 17:13; 29:5; Dan 2:35; Hos 13:3; Matt 3:12; Luke 3:17). Discriminatory judgment could be symbolized by the gathering of the grain into the barns, while the weeds (removed before reaping) or the chaff are burned (Matt 3:12; 13:30; Luke 3:17).[78] Hardly ever is the harvest as such, which would mean primarily the reaping, a negative image of judgment (Hosea 6:11 is perhaps the only biblical instance).[79] With reference to the eschatological consummation, reaping is always a positive image of bringing people into the kingdom (Mark 4:29; John 4:35-38). Modern urban readers, not used to thinking about unmechanized agricultural processes, do not naturally bother to discriminate among biblical harvest images. But ancient readers differed sharply from us in this respect. The actions depicted were very familiar to them. They would immediately notice that Revelation's picture of the grain harvest does not proceed to the processes which symbolized judgment, while that of the vintage does.

Secondly, the single action in the grain harvest is performed by 'one like a son of man' (ὅμοιον υἱὸν ἀνθρώπου) seated on a cloud and wearing a crown (14:14), whereas the two actions of the vintage are performed respectively by an angel (14:19) and one whose identity is not revealed until 19:11-16 depicts him as the divine warrior and judge. The figure who reaps the grain harvest is certainly Jesus Christ (cf. 1:13: ὅμοιον υἱὸν ἀνθρώπου)[80] and so is the one who treads the winepress, but the two images of Christ are deliberately different. The description of the figure on the cloud is a precise allusion to Daniel 7:13-

---

[78]2 Bar 70:2 uses the general image of the harvesting of the products of good and evil seeds.

[79]Hos. 6:11 LXX has τρυγᾶν, presumably translating a text which had בציר instead of קציר (MT). This means that Caird (1966) can correctly say that the LXX never uses θερισμός or θερίζω as an image for destructive judgment. But the Hebrew text of the Old Testament is more relevant to John's usage.

[80]The use of ἄλλος ἄγγελος in 14:15 does not mean that the 'one like a son of man' is also an angel: it refers back to the three angels of 14:6-9 (so van Schaik [1980]).

14,[81] the only verses in Daniel which refer to 'one like a son of man' (כבר אנש). They depict him coming on clouds to God (compare the relation of the cloud to the heavenly temple in Revelation 14:14-15) to receive 'dominion and glory and kingship over all peoples, nations and languages' (7:14; compare the golden crown, symbolizing kingship, which the figure in Revelation 14:14 wears).[82] Daniel 7 does not depict this figure as a judge or as concerned in the destruction of the beast. He simply receives his universal kingdom. This is also what he does in Revelation 14:14-16. He receives into his kingdom the nations which have been won from the beast's dominion for Christ's by the martyrs' conquest of the beast. Unlike the Gospel traditions in which Jesus is called 'the Son of Man' (ὁ υἱὸς τοῦ ἀνθρώπου), John carefully uses the exact phrase from Daniel, 'one like a son of man' (ὅμοιον υἱὸν ἀνθρώπου), and uses it only here and in 1:13. He does not associate Daniel 7:14-15 with Christ's parousia as judge, as some early Christian writers do, but restricts the christological reference of the passage to what it actually says, which closely related to his own interest in Christ's rule over all the nations. In 1:13 Christ is depicted as the one who has authority already over the churches, but as we now know he constituted the churches a kingdom for God only so that they, by their witness in the world, could participate in bringing all the nations into the kingdom of God and his Christ (11:15). He is 'one like a son of man' precisely in relation to the churches *as lampstands* (1:12-13), bearing light for the nations. In 14:14-16 we see Christ's kingdom extended from the church to the nations.

---

[81]Casey (1979) 148-149 denies this and regards the figure as an angel, while on pp. 144-145 he also denies that Rev 1:13 alludes to Dan 7:13, preferring, if anything, an allusion to Dan 10:16, 18. But this is to disregard the precision of John's allusions to the Old Testament text, as well as various contextual factors that point to dependence on Dan 7:13 in Rev 14:14. It may well be that, since most of the description of Christ in 1:13-15 derives from Dan 10:5-6, John associated כדמות בני אדם (Dan 10:16) and כמראה אדם (Dan 10:18) with כבר אנש (Dan 7:13), but it is the last phrase of which he gives a precise literal translation in Rev 1:13; 14:14.

[82]Perhaps cf. Ps 21:3. In a depiction of the parousia partly dependent on Dan 7:13, ApPet 6:2 says that God will place a crown on Christ's head. But here the thought is more of judgment than of rule.

So in 14:14-20 John depicts the outcome of history in two contrasting images—the positive 'harvest of the earth' and the negative 'vintage of the earth'. This is rather different from 11:13, where the story of the church's witness ends with the conversion of all who survive the warning judgments. The difference corresponds to the fact that in chapters 13-14 the power and deception of the beast have been presented and the ambiguity of the conflict between the beast and the martyrs highlighted. It is an open question whether the nations will accept the witness of the martyrs and perceive their death as victory over the beast or whether they will persist in delusion and continue to worship the beast who appears to triumph over the martyrs. The double conclusion to chapter 14 corresponds to the two possibilities opened by the proclamation of the angels (14:6-11). We shall return to this issue after considering the third and final passage in which Revelation depicts the effect of the witness of the martyrs in converting the nations (15:2-4).

7. The song of Moses (15:2-4)

In 11:3-13 the conversion of the nations, as a result of the church's witness, was portrayed under the image of the two prophets. In chapter 14 it was portrayed under the image of the harvest. In 15:2-4 it is the image of the new exodus, one of the dominant symbolic motifs of Revelation, which is used. In 15:2 the martyrs are seen to have come triumphantly out of their conflict with the beast.[83] Their passage through martyrdom to heaven is compared with the passage of the Israelites through the Red Sea, for the sea of glass in heaven (cf. 4:6) is now mingled with the fire of divine judgment (15:2). When they are said to be standing ἐπὶ τὴν θάλασσαν (15:2), there may be a deliberate ambiguity.[84] Since the sea of glass is the floor of

---

[83]This seems to be the sense of the difficult expression: τοὺς νικῶντας ἐκ τοῦ θηρίου. Cf. Beckwith (1919) 674; Charles (1920) 2.33; Caird (1966) 198.

[84]Mealy (1989) 99.

heaven, they stand on it. But the phrase also alludes to the Israelites who, having passed unharmed through the Red Sea, stood beside it and sang the song in which they celebrated Yahweh's great act of deliverance (Exod 15). Like the Israelites, the martyrs in heaven sing 'the song of Moses' (15:3), but it is also 'the song of the Lamb,' because the new exodus is a victory they have won by the blood of the new passover Lamb (cf. 7:14; 12:11).

However, the reference to the song of Moses has caused some difficulty and perplexity, since the words of the martyrs' song are not those of the song sung by Moses and the Israelites in Exodus 15:1-18. Some commentators therefore suggest that the song intended is not that of Exodus 15, but the song of Moses recorded in Deuteronomy 31:30-32:43.[85] But the proposed links with this song of Moses are very tenuous indeed, and cannot count against the allusions to the exodus and the Red Sea, which make it clear that it is the song in Exodus 15 that is intended. Thus, Schüssler Fiorenza sums up the consensus when she writes: 'the song which follows [in Rev 15:3-4] is not connected in any literary way with the song of Moses in Exodus 15 and Deuteronomy 32, but is an amalgam of various OT themes'.[86] But this, as we shall see, is a mistaken verdict. It leaps from the correct observation that none of the words of the song in Revelation 15:3-4 derive from Exodus 15:1-18, to the claim that therefore there is no literary connexion between the two passages. The literary connexion, as we shall see, is made, as it were, beneath the surface of the text by John's expert and subtle use of current Jewish exegetical method. Schüssler Fiorenza is typical of many scholars who, instead of studying John's allusions to the Old Testament in the light of the way the Old Testament was read and used in the learned Jewish exegesis of his time, assume that John 'does not interpret the OT but [merely] uses its words, images, phrases, and patterns as a language arsenal in order to make his own theological statement or express his own prophetic vision.'[87]

[85]E.g. Beckwith (1919) 677; Ford (1975) 247.
[86]Schüssler Fiorenza (1985) 135.
[87]Schüssler Fiorenza (1985) 135.

Nothing could be further from the truth. This failure to recognize that John conveys meaning by means of very precise allusions to the Old Testament is the root of a great deal of contemporary scholarly misunderstanding of his book. Even when it does not lead to misinterpretation, it leads to a shallow form of interpretation, which ignores the remarkable wealth of meaning John has packed into his dense text.

We may first of all observe that the notion of referring to a psalm or hymn to be found in the historical books of the Old Testament and then giving, not the words of the Old Testament text, but a new composition, is not unknown in the Jewish literature of the New Testament period. There is a major example in chapter 32 of the Biblical Antiquities of Pseudo-Philo. The opening words of the chapter reproduce the words which, in Judges 5:1, introduce the song of Deborah, but what follows is not the song of Deborah as given in Judges 5:2-31. It makes only very occasional and brief contact with the words of Judges 5:2-31. It is, in effect, the author's own, new version of the biblical song of Deborah, by which he expresses his own interpretation of the great deliverance of the Israelites from the army of Sisera. Like the biblical version of the song of Deborah, it celebrates that deliverance, but as a new version of the song of Deborah it can provide a fresh interpretation of the significance of that deliverance. Among other things, it presents the deliverance from Sisera as a kind of parallel to the deliverance from Pharaoh at the Red Sea. This makes it an interesting parallel to the way Revelation gives a new version of the song of Moses. The intention is rather similar: John writes a new version of the song of Moses in order to provide an interpretation of the deliverance at the Red Sea and its eschatological antitype. But, as we shall see, his version of the song of Moses is in fact much more closely linked to the text of its biblical precedent, than is Pseudo-Philo's version of the song of Deborah.[88]

---

[88]The version of the song of Hannah in LAB 51:3-6 is also a new version of the song, interpreting it as a prophecy of the ministry of Samuel, but it contains many allusions to the song of Hannah in 1 Sam 2.

An even more pertinent parallel, which John certainly knew well, is in Isaiah 12. The new salvation event of the future, foreseen in the latter part of the chapter 11, is represented there as a new exodus, explicitly compared with the exodus from Egypt (11:15-16). Therefore, on that great day of eschatological salvation, the Israelites will again sing the song they had sung at the Red Sea.[89] But the words of the song (or rather two songs) given in Isaiah 12:1-2, 4-6, are a new version of the song of Exodus 15:1-18. The two opening verses of the song in Exodus 15:1-2 are echoed in Isaiah 12:2b, 5a. But otherwise the words of the two songs of the new exodus are not those of Exodus 15:1-18. However, it should also be noticed that the opening of the second of the two songs (Isa 12:4) correspond *verbatim* to the first verse of Psalm 105. Moreover, there are further allusions to the psalm in 12:5 (זמרו: cf. Ps 105:2; בכל־הארץ: cf. Ps 105:7) and probably in 12:3 (בששון: cf. Ps 105:43).

The reason for the use of Psalm 105 in Isaiah 12 is no doubt partly because it is a psalm that celebrates the exodus, and so can be understood as appropriate to a celebration of the new exodus, along with Exodus 15. But it also has itself verbal links with Exodus 15:1-18, in verses 2 and 5:

> Sing to him (שירו־לו), sing praises to him;
> tell of all his wonderful works (בכל־נפלאות)....
> Remember the wonderful works he has done
> (נפלאותיו אשר־עשה).

The words given in Hebrew correspond to phrases in Exodus 15:1 (אשירה ליהוה) and 15:11 (עשה פלא). Jewish exegesis made much use of the principle that passages in which the same words and phrases occur can be used to interpret each other (roughly the principle known in later rabbinic exegetical terminology as *gezērâ šāwâ*).[90] Such verbal links between Exodus 15 and Psalm 105 can be understood to mean that the latter

---

[89]Cf. Wacholder (1988) 28-29.

[90]For *gezērâ šāwâ* in the Qumran texts, see Slomovic (1969-71) 5-10; Brooke (1985) 166, 320; for *gezērâ šāwâ* in Philo, see Brooke (1985) 22-24.

celebrates the same event of salvation as the former. Therefore, the new version of the Song at the Sea in Isaiah draws on Psalm 105 as well as Exodus 15. It should be noticed that the verbal links between Exodus 15 and Psalm 105 are not visible in the text of Isaiah 12: they occur in parts of the text of Exodus 15 and of Psalm 105 which are not quoted in Isaiah 12. This is a kind of implicit *gezērâ šāwâ* which is not uncommon in Jewish and Jewish Christian literature.[91]

The fact that Isaiah 12 draws on Psalm 105 as well as Exodus 15 has an important effect which is significant for comparison with Revelation 15:3-4. Exodus 15:14-16 says that the news of Yahweh's great act at the Red Sea came to the neighbouring peoples and speaks of its effect on them. This feature of the Song is paralleled in Isaiah 12 by language dependent on Psalm 105: 'make known his deeds among the peoples... let this be known in all the earth' (Isa 12:4-5; cf. Ps 105:1, 7). The result is that the song in Isaiah 12:4-6 is more universalistic in tone and expression than Exodus 15:14-16. God's great act of eschatological salvation for his people is to be made known to all the nations.

Isaiah 12 attests an eschatological interpretation of Exodus 15 which is continued in later Jewish literature.[92] The most notable instance is the interpretation of Exodus 15:17-18 in 4QFlorilegium 1:2-7, where the sanctuary is understood as the eschatological temple to be established in connexion with the eschatological reign of God. A similar eschatological interpretation of Exodus 15:18 may be presupposed by Psalm of Solomon 17:1, 3, 46. The echo of Exodus 15:11 in 1QM 10:8-9 ('O God of Israel, who is like thee in heaven or on earth?') has in view the great eschatological victory of Israel over her enemies, which will be like that at the Red Sea (cf. also 1 QM 13:13). That Revelation 15:3-4 belongs to this tradition of relating the song in Exodus 15 to the new exodus of the future is clear. It is probably significant, in this respect, that the song is there called 'the song of Moses, the servant of God' (15:3).

---

[91]Cf. Bauckham (1990A) 207.

[92]For rabbinic views, see Goldin (1971) 66, 102, 126, 128, 161, 190-191, 205-207.

This alludes to the verse in Exodus immediately preceding the song (15:30: 'the people... believed in the LORD and in his servant Moses'), but it also indicates that Moses was one of God's 'servants the prophets' to whom he announced the mystery of the coming of his kingdom (Rev 10:7).

In John's reading of the song in Exodus 15, the following points are likely to have been of significance:

(1) God's mighty act of judgment on his enemies, which was also the deliverance of his people (Exod 15:1-10, 12).

(2) God's mighty act of judgment demonstrated his incomparable superiority to the pagan gods:

Who is like you, O LORD, among the gods?
Who is like you, majestic in holiness,
awesome in splendour, doing wonders? (Exod 15:11).

(3) God's mighty act of judgment filled the pagan nations with fear (Exod 15:14-16).

(4) It brought his people into his temple (Exod 15:13, 17).

(5) The song concludes: 'The LORD shall reign forever and ever' (Exod 15:18).

The words with which the song ends (5) clearly connect with Revelation's overall theme of the establishment of God's eschatological kingdom, and so they have already been quoted at 11:15. The significance of the new exodus for John is ultimately that it leads to God's eternal kingdom. Point (1) is reflected in the references to God's deeds, ways and judgments in the song of the martyrs (Rev 15:3-4), and point (4) is fulfilled in the presence of the martyrs in the heavenly sanctuary (15:2: implied by the sea of glass, which is before the divine throne, according to 4:6). But it is notable that the deliverance of God's people, though presupposed, is not mentioned in Revelation's version of the song.

Point (2) is plainly relevant to Revelation's concern with demonstrating the incomparability of the one true God against the idolatrous pretensions of the beast. Therefore the words with which the whole world worships the beast in 13:4 are in fact a parody of these words from the song of Moses: 'Who is like the beast, and who can fight against it?' John

understands the new exodus as God's demonstration of his
incomparable deity to the nations, refuting the beast's claim
to deity.[93] Therefore also point (4) falls into place: God
demonstrates his deity so that the nations 'fear God and give
him glory' (14:7). This has become in fact the main point of
the interpretation of the song given by the version in Revelation
15:3-4. In Exodus 15, God's mighty act of judgment and
deliverance inspires terror in the pagan nations. This is
indeed, in the context, a recognition of his incomparable
deity, but its significance remains rather negative. John has
not only given this theme an emphatically universalistic
sense, as in Isaiah 12:4-5. He has also interpreted it in a
strongly positive sense, as referring to the repentance of all
the nations and their acknowledgement and worship of the
one true God.

The way in which he has arrived at this interpretation is by
skilled use of *gezērâ šāwâ*. We have seen that the version of the
song of Moses in Isaiah 12 draws extensively on the words
both of Exodus 15 and also of a passage which could be
associated with Exodus 15 by *gezērâ šāwâ* and so used to
interpret it. John's version of the song of Moses uses hardly
any of the words of Exodus 15 itself, but instead is composed
of allusions to three other Old Testament passages which
are connected with Exodus 15 by *gezērâ šāwâ*.

These passages are connected especially with Exodus 15:11,
evidently a key verse in the song both for John and for other
Jewish exegetes:

Who is like you, O Lᴏʀᴅ, among the gods?
(מי־כמכה באלם יהוה)
Who is like you, majestic in holiness,
awesome in splendour, doing wonders (עשׂה פלא)?

---

[93]Mekilta, Shirta 8, gives one interpretation of 'Who is like you, O LORD,
among the gods?' (Exod 15:11) as 'Who is like you among those who call
themselves divine?' and instances the biblical rulers who claimed divinity: Pharaoh,
Sennacherib, Nebuchadnezzar, and the prince of Tyre. Goldin (1971) 193,
regards this as polemic against the cult of the Roman Emperors.

With this verse John has associated the following two passages (in which the italics indicate the parallels with Exod 15:11, while the underlining indicates the allusions in Rev 15:3-4):

There is none *like you, O LORD* (מאין כמוך יהוה);
> you are great, and your name is great in might.
> <u>Who would not fear you, O King of the nations?</u>
> For that is your due (Jer 10:6-7a).

There is none *like you among the gods*, O Lord,
(אין־כמוך באלהים אדני)
> nor are there any works like yours.
> <u>All the nations</u> you have made <u>shall come</u>,
>> <u>and bow down before you</u>, O Lord,
>> <u>and shall glorify your name</u>.
> For you are great and *do wondrous things* (ועשה נפלאות);
>> <u>you alone are</u> God (Ps 86:8-10).

Not only the passage quoted from Jeremiah 10, but its whole context, makes it peculiarly appropriate to John's allusion to it. The context concerns the vindication of Yahweh as the one true, incomparable God, against the idols of the nations, which, unlike Yahweh, did not make the heavens and the earth (10:11-12). John's allusions to both passages in Revelation 15:3-4 are *verbatim*, with the exception of the last words of Psalm 86:10 ('you alone are God') which appear in Revelation 15:4 as 'you alone are holy' (μόνος ὅσιος).[94] The reason is that, since the psalm has just said that Yahweh is incomparable 'among the gods' (86:8: באלהים), it is odd to say that he alone is 'God' (86:10: אלהים). Therefore, the Septuagint translator rendered the end of 86(87):10: σὺ εἶ ὁ θεός μόνος ὁ μέγας. John solves the problem by translating אלהים here by ὅσιος. He evidently uses this word (here and in 16:5) in an unusual way, to refer to the uniquely divine holiness, the quality that characterizes God

---

[94]The discussion of this phrase by Jörns (1971) 130-131, along with much of his discussion of Revelation's Old Testament allusions, is marred by his unjustified assumption that John used the LXX and his failure even to refer to the Hebrew text of the Old Testament.

as the only true God, whereas ἅγιος refers to a quality that can be shared by God's creatures.

The concluding words of John's version of the song of Moses allude to Psalm 98:2, of which the context is:

> O sing to the LORD (שירו ליהוה) a new song,
>   for he has done wondrous things (ופלאות עשה).
> His *right hand* and his holy arm
>   have gotten him victory.
> The LORD has made known his victory;
>   he has *revealed his righteous acts* (צדקתו) in the sight of the
> nations (Ps 98:1-2).

The Massoretic pointing (צִדְקָתוֹ) gives צדקתו the meaning 'his righteousness' (or 'his vindication') but John has read it as צִדְקֹתָו ('his righteous acts') and translated: τὰ δικαιώματά σου (15:4). The points of contact between these verses of Psalm 98 and Exodus 15 are the Hebrew phrases given above in the first two lines (cf. Exod 15:1, 11) and the reference to Yahweh's right hand in the third line (cf. Exod 15:6, 12). As with the other two passages John has linked with Exodus 15, the links are especially with the key verse 15:11 and its immediate context (15:12). These points of contact would have identified Psalm 98, for John, as the 'new song' which celebrates the great salvation event of the new exodus, connecting it therefore with the 'new song' to which he refers in Revelation 5:9; 14:3, and to the important allusions to Psalm 96 (which begins with the same words) which, as we have seen in the last section, he makes in 14:6-7.

We have accounted for every word in Revelation's version of the song from ὁ βασιλεὺς τῶν ἐθνῶν onwards. The address to God which is in parallel with this phrase is κύριε ὁ θεὸς ὁ παντοκράτωρ, which is Revelation's characteristic term for God in his sovereignty, used seven times (1:8; 4:8; 11:17; 15:3; 16:7; 19:6; 21:22; cf. 16:14; 19:15) and especially in hymnic celebrations of the coming of God's kingdom (4:8; 11:17; 15:3; 16:7; 19:6). Its use here shows that the kingdom of God comes just as much through the worship of the nations as through the judgment of evil. This leaves the two parallel clauses in 15:3:

Μεγάλα καὶ θαυμαστὰ τὰ ἔργα σου... δίκαιοι καὶ ἀληθιναὶ αἱ ὁδοί σου... The first is probably John's paraphrase of the expression עֹשֵׂה פֶלֶא (Exod 15:11) or עֹשֵׂה נִפְלָאוֹת (Ps 86:10; 98:1; 105:5).[95] In this case, the opening words of Revelation's version of the song come close to being an actual allusion to Exodus 15:11. The second clause is probably John's own composition as a parallel to the first, with no specific Old Testament source.[96] δίκαιοι καὶ ἀληθιναὶ is typical of his usage (cf. 16:7; 19:2).

Thus John's version of the song takes as its starting point the key verse Exodus 15:11, which is taken for granted, without being quoted, because it is the common denominator which links the passages to which allusion is made (Jer 10:6-7; Ps 86:8-10; Ps 98:1-2). The controlling motif of this version of the song is therefore the incomparability of God ('Who is like you, O LORD, among the gods?') shown in his wondrous acts of deliverance ('doing wonders': Exod 15:11). By the use of other Old Testament passages which take up these themes, the victory of God, celebrated in the song of Moses, is presented as one which, by demonstrating God to be the one true God, brings all the nations to worship him. Remembering that this version of the song of Moses is sung by the martyrs in their triumph over the beast and that it is also called 'the song of the Lamb,' we can now understand more fully its relation to Revelation 13:4, which parodies the same verse of the song of Moses (Exod 15:11): 'Who is like the beast, and who can fight against it?' In 13:3-4, the worship of the beast, expressed in this acclamation, is the result of the impression made on the inhabitants of the world by the beast's recovery from its mortal wound. This is taken to demonstrate the beast's invincibility. In 15:2-4 we see how this proof of the beast's deity is refuted by the demonstration of the unique deity of the only true God. Just as the mortal wound and recovery of the beast are taken to

[95]Cf. also Mic 7:15, which could be related to the idea of a new exodus.
[96]Cf. Deut 32:4; Ps 145:17; Dan 4:37; LXX Dan 3:27. Ps 145:5-6 could be linked, by *gezērâ šāwâ*, to Exod 15:11, but these verses are too remote from Ps 145:17 to justify regarding the latter as a source for Rev 15:3.

demonstrate his deity, so the death and resurrection of the Lamb, witnessed by the martyrdom and vindication of his followers, demonstrates the deity of the true God. The vindication of the martyrs is the victory of God celebrated in the song of the Lamb, corresponding to the wondrous deeds done by Yahweh at the Red Sea. Just as the latter led to the awed recognition of his deity by the nations who heard of them (Exod 15:14-16), so the former leads to the repentance and worship of all the nations (Rev 15:4). The meaning of 15:2-4 therefore corresponds closely to that of 11:11-13.

Revelation's version of the song of Moses is not, as has usually been thought, a medley of Old Testament phrases with no relation to the song of Moses in Exodus 15. On the contrary, it is a careful interpretation of the song, achieved by skilful use of recognized exegetical methods. The effect is to interpret the song in line with the most universalistic strain in Old Testament hope: the expectation that all the nations will come to acknowledge the God of Israel and worship him. This has a most important bearing on the significance of the whole of the new exodus symbolism which is so prominent throughout Revelation. It shifts the emphasis in the significance of the new exodus, from an event by which God delivers his people by judging their enemies, to an event which brings the nations to acknowledge the true God. In 15:2-4 the martyrs celebrate the victory God has won through their death and vindication, not by praising him for their own deliverance, but by celebrating its effect on the nations, in bringing them to worship God. This gives a fresh significance to the earlier use of new exodus imagery with reference to the Lamb's victory, in which by his death he ransomed a people from all the nations to be a kingdom and priests for God (5:9-10). We now see that this redemption of a special people from all the peoples is not an end in itself, but has a further purpose: to bring all the peoples to acknowledge and worship God. The immediate effect of the Lamb's own victory was that his bloody sacrifice redeemed a people for God. But the intended ultimate effect is that this people's participation in his sacrifice, through martyrdom, wins all the peoples for God. This is how God's universal kingdom comes and the concluding verse of the song of Moses is fulfilled: 'The LORD will reign forever and ever' (Exod 15:18).

8. The New Jerusalem

The section we have just studied, in which the martyrs in heaven sing the song of Moses (15:2-4), is framed by the account of the preparation of the seven angels to pour out the seven last plagues, which complete the wrath of God on the sinful world (15:1, 5-8). The section also has verbal links with this account (15:3: μεγάλα καὶ θαυμαστά; cf. 15:1: μέγα καὶ θαυμαστόν) and also with the account of the seven plagues themselves (15:3: δίκαιαι καὶ ἀληθιναί; cf. 16:7: ἀληθιναί καὶ δίκαιαι). Moreover, the seven plagues are modelled on the plagues of Egypt, which relates them to the same new exodus motif that 15:2-4 employs. This poses the difficult question of the relationship between the song of Moses (15:3-4) and the seven plagues of God's wrath. Are the plagues the 'great and amazing deeds' (15:3) and the 'judgments' of God (15:4) to which the song refers? They certainly do not lead to the worship of God by all the nations which the song proclaims.

This problem cannot be solved by regarding the response of the nations in 15:4 as merely craven fear and enforced worship, an unwilling but unavoidable acknowledgment of God's sovereignty, to which they are reduced by God's final judgments. This would be to ignore the similarity between 15:4 and 11:13; 14:7 in the language used for the nations' response to God. Furthermore, the response of unrepentant sinners to the seven plagues is not craven fear and enforced worship.[97] On the contrary, they curse God. The description of their response in 16:9, 11, 21, is as deliberately antithetical to 15:3, as 11:13; 14:6 are parallel. In the subsequent account of the fall of Babylon, the parousia and the battle of Armageddon (chapters 18-19) there is never any suggestion that those who suffer final judgment finally acknowledge God's rule in enforced worship. Revelation seems to offer only two possibilities for the nations:

[97]E.g. Kiddle (1940) 309.

repentance, fear of God, genuine worship of God (11:13; 14:6; 15:4) or persistence in worshipping the beast, refusal to repent, refusal to worship, cursing of God, final opposition to God's rule, leading to final judgment (14:9-11; 16:9, 11, 21; 17:14; 19:17-21).

These two possibilities, it should be noticed, only emerge with the revelation of the content of the scroll. According to 9:20-21, as a result of the judgments of the seal-openings and the trumpets, the wicked fail to repent. The reaction of the unrepentant to the seven last plagues goes much further than this: they curse God (16:9, 11, 21) and gather for a determined last act of opposition to him (16:13-16; 17:14; 19:19). But the repentant nations worship him (11:13; 15:4). Those who curse God recognize who he is. As the parallel between the description of the Creator (14:7) and the first four of the seven plagues (16:2-11) indicates, the plagues themselves show him to be the Creator and the unrepentant cannot avoid recognizing this. But instead of responding to the invitation to worship the Creator (14:7), they curse him. Moreover, the title 'God of heaven', used only in 11:13 and 16:11, indicates the parallel and contrast between the two verses. In both cases there is recognition of God as the one true God, but whereas in 11:13 this leads to worship, in chapter 16 it leads to cusing.

These are two reactions to the same events: the judgments of God which accompany the church's witness to God and his call to repentance. The judgments of God, if recognized as vindications of the witness of the martyrs, lead to repentance and worship, but those who still refuse to heed this witness take up a position of stubborn opposition to God from which they cannot be converted. Therefore the same judgments, modelled on the plagues of Egypt and culminating in an earthquake, characterize the witness and vindication of the two witnesses (11:6, 13) and the seven last plagues (16:2-21). In the first case, they lead to the worship of God, in the second the response is cursing of God. To highlight this contrast (both to 11:3-13 and to 15:2-4) in people's response to the same judgments is the main purpose of chapter 16. This is why noone is said to die from the plagues of chapter 16, even though it is hard to see how, if we took them literally, some of these plagues would not result in death. The point is the response of those who finally harden themselves against all witness to the truth of God. The result of this hardening is their final assault against God's kingdom, in which they are destroyed so that God's kingdom may come.

The relationship of 15:2-4 to the rest of chapters 15-16 must be the same as that between the two images of the grain harvest (14:14-16) and the vintage (14:17-20). 15:2-4 portrays the conversion of the nations; chapter 16, further elaborated in chapters 17-19, portrays the judgment of the finally unrepentant. Both are portrayed in universal terms. According to the song of the martyrs, 'All nations shall come and worship before you' (15:4), while the birds invited to the great feast at Armageddon are offered 'the flesh of kings, the flesh of captains, the flesh of the mighty, the flesh of horses and their riders — flesh of all, both free and slave, both small and great' (19:18; cf. 6:15; Ezek 39:18, 20; Isa 66:16). This parallels the way the 'harvest of the earth' (14:15) and the 'vintage of the earth' (14:19) are juxtaposed. We do not take the images seriously if we allow either to qualify the other. The picture of universal judgment does not mean that the picture of the universal worship of God is not to be taken fully seriously, nor does the picture of the universal worship of God mean that the picture of universal judgment is not to be taken fully seriously. Because Revelation deals in images, it does not make the kind of statements which have to be logically compatible in order to be valid. Each picture portrays a valid aspect of the truth. The two pictures correspond to the choice presented to the nations by the three messages of the angels, which symbolize the effect of the martyrs' witness, in 14:6-11. It is no part of the purpose of John's prophecy to preempt this choice by predicting the degree of success the witness of the martyrs will have. One thing is certain: God's kingdom will come.

It might be thought that 15:5-19:21, which contains no hint of the conversion of the nations, cannot belong to the revelation of the scroll, whose essential message was summarized in 11:3-13. However, these chapters do portray the consequence of the church's witness. They could not have been written as they are immediately after 9:21. They show how the refusal to heed the church's witness hardens the world's opposition to God into a final climactic attempt to oppose the coming of God's kingdom. They also show how witness to the truth becomes evidence against those who reject it, the evidence which judges them. This is why the martyrs form the Lamb's army (17:14; 19:14) when he wages war with sword of his mouth (19:15), i.e. the evidence of his own faithful witness, continued by his followers, becomes his word of judgment on those who finally reject it.

However, 11:3-13, with its unqualified positive conclusion, gives the positive result of the witness of the martyrs the priority, in God's intention for the coming of his kingdom, over the negative. The theme of the conversion of the nations falls out of view after 15:4, while the visions of final judgment take their course, but it returns to prove its theological priority — and therefore eschatological ultimacy — in the vision of the New Jerusalem. The first part of the words of the heavenly voice (21:3-4), which explains the meaning of the descent of the New Jerusalem to earth in the new creation, is:

Ἰδοὺ ἡ σκηνὴ τοῦ θεοῦ μετὰ τῶν ἀνθρώπων,
καὶ σκηνώσει μετ᾽ αὐτῶν,
καὶ αὐτοὶ λαοὶ αὐτοῦ ἔσονται,
καὶ αὐτὸς ὁ θεὸς μετ᾽ αὐτῶν ἔσται.

Behold, the dwelling of God is with humanity,
and he will dwell with them;
and they will be his peoples,
and God himself will be with them (21:3).

The text given is the most probably original form of the text. The major variant readings (λαός for λαοί and the addition of θεός αὐτῶν after ἔσται) are explicable as attempts to conform the text to the standard Old Testament covenant declarations: 'They shall be my people, and I will be their God' (e.g. Ezek 37:23; Zech 8:8).

In a characteristic use of the Old Testament, Revelation 21:3 combines two sources:

My dwelling place (מִשְׁכָּנִי) shall be with them [Israel];

and I will be their God, and they shall be my people.
Then the nations shall know that I the LORD sanctify Israel,
when my sanctuary is among them forevermore (Ezek
37:27-28).

Sing and rejoice, O daughter of Zion!
For lo, I will come and dwell (וְשָׁכַנְתִּי) in your midst, says the
LORD.
Many nations shall join themselves to the LORD on that
day,
and shall be my people;
and I will dwell (וְשָׁכַנְתִּי) in your midst (Zech 2:10-11a [Heb
14-15a]).

Once again, Revelation takes up the most universalistic form of
the hope of the Old Testament. It will not be Israel alone that
will be God's people with whom he dwells. It will not even be
the eschatological Israel, redeemed from every nation. Rather,
as a result of the witness of the church called from every nation,
all nations will be God's peoples. In his statement of this hope,
John goes further even than Zechariah, who expects many
nations to join the elect people, Israel, as proselytes, thus
becoming 'my people'.[98] In Revelation 21:3, all humanity (τῶν
ἀνθρώπων) becomes God's peoples (λαοὶ αὐτοῦ). Other Old
Testament texts could also have influenced this formulation
(Isa 19:25; 25:6; 56:7; Amos 5:12; Ps 47:8-9; cf. Tob 14:6-7). We
should take τῶν ἀνθρώπων to mean, not just (some) human
beings as opposed to angels or animals, but the human race. It
has the universalistic sense which it commonly has in
Revelation's usage (8:11; 9:6, 10, 15, 18, 20; 13:13; 14:4; 16:8-9,
21; cf. 9:4; 11:13; 16:2).

Thus 21:3 declares all the nations to be God's covenant
peoples. In its combination of the language of God's commitment
to his covenant people with the most universalistic reference to all
humanity, this verse is programmatic for the whole account of the
New Jerusalem that follows. Two strands of language and symbolism
— referring respectively to the covenant people and to the

---

[98]Compare the probable allusion to Zech 2:15 LXX in JosAs 15:7.

312 The Climax of Prophecy

nations — run through the whole account. In the first place, the history of both Israel and the church comes to fulfilment in the New Jerusalem. The names of the twelve tribes of Israel are on its gates (21:12), as in Ezekiel's vision (Ezek 48:30-34), while the names of the twelve apostles are on its foundations (21:14). The structures and dimensions of the city are composed of the numbers symbolic of the people of God: twelve (21:12-14, 16, 19-21; cf. 22:2) and 144 (21:17; cf. 7:4; 14:1). It is, after all, the New *Jerusalem*. On the other hand, the nations walk by the city's light (21:24), the glory and honour of the nations are brought into it (21:26), and the kings of the earth bring their glory into it (21:24). These references to the relationship of nations and kings to the New Jerusalem are based on Isaiah's vision of the New Jerusalem ruling the world (Isa 60:3, 5, 11).

The combination of particularism (reference to the covenant people) and universalism (reference to the nations) in the account of the New Jerusalem could be explained in three ways. In the first place, it has been argued that throughout John intends to refer only to the covenant people redeemed from all the nations (5:9-10). When the rebellious nations have been judged, the covenant people inherit the earth and become the nations and kings of the earth in place of those who once served Babylon and the beast.[99] This explanation fails to take seriously 21:3, in which the overall meaning of the whole account is stated at the outset, as well as the evidence we have studied earlier in Revelation which indicates that the witness of the church is intended to bring about the conversion of the nations. Secondly, it might be thought that the covenant people are the inhabitants of the New Jerusalem itself (22:3b-5), while the nations and their kings live outside it and visit it (21:24-26). On this view, the eschatological blessings are shared with the nations, but the covenant people retain a special privilege. But this view also fails to take seriously the implication of 21:3, which declares all the nations to be covenant peoples. If the nations and the kings of the earth have to enter the city by its gates (21:24-26), so do the Christian martyrs (22:14). The image conveys the full inclusion of the nations in the blessings of the covenant, not their partial exclusion. The third explanation is the most probable: that the deliberate mixing of particular and universal imagery throughout the account is a way of maintaining the perspective given in 21:3. It brings together the Old Testament promises for the destiny of God's own people and the universal hope, also to be found in the Old Testament, that all the nations will become God's people. The history of the covenant people — both of the one nation Israel and of the church which is redeemed from all the nations — will find its eschatological fulfilment in the full inclusion of all the nations in its own covenant privileges and promises.[100]

Having established this general perspective, we now pay closer attention to some of John's Old Testament allusions in 21:24-22:3. 21:24 is a key verse for connecting the universal character of the New Jerusalem with the hope for the conversion of the nations earlier in Revelation. It is closely modelled on Isaiah 60:3:

Nations shall come to your light (והלכו גוים לאורך),
kings to the brightness of your dawn.

In Revelation, this becomes:

καὶ περιπατήσουσιν τὰ ἔθνη διὰ τοῦ φωτὸς αὐτῆς,
καὶ οἱ βασιλεῖς τῆς θέρουσιν τὴν δόξαν αὐτῶν εἰς αὐτήν.

The nations will walk by its light,
and the kings of the earth will bring their glory into it.

All the changes John has made to the text of Isaiah here are significant. In the first place, the indefinite 'nations' and 'kings' of Isaiah have become 'the nations' and 'the kings of

---

[100]This does not, of course, mean that Revelation expects the salvation of each and every human being. From 21:8, 27; 22:15, it is quite clear that unrepentant sinners have no place in the New Jerusalem. Attempts to see Revelation as predicting universal salvation (e.g. Maurice [1861] 400-405; Rissi [1972]) strain the text intolerably.

the earth'.[101] These are the terms John has used throughout Revelation to refer to all the nations and all the rulers of the world, depicted as united under the rule of Babylon and in alliance with the beast in opposition to God. Depicted as belonging to the beast's final resistance to the rule of God, both are destroyed at the parousia (12:5; 19:15, 21). In these references to them as opposing God's rule and therefore perishing under the judgment of his Messiah, allusions to Psalm 2 are dominant (cf. Ps 2:1-2, 9). But, even with reference to this psalm, we should not be too surprised that Revelation can also depict a positive destiny for the nations and even their rulers, converted to the fear and worship of God. Psalm 2:10-12 warns the rulers to submit to God's rule and so avoid judgment, while 2:8 promises the Messiah the nations as his inheritance. Thus John need not have seen this favourite psalm and his allusions to it as inconsistent with the hope that all the nations will worship God (Ps 86:9; Rev 15:4) and even the kings of the earth acknowledge his rule (Isa 49:7, 23; 60:3, 10-11, 16) and that of his Messiah (Ps 89:27; Rev 1:5). The close association of both terms with Babylon in chapters 17-18 (nations: 17:15; 18:3, 23; cf. 14:8; kings of the earth: 17:2, 18; 18:3, 9) is also significant. Babylon's universal dominion is here transferred to the New Jerusalem. This is one of a whole series of parallels and contrasts between the depiction of Babylon and that of the New Jerusalem.[102]

In Revelation's version of the first line of Isaiah 60:3, John seems to have translated והלכו לאורך by περιπατήσουσιν διὰ τοῦ φωτὸς αὐτῆς. This would be a reasonable translation of והלכו באורך, but not of והלכו לאורך. But John has not simply arbitrarily altered his source. He has employed, as often, *gezērâ šāwâ*. He has connected this phrase in Isaiah 60:3 with Isaiah 2:5: 'O house of Jacob, come, let us walk in the light of the LORD (לכו ונלכה באור יהוה).' Although these words are addressed to the house of Jacob, they conclude the vision of the eschatological pilgrimage of all the nations to the house of the Lord on the high mountain (cf. Rev 21:10). The exhortation to the house of Jacob in 2:5 parallels that to the nations in 2:3:

---

[101]Fekkes (1988) 282.
[102]See especially Deutsch (1987).

Come, let us go up (לכו ונעלה) to the mountain of the
LORD, to the house of the God of Jacob;
that he may teach us his ways
and that we may walk (ונלכה) in his paths.

The parallel enables John to apply 2:5 to the nations and to
connect it with Isaiah 60:3. The connexion is the easier because
he has already identified the New Jerusalem's light with the
glory of God (21:23; cf. Isa 60:1). But the result of this exegetical
procedure is significant. It means that John is able to portray
the relation between the nations and the New Jerusalem in a
more religiously significant way than a literal reading of Isaiah
60:3 would suggest. The glory of God as the light of the New
Jerusalem is not just a beacon that attracts the nations to it. It
is the light by which they live. The allusion to the image of the
New Jerusalem's glory in Isaiah 60:1-3 is combined with an
evocation of the theme of Isaiah 2:2-4 (cf. also Isa 51:4): that in
the last days not only Israel, but also all the nations will be
instructed in the will of Yahweh and live according to it.

John eschews the redundancy of synonymous parallelism.
What he says of the kings is drawn from the general sense of
what follows in Isaiah 60, but that chapter does not specifically
refer to anything brought into Jerusalem by the kings. The
reference to the 'glory' of the kings which they bring connects
with the pervasive theme of glory in the whole of the vision of
the New Jerusalem (cf. 21:11, 23, 26). The kings of the earth
offer their own glory to God's glory. In place of their old idolatrous
allegiance to the beast, they now give glory to God (cf. 11:13; 14:7;
15:4). When John goes on to say that 'the glory and honour of the
nations' are brought into the New Jerusalem (21:26), echoing
Isaiah 60:5, 11, he has again deliberately interpreted Isaiah in a
doxological sense.[103] The nations no longer claim glory and
honour independently for themselves, in idolatrous rejection of
the divine rule, but acknowledge that they come from and should
be given back in worship to God, to whom all glory and honour

---

[103]δόξα cannot translate חיל, which refers to the wealth of the nations in Isa 60:5,
11, but the wealth of the nations can also be called their כבוד (Isa 60:13; 61:6; 66:12).

belong. These two terms regularly appear in the doxologies of Revelation (4:11; 5:11, 13; 7:12; cf. 19:1).

John's interpretation of Old Testament prophecy in line with its most universalistic hopes for the inclusion of all the nations in the kingdom of God is further illustrated by the way that, in Revelation 22:2, he has adapted a prophecy which makes no reference to the nations in order to apply it to the nations. The description of the tree of life in 22:2 is based on Ezekiel 47:12, but whereas in Ezekiel the trees bear fruit every month, John has taken this to mean that they bear twelve kinds of fruit, and whereas in Ezekiel the leaves of the trees are simply said to be for healing (cf. also 4 Ezra 7:123), John specifies 'the healing of the nations'. Thus, in line with his purpose in the whole description of the New Jerusalem, he combines an allusion to the covenant people (the number twelve) with reference to the nations.

Finally, the statement which immediately follows in Revelation 22:3 should be closely connected with this healing of the nations by the leaves of the tree of life: 'and there shall no longer be any ban of destruction' (καὶ πᾶν κατάθεμα οὐκ ἔσται ἔτι). κατάθεμα here does not refer to the thing which is cursed (placed under the ban), as most translations have assumed. This would make the statement merely a repetition of the thought of the beginning of 21:27 and hardly appropriate at this point. κατάθεμα is the curse itself,[104] the Old Testament חרם in the sense of the sacred ban placed by Yahweh on enemies of his rule, requiring that they be utterly destroyed. This is the meaning of חרם in Zechariah 14:11, of four words of which John's Greek is a literal translation: וחרם לא יהיה־עוד ('there shall never again be a ban of destruction'). In the context in Zechariah, the reference is to Jerusalem in the eschatological age:

And they shall dwell in it [Jerusalem], and there shall never again be a ban of destruction, and Jerusalem shall dwell in security (Zech 14:11).

---

[104]So, e.g., Beckwith (1919) 766.

John has taken this to mean that the nations who dwell in the New Jerusalem, where they are healed of their idolatry and other sins by the leaves of the tree of life, will never again be subject to the destruction which God decrees for those nations who oppose his rule. This meaning of Revelation 22:3a also provides a good transition to the rest of the verse and the following verses. In the New Jerusalem, the nations will no longer resist God's rule and so there will never again be a ban of destruction. On the contrary, God's throne will be there and they will worship him in his presence and reign with him.

The fact that John has picked this statement out of Zechariah 14:11 as significant enough to include in his account of the New Jerusalem is probably to be explained by its connection with other prophetic passages which John used in his composition. In particular, there is a significant occurrence of חרם in Isaiah 34:1-2:

> Draw near, O nations, to hear;
>   O peoples, give heed!
> Let the earth hear, and all that fills it;
>   the world, and all that comes from it.
> For the LORD is enraged against all the nations.
>   and furious against all their hordes;
> he has doomed them (החרימם), has given them over for
>   slaughter.

This passage, unique in its reference to a ban imposed on all the nations, is followed in 34:5 by a reference to Edom as the people Yahweh has doomed (חרמי) to judgment. Isaiah 34 is a passage to which Revelation makes quite frequent allusion.[105] The imagery with which the day of the Lord is evoked in Revelation 6:13-14a comes from Isaiah 34:4. The oracle against Edom in Isaiah 34:8-17 is a major source for John's oracle against Babylon (Rev 18:2b: Isa. 34:11, 13b-14; Rev 19:3b: Isa 34:9-10a) and also supplies the imagery of the judgment of the worshippers of the beast (Rev 14:10b-11a: Isa 34:9-10a).

---

[105]According to Fekkes (1988) 296, it is one of four Isaianic passages which are especially prominent in Revelation's allusions to Isaiah.

Moreover, there are obvious connexions between Isaiah 34:5-7 and the prophecies in Isaiah 63:1-6 and Ezekiel 39:17-20, which supply important imagery to the picture of the judgment of the nations in Revelation 19:15-18. Clearly John read Isaiah 34 as a key prophecy of the eschatological judgment of all the nations, led in their opposition to God's kingdom by Rome (Edom). He would certainly have noticed the use of חרם in Isaiah 34:2. We should also notice that reference to a ban of destruction decreed by Yahweh against Babylon occurs in the oracle against Babylon in Jeremiah 50-51 (see 50:21, 26; 51:3), which was an even more important source of John's account of the fall of Babylon (Rev 17:1: Jer 51:13; Rev 17:4: Jer 51:7; Rev 18:4: Jer 51:45; Rev 18:5: Jer 51:9; Rev 18:6: Jer 50:15, 29; Rev 18:8: Jer 50:34; Rev 18:20: Jer 51:48; Rev 18:21: Jer 51:63-64). In Revelation 18:2, John depicts (in images from Isa 13:21; 34:11, 13-14; cf. Jer 50:39) the total destruction of Babylon which is the effect of the ban on her.

Thus Revelation 22:3a recalls the judgment of the nations that worshipped the beast and opposed God's kingdom, but declares that, with the coming of God's kingdom, the nations which have been converted to the worship of God and the acknowledgement of his rule need never again fear his judgment. In this way the vision of the New Jerusalem supersedes all the visions of judgment and brings to fulfilment the theme of the conversion of the nations which was set out in 11:13; 14:14-16; 15:4.

9. Testimonia (1:7; 22:16b)

We have seen how prominent the theme of the conversion of the nations is in Revelation, emerging first in chapter 11 and reaching its culmination in the New Jerusalem. But the theme also appears in a particular way in both the prologue (1:1-8) and the epilogue (22:6-21) to the book. In both cases John cites Old Testament prophecies from the *testimonia* tradition which would already have been familiar to his readers. The purpose is to indicate that the conversion of the nations is already part of the church's hope founded on the scriptures. Whereas the revelation of the way this hope is to be realised is novel — the content of the hitherto sealed scroll — the hope itself is not novel.

The traditional *testimonium* in the prologue is 1:7. Comparison with Matthew 24:30 shows this to be traditional:

Ἰδοὺ ἔρχεται μετὰ τῶν νεφελῶν,
καὶ ὄψεται αὐτὸν πᾶς ὀφθαλμὸς καὶ οἵ τινες αὐτὸν
  ἐξεκέντησαν,
καὶ κόψονται ἐπ' αὐτὸν πᾶσαι αἱ φυλαὶ τῆς γῆς
  (Rev 1:7).

καὶ τότε κόψονται πᾶσαι αἱ φυλαὶ τῆς γῆς
καὶ ὄψονται τὸν υἱὸν τοῦ ἀνθρώπου
ἐρχόμενον ἐπὶ τῶν νεφελῶν τοῦ οὐρανοῦ μετὰ δυνάμεως
  καὶ δόξης πολλῆς (Matt 24:30)

These two passages[106] both conflate Daniel 7:13 and Zechariah 12:10, 12, although they do so in different orders, and although Revelation quotes more of Zechariah than Matthew does, while Matthew quotes more of Daniel than Revelation does. Comparison with Zechariah 12:10, 12 LXX, will enable us to see that the agreement between Revelation and Matthew is not coincidental:

...καὶ ἐπιβλέψονται πρός με, ἀνθ' ὧν κατωρχήσαντο·
καὶ κόψονται ἐπ' αὐτὸν κοπετόν...
Καὶ κόψεται ἡ γῆ κατὰ φυλὰς φυλάς...

Revelation and Matthew agree against the Septuagint in the following respects: (1) in translating והביטו as ὄψεται / ὄψονται, while LXX has ἐπιβλέψονται; (2) in the phrase πᾶσαι αἱ φυλαὶ τῆς γῆς.[107] The latter in particular shows that either Revelation must be dependent on Matthew or both must be dependent on

---

[106]See the discussions in Lindars (1961) 122-127; Vos (1965) 60-71; Wilcox (1988) 201-202.

[107]This feature of the texts is oddly neglected by Lindars (1961) 123.

a common tradition of the text. Two considerations make the latter much more probable: (1) Revelation quotes more of Zechariah 12:10 (οἳ τινες αὐτὸν ἐξεκέντησαν... ἐπ' αὐτὸν) than does Matthew. If John referred independently to the Hebrew text of Zechariah, it is hard to see why he should have followed Matthew at all. (2) Revelation is also in striking agreement (against the LXX) with the form of the quotation from Zechariah 12:10 in John 19:37 (ὄψονται εἰς ὃν ἐξεκέντησαν).[108] This indicates that a Greek version of Zechariah 12:10, not dependent on the LXX, was current in early Christian tradition.[109] Since the conflated quotation from Daniel and Zechariah in Revelation 1:7 is a self-contained unit, whereas in Matthew the material is integrated into its context, it is a reasonable conclusion that the *testimonia* tradition included a conflated quotation in a form very similar to that in Revelation 1:7, whereas the quotation has been adapted by Matthew.

The most interesting aspect of this traditional *testimonium* is the concluding clause: καὶ κόψονται ἐπ' αὐτὸν πᾶσαι αἱ φυλαὶ τῆς γῆς. This has resulted, in the first place, from combining וספדו עליו ('they shall mourn for him': Zech 12:10) with וספדה הארץ משפחות משפחות ('the land shall mourn, family by family': Zech 12:12). The eschatological context in both Revelation and Matthew makes it clear that הארץ was taken to mean, not the land of Israel, but the earth, so that the families or tribes of Zechariah 12:12a are all the tribes of the earth. This need not mean that the meaning of the text was intentionally changed or that it was taken out of context, ignoring the rest of verses 12-13, with their references to Israelite families. Early Christian exegetes could have understood verse 12 to begin by referring to all the tribes of the earth, including those of Israel, and then to continue by referring specifically to Israelite

---

[108]ἐξεκέντησαν is used in Aquila's and Theodotion's versions of Zech 12:10.

[109]Lindars (1961) 124, quite plausibly reconstructs a text of Zech 12:10 lying behind Matt 24:30; John 19:37; and Rev 1:7:

καὶ ὄψονται εἰς ὃν ἐξεκέντησαν

καὶ κόψονται ἐπ' αὐτὸν πᾶσαι αἱ φυλαὶ τῆς γῆς.

Both Matthew and Revelation knew this associated with Daniel 7:13.

families as examples. What has gone largely unnoticed[110] in discussion of the early Christian use of this text is that the phrase πᾶσαι αἱ φυλαὶ τῆς γῆς is more than just a free translation of part of Zechariah 12:12. It is also an allusion to the promise to Abraham in Genesis 12:3, that 'in you all the tribes of the earth (כל משפחת האדמה) shall be blessed' (repeated in Gen 28:14). The two texts have been associated by *gezērâ šāwâ:* since האדמה משפחות occurs in both, the promise to Abraham can be used to interpret the prophecy of Zechariah.

This interpretative intrusion of the phrase πᾶσαι αἱ φυλαὶ τῆς γῆς into the text of a quotation from Zechariah has an interesting parallel in the Septuagint of Psalm 71 (72):17b. The Hebrew text says of the king who is the subject of the psalm:

In him all nations will be blessed,
and they will call him blessed.

The Sepuagint has:

καὶ εὐλογηθήσονται ἐν αὐτῷ πᾶσαι αἱ φυλαὶ τῆς γῆς·
πάντα τὰ ἔθνη μακαριοῦσιν αὐτόν.

Here the words ויתברכו בו כל־גוים (Ps 72:17) have been associated with והתברכו בזרעך כל גוים הארץ (Gen 22:18; 26:4) in a messianic interpretation of the psalm, identifying the king in the psalm with the offspring of Abraham to whom the promises referred. Therefore a reference to the more familiar form of the patriarchal promise which referred to כל משפחת האדמה (πᾶσαι αἱ φυλαὶ τῆς γῆς: Gen 12:3; 28:14) has been added to the psalm. It is worth noticing that Justin (*Dial.* 121.1-2) interpreted the psalm messianically and related this verse (in the Septuagint version) both to the patriarchal promise and to Zechariah 12:12. He is likely to be following an exegetical tradition, since his own usual interpretation of Zechariah 12:10, 12 applied it to the Jews in the sense of their repentance when it will be too late, at the parousia (*1 Apol.* 52.12; *Dial.* 14.8; 32.2; 64.7; 118.1; 126.1).[111]

---

[110]An exception is Wilcox (1988) 202.

[111]On these passages, see Skarsaune (1987) 76-78, 154, 280-282 (he thinks the repentance of the Jews is sincere and probably salvific: 281).

Since the phrase πᾶσαι αἱ φυλαὶ τῆς γῆς occurs in both
Matthew and Revelation, it was clearly part of the traditional
form of the conflated quotation from Daniel and Zechariah.
Since it alludes to the promise to Abraham that through him
and his offspring all the nations of the world would be blessed,
it follows that in early Christian use of this *testimonium* κόψονται
must have been understood in a positive sense, referring to
genuine repentance and faith in the crucified Christ. This
must settle the debate over whether κόψονται, in Revelation's
use of the quotation, has a positive sense and expects the
salvation of the nations.[112] John could take for granted his
readers' familiarity with this positive sense of the quotation,
and so could use the quotation to indicate, already in his
prologue, the central theme of his prophecy.

The conflation of Zechariah 12:10, 12 with Daniel 7:13 also
makes the conflated quotation peculiarly apposite to John's
central theme in Revelation. Daniel 7:13-14 portrays not simply
the parousia, but (as we noticed in section 6 with reference to
the allusion in Rev 14:14) the transfer of sovereignty over the
nations of the world to Jesus, the 'one like a son of man,' as the
one who exercises God's rule. The conflated quotation suggests
that the kingdom of God will come, not so much by the
destruction of the nations, as by their repentant
acknowledgement of God's rule over them.

The corresponding indication of this theme in the epilogue
is 22:16b: ἐγώ εἰμι ἡ ῥίζα καὶ ὁ γένος Δαυειδ, ὁ ἀστὴρ ὁ
λαμπρὸς ὁ πρωϊνός. This statement is notable for two reasons.
It is a declaration of his identity by Jesus Christ himself,
comparable only with 1:17-18 and 22:13. It also follows
immediately a statement in which Jesus declares himself to be
the source of the revelation which has been given to John for
the churches (22:16a), in terms which closely relate to those of
the book's title (1:1-2). This would lead us to expect 22:16b to
describe Christ in terms peculiarly appropriate to the central
message of John's prophecy. But commentators do not seem to
have been able to explain the significance of the two

---

[112]Cf. Sweet (1981) 111-112, who suggests a positive sense, but concludes:
'There is no proof that this is how John read Zechariah.'

designations for Christ in 22:16b in a way which explains the importance that seems to be attached to them in the context.

Both designations have occurred in shorter forms elsewhere in Revelation: ἡ ῥίζα Δαυειδ (5:5), τὸν ἀστέρα τὸν πρωϊνόν (2:28). The first alludes to Isaiah 11:10. ῥίζα is used, not to translate גזע or שׁרשׁ in Isaiah 11:1, but to translate שׁרשׁ in Isaiah 11:10. In other words, it is not the root from which the shoot grows, but the root — more appropriately, the shoot — that comes from David. This is made clear by the addition of ὁ γένος in Revelation 22:16. Thus, although the allusion could well be taken to refer to the whole of Isaiah 11:1-10, it is made in such a way as to allude specifically to Isaiah 11:10. This is the more striking, in view of the fact that the closest parallel to the term 'Root of David' is the term 'Branch of David' used in the Qumran literature (צמח דויד: 4QFlor 1:11; 4QPBless 3; 4QpIsaᵃ 7-10:3:22; cf. Isa 4:2; Jer 23:5; 33:15; Zech 3:8; 6:12).

The morning star (ἀστὴρ ὁ πρωϊνός) is generally taken, in both 2:28 and 22:16, to be an allusion to Numbers 24:17, where the star that comes out of Jacob was widely interpreted as a reference to the Davidic Messiah. In that case, Revelation displays an interesting pattern of combined allusions to pairs of prophecies of the Davidic Messiah:

2:26-28	Ps 2:9	+	Num 24:17
5:5	Gen 49:9	+	Isa 11:10
19:15	Ps 2:9	+	Isa 11:4
22:16	Isa 11:10	+	Num 24:17

These four Old Testament passages (counting Isa 11:4 and 11:10 as belonging to the same passage: 11:1-10) are all linked by the catchword שׁבט ('sceptre': Gen 49:10; Num 24:17; Ps 2:9; Isa 11:4), as well as being commonly associated in Jewish messianic expectation.[113] All make reference to destructive judgment on the nations (Gen 49:9;[114] Num 24:17b-19; Ps 2:9;

---

[113]Cf. PsSol 17:24-27; 4QPBless; 1QSb 5:20-29; TJud 24:1-6.
[114]The image of the lion, especially when associated with other biblical references to lions (as in 1QSb 5:29), gives this verse a warlike character: see chapter 6 above.

Isa 11:4b), and it is for the sake of this theme of messianic victory over the nations by war or judgment that allusions to them are made in Revelation 2:26-28; 5:5; 19:15. In 22:16, however, the intention is different.

In the case of the Isaianic allusion, the expanded form of the allusion in 22:16 (by comparison with 5:5) calls attention to Isaiah 11:10 as the verse that is especially in mind: 'On that day the root of Jesse shall stand as a signal to the peoples; the nations shall inquire of [or: seek] him, and his dwelling shall be glorious.' In this verse, the Davidic Messiah acquires a positive significance for the nations. Romans 15:12 shows that it was already, before Revelation, used in early Christianity with reference to the salvation of the Gentiles by Jesus Christ.[115] John could expect his allusion to it in 22:16 to carry this implication. By calling Jesus ἡ ῥίζα καὶ ὁ γένος Δαυείδ, he designates him the Messiah to whom the nations will rally, the Davidic king who will include all the nations in the kingdom of God.

Can the same significance attach to ὁ ἀστὴρ ὁ λαμπρὸς πρωϊνός? Certainly, it is hard to see a positive hope for the nations in Balaam's prophecy (Num 24:17-19). But Numbers 24:17 cannot account for the description of the star as ὁ λαμπρὸς πρωϊνός. There is other evidence that early Christians identified the messianic star of Numbers 24:17 with the morning star (Venus). 2 Peter 1:19 refers to the dawning of the eschatological age and the parousia of Jesus Christ, thus: 'until the day dawns and the morning star rises' (ἕως οὗ ἡμέρα διαυγάσῃ καὶ φωσφόρος ἀνατείλῃ). The first clause here may allude to Song of Songs 2:17; the second probably alludes to Numbers 24:17 (LXX: ἀνατελεῖ ἄστρον ἐξ Ἰαχώβ).[116] A star whose rising accompanies the dawn (the light of the eschatological age succeeding the darkness of this) would be naturally identified as the morning star. But there is probably also a connexion with Isaiah 60:1-3:

Arise, shine; for your light has come,
   and the glory of the LORD has risen (זרח; LXX
ἀνατέταλκεν) upon you.

[115]Cf. Lindars (1961) 202.
[116]Bauckham (1983) 225-226.

For darkness shall cover the earth,
> and thick darkness the peoples;

but the LORD will arise (זרח; LXX φανήσεται) upon
> you, and his glory will appear over you.

Nations shall come to your light,
> and kings to the brightness of your dawn (לנגה זרחך;
> LXX λαμπρότητι) (Isa 60:1-3).

זרח is commonly used of the rising of the sun, and so the image
of Yahweh in his glory rising over Jerusalem is that of the dawn.
But a reference to the morning star could be found in the last
phrase (לנגה זרחך), if it were read as referring not to the
brightness of the sun's rising, but to the brightness of a star that
accompanies the sun's rising. נגה can be used of the brightness
of stars (Joel 2:10; 4[3]:15) and so could designate the morning
star as the brightest of the stars.[117] Moreover, in the Aramaic of
the Targums (Tg Isa 14:12: כוכב נגהא; Tg II Est 2:7: כוכב נוגהא) and
in rabbinic Hebrew it is used (with כוכב expressed or understood)
for Venus, the morning star. It seems quite probable that
Revelation 22:16, alluding to Isaiah 60:3, shows that this usage
was already current in New Testament times.

In calling Jesus ὁ ἀστήρ <u>ὁ λαμπρὸς</u> ὁ πρωϊνός, John in
Revelation 22:16b makes clear that the allusion is principally to
Isaiah 60:3.[118] It is worth noticing that the last two words of
Isaiah 60:3, which are paraphrased by this designation of Jesus,
are precisely those which were omitted from John's adaptation
of Isaiah 60:3 in Revelation 21:24. He has saved them for this
designation of Jesus as the one who draws the nations into the
New Jerusalem.

Thus Revelation 22:16b alludes to two prophetic texts (Isaiah
11:10; 60:3) which, applied to Jesus, portray him as the one to
whom the nations come for salvation. This accounts for the
prominence given to these allusions, as self-designations of

---

[117]Note that הילל, the term used for the morning star in Isa 14:12, seems to mean
'shining one' (from הלל). There the morning star is called 'son of the dawn'
(בן־שחר).

[118]This makes unnecessary the rather speculative suggestion of Moore (1982),
who finds in Rev 22:16 an allusion to pagan worship of Venus.

Jesus, in close connexion with his attesting the revelation to John. As the Saviour of the nations, he has revealed to John the way in which his church in the last days is called to participate in his witness to the nations.

10. The fourfold formula for the nations

There is one very special way in which John makes reference to all the nations of the world. This is the fourfold phrase which occurs seven times in varying forms:

ἐκ πάσης φυλῆς καὶ γλώσσης καὶ λαοῦ καὶ ἔθνους (5:9)
ἐκ παντὸς ἔθνους καὶ φυλῶν καὶ λαῶν καὶ γλωσσῶν (7:9)
ἐπὶ λαοῖς καὶ ἔθνεσιν καὶ γλώσσαις καὶ βασιλεῦσιν
  πολλοῖς (10:11)
ἐκ τῶν λαῶν καὶ φυλῶν καὶ γλωσσῶν ἐθνῶν (11:9)
ἐπὶ πᾶσαν φυλὴν καὶ λαὸν καὶ γλῶσσαν καὶ ἔθνον (13:7)
ἐπὶ πᾶν ἔθνος καὶ φυλὴν καὶ γλῶσσαν καὶ λαὸν (14:6)
λαοὶ καὶ ὄχλοι εἰσὶν καὶ ἔθνη καὶ γλῶσσαι (17:15)

These passages are a remarkable example of the way John's subtle compositional techniques create a store of meaning hidden within his text for the discerning reader to discover. This is no ordinary case of John's tendency to repeat the same phrase in varying forms. Every detail of this formula's use and variation seems to be deliberately designed for a purpose. A detailed study of this formula will reveal how John has embodied his central prophetic conviction about the conversion of the nations in the most meticulous detail of his literary composition.

In a previous chapter[119] we noted these seven passages as an example of John's numerical composition. In Revelation, four is the number of the world, seven is the number of completeness. The sevenfold use of this fourfold phrase indicates that reference is being made to all the nations of the world. In the symbolic world of Revelation, there could hardly be a more emphatic indication of universalism.

[119]Chapter 1 section 3 above.

But there is much more to these passages. We should note initially that the same four nouns (φυλή, γλῶσσα, λαός, ἔθνος) are used in all cases except 10:11 and 17:15, where φυλή is replaced by βασιλεύς and ὄχλος respectively. But the order of the four nouns is never the same, nor is the order in any instance ever the reverse of another, nor is γλῶσσα ever placed first of the four. πᾶς is used only in the four cases where the list begins with φυλή or ἔθνος, not in the three cases where the list begins with λαός. These facts may already indicate that the order of the list is not varied haphazardly, as though all that mattered was that it should never be the same, but is varied according to certain principles of order.

We shall begin to understand the variation of order if we first consider the Old Testament sources of the list, which are two: Genesis 10 and Daniel. In Revelation 5:9-10, where the list first occurs in Revelation, John is interpreting Exodus 19:5-6, the well-known statement of the Sinai covenant constituting Israel God's chosen people. In Revelation this statement is applied to the church as the eschatological people of God, the people of the new Exodus, who have been redeemed by the blood of Christ, the eschatological Passover Lamb. The reference to Exodus 19:6 ('you shall be for me a priestly kingdom') in Revelation 5:10 ('you have made them a kingdom and priests to our God') is clear. Less often noticed is that 5:9 alludes to Exodus 19:5: 'you shall be my treasured possession out of all the peoples'. Instead of taking 'out of all the peoples' (מכל־העמים) to mean that God has chosen one of the peoples, John has taken it to mean that members have been drawn from all nations to constitute the church: 'by your blood you have purchased for God [people] from (ἐκ) every tribe and language and people and nation'. This is a grammatically quite legitimate interpretation of Exodus 19:5, which John must have thought now yielded its full meaning for the first time in the light of the international character of the New Testament people of God.

The Old Testament provides a definitive list of all of the nations of the world in the table of the nations in Genesis 10. The seventy nations listed as descendants of the three sons of Noah represent all the nations of the world, as John, with his penchant for number symbolism, would have been the first to appreciate. After the list of the descendants of each of Noah's sons occurs a refrain (10:5, 20, 31), which in the latter two cases uses the same four nouns in the same order: 'by their families, their languages, their lands, and their nations' (10:31: למשפחתם ללשנתם בארצתם לגויהם : LXX: ἐν ταῖς φυλαῖς αὐτῶν, κατὰ γλώσσας αὐτῶν, ἐν ταῖς χώραις αὐτῶν, καὶ ἐν τοῖς ἔθνεσιν αὐτῶν). This is in fact, the only fourfold phrase used in the Old Testament to describe the nations of the world.[120] John has used it to expand the phrase in Exodus 19:5: 'out of all the peoples'. He has combined the two phrases by substituting Exodus's 'peoples' (rendering עם appropriately by λαός) for Genesis's 'lands,' which must have seemed less appropriate than the other terms for describing the nations as such. The result is John's fourfold phrase in the order in which it is used in Revelation 5:9: ἐκ πάσης φυλῆς καὶ γλώσσης καὶ λαοῦ καὶ ἔθνους.

However, there is a very similar threefold phrase which the book of Daniel uses six times to describe all the nations of the world: 'all peoples, nations and languages' (Dan 3:4, 7, 31 [4:11]; 5:19; 6:25[26]; 7:14; cf. also 3:29).[121] This is always in the same form (Aramaic: כל עממיא אמיא ולשניא), except that 3:4 lacks 'all'. The Septuagint translation of Daniel expands this phrase, on its first occurrence at 3:4, into a fourfold phrase by adding χῶραι (ἔθνη καὶ χῶραι, λαοὶ καὶ γλῶσσαι), thereby producing a list of the same four nouns that are used in the Septuagint of Genesis 10:20, 31. Probably the translator had associated the Danielic phrase with the refrain in Genesis 10. Although it is unlikely that John used the Septuagint of Daniel, he is likely to have made the same association, for the Jewish exegetical technique of relating scriptural passages which contain the same phrases is one which he uses quite frequently. Moreover,

[120] 4 Ezra 3:7 uses a fourfold phrase to describe the descendants of Adam before the Flood: 'nations and tribes, peoples and clans' (*gentes et tribus et populi et cognationes*) (cf. also 3:12). This list may be based on Gen 10:5, 20, 31, but it includes neither 'languages' nor 'lands'.

[121] Judith 3:8 (referring to the worship of Nebuchadnezzar by all nations, languages and tribes: πάντα τὰ ἔθνη καὶ πᾶσαι αἱ γλῶσσαι καὶ πᾶσαι αἱ φυλαί) echoes this Danielic phrase, though it changes the order.

not only is Daniel one of John's major Old Testament sources, but Daniel 7 in particular is foundational for his work. He alludes to almost every part of that chapter at some point in Revelation, demonstrating that a consistent and complete exegesis of Daniel 7 lies behind his work. The threefold list occurs at the climactic point of the vision in Daniel 7:1-14 (before the explanation of the vision in the rest of the chapter). When the human-like figure ('one like a son of man') is presented before the Ancient of Days:

> To him was given dominion and glory and kingship,
> that all peoples, nations and languages should serve him
> (7:14a).

John alludes to Daniel 7:13 at Revelation 1:7, 13; 14:14, and probably to Daniel 7:14b at Revelation 11:15 (cf. also 1:6 with Daniel 7:14a). He must have related his fourfold phrase for the nations to Daniel 7:14a.[122] Moreover, the threefold phrase in Daniel is used to refer to the transfer of sovereignty over the world from the beasts, representing the succession of world empires, to 'one like a son of man,' representing the people of God. Accordingly, in its earlier occurrences in Daniel it describes the dominion of kings Nebuchadnezzar and Darius, who are represented (in a conventional hyperbole) as ruling the whole world. In chapter 3 it is associated with Nebuchadnezzar's attempt to impose the idolatrous worship of the great golden image on all his subject, an episode which must have seemed to John to prefigure the universal worship of the image of the beast.

It is this Danielic usage which most adequately explains the use of the fourfold phrase in Revelation from 10:11 onwards, though the association with Genesis 10 does not thereby become redundant. In the two earlier occurrences (5:9; 7:9) the nations themselves are not directly in view. The reference is rather to the church which is composed of people from all the nations. But from 10:11 onwards the phrase refers to the nations themselves, subject to the universal rule of the beast (13:7) and Babylon

---

[122]Cf. Beale (1984) 234-238.

(17:15). Thus it closely relates, in Revelation as in Daniel, to the issue of the coming of God's kingdom, which will occur when 'the kingdom of the world,' now ruled by the beast, becomes 'the kingdom of our Lord and his Messiah' (11:15). There is a sense, in Revelation as in Daniel, in which this is the kingdom also of God's people (Rev 5:10; 20:4, 6), but John takes the human-like figure of Daniel 7:14 to be Jesus Christ himself (Rev 1:13; 14:14). Thus his use of the fourfold phrase, recalling Daniel 7:14, implicitly indicates the expectation that all the nations, who currently worship the beast, are to serve Jesus Christ. It should be noted that John cannot have thought Daniel 7:14 fulfilled in the redemption of people from all nations in the church (5:9), for in his exegesis of Daniel these are 'the holy ones' whom the horn (Revelation's beast) fights and conquers (Daniel 7:21, to which Revelation 13:7a alludes), while still ruling the nations (13:7b). This persecution is that from which the people drawn from all nations emerge victorious in 7:9. But reading Daniel 7:14 as John must have read it, we are led to expect something more: the transfer of dominion over the nations themselves from the beast to Jesus Christ.[123]

The threefold Danielic phrase explains the precise form which John's fourfold phrase takes in Revelation 10:11: ἐπὶ λαοῖς καὶ ἔθνεσιν καὶ γλώσσαις καὶ βασιλεῦσιν πολλοῖς. The first three nouns here are John's translation of the three Aramaic terms in the same order as they occur in the Danielic phrase. (The Greek translations of Daniel differ in their translations of this phrase: Theodotion uses λαός, φυλή, γλῶσσα in all cases, LXX varies between ἔθνος, φυλή, γλῶσσα and ἔθνος, γλῶσσα, χώρα. But λαός, ἔθνος, γλῶσσα would be good equivalents of the Aramaic words.) In 10:11 John is told the subject of the rest of his prophecy. Hitherto he has not referred to the nations of the world as such, only to the church as drawn from them. From now on the church's witness to the nations and its conflict with the beast who rules the nations become the

---

[123]Cf. perhaps also Isa 66:18: 'I am coming to gather all nations and languages.' This verse is quoted in 2 Clem 17:4 in a way that assimilates it to the Danielic threefold phrase for the nations:Ἔρχομαι συναγαγεῖν πάντα τὰ ἔθνη, φυλὰς καὶ γλώσσας.

subject of John's visions. Therefore it is appropriate that at 10:11 the phrase should be used in its Danielic form. Moreover, since the issue is really that of sovereignty over the nations, John's prophecy is to concern not only the nations, described by the three terms from Daniel, but also 'kings', which form part of the fourfold phrase only in Revelation 10:11. These 'kings', symbolized by the beasts and the horns, feature prominently in Daniel 7 (explicitly at 7:17, 24). 'Many peoples and nations and languages and kings' is a good summary of one aspect of Daniel 7: the universal empires which are to be taken from their tyrannical, pagan rulers and transferred to the dominion of the 'one like a son of man' and the holy ones of the Most High. John's prophecy from 10:11 onwards concerns the way this transfer of sovereignty — the coming of the kingdom of God — is to happen.

The form of the fourfold formula in 10:11 not only coincides with the Danielic form. As we showed in section 3 of this chapter, it also alludes to Ezekiel 3:6: the 'many peoples' to whom Ezekiel was not sent but John is. This explains the unique occurrence of 'many' (πολλοῖς) in this version of the formula.

It is worth noticing that 'the kings of the earth,' who feature prominently in the vision of Babylon and her fall (17:2, 18; 18:3, 9), and the ten kings (17:12-13, 16-17), who derive from Daniel 7:24, are closely associated with the fourfold phrase when it occurs in 17:15. But on this occasion another term, ὄχλος, is substituted for the usual φυλή: λαοὶ καὶ ὄχλοι εἰσὶν καὶ ἔθνη καὶ γλῶσσαι. Here the first two terms are set apart from the latter two. Elsewhere in the vision of Babylon, ἔθνος is used for the nations over which she rules (18:3, 23; cf. 14:8; 16:19), but λαός and ὄχλος are used for the people of God: 'my people' (ὁ λαός μου), who are called to come out of Babylon (18:4), and the 'great multitude' (ὄχλος πολύς), who are the martyred Christians in heaven rejoicing over Babylon's fall (19:1, 6; cf. 7:9). Moreover, when the voice of the great multitude is said to be 'like the sound of many waters' (19:6; cf. 14:2), we are reminded that the fourfold phrase is used in 17:15 to explain the meaning of the 'many waters' (17:2) on which Babylon sits. Thus by placing λαός first in the fourfold formula and uniquely including ὄχλος, John has highlighted, in this form of the fourfold phrase, the contrast between the nations who serve Babylon and the people of God who suffer at her hands (17:6; 18:20, 24).

Just as in 10:11, allusion to the Danielic phrase is combined with allusion to Ezekiel 3:6, continuing the reference to Ezekiel's prophetic commissioning throughout chapter 10, so in 14:6 allusion to the Danielic formula is combined with allusion to Psalm 96:3. As we showed in section 6 of this chapter, 14:6-7 are based on this psalm, which in verse 3 speaks of declaring God's glory and saving activity among 'the nations' (גוים) and 'all the peoples' (כל־העמים). The order of the fourfold formula in 14:6 may be so designed as to place these two terms first and last, thus including the others within those mentioned in this verse of the psalm. (There is also a reference to 'the tribes of the peoples' [משפחות עמים] in Psalm 96:7.)

So far we have explained the order in which the terms in the fourfold formula occur in 5:9 and 10:11, and partially in 17:15 and 14:6. To understand the rationale for the variation in order between all seven of the occurrences of the phrase, we need to compare the order in all seven. If we take the order in 5:9 as normative and therefore number the four nouns in the order in which they occur there (1 = φυλή, 2 = γλῶσσα, 3 = λαός, 4 = ἔθνος), we find the following pattern (X and Y stand for βασιλεύς and ὄχλος in 10:11 and 17:15 respectively):

5:9	ἐκ πάσης	1 2 3 4
7:9	ἐκ παντός	4 1 3 2
10:11	ἐπι	3 4 2 X
11:9	ἐκ	3 1 2 4
13:7	ἐπὶ πᾶσαν	1 3 2 4
14:6	ἐπὶ πᾶν	4 1 2 3
17:15		3 Y 4 2

The four occurrences of the formula which include πᾶς can now be seen to form a carefully structured set of two pairs:

5:9	ἐκ πάσης	1 2 3 4
13:7	ἐπι πᾶσαν	1 2 3 4

7:9	ἐκ παντός	4 1 3 2
14:6	ἐπὶ πᾶν	4 1 2 3

Each pair consists of, firstly, a group drawn from (ἐκ) all the nations (5:9; 7:9), and, secondly, all the nations themselves. In each pair the fourfold phrase begins with the same noun (5:9; 13:7: φυλή; 7:9; 14:6: ἔθνος). Moreover, in each pair the order of the four nouns diverges only by the reversal of two adjacent nouns (the second and third in 5:9; 13:7, the third and fourth in 7:9; 14:6). This pattern relates the two members of each pair closely together. But there is also a correlation between the two pairs, because the order in 7:9 differs from that of 5:9 in the same way that the order of 14:6 differs from that of 13:7.

The close relationship between 5:9 and 13:7 is part of a deliberate pattern of ironic parallels between the Lamb's conquest and the beast's. John sees the Lamb 'as if slaughtered' (5:6: ὡς ἐσφαγμένον) and one of the beast's heads 'as if slaughtered' (13:3: ὡς ἐσφαγμένην). The Lamb has conquered (5:5); the beast was allowed to conquer the saints (13:7). The Lamb's conquest by his death leads to the worship of God and the Lamb by every creature (5:13); the beast's recovery from its mortal wound leads to the worship of the dragon and the beast by the whole world (13:3-4, 8). The Lamb has ransomed people from every tribe and language and people and nation, to make them a kingdom (5:9-10); the beast is allowed to rule over every tribe and people and language and nation (13:7). The ironic parallel between the Lamb and the beast is especially sharp in 13:7, where the saints whom the beast is allowed to conquer (13:7a) are, of course, precisely those whom the Lamb's conquest had won from every tribe and language and people and nation (5:9), and the beast's conquest of them is closely linked to the authority he is allowed to exercise over every tribe and people and language and nation (13:7b).

In 7:9 those whom the Lamb's conquest had won from all the nations are seen celebrating in heaven, as martyrs, the victory they in turn have won by participation in his victory (cf. 7:14). The link between 5:9 and 7:9 is clear enough: the Lamb's victory is continued by his people. The argument of the rest of this chapter explains the link between 7:9 and 14:6. The church's faithfulness in witness even as far as death is the way in which the nations are to be won from the worship of the beast to the worship of the true God. The message of the angel to every nation and tribe and language and people (14:6-7) dramatizes the effect of the victory of the martyrs on the nations: it calls them to repudiate the beast's rule (13:7) and worship God. Thus, whereas in 13:7 the beast's apparent victory over the saints (putting them to death) appears to consolidate his universal rule, in 14:6-7 it becomes clear that it is actually the means for the saints, by their suffering witness, to challenge his universal rule and to call the nations into the kingdom of God.

The remaining three occurrences of the formula have this pattern:

10:11	ἐπί	3 4 2 X
11:9	ἐκ	3 1 2 4
17:15		3 Y 4 2

All three begin the list of four nouns with λαός, but it is 11:9 and 17:15 which make a pair comparable with the two pairs we have just discussed. In these cases, as in 5:9; 13:7 and 7:9; 14:6, the order of the four nouns diverges only by the reversal of two adjacent nouns (the third and fourth), though the substitution of ὄχλος in 17:15 for φυλή in 11:9 creates a further divergence. Moreover, as in 5:9; 13:7 and 7:9; 14:6, the pair consists of, firstly, a group drawn from (ἐκ) the nations (11:9), and, secondly, the nations themselves (17:15). So we should probably regard 11:9 and 17:15 as a pair, and 10:11 as set apart from the three pairs into which the other six occurrences of the fourfold phrase fall. This is appropriate, since 10:11 has a special importance, as John's commission to give the prophetic revelation which is the central message of his book. The relationship between 11:9 and 17:15 is not hard to see. Both concern the nations as subjects of the great city, which is responsible for the murder of the prophetic witnesses of Jesus (cf. 17:6; 18:24).

It is not insignificant that only three of the four nouns which usually compose the fourfold phrase (φυλή, λαός, ἔθνος) are placed first in order, while γλῶσσα never occurs first. This corresponds to the fact that these three nouns are each used, outside the fourfold phrase, to refer to all the nations of the world, while γλῶσσα is not (outside the fourfold phrase it occurs only in its literal sense in 16:10). Moreover, the fact that πᾶς is used with the fourfold phrase only in the four cases where φυλή or ἔθνος head the phrase, not in the three cases where λαός heads the phrase, corresponds to the fact that, outside the fourfold phrase, πάντα is used with ἔθνη (12:5; 14:8; 15:4; 18:3, 23) and πᾶσαι with φυλαί (1:7), but πᾶς is not used with λαός or πάντες with λαοί (cf. 18:4; 21:3). This helps to show that the fourfold phrase is intended to be related to other references to the nations of the world which employ only one of the four nouns. Moreover, it gives the fourfold phrase a special relationship to three passages (1:7; 15:4; 21:3) which refer, as we have argued in sections 8 and 9 of this chapter, to the conversion and salvation of the nations. With occurrences of the fourfold phrase grouped in the three pairs we have distinguished they make the following pattern:

1:7	πᾶσαι αἱ φυλαί
5:9	ἐκ πάσης φυλῆς...
13:7	ἐπὶ πᾶσαν φυλήν...
7:9	ἐκ παντὸς ἔθνους...
14:6	ἐπὶ πᾶν ἔθνος...
15:4	πάντα τὰ ἔθνη
11:9	ἐκ τῶν λαῶν...
17:15	λαοί...
21:3	λαοί

That this pattern is not accidental seems clear from the further observation that each of the passages which do not use the fourfold phrase is in this way related to the occurrence of the fourfold phrase which is placed closest to it in the composition of the book (1:7 to 5:9; 15:4 to 14:6; 21:3 to 17:15). Furthermore, each of these three groups of passages has a thematic unity. The first group (1:7; 5:9; 13:7) is linked by reference to the sacrificial death of Christ. The second group (7:9; 14:6; 15:4) is linked by the theme of worship. The third group (11:9; 17:15; 21:3) is linked by the theme of the city: Babylon in 11:9 and 17:15, the New Jerusalem which replaces Babylon in 21:3. The pattern therefore indicates that (1) the Lamb by his sacrifice will win the allegiance of the nations which are now impressed by the bogus sacrifice of the beast; (2) the nations which now worship the beast will be won, through the witness of the martyrs, to the worship of God; (3) the nations which now serve Babylon will become, through the witness of the martyrs, God's peoples with whom he will be present in the New Jerusalem. Thus it becomes clear that, although the fourfold phrase is not itself used to describe the nations as converted and included in the kingdom of God, it is always used with this transfer of the nations from the beast's rule to God's in view. This is also implicit in the relationship of the phrase to the key verse Daniel 7:14.

Finally, we return to the numerical symbolism of the sevenfold use of the fourfold phrase. We have observed that this number 28 (7 for completeness x 4 for the world) indicates that the phrase refers to all the nations of the whole world. On its first occurrence (5:9) the phrase is closely linked to the Lamb and his conquest. It is certainly not accidental that the word 'Lamb' (ἀρνίον) is used of Christ 28 times in Revelation. Thus John indicates that the ultimate purpose of the Lamb's conquest is to win all the nations of the world, designated by the fourfold phrase, for his kingdom, as Daniel 7:14 predicts. Moreover, in the same passage in which the Lamb is first introduced, in relation to the fourfold phrase (5:6-10), we are told that the Lamb's seven horns and seven eyes are the seven Spirits of God sent out into all the earth (5:6). There are four references to the seven Spirits in Revelation (1:4; 3:1; 4:5; 5:6), matching the seven occurrences of the fourfold description of the nations. It is to all the nations of the world that the seven Spirits are sent out, in order, through the prophetic witness of the church, to win the nations to the worship of the true God. Thus the fourfold phrase we have been studying is tied into a pattern of numerical symbolism which encapsulates what we have seen to be John's central prophetic conviction about the coming of God's kingdom on earth: that the sacrificial death of the Lamb and the prophetic witness of his followers are God's strategy for winning all the nations of the world from the dominion of the beast to his own kingdom.

10

The Economic Critique of Rome in Revelation 18

The Book of Revelation is one of the fiercest attacks on Rome and one of the most effective pieces of political resistance literature from the period of the early empire. Its thorough-going criticism of the whole system of Roman power includes an important element of economic critique. This condemnation of Rome's economic exploitation of her empire is the most unusual aspect of the opposition to Rome in Revelation, by comparison with other Jewish and Christian apocalyptic attacks on Rome, and it has also received the least attention in modern study of the book. Though we shall have to refer briefly to other aspects of Revelation's critique of Rome, this chapter will focus on the economic aspect. In particular, a detailed study of the passage 18:9-19 will be offered. Finally, some comparable material in the Jewish Sibylline Oracles will be noticed.

1. The literary structure of the account of the fall of Babylon

The broad structure of the last seven chapters of Revelation[1] is as follows:

16:1-21   The seven last plagues leading to the fall of Babylon

[1]For this structure, see especially Giblin (1974).

The key to this structure is found in the clear parallelism between the major sections 17:1-19:10 and 21:9-22:9, which describe the two contrasting cities: Babylon the harlot and the New Jerusalem the bride of the Lamb. The introductions to each of these two sections, describing how the interpreting angel takes John to see in a vision each of the two women who represent the two cities (17:1-3; 21:9-10), are closely parallel. So are the conclusions to each of these two sections, again featuring the same interpreting angel with which each section began (19:9-10; 22:6-9). Between these parallel introductions and conclusions, however, these two major sections are rather different. In the second section (21:9-22:9) John merely describes his vision of the New Jerusalem. The first section (17:1-19:10) is more complex in structure. The vision of the harlot (17:1-6) is followed by a lengthy explanation of the vision by the interpreting angel (17:7-8). Then a further series of visions and auditions (18:1-19:8) serve to describe the fall of Babylon and its significance. This series of visions and auditions ends with a reference to the New Jerusalem (19:7-8) which serves to connect the two major sections on Babylon and the New Jerusalem. It indicates the relation between the two: that Babylon the harlot must fall in order to make way for the arrival of the New Jerusalem. That connexion having been established, the events which intervene between the fall of Babylon and the arrival of the New Jerusalem are described in the transitional section (19:11-21:8).

The passage with which we are here primarily concerned is the series of visions and auditions in 18:1-19:8 (though we shall also have to refer to the initial vision of Babylon in chapter 17). The structure of this passage 18:1-19:8 has been frequently misunderstood, but is important to grasp. It falls into four main parts:

A   18:1-3   An angel pronounces judgment on Babylon
B   18:4-20   A voice from heaven predicts the fall of
                Babylon
A¹   18:21-24   An angel pronounces judgment on Babylon
B¹   19:1-8   Voices in heaven praise God for the fall of
                Babylon

Although chapter 18 has often been treated as a unit in itself,[2] it should be clear that the scene of rejoicing in heaven in 19:1-8 is part of the depiction of the fall of Babylon and is needed to complete the unit. Moreover, just as there are links between the passages here labelled A and A¹,[3] so there are also between B and B¹, which show that the latter is the fourth part of a four-part unit. B depicts the mourning for Babylon by the kings of the earth, the merchants and the sailors (18:9-19) and ends by calling on the inhabitants of heaven to rejoice over Babylon's fall. This call is taken up in B¹, where the rejoicing in heaven over Babylon's doom contrasts with the mourning on earth in B.

But section B (18:4-20), which contains the material most relevant to our theme, needs to be further analyzed.[4] It is important to realise that the whole of this section is the words of the voice from heaven to which 18:4 refers.[5] Most interpreters and translations have supposed that the words of the voice from heaven end with verse 8, but there is no reason to suppose this. Rather, the prediction of Babylon's fall which begins in verses 7b-8 continues with the prediction of how the kings, the merchants and the sailors will mourn for her (vv. 9-19). John is not describing the mourning on his own account, but continuing to report the words of the heavenly voice. (The

---

[2]This is a mistake made by Strand (1982) and Shea (1982) (both following Farrer [1964] 189), who propose a chiastic structure for Revelation 18. They correctly recognize the parallelism between 18:1-3 and 18:21-24, but they miss the parallelism between 18:4-20 and 19:1-8. Moreover, their analysis of 18:4-20, which treats 4-8 as a unit, cannot be upheld (see below for my alternative analysis).

[3]Yarbro Collins (1980) 198-199.

[4]The following analysis largely agrees with Yarbro Collins (1980) 193-196.

[5]So Yarbro Collins (1980) 193; Yarbro Collins (1984) 117.

future tenses in vv. 9-10, 15 make clear that the account of the mourners is prediction; the vividness of the scene accounts for the present and past tenses in vv. 11, 14, 17-19; for the variation of tenses, cf. 11:7-13.[6]) Recognizing this removes the problems otherwise caused by verses 14 and 20. In verse 14 the account of the mourning of the merchants is interrupted by a comment addressed to Babylon, but the speaker does not change. Verse 20 is not part of the lament of the sailors (v. 19): it would be quite incongruous for the sailors who are lamenting the loss of their own livelihood through the fall of Babylon to continue by calling on the inhabitants of heaven to rejoice because of it. But on the other hand, there is no need to supply for verse 20 a new speaker not indicated in the text. Rather the heavenly voice, after quoting the sailors' lament in verse 19, turns to address the inhabitants of heaven in verse 20. The key to analysing the whole section B is to recognize the various addressees of various passages and to distinguish the passages addressed to various addressees from those which are predictions addressed to no specified hearers. The section can then be divided as follows:

4a	Introduction
4b-5	A call to the people of God to come out of Babylon
6-7a	A call to the agents of divine justice to execute vengeance on Babylon
7b-8	Prophecy of the fall of Babylon
9-10	Prophecy of the mourning for Babylon: First group of mourners
11-13	Prophecy of the mourning for Babylon: Second group of mourners (a)
14	Interjection addressed to Babylon
15-17a	Prophecy of the mourning for Babylon: Second group of mourners (b)
17b-19	Prophecy of the mourning for Babylon: Third group of mourners
20	Call to the inhabitants of heaven to rejoice over the fall of Babylon

[6]Cf. also Fekkes (1988) 221 n. 53.

In these divisions there is a logical progression. First, the people of God are warned to leave doomed Babylon lest they share her punishment. Then, the ministers of vengeance[7] are commanded to do their work. Then, the execution of vengeance, the fall of Babylon, is foreseen. Then, as Babylon burns, three groups of mourners are depicted lamenting her fall. Finally, heaven is called on to rejoice that God's judgment on Babylon has taken place.

The whole of chapter 18 is closely related to Old Testament prophecies of the fall of Babylon and the fall of Tyre, from which it borrows phrases, images, and ideas. But out of these deliberate echoes of the Old Testament John has created a fresh prophecy of considerable literary skill, which appears especially in the vivid portrayal of the three groups of mourners for Babylon (vv. 9-19). This is inspired by and borrows phrases from Ezekiel's prophecies of the fall of Tyre, which include dirges sung for Tyre by two different groups of mourners (26:15-18; 27:29-36) and also a catalogue of the merchandise from various lands in which Tyre traded (27:12-24). But with this inspiration from Ezekiel, John has produced a highly effective description of his own, in which the terms of the description are both repeated and varied in each of the three cases, creating parallelism while avoiding monotony.[8] The function of this description of the mourners will be discussed later, but it is appropriate to note here how the structure of the passage gives a special prominence to the merchandise which the merchants import to Rome. The two shorter accounts of the kings (vv. 9-10) and the sailors (vv. 17b-19) frame the longer account of the merchants (vv. 11-17a), which is broken in two by the interjection addressed to Babylon (v. 14). The merchandise is listed at length in the first part of the account of the merchants (vv. 12-13), is the topic of the interjection addressed to Babylon (v. 14), is mentioned again when the account of the merchants is resumed after the interjection

---

[7]These are unidentified, but are probably heavenly beings: Yarbro Collins (1980) 193.

[8]Vanhoye (1962); Yarbro Collins (1980) 199.

(v. 15) and is also portrayed symbolically, as the adornments of Babylon imagined as a woman, in the merchants' lament (v. 16), which ends by lamenting the destruction of so much wealth (v. 17a). We would be justified in supposing that in his account of the fall of Babylon John wished particularly to highlight the imported wealth which will perish with the city.

2. Rome as the harlot city

The book of Revelation uses two major, complementary images of the evil power of Rome. One is the sea-monster ('the beast'), introduced in chapter 13. It represents the imperial power, the Roman Emperors as a political institution, and in particular their *military might*, on which the Roman empire was founded. The other image is of the great city Babylon, first named in 14:8, and then portrayed as a woman, 'the great harlot,' in chapter 17. Babylon is the city of Rome (built on seven hills: 17:9) and in particular the city of Rome as a *corrupting influence* on the peoples of the empire. Chapter 17 brings the two images together: the harlot is enthroned on the seven heads of the beast (17:3, 9-10). In other words, Roman civilization, as a corrupting influence, rides on the back of Roman military power. The city of Rome grew great through military conquest, which brought wealth and power to the city, and its economic and cultural influence spread through the world in the wake of the imperial armies. John never forgets that Rome's power is founded on war and conquest, but he also recognizes that it cannot be reduced to this. As well as the irresistible military might of the beast, there are the deceptive wiles of the great harlot.

For John, the satanic, antichristian nature of Roman power, as exercised in his time, was demonstrated most obviously by the Roman state religion in which the power of the state was deified. It may be that John's use of the two distinct images of Roman power — the beast and the harlot-city — was assisted by a feature of this state religion. It included not only the worship of the divinized Emperors but also the worship of the goddess

Roma,[9] who was a kind of personification of the city of Rome.[10] It may be that in the woman of Revelation 17 John's readers would have recognized the goddess Roma,[11] revealed by the vision in her true character: a Roman prostitute, wearing her name on a headband on her forehead (17:5) as prostitutes did in the streets of Rome.[12]

John describes the impulse to the imperial cult in 13:14: people 'worshipped the beast saying, "Who is like the beast, and who can fight against it?"' The irresistible military might of Rome seems divine and attracts worship. The verse has a kind of parallel in 18:18, with reference to Babylon. Those who there lament her downfall cry, 'What city was like the great city?' Here the wealth and splendour of the city of Rome evoke admiration, just as her military might evoked spontaneous, if somewhat craven, worship. The point should not be pressed too far. If the picture of the great harlot owes something to the goddess Roma, John does not actually portray her as an object of worship, as he does the beast. His point is more that, through her corrupting influence, she promotes the idolatrous religion of Rome. But Babylon comes close to self-deification in her proud boast, 'A queen I sit, I am no widow, mourning I shall never see' (18:7), which echoes not only ancient Babylon's boast (Isa 47:7-8)[13] but also contemporary Rome's self-promoted reputation as the eternal city.[14] It was the city which believed, as an article of faith, that she could never fall, whose fall is announced in Revelation 18.

In order to understand why John portrays the city of Rome both as the city of Babylon and as a harlot, we must briefly consider his Old Testament sources. John is very conscious of

[9]See Court (1979) 148-152. For the cult of Roma in the cities of Asia, see Magie (1950) 1613-1614; Price (1984) 40-43, 252, 254; Mellor (1975) 79-82.

[10]Mellor (1975) 199: 'Roma was the deification of the *populus Romanus*.'

[11]So Court (1979) 148-152.

[12]Charles (1920) 2.65.

[13]For the dependence on Isaiah 47:7-9, see Fekkes (1988) 227-231. With Revelation 18:7 and 17:18, cf. Frontinus, *De aquis* 2.88.1: Rome as *regina et domina orbis*.

[14]Yarbro Collins (1980) 201.

writing in a long tradition of prophetic oracles[15] and so is constantly echoing and reapplying the oracles of his predecessors. His portrayal of the fall of Babylon is a remarkable patchwork of skilful allusions to Old Testament prophecies of the fall of Babylon and the fall of Tyre.[16] There are two major sources: Jeremiah's great oracle against Babylon (Jer 50-51) and Ezekiel's great oracle against Tyre (Ezek 26-28). But allusion is also made to all of the shorter oracles against Babylon and Tyre to be found in the Old Testament prophets (Babylon: Isa 13:1-14:23; 21:1-10; 47; Jer 25:12-38; Tyre: Isa 23).[17] It seems that John has quite deliberately fashioned a prophetic oracle against Rome which gathers up all that his prophetic predecessors had pronounced against the two cities of Babylon and Tyre. For John these oracles are more than a literary source. They are oracles which, because they applied to Rome's predecessors in evil, apply also to Rome. He sees Rome as the culmination of all the evil empires of history. Just as the beast, as portrayed in Revelation 13:1-2, combines in itself the features of all the beasts which in Daniel's vision symbolized the evil empires before Rome (Dan 7:3-8), so the Babylon of Revelation 17-18 combines in itself the evils of the two great evil cities of the Old Testament prophetic oracles: Babylon and Tyre.[18]

Of the two, Babylon is the city whose name John uses as a cipher for Rome. No Old Testament city could more truly be called, like Rome, 'the great city which has dominion over the kings of the earth' (Rev 17:18). Rome resembled Old Testament Babylon in being a proud, idolatrous, oppressive empire, and especially in being the power which conquered and oppressed the people of God. Rome declared itself the heir of Babylon by setting itself against God in its political and religious policies.

---

[15]See Mazzaferri (1989), especially ch. 10. His positive thesis—John's conscious continuity with Old Testament prophecy — is more convincing than his negative thesis: the contrast between Revelation and apocalyptic.

[16]Vanhoye (1962) 475-476; Charles (1920) 2.95-113; Fekkes (1988) 83-84.

[17]Fekkes (1988) 86-88.

[18]Cf. Beasley-Murray (1974) 264: 'This city summed up in itself and surpassed the wickedness of the tyrant-powers of the past.'

But it is important to notice that Ezekiel's oracle against Tyre contributes as much to John's account of the fall of Babylon as Jeremiah's and Isaiah's oracles against Babylon do. If Rome was the heir of Babylon in political and religious activity, she was also the heir of Tyre in economic activity. For Tyre was the greatest trading centre of the Old Testament period, notable not, like Babylon, for her political empire, but for her economic empire. So it is to focus his indictment of Rome for her *economic* exploitation and his pronouncement of judgment on Rome for *this* aspect of her evil, that John reapplies to Rome Ezekiel's oracle against Tyre. The Old Testament background therefore helps us to see how central the economic theme is to the condemnation of Rome in Revelation.

If Babylon gave Rome its name in John's oracle, it is probably Tyre that supplied the image of the harlot for Rome.[19] The Old Testament prophets do not portray Babylon as a harlot, but Isaiah 23:15-18 uses the image of the harlot for Tyre. The reference there is obviously to the vast trading activity through which the city of Tyre had grown rich. Tyre's commercial enterprise is compared with prostitution because it is association with other nations for the sake of profit. Thus we should expect the primary significance of John's portrayal of Rome as the great harlot to be economic. But since the way in which Tyre profited from her purely commercial empire was significantly different from the way in which Rome benefited economically from her political empire, John develops the image of the harlot to suit its specific reference to Rome. The significance he gives to it requires some careful unpacking.

The image of the harlot is so fundamental to John's understanding of Rome that even when he is speaking primarily of the city, as in chapter 18, he does not forget that the city is a harlot. Hence the terms of the description in 17:1-6 are echoed in 18:3, 9 (cf. 17:2) and 18:16 (cf. 17:4), while the image of the harlot recurs explicitly in 19:2. The basic notion, of course, is that those who associate with a harlot pay her for

---

[19]So Fekkes (1988) 219-220, who thinks Revelation 17:3b; 18:3b, 9a allude to Isaiah 23:17b.

the privilege. And Rome is no ordinary harlot: she is a rich courtesan, whose expensive clothes and jewelry (17:4) indicate the luxurious lifestyle she maintains at her lovers' expense. The meaning of the picture is unpacked for us when the harlot's clothing and jewels are described again, in the same terms, in 18:16. Here they are plainly a metaphor for the wealth of the city of Rome, for all the luxury goods listed in 18:12-13, brought to Rome by the great network of trade throughout her empire. In other words, Rome is a harlot because her associations with the peoples of her empire are for her own economic benefit. To those who associate with her she offers the supposed benefits of the *Pax Romana*, much lauded in the Roman propaganda of this period. Rome offered the Mediterranean world unity, security, stability, the conditions of prosperity. But in John's view these benefits are not what they seem: they are the favours of a prostitute, purchased at a high price. The *Pax Romana* is really a system of economic exploitation of the empire. Rome's subjects give far more to her than she gives to them.

There are, of course, those who have a vested interest in the power and the economic dominance of Rome: the kings, the merchants and the mariners (18:9-19). To these people, who share in Rome's profit, we shall return later. But many of Rome's subjects are in fact exploited by her, yet fail to see it. They are taken in by Roman propaganda. They are dazzled by Rome's glory and seduced by the promised benefits of the *Pax Romana*. This delusion John portrays by means of two additional metaphors, which extend the harlot image. When he refers to the harlot's influence, not on the ruling classes of the empire, but over the peoples of the empire, he says that she intoxicates them with the wine of her fornication (14:8; 17:2; 18:3) or that she deceives them with her sorceries (18:23). The latter probably refers to the magic arts used by a prostitute to entice her clients (as in Nah 3:4),[20] or may simply portray Rome in another guise:

[20]J. M. Powis Smith in Powis Smith, Hayes Ward and Brewer (1912) 338; Maier (1959) 302.

as a witch (cf. Isa 47:12). In any case, it is clear what John means. When Rome's subjects, the ordinary people of the empire, welcome her rule, it is because she has enticed and seduced them. They are taken in by the prostitute's wiles and the tricks of her trade.

We have seen, then, that the primary meaning of the harlot image in Revelation 17-18 is economic. But John was no doubt also aware of a much more common Old Testament use of harlotry as a metaphor.[21] In this usage, idolatrous religion is described as harlotry, because the people of God, when they adopted pagan religious practices, were being unfaithful to their husband, God, and 'played the harlot' with other gods (e.g. Jeremiah 3). This Old Testament sense of harlotry could strictly be applied only to the people of God, but it is very likely that John takes advantage of the traditional association of harlotry with idolatrous religion, when he refers to the *corrupting* influence of the harlot city (19:2). When the intoxicating draft from her golden cup is otherwise described as 'abominations and the impurities of her fornication' (17:4), and when she is described as 'the mother [i.e. the mother-city, the metropolis] of harlots and of the abominations of the earth' (17:5), the reference, following a familiar Old Testament use of the term 'abominations', is to idolatrous religion. *Religious* corruption is offered in the cup whose golden exterior symbolizes the attraction of Rome's wealth and splendour. John will be thinking primarily of the imperial cult. Part of the delusion of the *Pax Romana* — the intoxicating wine from the harlot's cup — was the people's sense of gratitude to the Emperor, who was worshipped as a divine Saviour for the blessings he had brought to his subjects. From John's Jewish Christian perspective, the political religion of Rome was the worst kind of false religion, since it absolutized Rome's claim on her subjects and cloaked her exploitation of them in the garb of religious loyalty. Thus, for John, Rome's economic exploitation and the corrupting influence of her state religion go hand in hand.

[21]Court (1979) 140-141.

Finally, the portrait of the harlot in Revelation 17:1-6 ends with a fresh and even more sinister use of the image of drunkenness: she who made the earth drunk with her seductive wiles is herself 'drunk with the blood of the saints and the blood of the witnesses of Jesus' (17:6). The accusation recurs, this time with a judicial image, in 18:24: 'in her was found the blood of prophets and of saints, and of all who have been slain on earth'. Here the prophets and saints are the Christian martyrs, and many commentators understand 'all who have been slain on earth' also as Christian martyrs, but this is not the natural sense, and it robs the verse of its climax. Rome is indicted not only for the martyrdom of Christians, but also for the slaughter of all the innocent victims of its murderous policies.[22] The verse expresses a sense of solidarity between the Christian martyrs and all whose lives were the price of Rome's acquisition and maintenance of power. John has not forgotten that Babylon rides on the beast with its bear's hug and its lion's teeth (13:2). He knows that the *Pax Romana* was, in Tacitus's phrase, 'peace with bloodshed,'[23] established by violent conquest, maintained by continual war on the frontiers, and requiring repression of dissent.[24] Like every society which absolutizes its own power and prosperity, the Roman empire could not exist without victims. Thus John sees a connexion between Rome's economic affluence, Rome's idolatrous self-deification, and Rome's military and political brutality. The power of his critique of Rome — perhaps the most thorough-going critique from the period of the early empire — lies in the connexion it portrays between these various facets of Rome's evil.

Thus it is a serious mistake to suppose that John opposes Rome only because of the imperial cult and the persecution of Christians. Rather this issue serves to bring to the surface evils which were deeply rooted in the whole system of Roman power. In John's perspective, the evils of Rome came to a head

[22]The fact that the verb σφάζω is used of the Lamb in 5:6, 9, 12; 13:8 and of Christian martyrs in 6:9, is no proof to the contrary, for it is also used of general slaughter in 6:4.

[23]Tacitus, *Ann.* 1.10.4.

[24]Cf. Wengst (1987) 11-19.

in her persecution of Christians, because here Rome's self-deification clashed with the lordship of the Lamb to which the Christian martyrs bore witness and so what was implicit in all of Rome's imperial policies here became explicit. Hence Revelation most often portrays the fall of Rome as vengeance for the death of the Christian martyrs (16:6; 18:24; 19:2; cf. 18:6). But this is certainly not the whole story: God's judgment of Rome is also attributed to her slaughter of the innocent in general (18:24; cf. 18:6), her idolatrous arrogance (18:8), and her self-indulgent luxury at the expense of her empire (18:7). The economic element in this critique is probably the one which has received the least attention in previous scholarship, but as we have noticed it is very prominent in chapter 18, and to the detail of it we now turn.

3. The list of cargoes (18:12-13)

John's list of twenty-eight items of merchandise imported by sea to the city of Rome has not received the attention it deserves. Although, of course, it lists no more than a small selection of Rome's imports in this period, it is, to my knowledge, much the longest extant list of Roman imports to be found in the literature of the early empire. This rather remarkable fact suggests that we pay rather careful attention to the significance of this list for Revelation's polemic against Rome.

Some commentators have been content to remark that the list is modelled on Ezekiel's list of forty foreign products in which the city of Tyre traded (27:12-24), as though John's list were sufficiently explained by this source.[25] No doubt it was Ezekiel's list which suggested the idea of a list of cargoes. It is true that a number of items of merchandise are common to both lists, but no more than would be practically inevitable in any two lengthy lists of items traded in the ancient world. Each list also has a significant number of items which do not occur in the other. But the feature of the lists which shows that John's

[25]Charles (1920) 2.103; Beckwith (1919) 715.

was formulated largely independently of Ezekiel's is that the principle by which each list is arranged is different. Ezekiel lists the products with which each named country traded with Tyre: the arrangement is geographical. John does not indicate the sources of the merchandise, but arranges his list according to types of cargo. Closer study of John's list will reveal that what he has done is to substitute for Ezekiel's, which is an accurate account of Tyre's trade in the sixth century B.C., a list which is just as accurate in representing the imports of the city of Rome in the first century A.D.

With the exception of William Barclay's popular commentary on Revelation,[26] H. B. Swete in his commentary of 1906[27] was the last New Testament scholar who made any attempt to gather information about individual items in the list and to comment on their significance as Roman imports.[28] No doubt this lack of interest in the concrete detail which John so deliberately provides, reflects, not only the average exegete's preference for theology over concrete history, but also a failure fully to recognize the thoroughly contextualized nature of John's prophetic message. For all its visionary symbolic form, John's attack on Rome is aimed at the concrete political and economic realities of the empire in his time.[29] The symbolism is not a way of abstracting from these realities but a means of prophetic comment on their significance. By neglecting the list of cargoes, interpreters of Revelation have neglected one of the best pieces of evidence for John's engagement with the realities of Roman power as experienced by his contemporaries.

In order to redress the balance, though still in a rather provisional way, we offer here some comment on each item in the list. Of particular importance will be evidence that the

[26]Barclay (1960) 220-212.
[27]Swete (1907) 232-235.
[28]Later commentators, such as Charles (1920) 2.103-105, and Beckwith (1919) 716-717, do no more than select information from that collected by Swete and, long before him, Wetstein. Mounce (1977) 329-331, gives more detail than most recent commentators, by following Barclay as well as Swete.
[29]Cf. Georgi (1986) 121-126, especially 123: 'John's work is anything but the product of an esoteric quietist piety. Here a prophetic consciousness which has a hold on historical reality expresses itself.'

merchandise in question was generally seen as a feature of the newly conspicuous wealth and extravagance of the rich families of Rome in the period of the early empire.

gold: Rome imported gold especially from Spain,[30] where most of the mines had become state property during the first century (Strabo 3.2.10), sometimes by highly dubious means of confiscation (Tacitus, *Ann.* 6.19). The use of gold was one of the commonly noticed features of the growth of extravagant luxury among the wealthy families of Rome in the first century (e.g. Tacitus, *Ann.* 3.53; Pliny, N.H. 33.39-40; Martial 10.49; 11.95), and in one of the periodic attempts to curb this, in 16 A.D., a law prohibiting the use of solid gold plate at private dinner parties was passed (Tacitus, *Ann.* 2.33). Pliny complains that now the ceilings of private houses are commonly covered in gold (N.H. 33.57), that today even slaves use gold for ornament (N.H. 33.23), and reports that since even plebeian women now wear shoe-buckles of gold, they are thought old-fashioned and silver ones are preferred by the aristocracy (N.H. 33.152). With the place of gold at the head of John's list, it is worth comparing the fact that it is the first object of Roman greed mentioned in Eumolpus' account of the insatiable desire for wealth and luxury which motivated Roman imperial expansion: 'if there were... any land that promised a yield of yellow gold, that place was Rome's enemy, fate stood ready for the sorrows of war, and the quest for wealth went on' (Petronius, *Sat.* 119). Pliny (N.H. 36.6) considered the private use of ivory, gold and precious stones the evidence of the luxury (*luxuria*) he so regularly condemns as moral degeneration in the Rome of his day.

silver: The case of silver, also imported mostly from Spain,[31] was similar to that of gold (cf, e.g., Tacitus, *Ann.* 3.53). Pliny strongly associates silver with the luxury of the Roman rich in his time, remarking on the fashions for silver-plated couches and baths made of silver, the common use of silver for serving food (cf. Martial 11.97), the rage not only for vast quantities of silver plate but also for silver art objects by particular artists

---

[30]T. Frank in Frank (1940) 292.
[31]Ibid.; J. J. van Nostrand in Frank (1937) 150-151, 158.

(Pliny, N.H. 33.145-153). In the use of gold and silver, as with so many of these imported luxuries, Nero and Poppaea provide examples of the current extravagance taken to absurd extremes (Pliny, N.H. 33.54, 140; Suetonius, *Nero* 30.3).

precious stones: Most came from India, as part of the eastern trade in luxuries which flourished from the reign of Augustus onwards.[32] Indian jewels were widely used in Rome throughout the first century.[33] That they came from beyond the bounds of the empire explains why the emperor Tiberius, in his letter to the Senate about Roman extravagance in 22 A.D., referred to 'that special feature of Roman extravagance, the transfer of Roman currency to foreign, often hostile nations, for the purchase of jewelry' (Tacitus, *Ann.* 3.53). But, of course, Rome owed it to her empire that she could afford these expensive imports from beyond the empire. Pliny, who thought that the fashion for the extravagant use of precious stones in Rome dated from Pompey's triumphs, in which fabulous jewels were exhibited (N.H. 37.11-13, 17), thought the human love of them had grown into a violent passion in his time (N.H. 37.2). They were not only worn by women in large quantities (cf. Pliny, N.H. 9.117-118 for an extreme example), but also set in rings for men (Pliny, N.H. 33.22; Martial 5.11) and frequently used to inlay expensive drinking vessels (Pliny, N.H. 33.5; 37.17; Juvenal 5.37-45; Martial 14.109, 110).

pearls: Inferior pearls came from the Red Sea, the finest quality from the Persian Gulf, the most abundant supplies from India. Pearls were one of the imports from India and the east which were increasing considerably in the later first century, and they may have made up the largest part of the oriental trade. Romans valued the pearl after the diamond, but for the largest and best would pay more than for any other piece of jewelry.[34] Pliny calls pearls the most costly product of the sea (N.H. 37.204). Nero, who scattered pearls among the people of Rome (Suetonius, *Nero* 11.2), exemplifies the Roman obsession with pearls (Pliny, N.H. 37.17), including the practice

---

[32]Warmington (1974) Part 2, ch. 3.
[33]Warmington (1974) 40, 90.
[34]Warmington (1974) 89, 167-171.

of swallowing them, dissolved in vinegar, at banquets for the sake of the thrill of consuming such vast expense at a single gulp (cf. Pliny, N.H. 9.121-122). During the first century it became common for wealthy Roman women to wear pearls in great quantities, to the fury, once again, of those who blamed feminine extravagance for the outflow of Roman currency from the empire (e.g. Pliny, N.H. 12.84). Pliny constantly treats pearls as the epitome of extravagant luxury (N.H. 9.105, 112-114, 117-122; 37.14-17; cf. Petronius, *Sat.* 55).

fine linen (βυσσίνου): During the first century linen was tending to replace wool as clothing in Rome. John refers to the expensive linen worn by the wealthy, imported mostly from Egypt, but also from Spain and Asia Minor.[35]

purple: The list of four textiles (fine linen, purple, silk, scarlet) is made up alternately of types of cloth (fine linen, silk) and cloths characterized by their dyes (purple, scarlet). Silk, linen and woollen cloths (in order of expense) were all died with purple, the expensive dye obtained from shell-fish which were fished in various places around the Mediterranean and which was much prized in the ancient world. Reinhold calls it 'the most enduring status symbol of the ancient world'.[36] Because of the vast number of tiny shell-fish needed to make small quantities of the purple dye, the dye was much more expensive than any of the materials which it was used to dye and accounts for the exorbitant price of purple cloth.[37] Because of its price, it was used not only as a mark of official status, political or cultic, but also by private individuals as a deliberate, conspicuous display of affluence. From the late Republic onwards, it was increasingly in evidence in Rome for this purpose, and regularly appears as a symbol of extravagance in writers of the first century B.C. and first century A.D.[38] From Julius Caesar to Nero, attempts were made to limit the use of purple, but after the death of Nero apparently no restrictions were in force.[39] According to Pliny, first-century Rome

---

[35]Frank in Frank (1940) 156; T. R. S. Broughton in Frank (1938) 822.

[36]Reinhold (1970) 71.

[37]For the price, see Raschke (1978) 624, 725 n. 305.

[38]Reinhold (1970) 41-44, 51-52, 72.

[39]Reinhold (1970) 45-47, 49-50.

developed an insane craze for purple clothing (*purpurae insania*: N.H. 9.127; cf. 8:197; 9.137), which, he says, 'the same mother, Luxury, has made almost as costly as pearls' (N.H. 9.124). Because both pearls and purple dyes derive from shell-fish, he calls shell-fish the greatest single source of moral corruption and luxury (N.H. 9.104). From at least the time of Nero, there was an imperial monopoly in the purple dye,[40] and an inscription from Miletus indicates that those involved in the purple trade were freedmen of the *familia Caesaris*.[41] This connection with the Emperors gives an extra significance to the appearance of purple in the list in Revelation. Moreover, in view of the geographical area to which the book of Revelation is addressed, it is worth noting that some of Rome's purple cloth would probably have come from the clothing and dyeing industries of Miletus, Thyatira, Laodicea and Hierapolis.[42]

silk: Silk,[43] imported at great expense[44] from China, some by the overland route through Parthia, most via the ports of northwest India, was used in Rome to any extent only from the reign of Augustus.[45] Romans, who thought silk grew on trees, considered nard and silk the most expensive things derived from trees.[46] The sumptuary laws of 16 A.D. prohibited, as an effeminate custom, the wearing of silk by men (Tacitus, *Ann.* 2.33), but the extent to which silk became common for both male and female dress (though clothing was not usually made wholly of silk[47]) is indicated by Josephus' account of Roman

[40]Horsley (1977) 26, 28, against Reinhold (1970) 72.

[41]Horsley (1977) 28.

[42]For these, see Hemer (1978) 53-54; Hemer (1986) 109, 181-182, 199-201; Broughton in Frank (1938) 817, 819-820; Pleket (1983) 141-142. As well as the true purple, the term was also used for less expensive dyes (Reinhold [1970] 52-53), such as that made from the roots of the madder plant in western Asia Minor: see Hemer (1978) 53-54, for the suggestion that it was in this that Lydia of Thyatira (Acts 16:14) traded.

[43]On the silk trade, see now especially Raschke (1978) 605-637. He denies that it was responsible for Rome's adverse balance of trade with the East.

[44]For the price of silk, see Raschke (1978) 624-625.

[45]Warmington (1974) 175.

[46]Warmington (1974) 177.

[47]Raschke (1978) 623.

soldiers dressed in silk at the triumphs of Vespasian and Titus (*BJ* 7.126).

scarlet (κοκκίνου): Since the scarlet dye was obtained especially from the kermes oaks (from the 'berry' [κόκκος] — in fact an insect parasite) in various parts of Asia Minor (the best was said to come from Galatia[48]), John may be thinking especially of the clothing industries of his own province of Asia. Petronius's Trimalchio, who represents the excesses of the first-century Roman rich taken to ludicrous absurdity,[49] had cushions with crimson (*conchyliatum:* a variety of the purple dyes derived from shellfish) or scarlet (*coccineum*) stuffing (*Sat.* 38). Typically, it is Nero who nearly matched this fictional absurdity in fact: the cords of his golden fishing net were of purple and scarlet thread (Suetonius, *Nero* 30.3).

all kinds of citrus wood (πᾶν ξύλον θύϊνον): The phrase may mean 'all articles made of citrus wood', or, since different specimens of the wood were valued for their various colours and the various patterns created by the veining (resembling the eyes of the peacock's tail, the spots of the panther or the stripes of the tiger: Pliny, N.H. 13.96-97; Martial 14.85), 'all kinds of citrus wood'.[50] The wood[51] came from the citrus tree (*Callitris quadrivalvis*), which grew along the whole north African coast from Cyrenaica westward, but had been much depleted so that by Pliny's time the best quality trees were largely confined to Morocco. Tables made from the wood became one of the most expensive fashions of early imperial Rome, indispensable at the banquets of the wealthy, so that largely with reference to these tables, Pliny could say that 'few things which supply the apparatus of a more luxurious life (*nitidioris*) rank with' the citrus tree (Pliny, N.H. 13.100). Seneca, contrary to his own principles, possessed five hundred

---

[48]See Pliny, N.H. 16.32; 9.141; Broughton in Frank (1938) 617.

[49]Trimalchio, a freedman who has made a fortune from sea-borne commerce, apes the ostentatious symbols of wealth of the Roman upper classes. On locating Trimalchio in his social and economic context, see D'Arms (1981) 97-120.

[50]So Swete (1907) 233; Beckwith (1919) 716.

[51]On Roman use of citrus wood, see especially Meiggs (1980) 185-186; Meiggs (1982) 286-292.

of them, with ivory legs (Dio 61.10.3). Because trees large enough to provide a table top in one piece took a very long time to reach that size and were rare, these tables were vastly expensive. Even Cicero paid 500,000 sesterces for his, which was said to have been the first recorded citrus wood table in Rome (Pliny, N.H. 13.102), while Petronius's Eumolpus writes of 'tables of citrus wood dug out of the soil of Africa and set up, the spots on them resembling gold which is cheaper than they, their polish reflecting hordes of slaves and purple clothes, to lure the senses' (Petronius, *Sat.* 119; cf. Martial 14.89: a table worth more than gold). Certainly, the record price which Pliny quotes for one table would have been enough to buy a large estate (Pliny, N.H. 13.95). These tables were therefore standard in references to first-century Roman excess. According to Pliny, when Roman women were accused of extravagance in pearls, they pointed out the equally extravagant mania of men for citrus wood tables (Pliny, N.H. 13.91). But the wood was also used on a smaller scale in furniture and works of art, doorposts (Statius, *Silvae* 1.3.35) or even writing-tablets (Martial 14.3).

all articles of ivory: The Roman consumption of ivory was one of the earliest stages of the process which now so notoriously threatens the survival of the elephant. In the first century A.D. the Syrian elephant (once one of the three species) was already well on the way to extinction (Juvenal 11.126-127 refers to Nabataean elephants as a source of ivory). When Pliny wrote (N.H. 8.7), the extravagant Roman use of ivory had led to the severe depletion of elephants within the accessible areas of north Africa, and the shortage of African ivory was made up by the increasing trade in Indian ivory throughout the first century.[52] As examples of its use found in ancient literature, Warmington lists statues, chairs, beds, sceptres, hilts, scabbards, chariots, carriages, tablets, bookcovers, table-legs, doors, flutes, lyres, combs, brooches, pins, scrapers, boxes, bird-cages, floors:[53]

[52]Warmington (1974) 40, 89, 162-165. Raschke (1978) 650, contests this, but probably incorrectly.

[53]Warmington (1974) 163.

a list to which it would be easy to add (e.g. Juvenal 11.131-134: dice, draughts, knife-handles; Suetonius, *Nero* 31.2: ceilings). For Pliny, it was a striking indication of modern luxury that ivory had replaced wood for making images of the gods and table-legs (Pliny, N.H. 12.5; cf. 36.6), while Juvenal complains that nowadays a rich man cannot enjoy his dinner unless the table is supported by a leopard carved in solid ivory (11.120-124). In their race for conspicuous luxury, the Roman rich of the early imperial period had whole articles of furniture covered in ivory. The increased use of ivory is reflected in the increased literary references to ivory in the late first century.[54] Lucian on one occasion regards gold, clothing, slaves and ivory as the constituents of wealth (*Dial. Meretr.* 9.2).

all articles of costly wood: Expensive woods might include ebony, from Africa and India, but there is hardly any evidence for its use in Rome.[55] The best maple wood, used for furniture, could be very expensive.[56] Cedar and cypress were used for furniture, boxes, sarcophagi, doors and sculpture.[57] The expensive woods were also used for veneering,[58] a practice Pliny regards as a new-fangled extravagance (N.H. 16.232; 33.146).

[all articles of] bronze: The reference will be especially to expensive works of art made from Corinthian bronze and perhaps also Spanish bronze.[59] Petronius' Eumolpus gave as an example of the way Romans acquired a decadent taste for luxuries from overseas: 'the soldier out at sea would praise the bronze of Corinth' (Petronius, *Sat.* 119). Pliny speaks of a mania for Corinthian bronze, which he claims is more valuable than silver, almost more valuable than gold (N.H. 34.1). The frequently mentioned 'Corinthian bronzes' were statuettes, which seem to have been a Roman fashion throughout the first

---

[54]Warmington (1974) 164.
[55]Meiggs (1982) 285-286, against Warmington (1974) 213-214.
[56]Meiggs (1982) 291-292.
[57]Meiggs (1982) 292-294; cf. R. M. Hayward in Frank (1938) 53.
[58]Meiggs (1982) 296-297.
[59]Van Nostrand in Frank (1937) 163.

century and vastly expensive (Pliny, N.H. 34.6-8, 36; 36.115; 37.49; Martial 9.59.11; 14.172, 177; Suetonius, *Aug.* 70.2; Petronius, *Sat.* 50). When Tiberius set price limits for household furnishings, his particular complaint was that the price of Corinthian bronze vessels had risen to an immense figure (Suetonius, *Tiberius* 34). Vastly expensive bronze lamp-stands (not of Corinthian bronze) were also popular, as were such items of furniture in bronze as banquetting couches (Pliny, N.H. 34.10-14).

[all articles of] iron: Articles of iron and steel would be, for example, cutlery, swords and other armaments, ornamental vessels, imported especially from Spain[60] and Pontus. The Seric iron mentioned by Pliny has often been thought to be high quality Indian steel, but Raschke thinks it more likely to be cast iron from China or central Asia.[61]

[all articles of] marble: Rome imported marble mainly from Africa,[62] Egypt[63] and Greece.[64] Augustus' famous boast that he found Rome brick and left it marble (Suetonius, *Aug.* 28.3) was relatively justified,[65] and heralded the beginning of a period of lavish use of fine marble in Rome, not only for public buildings but also for the ostentatious palaces of the rich (cf. Pliny, N.H. 17.6). The major marble quarries of the empire were annexed to imperial ownership in the early first century so that they might more efficiently supply the needs of Rome.[66] Of course, marble was used not only for building but also for such things as statuary, sarcophagi and baths (Martial 9.75). John's reference to articles of marble presumably refers to such articles, as well as, for example, to columns already cut and shaped in standard lengths before shipment to Rome.[67] Pliny treats the private use of marble as an absurd and indefensible luxury (N.H. 36.2-8, 48-51, 110, 125).

---

[60]Van Nostrand in Frank (1937) 162; Frank in Frank (1940) 292.
[61]Raschke (1978) 650-651, against Warmington (1974) 257-258.
[62]R. M. Hayward in Frank (1938) 53, 62; Ward-Perkins (1980) 326.
[63]*Ibid.*
[64]J. A. O. Larsen in Frank (1938) 488-489.
[65]Frank in Frank (1940) 19.
[66]Ward-Perkins (1980) 326-328.
[67]Ward-Perkins (1980) 327-328.

cinnamon: The term most likely refers both to cassia (the wood of the plant), which was often called cinnamon and formed the bulk of the trade in cinnamon, and also to cinnamon proper (the tender shoots and delicate bark), which was extremely expensive.[68] The common modern view is that they came from somewhere in south Asia (India, Ceylon, Indonesia or south China), but that the merchants of south Arabia, the middlemen in the trade, succeeded in keeping the Romans ignorant of the true source in order to keep the trade in their own hands, with the result that the Romans continued to believe that cinnamon came from Arabia or east Africa.[69] Raschke, however, maintains that ancient cassia and cinnamon were not the same spices as are known by those names today and that they probably did in fact come from east Africa (Somalia).[70] In any case, cinnamon was valued as incense, medicine, perfume and a condiment in wines. In common with the rest of the eastern trade, the trade in cinnamon probably increased considerably in the later first century A.D.[71]

amomum (ἄμωμον): This was another aromatic spice, certainly from south India, though the Romans thought it came from various places along its trade routes.[72]

incense: Incense, made in various parts of the east from a combination of ingredients, often very expensive, was not only used in religious rites, but also valued for perfuming the rooms and the funerals of the rich.

sweet-smelling ointment: Despite many translations, μύρον refers generally to aromatic ointment, not exclusively to that made from myrrh (σμύρνα). Myrrh, imported from the Yemen and Somalia at great expense,[73] was certainly one of the most prized of such perfumes (Pliny, N.H. 13.17), and was also an ingredient, as were cinnamon and amomum, in perfumes, some vastly expensive (Pliny, N.H. 13.15), made from a variety of

---

[68]For the reasons for the high prices of spices in Rome, see Raschke (1978) 670.
[69]V. M. Scramuzza in Frank (1937) 350-351; Frank in Frank (1940) 293.
[70]Raschke (1978) 652-655.
[71]Warmington (1974) 186-188.
[72]Warmington (1974) 184-185.
[73]van Beek (1960) 86-88.

ingredients. Such unguents were considered typical features of the good life in imperial Rome,[74] and therefore Pliny treats them as one of the expensive feminine — or, if used by men, effeminate — indulgences which were ruining the society of his time (N.H. 13.20-22; cf. 12.83-84).

frankincense: Frankincense from the Sabaeans (of southern Arabia) is one of Virgil's examples of the imports to Rome from distant parts of the world (*Georgics* 1.57). Like other aromatics, it was used as perfume. Frankincense and myrrh[75] are the prime examples of the perfumes of Arabia (Pliny, N.H. 12.51), on which Pliny blames in part the drain of Roman currency to the east (N.H. 12.82-84). They are also the kind of perfumes which were consumed in vast quantities at the funerals of the rich, illustrating for Pliny the *luxuria* of mankind even in the hour of death: 'the perfumes such as are given to the gods a grain at a time... are piled up in heaps to the honour of dead bodies'. As so often, Nero supplies the most outrageous example: Pliny thinks he must have used at the funeral of Poppaea more perfumes than Arabia produces in a whole year (N.H. 12.82-83). According to Warmington, 'So great was the use of aromatics at funerals that the death of any living thing tended to call forth from the poets reference to Indian and Arabian perfumes.'[76]

wine: Rome imported wine especially from Sicily[77] and Spain.[78] Trimalchio's first business enterprise was to send five ships loaded with wine from Asia to Rome: he lost thirty million sesterces when they were wrecked (Petronius, *Sat.* 76). However exaggerated the sum, it indicates that the wine trade with Rome could be considered highly profitable.[79] It seems that by

---

[74]See the revealing funerary inscriptions from Rome in Connolly (1979) 130-131.

[75]On frankincense and myrrh, see van Beek (1960) 70-95; Connolly (1979) 129-131; Raschke (1978) 652.

[76]Warmington (1974) 90.

[77]V. M. Scramuzza in Frank (1937) 350; Frank in Frank (1940) 293.

[78]van Nostrand in Frank (1937) 177-178; Frank in Frank (1940) 220, 297.

[79]The qualities of wine from various places are discussed in Athenaeus, *Deipnosophistae* 1.32-34, but the discussion is so literary it would be hazardous to conclude that they were all drunk in Rome.

the end of the first century A.D., the Empire had a serious problem of a surplus of wine and a shortage of grain (cf. Revelation 6:5-6). With the extension of the large estates (*latifundia*) owned by wealthy Romans in the provinces, vines were cultivated at the expense of corn, because the wine trade was the more profitable. An edict of Domitian therefore attempted to reduce by half the cultivation of vines in the provinces, but it was apparently quite ineffective in the face of commercial considerations.[80]

oil: Africa and Spain were at this time taking over from Italy as the major suppliers of olive oil to Rome.[81] Vast quantities were imported.[82]

fine flour: Although the other three items of food (wine, oil, wheat) grouped together in the list were staples for all inhabitants of Rome, it is noteworthy that the list's general emphasis on luxury is maintained by this reference to fine flour imported for the wealthy. According to Pliny, the Egyptian product was not as good as the Italian (N.H. 18.82), but the most esteemed fine flour was imported from Africa (N.H. 18.89).

wheat: The sheer size of first-century Rome's population (estimated at 800,000 to one million)[83] made its corn supply a vast economic operation. Under the early empire, Sardinia and Sicily declined in significance as suppliers of grain to Rome, while Africa and Egypt supplied the bulk of Rome's needs (cf. Josephus, *BJ* 2.283, 386). Thousands of ships must have been involved in shipping the grain across the Mediterranean.[84] As Tiberius put it, 'the very life of the Roman people is daily at the hazard of wind and wave' (Tacitus, *Ann.* 3.54). The immense importance of the corn supply meant that the state increasingly supervised the system, but private

---

[80]Wengst (1987) 224; Hemer (1986) 158.

[81]van Nostrand in Frank (1937) 177; R. M. Hayward in Frank (1938) 61; Frank in Frank (1940) 221, 292, 297. On the olive oil trade in Rome, see Panciera (1980) 235-250.

[82]For the volume of Spanish oil imported, see Garnsey and Saller (1987) 58.

[83]See Hopkins (1978) 96-98.

[84]Rickman (1980) 263-264.

merchants and shippers continued to run it.[85] It was financed not only by the sale of grain to consumers but also by the government which bought supplies to distribute as the free corn dole, though much of the latter was also made up of the supplies of corn which came from the provinces as tax in kind. This makes the inclusion of wheat in John's list significant, as well as inevitable. Whereas many other items in the list illustrate how the wealth which rich citizens of Rome gained from the empire was spent on conspicuous luxuries, this item shows how the general population of Rome survived only at the expense of the rest of the empire. A city of a million people — the largest city in the western world before eighteenth-century London — could not have grown and survived without the resources of the whole empire to support it.[86] This was one respect in which the harlot (the city of Rome) rode on the beast (the imperial power). There is some evidence of bread riots in the cities of Asia Minor around the time when Revelation was written,[87] and since Rome had first claim on Egyptian wheat, before the other cities of the empire,[88] resentment could well have been directed by the poor against the system of corn supply to Rome. The economic background to Revelation is in this respect vividly portrayed in Revelation 6:5-6: shortage of the most basic foodstuffs (wheat and barley), but a surplus of wine and oil.[89]

cattle: The import of animals to Rome by sea might at first sight seem surprising, but in fact methods of transporting livestock on ships must have been well developed in the imperial period, when large numbers of wild animals of all kinds were transported to Rome for the entertainments in the amphitheatres.[90] Wild bulls and wild sheep were among such animals,[91] but the references to cattle and sheep in the

---

[85]Rickman (1980) 268-272; Garnsey (1983) 126-128.

[86]Garnsey and Saller (1987) 83.

[87]Yarbro Collins (1984) 94-97; Wengst (1987) 224.

[88]Garnsey and Saller (1987) 98-99.

[89]Wengst (1987) 223-224; Hemer (1986) 158-159.

[90]Frayn (1984) 164.

[91]Bulls: Toynbee (1973) 149-151; Jennison (1937) 59, 70. Sheep: Frayn (1984) 42, 164; and cf. Columella 7.2.4.

Revelation are unlikely to be to these, since if the supply of animals to the amphitheatres were in mind, more obvious species such as elephants or lions would surely have been referred to. Nor is the import of cattle likely to have been for food:[92] beef was not a very important item even in the banquets of the rich.[93] Cattle were kept primarily as working animals and for milk. But one breed of cattle not native to Italy, the Epirote, was highly regarded by Roman farmers (Varro, *Res rust.* 2.5.10; Pliny, N.H. 8.45)[94] and cattle of this breed were imported from Greece to Italy for breeding purposes, to improve local breeds (Strabo 7.7.5, 12). The first century was the period in which Roman aristocracy had acquired large sheep and cattle ranches (*latifundia*) both in Italy and, by conquest and confiscation, in the provinces.[95] Cattle were also imported to Italy from Sicily (Strabo 6.2.7).

sheep: Since the reference is to the animals, it can hardly be the wool trade that is in mind.[96] Some sheep may have been shipped from Sicily to Rome for meat for the rich,[97] but the reference is probably again to the import of sheep for breeding purposes. Roman estate-owners were no doubt anxious to improve the amount and quality of the wool produced by their flocks and would import good foreign breeds for this purpose.[98] Although his meaning is not quite clear, Strabo (3.2.6) probably refers to the transport of rams from southwest Spain to Italy for breeding.[99] John's first readers might well have been familiar with the transport of sheep to Rome, since the Romans rated

[92] Pigs were shipped live from Spain to Rome: van Nostrand in Frank (1937) 181.
[93] White (1970) 276-277.
[94] Cf. White (1970) 279.
[95] Frayn (1984) 111-113, 164-165.
[96] For the wool trade, see Frayn (1984) 161-171. I am grateful to Dr Frayn for advice on this paragraph.
[97] V. M. Scramuzza in Frank (1937) 351-352; cf. Frayn (1984) 3, 24; Columella 7.2.1; 7.3.13.
[98] Cf. Frayn (1984) 32-33; and cf. Columella 7.2.4-5; Hilzheimer (1936) 205-206.
[99] Frayn (1984) 165. The context, referring to Turdetanian exports, favours this interpretation.

Milesian sheep as the third best in the world (Pliny, N.H. 8.190).[100]

horses: Race horses for chariot racing in the circuses were imported from Africa, Spain, Sicily, Cappadocia and parts of Greece famous for their horses (Laconia, Thessalia, Aetolia).[101] There were imperial stud farms in Spain and Cappadocia for the supply of such horses. Since Italy was short of the high quality pasture needed for breeding racing horses and the demand for them was considerable, there must have been a sizeable overseas trade.[102]

chariots (ῥεδῶν = Latin *raeda* or *reda*, apparently the same as the *carruca*: see Martial 3.47): These were the four-wheeled, horse-drawn, private chariots used by the rich for travel in Rome and to their country estates. Presumably the chariots themselves, like the word *raeda* (Quintilian 1.5.57), were imported from Gaul. In order to satisfy the taste for ostentatious extravagance, there were silver-plated (Pliny, N.H. 33.140) and gilt (Martial 3.62) chariots of this kind.

slaves: The significance of the way John refers to slaves and their place at the end of the list will be discussed below. Increasing numbers of slaves in Rome were a feature of the growing prosperity of the rich and the increasing size of the city.[103] The demand was by no means met by the offspring of existing slaves. The enslavement of prisoners taken in war, which had been the normal source of slaves under the Republic, continued to be important in the first century A.D., when wars on the frontiers continued and the Jewish war alone produced 70,000 slaves (Josephus, *BJ* 6.420), but it cannot have been as productive a source as it had been during the period of continuous foreign wars. Harris argues that of the other sources (foundlings, children sold by their parents, adults selling themselves into slavery, slavery through debt, victims of kidnapping, some criminals), much the most important source,

---

[100]Frayn (1984) 34, 167-168.
[101]van Nostrand in Frank (1937) 180; R. M. Hayward in Frank (1938) 52; J. A. O. Larsen in Frank (1938) 485; Frank in Frank (1940) 293; White (1970) 289.
[102]White (1940) 298.
[103]Hopkins (1978) ch. 1, discusses the increase in slaves in Italy generally.

because of the common practice of exposing children, must have been foundlings.[104] In any case, slave trading was a profitable business, and Asia Minor was evidently the most important source of those slaves who were not taken in war.[105] Ephesus, one of the seven cities of Revelation, must have played a major role in exporting slaves from Asia Minor to Rome.[106] It should be noted that, whereas slaves as such were certainly not regarded as a luxury, the vast numbers of slaves acquired by the Roman rich and the huge prices paid for slaves of particular beauty or skill were considered extravagances (e.g. Tacitus, *Ann.* 3.53; Juvenal 5.56-60; Martial 11.70).

These detailed notes on the merchandise enable us to draw some general conclusions about the list. In the first place, most of the items were among the most expensive of Rome's imports. At the end of his *Natural History* (37.204), Pliny has a list of the most costly products of nature in various categories. It has twenty-seven items in all, or twenty-nine if gold and silver, which he mentions as an afterthought, are included. Including gold and silver, thirteen of the twenty-eight cargoes in Revelation occur in this list of Pliny's (gold, silver, precious stones, pearls, purple, silk, scarlet, citrus wood, ivory, cinnamon, amomum, aromatic ointment, frankincense), and these in fact account for eighteen of the items in Pliny's list. These cargoes were expensive in themselves. Others in the list in Revelation (oil, wheat) were not expensive as such, but were imported in such vast quantities that in total they must have cost a very great deal. Thus the list is very representative of Rome's more expensive imports.

Again, while the list includes some items (wine, oil, wheat) which illustrate how the survival of the whole city depended on such imports, it features especially the luxury items which fed the vulgarly extravagant tastes of the rich. In this respect, perhaps the most surprising omission is a reference to the exotic foodstuffs imported from all over the empire for the

[104]Harris (1980) 118-124.
[105]Harris (1980) 122.
[106]Harris (1980) 127.

banquets of the rich, which are regularly the special target of Roman writers' complaints or satires on the excesses of first-century Roman indulgence (e.g. Petronius, *Sat.* 38; 55; 119; Juvenal, 5.80-119; 11.138-144; Seneca, *Ad Helviam* 10:2-11; *De vita beata* 11:4; *Ep.* 60.2; 89.22; Pliny, N.H. 12.4; 15.105). But it may be that no *single* item of this kind was important enough to belong in a list like this. However, the import of many of the luxury items which are listed had very considerably increased during the period since Augustus. It is not surprising that several of the items belong wholly or partly to the eastern trade with Arabia, east Africa, India and beyond (jewels, pearls, silk, ivory, iron, cinnamon, amomum, incense, aromatic ointment, frankincense), which flourished especially under the early empire.[107] Imports from the east are regularly prominent among the luxury goods mentioned by Roman writers critical of the conspicuous extravagance of the Roman rich in that period. It is true that Tacitus claims (*Ann.* 3.55) that the fashion for expensive excess gave way to simpler tastes again from the time of Vespasian, but neither the literary nor other evidence (e.g. in 92 Domitian constructed warehouses for oriental spices in Rome)[108] bears this out, at least with regard to the kind of items included in the list in Revelation.[109] As a critique of Roman wealth, John's list will still have accurately made its point in the reign of Domitian (if we accept this traditional and most widely accepted date for Revelation).[110]

As the notes on each cargo have shown, many of the items in the list are specifically mentioned as prime examples of luxury and extravagance by Roman writers critical of the decadence, as they saw it, of the wealthy families of Rome in the early imperial period (gold, silver, jewels, pearls, purple, silk, scarlet, citrus wood, bronze, marble, cinnamon, amomum,

---

[107]Warmington (1974) 79-80.

[108]Warmington (1974) 89-90.

[109]According to Griffin (1984) 206-207, what happened under Vespasian was a change of imperial style (away from extravagance), a change later reversed under Domitian.

[110]For recent defences of this date, see Yarbro Collins (1984) ch. 2; Hemer (1986) 2-12.

aromatic ointment, frankincense, slaves). This same verdict is
effectively expressed in the comment on the list which is made
by the voice from heaven in Revelation 18:14:

> The ripe fruit (ὀπώρα) which your soul craves has gone
> from you,
> and all your luxuries (λιπαρά) and your glittering prizes
> (λαμπρά) are lost to you, never to be found again
> (my translation).

The first line evokes Rome's addiction to consumption, while
the two words chosen for the merchandise in the second line
suggest both the self-indulgent opulence (λιπαρά) and the
ostentatious display (λαμπρά) of Roman extravagance.

This is not to say that John's objections to Roman luxury are
necessarily the same as those of Roman moralists. The list in
Revelation is part of a thorough-going, comprehensive critique
of the Roman empire as such. Many of the Roman writers we
have mentioned were primarily concerned with the way wealth
has corrupted the upper classes of Rome. They are nostalgic
for the traditional austerity and simplicity of the old Roman
aristocratic lifestyle. This is not likely to be John's perspective.
Nor will he have shared the anxieties of Pliny and the emperor
Tiberius about the empire's disadvantageous balance of trade
with the lands to the east. But occasionally the Roman sources
indicate moral sensitivity to the fact that the wealth of the
Roman rich derived from the conquest and plunder of the
empire and that the economic exploitation of the empire was
by no means always to the advantage of the people of the
empire (e.g. Petronius, *Sat.* 119). Lucan, for example, clearly
recognizes that it was not the ordinary people of Mauretania
who benefitted from the high price of the tables made from the
citrus trees they themselves had valued only as shade from the
sun (9.426-430). Seneca inveighs against 'the wretches whose
luxury overleaps the bounds of an empire that already stirs too
much envy' (*Ep.* 10.2), and rather similarly suggests the danger
to Rome from greed for the spoils of conquered nations:
'whatever one people has snatched away from all the rest may
still more easily be snatched by all away from one' (*Ep.* 87.41).

That John saw Rome's wealth as her profit from her empire, enjoyed at the expense of the peoples of the empire, is left in no doubt by the literary connexion between the list of cargoes and his portrait of the harlot Babylon. In 17:4 he had described the harlot as

περιβεβλημένη πορφυροῦν καὶ κόκκινον, καὶ κεχρυσωμένη χρυσίῳ καὶ λίθῳ τιμίῳ καὶ μαργαρίταις.

In 18:16 the merchants, in their lament for the great city, describe her (implicitly as a woman who is)

περιβεβλημένη βύσσινον καὶ πορφυροῦν καὶ κόκκινον, καὶ κεχρυσωμένη ἐν χρυσίῳ καὶ λίθῳ τιμίῳ καὶ μαργαρίτῃ.

The description is practically identical in each case except for the addition of βύσσινον (fine linen) in 18:6. The addition of βύσσινον serves to link the description in 18:16 more closely with the list of Roman imports in 18:12-13. All the six items of finery mentioned in 18:16 occur among the first eight items in the list of cargoes (18:12). (The addition of βύσσινον also serves to link 18:16 with 19:8: just as Babylon, the harlot, is clothed in fine linen, so is the New Jerusalem, the bride of the Lamb, but the varying significance of the fine linen highlights the contrast between the two cities.)

Clearly the expensive adornments of the harlot (17:4; 18:16) represent symbolically the imports listed in 18:12-13, the wealth of Rome (18:17a). The luxuries Rome imports are like the extravagant lifestyle which a rich courtesan maintains at the expense of her clients. They are the price which the kings of the earth have paid for the favours of the harlot (17:2; 18:3). But we must assume that while it is the kings who associate with the harlot — bringing their lands under her dominion and ruling in collaboration with her — the price is actually paid by their peoples. In the case of some of the items of merchandise, the trade was probably perceived by most provincials who, like John, did not benefit from it as directly exploitative, drawing resources to Rome which were needed in the provinces (such as wheat and slaves) or using local labour to extract expensive products at little benefit to local people (for example, marble). We shall later find evidence that anti-Roman sentiment in Asia Minor perceived the slave trade in that way (SibOr 3:353-355, discussed in section 5 below). But the trade with the east cannot have been seen as part of Rome's exploitation of the empire in that way. Rather the point will be that the wealth Rome squanders on luxuries from all over the world was obtained by conquest, plunder and taxation of the provinces. Rome lives well at her subjects' expense. Of course, John recognizes that some of her subjects also benefitted from the vast network of trade which fed the huge appetite and expensive tastes of the capital. To those beneficiaries we shall shortly turn.

The way in which the list of cargoes ends still requires comment. The last cargo, slaves, is described thus: σωμάτων, καὶ ψυχὰς ἀνθρώπων. σώματα was in common use with the meaning 'slaves', and John has taken ψυχὰς ἀνθρώπων from Ezekiel 27:13 (MT: אדם בנפש LXX: ἐν ψυχαῖς ἀνθρώπων),[111] where it also refers to slaves. It is just possible that John intends two categories of cargo ('slaves and human lives') and that whereas the former refers to the regular slave trade, the latter refers to those slaves who, along with some prisoners of war and certain criminals, were destined to die fighting for their lives in the amphitheatres of Rome. This would make a telling climax, but more probably, as most commentators and translations agree, the καί is epexegetical: 'slaves, that is, human persons.' This gives considerable emphasis to the reference to slaves at the end of the list. That John gives both the common term for slaves in the slave markets (σώματα) and a scriptural description of slaves (ψυχαὶ ἀνθρώπων) must mean that he intends a comment on the slave trade. He is pointing out that slaves are not mere animal carcasses to be bought and sold as property, but are human beings. But in this emphatic position at the end of the list, this is more than just a comment on the slave trade.

---

[111]This phrase is a literal Greek rendering of the Hebrew, with which John agrees by coincidence. Revelation 18 is not dependent on the LXX of Ezekiel: see Vanhoye (1962) 447, 449-450, 453. For Revelation's general dependence on the MT rather than the LXX, see Mazzaferri (1989) 42-45.

It is a comment on the whole list of cargoes.[112] It suggests the inhuman brutality, the contempt for human life, on which the whole of Rome's prosperity and luxury rests.

4. The mourners (18:9-19)

Some commentators on Revelation suppose that in 18:9-19 John betrays some admiration for the opulence of Rome and some regret at its destruction: 'it is with infinite pathos that John surveys the loss of so much wealth' (Caird).[113] That this is a misunderstanding is already made likely by our study of the list of cargoes. It becomes quite certain when we observe that John attributes the laments for Rome's destruction to three very definite classes of people: the kings of the earth (v. 9), the merchants of the earth (v. 11), and the mariners (v. 17). These are precisely the people who themselves benefitted from Rome's economic exploitation of her empire. What they lament is the destruction of the source of their own wealth.

'The kings of the earth' — whom John brands as having 'committed fornication with' the harlot (17:2; 18:3, 9) — is a stock phrase in Revelation (1:5; 6:15; 17:2, 18; 18:3, 9; 19:19; 21:24; cf. 16:14), with which John probably intends an allusion to Psalm 2:2. Psalm 2, with its account of the victory of God's Messiah over the nations who set themselves against God and his Messiah, is one of the Old Testament texts which John made fundamental to his work and to which he alludes throughout it (cf. 2:26-27; 11:15, 18; 12:5; 14:1; 19:15). He may also have noticed the occurrence of the same phrase in Ezekiel's oracle against Tyre (27:33: 'with your abundant wealth and merchandise you enriched the kings of the earth'; cf. also Isa 24:21). Thus the phrase itself is determined by its scriptural sources; the class of people John uses it to designate need not

---

[112]Sweet (1979) 271.
[113]Caird (1966) 227. Against this view, see Yarbro Collins (1980), especially 203; also Boesak (1987) 121-122.

be literally kings.[114] It will refer not just to the client kings who put their kingdoms under the umbrella of the Roman empire, but more generally to the local ruling classes whom throughout the empire Rome coopted to a share in her rule. John's readers in the province of Asia Minor will have thought most obviously of the local aristocracy who sat on the councils of their cities. For such people Roman authority served to prop up their own dominant position in society. Naturally, therefore, it is the destruction of Rome's *power* that they lament (v. 10), whereas the other two laments mention her wealth (vv. 17, 19).

However, the power they shared with Rome certainly had economic advantages,[115] to which John alludes in verse 9: οἱ μετ' αὐτῆς πορνεύσαντες καὶ στρηνιάσαντες ('committed fornication and indulged themselves with her'). As part of the metaphor, along with πορνεύσαντες, στρηνιάσαντες may here refer to the sensual indulgence of the harlot's clients, but it will also suggest the luxury of material wealth. This is the sense of ἐστρηνίασεν in verse 7, where it refers to Babylon's own indulgence in luxury, while in verse 3 στρῆνος is used of Babylon's luxury which has enriched the merchants of the earth (τῆς δυνάμεως τοῦ στρήνους αὐτῆς: 'her excessive luxury'). Thus in verse 9 the meaning must be that the kings' association with Roman power brings them a share in Rome's luxury. It may be worth remembering here that the aristocracies of the cities of the empire, while they did not engage directly in commerce like the merchants of verse 11, often invested in and profited from trading enterprises.[116] So they too had a direct stake in the vast trade with Rome which is described in connection with the second group of mourners, the merchants. Roman rule increased the prosperity of the cities of the eastern Empire, but it was only the ruling classes who benefited and the gap between rich and poor widened.[117]

[114]Note also that in Psalm 2:2 (cf. 10) 'the kings of the earth' appear in parallel with 'the rulers'.

[115]Cf. Wengst (1987) 26.

[116]Pleket (1983) 131-144; Raschke (1978) 646. Note the example of Damian in mid-second-century Ephesus: D'Arms (1981) 164-165.

[117]Cf. Walton (1929) 51-52: the resulting discontent of the poor evidently increased under the Flavians.

The 'merchants of the earth' (18:3, 11) are also described as
'your [i.e. Babylon's] merchants' (18:23). This does not mean
that they were Romans, but simply that they did business with
the city of Rome. Most of the merchants engaged in the trade
with Rome, even those resident in Puteoli, Ostia and Rome,
were provincials, citizens of the exporting cities from which the
merchandise came[118] (though some of these would be Roman
citizens[119]). Thus citizens of the cities where John's readers
lived, especially Ephesus, will be included. It is also relevant to
note that even the eastern trade, which is prominent in the list
of imports, was largely in the hands of Roman subjects.[120]
John's term for the merchants (ἔμποροι) no doubt includes
both the *negotiatores* and the *navicularii* (ναύκληροι), i.e. the
independent shipowners who bought and sold their cargoes at
the ports. (Thus the *shipowners* are not included among the
seafarers of verse 17, who are all their employees.) According
to verse 23, Babylon's merchants were 'the great men
[μεγιστᾶνες] of the earth.' The phrase is drawn from Isaiah's
oracle against Tyre (23:8: 'whose merchants were princes,
whose traders were the honoured of the earth'),[121] but John
must have selected it as corresponding to the reality of the
Roman empire. Although merchants were not of high social
status,[122] John refers accurately to their wealth, which put many
of them among the richest men of their time, and to their
considerable economic power, as banded together in the
trading companies and associations.[123]

The third group of mourners are so described as to include
all who were employed in the maritime transport industry (v.
17). When they refer in their lament to the fact that 'all who
had ships at sea grew rich by her wealth' they are probably
referring to the shipowners who employed them. They

[118]Frank in Frank (1940) 242.
[119]Raschke (1978) 833 n. 770.
[120]Raschke (1978) 643-645.
[121]For the dependence on Isaiah 23:8, see Fekkes (1988) 231-233.
[122]A few merchants in highly profitable trades did rise into the urban elites:
Pleket (1983) 139-143.
[123]Rostovtzeff (1960) 264; Rickman (1980) 270-271; D'Arms (1981) 167-168.

themselves made a living, but presumably not a fortune, from the trade with Rome. Of course, partly for obvious geographical reasons and partly because transport by land was much more expensive than transport by sea, all the imports listed in verses 12-13 reached Rome by sea,[124] in John's time mostly through the port of Ostia whose harbour had been constructed by Claudius.[125] The mariners' sense of indebtedness to Rome for their livelihood, expressed in their lament, finds an interesting parallel in a story Suetonius tells about the emperor Augustus shortly before his death. He happened to sail into the gulf of Puteoli just as a ship from Alexandria was docking. The passengers and the crew honoured him with festal dress, incense and the highest praise, 'saying that it was through him that they lived, through him that they sailed the seas, and through him that they enjoyed liberty and their fortunes (*fortunis*)' (*Aug.* 98.2).[126]

Thus verses 9-19 allow us to see the fall of Rome from a very definite perspective which was certainly not John's: the perspective of those who depended for power and wealth or simply for a living on their involvement with Rome and her economic system. For such people, of course, Rome's downfall is also their own, and their lamentation is only to be expected. The perspective John shares is not that of these people of the *earth* and the *sea* (vv. 9, 11, 17), but that of heaven (18:20; 19:1), where Rome's victims the martyrs rejoice in the triumph of God's justice over Rome's exploitation of the earth.

In the last section, we cited evidence from Roman writers who shared something, if not all, of John's condemnation of Rome's luxury imports. But admiration for the wealth and luxury which Rome drew from all over the known world, such is expressed in the laments John attributes to provincials who benefited from it, can also be paralleled, significantly in writers from the provinces. For example, Plutarch refers to

---

[124]Cf. Aelius Aristides, *Oratio* 26.11-13, quoted below. Wengst's comments ([1987] 130) on the Mediterranean sea as a negative image in Revelation are worth considering in this connexion.

[125]Frank in Frank (1940) 236-241.

[126]I owe this reference to Dr Samuel Barnish.

all the things which the earth contributes, and the earth
and the sea and islands, continents, rivers, trees, living
creatures, mountains, mines, the first-fruits of everything,
vying for beauty in the aspect and grace that adorns this
place (*Mor.* 325e).

It is worth quoting at some length from Aelius Aristides the
orator, who came from Smyrna, one of the cities of Revelation.
In a speech (*Oratio* 26) delivered before the imperial court in
Rome, probably in 155 A.D.,[127] his admiration for the city of
Rome was naturally unbounded. But he is especially impressed
by the visual evidence of its character as 'the common trading
center of mankind and the common market of the produce of
the earth' (26.7), a description which rather obscures the fact
that Rome was the consumer of all the goods which arrived at
Ostia and the exporter of rather few. But Aristides continues:

Here is brought from every land and sea all the crops of
the seasons and the produce of each land, river, lake, as
well as of the arts of the Greeks and barbarians, so that if
someone should wish to view all these things, he must
either see them by travelling over the whole world or be
in this city.... So many merchants' ships arrive here,
conveying every kind of goods from every people every
hour and every day, so that the city is like a factory
common to the whole earth.[128] It is possible to see so many
cargoes from India and even from Arabia Felix, if you
wish, that one imagines that for the future the trees are
left bare for the people there and that they must come
here to beg for their own produce if they need anything.
Again there can be seen clothing from Babylon and
ornaments from the barbarian world beyond, which arrive
in much larger quantity and more easily than if
merchantmen bringing goods from Naxus or Cythnus
had only put into Athens. Your farmlands are Egypt, Syria,

[127]Behr (1981) 373.
[128]On this expression (a rhetorical topos), see Klein (1983) 71.

and all of Africa which is cultivated. The arrivals and departures of the ships never stop, so that one would express admiration not only for the harbor,[129] but even for the sea. Hesiod said about the limits of the Ocean, that it is a place where everything has been channeled into one beginning and end. So everything comes together here, trade, seafaring, farming, the scourings of the mines, all the crafts that exist or have existed, all that is produced or grown. Whatever one does not see here, is not a thing which has existed or exists, so that it is not easy to decide which has the greater superiority, the city in regard to present day cities, or the empire in regard to the empires which have gone before (26.11-13).[130]

This is, as it were, Revelation's list of imports to Rome seen from the perspective of the kings and the merchants.

Why then does John give us the perspective of Rome's collaborators in evil: the ruling classes, the mercantile magnates, the shipping industry? Part of the reason may be that, although the perspective was certainly not John's, it could rather easily be that of some of his readers. If it is not likely that many were among the ruling classes, it is not unlikely that John's readers would include merchants and others whose business or livelihood was closely involved with the Roman political and economic system. For such readers John has set a kind of hermeneutical trap. Any reader who finds himself sharing the perspective of Rome's mourners — viewing the prospect of the fall of Rome with dismay — should thereby discover, with a shock, where he stands, and the peril in which he stands. And for such readers, it is of the utmost significance that, prior to the picture of the mourners, comes the command:

Come out of her my people,
lest you take part in her sins,
lest you share in her plagues (18:4).

[129]i.e. of Ostia.
[130]Translation from Behr (1981) 74-76.

The command, whose language is borrowed from Jeremiah 51:45 (cf. 50:8; 51:6, 9; Isa 48:20), is not meant in the literal geographical sense it had in Jeremiah. None of John's first readers lived in the city of Rome. The command is for the readers to *dissociate* themselves from Rome's evil,[131] lest they share her guilt and her judgment. It is a command not to be in the company of those who are then depicted mourning for Babylon.

Revelation's first readers, as we know from the seven messages to the churches in chapters 2-3, were by no means all poor and persecuted, like the Christians at Smyrna. Many were affluent, self-satisfied and *compromising*, and for them John intended an urgent revelation of the requirements and the peril of their situation. Most of the seven cities were prosperous communities with significant stakes, as ports or as commercial, administrative and religious centres, in Roman rule and Roman commerce.[132] But in order to participate in the business and social life of these cities, and so in the prosperity of their wealthier citizens, Christians had to participate also in idolatrous religion, including the Roman state religion. The Nicolaitans, apparently active in several of the churches (2:6, 15), and the prophetess Jezebel in Thyatira, were evidently advocating that such compromise was quite permissible (2:14, 20).[133]

We should note, as the Christians at Thyatira would certainly have noticed, the resemblance between Jezebel, as John portrays her in the message to Thyatira, and the harlot Babylon, as he portrays her in chapters 17-18. Of course, Jezebel is John's symbolic name for the prophetess, just as Babylon is his symbolic name for Rome. It serves to compare her with the Old Testament queen who seduced Israel into idolatry in the time of Elijah. Once reminded of Old Testament Jezebel's 'harlotries and sorceries' (2 Kings 9:22) and her slaughter of the prophets of the Lord (1 Kings 18:13), we can see that the harlot of

---

[131]Note that the reference to Babylon's *sins* here is not in John's Old Testament sources but has been deliberately added by him: cf. Kiddle (1940) 363.

[132]See especially Hemer (1986).

[133]Hemer (1986) 87-94, 117-123.

Babylon is also in part modelled on Jezebel (cf. 18:7, 23, 24).[134] Thus it appears that the Thyatiran prophetess, who was encouraging her followers to participate without qualms of conscience in the thriving commercial life of the city,[135] was, so to speak, the local representative of the harlot of Babylon within the church at Thyatira. Through her the seductive power of Rome's alliance of commerce and idolatrous religion was penetrating the church. Some of her followers—who have 'committed adultery with' her (2:22) — might therefore find themselves, with a salutary shock of recognition, among 'the merchants of the earth [who] have grown rich with the wealth of [Babylon's] wantonness' (18:3).[136] Thus John's prophecy against Rome could also become a painful and demanding challenge to some of his Christian readers, who needed to 'come out of her'.

John's critique of Rome therefore did more than voice the protest of groups exploited, oppressed and persecuted by Rome. It also required those who could share in her profits to side with her victims and become victims themselves. But those who from the perspective of the earth and the sea were Rome's victims John saw from the perspective of heaven to be the real victors. Hence his account of the fall of Babylon climaxes not in the laments of the kings, the merchants and the mariners, but in the joyful praises of the servants of God in heaven (19: 1-8).

5. Additional note on the economic critique of Rome in the Jewish Sibylline Oracles

Jewish apocalypses roughly contemporary with Revelation, which also predict the fall of Rome, criticize Rome for her

---

[134]It may also be relevant to remember Jezebel's connexion with Tyre (1 Kings 16:31: daughter of the king of Sidon), the Old Testament city which Revelation takes as typical of Rome's economic evil.

[135]Cf. Ramsay (1909) 316-353; Hemer (1986) 120-123.

[136]One could also link the complacent, arrogant affluence of the church at Laodicea (Rev 3:17) with that of Babylon (18:7): cf. Yarbro Collins (1980) 202.

violence, oppression and pride (4 Ezra 11:40-46; 2 Bar 36:8; 39:5), but not for her wealth (though cf. 4 Ezra 3:2). For any parallels at all, in prophetic oracles, to John's economic critique of Rome we must turn to the Sibylline Oracles.

The most important passage is Sibylline Oracle 3:350-380, of which it will be sufficient here to quote lines 350-368:

> However much wealth Rome received from tribute-bearing Asia,
> Asia will receive three times that much again
> from Rome and will repay her deadly arrogance to her.
> Whatever number from Asia served the house of Italians,
> twenty times that number of Italians shall be serfs
> in Asia, in poverty, and they will be liable to pay ten-thousandfold.
> O luxurious golden offspring of Latium, Rome,
> virgin, often drunken with your weddings with many suitors,
> as a slave will you be wed, without decorum.
> Often the mistress will cut your delicate hair
> and, dispensing justice, will cast you from heaven to earth,
> but from earth will again raise you up to heaven,
> because mortals are involved in a wretched and unjust life.
> Samos will be sand, and Delos will become inconspicuous,
> Rome will be a street. All the oracles will be fulfilled.
> Smyrna will perish and there will be no mention of it.
>   There will be an avenger,
> but for the bad counsels and the wickedness of its leaders...
> Serene peace will return to the Asian land,
> and Europe will then be blessed.[137]

With the exception of Nikiprowetzky, all scholars regard this as an independent oracle, inserted into the third book of the Sibylline Oracles along with other independent oracles (381-488) which did not belong originally with the bulk of the

---

[137]Translation from Collins (1983) 370.

material in this book.[138] The latter is a product of Egyptian Judaism, probably of the second century B.C.[139] The oracle in lines 350-380 has been assigned to two specific geographical and historical contexts, both in the first century B.C. Collins argues for a context in Cleopatra VII's campaign against Rome,[140] but there seems no sufficient evidence for this view. The 'mistress' of line 359 need not be Cleopatra identified with Isis,[141] but can be understood as either Asia or Fortune.[142] The former is the most obvious reading of the passage: line 359 depicts a reversal of the situation in which Rome is the mistress and Asia the slave. Moreover, although Collins does produce evidence that the conflict between Cleopatra and Octavian was perceived in terms of the traditional theme of the conflict between East and West, Asia and Europe,[143] and so is able to explain the use of the name Asia in lines 350-355 as a reference to the East led by Cleopatra,[144] he ignores the placenames in lines 363, 365, which make a reference to Asia Minor much more plausible. Even if the oracle in lines 363-364, with its wordplay on the three names Samos, Delos and Rome (Σάμος ἄμμος... Δῆλος ἄδηλος... Ῥώμη ῥύμη), was already known in the Sibylline literature (it recurs in 8:165-166) and was inserted here for the sake of its reference to Rome, the specific mention of Smyrna in line 365 would be strange in an oracle originating in Egypt. Moreover, the oracle in lines 400-488, with its many references to places in Asia Minor, can be located with some confidence in Asia Minor and probably assigned to the Erythrean Sibyl.[145] It would not be difficult to suppose that 350-380 comes from the same geographical area.

The alternative proposal locates the oracle in Asia Minor in the context of the campaign of Mithridates VI against Rome.[146]

[138]See Collins (1974) 21-24, 27-28.
[139]Collins (1974) 28-33.
[140]Collins (1974) 57-64; followed by Yarbro Collins (1984) 91.
[141]Collins (1974) 61-62.
[142]Nikiprowetzky (1970) 342.
[143]On this theme in the Jewish Sibyllines, see Kocsis (1982).
[144]Collins (1974) 59-60.
[145]Collins (1974) 27-28.
[146]McGing (1986) 102, 105; followed by Parke (1988) 136-137, 148 n. 1. Cf. also Fuchs (1964) 36.

The strength of this proposal is that lines 350-355 do resemble a theme of Mithridates' anti-Roman propaganda: the depiction of the Romans as *latrones gentium,* driven in their imperial conquests by not only the love of power but also greed for material gain. The prediction of peace and reconciliation for Asia and Europe beyond the conflict (367-368) would also fit Mithridates' campaign against Rome, in which he stressed his role as a unifier of East and West. However, it is perhaps, as Collins points out, more difficult to place the prediction of Rome's restoration after destruction (361) in the context of Mithridates' campaign.[147]

The association of the oracle with Mithridates' campaign is probably too specific. The oracle makes no reference to a king. There is no reason to connect it with any specific historical occasion. But the parallel with Mithridates' propaganda is illuminating. Both Mithridates and the oracle no doubt take up popular resentment in Asia Minor against Roman plunder and taxation.[148] In view of the large numbers of slaves which Asia Minor supplied the Roman slave trade, lines 353-355 would be particularly appropriate in an anti-Roman oracle from Asia Minor. It is not entirely clear whether the oracle is pagan or Jewish in origin. The Jewish Sibylline Oracles were deliberately written within the same literary tradition as pagan Sibylline Oracles, and some fragments of the latter have very probably been incorporated into the extant Jewish Sibyllines.[149] However, lines 357-360 do seem to contain echoes of Old Testament prophecies of the fall of Babylon (Isa 47:1; Jer 51:7; Isa 14:12; Isa 47:5, 7).[150] None of these can be regarded as

[147]Collins does not advance this argument against the Mithridatic origin of the passage in (1974) 60-61, but does in (1983) 358.

[148]Cf. also Antisthenes' story of the Roman consul's prophecy after the Roman victory over Antiochus III at Thermopylae (191 B.C.), predicting that a great army from Asia would defeat Rome, devastate Italy, and take women, children and wealth as booty to Asia: Fuchs (1964) 6-7; Yarbro Collins (1984) 89.

[149]Parke (1988) 13, 132-133. The fall of Rome was predicted even in Sibylline oracles which circulated in first-century Rome: Parke (1988) 142-143.

[150]Other parallels suggested by Nikiprowetzky (1970) 342, are even less close. For Isaiah 14:12 applied to Rome, cf. Sibylline Oracles 5:177-178; 8:101.

certain allusions which definitely establish the oracle as Jewish, but in combination they make it likely.

As happens not infrequently in the Sibylline Oracles, this oracle is echoed or imitated in later books, especially in 4:145-148:

> Great wealth will come to Asia, which Rome itself
> once plundered and deposited in her house of many
>   possessions.
> She will then pay back twice as much and more
> to Asia, and then there will be a surfeit of war.[151]

In its present form at least, the fourth Sibylline Oracle is a Jewish work of the late first century A.D., more or less contemporary with Revelation.[152] If this passage is dependent on 3:350-365, it shows that the latter was known in Jewish circles by the time John wrote. It is also of interest that the fourth Sibylline Oracle uses, in close connexion with the passage just quoted, the legend of the return of Nero (4:137-139), which is also connected with the fall of Rome in Revelation (16:12-14; 17:11-13, 16-17).

A Sibylline passage later than Revelation (8:68-72, which probably refers to and should be dated in the reign of Marcus Aurelius)[153] predicts that the wealth Rome has taken from Asia will be restored to her by the returning Nero:

> One, an old man, will control dominions far and wide,
> a most piteous king, who will shut up and guard all the
>   wealth
> of the world in his home, so that when the blazing
> matricidal exile returns from the ends of the earth
> he will give these things to all and award great wealth to
>   Asia.[154]

---

[151]Translation from Collins (1983) 387-388.
[152]Collins (1983) 382.
[153]Collins (1983) 416.
[154]Translation from Collins (1983) 419.

Another fragmentary passage in the same eighth book evidently referred to Rome's sumptuousness (8:123-124) and predicts that, when destroyed, Rome will have to repay all she has taken (129). Sibylline Oracles 2:18-19 and 8:40 merely predict that, in Rome's coming destruction by fire, her great wealth will perish. We may further note that the adjective χλιδανή (luxurious), applied to Rome in both 3:356 and 8:50, appears to be part of the Sibylline tradition of criticism of Rome's luxury. Finally, the picture of the people of Rome foreseeing her imminent fall and mourning for her with dirges by the banks of the Tiber (8:60-64) is reminiscent of Revelation 18:9-19, but contains no reference to Rome's wealth (and might be dependent on Revelation 18).[155]

Some contact between Revelation and the Jewish Sibylline tradition of criticism of Rome's economic oppression of Asia is therefore possible, but no parallel exists in the latter for Revelation's focus on trade with Rome.[156]

[155]Cf. also 4 (6) Ezra 15:44.
Some of the material in this chapter was published in a more popular form as chapter 6 of Bauckham (1989).

[156]This confirms the verdict of Georgi (1986) 125: 'The recognition of Rome as a world trade center in the Book of Revelation is a new idea in early Christian literature and has no parallels in Jewish apocalypses.'

11

Nero and the Beast

Although the emperor Nero is not named in Revelation, his name plays a key role in it. For Nero Caesar is the name of the beast (13:17; 15:2). To justify this statement we must unravel the numerology of the beast, which will involve not only the number 666 (13:18) but all the numbers associated with the figure of the beast in Revelation (section 1). Insight into Revelation's numerology will highlight the importance of Nero for John's portrayal of the beast, but will not in itself explain why or in what sense John identified the beast with Nero. To understand that we must first trace the origin and forms of the pagan and Jewish expectation of the return of Nero (section 2) and then examine precisely how John has taken up and transformed the Nero legend. As Revelation 13:18 indicates, the history and legend of Nero will illuminate much that is otherwise enigmatic about the apocalyptic beast. But the real key to Revelation's accounts of the beast will be found to be not Nero alone, but the parallel and contrast, the historical and eschatological confrontation between Nero Caesar and Jesus Christ.

1. The numbers of the beast

The majority of modern scholars find a reference to Nero in Revelation 13:18, where the number of the beast is said to be 666. Since this number is also called 'the number of his name' (13:17; 15:2), John has usually and rightly been supposed to be employing the ancient practice of gematria, whereby any word could be given a numerical value. Since the letters of both the Greek and the Hebrew alphabets were all used as numbers, it is possible to add up the numerical value of each letter of any Greek or Hebrew word and obtain the 'number' of the word. This, it is generally supposed, is what it would be to 'calculate (ψηφισάτω) the number of the beast' (13:18): John is inviting the reader 'who has intelligence' (ὁ ἔχων νοῦν) to reckon the numerical value of the beast's name and find it to be 666.

The practice of gematria is well attested in both Jewish and pagan circles in the ancient world.[1] It was used in various ways. Most relevant, because of Revelation's specific phrase 'the number of his name', are cases where a *name* is given a numerical value.[2] Sometimes, the number functions as a code to conceal the name or to pose a riddle for the reader to solve. A graffito found in Pompeii reads: 'I love the girl whose number is 545' (φιλῶ ἧς ἀριθμός φμε).[3] Presumably the beloved herself is expected to recognize the numerical value of her name, but few others would take the trouble to work out which name was this numerical value (as most probably several Greek feminine names have). The Jewish and Christian Sibylline Oracles use gematria in order to provide a degree of mystery or obscurity of reference appropriate in a prophetic text. For example, a prophecy of all the Roman Emperors from Julius Caesar to Hadrian gives none of their names but provides the numerical value of the first letter of each of their names (SibOr 5:12-51; cf. also 11:256, 266; 12:16-271). A riddle concealing a name of God by gematria (SibOr 1:141-145) remains still unsolved. The name of the incarnate Son of God is said to be 888 (1:324-330), the sum of the Greek letters of the name Jesus (ι = 10 + η = 8 + σ = 200 + o = 70 + υ = 400 + σ = 200). Anyone familiar with the Christian claim about Jesus would not find this difficult to solve. But in another instance in the Sibylline

---

[1] Dornseiff (1922) 91-113.

[2] Compare the phrase ἡ ψῆφος τοῦ ὀνόματι ('the reckoning of the name') used in TSol 15:11 (cf. 6:8; 11:6) and 13:6 (MS. P) to indicate the numerical value, by gematria, of the names Emmanuel and Raphael.

[3] Deissmann (1910) 276.

Oracles gematria is used rather differently.[4] The numerical value of the name Rome (948) is taken to indicate the number of years the city of Rome will last from its foundation to its destruction at the hands of Nero returning in the future (8:148-149). Here the point is not mystery and the number is not a code: Rome is openly named (8:145). Rather the 'number' of Rome is taken to reveal something significant about the city.

We should also note the method (known as *isopsephism*) of establishing a connexion between two different words by showing that their numerical values are the same (the two words are then said to be ἰσόψηφα).[5] It is interesting to observe that this method is employed in one of the Greek verses lampooning Nero which Suetonius (*Nero* 39) says circulated during his reign:[6]

Νεόψηφον· Νέρων ἰδίαν μητέρα ἀπέκτεινε·
A new calculation: Nero killed his own mother.

The word νεόψηφον (not otherwise known[7]) must invite the reader to discover that the numerical value of the name Nero (1005) is the same as that of 'killed his own mother'. Thus the popular rumour, following the death of Agrippina, that Nero had been responsible for her murder is confirmed by isopsephism.

Isopsephism was also used in Jewish exegesis. One rabbinic tradition about the name of the Messiah maintained that the Messiah would be called Menahem ('comforter': cf. Lam 1:16) because this name (מנחם) has the same numerical value (138) as the word צמח ('branch') which is the title of the Davidic

---

[4]This example is missed by Yarbro Collins (1984) 1270-1271, who, relying only on SibOr 1-2 and 5, explains the use of gematria in the Sibylline Oracles only for cryptograms.

[5]Dornseiff (1922) 96-97.

[6]For the dating of these lampoons, see Townend (1960) 104, who thinks they must date from the very last years of Nero's reign, and Bradley (1978) 239, who thinks, to the contrary, that the references to Agrippina's murder must have appeared soon after the event.

[7]Cf. Bücheler (1906).

Messiah in Zechariah 3:8; 6:12 (y. Ber. 5a; Lam. R. 1:16).[8]
Another tradition found a reference to the angel Gabriel in
Ezekiel 43:2, because the phrase 'many waters' (מים רבים) has
the same numerical value (342) as the phrase 'the angel
Gabriel' (המלאך גבריאל).[9]

The solution to the riddle of 666 which has been most widely
accepted since it was first suggested in 1831[10] is that 666 is the
sum of the letters of Nero Caesar written in Hebrew characters
as נרון קסר (נ = 50 + ר = 200 + ו = 6 + ן = 50 + ק = 100 + ס = 60 +
ר = 200). Few of the many other solutions by gematria which
have been proposed[11] offer a *name*, which the phrase 'the
number of his name' (Rev 13:17; 15:2) requires,[12] and of those
few which do this seems eminently the most preferable. It has
also been suggested that the variant reading 616 can be
explained by the same proposal, since if the Latin form Nero,
rather than the Greek form Νέρων, is transliterated into Hebrew,
so that the final ן is omitted from נרון, the numerical value
becomes 616.[13]

---

[8]If, as has frequently been suggested, the tradition of the name Menahem ben
Hezekiah for the Messiah originated from the name of the Zealot leader Menahem,
the grandson of Hezekiah (cf. Hengel [1989A] 293-297), then it is *possible* that this
example of isopsephism originated at the time of the first Jewish revolt, as a way of
demonstrating Menahem to be the Messiah.

[9]*Abot de Rabbi Natan*, quoted and discussed in Goldin (1988) 326-329.

[10]It was apparently suggested independently by four German scholars in 1831
(O. F. Fritsche), 1836 (F. Benary) and 1837 (F. Hitzig, E. Reuss): see Peake (1920)
323; Brady (1983) 292.

[11]For the most important of these, see Peake (1920) 319-324; Beckwith (1919)
404-405. Many older suggestions are recounted and discussed in Brady (1983); cf.
also Sanders (1918). Among other modern suggestions, note also Couchoud
(1932) 140 ('Αττει); Giet (1957) 76-79 (sum of the initials of the emperor's names
from Julius Caesar to Vespasian); Stauffer (1947) (abbreviation of the full imperial
title of Domitian).

[12]Beckwith (1919) 403.

[13]Charles (1920) 1:367; Rühle (1964) 463; Yarbro Collins (1976) 175.
Alternatively, 616 may represent a different solution: Gaius Caesar (i.e. Caligula)
in Greek (γ = 3 + α = 1 + ι = 10 + ο = 70 + σ = 200 + κ = 20 + α = 1 + ι = 10 + σ = 200
+ α = 1 + ρ = 100) (Swete [1907] 176). Some early copyist, unable to make sense of
666, substituted this rather plausible identification of the beast as the emperor
Caligula.

There have been two major objections to the suggestion that 666 = קסר נרון. One is that the spelling קסר (instead of קיסר) is defective.[14] As Peake pointed out,[15] the abnormal spelling could be accepted if we assume that John had some *other* reason for wanting the sum to come to 666. We shall shortly discover that he did have at least one reason for wanting precisely this number to be Nero's. But, in fact, that the defective spelling was used for Nero himself has now been shown by a papyrus document in Aramaic from Murabba'at, which is dated in the second year of Nero Caesar (לנרון קסר).[16] The second objection is that John, writing in Greek for Greek-speaking readers (hearers) in the cities of Asia, would not have done his gematria in Hebrew.[17] To this it may be replied that he could count on having at least some readers (hearers) who knew some Hebrew in each of the churches, and that if John found special significance in the numerical value of a name he may well, as a Jewish Christian, have expected this significance to inhere in Hebrew rather than Greek letters. Moreover, we shall later suggest that John probably inherited the number 666, as equivalent to קסר נרון, from Jewish Christian apocalyptic tradition.

While נרון קסר is probably part of the solution to John's riddle, it is not the whole solution. We may suspect that John intends not merely to cloak a reference to Nero in mystery, but to point out that the numerical value of Nero's name has significance. The parallel with the verse about Nero quoted by Suetonius suggests that John may be employing isopsephism, and, once alerted to that possibility, we can see that in fact he says as much: 'let him who has intelligence calculate the number of the beast (τοῦ θηρίου), for it is the number of a man'

[14]It was already rejected (before anyone else proposed it) on these grounds by Ewald in 1828: Peake (1920) 323. Others pointed out that the defective spelling is attested in rabbinic literature: Beckwith (1919) 406.

[15]Peake (1920) 326.

[16]Mur 18 line 1: Benoit, Milik & de Vaux (1961) 101. This was pointed out by Hillers (1963).

[17]Farrer (1964) 158.

(13:18). The number of the beast is *also* the number of a man.[18]
If 'the number of a man' is the numerical value of Nero Caesar
(נרון קסר), what is 'the number of the beast'? It so happens that
the Greek word θηρίον (beast), when transliterated into Hebrew
as תריון, has the numerical value 666 (ת = 400 + ר = 200 + י = 10
+ ו = 6 + ן = 50).[19]

This way of practising gematria — by calculating the value of
a Greek word written in Hebrew letters — is also found in the
Greek Apocalypse of Baruch (3 Baruch), which may well be
roughly contemporary with or somewhat later than Revelation
and, like Revelation, was written in Greek. In 3 Baruch 4:3-7,
Baruch is shown a snake (δράκων) which drinks one cubit of
water a day from the sea, but he is told that the sea is never
diminished because it is replenished by 360 rivers. The figure
is probably derived from the fact that the numerical value of
δράκων written in Hebrew characters is 360 (ד = 4 + ר = 200 + ק
= 100 + ו = 6 + ן = 50). In 4:10 the number of the giants who
perished in the Flood (κατακλυσμός) is said to have been
409,000, corresponding, no doubt, to the fact that the numerical
value of κατακλυσμός written in Hebrew characters is 409 (ק =
100 + ט = 9 + ק = 100 + ל = 30 + י = 10 + ס = 60 + מ = 40 + ס = 60).[20]
The use of gematria in 3 Baruch is rather less subtle than in
Revelation, but shows that John must be following a method of
doing gematria which was accepted in the circles which
produced the Jewish and Jewish Christian apocalypses.

Thus John is saying that the number of the *word* beast (תריון)
is also the number of a man (נרון קסר). The gematria does not
merely assert that Nero is the beast: it demonstrates that he is.
Nero's very name identifies him by its numerical value as the
apocalyptic beast of Daniel's prophecy (just as rabbinic tradition

---

[18]Corssen (1902), followed by Peake (1920) 325-326, recognized this but was
not able to explain satisfactorily how 666 is the number of the *beast*. He supposed
it was an ancient apocalyptic number handed down by tradition (cf. Beckwith
[1919] 406), and referred to Gunkel's view that it designated the primeval chaos
monster (תהום קדמוניה, 'primal chaos' = 666).

[19]Rühle (1964) 463. For the spelling תריון, as a plausible transliteration, rather
than תיריון, see Rosůn (1963) 65.

[20]Bohak (1990) 119-120.

used isopsephism to demonstrate that Menahem is the name of the messianic 'branch' of Zechariah's prophecy). Surprisingly, the variant reading 616 can also yield the same information. If the number 616 is simply written in Hebrew letters, it is תריו (600 = תר, 10 = י, 6 = ו), which transliterates θηρίου, the genitive form which appears in the phrase τὸν ἀριθμὸν τοῦ θηρίου in Revelation 13:18.[21] The variant reading seems to represent a genuine alternative tradition about the number of the beast, which also yields the identification of Nero with the apocalyptic beast.

If, as the manuscript evidence strongly suggests, John himself preferred the number 666, this was probably because there are further mysteries hidden in this number. Unlike 616, 666 has peculiar mathematical characteristics. It is a doubly triangular number, though it seems that it was not until 1912 that this was first recognized.[22] Ancient mathematics inherited from the Pythagorean tradition an interest in numbers conceived as corresponding to geometrical figures. Those corresponding to two-dimensional figures are known as plane numbers. These can be divided into two types: those corresponding to figures with equal sides (triangular, square, pentagonal, hexagonal etc.) and those corresponding to figures with unequal sides, of which the most important are the rectangular numbers. Of all these plane numbers, much the most important were the triangular numbers (τρίγωνοι), the square numbers (τετράγωνοι) and the rectangular numbers (ἑτερομήκεις).[23] These three types of numbers are closely related to each other and were frequently discussed in relation to each other, as, for example, in the mathematical works of Theon of Smyrna[24] and

---

[21]Oberweis (1986) 236.

[22]van den Bergh van Eysinga (1912). His further conclusion that therefore 666 represents the Gnostic figure of Sophia is implausible.

[23]There is no satisfactory translation of ἑτερομήκης. It describes a rectangular figure of which one side is precisely one unit longer than the other, and so the terms 'rectangular' and 'oblong' are not really sufficiently specific. D'Ooge's translation of Nichomachus (D'Ooge [1926]) uses 'heteromecic'. For convenience I follow Menken (1985) 27-28, in referring to 'rectangular numbers'.

[24]See D'Ooge (1926) 39.

Nicomachus of Gerasa.[25] Although these mathematicians were writing in the second century A.D.,[26] many of their ideas about plane numbers were known to Philo of Alexandria and so can be presumed to have been commonly known to educated people in the late first century A.D.[27] Discussions of John's use of the number 666 which recognize it as a triangular number have usually treated triangular numbers in isolation.[28] We shall appreciate the significance of 666 better if we recognize the relationships between triangular, square and rectangular numbers.

Pythagorean arithmetic represented numbers by figures made with pebbles (ψῆφοι: hence the verb ψηφίζω in the sense of 'to count up, to calculate,' as used in Rev 13:18). The three types of numbers — triangular, square, and rectangular — are conceived as triangular, square and rectangular shapes.[29] A triangular number is the sum of successive numbers $(1 + 2 + 3 +...)$. Thus ten is the 'triangle' of 4, i.e. it is the sum of all the numbers up to 4 $(1 + 2 + 3 + 4 = 10)$. The first four triangular numbers $(1, 3, 6, 10)$ can be represented as equilateral triangles thus:

```
 α          α          α            α
          α α        α α          α α
                   α α α        α α α
                              α α α α
```

Each triangle is formed by the series of numbers to be added, and the side of each triangle is equal to the last number in the

[25]*Introduction to Arithmetic* 2.12.1-4; 2.17.2-3; 2.19.1-2.20.3. The *Introduction to Arithmetic* is translated with introduction and notes in D'Ooge (1926); Bertier (1978). On Nichomachus, see also Dillon (1977) 352-361; O'Meara (1989) 14-23.

[26]For Nichomachus' date, see Bertier (1978) 7; for Theon, see D'Ooge (1926) 36, 72.

[27]D'Ooge (1926) 31-32; Menken (1985) 27-28; cf. Collins (1984) 1257.

[28]The only notable exception is Colson (1915); but cf. Farrer (1964) 159, followed by Sweet (1979) 219 (triangle and square).

[29]The information which follows is set out as simply as possible for the benefit of readers who (like the author) have no mathematical inclinations.

series. The number of units in each case is the triangular number.

A square number is the sum of successive *odd* numbers (1 + 3 + 5 +...). Thus 16 is the sum of all the odd numbers up to 7 (1 + 3 + 5 + 7 = 16). Such a number is represented as a square, so that the first four square numbers (1, 4, 9, 16) can be represented thus:

```
α        α α        α α α        α α α α
         α α        α α α        α α α α
                    α α α        α α α α
                                 α α α α
```

Each number added (after 1) forms two sides of the square. So in this case the side of each square is not the last number in the series, but what we call the square root. 16 is the sum of the odd numbers up to 7, but it is the square of 4.

A rectangular number is the sum of successive *even* numbers (2 + 4 + 6 +...). Thus 20 is the sum of all the even numbers up to 8 (2 + 4 + 6 + 8 = 20). Such numbers can be represented as rectangles in which one side is one unit longer than the other, so that the first four (2, 6, 12, 20) can be represented thus:

```
α α      α α α      α α α α      α α α α α
         α α α      α α α α      α α α α α
                    α α α α      α α α α α
                                 α α α α α
```

Hence a rectangular number can be thought of as the product of two successive numbers (2 x 3 = 6, 3 x 4 = 12, 4 x 5 = 20).

Not only did these three classes of numbers represent an obvious group (the sum of successive numbers, the sum of successive odd numbers, the sum of successive even numbers), but also they were thought of in corresponding numbered series (e.g. the 3rd triangular number corresponding to the 3rd square number and the 3rd rectangular number). The first 36 numbers in the three series are as follows:

	1st[30]	2nd	3rd	4th	5th	6th	7th	8th	9th
triangles	1	3	6	10	15	21	28	36	45
squares	1	4	9	16	25	36	49	64	81
rectangulars	2	6	12	20	30	42	56	72	90

	10th	11th	12th	13th	14th	15th	16th	17th	18th
triangles	55	66	78	91	105	120	136	153	171
squares	100	121	144	169	196	225	256	289	324
rectangulars	110	132	156	182	210	240	272	306	342

	19th	20th	21st	22nd	23rd	24th	25th	26th	27th
triangles	190	210	231	253	276	300	325	351	378
squares	361	400	441	484	529	576	625	676	729
rectangulars	380	420	462	506	552	600	650	702	756

	28th	29th	30th	31st	32nd	33rd	34th	35th	36th
triangles	406	435	465	496	528	561	595	630	666
squares	784	841	900	961	1024	1089	1156	1225	1296
rectangulars	812	870	930	992	1056	1122	1190	1260	1332

The relationships between these series make it quite easy to calculate the corresponding triangular, square and rectangular numbers. Thus, every rectangular number is double its corresponding triangle: e.g., 1332, the 36th rectangular, is twice 666, the 36th triangle. A square added to the number of its place in the series (which is the same as its square root) makes the corresponding rectangular: e.g. 1296 + 36 = 1332. Two consecutive triangular numbers make the square corresponding to the second of them: e.g. 630 + 666 = 1296. It is important to realise that a quite elementary acquaintance with these principles would make these numbers and their relationships easily accessible.

For this way of understanding arithmetic, 666 is a remarkable number. In the first place, it is a *doubly* triangular number. In other words, it is the 'triangle' of 36 (1 + 2 + 3 ... + 36 = 666), and

---

[30]Nichomachus, *Introduction* 2.8.2-3; 2.9.2-3, calls one 'potentially' the first triangular number and 'potentially' the first square.

36 is also a triangular number, the 'triangle' of 8 (1 + 2 + 3...
+ 8 = 36). Such doubly triangular numbers are rare: the series
runs 1, 6, 21, 55, 120, 231, 406, 666, 1035, 1540.... It seems
rather unlikely that the number of the beast should be one of
these numbers purely accidentally. Moreover, uniquely among
these doubly triangular numbers, 666 *looks* like a doubly
triangular number. (The Greek number written as χξϛ would
not make the impression of our three repeated digits, but
written or said as ἑξακόσιοι ἑξήκοντα ἕξ the repetition of ἕξ
would be apparent.) Two triangles have six sides! But thirdly,
666 is the 'triangle' of a number (36) which is not only
triangular but also square (6 x 6 = 36). Numbers which are both
triangular and square are even rarer than doubly triangular
numbers: the first three are 1, 36, 1225. That 666 is the
'triangle' of such a number makes it a very remarkable number
indeed. The next such number is 750925 (the 'triangle' of
1225)!

These peculiarities of 666 would be of no importance to us
if we could not show that John was aware of them and has
exploited them. In fact, he has given some clues to the
significance they had for him in the literary connexions between
13:18 and other passages of his work. Firstly, there is a connexion
between 13:18 and 17:9. In 13:18 the number of the beast is
introduced thus: ὧδε ἡ σοφία ἐστιν. ὁ ἔχων νοῦν ψηφισάτω...
('Here is wisdom. Let him who has intelligence calculate...').
A similar introduction is given in 17:9 to the interpretation of
the seven heads of the beast: ὧδε ὁ νοῦς ὁ ἔχων σοφίαν ('Here
[is] the intelligence which has wisdom'). The resemblance
between the two passages is clearly deliberate, and the variation
between them typical of John's stylistic habit of varying the
precise form of expressions he repeats. By omitting ἐστιν and
exchanging the synonyms νοῦς and σοφία, the first seven words
of 13:18 become the first six words of 17:9. John must have
intended the formula to make a link between the two passages,
which are in any case closely related. Chapter 13, which the
riddle of the number of the beast (13:18) concludes, introduces
the figure of the beast from the sea (assisted in the latter part
of the chapter by the beast from the land). But two features of
the description of the beast remain unexplained in chapter 13:

his seven heads and ten horns (13:1). Even though the mortal wound received by one of the heads (13:3) is a key event in chapter 13, the reader is not told what the heads represent or which of them is wounded. Explanation of the heads and the horns of the beast is reserved from 17:7-17, which is the second major passage about the beast in Revelation. The explanation of the heads and the horns of the beast is introduced at this point because it is necessary for explaining the judgment of the harlot who rides on the beast. This will occur when the beast (more precisely the beast which is 'the eighth and of the seven' heads: 17:11) and his allies the ten horns turn against the harlot and destroy her (17:16-17).

Thus the repeated formula in 13:18; 17:9 links the two major, complementary passages about the beast and in each case introduces an explanation which involves numerical calculation. In 17:9 the seven heads of the beast are explained as seven hills on which the woman sits. Just as in 13:18 the formula may at first seem to introduce a riddle which conceals the identification of the beast as Nero, so in 17:9 it may at first seem to introduce a riddle which conceals the identification of the harlot as the city of Rome, built on seven hills. But, as in 13:18 so in 17:9, we soon see that mystery is not the real point. That Rome was built on seven hills was extremely well-known. So the indication of the harlot's identity required no great intelligence. By referring to its seven hills John was not concealing Babylon's identity as Rome but making it obvious. But, just as when we look more closely at 13:18 we see that more than a riddling *reference* to Nero is involved, so 17:9 leads on in 17:10-11 to a further identification of the seven heads of the beast as seven kings and the beast himself as an eighth which also belongs to the seven. This is the point at which intelligence is really required and at which the link between the two passages (13:18 and 17:9) becomes important. As we have noticed, the number 666 is the 'double triangle' of 8 (i.e. 666 is the 'triangle' of 36, which is the 'triangle' of 8). Or to put the same point in a perhaps more relevant way, 666 is the *eighth* 'doubly triangular' number (in the series: 1, 6, 21, 55, 120, 231, 406, 666). We have noted that numbers of this kind were thought of in a numbered series and according to their place in that series. Thus Nero's number 666 not only reveals by isopsephism that he is the beast; it also, as the eighth 'doubly triangular' number, reveals that he is 'the eighth' and thus related to the seven heads of the beast as an eighth. Perhaps — though it is impossible to be sure of this — John also noticed that one of the first seven 'doubly triangular' numbers is 6, so that in this sense it could be said that the eighth number (666) is also one of the first seven, as the beast is an eighth and also 'of the seven' (17:11). But the main point of the numerological connection between 666 and 8 must be to demonstrate Nero's relationship to the seven heads as an eighth.

Of course, as we shall see later in more detail, John is making use of the legend of the return of Nero: Nero, one of the seven emperors of Rome, will return as the final Antichrist, the eighth. But we shall also see later that in his use of this legend in chapter 17, John is especially interested in presenting the return of Nero as a parody of the parousia of Jesus Christ. The beast who 'was and is not and is to come' (17:8, cf. 11) is the demonic parody of God as he 'who was and is and is to come' in the parousia of his Christ (4:8; cf. 11:17; 16:5). This makes it not improbable that John attached to the number eight the eschatological significance which it certainly already had in John's time. Eight represented the eighth day of new creation following the seven days of the old creation's history (2 Enoch 33:1-2; Barn. 15:9). The fact that Noah could be called 'the eighth' (along with his seven relatives in the ark)[31] was seen as significant for this reason: emerging from the ark into the new postdiluvian world, he was a type of the new creation after the last judgment (SibOr 1:280-281; cf. 2 Pet 2:5). Early Christians associated the eschatological symbolism of the eighth with Sunday as 'the eighth day' (Barn. 15:9; Justin, *Dial.* 24:1; 41:4; 138:1). Revelation's use not simply of the number eight but of the idea of an eighth which follows seven makes an allusion to the sabbatical eschatology of an eighth day of creation after the seven quite plausible. It is tempting to see in the eighth which is one of the seven a parallel to the Christian eighth day,

[31]Cf. Bauckham (1983) 250.

Sunday, which is also (as the first day of the week) one of the seven, but since John had other reasons for making his eighth one of the seven heads we cannot be sure that he intended this parallel. The nature of numerological symbolism means that we can attempt to identify the principal significance which John saw in his numbers, but we cannot set a limit to the chain of further significance which the numbers could have generated. John was setting his readers thinking. Given the ancient attitude to the significance of numbers, he would probably not have denied dimensions of significance to his numbers which he himself had not discovered but which his readers might discover.

This uncertainty about how far John himself pursued the significance of his numbers must apply to a further aspect of the number eight. Very probably, it designates the beast (Nero returning) as the demonic rival to Christ in his eschatological coming to judgment. But at this point we are reminded of the curious circumstance that the numerical value of the name Jesus in Greek is 888 ($\iota = 10 + \eta = 8 + \sigma = 200 + o = 70 + \upsilon = 400 + \sigma = 200$). Knowledge and use of this example of gematria is attested, some time after Revelation, in Sibylline Oracle 1:323-331, but Christians interested in gematria would surely have worked out the numerical value of the name Jesus at an early date. Of course, 666 is the value of Nero Caesar in Hebrew, whereas 888 is the value of Jesus in Greek. John may not have practised or valued gematria in Greek. So it must remain quite uncertain whether he noticed or saw significance in the correspondence between 666 as the number of the beast and 888 as the number of Jesus. But if he did, the significance would probably be connected with the fact that 666 reduces to the eschatological number 8.

We may return to more solid ground by observing a second literary connexion between 13:18 and another part of the book. In 13:18 the one who has intelligence is invited to 'calculate the number of the beast, for it is the number of a human being' (ψηφισάτω τὸν ἀριθμόν τοῦ θηρίου· ἀριθμὸς γὰρ ἀνθρώπου ἐστίν), and the figure 666 is then given as the beast's number. In 21:17 we are told that the angel who showed John the new Jerusalem 'measured its wall, 144 cubits by the measure of a human being, that is, of an angel' (ἐμέτρησεν τὸ τεῖχος αὐτῆς ἑκατὸν τεσσεράκοντα τεσσάρων πηχῶν, μέτρον ἀνθρώπου, ὅ ἐστιν ἀγγελου). There is not only the parallel between the phrases ἀριθμὸς ἀνθρώπου and μέτρον ἀνθρώπου, but also the contrast between the identification of the first with the number of the beast and that of the second with the measure of an angel. In the first text the beast's number is said to be that of a human being, in the second the measure of a human being is said to be that of an angel. The parallel and contrast surely suggest that whereas the beast is humanity debased, the new Jerusalem represents humanity exalted to the position of the angels. Of course, 21:17 is inspired by Ezekiel 40:5, which refers to the angel as a man and explains that the kind of cubits his measuring rod measures are the long rather than the common cubit. But unlike Ezekiel's explanation, John's does not enable us to calculate the literal width — or is it the height? — of the wall. By telling us that the cubits are according to the measure of a man, that is an angel, John intends something less prosaic: an indication that the calculation is in some sense the obverse of that in 13:18.

The parallel and contrast between 13:18 and 21:17 invite us to relate the *numbers* given in the two texts: 666 and 144. Just as 666 is the numerical value of θηρίον ('beast') written in Hebrew characters, so 144 is the numerical value of ἀγγέλος ('angel') written in Hebrew characters (א = 1 + ג = 50 + ג = 3 + ל = 30 + ס = 60).[32] Thus the contrast we have already discerned — between

---

[32]Bohak (1990) 121. Topham (1989) offers an alternative explanation: 144 is the numerical value of 'son of God', written in Hebrew as בן אלהים. But Bohak's explanation coheres with the fact that in 13:18 the gematria depends on writing a Greek word in Hebrew letters. Moreover, since 'son of God' is a christological title in Revelation (2:18), John is unlikely to have used it as a term for an angel, while a reference to Christ by gematria in 21:17 is not appropriate. Revelation does not portray Christ as the builder of the New Jerusalem, and so the suggested parallel with an inscription of Sargon II of Assyria (c. 712 B.C.), which points out that the numerical value of Sargon's name is the number of cubits in the length of a city wall he has built (Simon [1909] 99-100), seems less relevant than Topham claims.

Friesenhahn (1935) 245, gives ἡ ἀγία 'Ιεροσόλυμα (cf. Rev 21:1, 10) the numerical value of 144, but he does this (as in most of the calculations in his book)

the bestial and the angelic — is confirmed and reinforced by the gematria indicated in the two texts. But there is also an obvious arithmetical contrast between the two numbers: 666 is triangular, 144 is square. In fact, 144 is the twelfth square number, that is, it is the square of 12. As such, it is the number which best represents the new Jerusalem. In the first half of 21:16 John carefully indicates that the new Jerusalem is square, before going on in the second half of the verse to show that it is also a cube. The number 12 is reiterated throughout the account of the new Jerusalem (21:12-22:2). Thus whereas humanity debased to the level of the beast bears the triangular number 666, humanity raised to the level of the angels in the new Jerusalem is surrounded by the square of 12.

The measurements of the city and its wall — 12,000 stadia (21:16), 144 cubits (21:17) — certainly also relate to the people of God who are reckoned by the symbolic number of 144,000 in 7:4-8 (where the 12,000 from each of the twelve tribes is formulaically declared) and 14:1. These are the people who will find their home in the new Jerusalem, with its dimensions of 12,000 stadia and its wall of 144 cubits. Moreover, the reference to the 144,000 in 14:1 certainly relates closely to the account of the beast which climaxes by giving his number at the end of chapter 13. Chapter 13 describes how the beast, the agent of the dragon, is victorious over the saints. In 14:1 we see the Lamb with his army of saints, the 144,000, standing to oppose the beast on mount Zion. Whereas all who worship the beast have its name or the number of its name marked on the right hand or the forehead (13:16-17), the 144,000 have the Lamb's name and that of his Father written on their foreheads (14:1; cf. 7:3). There is a clear parallel, but it is unlikely that John intends to suggest that the saints have 888, the number of Jesus, written on their foreheads, as the worshippers of the beast have 666. He does not suggest that the name of the Lamb

---

only by using a system of numbering the letters of the Greek alphabet which is different from the usual one. For this system, in which the letters are simply numbered consecutively 1-24 and ἐπίσημα are not used (so α = 1, ω = 24), he claims some evidence that it was an earlier one than the usual system (p. 84), but gives no evidence for its use in gematria or in the first century A.D.

has a number, and insists that the 144,000 have the names of both the Lamb and his Father on their foreheads.[33] (It is possible that the name of the Lamb and the name of his Father are the same name: the divine name of God borne also by Christ; cf. 22:4.) Instead, he allows 666 to stand in contrast to 144,000. The latter is not, of course, a square number, but it is the square of 12 multiplied by a thousand. Here and in 7:4-8 John needed a number large enough to suggest a large army, but by making it an obvious multiple of the square of 12, he allows the square of the people of God to stand in contrast to the triangle of the beast. However, the relation between 666 in 13:18 and 144,000 in 14:1 is clear only in the light of the relation between 13:18 and 21:17, the only place where John uses the square number 144 itself.

Our argument that John is playing a serious game with triangular and square numbers — the triangular representing the beast, the square the people of God — is strengthened by the observation that he also uses the third, related class of numbers, the rectangular numbers, for a specific purpose. The numbers 42 and 1260, which he uses to designate the apocalyptic period of the end-time as forty-two months or 1260 days (11:2, 3; 12:6; 13:5), are rectangular numbers. This is the period of the reign of the beast, in which he persecutes the saints (13:5-7). It is the period in which the woman (who represents the heavenly reality of the people of God) is protected by God in the wilderness (12:6, 14): that is, the church is kept spiritually safe while outwardly persecuted. The image of 11:1-2 — the Gentiles trample the holy city for forty-two months but the sanctuary is protected — has the same meaning: the forces of evil persecute the church but her true spiritual reality with God is unharmed. Finally, the same period is that in which the two

---

[33]Skehan (1948) suggests that just as the number of the name of the beast is 666, so the number of the name of the beast's conqueror, given in Rev 19:16 (cf. 18:14) as 'king of kings and lord of lords,' is 777. The calculation is done by omitting the 'and', and translating the two titles into Aramaic (מלך מלכין מרא מרון), in which their combined numerical value is 777. It is conceivable that this name could be regarded as not only the Lamb's name but also his Father's (cf. Dan 2:47). But whether John intended this gematria must be very uncertain.

witnesses prophesy (11:3), that is, the church bears prophetic witness to the world against the powers of evil. Thus the period in question belongs in a sense both to the beast and to the people of God. It is the period of the beast's reign and of the church's witness. It is the period of his victory over the saints (13:7) and of their victory over him (15:2). If a triangular number represents the beast and a square number the saints, then it may seem appropriate for the third class of number, the rectangular, to designate this ambiguous period in which the beast and the saints oppose each other. Moreover, since 12 and 30 (the numbers which divide the year into months and the months into days, and by which John is able to make three and a half years equivalent to 42 months or 1260 days) are also rectangular numbers, rectangular numbers may have seemed the appropriate kind of numbers for periods of time.

The period itself is borrowed from Daniel, whose phrase 'a time, times, and half a time' (Dan 7:25; 12:7), John uses, to make the connexion with Daniel clear, in 12:14. But the alternative specifications of the same period to be found in Daniel are 1290 days (12:11) and 1335 days (12:12). It has never been satisfactorily explained why John ignored these numbers — which had scriptural authority — and chose instead to convert the period of three and a half years into both 42 months and 1260 days. The calculation, after all, is artificial, in that it requires years of just 12 months of just 30 days each, allowing neither some longer months nor intercalated months. The reason, we have suggested, is that John preferred rectangular numbers. But furthermore he must surely have noticed that these are not just any rectangular numbers but rather special ones. Here are their places in the series and their corresponding square numbers:

	6th	35th
square	36	1225
rectangular	42	1260

As a rectangular number 42 is 6 x 7, and the sum of the even numbers up to 12, while 1260 is 35 x 36 and the sum of the even numbers up to 70. 12 and 70 are both special numbers for

Jewish thought. But even more significant are the square numbers to which these rectangular numbers correspond. 36 is the triangular root of the beast's number 666, and we have already noticed its peculiarity in being both a square and a triangular number. It is the first such number after 1, and the next such number after it is 1225, the square which corresponds to the rectangular 1260. 1225 itself is the triangle of 49, the 'jubilee' number of 7 x 7, again a special number in Jewish thought.

The two numbers 42 and 1260 thus prove so numerologically suggestive it is difficult to be sure what symbolic significance John may particularly have seen in them. As with 666, he was probably aware of using numerologically rather extraordinary numbers whose significance his readers could explore but which he need not have thought he had himself exhausted. But the link between 42 and 36 is surely very significant. We should note that when John uses the figure 42 months he designates the apocalyptic period as the beast's time — for trampling and rule (11:2; 13:5), whereas when he uses the figure 1260 days he designates it as the church's time — for prophesying and protection (11:3; 12:6). This may be because 42 is the sixth rectangular number and corresponds to 36, the triangular root of 666, and so is more closely associated with the beast, whereas both 1260 and its corresponding square 1225 relate to the number of the people of God, 12 (though this is not so obvious in John's Greek). But both numbers have some ambiguity in this respect, appropriate to the ambiguity of this period of confrontation between the beast and the saints: 42 is the sum of the even numbers up to 12, whereas 1260 ends with 60, part of the beast's number 666. Even more significant, however, is the fact that the two squares (36 and 1225) are remarkable precisely as squares which are also triangles: thus they symbolize the confrontation between the triangle of the beast and the square of the people of God. The rectangles which correspond to them are the appropriate numbers to designate the period in which the beast and the saints are in conflict.

The Danielic apocalyptic period of three and a half years also appears in a passage in the Ascension of Isaiah (4:2-14) which, as we shall see in the next section, reproduces Christian apocalyptic tradition about the Antichrist as the returning Nero similar to the traditional material which John must have used. Here it is said that the Antichrist will reign for 3 years, 7 months and 27 days (4:12). Later the period is specified, in the extant Ethiopic text, as 332 days (4:14). The figure must originally have been 1332 days, which is equivalent to 3 years, 7 months, 27 days (3 years of 365 days + 7 months of 30 days + 27 days).[34] 1332 seems to be a variation of the figure of 1335 days in Daniel (12:12), just as 1260 in Revelation is a variation of the figure of 1290 days in Daniel (12:11), and for a similar reason. 1332 is the next rectangular number after 1260, and if we correlate it this time with its corresponding triangular number the reason for its use in Ascension of Isaiah 4:14 becomes very clear:

	36th
triangular	666
rectangular	1332

A rectangular number is always double its corresponding triangular, but in view of Revelation's use of rectangular numbers for the Danielic period it is likely that 1332 is used in the Ascension of Isaiah because it is the rectangular number related to 666, not simply because it is double 666.[35] The number of the beast itself does not appear in the Ascension of Isaiah, but the conclusion that it lies behind the text is surely necessary. Evidently, numerological speculation relating Nero's

[34]Bosse (1909) 321. The period given in 4:12 can be calculated as 1335 days if three months of 31 days are included, as in the Julian calendar they would be. Dillmann (1877) 69, and Charles (1900) 33, therefore correct the text of 4:14 to 1335, agreeing with this calculation and with the Danielic number of 1335 days (Dan 12:12). George Cedrenus, *Historiarum compendium* (PG 121:152C, quoted in Tisserant [1909] 121; Charles [1900] 29), quotes the period in AscIsa 4:12 as only three years and seven months, which he then calculates (3 years of 360 days + 7 months of 30 days) as 1290 days. Presumably this is an attempt to bring the text into line with Dan 12:11. Cedrenus doubtless knew the text of AscIsa 4:12 only indirectly through earlier chronographers: Acerbi (1984) 64.

[35]Bosse (1909) 322-323. Reicke (1972) 188, suggests that the doubled 666 indicates that it is a question of the eschatological return of Nero.

number 666 to the traditional apocalyptic period for the rule of Antichrist lies behind both Revelation and the Ascension of Isaiah in the Christian apocalyptic tradition on which they depend.[36] The respective authors have chosen different, though related, possibilities. John could have chosen the rectangular number directly related to 666 (and for such numerological thinking the relationship is so simple and obvious he could hardly have missed this possibility). His preference for the numbers 42 and 1260 must have been because of their greater symbolic value.

In order to complete our discussion of numbers associated with the beast, two numbers remain to be considered: seven and ten. These are the numbers of the heads and the horns of the beast (13:1; 17:3). That John's beast has seven heads and ten horns results from the fact that it combines the characteristics of all four beasts of Daniel's vision (Dan 7:3-7; cf. Rev 13:2).[37] It sums up and surpasses the evil empires of history in itself. Daniel's four beasts have seven heads between them, since the fourth has four (Dan 7:6), while none has horns except the fourth, which has ten (Dan 7:7). Nevertheless, John would not have given his beast seven heads and ten horns purely for this reason. He uses the imagery he takes over from Daniel fairly freely. He does not, for example, take over the four wings of Daniel's fourth beast (Dan 7:6), for which he evidently had no symbolic use. Whereas Daniel's individual 'Antichrist' figure is one of the ten horns (Dan 7:8, 20-21), John's is one of the heads of the beast.

The seven heads and the ten crowned horns link the beast with its master and source of power, the dragon (12:3). We have already noted the equation of the seven heads of the beast with the seven hills of Rome (17:9) and with seven kings of which one is also an eighth (17:9-11). Here the number seven is linked to the number eight, whose relationship to 666 and eschatological symbolism we have explored. But there is a little more to be said about this use of the number seven in connexion

---

[36]So, rightly, Reicke (1972) 188-189, followed by Robinson (1976) 240 n. 98.
[37]Farrer (1964) 152.

with eight. Seven is the number of totality. It is sometimes said to be the number of perfection, but if this is meant to indicate value, rather than simply quantity, it is misleading and would make it puzzling that John gives evil powers, the dragon and the beast, seven heads. Seven is better understood as the number of totality.[38] The seven heads, interpreted as seven kings, represent the complete series of evil, antichristian rulers of Rome. How then can there be an eighth? Perhaps because he is one of the seven recurring as a kind of final excess of evil. In him completeness becomes excess. But in John's use here of the numbers seven and eight there may also be a reflection of the Hebrew idiom, the 'graded numerical saying,' which uses two consecutive numbers in parallel.[39] In some cases this idiom indicates that the enumeration is illustrative rather than exhaustive (Prov 6:16; 30:15, 18, 21, 29),[40] but when the numbers seven and eight are used in this way, they seem to indicate an indefinite but adequate number (Eccl 11:2; Mic 5:4[5]). The latter text which speaks specifically of rulers ('seven shepherds and eight installed as rulers') is especially relevant. This usage may confirm what we would be justified in suspecting in any case: that John's numbers seven and eight are not to be taken literally, as defining how many Roman emperors there will actually be before the parousia, but as symbolizing all the evil, antichristian emperors there can be before their excess of evil brings its own destruction.

Of course, it cannot be denied that 17:9-11 provides in some sense a numbered sequence of emperors and locates the time of writing within this sequence. Consequently a great deal of inconclusive discussion has attempted to determine from this passage which emperor was reigning when Revelation was written.[41] Such attempts have been inconclusive because it

---

[38]So Corsini (1983) 42-44. Yarbro Collins (1984) 1276-1279, argues that seven is a principle of order rather than totality, but the Old Testament evidence of seven as the number of fullness or totality is strong: see Schmitz (1976) 690.

[39]See Towner (1973) 6-8.

[40]But according to Roth (1965) 6, the second number is the one intended.

[41]Notable recent discussions include Strobel (1963-64); Reicke (1972); Court (1979) 125-138; Yarbro Collins (1981); Ulrichsen (1985).

seems impossible to be sure with which emperor the sequence should begin or whether all emperors should be counted. The only obvious procedure would be to begin with Julius Caesar, with whom contemporary reckonings of the emperors begin,[42] and count all reigning emperors. But this would make the sixth head, the emperor now reigning (17:10), Nero. This cannot be correct, because, as we shall see later, Revelation certainly presupposes the death of Nero as an event of the past. Nero, who is also the eighth (17:11), has to be one of the five who have fallen (17:10). But if the obvious way of identifying the heads is thus excluded, there seem to be no conclusive arguments for any particular alternative reckoning.

In fact, we should not have expected to be able to use this text to identify the emperor in whose reign Revelation was written. It was never designed to be so used. Revelation's first readers knew perfectly well who the sixth head, the reigning emperor, was, and did not need to work it out.[43] They did not need to know where to start counting the sequence of seven from the beginning and would hardly be interested in doing so. Even John did not need to discover that there were to be seven emperors by counting them: he knew there had to be seven, because that is the number of completeness. Whether he actually did count six emperors up to and including the present one, by beginning from an emperor later than Julius Caesar and/or by omitting some emperors, it is impossible to be sure. All that 17:10 is intended to tell his readers is how far they are from the *end* of the sequence of seven, that is, of the full sequence of emperors of Rome. It tells them there is only one short reign to go before the end of Roman imperial dominance of the world.[44] It tells them, as Revelation frequently

[42]Cf. 4 Ezra 11:12-17 (the second wing has to be Augustus and so the first is Julius Caesar); SibOr 5:12-13; Suetonius, *Vit. Caes.*

[43]The idea that Revelation is backdated to the reign of the emperor before the actually reigning one is implausible precisely because the readers are given no indication of how to count the sequence of seven from the beginning. They have no means of knowing that the sixth head is other than the emperor presently reigning. On the thesis of backdating, see also Schüssler Fiorenza (1985) 41-42.

[44]Cf. Beckwith (1919) 708.

does, that the end is near. But it distances the end by the conventional period of apocalyptic imminence: 'a little while' (cf. 6:11).[45] In much the same way, the vision of the Roman eagle (4 Ezra 11-12) in the near-contemporary Jewish apocalypse of 4 Ezra, after forcing the sequence of Roman emperors up to and including Domitian into the pattern of twelve wings and three heads, indicates that following Domitian the empire will endure a little longer before its destruction by the Messiah: 'the two wings... arose and set themselves up to reign, and their reign was brief and full of tumult' (4 Ezra 12:2, cf. 39).

Finally, the ten horns symbolize the ten kings which are to be the beast's allies in making war on the Lamb and destroying Babylon (17:12-14, 16-17). John may well have noticed that ten is a triangular number and so an appropriate number for the allies of the beast. It is the triangle of four. Since this is the number of the earth with its four corners (7:1), it might identify the ten kings with 'the kings of the earth' to which Revelation frequently refers (with allusion to Ps 2:2). However, it is more likely that the ten kings are 'the kings of the east' (16:12), who must cross the Euphrates because, as we shall see in the two following sections, according to the legend of Nero's return, they accompany the returning Nero on his return from Parthia (cf. SibOr 5:109). In that case there may be a link with the four angels bound at the river Euphrates (9:14).

2. The legend of Nero's return

We have seen that the number 666 in some sense identifies the beast with Nero. This identification, as has long been recognized by scholars, undoubtedly has something to do with the legend of Nero's return,[46] which was current in more than one form when John wrote his Apocalypse. In order to understand the

[45]Cf. Brun (1927) 150.

[46]On this, see Charles (1900) lvii-lxxiii; Beckwith (1919) 400-403; Charles (1920) 2.76-87; Prigent (1974) 229-232; Collins (1974) 80-87; Yarbro Collins (1976) 176-183; Kreitzer (1988); Bodinger (1989).

origin and various interpretations of this legend, it is important, first, to appreciate the ambiguity of the historical Nero's reputation after his death. The image of a vicious and murderous tyrant, which later Jewish and Christian sources, as well as the extant Roman historians, present, was part of this reputation but it was not the whole story. It had a lurid enough basis in the long series of political murders in which Nero indulged and of which the most shocking, the murder of his mother Agrippina, became one of the most notorious of all crimes. To evoke the image of the bloodthirsty, unnatural, hated tyrant it was sufficient to call Nero the matricide.[47] Nero's strong and increasing tendency to absolutism, no doubt connected with his self-indulgent personality, provoked the opposition of the Roman senatorial aristocracy, which led to his downfall, and it was historians, notably Tacitus, with Roman republican sympathies who continued this opposition in the form of the historiographical tradition. On the other hand, Nero was popular with the populace of Rome. More important, his philhellenism,[48] which showed itself in his passion for and personal dedication to music and the games, alienated the Roman aristocracy, whose traditional *mores* it offended, but endeared him to the hellenistic East. Attempts to show that Nero tried to develop his position as emperor in the direction of oriental divine monarchy[49] have probably been much exaggerated,[50] but that he was seen in this light in the eastern provinces of the empire, where he was worshipped as a living god in the imperial cult, is not to be doubted.[51] His tour of Greece in 66-67,[52] not long before his death, evidently sealed his popularity in Greece. He took part in the various games, inaugurated the work on the canal through the isthmus of Corinth, and also at Corinth proclaimed the freedom of

[47]E.g. Philostratus, *Vit. Apoll.* 4.32; SibOr 5:363; 8:71.
[48]On Nero's philhellenism, see Griffin (1984) 208-220.
[49]Cizek (1972) 209-213, 220-224, 242-243; Bodinger (1989) 25-30.
[50]Griffin (1984) 215-219.
[51]Momigliano (1934) 732.
[52]On the tour, see Cizek (1972) 213-220; Griffin (1984) 161-163, 211.

Greece.[53] On this last occasion the priest of the imperial cult responded by calling him 'the mightiest emperor, philhellene, Nero Zeus god of freedom.'[54] Finally, Nero was evidently held in considerable respect by the Parthians, with whom he concluded a peace over Armenia. At a splendid ceremony in Rome, Nero crowned the Parthian prince Tiridates king of Armenia and Tiridates worshipped Nero as the god Mithras. After his death the Parthian king requested the Senate to honour his memory.

Nero's popularity in the East is as important for understanding Revelation as is the memory of his murderous cruelty. A nice illustration of the ambiguity of the memory of Nero is provided by Plutarch, who judged Nero a criminal and a tyrant who almost ruined the empire. In his account of the visit of Thespesius to Hades, Thespesius sees the soul of Nero being tortured for his crimes. He was to be reincarnated, as further punishment, in the form of an animal. But instead of the proposal that he become a viper that will eat its way out of its mother's womb, a divine voice decrees that he must now be treated mercifully, since 'he had paid the penalty for his crimes, and a piece of kindness too was owing him from the gods, since to the nation which among his subjects was noblest and most beloved of heaven [i.e. the Greeks] he had granted freedom.' So he would become a frog, singing in the marshes and ponds (*De sera* 32).[55]

It is worth noticing that in the tradition which remembered Nero as a monster of vice, he could be called a beast, quite independently of the Jewish apocalyptic tradition of apocalyptic symbolism. According to the emperor Marcus Aurelius, 'To be violently drawn and moved by the lusts of the soul is proper to wild beasts and monsters, such as Phalaris and Nero were.'[56] Philostratus, in his life of the first-century philosopher Apollonius of Tyana, represents Apollonius of Tyana arriving in Rome during the reign of Nero and speaking of the emperor

[53]Hence the strong association of Nero with Corinth in SibOr 5:214-219.
[54]Quoted Griffin (1984) 210.
[55]Cf. also Philostratus, *Vit. Apoll.* 5.41.
[56]Quoted Henderson (1903) 419.

in terms astonishingly reminiscent of Daniel 7:3-7 and Revelation 13:2:

> In my travels, which have been wider than ever man yet accomplished, I have seen many, many wild beasts of Arabia and India; but this beast (θηρίον), that is commonly called a tyrant, I know not how many heads it has, nor if it be crooked of claw, and armed with horrible fangs. However, they say it is a civil beast, and inhabits the midst of cities; but to this extent it is more savage than the beasts of mountain and forest, that whereas lions and panthers can sometimes by flattery be tamed and change their disposition, stroking and petting this beast does but instigate it to surpass itself in ferocity and devour at large. And of wild beasts you cannot say that they were ever known to eat their own mothers, but Nero has gorged himself on this diet.[57]

The reference to Nero (on his return) as 'the great beast' (θῆρα μέγαν) in Sibylline Oracle 8:157 may be influenced by apocalyptic symbolism, but it may also belong to this more ordinary tradition,[58] as does the younger Pliny's description of Domitian, who was often considered a second Nero[59] on account of his cruel tyranny, as 'the most monstrous beast' (*immanissima belua: Panegyricus* 48.3).[60]

The Jewish war broke out in Nero's reign and he sent Vespasian to quell it. Thus Jews could hold him responsible for the destruction of the temple and Jerusalem (SibOr 5:150-151). But it was mainly Vespasian and Titus who were the objects of Jewish hatred on this account, and it is probable that Nero only assumed special significance for Jews in the light of the legend of his return, as we shall see. For Christians,

---

[57]Philostratus, *Vit. Apoll.* 4.38, quoted from J. S. Phillimore's translation in Robinson (1976) 235-236.

[58]Cf. also SibOr 5:343, where the 'destructive beast' (ὀλοὸν δάκος) is most likely Nero.

[59]Juvenal 4.38; cf. Swete (1907) 221 for other references.

[60]Cf. Scott (1936) 132.

however, it was a very different matter. Nero was the first emperor to persecute the church.[61] His persecution, though confined to the city of Rome, was a traumatic experience for the whole church, it seems, not least because Peter and Paul were martyred during it. It was most likely understood by many as the final Antichrist's onslaught against the people of God, and the civil wars which threatened the very survival of the empire at the time of and following Nero's death (contemporaneously with the Jewish war) may well have seemed the final internecine strife in which, according to some apocalyptic expectations, the enemies of God's people were to slaughter each other immediately before the end (e.g. Zech 14:13; 1 Enoch 56:7; 100:1-4). A Christian apocalyptic tradition which had identified Nero as the Antichrist would be able to maintain this identification after his death by taking up the later expectation of Nero's return.

Two Christian apocalyptic passages from the early second century refer to Nero's historical persecution of the church in the context of the expectation of his eschatological return as the final Antichrist and probably still contain an echo of the way the historical Nero was perceived by Christians at the time of his persecution of the church. One, from a passage we shall later have occasion to consider in detail, is Ascension of Isaiah 4:2-3, where Nero is identified as 'a lawless king, a matricide... who will persecute the plant which the twelve apostles of the Beloved have planted [i.e. the church], and one of the twelve [i.e. Peter] will be delivered into his hands.' In Apocalypse of Peter 14:11 (according to the Greek text in the Rainer fragment) the risen Christ instructs Peter: 'Go to the city which rules the west and drink the cup which I have promised you at the hands of the son of one who is in Hades so that his disappearance (ἀφάνεια) may receive a beginning.' Here Nero seems to be described as the son of the devil, though it is unusual to locate

---

[61]On Nero's persecution, see Beaujeu (1960); Garzetti (1974) 614-617, 745-746 (bibliography); Keresztes (1979) (with bibliography); Smallwood (1976) 217-219; Keresztes (1984).

the devil in Hades at this date.[62] Although ἀφάνεια could be translated 'destruction', as in the Ethiopic version, it probably contains an allusion to the idea that Nero did not die but disappeared to some place of hiding pending his return.[63] Peter's martyrdom is seen as instrumental in Nero's downfall, according to the apocalyptic notion that martyrdom brings down judgment on the persecutor.

Revelation says nothing explicitly about the historical Nero, but it probably alludes to the Neronian persecution (Rev 17:6; 18:24; 19:2; cf. 6:9-10). We can well imagine that John would have seen the historical Nero as the figure in whom the imperial power had so far shown most clearly its antichristian tendency: as self-deifying absolutism which sets itself against God and murders his witnesses (cf. 11:7; 13:5-7). The impending confrontation between the beast and the followers of the Lamb would appear to John as an apocalyptic extension and intensification of the Neronian persecution.

Given Nero's popularity in some quarters, the rather mysterious circumstances of Nero's death could easily have given rise to the rumour that he was still alive. Suetonius says that when he realised he must flee from Rome, he thought, among other possibilities, of fleeing to the Parthians (*Nero* 47). When he did flee, he may well have intended to try to escape to the East, where he would find support, but in fact he got no further than the suburban villa of his freedman Phaon, where, on hearing the news that the Senate had declared him a public enemy and that troops were on their way to take him captive, he killed himself with a dagger in the throat (Suetonius, *Nero* 49; Josephus, *BJ* 4.493). Although Suetonius says that his funeral was expensive, it was presumably not permitted to be a public event, and he was buried privately in the family tomb of the Domitii, not in the mausoleum of Augustus (*Nero* 50). These evidences of his death could easily have been dismissed

---

[62]Cf. Bauckham (1990).

[63]For the notion of Nero's disappearance or invisibility, a persistent feature of the tradition about his return, see SibOr 4:120; 5:33, 150; John of Antioch, fr. 104 (quoted below); Commodian, *Carmen de duobus populis* 831; Lactantius, *De Mort. Pers.* 2.7.

as the pretences of his enemies, if the rumour-mongers needed to counter them, but in the East, where the rumours of his survival flourished, they may not even have been known (cf. Tacitus, *Hist.* 2.8). Much later, it seems, it was supposed that Nero had no grave at all (Lactantius, *De Mort. Pers.* 2.7).

The first of the imposters claiming to be Nero[64] appeared only about a year after his death (c. July 69), during the period of conflict and confusion in which it must have seemed possible for a reappearing Nero to win the allegiance of the eastern provinces. The imposter, whom some said was a runaway slave[65] from Pontus, others a freedman from Italy, had the advantages not only of looking remarkably like Nero, but also of being able to sing and to play the lyre. He appeared in Greece, where he mustered some support, set sail for Syria, but was forced by a storm to put in at the island of Cythnos in the Cyclades, where he was captured and killed. His dead body was taken to Rome via Asia (Tacitus, *Hist.* 2.9).

The second 'false Nero', who appeared in 80 A.D. and whose real name was Terentius Maximus, also apparently resembled Nero. He claimed that he had been living in concealment (ἐν ἀφανεῖ) somewhere up to that time (John of Antioch fr. 104). He appeared in the province of Asia, where he acquired a few followers, but gained far more followers as he marched east towards the Euphrates. There he won the support of Artapanus IV, a pretender to the Parthian throne who supported him against the emperor Titus presumably because of the latter's refusal to back his own claim. It is not known how the matter ended.

[64]On the false Neros, see Pappano (1937); Walter (1957) 257-258; Bastomsky (1969); Gallivan (1973); MacMullen (1966) 143-145. The sources, for the three pretenders are:

(1) Tacitus, *Hist.* 2.8-9; Dio Cassius (epitome) 63.9.3; Zonaras 11.15;

(2) Dio Cassius 66.19.3; Zonaras 11:18; John of Antioch, fr. 104 (ed. Mueller);

(3) Suetonius, *Nero* 57.2; Tacitus, *Hist.* 1.2.1.

[65]This report (Tacitus, *Hist.* 2.8.1) may have influenced SibOr 4:119, 123, which represents Nero fleeing like a runaway slave from Italy to Parthia.

At least one more pretender appeared, in the reign of Domitian, c. 88/89 A.D.[66] This one apparently gained the support of the Parthian king Pacorus II and posed a serious threat to the empire.[67] On the most probable dating of Revelation, these events would have been fresh in the memory of John and his first readers. The association of both the latter two pretenders with the Parthians is noteworthy because it is a prominent feature also in the Jewish literary tradition of the return of Nero, as we shall see. The last we hear of pagan expectations of Nero's return is a remark by Dio Chrysostom,[68] writing in Asia Minor probably at the end of the first century: 'even now everyone wishes he were alive, and most believe that he is' (*Orat.* 21.10).[69] No doubt this is rhetorical exaggeration, but it nevertheless testifies to the continuing popularity both of Nero himself and of the expectation of his return. So far from discrediting the legend, the pretenders seem to have helped keep it alive.

The legend of Nero's return acquired literary form first in the Jewish Sibylline Oracles. It is noteworthy that there is nowhere any trace of it in the Jewish apocalypses. It was the diaspora Jewish authors of the Sibyllines, engaged in Jewish propaganda for the hellenistic world, who took up this popular pagan idea and adapted it to Jewish eschatological purposes. We need to distinguish three forms in which it appears in the Sibyllines.[70]

The earliest, in the fourth Sibylline Oracle, is closest to the pagan legend, but it is also closely integrated into a Jewish view of the Jewish war and the Roman destruction of Jerusalem.

---

[66]The view that Suetonius, *Nero* 57.2, refers to a third pretender in 88/89, not to the second pretender of 80, is convincingly defended by Gallivan (1973) 365. Tacitus, *Hist.* 2.8.1, referring to 'others' between the pretender of 69 and the death of Domitian, may even imply that there were more than three false Neros in all.

[67]Gallivan (1973) 365.

[68]The reference by Kreitzer (1988) 97, to Dio Chrysostom as a Christian writer who associates the Nero myth with the figure of Belial is, of course, quite mistaken. Presumably he has confused him with John Chrysostom.

[69]Cf. also Lucian, *Adv. indoct.* 20.

[70]Collins (1974) 80-87, also distinguishes these three forms, but I disagree with his view of them as three consecutive stages of development.

Following a prophecy of the beginning of the Jewish war, Nero's supposed flight to the east in 68 is thus described (lines 119-124):

> Then a great king will flee from Italy like a runaway slave
> unseen and unheard over the channel of the Euphrates,
> when he dares to incur a maternal curse for repulsive
>   murder
> and many other things, confidently, with wicked
>   hand.
> When he runs away, beyond the Parthian land,
> many will bloody the ground for the throne of Rome.[71]

Following this allusion to the year of the four emperors (69 A.D.), Titus' destruction of Jerusalem is predicted (lines 125-127). The eruption of Vesuvius (79 A.D.) is prophesied as a signal of divine vengeance against the people of Italy for their treatment of the Jewish people (lines 130-136). Nero's return is then portrayed as retribution for Rome (lines 137-139):

> Then the strife of war being aroused will come to the west,
> and the fugitive from Rome will also come, brandishing a
>   great spear,
> having crossed the Euphrates with many myriads.

His warlike progress west will destroy Antioch and Cyprus en route (lines 140-144), and his sack of Rome is implied in the reference to its result (lines 145-148):

> Great wealth will come to Asia, which Rome itself
> once plundered and deposited in her house of many
>   possessions.
> She will then pay back twice as much and more
> to Asia, and then there will be a surfeit of war.

These last lines evoke the standard theme of the conflict of east and west, and the hope for a reversal of Rome's domination of

---

[71]This and all further translations from the Sibylline Oracles are by Collins (1983).

the east by a triumph of Asia over Rome.[72] Possibly a pagan Sibylline oracle is here being used by the Jewish writer. At any rate, it looks as though he has here preserved the terms in which pagans in the eastern empire embraced the hope of Nero's return as a kind of saviour figure to wreak the revenge of the east on the west. The Jewish author has taken over this theme and made it his own, by understanding the revenge as God's retribution on Rome for the sack of Jerusalem. But this has meant that Nero no longer appears in the good light in which presumably he was remembered in the pagan expectation of his return. His crimes, evoked especially by the reference to the matricide, are emphasized. Nero the monster of evil has become a bogey with which to threaten Rome.

This passage (and the final redaction of the fourth Sibylline) must date from soon after 79 A.D., since the eruption of Vesuvius is the last historical event which is prophesied.[73] Gallivan thought the prophecy of Nero's return actually refers to the false Nero (Terentius Maximus) of 80 A.D.[74] In that case, the Oracle would have to be dated at the brief moment when this pretender looked as though he might succeed. But the Oracle's expectation of Nero's return from beyond the Euphrates with a vast army does not fit what we know of this historical false Nero, who appeared in the province of Asia and then marched to the Euphrates. Probably, therefore, the Oracle reflects the expectation of Nero's return around the same time as Terentius Maximus attempted to exploit that expectation, but does not specifically refer to him.

In the fifth Sibylline oracle, which contains five passages about Nero (lines 28-34, 93-110, 137-154, 214-227, 361-380), we find the second Jewish form of the Nero legend. The same idea of Nero's secret flight from Italy to the east is found (lines 143, 216, 364), and his taking refuge with 'the Medes and the kings of the Persians' is explained by his good relations with

---

[72]For this theme, also with reference to the wealth Rome gained from Asia, see SibOr 3:350-355. SibOr 8:70-73, which prophesies the return of Nero in the time of Marcus Aurelius, also uses this theme: it echoes SibOr 5:363-364 and 4:145.

[73]Cf. Collins (1983) 382.

[74]Gallivan (1973) 364 n. 7.

them during his reign (line 147). There is considerable emphasis on the characteristics and deeds of the historical Nero (lines 29-32, 138-151, 217-218, 363), and to some extent Nero's future behaviour at his return is modelled on his historical behaviour during his reign. As he was destructive then (lines 30, 142, 145), so he will be when he returns (lines 33, 94, 97, 102, 107, 219, 365, 368). As he opposed the Jews during his reign (lines 150-151), so he will when he returns (line 107). As he cut the canal through the isthmus at Corinth, so he will appear there and destroy Corinth (lines 214-219).[75]

Nero is now so identified with Parthia and the traditional threat to the empire from the Parthians that he is called 'the Persian' (line 93) and 'the one who has obtained the land of the Persians' (line 101), though he is also said to return 'from the ends of the earth' (line 363). As in the fourth Sibylline, his return will bring about the destructive war (line 365) which will be divine vengeance on the empire, especially for the destruction of Jerusalem (lines 225-227). The Oracle seems to envisage him first capturing Rome (line 367), though Rome's destruction is ascribed to supernatural agency (lines 155-161), and then coming from the West with a vast army (lines 97, 104, 371-373) to destroy Egypt and generally wreak destruction (lines 93-105, 214-221, 365-374). Finally, having conquered the whole empire, he will attack Jerusalem, but God will send the messianic king against him and the final judgment will take place (lines 106-110, cf. 374-380).

What distinguishes the account of Nero's return in the fifth Sibylline from that in the fourth is that features of Jewish apocalyptic expectation have been added to the former. In particular, Nero has been assimilated to the eschatological adversary of the people of God, the tradition about whom was modelled on the prophecies in Daniel which originally portrayed Antiochus Epiphanes. This accounts for the returning

---

[75]Perhaps SibOr 5:369 ('he will set fire to all men as no one else ever did') reflects the burning of the people of Jerusalem (5:150), the fire of Rome (though this never appears in references to Nero in the Sibylline Oracles), or Nero's use of Christians as human torches (Tacitus, *Ann.* 15.44).

Nero's attempt to 'destroy the city of the blessed ones' (line 107) which precipitates the coming of the messianic king and the final judgment. It also explains lines 33-34: 'he will return declaring himself equal to God. But he [God] will prove that he is not' (cf. also line 139). This claim to equality with God is not connected with the imperial cult of the historical Nero, but is a traditional feature of the eschatological adversary (cf. Dan 7:25; 8:11-12; 11:36-37; 2 Thes 2:4; Did 16:4). Other apocalyptic features are that the returning Nero will kill two-thirds of humanity (lines 102-103; cf. Zech 13:8; Rev 9:15, 18), probably the strong emphasis on his destructiveness (cf. Dan 8:24-25), and his unsurpassed cunning (line 363, 366; cf. Dan 8:25). Whatever the meaning of the obscure description of his 'cutting off the roots from three heads' (lines 222-224), it certainly alludes to Daniel 7:8.[76] The returning Nero's destruction of Egypt (lines 93-98) may well be based on Daniel 11:42.[77] Thus the account of Nero in the fifth Sibylline is the result of combining the existing legend of his return with the apocalyptic tradition about an eschatological adversary of the people of God.[78]

The final redaction of the fifth Sibylline Oracle must have taken place in the reign of Marcus Aurelius, to whom line 51 refers. But this line is very probably a later addition to the sequence of Roman emperors in lines 12-51. In that case, the collection of oracles dates from the reign of Hadrian (lines 46-48), before the Jewish revolt of 132 A.D., since the reference to Hadrian is extremely favourable.[79] The oracles about Nero may themselves be earlier.

[76]Cf. Barn. 4:4-5.

[77]SibOr 5:155 ('after the fourth year') may allude to the Danielic apocalyptic time-period of three and a half years, but how this is connected with Nero is obscure.

[78]The prophecies of the return of Nero in SibOr 8:70-72, 140-159, which date from the reign of Marcus Aurelius (see lines 68-72 and 148-150), are probably dependent on the fourth and fifth Sibylline Oracles (cf. 8:70-71 with 5:363-364; and 8:72 with 4:145; and 8:155 with 5:138, 217-218). But they fall, like the fourth Sibylline, into the first of our three categories, rather than, like the fifth Sibylline, into our second category. Their overwhelming concern with the destruction of Rome by Nero has excluded any features of the eschatological adversary.

[79]Cf. Collins (1983) 390.

The third Jewish form of the legend of Nero's return is found in Sibylline Oracle 3:63-74:

> Then Beliar will come from the *Sebastēnoi*
> and he will raise up the mountains, he will raise up the sea,
> the great fiery sun and shining moon,
> and he will raise up the dead, and perform many signs
> for men. But they will not be effective in him.
> But he will, indeed, also lead men astray, and he will lead
>   astray
> many faithful, chosen Hebrews, and also other lawless
>   men
> who have not yet listened to the word of God.
> But whenever the threat of the great God draws nigh
> and a burning power comes through the sea to land
> it will also burn Beliar and all overbearing men,
> as many as put faith in him.

The cryptic phrase ἐκ δὲ Σεβαστήνῶν, though it could mean 'from the inhabitants of Sebaste (Samaria)', should almost certainly be understood to mean 'from the line of Augustus,'[80] and so to identify Beliar with Nero, the last emperor of the line of Augustus. A future figure from the line of Augustus would have to be the returning Nero. But although this passage thus identifies the eschatological adversary, understood as the evil spirit Beliar in human form, with the returning Nero, it draws on the legend of the returning Nero in no other way. It reflects no features of the historical Nero and his reputation and makes no reference to any of the distinctive features of the legend of his return. Its account draws exclusively on the apocalyptic tradition of the eschatological adversary, who will perform miracles to deceive people so that they believe in him (cf. Matt 24:11, 24; Mark 13:22; 2 Thes 2:9-12; Did 16:4; SibOr 2:167-168; ApPet 2:12; ApEl 3:7). The depiction, in fact, is of the false prophet (cf. Deut 13:1-5; LAB 34), rather than the conquering king. Thus, in this form of the legend, the

---

[80]Collins (1974) 86.

apocalyptic expectation has simply been attached to the idea of Nero's return, without drawing at all on the content of the legend of Nero's return.

The date of the third Sibylline as a whole and of this passage in particular cannot be determined with any assurance. This passage itself could date from any time after 69 A.D. There is no need to see this third Jewish form of the Nero expectation as a further development subsequent to the second form, going further in the direction of apocalyptic mythicization of the legend. The second and third forms of the expectation are simply alternative Jewish appropriations of the legend, both of which could have occurred at any time once the pagan legend itself was current. In one, features of the legend have been amalgamated with features of the apocalyptic tradition of the eschatological adversary; in the other, the apocalyptic tradition (in one form) has been reproduced along with the merest indication that the expected figure will be Nero.

That Sibylline Oracle 3:63 does allude to the legend of Nero's return is confirmed by the Christian apocalyptic passage in Ascension of Isaiah 4:2-14. Here too the reference is to Beliar coming in human form (4:2-4). The identification with Nero is fuller and more explicit (4:2-3: Beliar will come 'in the form of a man, a lawless king, a matricide... who persecuted the plant which the twelve apostles of the Beloved had planted and one of the twelve was delivered into his hand'). But the account of the returning Nero then draws exclusively on the apocalyptic tradition of the eschatological adversary, and makes no use at all of the features distinctive to the Nero legend. It is a somewhat fuller version of the same tradition as is found in the third Sibylline. Beliar in the form of Nero performs nature miracles similar to those of Sibylline Oracle 3:64-65 (AscIsa 4:5, 10), by which he will deceive the world and even some erstwhile Christian believers (4:7, 9). He will claim to be God and will be worshipped as such (4:6, 8). He will rule for the apocalyptic period of 1332 days (4:12, 14; cf. Dan 7:25; 12:12) and be cast into Gehenna by Christ at his coming (4:14). One feature seems influenced by the imperial cult: 'he will set up his image before him in every city' (4:11). But this is nowhere associated with the Nero legend as such. It is simply an elaboration, from the contemporary ruler cult in the Roman east, of the tradition that the eschatological adversary would claim divinity. Thus the account of the returning Nero in the Ascension of Isaiah is a Christian form of the third Jewish form of the Nero legend.

Before considering the use of such traditions in Revelation, a final issue with regard to the Nero legend must be addressed. Scholars have frequently referred to the legend of Nero's return as the Nero *redivivus* myth. This term is misleading, since it implies a belief that Nero had died and would return from death. The sources we have examined attest that the belief, up to at least the end of the first century, was that Nero had not died but was still alive, in hiding somewhere in the east, and would return across the Euphrates. The theme of Nero's disappearance and secret flight deliberately takes the place of any reference to his death. There is only one passage which might suggest otherwise: in Sibylline Oracle 5:363-367:

> A man who is a matricide will come from the ends of the
> earth
> in flight and devising penetrating schemes in his mind...
> He will immediately seize the one because of whom he
> himself perished.

Lines 363-364 here allude to the common notion that Nero did not die but fled to the far east (cf, e.g., 4:119-123; and for the persistent description, in the tradition about Nero's return, of Nero as a fugitive, cf. SibOr 4:138; 5:153, 215; 8:71; 12:93; Commodian, *Carmen de duobus populis* 869). But line 367 (ἧς χάριν ὤλετό τ' αὐτός, ἐλεῖ ταύτην παραχρῆμα), which must refer to the city of Rome, appears to say that he will seize the city on account of which he died (ὤλετο). This is so anomalous that Yarbro Collins argues that ὤλετο must here mean 'was ruined' rather than 'was destroyed' in the sense of 'died'.[81] However, this argument is rather difficult to accept, since ὄλλυμι used of people normally refers to violent death and is frequently used in this sense in the fifth Sibylline Oracle (lines 30, 94, 109, 116,

[81]Yarbro Collins (1976) 181.

132, 145, 153, 174, 380, 467, 509). Indeed Nero's own final destruction is called ὄλεθρον in line 374, while ὤλετο describes Titus' death in line 411. The most that is conceivable is that in line 367 it is deliberately ambiguous, alluding to the view that Nero did die in 68 A.D. but allowing the interpretation that he merely fell from power. Alternatively, we must suppose that this line is inconsistent with the rest of this Oracle's account of Nero.

If this line does suggest that Nero is to return from the dead, it is an isolated and wholly uncharacteristic suggestion. It is quite mistaken to suppose, as has often been done,[82] that with the passage of time the expectation that Nero would return was bound to change from the belief that he never died to the belief that he would return from the dead. In world folklore figures of this kind are frequently envisaged to be hidden somewhere, without dying, for periods much longer than a natural lifetime. This is what in fact happened in the case of Nero. Lactantius, reporting the views of Christians in the early fourth century who believed in Nero's return, does not mention the idea of his resurrection, but only the view that he had not died but had been 'borne away and kept alive' (*translatum ac vivum reservatum*), drawing a parallel with Enoch and Elijah (*De Mort. Pers.* 2.7-9). Commodian reflects the same tradition: he does say that Nero will return from the underworld (probably under the influence of Rev 17:8), but this does not mean that he died, since Commodian immediately adds that Nero will return from secret places where he has been preserved for a long time in his original body (*Carmen de duobus populis* 825-830). Early in the fifth century Augustine reports that some do expect Nero to rise from the dead, but others think he is still living at the same age at which he was supposed to have died (*De Civ. Dei* 20.19). The view that he would rise from the dead probably derives simply from exegesis of Revelation 13:3, 12, 14 as referring to Nero, as is patently the case in Sulpicius Severus (*Chron.* 2.29). In view of these passages in Revelation, the striking fact about the later tradition is that belief in Nero's

---

[82]E.g. Charles (1920) 2.85; Beasley-Murray (1974) 210-211.

resurrection was not the form the tradition generally took. Thus there is even less ground for supposing that at the time when John wrote the Apocalypse the legend of Nero's return was current in a form which envisaged Nero's death and resurrection.[83] This is a most important conclusion for understanding John's use of the legend.

3. The returning Nero traditions in Revelation

A major key to understanding John's use of the legend of the return of Nero, hitherto unrecognized, is to see that he uses two distinct forms of the legend. In chapter 13 he uses what we have described as the third Jewish form of the tradition (also found in the Ascension of Isaiah), while in chapter 17 he uses the second Jewish form of the tradition (as in the fifth Sibylline Oracle). Chapter 16 forms a bridge between the two.

In order to appreciate John's use of the tradition in chapter 13, we must first of all recognize that the context into which he has here incorporated it is unique. Nowhere else is the expectation of the return of Nero connected with a visionary interpretation of the fourth beast of Daniel 7.[84] But John's vision of the beast (13:1-2) is paralleled in Jewish apocalypses contemporary with Revelation. Both 4 Ezra 11-12 and 2 Baruch 36-40 reflect Daniel 7 and interpret Daniel's fourth beast as the contemporary Roman Empire, which is shortly to be destroyed by the Davidic Messiah.[85] In 4 Ezra the reference to Daniel is quite explicit (11:39-40; 12:11), but what Ezra sees is a different symbolic vision of the same reality (the Roman Empire) as Daniel had seen in the form of his fourth beast. Ezra's vision is of an eagle with twelve wings and three heads. The eagle is an obviously appropriate symbol for the Roman Empire. The

---

[83]Yarbro Collins (1976) 183, is very unusual in recognizing this point.

[84]Reicke (1972) 186, comparing Barn. 4:4-5 (which quotes Dan 7:7-8, 24) with SibOr 5:220-227, thinks it refers to the overthrow of the three Flavian emperors by the returning Nero. But this is very conjectural.

[85]For the dependence of these passages on Daniel 7, see Beale (1984) 112-129, 144-153.

wings and the heads represent Roman emperors, and are given a very elaborate (and in part impenetrably obscure) interpretation. In its attempt to represent the succession of the Caesars from Julius Caesar until the time of writing (c. 100 A.D.) and a little way into the future, up to the imminent end, this vision is much more elaborate than John's, but provides a parallel to John's interpretation of the seven heads of his beast as representing Roman emperors (Rev 17:9-14). But it contains no hint of the legend of the return of Nero.

Daniel 7 is one of the key Old Testament texts on which Revelation is based and to which it frequently alludes.[86] It depicts in vivid visionary form one of the key eschatological expectations of Revelation: that 'the kingdom of the world' will become 'the kingdom of our Lord and of his Christ' (Rev 11:15). In chapter 13 John naturally turns to it for an account of the great anti-God power of his day, the Roman Empire. But like Ezra's, John's vision of the beast (13:1-2) is a new vision, inspired by but not identical with Daniel's. It is composed of features of all four of Daniel's beasts (cf. Dan 7.3-6), indicating that the Roman imperial power is the culmination of all the evil empires of history. John's account of the beast continues to allude to Daniel 7 down to verse 7 of chapter 13. In doing so, it draws on Daniel's account of the 'little horn,' which appears on the head of the fourth beast and represents the king who is the final adversary of God and his people. The major allusions are as follows:[87]

Revelation	13:1	Daniel	7:2-3, 7
	13:2		7:3-6
	13:4		7:6, 12
	13:5a		7:8, 25

[86]Beale (1984) 154-267, though he does not discuss allusions to Daniel 7 outside chapters 1, 4-5, 13 and 17 of Revelation. Cf. also Fekkes (1988) 78-82, 98-99.

[87]Beale (1984) 229-244 lists allusions to Daniel in Revelation 13 in three categories: 'clear allusion,' 'probably allusion' and 'possible allusion or echo.' My estimate of allusions to Daniel 7 differs somewhat from his, but most of those I list occur in his first and second categories.

13:5b	7:25 (cf. 12:7, 11-12)
13:6	7:25 (cf. 8:10-11; 11:36)
13:7a	7:21
13:7b	cf. 7:14

At 13:7 allusions to Daniel 7 run out.[88] The rest of John's vision of the beast in this chapter derives from a different source: an apocalyptic tradition, which also appears in Ascension of Isaiah 4:2-14, about the eschatological adversary, identified with the returning Nero. Since the apocalyptic tradition of the eschatological adversary derived in part from Daniel's depiction of the little horn, it was entirely appropriate for John to use it to fill out and develop the picture derived from Daniel 7. The two sources in fact overlapped and John has closely integrated them in creating his own account of the beast.

The extent to which John is indebted to the same tradition as appears in Ascension of Isaiah 4:2-14 can best be seen by indicating the parallels to the latter in Revelation 13 (with some also in Rev 12):

Ascension of Isaiah 4:2-14[89]   Revelation

(2)... Beliar will descend, the great angel [ruler], the king of this world, which he has ruled ever since it existed. He will descend from his firmament in the form of a man, a lawless king, a matricide, who himself, this king, (3) will persecute the plant which the twelve apostles of the Beloved have planted,

[88]Beale (1984) 241, claims that 'beginning with v. 11a there is a renewed focus on Daniel 7'. But this is misleading. He himself lists no clear allusions to Daniel 7 after v. 7. For v. 11 he lists as probable allusions Daniel 7:17 and 8:3. But John's second beast is not a king (as in Dan 7:17), and the phrase ἀναβαῖνον ἐκ τῆς γῆς in 13:11 is probably formed by analogy and contrast with 13:1, rather than by influence from Daniel 7:17.

[89]The original Greek of this passage is extant only for vv. 2b-4a. I give my own translation of the Greek. The rest of the passage is given in Knibb's translation of the Ethiopic: Knibb (1985) 161-162.

and one of the twelve will be delivered into his
hands — (4) this ruler will come in the form of
that king, and with him will come all the powers
of this world, and they will obey him in every
wish. (5) By his word he will cause the sun to   13:13
rise by night, and the moon also he will make
to appear at the sixth hour. (6) And he will do
everything he wishes in the world; he will act
and speak like the Beloved, and will say, 'I am
the Lord, and before me there was no one.' (7)   13:5a, 6
And all men in the world will believe in him. (8)   13:3b
They will sacrifice to him and will serve him,   13:4, 8
saying, 'This is the Lord, and besides him there
is no other.' (9) And the majority of those who
have associated together to receive the Beloved   13:13
he will turn aside after him. (10) And the power
of his miracles will be in every city and district.
(11) and he will set up his image before him   13:14-15
in every city. (12) And he will rule for three   13:5b
years and seven months and twenty-seven days. (cf. 13:18)
(13) And many faithful and saints, when they
saw him for whom they were hoping, who was
crucified, Jesus the Lord Christ...[90] and who
believed in him, of these few will be left in those
days as his servants, fleeing from desert to desert   12:6, 14
as they await his coming. (14) And after [one
thousand] three hundred and thirty-two days   12:6, 14
the Lord will come with his angels and with   17:14;
the host of the saints from the seventh heaven,   19:11-14
with the glory of the seventh heaven, and will
drag Beliar, with his hosts also, into Gehenna.   19:20

The following points will elucidate the relationship between
Ascension of Isaiah 4:2-14 and Revelation 13. (1) Ascension of
Isaiah 4:2-14 and Daniel 7 agree on two points which are also
found in Revelation: the blasphemies of the eschatological

---

[90]Words in the Ethiopic text which are very probably a gloss are omitted here.

adversary (AscIsa 4:6; Dan 7:25; Rev 13:5-6) and the time period, which both the Ascension of Isaiah and Revelation have adapted from Daniel (AscIsa 4:12, 14; Dan 7:25; Rev 13:5). But Ascension of Isaiah 4:2-14 and Revelation share features not found in Daniel: the whole earth worships the adversary (AscIsa 4:7-8; Rev 13:4, 8); the miracles (AscIsa 4:11; Rev 13:13-14); his image (AscIsa 4:11; Rev 13:14-15).[91] Moreover, both Ascension of Isaiah 4 and Revelation 13 represent the adversary as imitating Christ, though, as we shall see, they develop this theme differently. Thus the two passages clearly share common tradition which goes beyond the common dependence on Daniel.

(2) Other texts reflecting the apocalyptic tradition about the eschatological adversary (notably SibOr 2:167-168; 3:63-74; 2 Thes 2:3-12; Did 16:4) evidence many of the themes common to Ascension of Isaiah 4:2-14 and Revelation 13. But only these two texts speak of the *setting up of the image* of the adversary. Moreover, only these two texts share the tradition about the *number 666*, which, though not explicitly mentioned in Ascension of Isaiah 4, lies behind the figure of 1332 days for the adversary's reign. As we saw in section 1, both Revelation and the Ascension of Isaiah have adapted the Danielic time-period under the influence of the number 666, which both must have known as the gematrial number of Nero. Thus the tradition common to both was not only very close in its account of the eschatological adversary, but it had also already identified the eschatological adversary with the returning Nero.

(3) The relationship between the two passages is not one of direct literary dependence but of use of common tradition. This can be shown from the fact that in two cases a common idea has been developed in two distinct ways: (a) As we have already noticed, both texts have adapted the apocalyptic time-period of Daniel (three and a half years or 1290 days or 1335

---

[91] In Revelation 13:13-14 the miracles are performed not by the eschatological adversary himself (as in AscIsa 4:11) but by the second beast. Similarly in Revelation 13:14-15 it is the second beast who procures the setting up of the image of the first beast, whereas in Ascension of Isaiah 4:11 the adversary sets up his own image himself. These differences will be discussed below.

days) in such a way as to relate it to the number 666. But they have done so in different ways: 1332 days in the Ascension of Isaiah, 42 months or 1260 days in Revelation.[92] (b) Both have the idea of the adversary as imitating Christ. In the Ascension of Isaiah this is developed as a parallel between Belial's incarnation as the returning Nero and the Beloved's incarnation as Jesus. Ascension of Isaiah 4:2 (Beliar will descend from his firmament in the form of a man [ἐν εἴδει ἀνθρώπου]) echoes 3:13 (the Beloved will descend from the seventh heaven in the form of a man [ἐν εἴδει ἀνθρώπου]).[93] Then the adversary's divine claim and his miracles parallel those of Christ (AscIsa 4:6). In Revelation 13 the parallels between the beast and Christ are, as we shall see, quite different.

Thus it seems that in Ascension of Isaiah 4:2-14 we are fortunate to have a passage which is roughly contemporary with Revelation[94] and which is closely dependent on the same apocalyptic tradition that John used in Revelation 13. The tradition was one in which the eschatological adversary retained his traditional features (to be seen in other passages such as 2 Thes 2:3-12; SibOr 3:63-74). Though he remained a figure of the future, some influence from the contemporary imperial cult can be detected in the way his claim to divinity is depicted: he sets up his image in every city (AscIsa 4:11).[95] Finally, he had been identified with the returning Nero and related to the number 666, but the portrayal of him has not been otherwise affected by the legend of Nero's return.

[92]For the relation of these numbers to 666, see section 1 above.

[93]It is not necessary to discuss here the question of sources incorporated in the Ascension of Isaiah. My own view is that the work was composed as a unity. But the more common division of the work into distinct sources, of which the present work is merely a compilation, usually treats the section 3:13-4:22 as a unity.

[94]For the date of the Ascension of Isaiah or this section of it, see Charles (1900) xliv (late 1st century); Knibb (1985) 147 (late 1st century); Hall (1990) (early 2nd century).

[95]For the importance of images in the imperial cult, see Price (1984) 170-206; Botha (1986) 94-96. Ascension of Isaiah 4:8 also refers to sacrifices to Belial/Nero. Sacrifices were made to the emperor in the imperial cult, though sacrifices to the gods on behalf of the emperor were more common: Price (1984) 207-222.

The result of John's use of this form of the Nero legend in chapter 13, along with the fact that he has used it to develop an account of Roman imperial power inspired by Daniel 7, is that the beast in Revelation 13 differs very significantly from the figure of the returning Nero as it appeared in the pagan legend and in the first and second Jewish forms of the legend. In the pagan legend Nero is a threat to the Empire, returning to wreak vengeance on the city of Rome that had brought about his downfall. He embodies the hopes of the east for reversing the supremacy of west over east. In the Jewish forms of the legend, this picture is continued and Nero is seen as instrument of divine vengeance on Rome, destroying the city of Rome and conquering the empire. In Revelation 13 it is quite the contrary: the beast's recovery from its mortal wound is not the overturning of the beast's power but the restoration and enhancement of the beast's power. The implication of the identification of the eschatological adversary with Nero is not here to identify the eschatological adversary with the threat to Rome but to identify the eschatological adversary with the imperial power of Rome. The chapter is not concerned with the downfall of the Roman Empire, but with its apparent ability to oppose God and to persecute his people with impunity. In this respect, chapter 17 is quite different. Here John is primarily concerned with the fall of Babylon (the city of Rome) and also, by way of anticipation of 19:11-21, with the destruction of the beast at the parousia. The form of the Nero legend which is echoed in 17:7-18 is therefore, appropriately, one which portrays the returning Nero and his allies from the east as hating and destroying the city of Rome.

The form of the legend that John uses in chapter 17 is the one found in the fifth Sibylline Oracle. The ten kings, who 'yield their power and authority to' the returning Nero (17:13), are no doubt 'the kings of the east,' for whose march from Parthia into the Roman Empire the river Euphrates was dried up (16:12). We are reminded that in the fifth Sibylline, not only did Nero flee 'to the Medes and to the kings of the Persians' (line 147), but also he returns as ruler of the Persian empire (line 101): the princes, the satraps and the client kings of Parthia have put themselves under his authority.[96] In Revelation 17, we are presumably to envisage them conquering the Roman Empire as the returning Nero's allies and in this sense receiving 'authority as kings... together with the beast' (17:12). Though already rulers of the east, it is only when they conquer the Roman Empire that they become the ten horns of the beast, i.e. participate in the imperial power of Rome that the beast symbolizes. The seventh head of the beast, returning as an eighth, conquers the empire and rules it along with the ten horns for a very short period (17:12: 'one hour'). The principal act of their conquest of the empire is the sacking of the city of Rome (17:16).[97] All this might be indebted simply to the pagan legend or to its Jewish adaptation in the fourth Sibylline. What aligns Revelation 17 with the form of the legend found in the fifth Sibylline is that the destruction of Rome and the conquest of the empire are not the returning Nero's ultimate objective. His final purpose is to assemble the forces of the whole world — east and west — for battle against God and his Messiah (16:13-14, 16; 17:14; 19:19). This is why his rule over the empire is so short, for it ends in his destruction at the parousia (17:12-14; 19:20-21; cf. SibOr 5:106-110).

Thus, whereas, as we saw in section 1, it is Nero in the form of his number 666 who links the 'eighth' beast of chapter 17 to the beast that recovers from its mortal wound in chapter 13, John has taken up two different forms of the Nero legend for two different purposes in the two chapters. In chapter 13 he has used one form of the legend to portray the power and success of the Roman Empire in its opposition to God and his people; in chapter 17 he has used another form to portray the ultimate downfall of the empire. These two distinct uses of the Nero legend need to be investigated further in the next two sections. The bridge between them is formed by chapter 16. In

[96]Note also 1 Enoch 56:5, which is not connected with the Nero legend, but, in referring to an invasion by 'the Parthians and Medes,' speaks of 'the kings'.

[97]Note that SibOr 5:143, 149, calls Rome Babylon, as in Revelation. In the *burning* of Rome in Revelation 17:16 there may be a reminiscence of the great fire of Rome, for which Nero was popularly held responsible.

verse 2 it is those who have received the mark of the beast and worshipped its image (cf. 13:15-16; 14:9-11) who are judged. In verse 13, the 'satanic trinity' of the dragon, the beast and the false prophet (the second beast) reappear for the first time after chapters 12-13, but they do so in the context of a passage (16:12-16) which prepares for and points forward to 17:7-18 and 19:11–21. In this way John has integrated the two traditions with each other and into the overall structure of his work.

4. Christological parody

We have yet to take account of one extremely important way in which both chapters 13 and 17 of Revelation differ from the Nero legend as elsewhere attested in the late first century A.D. In the legend Nero did not die; he merely disappeared. He fled secretly from Italy to Parthia, whence he will return. Chapters 13 and 17 of Revelation speak quite differently from the legend about the disappearance and reappearance of the beast. But it is equally important to notice that the way chapter 13 speaks of this is quite different from the way chapter 17 speaks of it. This is another important difference between John's use of the Nero legend in the two chapters.

In chapter 13 the expressions used are:

'One of its [the beast's] heads seemed to have received a death-blow (ὡς ἐσφαγμένην εἰς θάνατον), but its [the beast's] mortal wound (ἡ πληγὴ τοῦ θανάτου αὐτοῦ) had been healed' (13:3);

'the first beast, whose mortal wound had been healed' (13:12);

'the beast that had been wounded by the sword and had come to life (ἔχει τὴν πληγὴν τῆς μαχαίρης καὶ ἔζησεν) (13:14).

In chapter 17 the expressions used are:

'The beast that you saw was, and is not, and is going to ascend from the abyss and goes to destruction' (17:8a);

'it was and is not and is to come' (17:8b);

'The beast that was, and is not, is also an eighth but it
belongs to the seven, and it goes to destruction' (17:11).

In each case essentially the same expression occurs three
times in somewhat different forms, but the expression used in
one chapter has nothing in common with that used in the
other.[98] We may defer for the moment the question whether
both are intended to refer to the same events in the history of
the Roman Empire, and focus on the significance of each
expression. Each is formed by analogy with expressions John
elsewhere uses of Christ or God. Each embodies the idea that
the beast is an imitation or satanic parody of Christ.

In 13:3 the phrase ὡς ἐσφαγμένην echoes 5:6, where the
same phrase is used of the Lamb on his first appearance in
Revelation. It is clearly intended to create a parallel between
Christ's death and resurrection, on the one hand, and the
beast's mortal wound and its healing, on the other. Since the
use of ὡς in 5:6 certainly does not imply that the Lamb only
seemed to have died but had not really, its use in the same
phrase in 13:3 cannot mean that the beast's head only appeared
to be mortally wounded. The use of ὡς is a feature of John's
visionary style (though not elsewhere used with a participle: cf.
4:6; 8:8; 9:7; 15:2; 19:6) which may here indicate that neither
the Lamb nor the beast is actually dead when John sees it in his
vision, because it has already come to life again.[99] If 13:3
stresses, by the allusion to 5:6, the beast's parallel to Christ's
death, 13:14 stresses, by the use of ἔζησεν, the beast's parallel
to Christ's resurrection. It echoes 2:8, where Christ is 'the first
and the last, who was dead and came to life (ἔζησεν)' (cf. 1:18).
There is an interesting complementarity between 13:3 and
13:14. In 13:3 the beast's death is described in terms which
allude to the Lamb's (ὡς ἐσφαγμένην εἰς θάνατον), but his
'resurrection' is described in terms which distinguish it from
the Lamb's ('his mortal wound was healed'). In 13:14 the
beast's 'resurrection' is described in terms which allude to

---

[98]It is extraordinary that Beckwith (1919) 696, can say: 'The language is similar'.
[99]Charles (1920) 141, 349.

Christ's (ἔζησεν), but his death is described in terms which distinguish it from the Christ's ('had been wounded by the sword'). By this means John is able to suggest that the beast's death and resurrection are and are not like Christ's. In other words, they are deceitful imitation.

Given the reference to Nero which we know from the number 666 there must be, the sword (13:14) must allude to Nero's suicide with a dagger (Suetonius, *Nero* 49). But it is by no means improbable that it also suggests the sword of divine judgment (cf. especially Isa 27:1, in view of the verse's relation to Rev 12) which is the judicial word of God issuing from Christ's mouth (Rev 1:16; 2:12, 16; 19:15, 21). The hint that the beast's mortal wound is an act of divine judgment seems confirmed by the use of the word πληγή (13:3, 12, 14). Though this is a quite natural usage for a fatal wound inflicted by a sword, the word is elsewhere used in Revelation in the sense of a blow of divine judgment, a 'plague' (9:18, 20; 11:6; 15:1, 6, 8; 16:9, 21; 18:4, 8; 21:9; 22:18).[100] Thus Nero's downfall is a divine judgment from which the beast appears to recover. The beast's own claim to divinity seems validated by this recovery. Just as Jesus, crucified by Roman power, was vindicated by his resurrection, as Christians saw it, so the beast, struck down by divine judgment, was vindicated by his recovery, as the world in general saw it (13:3-4).[101]

Thus John's divergence from the Nero legend as it was current in his time, referring to Nero's mortal wound and recovery instead of his escape from death, serves his purpose of portraying the beast's claim to divinity as a parody of Christ's

---

[100]Cf. Minear (1968) 253. A number of scholars also see an allusion to Genesis 3:15 (the woman's offspring will 'strike' [some MSS of LXX: πλήξει] the serpent's head): see Farrer (1949) 289; Farrer (1964) 153; Minear (1968) 259; Sweet (1979) 207, 210. Again, the allusions to this verse in Revelation 12 (the dragon, the woman and her offspring: cf. especially 12:9, 17: and cf. Gollinger [1971] 137) make this quite probable.

[101]It is possible that the mortal wound of the beast coincides with the dragon's fall from heaven (12:9-12), since the dragon was conquered by the witness of the martyrs, presumably under Nero (12:10-11), and his subsequent determination to make war on the saints (12:17) seems to be carried out by the beast after its recovery from the mortal wound (13:7).

death and resurrection. This is the central parallel between
Christ and the beast in chapter 13, but other parallels follow
from it. The universal worship of the beast (13:4, 8), following
the portrayal of his head as ὡς ἐσφαγμένην (13:3), parallels the
universal worship of the Lamb (5:8-14), following his portrayal
as ὡς ἐσφαγμένην (5:6). That the dragon gives the beast his
power, throne and authority (13:2) parallels the Father's gift of
authority and a place on his throne to Christ (2:28; 3:21).

The introduction of the second beast (13:11)[102] is at least
partly intelligible through the theme of christological parody.
Whereas in Ascension of Isaiah 4, the adversary himself performs
miracles to induce belief in him and sets up his own image, in
Revelation these things are performed on behalf of the beast
by the second beast. In fact, the adversary in the Ascension of
Isaiah is an amalgam of the self-deifying king and the false
prophet. John has separated these functions, portraying the
beast as the king who claims divinity and the second beast as his
prophet (cf. 16:13; 19:20) who proclaims the first beast's
divinity and organizes his worship. John may well have made
this distinction on the basis of tradition. He may have known
the Synoptic apocalyptic tradition which predicted 'false Christs'
and 'false prophets' (Matt 24:24; Mark 13:22). But the
distinction also enables him to create a satanic trinity: the
dragon from heaven, the beast from the sea and the beast from
the earth. The dragon relates to the first beast as God the
Father to Christ. The second beast relates to the first beast not
as the Holy Spirit to Christ, but as the Christian prophets,
inspired by the Spirit, relate to Christ.[103] The second beast acts
on behalf of (ἐνώπιον) the first beast (13:12, 14) as the prophets
stand before (ἐνώπιον) the true Lord of the earth (11:4). It
testifies to the beast's divinity with signs (13:3-4), as the prophets

---

[102]No doubt the idea of the two beasts was suggested by the myth of Leviathan
and Behemoth, as monsters respectively of sea and land: cf. Yarbro Collins (1976)
164-165. But this accounts for the portrayal of the false prophet *as a beast from the
land*, corresponding to the beast from the sea, not for the introduction of the
figure at all.

[103]The parallel between the second beast and the two witnesses of Revelation
11:3-13 is well brought out by Kiddle (1940) 252-256.

accompany their testimony to Christ with miracles (11:6). Finally, the mysterious mark of the beast, his name or his number on the right hand or the forehead of those who worship him (13:16-17) is parallel to the seal (7:3; 9:4) or the name (14:1; 22:4) on the foreheads of the followers of the Lamb.[104]

In chapter 17, the christological parody is again focused on the theme of the beast's disappearance and reappearance, but just as the way the latter is expressed is quite different from chapter 13, so the christological parody is quite different. That the beast 'was and is not and is to come' (17:8: ἦν καὶ οὐκ ἔστιν καὶ παρέσται) clearly parodies one of Revelation's key designations for God: 'he who was and who is and who is to come' (4:8: ὁ ἦν καὶ ὁ ὢν καὶ ὁ ἐρχόμενος; cf 1:4, 8).[105] It may even be deliberate that, just as this threefold designation of God occurs, with variation, three times in Revelation, so the corresponding threefold designation of the beast occurs, with variation, three times (17:8a, 8b, 11). The divine designation uses, instead of a mere future tense of the verb to be, a reference to God's 'coming', which is his coming to the world in judgment and salvation, to bring in his kingdom, at the end. This divine coming is nothing other than the 'coming' of Jesus Christ (cf. 1:7: ἔρχομαι),[106] who in Revelation declares seven times 'I am coming' (ἔρχομαι: 2:5, 16; 3:11; 16:15; 22:6, 12, 22; cf. also 3:3). Thus, although the beast's designation parodies a divine designation, it is no less a christological parody: it makes the return of the beast a parody of the eschatological coming of Jesus Christ.

The threefold formula as used of the beast differs, of course, significantly from the divine designation. In the first place, the middle term, which refers to the present, is negative (οὐκ ἔστιν). Unlike God, the beast is not eternal. Therefore whereas the future coming of the eternal God will bring his eternal

---

[104]For this parallel, see especially Cruz (1973) 86-90, 92-96.

[105]This has, of course, been noticed — e.g. by Farrer (1964) 184; Yarbro Collins (1976) 185; Sweet (1979) 255, 258 — but has not been fully explored.

[106]Cf. Comblin (1965) 50-54.

kingdom, this cannot be expected of the future coming of the beast. He has perished once already. His coming in the future is not likely to establish his sovereignty. It should be observed how differently the theme of the disappearance and reappearance of the beast functions in chapters 13 and 17. In chapter 13 the fact that the beast dies and recovers parallels the death and resurrection of Christ, but in chapter 17 the beast's temporary non-existence contrasts with the eternity of God. Both contradict the Nero legend's belief in Nero's continuing to live without dying, but they assert a break in the beast's life in quite different ways and for quite different purposes.

The third term in the threefold designation of the beast also varies from the corresponding term in the divine designation. It seems that the verb ἔρχομαι, despite its ordinariness, was in such a context in Revelation christologically charged. This verb is avoided in the beast's case, to distinguish his coming from the eschatological coming of Christ. Thus the simplest version of the formula has: καὶ πάρεσται (17:8b). (The word παρουσία, from this verb πάρειμι, was widely used of the coming of Christ, but not in Revelation.) The first occurrence of the formula ends: 'and is going to ascend from the abyss and goes to destruction' (17:8a). Here the eschatological coming of the beast, as an ascent from the abyss, contrasts with the eschatological coming of Christ, who descends from heaven (19:11). The reference to the abyss is probably not to the place of the dead (which in Revelation is Hades), but rather to the place of the demonic, from which all evil arises (9:1-2, 11; 20:1). It is in fact the same as the sea — the primeval chaos — from which the beast rises in 13:1.[107] Therefore the point in 17:8 is not really that the dead Nero returns to life, but rather that the beast rises again from the abyss from which the dragon originally

---

[107]Cf. Yarbro Collins (1976) 165-166, 170-171. Revelation 13:1 refers to the sea, rather than the abyss, because it alludes to Daniel 7:3 and because it fits into the scheme of heaven, earth and sea (12:12) which is used in Revelation 12-13: the dragon from heaven, the beast from the sea, the second beast from the earth. But because the abyss and the sea are identical, 11:7, where the beast is first introduced as 'the beast that ascends from the abyss,' need not refer to the beast's 'second coming' (17:8) but can refer to the beast's origin from the abyss (13:1).

called it (13:1). Once again the language is controlled not by the Nero legend but by the needs of the christological parody: to represent Nero's return as the evil counterpart of Christ's coming. That the beast 'goes to destruction' suffices as the third term in the third occurrence of the formula (17:11). The beast's destiny is not to reign (cf. 11:17) but to perish.

Thus whereas in chapter 13 the Nero legend is adapted to give the beast a parodic counterpart to the death and resurrection of Christ, in chapter 17 another form of the Nero legend is adapted to give the beast a parodic counterpart of the future coming of Christ. With this contrast is connected another striking contrast between the two chapters: in chapter 13 the beast makes war on the saints and conquers them (13:7), whereas in chapter 17 the beast makes war on the Lamb and is conquered by him (17:14). Chapter 13 portrays the beast's success. Struck down by divine judgment, he miraculously recovers, vindicating his claim to divinity. He pursues his opposition to God by making war on the followers of Christ and wins! All who will not worship the beast die. Of course, it is only from the perspective of the beast and his worshippers that this is victory. Elsewhere, John refers to the same occurrence — the saints' faithful witness to death at the hands of the beast — as their victory over him (15:2). But in chapter 13 he portrays the beast's public and publicly acclaimed success in advancing his own divinity against that of the true God and his Christ. In chapter 17 he portrays the beast's inevitable, ultimate failure. Unlike his resurrection, his eschatological coming fails to vindicate his divinity. He comes only to go to destruction. He cannot establish his kingdom eternally. Public victory now belongs to Christ, whose witnesses, the victims of the beast, are also now publicly vindicated with Christ at his coming (17:14). This pattern of success for the beast in chapter 13 and failure in chapter 17 also corresponds to the fact that in the parallel with Christ the emphasis in chapter 13 is on the similarity between the beast's 'death' and 'resurrection' and Christ's, while in chapter 17 the emphasis is on the difference between the beast's 'parousia' and Christ's.

The theme of christological parody indicates that John has constructed a *history* for the beast which parallels that of Christ.

The beast, like Christ, has his death, his resurrection and his parousia. This has not hitherto been recognized,[108] because exegetes who recognize the influence of the Nero legend on chapters 13 and 17 have supposed that the healing of the beast's mortal wound in chapter 13 must be the same event as the beast's coming up from the abyss in chapter 17. They have supposed this because they have assumed that the Nero legend controls John's thinking. The Nero legend envisages only one event of Nero's return, not two distinct events: resurrection and parousia. But we have found plenty of evidence that it is John's creative thinking that controls his use of the Nero legend. He has used two quite different forms of it in chapters 13 and 17 in order to develop two quite different aspects of his understanding of the beast. Moreover, in both cases he has significantly reformulated the Nero legend. This supplied him neither with the idea of the beast's miraculous recovery from a mortal wound nor with the idea of the beast's reemergence from the abyss. Consequently there is no need to suppose that he intended these two ideas to refer to the same event. He has not reproduced the Nero legend, but has drawn on it in order to construct his own vision of the beast's history.

The view that the healing of the beast's mortal wound in chapter 13 is the same event as the beast's reemergence from the abyss in chapter 17 has, in any case, grave difficulties of its own. It would mean that Nero, recovered from his mortal wound or returning from the abyss, will rule the Roman Empire for the three-and-a-half year apocalyptic period (13:5) prior to the coming of the kings of the east across the Euphrates (16:12) and the 'one hour' (17:13) in which they rule the Roman Empire together with Nero (17:12) and sack the city of Rome (17:16). This sequence would be necessary, because 16:2 indicates that the setting up of the image of the beast and

---

[108]Cf., e.g., Yarbro Collins (1976) 185-186. On p. 185 she recognizes that the 'second coming' of Nero in 17:8 parodies the parousia of Christ, but immediately on p. 186 she assimilates 17:8 to 13:3 and regards both as parodies of the resurrection of Christ. This is because, despite her recognition of the theme of christological parody, she allows the Nero legend a controlling influence on interpretation even against the evidence of the text itself.

the marking of those who worship it, events which follow the beast's recovery from his mortal wound (13:14-17), precede the arrival of the kings of the east from beyond the Euphrates (16:12). Moreover, even though the 'one hour' of 17:12 can scarcely be taken literally, it must indicate that the period in which the beast rules together with the ten kings is very much shorter than the forty-two months of his rule to which 13:5 refers. Therefore the returning Nero would not return across the Euphrates with the kings of the east, as in the Nero legend, but would already have ruled the empire from Rome for some time before the Parthian invasion which supports him. Since Revelation does not explicitly say that the beast comes from the east with the ten kings, this is a possible interpretation, but one which requires that John has considerably reformulated the Nero legend. Thus the idea that the Nero legend *controls* John's thinking and that therefore strict conformity with the Nero legend must be an exegetical principle for interpreting Revelation 13 and 17 must be abandoned by this line of interpretation too. On any showing it is clear that John has reworked the Nero legend freely for his own purposes.

However, the reconstruction just suggested, which postulates one future event of Nero's resurrection/return from the abyss, is incoherent because it portrays Nero *redivivus*, already secure in his totalitarian rule over the empire (chapter 13), then subsequently allied with the invading Parthians in conquering the empire and destroying the city of Rome (chapter 17). In other words, it fails to recognize a crucial distinction between chapters 13 and 17: that in chapter 13 the beast's recovery from his mortal wound consolidates the imperial power of Rome, whereas in chapter 17 the beast's return from the abyss is a threat to the empire which leads to the destruction of its capital. Rather than imagining — with no help from the text — a Nero *redivivus* who unaccountably follows his own successful rule of the empire by turning against it in alliance with the Parthians, it would be better to recognize that the healing of the beast's mortal wound in chapter 13 is a different event, prior to the beast's return from the abyss in chapter 17. This involves recognizing also that the beast which recovers from its mortal wound and the beast which returns from the abyss cannot both be *literally* Nero *redivivus*, though both are the imperial power whose full potential for opposing God and his people first appeared in the historical Nero.

Apart from the supposedly controlling influence of the Nero legend, there is one textual feature of John's accounts of the healing of the beast's mortal wound and of the return of the beast from the abyss which has sometimes been supposed to indicate that these events are identical.[106] The world's immediate reaction to the healing of the beast's mortal wound is described in 13:3: 'the whole earth followed the beast in amazement' (ἐθαυμάσθη ὅλη ἡ γῆ ὀπίσω τοῦ θηρίου). In 17:8 the same reaction greets the reappearance of the beast from the abyss: 'the inhabitants of the earth, whose names have not been written in the book of life from the foundation of the world [cf. 13:8], will be amazed when they see the beast (θαυμασθήσονται... βλεπόντων τὸ θηρίον), because it was and is not and is to come.' Certainly, 17:8 is intended to recall 13:3 and 13:8, but it need not describe the same event. Rather it may indicate the continuity in the beast's blasphemous pretensions to divinity and its success in persuading the world to believe them. The 'resurrection' and the 'parousia' of the beast are both attempts to vindicate and establish his rule as divine. Just as the resurrection and the parousia of Christ both vindicate him as divine victor and ruler, despite his apparent defeat on the cross (cf. 1:5, 7), so the 'resurrection' and the 'parousia' of the beast are both seen by the world as proving him the invincible divine ruler of the world, despite his previous downfall.

Thus, the way in which John has adapted the two forms of the Nero legend in the interests of the theme of christological parody strongly indicates that he understands the 'resurrection' of the beast in chapter 13 as a distinct event from his 'parousia' in chapter 17. But John's account of the beast is not just an imaginative creation. It is a theological reading of the history and future of the Roman Empire of his day. He was not simply projecting the theme of christological parody onto the empire.

---

[109]Beckwith (1919) 695-696.

He saw certain definite features of the empire as constituting a divine and messianic claim that rivalled Christ's. So in order to confirm and to complete our interpretation of John's use of the Nero legend we must turn to the question of the historical reference he intended his images to have.

5. Historical reference

If the healing of the beast's mortal wound represents the personal return of Nero, a future event from the perspective of Revelation, then everything Revelation says about the beast from 13:3 onwards belongs to the future. There should then be no question of identifying the second beast, the false prophet, with a reality contemporary with John, such as the Asiarchs or the imperial priesthood, for the second beast appears only in connection with the beast whose mortal wound has been healed (13:12), i.e. on this view the Nero *redivivus* of the future. The imperial cult as it existed in John's time should not, on this view, be what he depicts in 13:12-15, though he could have modelled the future cult of Nero *redivivus* on the imperial cult as he knew it. The beast's persecution of Christians (13:7) can, on this view, refer neither to persecution taking place in John's time nor to persecution immediately impending, but only to what will happen when the present emperor's successor is succeeded by Nero *redivivus* (17:9-11). Commentators are by no means always consistent in following through these implications of the view that 13:3 refers literally to the future return of Nero from the grave,[110] but they are clearly necessary.

Thus the interpretation of the beast's 'resurrection' is closely connected with the question whether 13:3-17 refers to the present, the near future, the rather more distant future, or some combination of present and future. It also involves the question of the relation between the beast and its heads. In

---

[110]E.g. Charles (1920) 1.348-364; Beasley-Murray (1974) 206-219. Beckwith (1919), while carrying through the future interpretation of chapter 13 as referring to Nero *redivivus* fairly consistently, still identifies the second beast with the imperial priesthood (409, 639-640).

13:3 it is one of the beast's seven heads that is wounded to death, but the head itself is never again referred to in this chapter. Immediately within the same verse the mortal wound is said to be the beast's: 'its [αὐτοῦ] mortal wound was healed,' where αὐτοῦ must refer to θηρίον, not κεφαλή.[111] In other words, although it is one of the heads that receives the mortal wound, it is not said that the head recovers, but that the beast recovers from what was a mortal wound to the beast itself. Subsequent references are to the beast's wound and recovery: 'the first beast, whose mortal wound had been healed' (13:12), 'the beast that had been wounded by the sword and came to life again' (13:14). If the head is Nero, as it most likely is, and if the recovery is also Nero's, then we must suppose that from 13:3 onwards 'the beast' designates Nero *redivivus*. Such a usage could certainly be supported from chapter 17,[112] where the seventh head of the beast who returns as the eighth is consistently described as 'the beast that was and is not and...' (17:8a, 8b, 11). The reason for this is probably not simply that each emperor (head) in a sense *is* the imperial power (the beast) during his reign. The reason is rather that, for John, Nero (the head that will return as the eighth) was the emperor who incarnated and demonstrated most fully the demonic nature of the beast in its opposition to God and his people.

Yet, if chapter 13 is read in its own terms and if we are not already convinced that the healing of the mortal wound must represent Nero's own resurrection, the most natural way to read 13:3, 12, 14 is to understand that the mortal wound sustained by Nero (the head) was also a mortal wound to the imperial power as such (the beast) and that it was the imperial power, not Nero himself, which recovered. Such an interpretation can give the image an obvious historical reference. Nero's suicide, which was also the end of the Julio-Claudian dynasty, was a death-blow to the imperial power,

---

[111]Charles (1920) 1.349, strangely insists that αὐτοῦ shows the text 'to refer to the healing of the wounded head and not to the healing of the Beast itself with seven heads'. He seems to have influenced not a few subsequent interpretations of this verse.

[112]Cf. Yarbro Collins (1976) 171-172.

because it coincided with the beginning of the period of chaos, the so-called 'year of the four emperors,' in which more than one claimant was contesting the imperial title, in which various provinces hoped to be able to throw off Roman rule, and in which the survival of the empire was put in very serious question.[113] Jews and Christians alike must have hoped that this near-disintegration of the empire was the divine judgment from which Rome would never recover. But the imperial power in fact fully recovered under Vespasian, the Jews in Judaea and other movements of revolt were utterly quashed, and the subjects of the Empire were impressed even more than before with its apparent invincibility: 'Who is like the beast, and who can fight against it?' (13:4).

The year 69 threatened the survival of the empire and ruptured the empire's history in a way which made a deep impression on those who lived through it and which fully justifies a description of it as a mortal wound from which the imperial power miraculously recovered. As Josephus put it, in the context of Vespasian's acclamation as emperor in Alexandria, 'the Roman state [was] saved beyond expectation' (*BJ* 4.657). In the interpretation of Ezra's vision of the Roman eagle, which is comparable in significant ways with John's vision of the beast, he is told: 'In the midst of the time of that kingdom great struggles shall arise, and it shall be in danger of falling; nevertheless it shall not fall then, but shall regain its former power' (4 Ezra 12:18). The Sibyllines refer to the events of the year 69 as following Nero's 'disappearance':

When he runs away, beyond the Parthian land,
many will bloody the ground for the throne of Rome
(SibOr 4:123-124).

For on his [Nero's] [dis]appearance[114] the whole creation
was shaken and kings perished... (SibOr 5:152-153).

---

[113] See Greenhalgh (1974); Wellesley (1975).

[114] The manuscript reading τούτου γὰρ φανέντος leaves the line a syllable short. Suggested emendations are προφανέντος, τε φανέντος (Geffcken [1902] 111), θανεόντος (Lanchester, cited Collins [1983] 396). But the context demands a

Minear objects that the civil unrest was not the consequence of Nero's death, but preceded it (since it was revolt in the provinces and the Senate's declaring him a public enemy which precipitated his suicide). Moreover, 'his death did not jeopardize the power of the empire, because he died as a fugitive and enemy of the state. Imperial authority was not threatened by his death; rather, his death demonstrated the superior power of the state.'[115] But the latter is a Roman legalistic view of the matter not likely to be taken by provincials in the east. To all appearances it was Nero's downfall, ending the only dynasty that had ruled as Roman emperors, which opened the way for revolt and civil war. Strictly speaking, one might say that the civil unrest that began before Nero's death was the consequence of his loss of imperial authority. His death itself was only the final point of his downfall, though as that it certainly contributed to the disorder that followed. But it is entirely understandable that John should find in Nero's suicide an appropriate *symbol* for the mortal blow to the empire that occurred at the end of his reign, especially as the image of a fatal wound with a sword could also hint at an act of divine judgment.[116]

If this interpretation is correct, it follows that in chapter 13 John has *historicized* the apocalyptic tradition of the eschatological adversary identified with the returning Nero. He sees it already being fulfilled in the Flavian dynasty which reestablished the imperial power. The forms of the Nero legend which are found in the Sibylline Oracles (Nero returning with the Parthians to conquer the empire and destroy Rome) could not have been so historicized. But this is why it is not those forms of the legend which John uses in chapter 13, but

reference neither to Nero's appearance nor to his death (for according to SibOr 5:143 Nero did not die, but fled), but to his disappearance. I suggest therefore that μή should be supplied before φανέντος.

[115]Minear (1968).

[116]Yarbro Collins (1976) 174, has a different objection to this interpretation: 'The force of the [christological] parody requires an individual who not only died but also rose from the dead.' But this is not a cogent objection, since it is precisely not an individual, but the imperial power exercised by a succession of emperors, that John sees as usurping the divine rule of Christ.

the form which is found in Ascension of Isaiah 4. This tradition also provided him with the notion that the eschatological adversary imitates Christ, which no doubt served as the hint from which he was able to interpret Nero's death and the subsequent recovery of the imperial power as a parody of Christ's death and resurrection.

Since in chapter 13 John is interpreting already existing apocalyptic tradition as fulfilled in the history of the Roman Empire in the first century, we should not expect it to read like an allegory composed to correspond precisely to the events it symbolizes. But we can see that in various ways John has modified the tradition in the interests of presenting a more realistic picture of the imperial cult as he knew it under the Flavians:

(1) 13:4: 'They worshipped the dragon, for he had given his authority to the beast, and they worshipped the beast...' This does not just mean that by worshipping the emperor people were implicitly worshipping Satan.[117] Rather, John recognizes that in the imperial cult the emperor was worshipped in association with the traditional pagan gods.[118] Though sacrifices were offered to the emperor, they were more often offered for the emperor to the gods, expressing gratitude to the gods for the benefits of the emperor's rule.[119]

(2) 13:4: '... they worshipped the beast, saying, "Who is like the beast, and who can fight against it?"' John knows that in the Greek east the imperial cult was not imposed from above, but organized by the cities and provinces themselves,[120] though the establishment of the cult had always to be negotiated with Rome.[121] Above all, John knows that the imperial cult was a reaction to power. The Roman empire as a power external to the Greek cities, to which they were subject, was represented

[117]So, e.g., Mounce (1977) 253.
[118]Cf. Price (1984) 103, 109.
[119]Price (1984) 210-220; Botha (1988) 96-97.
[120]Botha (1988) 90-91; Price (1984) 53-58.
[121]Price (1984) 65-77.

within the life of the cities by assimilation to the gods.[122] The temples, altars, images, festivals and rituals of the imperial cult represented at the heart of their civic life the cities' willing acceptance of subjection to Rome. The imperial power was treated as godlike to the extent that it appeared as godlike in its power, requiring subjection, and in the benefits of its rule, requiring gratitude. Thus, if the threatened collapse of the empire in 69 might have discredited its pretensions to godlike power, its recovery under the Flavians reestablished its claims to be worshipped. The iconography of the imperial cult under the Flavians frequently features symbols of military power and victory.[123]

(3) The second beast (13:11-17) should probably not be individualized as the high priest of the imperial cult in the province of Asia[124] or limited to the provincial assembly. It most appropriately represents the imperial priesthood generally, composed also of prominent members of the élite of the cities.[125]

John has transferred to the second beast functions which in the tradition, as represented by Ascension of Isaiah 4:5, 11, were performed by the eschatological adversary himself: miraculous signs attesting his divinity and the setting up of his image. John correctly sees these as functions of those who instigated, encouraged and officiated at the imperial cult at the local level. Imperial images were very rarely erected by Roman officials; they were most commonly erected by the city itself,[126] and no doubt the imperial priests on the city assembly would take the lead in proposing such matters (cf. 13:14). As Scherrer has shown, the signs performed by the second beast (13:13-14), as well as his giving voice to the image of the beast

---

[122]This is Price's view of the cults of Roman power in the republican period: Price (1984) 43, 52. He stresses that from the reign of Augustus the imperial cult developed at the provincial as well as the civic level: 54-56. But for the continuing validity of the essential point, see 235, 239.

[123]Botha (1988) 94.

[124]Barnett (1989) 116.

[125]Price (1984) 62-64.

[126]Price (1984) 174.

(13:15), are credible as references to the imperial cult.[127] In Ascension of Isaiah 4:5 the signs of the Antichrist are his ability to affect the movements of the sun and the moon (and cf. SibOr 3:64-65, which confirms that stupendous nature miracles of this kind belonged to the tradition). If John has deliberately substituted the sign of fire from heaven (13:14), this may not only be to make the second beast the satanic counterpart of the prophet Elijah (1 Kgs 18:38; 2 Kgs 1:10-14; Luke 9:54), but also to approximate the sign to the kind of miracle actually engineered in the imperial cult.[128]

(4) The universal enforcement of worship of the beast, on pain of death, together with the mark of the beast, however that is to be interpreted (13:15-17), are probably not intended to represent contemporary reality. The seven messages to the churches do not indicate that persecution of Christians who refused to participate in the imperial cult had been anything more than sporadic. In these verses John foresees the way things are going. But they correctly represent the pressure as occurring at the local level,[129] not on the orders of the beast from Rome, but at the instigation of the second beast, his local propagandists. Pressure on Christians and animosity against them for their refusal to join in the corporate expression of religio-political loyalty would come at such times as the city's celebration of festivals dedicated to the imperial cult,[130] at which all were expected, by public opinion if nothing else, to turn out[131] and Christians who did not would be easily conspicuous to their neighbours by their absence. Price argues that large numbers of small altars dedicated to the emperor, found, for example, at Pergamum, indicate a city decree instructing all citizens to provide their own altars for sacrificing outside their houses as the festival procession passed.[132] It was

[127]Scherrer (1984); cf. also Scherrer (1979) 84-125; Botha (1988) 95-96.

[128]Cf. Scherrer (1984) 604-609. It is probably significant that the sign differs from those of the two witnesses (11:5-6), which are modelled on those of Elijah and Moses.

[129]Cf. Botha (1988) 97-98; Price (1984) 123-124, 198.

[130]On these, see Price (1984) 101-132.

[131]Cf. Price (1984) 102-103, 108, 113-114.

[132]Price (1984) 112.

by such local actions that things might move, for John's readers, in the direction envisaged by 13:15-17. At any rate, John shows an accurate sense of the dynamics of local pressure on Christians to participate in the imperial cult.

The account of the beast's rule in 13:3-17 is, of course, a mythic heightening of contemporary reality, intended to highlight its true nature as John the prophet perceives it, and in part at least an apocalyptic heightening of contemporary reality, pointing the direction in which things are to develop as the conflict between God and his demonic opponents comes to a head. It is for these purposes that John develops apocalyptic traditions instead of offering a prosaic description of contemporary reality. But he has developed apocalyptic traditions in a way which reflects the real historical situation in which he lived. It is plausible to say that in this chapter he has historicized apocalyptic traditions, relating them in such a way as to indicate their fulfilment in the Roman Empire since Nero.

The way in which John has historicized the tradition about the eschatological adversary identified with the returning Nero has an interesting parallel in chapter 11. In the story of the two witnesses (11:3-13) John is undoubtedly dependent on an apocalyptic tradition about the two prophets of the last days, who were expected to be Moses and Elijah returning to earth.[133] The story of the two witnesses, as John tells it, clearly alludes to the Old Testament accounts of Moses and Elijah, while also reflecting the story of Jesus himself. But John has historicized the tradition. The two witnesses are not two individual prophets of the future, still less Moses and Elijah in person. They are the churches in their prophetic and suffering witness during the period of conflict with the beast. The story models symbolically the vocation to which John's readers are called,[134] in the last days in which they already live, and the fate

---

[133] As attested elsewhere, the tradition concerns *Enoch* and Elijah: see Bauckham (1976); Berger (1976B); Black (1978). John may have used a variant of this tradition or may himself have substituted Moses for Enoch.

[134] See chapter 9 section 5 above; cf. Giblin (1984) 441-443.

they must expect if they prove faithful witnesses, in the coming crisis of conflict with the imperial cult. This parallel to John's historicization of the expectation of Nero's return is of special interest because, as the apocalyptic time period (11:2-3; cf. 13:5) indicates, chapter 11 tells from a different point of view the same story as chapter 13 tells. The story of the witnesses whom the beast conquers (11:7) is the obverse, as it were, of the story of the beast who conquers the saints (13:7). The imperial power of the Flavians is Nero *reditus* in the same sense as the church under the Flavians is Moses and Elijah *rediti*.[135] It follows that the time period of the beast's reign and the witnesses' testimony cannot be taken literally. But since the 'one hour' of the reign of the ten kings with the beast (17:12) could not conceivably be intended literally, we should not expect any of the time periods in Revelation to be literal.

If in chapter 13 John historicizes the Nero legend, it is otherwise in chapter 17, where his concern is exclusively with the future. By contrast with his depiction of the empire's apparently miraculous recovery and apparently divine success in chapter 13, in chapter 17 John must show how the empire had only temporarily escaped the divine judgment which Nero's death had symbolized and only temporarily recovered its strength under the Flavians. So in 17:7-18 the contemporary realities reflected are not events but expectations. On the one hand, there was the religious faith, propagated and expressed in the imperial cult, that Rome's godlike rule would be eternal. A graffito found in a private house in Ephesus expresses it well: 'Rome, ruler of all, your power will never die.'[136] John must confront this expectation with the Christian eschatological hope that the kingdom of Christ, the true ruler of all, is coming. But on the other hand, there was also the popular pagan expectation of the return of Nero. For much of the population of the eastern provinces of the empire, it seems (especially from Dio Chrysostom's comment, quoted in section 2 above) that Nero's return was not merely an object of

---

[135]Cf. Beckwith (1919) 408.
[136]Price (1984) 120.

expectation but an object of eager hope. The philhellene emperor, friendly to the Parthians, had acquired the mythic image of a messianic saviour figure, who would wreak the vengeance of the east on the west and reestablish the rule of the east. This expectation John must confront with the Christian eschatological hope for the coming of the true Messiah, Jesus Christ.

John's prophecy exploits the contradiction between these two pagan expectations: the admiring belief in Rome's eternal destiny to rule the world and the rebellious hope of a conqueror from the east who would destroy Rome. It also exploits the fact that, because the latter was expected to be Nero, both expectations were attached to the Roman imperial succession. Thus the pagan messiah appears as one of the seven heads of the beast returning as an anomalous, supernumerary eighth, leading the enemies of Rome against it. The prophecy plays off the two pagan expectations against each other and both against the Christian hope of the coming of Christ. The parousia of the beast, the returning Nero, is seen as the last and most far-reaching attempt by the beast to establish his kingdom over all. In this attempt he destroys the eternal city itself, contradicting the idolatrous faith in the eternity of Roman rule. But the returning Nero's attempt to establish, on the ruins of Rome, a truly universal empire in opposition to the rule of God and his Messiah is doomed to failure. For he is the emperor who has already perished under the judgment of God. His parousia must prove a fraud, the last gasp of the demonic will to godlike power which is already doomed.

6. The hermeneutical question

It makes little sense to ask whether in chapter 17 John took the future return of Nero literally. Prophecy can only *depict* the future in terms which make sense to its present. It clothes the purpose of God in the hopes and fears of its contemporaries. The legend of Nero's return proved useful to John because he could adapt it to the needs of his prophetic vision of the triumph of the kingdom of God over the Roman Empire's pretensions to divine rule. He uses it to expose the inherent instability of the latter and to portray its ultimate failure as it clashes with the truly eternal kingdom of Christ. Like all prophets, John *perceives* the future in the *images* he uses to depict it. It is only as the historical relativity of the images becomes apparent to later generations that the impulse to state what the images essentially express arises. Late twentieth-century readers who are serious in their attempt to understand John's prophecy inevitably feel that impulse. But we need to direct it, not into an attempt to replace the images by a supposedly more permanent message, but into an attempt to make the images accessible to ourselves once more. This, after all, is what John himself did with the images of the ancient prophecies of the Old Testament which he was constantly reappropriating for his contemporaries.

The images of the beast will probably become most easily accessible to us as we realise that it was primarily in developing the theme of christological parody that John found the Nero legend useful. It enabled him to construct a history of the beast as paralleling the death, the resurrection and the parousia of Jesus Christ. Some interpretation of Revelation has made the theme of christological parody seem a mere creative fantasy which John projects onto the Roman Empire, which of course had no intention of aping the Christian story of Jesus. In fact, as we have seen, the christological parody corresponds to real features of the history of the empire, to the character of the imperial cult, and to contemporary expectations of the future of the empire. It is a profound prophetic interpretation of the contemporary religio-political image of the empire, both in Rome's own propaganda and in its subjects' profoundest responses to Roman rule. This religio-political ideology, which John sees as a parody of the Christian claims about Christ, was no mere cover for the hard political realities: it entered deeply into the contemporary dynamics of power as they affected the lives of John's contemporaries. He sees it as a deification of power. The empire's success is founded on military might and people's adulation of military might. By these standards Christ and the martyrs are the unsuccessful victims of the empire. Instead of worshipping the risen Christ who has won his victory by suffering witness to the truth, the world worships the beast whose 'resurrection' is the proof that this military might is invincible. The parallel between the 'death' and 'resurrection' of the beast and the death and resurrection of Jesus Christ poses the issue of what is truly divine. Is it the beast's apparent success which is worthy of religious trust and worship? Or is the apparent failure of Christ and the martyrs the true witness to the God who can be ultimately trusted and may alone be worshipped?

The ambiguity of the period of the beast's reign, in which to earthly appearances the beast's 'resurrection' has established his eternal kingdom, while those who acknowledge God's rule are slaughtered by the beast, cannot be permanent. God's kingdom must come. The parallel between the beast's 'parousia' and Christ's poses the issue of what will turn out ultimately to be divine, whose kingdom will prevail in the end. The cult of military power contains its own contradiction: the city which lived by military conquest will fall by military conquest. But beyond that, military power which aims only at its own absolute supremacy must prove a false messiah. It overreaches itself because it is the merely human grasping for what is truly only divine. It is only the parousia of Christ that can establish an eternal kingdom, because it is truly the coming of the eternal God who alone can be trusted with absolute supremacy.

The riddle of the number of the beast pointed specifically to Nero as the figure whose history and legend displayed, to those who had wisdom, the nature of the Roman Empire's attempt to rival God. Any contemporary reappropriation of Revelation's images that aims to expose the dynamics of power in the contemporary world in the light of the Gospel would also have to be specific.

Abbreviations

Abbreviations for ancient Jewish and Christian literature

ActsThom	Acts of Thomas
ApConst	Apostolic Constitutions
ApAbr	Apocalypse of Abraham
ApEl	Apocalypse of Elijah
1ApJas	First Apocalypse of James (CG V,3)
ApMos	Apocalypse of Moses
ApocrJn	Apocryphon of John
ApPaul	Apocalypse of Paul
ApPet	Apocalypse of Peter
ApSedr	Apocalypse of Sedrach
ApZeph	Apocalypse of Zephaniah
AscIsa	Ascension of Isaiah
b. 'Abod. Zar.	Babylonian Talmud tractate 'Abodah Zarah
2 Bar	Syriac Apocalypse of Baruch
3 Bar	Greek/Slavonic Apocalypse of Baruch
4 Bar	4 Baruch (or Paralipomena of Jeremiah)
Barn.	Epistle of Barnabas
b. B. B.	Babylonian Talmud tractate Baba Batra
Bel	Bel and the Dragon (LXX Additions to Daniel)
b. Giṭṭ.	Babylonian Talmud tractate Giṭṭin
b. Ḥag.	Babylonian Talmud tractate Ḥagigah
b. Ḥull.	Babylonian Talmud tractate Ḥullin
b. Kidd.	Babylonian Talmud tractate Kiddushin
b. Men.	Babylonain Talmud tractate Menaḥot

b. Shabb.	Babylonian Talmud tractate Shabbat
b. Sanh.	Babylonain Talmud tractate Sanhedrin
Cant	Canticles (Song of Songs)
CD	Damascus Rule
CG	Nag Hammadi codices
1 Chron	1 Chronicles
2 Chron	2 Chronicles
1 Clem	1 Clement
2 Clem	2 Clement
Col	Colossians
1 Cor	1 Corinthians
2 Cor	2 Corinthians
Dan	Daniel
Deut	Deuteronomy
Did	Didache
Eccl	Ecclesiastes (Qohelet)
2 Enoch (A, J)	Slavonic Apocalypse of Enoch (MSS A [shorter recension] and J [longer recension])
Eph	Ephesians
1 Esd	1 Esdras (LXX)
Est	Esther
Exod	Exodus
Exod. R.	Midrash Rabbah on Exodus
Ezek	Ezekiel
4 Ezra	Apocalypse of Ezra (2 Esdras)
5 Ezra	Chapters 1-2 of 4 Ezra
6 Ezra	Chapters 15-16 of 4 Ezra
Fragm. Tg.	Fragment Targum
Gen	Genesis
Gen. R.	Midrash Rabbah on Genesis
GkApDan	Greek Apocalypse of Daniel
GkApEzra	Greek Apocalypse of Ezra
GThom	Gospel of Thomas (CG II,2)

Hab	Habakkuk
Hag	Haggai
Heb	Hebrews
Hek. Rab.	Hekhalot Rabbati
Hek. Zuṭarti	Hekhalot Zuṭarti
Hos	Hosea
Isa	Isaiah
Jas	James
Jdt	Judith
Jer	Jeremiah
Jon	Jonah
JosAs	Joseph and Aseneth
Josh	Joshua
j. Sanh.	Palestinian Talmud tractate Sanhedrin
Jub	Jubilees
Judg	Judges
1 Kgs	1 Kings
2 Kgs	2 Kings
LAB	Pseudo-Philo, *Liber Antiquitatum Biblicarum*
LAE	Life of Adam and Eve
LadJac	Ladder of Jacob
Lam	Lamentations
Lam. R.	Midrash Rabbah on Lamentations
Lev	Leviticus
Lev. R.	Midrash Rabbah on Leviticus
LivPro	Lives of the Prophets
LXX	Septuagint
1 Macc	1 Maccabees
2 Macc	2 Maccabees
3 Macc	3 Maccabees
4 Macc	4 Maccabees
m. B. B.	Mishnah tractate Baba Batra
m. Ber.	Mishnah tractate Berakot

m. Giṭṭ.	Mishnah tractate Giṭṭin
Mic	Micah
m. Sanh.	Mishnah tractate Sanhedrin
MT	Massoretic text of the Hebrew Bible
m. Tam.	Mishnah tractate Tamid
Mur	Muraba'at texts
m. Yom.	Mishnah tractate Yoma
Nah	Nahum
Neh	Nehemiah
Num	Numbers
Num. R.	Midrash Rabbah on Numbers
OdesSol	Odes of Solomon
1 Pet	1 Peter
2 Pet	2 Peter
Prov	Proverbs
Ps, Pss	Psalms
PsSol	Psalms of Solomon
4QBer[a]	Benedictions from Qumran Cave 4
4QFlor	Florilegium from Qumran Cave 4
1QGenApoc	Genesis Apocryphon from Qumran Cave 1
1QH	Hodayot (Thanksgiving Hymns) from Qumran Cave 1
4QJub[a]	Jubilees MS from Qumran Cave 4
1QM	Milḥamah (War Scroll) from Qumran Cave 1
4QPBless	Blessings of Jacob (Patriarchal Blessings) from Qumran Cave 4
4QShirShabb	Songs of the Sabbath Sacrifice from Qumran Cave 4
1QpHab	Pesher on Habakkuk from Qumran Cave 1
4QpIsa[a]	Pesher on Isaiah from Qumran Cave 4
1QSa	Messianic Rule from Qumran Cave 1
1QSb	Blessings from Qumran Cave 1
QuEzra	Questions of Ezra

Rev	Revelation
Rom	Romans
1 Sam	1 Samuel
2 Sam	2 Samuel
SibOr	Sibylline Oracles
Sir	Ben Sira (Ecclesiasticus)
TAbr (A, B)	Testament of Abraham (Recensions A and B)
TAdam	Testament of Adam
TAsher	Testament of Asher
TDan	Testament of Dan
Tg.	Targum
Tg. Neof.	Targum Neofiti
Tg. Ps-Jon.	Targum of Pseudo-Jonathan
1 Thes	1 Thessalonians
2 Thes	2 Thessalonians
1 Tim	1 Timothy
2 Tim	2 Timothy
TIsaac	Testament of Isaac
TJob	Testament of Job
TJos	Testament of Joseph
TJud	Testament of Judah
TLevi	Testament of Levi
TMos	Testament of Moses
TNapht	Testament of Naphtali
Tob	Tobit
TSol	Testament of Solomon
Wisd	Wisdom of Solomon
y. Ber.	Palestinian Talmud tractate Berakot
y. Sanh.	Palestinian Talmud tractate Sanhedrin
y. Ta'an.	Palestinian Talmud tractate Ta'anit
Zech	Zechariah

Abbreviations for serial publications

AARSR	American Academy of Religion Studies in Religion
AB	Anchor Bible
AGJU	Arbeiten zur Geschichte des antiken Judentums und des Urchristentums
AnBib	Analecta Biblica
ANCL	Ante-Nicene Christian Library
Aug	*Augustinianum*
AUSS	*Andrews University Seminary Studies*
BA	*Biblical Archaeologist*
BASOR	*Bulletin of the American Schools of Oriental Research*
BEATAJ	Beiträge zur Erforschung des Alten Testaments und des Antiken Judentums
BETL	Bibliotheca ephemeridum theologicarum Lovaniensium
BGBE	Beiträge zur Geschichte der biblischen Exegese
BHT	Beiträge zur historischen Theologie
Bib	*Biblica*
BibOr	Biblica et Orientalia
BNTC	Black's New Testament Commentaries
BR	*Biblical Research*
BZNW	Beihefte zur *ZNW*
CBQ	*Catholic Biblical Quarterly*
CBQMS	*Catholic Biblical Quarterly* Monograph Series
CChrSL	Corpus Christianorum: Series Latina
CH	*Church History*
CJ	*Classical Journal*
CNT	Commentaire du Nouveau Testament
ConB(NT)	Coniectanea Biblica (New Testament Series)
ConNt	*Coniectanea neotestamentica*
CRHPR	Cahiers de la *Revue d'histoire et de philosophie religieuse*

CrSt	*Cristianesimo nella Storia*
DJD	Discoveries in the Judaean Desert
DOS	Dumbarton Oaks Studies
EQ	*Evangelical Quarterly*
EtJ	Études juives
EvT	*Evangelische Theologie*
ExpT	*Expository Times*
FRALNT	Forschungen zur Religion und Literatur des Alten und Neuen Testament
GCS	Griechische christliche Schriftsteller
GNS	Good News Studies
HDR	Harvard Dissertations in Religion
Hist	*Historia*
HNT	Handbuch zum Neuen Testament
HSM	Harvard Semitic Monographs
HSS	Harvard Semitic Studies
HTR	*Harvard Theological Review*
HUCA	*Hebrew Union College Annual*
ICC	International Critical Commentary
Int	*Interpretation*
JAOS	*Journal of the American Oriental Society*
JBL	*Journal of Biblical Literature*
JJS	*Journal of Jewish Studies*
JQR	*Jewish Quarterly Review*
JRS	*Journal of Roman Studies*
JSJ	*Journal for the Study of Judaism in the Persian, Hellenistic and Roman Period*
JSNT	*Journal for the Study of the New Testament*
JSNTSS	*Journal for the Study of the New Testament* Supplement Series
JSOTSS	*Journal for the Study of the Old Testament* Supplement Series

JSP	*Journal for the Study of the Pseudepigrapha*
JSPSS	*Journal for the Study of the Pseudepigrapha* Supplement Series
JSS	*Journal of Semitic Studies*
JTS	*Journal of Theological Studies*
JU	Judentum und Umwelt
Lat	*Latomus*
LD	Lectio Divina
LUA	Lunds universitets arsskrift
MNTC	Moffat's New Testament Commentary
NCB	New Century Bible
Neot	*Neotestamentica*
NICNT	New International Commentary on the New Testament
NovT	*Novum Testamentum*
NovTSup	Supplements to *Novum Testamentum*
NTS	*New Testament Studies*
OCP	*Orientalia Christiana Periodica*
OTL	Old Testament Library
RB	*Revue biblique*
RechSR	*Recherches de science religieuse*
REAug	*Revue des études augustinennes*
RESl	*Revue des études slaves*
RevQ	*Revue de Qumran*
RHPR	*Revue d'histoire et de philosophie religieuse*
RHR	*Revue de l'histoire des religions*
RMP	*Rheinisches Museum für Philologie*
RSBS	*Rivista di Studi Bizantini e Slavi*
RSR	*Revue des sciences religieuses*
RTP	*Revue de théologie et de philosophie*
SBLDS	SBL Dissertation Series
SBLSCS	SBL Septuagint and Cognate Studies
SBM	Stuttgarter biblische Monographien

SBS	Stuttgarter Bibelstudien
SBT	Studies in Biblical Theology
SC	Sources chrétiennes
ScEs	*Science et Esprit*
Sem	*Semeia*
Semit	*Semitica*
SHR	Studies in the History of Religions
SJLA	Studies in Judaism in Late Antiquity
SJOT	*Scandinavian Journal of the Old Testament*
SNTSMS	Society for New Testament Studies Monograph Series
SPB	Studia Postbiblica
SSN	Studia Semitica Neerlandica
ST	*Studia Theologica*
STDJ	Studies on the Texts of the Desert of Judah
StNT	Studien zum Neuen Testament
SUNT	Studien zur Umwelt des Neuen Testament
SVTP	Studia in Veteri Testamenti Pseudepigrapha
TC	Torch Commentaries
TextsS	Texts and Studies
Them	*Themelios*
Theol	*Theology*
TDNT	G. Kittel and G. Friedrich ed., *Theological Dictionary of the New Testament*, 10 vols. (tr. G. W. Bromiley; Grand Rapids: Eerdmans, 1964-1976)
TNTC	Tyndale New Testament Commentaries
TSAJ	Texte und Studien zum antiken Judentum
TU	Texte und Untersuchungen
TynB	*Tyndale Bulletin*
UCOP	University of Cambridge Oriental Publications
UUA	Uppsala Universitetsarsskrift
VT	*Vetus Testamentum*

VTSup   Supplements to *Vetus Testamentum*

WBC   Word Biblical Commentary
WUNT   Wissenschaftliche Untersuchungen zum
                     Neuen Testament

YJS   Yale Judaica Series

ZAW   *Zeitschrift für die alttestamentliche Wissenschaft*
ZBK   *Zürcher Bibelkommentar*
ZNW   *Zeitschrift für die neutestamentliche
                     Wissenschaft*
ZTK   *Zeitschrift für Theologie und Kirche*

Bibliography

Abelson, J. *The immanence of God in rabbinical literature.* London: Macmillan, 1912.

Acerbi, A. *Serra Lignea: Studi sulla Fortuna della* Ascensione di Isaia. Rome: Editrice A.V.E., 1984.

Acerbi, A. *L'Ascensione di Isaia: Cristologia e profetismo in Siria nei primi decenni del II secolo.* Studia Patristica Mediolanensia 17. Milan: Vita e Pensiero, 1989.

Alexander, P. J. *The Oracle of Baalbek: The Tiburtine Sibyl in Greek Dress.* DOS 10. Washington, D.C.: Dumbarton Oaks Centre for Byzantine Studies, 1967.

Alexander, P. J. *The Byzantine Apocalyptic Tradition.* Ed. D. deF. Abrahamse. Berkeley/Los Angeles/London: University of California Press, 1985.

Alexander, P. S. 'The Historical Setting of the Hebrew Book of Enoch,' *JJS* 28 (1977) 156-180.

Alexander, P. S. '3 (Hebrew Apocalypse of) Enoch,' in J. H. Charlesworth ed., *The Old Testament Pseudepigrapha,* vol. 1 (London: Darton, Longman & Todd, 1983) 223-315.

Alexander, P. S. '3 Enoch and the Talmud,' *JSJ* 18 (1987) 40-68.

Alexander, P.S. 'Prayer in the Hekhalot Literature,' in R. Goetschel ed., *Prière, Mystique et Judaïsme: Colloque de Strasbourg (10-12 septembre 1984)* (Travaux du Centre d'Histoire des Religions de Strasbourg 11; Paris: Presses Universitaires de France, 1987) 43-64. (1987A)

Allison, D. C. 'The Pauline Epistles and the Synoptic Gospels: The Pattern of the Parallels,' *NTS* 28 (1982) 1-32.

Allison, D. C. '*4 Q 403* fragm. 1, col. 1, 38-46 and the Revelation to John,' *RevQ* 12 (1986) 409-414.

Allison, D. C. 'The Silence of Angels: Reflections on the Songs of the Sabbath Sacrifice,' *RevQ* 13 (1988) 189-197.

Allo, E.-B. *Saint Jean: L'Apocalypse.* Paris: Lecoffe, [2]1921.

Aptowitzer, V. 'The Celestial Temple as Viewed in the Aggadah,' in J. Dan ed., *Binah: Studies in Jewish History, Thought, and Culture*, vol. 2 (New York: Praeger, 1989) 1-29.

Atchley, E. G. C. F. *A History of the Use of Incense in Divine Worship.* Alcuin Club Collections 13. London: Longmans, Green, 1909.

Audet, J.-P. *La Didachè: Instructions des Apôtres.* Paris: Gabalda, 1958.

Aune, D. E. 'The Social Matrix of the Apocalypse of John,' *BR* 24 (1981) 16-32.

Aune, D. E. 'The Odes of Solomon and Early Christian Prophecy,' *NTS* 28 (1982) 435-460.

Aune, D. E. *Prophecy in Early Christianity and the Ancient Mediterranean World.* Grand Rapids: Eerdmans, 1983.

Aune, D. E. 'The Influence of Roman Imperial Court Ceremonial on the Apocalypse of John,' *BR* 28 (1983) 5-26. (1983A)

Aune, D. E. 'The Apocalypse of John and the Problem of Genre,' *Sem* 36 (1986) 65-96.

Aune, D. E. 'The Prophetic Circle of John of Patmos and the Exegesis of Revelation 22.16,' *JSNT* 37 (1989) 103-116.

Aune, D. E. 'The Form and Function of the Proclamations to the Seven Churches (Revelation 2-3),' *NTS* 36 (1990) 182-204.

Barclay, W. *The Revelation of John*, vol. 2. Daily Study Bible. Edinburgh: Saint Andrew Press, ²1960.

Barnard, L. W. *Justin Martyr: his life and thought.* Cambridge: Cambridge University Press, 1967.

Barnett, P. 'Polemical Parallelism: Some Further Reflections on the Apocalypse,' *JSNT* 35 (1989) 111-120.

Barr, D. L. 'The Apocalypse as a Symbolic Transformation of the World: A Literary Analysis,' *Int* 38 (1984) 39-50.

Barr, D. L. 'The Apocalypse of John as Oral Enactment,' *Int* 40 (1986) 243-256.

Bastomsky, S. J. 'The Emperor Nero in Talmudic Legend,' *JQR* 59 (1968-69) 321-325.

Bauckham, R. J. 'The Great Tribulation in the *Shepherd* of Hermas,' *JTS* 25 (1974) 27-40.

Bauckham, R. J. 'The Martyrdom of Enoch and Elijah: Jewish or Christian?' *JBL* 95 (1976) 447-458.

Bauckham, R. J. 'The rise of apocalyptic,' *Them* 3/2 (1978) 10-23.

Bauckham, R. J. 'The Delay of the Parousia,' *TynB* 31 (1980) 3-36.

Bauckham, R. J. *Jude, 2 Peter.* WBC 50. Waco, Texas: Word Books, 1983.

Bauckham, R. J. 'Enoch and Elijah in the Coptic Apocalypse of Elijah,' in *Studia Patristica* 16/2, ed. E. A. Livigstone (Berlin: Akademie-Verlag, 1985) 69-76.

Bauckham, R. J. 'The Two Fig Tree Parables in the Apocalypse of Peter,' *JBL* 10 (1985) 269-287. (1986A)

Bauckham, R. J. 'The Study of Gospel Traditions Outside the Canonical Gospels: Problems and Prospects,' in D. Wenham ed., *Gospel Perspectives 5: The Jesus Tradition Outside the Gospels* (Sheffield: JSOT Press, 1985) 369-403. (1985B)

Bauckham, R. J. 'The Apocalypses in the New Pseudepigrapha,' *JSNT* 26 (1986) 97-117.

Bauckham, R. J. *The Bible in Politics: How to read the Bible politically.* London: SPCK/Louisville, Kentucky: Westminster/John Knox Press, 1989.

Bauckham, R. J. 'Early Jewish Visions of Hell,' *JTS* 41 (1990) 355-385.

Bauckham, R. J. *Jude and the Relatives of Jesus in the Early Church.* Edinburgh: T. & T. Clark, 1990. (1990A)

Bauckham, R. J. 'The List of the Tribes in Revelation 7 Again,' *JSNT* 42 (1991) 99-115.

Bauckham, R.J. 'Jesus, Worship of,' in D.N. Freedman ed., *The Anchor Bible Dictionary,* vol. 3 (Garden City, New York: Doubleday, 1992) 812-819.

Bauckham, R. J. *The Theology of the Book of Revelation.* Cambridge: Cambridge University Press, 1993.

Bauckham, R. J. 'Resurrection as Giving Back the Dead: A Traditional Image of Resurrection in the Pseudepigrapha and the Apocalypse of John,' in J. H. Charlesworth and C. A. Evans ed., *The Pseudepigrapha and the New Testament* (JSPSS; Sheffield; JSOT Press, forthcoming 1993). (1993A)

Bauckham, R. J. *L'Apocalypse de Pierre: Une Apocalypse Judéo-Chrétienne du Temps de Bar Kokhba.* Paris: Brepols, forthcoming 1993. (1993B)

Bauckham, R. J. 'Papias and Polycrates on the Origin of the Fourth Gospel,' forthcoming in *JTS.* (1993C)

Bauer, W., Arndt, W. F. and Gingrich, F. W. *A Greek-English Lexicon of the New Testament and Other Early Christian Literature,* revised F. W. Gingrich and F. W. Danker from W. Bauer's fifth edition, Chicago/London: University of Chicago Press, 1979.

Baumgarten, J. M. 'The Qumran Sabbath Shirot and Rabbinic Merkabah Traditions,' *RevQ* 13 (1988) 199-213.

Beale, G. K. *The Use of Daniel in Jewish Apocalyptic Literature and in the Revelation of St John.* Lanham/New York/London: University of America Press, 1984.

Beale, G. K. 'Revelation,' in D. A. Carson and H. G. M. Williamson ed., *It Is Written: Scripture Citing Scripture: Essays in Honour of Barnabas Lindars, SSF* (Cambridge: Cambridge University Press, 1988) 318-336.

Beasley-Murray, G. R. *A Commentary on Mark Thirteen.* London: Macmillan, 1957.

Beasley-Murray, G. R. *The Book of Revelation.* NCB. London: Marshall, Morgan & Scott, 1974.

Beaujeu, J. 'L'incendie de Rome en 64 et les Chrétiens,' *Lat* 19 (1960) 65-80, 291-311.

Beckwith, I. T. *The Apocalypse of John.* Grand Rapids, Michigan: Baker Book House, 1967 (reprint of 1919 edition).

Behr, C. A. (tr.) *P. Aelius Aristides: The Complete Works.* vol. 2. Leiden: Brill, 1981.

Benoit, P., Milik, J. T. and de Vaux, R. *Les Grottes de Murabba'at.* DJD 2. Oxford: Clarendon Press, 1961.

Bensly, R. L. *The Fourth Book of Ezra.* TextsS 3/2. Cambridge: Cambridge University Press, 1895.

Berger, K. *Die Griechische Daniel-Diegese: Eine altkirchliche Apokalypse.* SPB 27. Leiden: Brill, 1976. (1976A)

Berger, K. *Die Auferstehung des Propheten und die Erhöhung des Menschensohn.* SUNT 13. Göttingen: Vandenhoeck & Ruprecht, 1976. (1976B)

Bergmeier, R. 'Die Buchrolle und das Lamm (Apk 5 und 10),' *ZNW* 76 (1985) 225-242.

Bergmeier, R. 'Die Erzhure und das Tier: Apk 12 18-13 18 und 17f.: Eine quellen- und redaktionskritische Analyse,' in W. Haase ed., *Aufstieg und Niedergang der römischen Welt,* vol. 2/25/2 (Berlin/New York: de Gruyter, 1988) 3899-3916.

Bertier, J. *Nicomaque de Gérase: Introduction Arithmétique.* Histoire des Doctrines de l'Antiquité Classique 2. Paris: Librairie Philosophique J. Vrin, 1978.

Beskow, P. *Rex Gloriae: The Kingship of Christ in the Early Church.* Stockholm/Göteborg/Uppsala: Almquist & Wicksell, 1962.

Best, E. *A Commentary on the First and Second Epistles to the Thessalonians.* BNTC. London: A. & C. Black, 1972.

Betz, O. 'The Eschatological Interpretation of the Sinai-Tradition in Qumran and in the New Testament,' *RevQ* 6 (1967) 89-107.

Betz, O. 'στίγμα,' in TDNT 7 (1971) 657-664.

Binger, T. 'Fighting the Dragon: Another Look at the Theme in the Ugaritic Texts,' *SJOT* 6 (1992) 139-149.

Black, M. 'The "Two Witnesses" of Rev. 11:3f. in Jewish and Christian Apocalyptic Tradition,' in E. Bammel, C. K. Barrett and W. D. Davies ed., *Donum Gentilicium: New Testament Studies in Honour of David Daube* (Oxford: Clarendon Press, 1978) 227-237.

Black, M. '"Not peace but a sword": Matt. 10:34ff; Luke 12:51ff,' in E. Bammel and C. F. D. Moule ed., *Jesus and the Politics of His Day* (Cambridge: Cambridge University Press, 1984)

Black, M. *The Book of Enoch or I Enoch: A New English Edition.* SVTP 7. Leiden: Brill, 1985.

Blaiklock, E. M. *Cities of the New Testament.* London, 1965.

Blumenthal, D. R. *Understanding Jewish Mysticism: A Source Reader.* New York: Ktav, 1978.

Böcher, O. 'Die Johannes-Apokalypse in der neueren Forschung,' in W. Haase ed., *Aufstieg und Niedergang der römischen Welt,* vol. 2/25/2 (Berlin/New York: de Bruyter, 1988) 3850-3893.

Bockmuehl, M. N. A. *Revelation and Mystery in Ancient Judaism and Pauline Christianity.* WUNT 2/36. Tübingen: Mohr (Siebeck), 1990.

Bodinger, M. 'Le mythe de Néron de l'Apocalypse de saint Jean au Talmud de Babylone,' *RHR* 206 (1989) 21-40.

Boesak, A. A. *Comfort and Protest: Reflections on the Apocalypse of John of Patmos.* Edinburgh: Saint Andrew Press, 1987.

Bogaert, P.-M. *L'Apocalypse syriaque de Baruch.* vol. 1. SC 144. Paris: Cerf, 1969.

Bogaert, P.-M. *L'Apocalypse syriaque de Baruch.* vol. 2. SC 145. Paris: Cerf, 1969. (1969A)

Bogaert, P.-M. 'Les apocalypses contemporains de Baruch, d'Esdras et de Jean,' in J. Lambrecht ed., *L'Apocalyptique johannique et l'Apocalyptique dans de Nouveau Testament* (BETL 53; Gembloux: Duculot/Leuven: University Press, 1980) 77-104.

Bohak, G. 'Greek-Hebrew Gematrias in *3 Baruch* and in Revelation,' *JSP* 7 (1990) 119-121.

Bonsirven, J. *L'Apocalypse de Saint Jean.* Paris: Beauchesne, 1951.

Bonwetsch, G. N. *Methodius.* GCS 27. Leipzig: Hinrichs, 1917.

Bori, P. C. 'L'estasi del profeta: *Ascensio Isaiae 6* e l'antico profetismo cristiano,' *CrSt* 1 (1980) 367-389.

Bori, P. C. 'L'esperienza profetica nell'*Ascensione di Isaia,*' in M. Pesce ed., *Isaia, il Diletto e la Chiesa: Visione ed esegesi profetica cristiano-primitiva nell'Ascensione di Isaia* (Brescia: Paideia, 1983) 133-154.

Boring, M. E. 'How May We Identify Oracles of Christian Prophets in the Synoptic Tradition: Mark 3:28-29 as a Test Case,' *JBL* 91 (1972) 501-521.

Boring, M. E. 'The Theology of Revelation: "The Lord Our God the Almighty Reigns,"' *Int* 40 (1986) 257-269.

Boring, M. E. *Sayings of the Risen Jesus: Christian Prophecy in the Synoptic Tradition.* SNTSMS 46. Cambridge: Cambridge University Press, 1983.

Bosse, A. 'Zur Erklärung der Apokalypse der Asc. Jesaiae,' *ZNW* 10 (1909) 320-323.

Botha, P. J. J. 'God, emperor worship and society: Contemporary experiences and the book of Revelation,' *Neot* 22 (1988) 87-102.

Bousset, W. *The Antichrist Legend: A Chapter in Christian and Jewish Folklore.* Tr. A. H. Keane. London: Hutchinson, 1896.

Bousset, W. *Die Offenbarung Johannes.* Göttingen: Vandenhoeck & Ruprecht, 1906.

The Climax of Prophecy

Bradley, K. R. *Suetonius' Life of Nero: An Historical Commentary*. Collection Latomus 157. Brussels: Latomus, 1978.

Brady, D. *The Contribution of British Writers between 1560 and 1830 to the Interpretation of Revelation 13.16-18 (The Number of the Beast)*. BGBE 27. Tübingen: Mohr (Siebeck), 1983.

Braude, W. G. *The Midrash on Psalms*. Vol. 1. YJS. New Haven: Yale University Press, 1959.

Braude, W. G. *Pesikta Rabbati*. YJS 18. New Haven: Yale University Press, 1968.

Brooke, G. J. *Exegesis at Qumran: 4QFlorilgeium in its Jewish Context*. JSOTSS 29. Sheffield: JSOT Press, 1985.

Brown, J. P. 'Synoptic Parallels in the Epistles and Form-History,' *NT* 10 (1963) 27-48.

Brownlee, W. H. 'From Holy War to Holy Martyrdom,' in H. B. Huffmon, F. A. Spina, A. R. W. Green ed., *The Quest for the Kingdom of God: Studies in honor of G. E. Mendenhall* (Winona Lake: Eisenbrauns, 1983).

Bruce, F. F. 'The Spirit in the Apocalypse,' in B. Lindars and S. S. Smalley ed., *Christ and Spirit in the New Testament: In Honour of Charles Francis Digby Moule* (Cambridge: Cambridge University Press, 1973) 333-344.

Brun, L. 'Die römischen Kaiser in der Apokalypse,' *ZNW* 26 (1927) 128-151.

Buchanan, G. W. *Revelation and Redemption: Jewish Documents of Deliverance from the Fall of Jerusalem to the Death of Naḥmanides*. Dillsboro, North Carolina: Western North Carolina Press, 1978.

Bücheler, F. 'Νεόψηφον,' *RMP* 61 (1906) 307-308.

Buchholz, D. D. *Your Eyes Will Be Opened: A Study of the Greek (Ethiopic) Apocalypse of Peter*. SBLDS 97. Atlanta, Georgia: Scholars Press, 1988.

Budge, E. A. W. *Miscellaneous Coptic Texts in the Dialogue of Upper Egypt*. London: Trustees of the British Museum, 1915.

Budge, E. A. W. *The Contendings of the Apostles*. London: Oxford University Press/Humphrey Milford, 1935.

Bultmann, R. *Theology of the New Testament*. Tr. K. Grobel. Vol. 2. London: SCM Press, 1955.

Bultmann, R. *The history of the Synoptic tradition*. Tr. J. Marsh. Oxford: Blackwell, 1963.

Burchard, C. 'Joseph and Aseneth,' in J. H. Charlesworth ed., *The Old Testament Pseudepigrapha*, vol. 2 (London: Darton, Longman & Todd, 1985) 177-247.

Burkert, W. *Lore and Science in Ancient Pythagoreanism*. Tr. E. L. Minar, Jr. Cambridge, Massachusetts: Harvard University Press, 1972.

Burkitt, F. C. *Jewish and Christian Apocalypses*. Schweich Lectures 1913. London: Oxford University Press, 1914.

Buttenweiser, M. *Die hebräische Elias-Apokalypse und ihre Stellung in der apokalyptischen Litteratur des rabbinischen Schrifttums und der Kirche.* Leipzig: Pfeiffer, 1897.

Caird, G. B. *A Commentary on the Revelation of St. John the Divine.* BNTC. London: A. & C. Black, 1966.

Caquot, A. 'Léviathan et Behémoth dans la troisième "Parabole" d'Hénoch,' *Semit* 25 (1975) 111-122.

Carmignac, J. *La Règle de la Guerre des Fils de Lumière contre les Fils de Ténèbres.* Paris: Letouzey et Ané, 1958.

Carnegie, D. R. 'Worthy is the Lamb: The Hymns in Revelation,' in H. H. Rowdon ed., *Christ the Lord: Studies in Christology presented to Donald Guthrie* (Leicester: Inter-Varsity Press, 1982) 243-256.

Carrington, P. *The Meaning of the Revelation.* London: SPCK, 1931.

Casey, M. *Son of Man: The interpretation and influence of Daniel 7.* London: SPCK, 1979.

Charles, R. H. *The Ascension of Isaiah.* London: A. & C. Black, 1900.

Charles, R. H. *The Book of Enoch.* Oxford: Clarendon Press, ²1912.

Charles, R. H. *A Critical and Exegetical Commentary on the Revelation of St. John.* ICC. 2 vols. Edinburgh: T. & T. Clark, 1920.

Charles, R. H. *A Critical and Exegetical Commentary on the Book of Daniel.* Oxford: Clarendon Press, 1929.

Charlesworth, J. H. *The Pseudepigrapha and Modern Research with a Supplement.* SBLSCS 7S. Chico, California: Scholars Press, 1981.

Charlesworth, J. H. ed. *The Old Testament Pseudepigrapha.* Vol. 1. London: Darton, Longman & Todd, 1983.

Charlesworth, J. H. ed. *The Old Testament Pseudepigrapha.* Vol. 2. London: Darton, Longman & Todd, 1985.

Charlesworth, J. H. *The Old Testament Pseudepigrapha and the New Testament.* SNTSMS 54. Cambridge: Cambridge University Press, 1985. (1985A)

Charlesworth, M. P. 'Some Observations on the Ruler-Cult, especially in Rome,' *HTR* 28 (1935) 5-44.

Chester, A. 'Citing the Old Testament,' in D. A. Carson and H. G. M. Williamson ed., *It Is Written: Scripture Citing Scripture: Essays in Honour of Barnabas Lindars, SSF* (Cambridge: Cambridge University Press, 1988) 141-169.

Cizek, E. *L'époque de Néron et ses controverses idéologiques.* Leiden: Brill, 1972.

Cohn, R. L. *The Shape of Sacred Space: Four Biblical Studies.* AARSR 23. Chico, California: Scholars Press, 1981.

Collins, J. J. *The Sibylline Oracles of Egyptian Judaism.* SBLDS 13. Missoula, Montana: Scholars Press, 1974.

Collins, J. J. 'The mythology of holy war in Daniel and the Qumran war scroll: a point of transition in Jewish apocalyptic,' *VT* 25 (1975) 596-612.

Collins, J. J. *The Apocalyptic Vision of the Book of Daniel.* HSM 16. Missoula, Montana: Scholars Press, 1977.

Collins, J. J. 'Sibylline Oracles,' in J. H. Charlesworth ed., *The Old Testament Pseudepigrapha*, vol. 1 (London: Darton, Longman & Todd, 1983) 317-472.

Collins, J. J. *The Apocalyptic Imagination: An Introduction to the Jewish Matrix of Christianity.* New York: Crossroad, 1984.

Colson, F. H. 'Triangular Numbers in the New Testament,' *JTS* 16 (1915) 67-76.

Comblin, J. *Le Christ dans l'Apocalypse.* Bibliothèque de Théologie: Théologie biblique 3/6. Paris: Desclée, 1965.

Commodian. 'Commodiani Carmina,' ed. J. Martin, in *Commodianus; Claudius Marius Victorinus* (CChrSL 108; Turnhout: Brepols, 1960).

Connolly, A. L. 'Frankincense and Myrrh,' in G. H. R. Horsley ed., *New Documents Illustrating Early Christianity 1979* (Macquarie University, NSW: The Ancient History Documentary Research Centre, 1987) 129-131.

Corsini, E. *The Apocalypse: The Perennial Revelation of Jesus Christ.* Tr. F. J. Moloney. Dublin: Veritas/Wilmington, Delaware: Glazier, 1983.

Corssen, P. 'Noch einmal die Zahl des Tieres in der Apokalypse,' *ZNW* 3 (1902) 238-242.

Couchoud, P. L. *The Book of Revelation: A Key to Christian Origins.* Tr. C. B. Bonner. London: Watts, 1932.

Court, J. M. *Myth and History in the Book of Revelation.* London: SPCK, 1979.

Cruz, W. A. *The Mark of the Beast: A Study of XAPAΓMA in the Apocalypse.* Amsterdam: Academische Pers N.V., 1973.

Daniélou, J. *A History of Early Christian Doctrine before the Council of Nicaea.* Vol. 1: *The Theology of Jewish Christianity.* Tr. J. A. Baker. London: Darton, Longman & Todd, 1964.

Daniélou, J. 'La Vision des ossements desséchés (Ezech. 37, 1-14) dans les *Testimonia*,' *RechSR* 53 (1965) 220-233.

Daniélou, J. *A History of Early Christian Doctrine before the Council of Nicaea.* Vol. 3: *The Origins of Latin Christianity.* Tr. D. Smith and J. A. Baker. London: Darton, Longman & Todd, 1977.

D'Arms, J. H. *Commerce and Social Standing in Ancient Rome.* Cambridge, Massachusetts/London: Harvard University Press, 1981.

Davids, P. H. 'James and Jesus,' in D. Wenham ed., *Gospel Perspectives 5: The Jesus Tradition Outside the Gospels* (Sheffield: JSOT Press, 1985) 63-84.

Davies, P. R. *1QM, the War Scroll from Qumran: Its Structure and History.* BibOr 32. Rome: Biblical Institute Press, 1977.

Davies, P. R. 'Dualism and Eschatology in the Qumran War Scroll,' *VT* 28 (1978) 28-36.

Davies, W. D. *Paul and Rabbinic Judaism.* London: SPCK, 1948.

Day, J. 'Echoes of Baal's seven thunders and lightnings in Psalm xxix and Habakkuk iii 9 and the identity of the seraphim in Isaiah vi,' *VT* 29 (1979) 143-151.

Day, J. *God's conflict with the dragon and the sea: Echoes of a Canaanite myth in the Old Testament.* UCOP 35. Cambridge: Cambridge University Press, 1985.

Dean-Otting, M. *Heavenly Journeys: A Study of the Motif in Hellenistic Jewish Literature.* JU 8. Frankfurt am Main/Bern/New York: Peter Lang, 1984.

Dehandschutter, B. 'The Meaning of Witness in the Apocalypse,' in J. Lambrecht ed., *L'Apocalyptique johannique et l'Apocalyptique dans le Nouveau Testament* (BETL 53; Gembloux: Duculot/Leuven: University Press, 1980) 283-288.

Deissman, A. *Light from the Ancient East.* Tr. L. R. M. Strachan. London: Hodder, 1910.

de Jonge, M. 'The Use of the Expression ὁ χριστός in the Apocalypse of John,' in J. Lambrecht ed., *L'Apocalyptique johannique et l'Apocalyptique dans le Nouveau Testament* (BETL 53; Gembloux: Duculot/Leuven: University Press, 1980) 267-281.

Delay, E. 'A qui s'addresse la prière chrétienne?', *RTP* 37 (1949) 189-201.

Delcor, M. 'Mythologie et Apocalyptique,' in L. Monloubou ed., *Apocalypses et Théologie de l'Espérance: Congrès de Toulouse (1975)* (LD 95; Paris: du Cerf, 1977) 143-177.

de Santos Otero, A. *Los Evangelios Apócrifos.* Madrid: La Editorial Católica, ⁶1988.

Deutsch, C. 'Transformation of Symbols: The New Jerusalem in Rv. 21³-22⁵,' *ZNW* 78 (1987) 106-126.

Diebner, B. J. 'Die sogennante Zephanie-Apokalypse — eine jüdische oder eine christliche Schrift? Erwägungen zu Kritieren für eine Beantwortung der Frage,' forthcoming in *Apocrypha.*

Dieterich, A. *Abraxas: Studien zur Religionsgeschtliche des spätern Altertums.* Leipzig: Teubner, 1923.

Dillmann, A. *Ascensio Isaiae: Aethiopice et Latine.* Leipzig: Brockhaus, 1877.

Dillon, J. *The Middle Platonists: A Study of Platonism 80 B.C. to A.D. 220.* London: Duckworth, 1977.

Dimant, D. 'Qumran Sectarian Literature,' in M. E. Stone ed., *Jewish Writings of the Second Temple Period* (Compendia Rerum Iudaicarum ad Novum Testamentum 2/2; Assen: Van Gorcum/Philadelphia: Fortress, 1984) 483-550.

Dix, G. 'The Seven Archangels and the Seven Spirits,' *JTS* 28 (1926) 233-250.

Dodd, C. H. 'The primitive catechism and the sayings of Jesus,' in A. J. B. Higgins ed., *New Testament Essays: Studies in memory of Thomas Walter*

Manson 1893-1958 (Manchester: Manchester University Press, 1959) 106-118.

Dodd, C. H. *The Parables of the Kingdom.* London: Collins, ²1961.

Donaldson, T. L. 'Proselytes or "Righteous Gentiles?" The Status of Gentiles in Eschatological Pilgrimage Patterns of Thought,' *JSP* 7 (1990) 3-27.

D'Ooge, M. L. *Nicomachus of Gerasa: Introduction to Arithmetic.* University of Michigan Studies: Humanistic Series 16. New York: Macmillan, 1926.

Dornseiff, F. *Das Alphabet in Mystik und Magie.* Στοιχεῖα: Studien zur Geschichte des antiken Weltbildes und der griechischen Wissenschaft 7. Leipzig/Berlin: Teubner, 1922.

Draper, J. 'The Jesus Tradition in the Didache,' in D. Wenham ed., *Gospel Perspectives 5: The Jesus Tradition Outside the Gospels* (Sheffield: JSOT Press, 1985) 269-287.

Dudley, G. *The Recovery of Christian Myth.* Philadelphia: Westminster Press, 1967.

Duensing, H. 'The Fifth and Sixth Books of Esra,' in E. Hennecke, W. Schneemelcher, R. McL. Wilson ed., *New Testament Apocrypha,* vol. 2 (London: Lutterworth, 1965) 689-703.

Duensing, H. 'Apocalypse of Paul,' in E. Hennecke, W. Schneemelcher, R. McL. Wilson ed., *New Testament Apocrypha,* vol. 2 (London: Lutterworth, 1965) 755-798. (1965A)

Duhaime, J. 'La Règle de la Guerre de Qumrân et l'apocalyptique,' *ScEs* 36 (1984) 67-88.

Duhaime, J. 'The War Scroll from Qumran and the Greco-Roman Tactical Treatises,' *RevQ* 13 (1988) 133-151.

Dumbrell, W. J. *The End of the Beginning: Revelation 21-22 and the Old Testament.* Homebush West, NSW: Lancer Books/Exeter: Paternoster, 1985.

Dungan, D. L. *The sayings of Jesus in the churches of Paul.* Oxford: Blackwell, 1971.

Dunn, J. D. G. *Jesus and the Spirit.* London: SCM Press, 1975.

Dunn, J. D. G. 'Prophetic "I"- Sayings and the Jesus Tradition: The Importance of Testing Prophetic Utterances within Early Christianity,' *NTS* 24 (1978) 175-198.

Dunn, J. D. G. *Christology in the Making:* London: SCM Press, 1980.

Dunn, J. D. G. *The Partings of the Ways: Between Christianity and Judaism and their Significance for the Character of Christianity.* London: SCM Press/Philadelphia: Trinity Press International, 1991.

Dupont, J. 'La parabole du maître qui rentre dans la nuit (Mc 13, 34-36),' in A. Descamps and A. de Halleux ed., *Mélanges Bibliques en hommage au R. P. Béda Rigaux* (Gembloux: Duculot, 1970) 89-116.

Efron, J. *Studies on the Hasmonean Period*. SJLA 39. Leiden: Brill, 1987.

Elior, R. 'The Concept of God in the Hekhalot Literature,' in J. Dan ed., *Binah: Studies in Jewish History, Thought, and Culture*, vol. 2 (New York: Praeger, 1989) 97-120.

Emerton, J. A. 'Leviathan and *ltn*: the vocalization of the Ugaritic word for the dragon,' *VT* 32 (1982) 327-331.

Enroth, A.-M. 'The Hearing Formula in the Book of Revelation,' *NTS* 36 (1990) 598-608.

Erbetta, M. *Gli Apocrifi del Nuovo Testamento*, vol. 3: *Lettere e apocalissi*. Casale Monferrato: Marietti, 1981.

Farrer, A. *A Rebirth of Images: The Making of St John's Apocalypse*. Westminster: Dacre Press, 1949.

Farrer, A. *The Revelation of St John the Divine*. Oxford: Clarendon Press, 1964.

Fawcett, T. *The Symbolic Language of Religion*. London: 1970.

Fehrenbach, E. 'Encens,' in F. Cabrol and H. Leclercq ed., *Dictionnaire d'Archéologie Chrétienne et de Liturgie*, vol. 5/1 (Paris: Letouzey & Ané, 1922) cols. 2-21.

Fekkes, J. *Isaiah and Prophetic Traditions in the Book of Revelation: Visionary Antecedents and their Development*. Ph.D. thesis, University of Manchester, 1988.

Fekkes, J. '"His Bride has Prepared Herself": Revelation 19-21 and Isaian Nuptial Imagery,' *JBL* 109 (1990) 269-287.

Foerster, W. *Gnosis: A Selection of Gnostic Texts*. Tr. R. McL. Wilson. Vol. 2. Oxford: Oxford University Press, 1974.

Fontenrose, J. *Python: A Study of Delphic Myth and its Origins*. Berkeley/Los Angeles/London: University of California Press, ²1980.

Ford, J. M. *Revelation*. AB 38. Garden City, New York: Doubleday, 1975.

France, R. T. 'The Worship of Jesus: A Neglected Factor in Christological Debate?,' in H. H. Rowdon ed., *Christ the Lord: Studies in Christology presented to Donald Guthrie* (Leicester: Inter-Varsity Press, 1982) 17-36.

Frank, T. ed. *An Economic Survey of Ancient Rome*. vol. 3. Baltimore: John Hopkins Press, 1937.

Frank, T. ed. *An Economic Survey of Ancient Rome*. vol. 4. Baltimore: John Hopkins Press, 1938.

Frank, T. ed. *An Economic Survey of Ancient Rome*. vol. 5. Baltimore: John Hopkins Press, 1940.

Frayn, J. M. *Sheep-rearing and the Wool Trade in Italy during the Roman period*. ARCA Classical and Medieval Texts: Papers and Monographs 15. Liverpool: Francis Cairns, 1984.

Freedman, H. and Simon, M. *Midrash Rabbah*. Vol. 9. London: Soncino Press, 1939.

Friedlander, G. *Pirkê de Rabbi Eliezer*. New York: Hermon Press, ²1965.

Friesenhahn, P. *Hellenistische Wortzahlenmystik im Neuen Testament*. Leipzig/ Berlin: Teubner, 1935.

Fuchs, H. *Der geistige Widerstand gegen Rom in der antiken Welt*. Berlin: de Gruyter, 1964.

Gallivan, P. A. 'The False Neros: A Re-examination,' *Hist* 22 (1973) 364-365.

Garnsey, P. 'Grain for Rome,' in P. Garnsey, K. Hopkins and C. R. Whittaker ed., *Trade in the Ancient Economy* (London: Chatto & Windus/ Hogarth Press, 1983) 118-130.

Garnsey, P. and R. Saller. *The Roman Empire: Economy, Society and Culture*. London: Duckworth, 1987.

Gärtner, B. *The Theology of the Gospel of Thomas*. Tr. E. J. Sharpe. London: Collins, 1961.

Garzetti, A. *From Tiberius to the Antonines: A History of the Roman Empire AD 14-192*. Tr. J. R. Foster. London: Methuen, 1974.

Geffcken, J. *Die Oracula Sibyllina*. GCS. Leipzig: Hinrichs, 1902.

Georgi, D. 'Who is the True Prophet?' *HTR* 79 (1986) 100-126.

Geyser, A. 'The Twelve Tribes in Revelation: Judean and Judeo-Christian Apocalypticism,' *NTS* 28 (1982) 388-99.

Giblin, C. H. 'Structural Patterns in Jos 24, 1-25,' *CBQ* 26 (1964) 50-69.

Giblin, C. H. 'Revelation 11.1-13: Its Form, Function and Contextual Integration,' *NTS* 30 (1984) 433-459.

Giblin, C. H. 'Structural and Thematic Correlations in the Theology of Revelation 16-22,' *Bib* 55 (1974) 487-504.

Giblin, C. H. *The Book of Revelation: The Open Book of Prophecy*. GNS 34. Collegeville, Minnesota: Liturgical Press, 1991.

Giet, S. *L'Apocalypse et l'Histoire*. Paris: Presses Universitaires de France, 1957.

Ginzberg, L. *The Legends of the Jews*. 7 vols. Philadelphia: Jewish Publication Society of America, 1913-1938.

Goldin, J. *The Song at the Sea: being a Commentary on a Commentary in Two Parts*. New Haven/London: Yale University Press, 1971.

Goldin, J. 'A Short Note on the Archangel Gabriel,' in J. Goldin, *Studies in Midrash and Related Literature*, ed. B. L. Eicher and J. H. Tigay (Philadelphia/New York/Jerusalem: Jewish Publication Society, 1988) 325-330.

Goldingay, J. E. *Daniel*. WBC 30. Dallas, Texas: Word Books, 1989.

Gollinger, H. *Das "grosse Zeichen" von Apokalypse 12*. SBM 11. Würzburg: Echter/Stuttgart: Katholisches Bibelwerk, 1971.

Goodenough, E. R. *Jewish Symbols in the Graeco-Roman World*. New York: Pantheon Books/Princeton University Press, 1952-1968. 13 vols.

Grant, R. M. and Graham, H. H. *The Apostolic Fathers II: First and Second Clement.* New York: Nelson, 1965.

Greenhalgh, P. A. L. *The Year of the Four Emperors.* London: Weidenfeld & Nicolson, 1975.

Greeven, H. 'προσκυνέω, προσκυνητής,' in TDNT, vol. 6 (1968) 758-766.

Griffin, M. T. *Nero: The End of a Dynasty.* London: Batsford, 1984.

Griffiths, J. G. *The Conflict of Horus and Seth.* Liverpool: Liverpool University Press, 1960.

Grözinger, K. E. *Musik und Gesang in der Theologie der frühen jüdischen Literatur.* TSAJ 3. Tübingen: Mohr (Siebeck), 1982.

Gruenwald, I. 'New Passages from the Hekhalot Literaure,' *Tarbiṣ* 38 (1969) 354-372.

Gruenwald, I. *Apocalyptic and Merkavah Mysticism.* AGJU 14. Leiden: Brill, 1980.

Gruenwald, I. 'Angelic Songs, the Qedushah and the Problem of the Origin of the Hekhalot Literature,' in I. Gruenwald, *From Apocalypticism to Gnosticism: Studies in Apocalypticism, Merkavah Mysticism and Gnosticism* (BEATAJ 14; Frankfurt am Main/Bern/New York/Paris: Peter Lang, 1988) 145-173.

Gundry, R. H. 'The New Jerusalem: People as Place, not Place for People,' *NovT* 29 (1987) 254-264.

Haas, C. 'Job's perseverance in the Testament of Job,' in M. A. Knibb and P. W. van der Horst eds., *Studies on the Testament of Job* (SNTSMS 66; Cambridge: Cambridge University Press, 1989) 117-154.

Hagner, D. A. *The Use of the Old and New Testaments in Clement of Rome.* NovTSup 34. Leiden: Brill, 1973.

Hall, R. G. 'The *Ascension of Isaiah*: Contemporary Situation, Date and Place in Early Christianity,' *JBL* 109 (1990) 289-306.

Hall, R. G. 'Living Creatures in the Midst of the Throne: Another Look at Revelation 4.6,' *NTS* 36 (1990) 609-613. (1990A)

Halperin, D. J. *The Faces of the Chariot: Early Jewish Responses to Ezekiel's Vision.* TSAJ 16. Tübingen: Mohr (Siebeck), 1988.

Hanson, P. D. *The Dawn of Apocalyptic.* Philadelphia: Fortress, 1975.

Harnisch, W. *Eschatologische Existenz.* FRLANT 110. Göttingen: Vandenhoeck & Ruprecht, 1973.

Harrington, D. J. 'Interpreting Israel's History: The *Testament of Moses* as a Rewriting of Deut. 31-34,' in G. W. E. Nickelsburg ed., *Studies on the Testament of Moses* (SBLSCS 4; Cambridge, Mass.: Scholars Press, 1973) 59-68.

Harris, W. V. 'Towards a Study of the Roman Slave Trade,' in J. H. D'Arms and E. C. Kopff ed., *The Seaborne Commerce of Ancient Rome: Studies in Archaeology and History* (Memoirs of the American Academy in Rome

36; Rome: American Academy in Rome, 1980) 117-140.

Harris, R. and Mingana, A. *The Odes and Psalms of Solomon.* Vol. 2. Manchester: Manchester University Press/ London/New York: Longmans, Green, 1920.

Hartman, L. *Prophecy Interpreted: The Formation of Some Jewish Apocalyptic Texts and of the Eschatological Discourse Mark 13 par.* ConB(NT) 1. Lund: Gleerup, 1966.

Hartman, L. 'Form and Message: A Preliminary Discussion of "Partial Texts" in Rev 1-3 and 22,6ff.,' in J. Lambrecht ed., *L'Apocalyptique johannique et l'Apocalyptique dans le Nouveau Testament* (BETL 53; Gembloux: Duculot/Leuven: University Press, 1980) 129-149.

Hartman, L. F. and Di Lella, A. *The Book of Daniel.* AB 23. Garden City: New York: Doubleday, 1978.

Hayman, P. 'M .10theism — A Misused Word in Jewish Studies?' *JJS* 42 (1991) 1-15.

Head, B. V. *Catalogue of the Greek Coins of Lydia.* London: Trustees of the British Museum, 1901.

Head, B. V. *Catalogue of the Greek Coins of Phrygia.* London: Trustees of the British Museum, 1906.

Heard, W. J. 'The Maccabean Martyrs' Contribution to Holy War,' *EQ* 58 (1986) 291-318.

Hedrick, W. K. *The Sources and Use of the Imagery in Apocalypse 12.* Th.D. thesis, Graduate Theological Union, Berkeley, 1971.

Hellholm, D. 'The Problem of Apocalyptic Genre and the Apocalypse of John,' *Sem* 36 (1986) 13-64.

Helmbold, A. K. 'Gnostic Elements in the "Ascension of Isaiah,"' *NTS* 18 (1971-72) 222-227.

Hemer, C. J. 'The Cities of the Revelation,' in G. H. R. Horsley ed., *New Documents Illustrating Early Christianity 1978* (Macquarie University, NSW: Ancient History Documentary Research Centre) 51-58.

Hemer, C. J. *The Letters to the Seven Churches of Asia in their Local Setting.* JSNTSS 11. Sheffield: JSOT Press, 1986.

Henderson, B. W. *The Life and Principate of the Emperor Nero.* London: Methuen, 1903.

Hendrikson, W. *More than Conquerors: An Interpretation of the Book of Revelation.* London: Inter-Varisty Press, 1962.

Hengel, M. 'Hymns and Christology,' in M. Hengel, *Between Jesus and Paul* (tr. J. Bowden; London: SCM Press, 1983) 78-96.

Hengel, M. *The 'Hellenization' of Judaea in the First Century after Christ.* Tr. J. Bowden. London: SCM Press, 1989.

Hengel, M. *The Zealots: Investigations into the Jewish Freedom Movement in the Period from Herod I until 70 A.D.* Tr. D. Smith. Edinburgh: T. & T. Clark, 1989. (1989A)

Hill, D. *Greek Words and Hebrew Meanings: Studies in the Semantics of Soteriological Terms.* Cambridge: Cambridge University Press, 1967.

Hill, D. 'Prophecy and Prophets in the Revelation of St John,' *NTS* 18 (1972) 401-418.

Hill, D. 'On the Evidence for the Creative Role of Christian Prophets,' *NTS* 20 (1974) 262-274.

Hillers, D. R. 'Rev 13:18 and a Scroll from Murabba'at,' *BASOR* 170 (1963) 65.

Hills, J. *Tradition and Composition in the Epistula Apostolorum.* HDR 24. Minneapolis: Fortress Press, 1990.

Hilzheimer, M. 'Sheep,' *Antiquity* 10 (1936) 195-206.

Himmelfarb, M. *Tours of Hell: An Apocalyptic Form in Jewish and Christian Literature.* Philadelphia: University of Pennsylvania Press, 1983.

Himmelfarb, M. 'The Experience of the Visionary and Genre in the Acension of Isaiah 6-11 and the Apocalypse of Paul,' *Sem* 36 (1986) 97-111.

Himmelfarb, M. 'Heavenly Ascent and the Relationship of the Apocalypses and the *Hekhalot* Literature,' *HUCA* 59 (1988) 73-101.

Himmelfarb, M. 'Revelation and Rapture: The Transformation of the Visionary in the Ascent Apocalypses,' in J. J. Collins and J. H. Charlesworth ed., *Mysteries and Revelations: Apocalyptic Studies since the Uppsala Colloquium* (JSPSS 9; Sheffield: JSOT Press, 1991) 79-90.

Holl, K. *Epiphanius (Ancoratus und Panarion).* Vol. 3. GCS 37. Leipzig: Hinrichs, 1933.

Holtz, T. *Die Christologie der Apokalypse des Johannes.* TU 85. Berlin: Akademie Verlag, 1962.

Holtz, T. 'Gott in der Apokalypse,' in J. Lambrecht ed., *L'Apocalyptique johannique et l'Apocalyptique dans le Nouveau Testament* (BETL 53; Gembloux: Duculot/Leuven: University Press, 1980) 247-265.

Hopkins, K. *Conquerors and Slaves.* Sociological Studies in Roman History 1. Cambridge: Cambridge University Press, 1978.

Horsley, G. H. R. 'The purple trade, and the status of Lydia of Thyatira,' in G. H. R. Horsley ed., *New Documents Illustrating Early Christianity 1977* (Macquarie University, NSW: Ancient History Documentary Research Centre) 25-32.

Hurtado, L. W. 'Revelation 4-5 in the Light of Jewish Apocalyptic Analogies,' *JSNT* 25 (1985) 105-124.

Hurtado, L. W. *One God, One Lord: Early Christian Devotion and Ancient Jewish Monotheism.* Philadelphia: Fortress Press, 1988.

Isaac, E. '1 (Ethiopic Apocalypse of) Enoch,' in J. H. Charlesworth ed., *The Old Testament Pseudepigrapha,* vol. 1 (London: Darton, Longman & Todd, 1983) 5-89.

Isaac, E. 'New Light Upon the Book of Enoch from Newly-Found Ethiopic NSS,' *JAOS* 103 (1983) 399-411. (1983A)

Jacobs, I. 'Elements of Near-Eastern Mythology in Rabbinic Aggadah,' *JJS* 28 (1977) 1-11.

James, M. R. *Apocrypha Anecdota: A Collection of Thirteen Apocryphal Books and Fragments.* TextsS 2/3. Cambridge: Cambridge University Press, 1893.

James, M. R. *The Lost Apocrypha of the Old Testament.* London: SPCK, 1920.

Jeansonne, S. P. *The Old Greek Translation of Daniel 7-12.* CBQMS 19. Washington, D.C.: Catholic Biblical Association of America, 1988.

Jennison, P. *Animals for Show and Pleasure in Ancient Rome.* Manchester: Manchester University Press, 1937.

Jeremias, J. *Jesus' Promise to the Nations.* Tr. S. H. Hooke, SBT 24. London: SCM Press, 1958.

Jeremias, J. 'θύρα,' in TDNT, vol. 3 (1965) 173-180.

Jeremias, J. *New Testament Theology: Part One: The proclamation of Jesus.* Tr. J. Bowden. London: SCM Press, 1971.

Jeremias, J. *The Parables of Jesus.* Tr. S. H. Hooke. London: SCM Press, ³1972.

Jeske, R. L. 'Spirit and Community in the Johannine Apocalypse,' *NTS* 31 (1985) 452-466.

Jongeling, B. *Le Rouleau de la Guerre des Manuscrits de Qumrân.* SSN 4. Assen: Van Gorcum, 1962.

Jörns, K.-P. *Das hymnische Evangelium: Untersuchungen zu Aufbau, Funktion und Herkunft der hymnischen Stücke in der Johannesoffenbarung.* StNT 5. Gütersloh: Mohn, 1971.

Joüon, P. 'Apocalypse, 1,4,' *RSR* 21 (1931) 486-487.

Jungmann, J. *The Place of Christ in Liturgical Prayer.* Tr. A. Peeler. London/Dublin: Chapman, ²1965.

Kaiser, O. *Isaiah 13-39: A Commentary.* Tr. R. A. Wilson. OTL. London: SCM Press, 1974.

Käsemann, E. *New Testament Questions of Today.* London: SCM Press, 1969.

Karrer, M. *Die Johannesoffenbarung als Brief: Studien zu ihrem literarischen, historischen und theologischen Ort.* FRLANT 140. Göttingen: Vandenhoeck & Ruprecht, 1986.

Keresztes, P. 'The Imperial Roman Government and the Christian Church: I. From Nero to the Severi,' in W. Haase ed., *Aufstieg und Niedergang der römischen Welt,* vol. 2/23/1 (Berlin/New York: de Gruyter, 1979) 247-315.

Keresztes, P. 'Nero, the Christians and the Jews in Tacitus and Clement of Rome,' *Lat* 43 (1984) 404-413.

Kiddle, M. *The Revelation of St John*. MNTC. London: Hodder & Stoughton, 1940.

Kiessling, N. K. 'Antecedents of the Medieval Dragon in Sacred History,' *JBL* 89 (1970) 167-177.

Kirby, J. T. 'The Rhetorical Situations of Revelation 1-3,' *NTS* 34 (1988) 197-207.

Klein, R. *Die Romrede des Aelius Aristides*. Texte zur Forschung 45. Darmstadt: Wissenschaftliche Buchgesellschaft, 1983.

Klijn, A. F. J. '2 (Syriac Apocalypse of) Baruch,' in J. H. Charlesworth ed., *The Old Testament Pseudepigrapha*, vol. 1 (London: Darton, Longman & Todd, 1983) 615-652.

Klostermann, E. *Analecta zur Septuaginta, Hexapla und Patristik*. Leipzig: Deichert, 1895.

Knibb, M. A. *The Ethiopic Book of Enoch*. vol. 2. Oxford: Clarendon Press, 1978.

Knibb, M. A. 'The Date of the Parables of Enoch,' *NTS* 25 (1980) 344-357.

Knibb, M. A. 'Martyrdom and Ascension of Isaiah,' in J. H. Charlesworth ed., *The Old Testament Pseudepigrapha*, vol. 2 (London: Darton, Longman & Todd, 1985) 143-176.

Knight, J. M. *Disciples of the Beloved One: A Study in the Ascension of Isaiah, with reference to its christology, social setting, and relevance for New Testament Interpretation*. Unpublished Ph.D. thesis, Cambridge, 1991.

Koch, K. *The Rediscovery of Apocalyptic*. Tr. M. Kohl. SBT 2/22. London: SCM Press, 1972.

Kocsis, E. 'Ost-West Gegensatz in den jüdischen Sibyllinen,' *NovT* 5 (1982) 105-110.

Kraft, H. *Die Offenbarung des Johannes*. HNT 16a. Tübingen: Mohr [Siebeck], 1974.

Kreitzer, L. 'Hadrian and the Nero *Redivivus* Myth,' *ZNW* 79 (1988) 92-115.

Kretschmar, G. *Studien zur frühchristlichen Trinitätstheologie*. BHT 21. Tübingen: Mohr (Siebeck), 1956.

Kümmel, W. G. *Promise and Fulfilment*. London: SCM Press, 1957.

Lacocque, A. *The Book of Daniel*. Tr. D. Pellauer. London: SPCK, 1979.

Lambrecht, J. 'A Structuration of Revelation 4,1-22,5,' in J. Lambrecht ed., *L'Apocalyptique johannique et l'Apocalyptique dans le Nouveau Testament* (BETL 53; Gembloux: Duculot/Leuven: University Press, 1980) 77-104.

Lawrence, D. H. *Apocalypse*. Harmondsworth: Penguin, ²1974.

Legrand, E. *Les Oracles de Léon le Sage, La Bataille de Varna, La Prise de Constantinople: Poëmes en grec vulgaire*. Collection de Monuments pour servir à l'étude de la langue néo-hellénique, NS 5. Paris: Maissonneuve/ Athens: Coromilas, 1875.

Leivestad, R. *Christ the Conqueror: Ideas of Conflict and Victory in the New Testament.* London: SPCK, 1954.

Lewis, R. 'An Apocalyptic Vision of Islamic History,' *BSOAS* 13 (1950) 308-338; reprinted as chapter 5 in B. Lewis, *Studies in Classical and Ottoman Islam (7th-16th Centuries)* (London: Variorum, 1976).

Lewis, R. 'On That Day: A Jewish apocalyptic poem on the Arab conquests,' in *Mélanges d'Islamologie, volume dédié à la mémoire de Armand Abel* (Leiden: Brill, 1974) 197-200; reprinted as chapter 6 in B. Lewis, *Studies in Classical and Ottoman Islam (7th-16th Centuries)* (London: Variorum, 1976).

Lidzbarski, M. *Ginzā: Der Schatz oder das grosse Buch der Mandäer.* Quellen der Religionsgeschichte 13. Göttingen: Vandenhoeck & Ruprecht/ Leipzig: Hinrichs, 1925.

Lieberman, S. *Texts and Studies.* New York: Ktav, 1974.

Lindars, B. *New Testament Apologetic: The Doctrinal Significance of the Old Testament Quotations.* London: SCM Press, 1961.

Lindars, B. 'A Bull, a Lamb and a Word: I Enoch xc.38,' *NTS* 22 (1976) 483-486.

Lindijer, C. H. 'Die Jungfrauen in der Offenbarung des Johannes xiv,' in *Studies in John Presented to Professor J. N. Sevenster* (NovTSup 24; Leiden: Brill, 1970).

Lohmeyer, E. *Die Offenbarung des Johannes.* Tübingen: Mohr, 1953.

Lohse, E. *Die Offenbarung des Johannes.* Göttingen: Vandenhoeck & Ruprecht, 1960.

Lövestam, E. *Spiritual Wakefulness in the New Testament.* LUA 1/55/3. Lund, 1963.

Lunt, H. G. 'Ladder of Jacob,' in J. H. Charlesworth ed., *The Old Testament Pseudepigrapha*, vol. 2 (London: Darton, Longman & Todd, 1985) 401-411.

Lust, J. 'The Order of the Final Events in Revelation and in Ezekiel,' in J. Lambrecht ed., *L'Apocalyptique johannique et l'Apocalyptique dans le Nouveau Testament* (BETL 53; Gembloux: Duculot/Leuven: University Press, 1980) 179-183.

McGing, B. C. *The Foreign Policy of Mithridates VI Eupator King of Pontus.* Mnemosyne Supplements 89. Leiden: Brill, 1986.

MacMullen, R. *Enemies of the Roman Order.* Cambridge, Massachusetts: Harvard University Press, 1966.

McNamara, M. *The New Testament and the Palestinian Targum to the Pentateuch.* AnBib 27. Rome: Pontifical Biblical Institute, 1966.

McNamara, M. *Targum and Testament: Aramaic Paraphrases of the Hebrew Bible: A Light on the New Testament.* Shannon: Irish University Press, 1972.

Magie, D. *Roman Rule in Asia Minor to the End of the Third Century after Christ.* Princeton: Princeton University Press, 1950.

Maier, W. A. *The Book of Nahum.* St Louis: Concordia Publishing House, 1959.

Mango, C. 'The Life of St Andrew the Fool Reconsidered,' *RSBS* 2 (1982) 297-313.

Martin, R. P. *Worship in the Early Church.* London: Marshall, Morgan & Scott, 1964.

Marx, A. 'Les racines du célibat essénien,' *RevQ* 7 (1971) 323-42.

Mastin, B. A. 'Daniel 2^{46} and the Hellenistic World,' *ZAW* 85 (1973) 80-93.

Maurice, F. D. *Lectures on the Apocalypse.* Cambridge: 1861.

Mazzaferri, F. D. *The Genre of the Book of Revelation from a Source-Critical Perspective.* BZNW 54. Berlin/New York: de Gruyter, 1989.

Mealy, J. W. *After the Thousand Years: Resurrection and Judgment in Revelation 20.* Ph.D. thesis, University of Sheffield, 1989.

Meiggs, R. 'Sea-borne Timber Supplies to Rome,' in J. H. D'Arms and E. C. Kopff ed., *The Seaborne Commerce of Ancient Rome: Studies in Archaeology and History* (Memoirs of the American Academy in Rome 36; Rome: American Academy in Rome, 1980) 185-196.

Meiggs, R. *Trees and Timber in the Ancient Mediterranean World.* Oxford: Clarendon Press, 1982.

Mellor, R. ΘΕΑ ΡΩΜΗ: *The Worship of the Goddess Roma in the Greek World.* Hypomnemata 42. Göttingen: Vandenhoeck & Ruprecht, 1975.

Melton, L. D. *A Critical Analysis of the Understanding of the Imagery of the City in the Book of Revelation.* Ph.D. thesis, Southern Baptist Theological Seminary, 1978.

Menken, M. J. J. *Numerical Literary Techniques in John: The Fourth Evangelist's Use of Numbers of Words and Syllables.* NovTSup 55. Leiden: Brill, 1985.

Milik, J. T. '"Prière de Nabonide" et autres écrits d'un cycle de Daniel,' *RB* 63 (1956) 407-415.

Milik, J. T. *The Books of Enoch: Aramaic Fragments of Qumrân Cave 4.* Oxford: Clarendon Press, 1976.

Milligan, G. *The Book of Revelation.* London: Hodder & Stoughton, ^{9}1906.

Minear, P. S. 'Ontology and Ecclesiology in the Apocalypse,' *NTS* 12 (1966) 89-105.

Minear, P. S. *I Saw a New Earth: An Introduction to the Visions of the Apocalypse.* Washington/Cleveland: Corpus, 1968.

Momigliano, A. 'Nero,' in S. A. Cook, F. E. Adcock, M. P. Charlesworth ed., *Cambridge Ancient History,* vol. 10 (Cambridge: Cambridge University Press, 1934) 702-742.

Montgomery, J. A. *A Critical and Exegetical Commentary on the Book of Daniel.* ICC. Edinburgh: T. & T. Clark, 1927.

Moore, C. A. 'On the Origins of the LXX Additions to the Book of Esther,' *JBL* 92 (1973) 382-393.

Moore, C. A. *Daniel, Esther and Jeremiah: The Additions.* AB 44. Garden City, New York: Doubleday, 1977.

Moore, M. S. 'Jesus Christ: "Superstar" (Revelation xxii 16b),' *NovT* 24 (1982) 82-91.

Morray-Jones, C. R. A. 'Hekhalot Literature and Talmudic Tradition: Alexander's Three Test Cases,' *JSJ* 22 (1991) 1-39.

Morris, L. *The Revelation of St John.* TNTC. London: Tyndale Press, 1969.

Moule, C. F. D. 'The Use of Parables and Sayings as illustrative Material in early Christian Catechesis,' *JTS* 3 (1952) 75-79.

Moule, C. F. D. *The Origin of Christology.* Cambridge: Cambridge University Press, 1977.

Moule, C. F. D. *Essays in New Testament Interpretation.* Cambridge: Cambridge University Press, 1982.

Mounce, R. H. *The Book of Revelation.* NICNT. Grand Rapids: Eerdmans, 1977.

Mowry, L. 'Revelation 4-5 and Early Christian Liturgical Usage,' *JBL* 71 (1952) 75-84.

Müller, H. P. 'Die himmlische Ratsversammlung: Motivgeschichtliches zu Apk. 5,1-5,' *ZNW* 54 (1963) 254-267.

Murtonen, A. 'The Figure of MEṬAṬRÔN,' *VT* 3 (1953) 409-411.

Mussies, G. *The Morphology of Koine Greek as used in the Apocalypse of St. John: A Study in Bilingualism.* NovTSup 27. Leiden: Brill, 1971.

Mussies, G. 'The Greek of the Book of Revelation,' in J. Lambrecht ed., *L'Apocalyptique johannique et l'Apocalyptique dans le Nouveau Testament* (BETL 53: Gembloux: Duculot/Leuven: University Press, 1980) 167-177.

Myers, J. M. *I and II Esdras.* AB 42. Garden City, New York: Doubleday, 1974.

Neubauer, A. 'Where are the Ten Tribes?' *JQR* 1 (1889) 14-28, 95-114, 185-201, 408-23.

Newsom, C. *Songs of the Sabbath Sacrifice: A Critical Edition.* HSS 27. Atlanta, Georgia: Scholars Press, 1985.

Newsom, C. 'Merkabah Exegesis in the Qumran Sabbath Shirot,' *JJS* 38 (1987) 11-30.

Nickelsburg, G. W. E. *Jewish Literature between the Bible and the Mishnah.* London: SCM Press, 1981.

Nikiprowetzky, V. *La troisième Sibylle.* EtJ 9. Paris/La Haye: Mouton, 1970.

Norelli, E. 'La resurrezione di Gesu nell'*Ascensione di Isaia*,' CrSt 1 (1980) 315-366.

Norelli, E. 'La sabbia e le stelle: *Gen* 13,16; 15,5; 22,17 nell' esegesi cristiana dei prima tre secoli,' *Aug* 22 (1982) 285-312.

Norelli, E. 'Sulla pneumatologia dell'*Ascensione di Isaia*,' in M. Pesce ed., *Isaia, il Diletto e la Chiesa: Visione et esegesi profetica cristiano-primitiva nell'Ascensione di Isaia* (Brescia: Paideia, 1983) 211-276.

Norelli, E. 'Interprétations nouvelles de l'Ascension d'Isaïe,' *REAug* 37 (1991) 11-22.

Oberweis, M. 'Die Bedeutung der neutestamentlichen "Rätselzahlen" 666 (Apk 13[18]) und 153 (Joh 21[11]),' *ZNW* 77 (1986) 226-241.

Odeberg, H. *3 Enoch, or The Hebrew Book of Enoch*. Cambridge: Cambridge University Press, 1928.

O'Meara, D. J. *Pythagoras Revised: Mathematics and Philosophy in Late Antiquity*. Oxford: Clarendon Press, 1989.

O'Rourke, J. J. 'The Hymns of the Apocalypse,' *CBQ* 30 (1968) 399-409.

Otto, R. *The Idea of the Holy*. Oxford: Oxford University Press, 1923.

Panciera, S. '*Olearii,*' in J. H. D'Arms and E. C. Kopff ed., *The Seaborne Commerce of Ancient Rome: Studies in Archaeology and History* (Memoirs of the American Academy in Rome 36; Rome: American Academy in Rome, 1980) 235-250.

Pappano, A. E. 'The False Neros,' *CJ* 32 (1937) 385-392.

Parke, H. W. *Sibyls and Sibylline Prophecy in Classical Antiquity*. London/ New York: Routledge, 1988.

Paton, L. B. *A critical and exegetical commentary on the Book of Esther*. ICC. Edinburgh: T. & T. Clark, 1908.

Peake, A. S. *The Revelation of John*. London: Holborn Press, n.d. (1920?).

Perrin, N. *Rediscovering the Teaching of Jesus*. London: SCM Press, 1967.

Pesce, M. 'Presupposti per l'utilizzazione storica dell'*Ascensione di Isaia*: Formazione e tradizione del testo; genere letterario; cosmologia angelica,' in M. Pesce ed., *Isaia, il Diletto e la Chiesa: Visione ed esegesi profetica cristiano-primitiva nell'Ascensione de Isaia* (Brescia: Paideia, 1983) 13-76.

Petermann, H. *Thesaurus s. Liber Magnus vulgo "Liber Adami" appellatus opus Mandaeorum summi ponderis*. 2 vols. Leipzig: Weidel, 1867.

Piper, O. A. 'The Apocalypse of John and the Liturgy of the Ancient Church,' *CH* 20 (1951) 10-22.

Pleket, H. W. 'Urban elites and business in the Greek part of the Roman Empire,' in P. Garnsey, K. Hopkins and C. R. Whittaker ed., *Trade in the Ancient Economy* (London: Chatto & Windus/Hogarth Press, 1983) 131-144.

Pope, M. H. *Job*. AB 15. Garden City, New York: Doubleday, 1965.

Powis Smith, J. M., Hayes Ward, W. and Brewer, J. A. *A Critical and Exegetical Commentary on Micah, Zephaniah, Nahum, Habakkuk, Obadiah and Joel.* ICC. Edinburgh: T. & T. Clark, 1912.

Preston, R. H. & Hanson, A. T. *The Revelation of Saint John the Divine.* TC. London: SCM Press, 1949.

Price, S. R. F. *Rituals and Power: The Roman imperial cult in Asia Minor.* Cambridge: Cambridge University Press, 1984.

Prigent, P. 'Au Temps de l'Apocalypse,' *RHPR* 54 (1974) 455-483; 55 (1975) 215-235, 341-363.

Prigent, P. *L'Apocalypse de Saint Jean.* CNT 14. Lausanne: Delachaux & Niestlé, 1981.

Quispel, G. *The Secret Book of Revelation: The Last Book of the Bible.* Tr. P. Staples. London: Collins, 1979.

Rainbow, P. A. 'Jewish Monotheism as the Matrix for New Testament Christology: A Review Article,' *NovT* 33 (1991) 78-91.

Ramsay, W. M. *The Cities and Bishoprics of Phrygia.* Vol. 1. Oxford: Clarendon Press, 1895.

Ramsay, W. M. *The Letters to the Seven Churches of Asia.* London: Hodder & Stoughton, 1909.

Raschke, M. G. 'New Studies in Roman Commerce with the East,' in H. Temporini ed., *Aufstieg und Niedergang der römischen Welt,* vol. 2/9/2 (Berlin/New York: de Gruyter, 1978) 604-1378.

Rawlinson, A. E. J. *The New Testament Doctrine of the Christ.* London: Longmans, Green, 1926.

Reddish, M. G. 'Martyr Christology in the Apocalypse,' *JSNT* 33 (1988) 85-95.

Reicke, B. 'Die jüdische Apokalyptik und die johanneische Tiervision,' *RechSR* 60 (1972) 173-192.

Reicke, B. 'The Inauguration of Catholic Martyrdom according to St John the Divine,' *Aug* 20 (1980) 275-283.

Reinhold, M. *History of Purple as a Status Symbol in Antiquity.* Collection Latomus 116. Brussels: Latomus, 1970.

Rengstorf, K. H. *Die Anfänge der Auseinandersetzung zwischen Christusglaube und Asklepiosfrömmigkeit.* Münster, 1953.

Resch, A. *Aussercanonische Paralleltexte zu de Evangelien.* Vol. 3. TU 10/3. Leipzig: Hinrichs, 1895.

Resch, A. *Der Paulinismus und die Logia Jesu in ihrem gegenseitigem Verhältnis untersucht.* TU 12. Leipzig: Hinrichs, 1904.

Ri, S.-M. 'Le Testament d'Adam et la Caverne des Trésors,' *OCP* 236 (1990) 111-122.

Richardson, P. and Gooch, P. 'Logia of Jesus in 1 Corinthians,' in D. Wenham ed., *Gospel Perspectives 5: The Jesus Tradition Outside the Gospels* (Sheffield: JSOT Press, 1985) 39-62.

Rickman, G. 'The Grain Trade Under the Roman Empire,' in J. H. D'Arms and E. C. Kopff ed., *The Seaborne Commerce of Ancient Rome: Studies in Archaeology and History* (Memoirs of the American Academy in Rome 36; Rome: American Academy in Rome, 1980) 261-176.

Riesenfeld, H. 'τηρέω, τήρησις παρατηρέω, παρατήρησις διατηρέω, συντηρέω,' in TDNT, vol. 8 (1972) 140-151.

Rissi, M. *Time and History: A Study on the Revelation.* Tr. G. C. Winsor. Richmond, Virginia: John Knox Press, 1966.

Robinson, J. A. T. *Redating the New Testament.* London: SCM Press, 1976.

Robinson, J. M. ed. *The Nag Hammadi Library in English.* Leiden: Brill, 1977.

Robinson, S. E. *The Testament of Adam: An Examination of the Greek and Syriac Traditions.* SBLDS 52. Chico, California: Scholars Press, 1982.

Robinson, S. E. 'The Testament of Adam and the Angelic Liturgy,' *RevQ* 12 (1985) 105-110.

Robinson, S. E. 'Testament of Adam,' in J. H. Charlesworth ed., *The Old Testament Pseudepigrapha,* vol. 1 (London: Darton, Longman & Todd, 1983) 989-995.

Robinson, S. E. 'The Testament of Adam: An Updated Arbeitsbericht,' *JSP* 5 (1989) 95-100.

Roloff, J. *Die Offenbarung des Johannes.* ZBK NT 18. Zürich: Theologischer Verlag, 1984.

Rosén, H. B. 'Palestinian κοινή in Rabbinic Illustration,' *JSS* 8 (1963) 56-71.

Rostovtzeff, M. *Rome.* New York: Oxford University Press, 1960.

Roth, W. M. W. *Numerical Sayings in the Old Testament: A Form-Critical Study.* VTSup 13. Leiden: Brill, 1965.

Rowland, C. *The Influence of the First Chapter of Ezekiel on Jewish and Early Christian Literature.* Unpublished Ph.D. thesis, Cambridge, 1975.

Rowland, C. 'The Visions of God in Apocalyptic Literature,' *JSJ* 10 (1979) 137-154.

Rowland, C. 'The Vision of the Risen Christ in Rev. i. 13ff.: The Debt of an Early Christology to an Aspect of Jewish Angelology,' *JTS* 31 (1980) 1-11.

Rowland, C. *The Open Heaven: A Study of Apocalyptic in Judaism and Early Christianity.* London: SPCK, 1982.

Rowland, C. 'Apocalyptic Visions and the Exaltation of Christ in the Letter to the Colossians,' *JSNT* 19 (1983) 73-83.

Rowland, C. 'A Man Clothed in Linen: Daniel 10.6ff. and Jewish Angelology,' *JSNT* 24 (1985) 99-110.

Rühle, O. 'ἀριθμέω, ἀριθμός,' TDNT, vol. 1 (1964) 461-464.

Russell, D. S. *The Method and Message of Jewish Apocalyptic.* London: SCM Press, 1964.

Saffrey, H. D. 'Relire l'Apocalypse à Patmos,' *RB* 82 (1975) 385-417.

Sanders, E. P. *Judaism: Practice and Belief 63BCE-66CE.* London: SCM Press/Philadelphia: Trinity Press International, 1992.

Sanders, H. A. 'The Number of the Beast in Revelation 13, 18,' *JBL* 37 (1918) 95-99.

Schäfer, P. *Die Bar-Kokhba-Aufstand: Studien zum zweiten jüdischen Krieg gegen Rom.* TSAJ 1. Tübingen: Mohr (Siebeck), 1981.

Schäfer, P. *Synopse zur Heikhalot-Literatur.* TSAJ 2. Tübingen: Mohr (Siebeck), 1981.

Schäfer, P. *Synopse zur Heikhalot-Literatur.* TSAJ 2. Tübingen: Mohr (Siebeck), 1981. (1981A)

Schäfer, P. *Übersetzung der Hekhalot-Literatur II, §§81-334.* Tübingen: Mohr (Siebeck), 1987.

Scherrer, S. J. *Revelation 13 as an Historical Source for the Imperial Cult under Domitian.* D. Th. thesis, Harvard University, 1979.

Scherrer, S. J. 'Signs and Wonders in the Imperial Cult: A New Look at a Roman Religious Institution in the Light of Rev 13:13-15,' *JBL* 103 (1984) 559-610.

Schmidt, F. 'Une source essénniene chez Commodien,' in M. Philonenko, J.-C. Picard, J.-M. Rosenthal, F. Schmidt, *Pseudépigraphes de l'Ancien Testament et manuscrits de la Mer Morte* 1 (CRHPR 41; Paris: Presses Universitaires de France, 1967) 11-26.

Schmitz, E. D. 'ἑπτά,' in C. Brown ed., *The New International Dictionary of New Testament Theology,* vol. 2 (Exeter: Paternoster, 1976) 690-692.

Schneider, G. *Parusiegleichnisse im Lukas-Evangelium.* SBS 74. Stuttgart: Katholisches Bibelwerk, 1975.

Scholem, G. *Major Trends in Jewish Mysticism.* London: Thames & Hudson, 1955.

Scholem, G. *Jewish Gnosticism, Merkabah Mysticism, and Talmudic Tradition.* New York: Jewish Theological Seminary of America, ²1965.

Schrage, W. 'Die Stellung zur Welt bei Paulus, Epiktet und in der Apokalyptik: Ein Beitrag zu 1 Kor 7, 29-31,' *ZTK* 61 (1964) 139-154.

Schrage, W. *Das Verhältnis des Thomas-Evangelium zur synoptischen Tradition und zu den koptischen Evangelienübersetzungen.* BZNW 29. Berlin: Töpelmann, 1964. (1964A).

Schürer, E. *The History of the Jewish People in the Age of Jesus Christ (175 B.C.- A.D. 135).* Revised version by G. Vermes, F. Millar, M. Black. Vol. 2. Edinburgh: T. & T. Clark, 1979.

Schürer, E. *The History of the Jewish People in the Age of Jesus Christ (175 B.C.- A.D. 135).* Revised version by G. Vermes, F. Millar, M. Goodman. Vol. 3/1. Edinburgh: T. & T. Clark, 1986.

Schüssler Fiorenza, E. 'Apocalyptic and Gnosis in the Book of Revelation and Paul,' *JBL* 92 (1973) 565-581.

Schüssler Fiorenza, E. 'Redemption as Liberation: Apoc. 1:5f. and 5:9f.,' *CBQ* 36 (1974) 220-232.

Schüssler Fiorenza, E. 'Cultic Language in Qumran and in the New Testament,' *CBQ* 38 (1976) 159-177.

Schüssler Fiorenza, E. *The Book of Revelation: Justice and Judgment.* Philadelphia: Fortress, 1985.

Schweizer, E. 'Die sieben Geister in der Apokalypse,' *EvT* 6 (1951-52) 502-512.

Scott, E. F. *The Book of Revelation.* London: SCM Press, ⁴1941.

Scott, K. *The Imperial Cult under the Flavians.* Stuttgart/Berlin: Kohlhammer, 1936.

Segal, A. F. *Two Powers in Heaven: Early Rabbinic Reports about Christianity and Gnosticism.* SJLA 25. Leiden: Brill, 1977.

Shea, W. H. 'Chiasm in Theme and by Form in Revelation 18,' *AUSS* 20 (1982) 249-256.

Shepherd, M. H. *The Paschal Liturgy and the Apocalypse.* Richmond, Virginia: John Knox Press, 1960.

Simon, Max. *Geschichte der Mathematik im Altertum.* Berlin: B. Cassirer, 1909.

Simon, Marcel. 'Remarques sur l'angélolâtrie juive au début de l'ère chrétienne,' *Académie des inscriptions et belles-lettres: Comptes rendus des séances de l'année 1971*, 120-132.

Simonetti, M. 'Note sulla cristologia dell' *Ascensione di Isaia,*' in M. Pesce ed., *Isaia, il Diletto e la Chiesa: Visione ed esegesi profetica cristiano-primitiva nell'Ascensione di Isaia* (Brescia: Paideia, 1983) 185-209.

Sjöberg, E. 'רוח in Palestinian Judaism,' in TDNT, vol. 6 (1968) 375-389.

Skarsaune, O. *The Proof from Prophecy: A Study in Justin Martyr's Proof-Test Tradition.* NovTSup 56. Leiden: Brill, 1987.

Skehan, P. W. 'King of Kings, Lord of Lords (Apoc. 19:16),' *CBQ* 10 (1948) 398.

Skrinjar, A. 'Les sept Ésprits (Apoc. 1:4; 3:1; 4:5; 5:6),' *Bib* 16 (1935) 1-25, 113-140.

Slomovic, E. 'Towards an Understanding of the Exegesis in the Dead Sea Scrolls,' *RevQ* 7 (1969-71) 3-15.

Smallwood, E. M. *The Jews under Roman Rule: From Pompey to Diocletian.* SJLA 20. Leiden: Brill, 1976.

Smith, C. R. 'The Portrayal of the Church as the New Israel in the Names and Order of the Tribes in Revelation 7.5-8,' *JSNT* 39 (1990) 111-118.

Smith, J. Z. 'Prayer of Joseph,' in J. H. Charlesworth ed., *The Old Testament Pseudepigrapha*, vol. 2 (London: Darton, Longman & Todd, 1985) 699-714.

Smitmans, A. 'Das Gleichnis vom Dieb,' in H. Feld and J. Nolte ed., *Wort Gottes in der Zeit: Festschrift Karl Hermann Schelkle* (Düsseldorf: Patmos-Verlag, 1973) 43-68.

Stauffer, E. '666 (Apoc. 13, 18),' *ConNT* 11 (1947) 237-241.

Stauffer, E. *Christ and the Caesars.* Tr. K. and R. Gregor Smith. London: SCM Press, 1955.

Stead, C. 'The Origins of the Doctrine of the Trinity, 1,' *Theol* 77 (1974) 508-517.

Steindorff, G. *Die Apokalypse des Elias, eine unbekannte Apokalypse und Bruchstücke der Sophonie-Apokalypse.* TU 17/3a. Leipzig: Hinrichs, 1899.

Stemberger, G. *Der Leib der Auferstehung: Studien zur Antropologie und Eschatologie des palästinischen Judentums im neutestamentlichen Zeitalter (ca. 170 v. Chr. — 100 n. Chr.).* AnBib 56. Rome: Biblical Institute Press, 1972.

Stone, M. E. 'The Concept of the Messiah in 4 Ezra,' in J. Neusner ed., *Religions in Antiquity: E. R. Goodenough Memorial* (SHR 14; Leiden: Brill, 1968) 295-312.

Stone, M. E. *Armenian Apocrypha relating to the Patriarchs and Prophets.* Jerusalem: Israel Academy of Sciennes and Humanities, 1982.

Stone, M. E. *Fourth Ezra.* Hermeneia. Minneapolis: Fortress Press, 1990.

Stone, M. E. 'On Reading an Apocalypse,' in J. J. Collins and J. H. Charlesworth ed., *Mysteries and Revelations: Apocalyptic Studies since the Uppsala Colloquium* (JSPSS 9; Sheffield: JSOT Press, 1991) 65-78.

Strand, K. A. *Interpreting the Book of Revelation: Hermeneutical Guidelines with Brief Introduction to Literary Analysis.* Worthington, Ohio: Ann Arbor Publishers, 1976.

Strand, K. A. 'Two Aspects of Babylon's Judgment Portrayed in Revelation 18,' *AUSS* 20 (1982) 53-60.

Strobel, A. 'Abfassung und Geschichtstheologie der Apokalypse nach Kp 17, 9-12,' *NTS* 10 (1963-64) 433-445.

Suter, D. 'Fallen Angel, Fallen Priest: The Problem of Family Purity in 1 Enoch 6-16,' *HUCA* 50 (1979) 115-35.

Sweet, J. P. M. *Revelation.* SCM Pelican Commentaries. London: SCM Press, 1979.

Sweet, J. P. M. 'Maintaining the Testimony of Jesus: the suffering of Christians in the Revelation of John,' in W. Horbury and B. McNeil ed., *Suffering and Martyrdom in the New Testament: Studies presented to G. M. Styler* (Cambridge: Cambridge University Press, 1981) 101-117.

Swete, H. B. *The Apocalypse of St John.* London: Macmillan, ²1907.

Talbert, C. H. 'The Myth of a Descending-Ascending Redeemer in Mediterranean Antiquity,' *NTS* 22 (1976) 418-440.

Taylor, L. R. *The Divinity of the Roman Emperor.* Middletown: American Philological Association, 1931.

Taylor, V. *The Gospel according to St Mark.* London: Macmillan, ²1966.

Thompson, L. L. *The Book of Revelation: Apocalypse and Empire.* New York/

Oxford: Oxford University Press, 1990.

Tisserant, E. *Ascension d'Isaïe*. Documents pour l'étude de la Bible. Paris: Letouzey & Ané, 1909.

Topham, M. "'A human being's measurement, which is an angel's,'" *ExpT* 100 (1989) 217-218.

Townend, G. B. 'The Sources of the Greek in Suetonius,' *Hermes* 88 (1960) 98-120.

Towner, W. S. *The Rabbinic "Enumeration of Scriptural Examples": A Study of a Rabbinic Pattern of Discourse with Special Reference to* Mekhilta d' R. Ishmael. SPB 22. Leiden: Brill, 1973.

Toynbee, J. M. C. *Animals in Roman Life and Art.* London: Thames & Hudson, 1973.

Trites, A. A. *The New Testament Concept of Witness.* SNTSMS 31. Cambridge: Cambridge University Press, 1977.

Trudinger, L. *The Text of the Old Testament in the Book of Revelation.* Th.D. dissertation, Boston University School of Theology, 1963.

Tuckett, C. M. '1 Corinthians and Q,' *JBl* 102 (1983) 607-619.

Uehlinger, C. 'Leviathan und die Schiffe in Ps 104, 25-26,' *Bib* 71 (1990) 499-526.

Ulfgard, H. *Feast and Future: Revelation 7:9-17 and the Feast of Tabernacles.* ConB(NT) 22. Stockholm: Almqvist & Wiksell, 1989.

Ulrichsen, J. H. 'Die sieben Häupter und die zehn Hörner: Zur Datierung der Offenbarung des Johannes,' *ST* 39 (1985) 1-20.

Urbach, E. E. *The Sages: Their Concepts and Beliefs.* 2 vols. Tr. I. Abrahams. Jerusalem: Magnes Press. 1975.

Vaillant, A. 'Un apocryphe pseudo-bogomile: la Vision d'Isaïe,' *RESl* 42 (1963) 109-121.

van Beek, G. W. 'Frankincense and Myrrh,' *BA* 23 (1960) 70-95.

van den Bergh van Eysinga, A. 'Die in der Apokalypse bekämpfte Gnosis,' *ZNW* 13 (1912) 293-305.

VanderKam J. C. and Milik, J. T. 'The First *Jubilees* Manuscript from Qumran Cave 4: A Preliminary Publication,' *JBL* 110 (1991) 243-270.

van der Ploeg, J. *Le Rouleau de la Guerre.* STDJ 2. Leiden: Brill, 1959.

Vanhoye, A. 'L'utilisation du livre d'Ezéchiel dans l'Apocalypse,' *Bib* 43 (1962) 436-477.

Vanni, U. *La Struttura Letteraria dell'Apocalisse.* Rome: Herder, 1971.

Vanni, U. 'L'Apocalypse johannique: État de la question,' in J. Lambrecht ed., *L'Apocalyptique johannique et l'Apocalyptique dans le Nouveau Testament* (BETL 53; Gembloux: Duculot/Leuven: University Press, 1980) 21-46.

van Schaik, A. P. 'Ἄλλος ἄγγελος in Apk 14,' in J. Lambrecht ed., *L'Apocalyptique johannique et l'Apocalyptique dans le Nouveau Testament* (BETL 53; Gembloux: Duculot/Leuven: University Press, 1980) 217-228.

van Unnik, W. C. 'Die "Zahl der vollkommenen Seelen" in der Pistis Sophia,' in O. Betz, M. Hengel and P. Schmidt ed., *Abraham unser Vater: Juden und Christen im Gespräch über die Bibel: Festschrift für Otto Michel* (Leiden: Brill, 1963) 467-477.

van Unnik, W. C. '"Worthy is the Lamb": The Background of Apoc. 5,' in A. Descamps and A. de Halleux ed., *Mélanges bibliques en hommage au R. P. Béda Rigaux* (Gembloux: Duculot, 1970) 445-461.

Verheyden, J. 'L'Ascension d'Isaïe et l'Évangile de Matthieu: Examen de AI 3,13-18,' in J.M. Sevrin ed., *The New Testament in Early Christianity: La réception des écrits néotestamentaires dans le christianisme primitif* (BETL 86; Leuven: Leuven University Press/Peeters, 1989) 247-274.

Vermes, G. *The Dead Sea Scrolls in English.* London/Harmondsworth: Penguin, ³1987.

Vögtle, A. 'Der Gott der Apokalypse: Wie redet die christliche Apokalypse von Gott,' in J. Coopens ed., *La Notion biblique de Dieu: Le Dieu de la Bible et le Dieu des philosophes* (BETL 41; Gembloux: Duculot/Leuven: University Press, 1976) 377-398.

von der Osten-Sacken, P. *Gott und Belial: Traditionsgeschichtliche Untersuchungen zum Dualismus in den Texten aus Qumran.* SUNT 6. Göttingen: Vandenhoeck & Ruprecht, 1969.

Vos, L. A. *The Synoptic Traditions in the Apocalypse.* Kampen: J. H. Kok, 1965.

Wacholder, B. Z. 'David's Eschatological Psalter 11Q Psalmsª,' *HUCA* 59 (1988) 23-72.

Wakeman, M. K. *God's Battle with the Monster: A Study in Biblical Imagery.* Leiden: Brill, 1973.

Walker, A. *Apocryphal Gospels, Acts, and Revelations.* ANCL 16. Edinburgh: T. & T. Clark, 1873.

Wallace, H. 'Leviathan and the Beast in Revelation,' *BA* 11 (1948) 61-68.

Walter, G. *Nero.* Tr. E. Craufurd. London: Allen & Unwin, 1957.

Walton, C. S. 'Oriental Senators in the Service of Rome: A Study of Imperial Policy down to the Death of Marcus Aurelius,' *JRS* 19 (1929) 38-66.

Ward-Perkins, J. 'The Marble Trade and its Organization: Evidence from Nicomedia,' in J. H. D'Arms and E. C. Kopff ed., *The Seaborne Commerce of Ancient Rome* (Memoirs of the American Academy in Rome 36; Rome: American Academy in Rome, 1980) 325-338.

Warmington, E. H. *The Commerce between the Roman Empire and India.* London: Curzon Press/New York: Octagon Books, ²1974.

Wellesley, K. *The Long Year A.D. 69.* London: Elek, 1975.

Wengst, K. *Pax Romana and the Peace of Jesus Christ.* Tr. J. Bowden. London: SCM Press, 1987.

Wenham, D. 'Paul and the Synoptic Apocalypse,' in R. T. France and D.

Wenham ed., *Gospel Perspectives 2: Studies of History and Tradition in the Four Gospels* (Sheffield: JSOT Press, 1981) 345-375.

Wenham, D. 'Paul's Use of the Jesus Tradition: Three Samples,' in D. Wenham ed., *Gospel Perspectives 5: The Jesus Tradition Outside the Gospels* (Sheffield: JSOT Press, 1985) 7-37.

Werner, M. *The formation of Christian dogma.* Tr. S. G. F. Brandon. London: A. & C. Black, 1957.

White, K. D. *Roman Farming:* London: Thames & Hudson, 1970.

Whittaker, M. *Die Apostolischen Väter: I. Der Hirt des Hermas.* GCS 48. Berlin: Akademie-Verlag, 1956.

Widengren, G. *Literary and Psychological Aspects of the Hebrew Prophets.* UUA 1948:10. Uppsala, 1948.

Wilcox, M. 'Tradition and Redaction in Rev 21,9-22,5,' in J. Lambrecht ed., *L'Apocalyptique johannique et l'Apocalyptique dans le Nouveau Testament* (BETL 53; Gembloux: Duculot/Leuven: University Press, 1980) 205-215.

Wilcox, M. 'Text form,' in D. A. Carson and H. G. M. Williamson ed., *It Is Written: Scripture Citing Scripture: Essays in Honour of Barnabas Lindars, SSF* (Cambridge: Cambridge University Press, 1988) 193-204.

Williams, A. L. 'The Cult of Angels at Colossae,' *JTS* 10 (1909) 413-438.

Winkle, R. E. 'Another Look at the List of Tribes in Revelation,' *AUSS* 27 (1989) 53-67.

Wintermute, O. S. 'Apocalypse of Zephaniah,' in J. H. Charlesworth ed., *The Old Testament Pseudepigrapha,* vol. 1 (London: Darton, Longman & Todd, 1983) 497-515.

Witt, R. E. *Isis in the Graeco-Roman World.* London: Thames & Hudson, 1971.

Wroth, W. *Catalogue of the Greek Coins of Mysia.* Ed. R. S. Poole. London: Trustees of the British Museum, 1892.

Yarbro Collins, A. *The Combat Myth in the Book of Revelation.* HDR 9. Missoula, Montana: Scholars Press, 1976.

Yarbro Collins, A. 'The Political Perspective of the Revelation to John,' *JBL* 96 (1977) 241-56.

Yarbro Collins, A. 'Revelation 18: Taunt-Song or Dirge?' in J. Lambrecht ed., *L'Apocalyptique johannique et l'Apocalyptique dans le Nouveau Testament* (BETL 53; Gembloux: Duculot/Leuven: University Press, 1980) 185-204.

Yarbro Collins, A. 'Myth and History in the Book of Revelation: the Problem of its Date,' in B. Halpern and J. D. Levenson ed., *Traditions in Transformation: Turning Points in Biblical Faith* (Winona Lake: Eisenbrauns, 1981) 377-403.

Yarbro Collins, A. 'Persecution and Vengeance in the Book of Revelation,' in D. Hellholm ed., *Apocalypticism in the Mediterranean World and the Near East: Proceedings of the International Colloquium on Apocalypticism: Uppsala, August 12-17, 1979* (Tübingen: Mohr [Siebeck], 1983) 729-749.

Yarbro Collins, A. 'Numerical Symbolism in Jewish and Early Christian Apocalyptic Literature,' in W. Haase ed., *Aufstieg und Niedergang der römischen Welt,* vol. 2/21/1 (New York/Berlin: de Gruyter, 1984) 1221-1287. (1984A)

Yarbro Collins, A. *Crisis and Catharsis: The Power of the Apocalypse.* Philadelphia: Westminster Press, 1984. (1984B)

Yarbro Collins, A. 'Reading the Book of Revelation in the Twentieth Century,' *Int* 40 (1986) 229-242.

Yadin, Y. *The Scroll of War of the Sons of Light against the Sons of Darkness.* Oxford: Oxford University Press, 1962.

Zeron, A. 'The Martyrdom of Phineas-Elijah,' *JBL* 98 (1979) 99-100.

Zervos, G. T. 'Apocalypse of Daniel,' in J. H. Charlesworth ed., *The Old Testament Pseudepigrapha,* vol. 1 (London: Darton, Longman & Todd, 1983) 755-770.

Index of Passages Cited

39:5	379
39-40	182
40:1	211
42:8	57-70
44-46	90
48:6	52
48:32	239
48:40	239
50	66
50:2	58-70
53	177
53:1	158
54:1	239
55:2	239
56-74	177
59:3	208
70:2	239, 294
70:8	201-202
72:6	211
70:10	239
78:5-7	219
81:3	51

3 Baruch	72, 141, 145, 177, 389
2:1-2	154
4:3-7	389
5:1	121
5:3	144
6-8	75
6:4	121
6:9	121
6:12	144
7:2	144
7:5	123
11-16	81
11:2	121, 144
11:3	121
11:8	121
12:2	121
16:4 (Slav)	142, 144

4 Baruch	
9:25-32	169

Book of Eldad and Modad	220

1 Enoch	38
6:6	189
7:1	231
9:1	128
9:8	231
10:1	128
10:11	231
10:20-21	243
14:8	154, 155
14:9	123
14:13-14	123
14:20	126
14:21	142
14:24	122
15:3	231
15:4	231
20 [Greek]	162
20:6	128
20:7	191
24	189
37:2	239
27:5	239
39:3	154
39:3-4	155
39:9-10	141
39:12	71
39:12-13	138
40:6	239
40:7	239
41:7	71
47:1-2	81
47:1-4	48-56
47:3-4	53
48:5	138, 239
49:3	214
51:1	56-70
52:1	155
54:6	239
54:9	239
55:1	239
55:2	239
56:5	430

V. DEAD SEA SCROLLS

VI. HELLENISTIC JEWISH
AUTHORS

VIII. CLASSICAL GREEK AND LATIN AUTHORS

XI MISCELLANEOUS

Index of Ancient Persons and Places

Index of Modern Authors